The Works of Mark Twain

VOLUME 19

WHAT IS MAN?
AND OTHER PHILOSOPHICAL WRITINGS

The Works of Mark Twain

The Works of Mark Twain

WHAT IS MAN?

AND OTHER PHILOSOPHICAL WRITINGS

Edited with an Introduction by

PAUL BAENDER

PUBLISHED FOR

THE IOWA CENTER FOR TEXTUAL STUDIES

BY THE

UNIVERSITY OF CALIFORNIA PRESS

BERKELEY, LOS ANGELES, LONDON

1973

CENTER FOR EDITIONS OF
AMERICAN AUTHORS
AN APPROVED TEXT
MODERN LANGUAGE
ASSOCIATION OF AMERICA
®

The research reported herein was performed pursuant to a contract with the United States Office of Education, Department of Health, Education, and Welfare, under the provisions of the Cooperative Research Program.

All collations were done and factual data were checked at Berkeley and Iowa City. Assistants at Berkeley under the direction of

BERNARD L. STEIN
were
RALPH DICKEY
VICTOR FISCHER
MARIAM KAGAN

Assistants at Iowa City, under the direction of the volume editor, were

SIDNEY BERGER
JUDITH HALE CROSSETT
LINDA ELLINGER
TERRY FIRKINS
CYNTHIA KUHN
HOPE LANDRES

ACKNOWLEDGMENTS

SEVERAL individuals and institutions have helped in the preparation of this volume. For assistance in collation and in checking the text the editor is indebted to the late Emily Anderson, Judy Clark, Dorotha Dilkes, Robert H. Hirst, Karen Keres, Murray Ross, Kenneth M. Sanderson, Jack Vanden Berg, Thomas Zolnay. For research assistance and preparation of copy: Evan Alderson, the late Billie Batchelor, Bruce T. Hamilton, Haydon Weihe. For information and facilitation of research: Howard G. Baetzhold; University of California Library, Berkeley; Julia Bartling; Walter Blair; Brown University Library; Louis J. Budd; Buffalo and Erie County Public Library; The First Church of Christ, Scientist in Boston, Massachusetts (Lee Z. Johnson, Archivist); John C. Gerber; William M. Gibson; Interlibrary Loan Office, University of Iowa Library; George N. Meissner Collection, Rare Book Department, Olin Library, Washington University, St. Louis; Memorial Library, University of Wisconsin; New York Public Library; Oriental Institute, University of Chicago (Klaus Baer); Roger Salomon; Jean Shaw; Martha Stocker; Ada M. Stoflet; The Stark Library, University of Texas; William B. Todd; John S. Tuckey; Yale University Library. For financial assistance: The Graduate College, University of Iowa. For permission to publish: The Collection of American Literature, Yale University, for the frontispiece; Elmira College Library, for "Contract with Mrs. T. K. Beecher"; The Clifton Waller Barrett Library of the University of Virginia Library, for material relating to

Christian Science; Memorial Library, University of Wisconsin, for readings in " 'The Turning Point of My Life' "; University of California, Berkeley, for items in the Supplements and the Textual Notes.

The editor is grateful for invaluable consultations with Fredson Bowers and Bernard L. Stein, and for the generous assistance of Frederick Anderson throughout the preparation of this volume.

CONTENTS

Titles in brackets are editorial; the works
were untitled or their titles have been lost.

ABBREVIATIONS

The following abbreviations and location symbols have been used in annotations. Unless otherwise indicated, all materials quoted in the documentation are transcribed from originals in the Mark Twain Papers, Bancroft Library, University of California, Berkeley. "DV" and "Paine" numbers are catalog numbers in the Mark Twain Papers. Volume numbers for multi-volume works appear before the abbreviation, thus, "37Z."

MT	Mark Twain
MTP	Mark Twain Papers, Bancroft Library, University of California (Berkeley)
SLC	Samuel L. Clemens
TS	Typescript

PREVIOUSLY PUBLISHED TEXTS

A1911	Anderson Auction Company, catalogue no. 892–1911 ("The Library and Manuscripts of Samuel L. Clemens")
BAL	Jacob Blanck, *Bibliography of American Literature* (New Haven: Yale University Press, 1957), vol. 2
CG	*Contributions to* The Galaxy *1868–1871 by Mark Twain*, ed. Bruce R. McElderry Jr. (Gainesville, Florida: Scholars' Facsimiles & Reprints, 1961)
C1951	"Mark Twain Library Auction," Los Angeles, 10 April 1951

DAB　　　　　*Dictionary of American Biography* (New York: Charles Scribner's Sons, n.d.)

Europe　　　　*Europe and Elsewhere* (New York: Harper & Brothers, 1923)

HH&T　　　　*Mark Twain's Hannibal, Huck & Tom*, ed. Walter Blair (Berkeley and Los Angeles: University of California Press, 1969)

LE　　　　　　*Letters from the Earth*, ed. Bernard DeVoto (New York: Harper & Row, 1962)

LLMT　　　　*The Love Letters of Mark Twain*, ed. Dixon Wecter (New York: Harper & Brothers, 1949)

MTA　　　　　*Mark Twain's Autobiography*, ed. Albert Bigelow Paine (New York: Harper & Brothers, 1924)

MTB　　　　　Albert Bigelow Paine, *Mark Twain: A Biography* (New York: Harper & Brothers, 1912)

MTCor　　　　*Mark Twain: San Francisco Correspondent*, ed. Henry Nash Smith and Frederick Anderson (San Francisco: Book Club of California, 1957)

MTE　　　　　*Mark Twain in Eruption*, ed. Bernard DeVoto (New York: Harper & Brothers, 1940)

MTH　　　　　Walter Francis Frear, *Mark Twain and Hawaii* (Chicago: Lakeside Press, 1947)

MTHHR　　　*Mark Twain's Correspondence with Henry Huttleston Rogers*, ed. Lewis Leary (Berkeley and Los Angeles: University of California Press, 1969)

MTHL　　　　*Mark Twain-Howells Letters*, ed. Henry Nash Smith and William M. Gibson (Cambridge, Massachusetts: Harvard University Press, Belknap Press, 1960)

MTL　　　　　*Mark Twain's Letters*, ed. Albert Bigelow Paine (New York: Harper & Brothers, 1917)

MTN　　　　　*Mark Twain's Notebook*, ed. Albert Bigelow Paine (New York: Harper & Brothers, 1935)

NF   Kenneth R. Andrews, *Nook Farm: Mark Twain's Hartford Circle* (Cambridge, Massachusetts: Harvard University Press, 1950)

RP   *Report from Paradise*, ed. Dixon Wecter (New York: Harper & Brothers, 1952)

S&B   *Mark Twain's Satires & Burlesques*, ed. Franklin R. Rogers (Berkeley and Los Angeles: University of California Press, 1967)

SCH   Dixon Wecter, *Sam Clemens of Hannibal* (Boston: Houghton Mifflin Co., 1952)

WIM   *What Is Man? and Other Essays* (New York: Harper & Brothers, 1917)

WWD   *Mark Twain's Which Was the Dream? and Other Symbolic Writings of the Later Years*, ed. John S. Tuckey (Berkeley and Los Angeles: University of California Press, 1967)

Z   *The Definitive Edition of the Writings of Mark Twain*, 37 vols. (New York: Gabriel Wells, 1922–1925)

INTRODUCTION

Development of the Ideas

IN January 1870, writing with romantic eloquence to his fiancée, Olivia Langdon, Samuel L. Clemens exclaimed that "the world we are so proud of is to the universe of careening globes as is one mosquito to the winged & hoofed flocks & herds. . . ." [1] He went on to ask: "Verily, What is Man, that he should be considered of God?" Soon after his marriage he was more sardonic:

> The difference between [the biblical] universe and the modern one revealed by science is as the difference between a dust-flecked ray in a barn and the sublime arch of the Milky Way in the skies. Its God was strictly proportioned to its dimensions. His sole solicitude was about a handful of truculent nomads. . . .
> To trust the God of the Bible is to trust an irascible, vindictive, fierce and ever fickle and changeful master. . . . [2]

Despite his attempts at piety during the recent courtship, Mark Twain reverted to an antagonism against Christianity he had already expressed. It had shown itself in San Francisco four years earlier, when he had assumed Bohemian attitudes of flippancy and disdain toward religious gentility ("Sabbath Reflections" and

1. SLC to Olivia Langdon, 8 January [1870], *LLMT*, pp. 133–134.
2. *MTB*, p. 412; Paine 60, MTP. This and another manuscript ("Letters from a Dog," DV344) are scheduled for publication among The Mark Twain Papers. All manuscript materials not otherwise designated are in MTP. "DV" and "Paine" numbers are catalog numbers in MTP.

"Reflections on the Sabbath," 1866).[3] A decade still earlier he had burlesqued conventional observances through the image of an insect congregation.[4] Like Robert G. Ingersoll and many others with Calvinist backgrounds, this "Brevet Presbyterian" turned against Christianity as such in rejecting the stern form of it he had known as a child.

But until the 1880s Mark Twain's hostility was fitful, and the record of his opinions for the previous years indicates, on the whole, an easy tolerance concerning religion. Because of his agreement with the tenets and aims of American secular culture, he could admire missionaries who propagated it: "[They] have clothed [the Sandwich Islanders], educated them, broken up the tyrannous authority of their chiefs. . . . the wonderful benefit conferred upon this people by the missionaries is so prominent, so palpable and so unquestionable. . . ."[5] And in 1870, immediately after denouncing "the God of the Bible," he posited a "true God" whose "beneficent, exact, and changeless ordering of the machinery of his colossal universe is proof that he is at least steadfast to his purposes; whose unwritten laws, so far as they affect man, being equal and impartial, show that he is just and fair. . . . "[6] At times what may seem to have been attacks on Christian institutions were really Mark Twain's attempts to discriminate the worst from the best in the national culture while he was establishing his own place as member and spokesman. His hatred of snobbish and sanctimonious clergymen in "Mr. Beecher and the Clergy" (1869), "About Smells" (1870), and "The Indignity Put upon the Remains of George Holland by the Rev. Mr. Sabine" (1871) was a response to their denials of democratic principles, especially offensive because of the clergy's elite status. While moving up in

3. Dates after titles are those of publication and, for works unpublished in Mark Twain's lifetime, of composition. Dates of works not in this volume appear only when they are obscure or important.

4. SLC to Annie Taylor, 25 May [1856], cited in *Selected Shorter Writings of Mark Twain*, ed. Walter Blair (Boston: Houghton Mifflin Co., 1962), pp. 3–4.

5. *MTH*, p. 289.   6. *MTB*, p. 412.

his culture Mark Twain believed the best of it. Intolerance, superstition, and other religious vices were only deviations from an enlightenment he thought characteristic of America.

In the early 1880s Mark Twain set down his religious principles in a group of brief manifestos ("Three Statements of the Eighties"). He declared that there was a God, yet that He never communicated with man or intervened in human affairs through Special Providences. The idea of eternal punishment was incredible because such punishment could accomplish no good end; moral laws were the product of human experience, and human action whether good or bad could not affect God. Certain harsh and contradictory passages in the Bible indicated that it was not the work of God but of incompetent men, and although latter-day Protestantism had reared highly moral individuals on its humane passages, the Bible nevertheless still contained sanctions for atrocities. These three papers, together with many of Mark Twain's notebook entries, letters, and book acquisitions, show that throughout the decade he felt dismayed curiosity at the creeds and disciplines of Christianity. He took a contemptuous interest in the beliefs of other men, ranging from past theologians like Samuel Clarke and Cotton Mather to his contemporaries George Washington Cable and Andrew Langdon. He read books that supported skepticism, for instance *The Autobiography of Mark Rutherford*, but he was more concerned with those he disapproved, such as Mather's *Magnalia Christi Americana*.[7] Meanwhile he became fond of cosmological images that countered the egoistic myth of Christianity, particularly entertaining

7. A1911, pp. 16, 49, lists Clarke's *Mirror or Looking Glass both for Saints and Sinners*, edition of London, 1671, and Mather's *Magnalia Christi Americana*, edition of Hartford, 1820, both containing heated marginalia. A reference to President Garfield's death in the Clarke marginalia cannot be earlier than 19 September 1881; Mark Twain dated both Mather volumes November 1881. For his opinion of Cable's religion see, for example, *MTHL*, p. 520; for his opinion of Langdon's see "Letter from the Recording Angel." He acquired *The Autobiography of Mark Rutherford* in 1886 (A1911, p. 61).

the fancy that "we are only the microscopic trichina concealed in the blood of some vast creature's veins, and it is that vast creature whom God concerns Himself about and not us."[8]

In the 1880s Mark Twain also wrote preliminary statements of his psychological theories, which have been considered emergences of the old Calvinism in secular form. On 19 February 1883, before the Hartford Monday Evening Club, he delivered "What Is Happiness?," which he later recalled as a harbinger of *What Is Man?*:

That was the chapter denying that there is any such thing as personal merit; maintaining that a man is merely a machine . . . no machine is entitled to praise for any of its acts. . . . the human machine gets all its inspirations from the outside and is not capable of originating an idea of any kind in its own head . . . no man ever does a duty for duty's sake but only for the sake of the satisfaction he personally gets out of doing the duty. . . .[9]

Later, in "The Character of Man" (1885), he stated these ideas more violently and added that man had instincts of malice, cruelty, servility, and nastiness. He once planned to read even this attack before the Monday Evening Club. At the end of the decade he made his tenets public through Hank Morgan in *A Connecticut Yankee*:

Training—training is everything; training is all there is *to* a person. . . . there is no such thing as nature; what we call by that misleading name is merely heredity and training. We have no thoughts of our own, no opinions of our own; they are transmitted to us, trained into us.

8. *MTN*, p. 170; 12 August 1883. In that period the image also appears in 1884 and 1886: Notebook 18, TS p. 7, and Notebook 21, TS p. 14.

9. *MTE*, p. 240. For the date of Mark Twain's paper see *The List of Members of the Monday Evening Club Together with the Record of Papers Read at their Meetings 1869–1954*, intro. Howell Cheney (Hartford: Privately Printed, 1954), p. 37.

In that decade, which he came to regard as the time of his enlight-enment concerning human nature,[10] Mark Twain used these notions for purposes of attack and reidentification. They were ways of measuring the illusoriness of a faith in man that he was giving up but that his culture continued to propagate. At the same time, his deterministic principles accounted for the pervas-iveness of the opposite faith in a way that discredited it: where many men believed in human goodness, free will, and personal merit, they were directed by heredity and training toward their belief. In those early days of his theorizing Mark Twain thought his knowledge relocated him on the side of a superior conscious-ness, reserved for the honest few. Later, though he often enjoyed a grim satisfaction in his awareness, he would remind himself that there was no escape from the natural imprisonment, not even for someone who recognized it.

In his remaining years, especially from 1897 through 1909, Mark Twain enlarged upon his basic ideas in numerous works and fragments. His reluctance to disclose his opinions to the public led him to seek indirect ways of presenting them; yet he left many manuscripts incomplete, and he suppressed almost all that he finished, probably because he was unsure of the safety of his de-vices and doubted their power to persuade his unreceptive con-temporaries. One of his devices of indirection was what may be termed the rhetorical occasion. He would often assume the pose that only the stimulus of recent events and current topics made him reveal his beliefs. The occasion of "Man's Place in the Animal World" (1896), war atrocities in Crete, allowed him to justify indictments he had already expressed in previous manuscripts. He introduced other occasions as if they were to be his subjects but then offhand, by what seemed to be accidents of his material, turned to his arguments on determinism or the "damned human

10. In the Autobiographical Dictations of 11 August and 4 September 1906 Mark Twain says he has been studying man with "close attention" for twenty-five years.

race." The most deceptive of such pieces was "Macfarlane" (1894?), which Albert Bigelow Paine and critics after him read as a factual narrative about a man whose pessimistic philosophy influenced young Sam Clemens, rather than as an expression through this character of Mark Twain's own beliefs, formulated in maturity. If the manuscript is incomplete, as it seems, the resulting imbalance of narrative over argument may help account for the traditional interpretation.[11] The opportunity to present what was probably the most effective of these arguments from occasion came in 1909, when he was asked to contribute to a series projected by *Harper's Bazar* in which famous people would discuss the turning points of their lives. In his contribution, " 'The Turning Point of My Life' " (1910), Mark Twain immediately disputed the notion of singular crises and then used well-known details of his early years to show that circumstances and temperament had made him a writer. The career was unplanned, he contended, and there were thousands of equally important turning points: "Circumstance furnished the capital, and my temperament told me what to do with it." This article gave him his best opportunity to present his theories without fear of resentment, for they appeared to be both a common-sense response to the premise of the series and the engaging humility of a great man deprecating his accomplishments.

Another device of indirection, by far his favorite, was the use of spokesmen to deliver his arguments. These were generally characters who, often because of a remarkable superiority or inferiority, seemed outside of middle-class culture, in some cases alien to the human race. In 1882 he wrote a fragment of dialogue in which two Negroes argue about God's responsibility for man's sins. One of them reasons that if God made man capable of sin and yet holds him accountable, it shows:

dat a man is a powful sight mo' juster en what de Lawd is! Kase de Lawd take en buil' up a man so he jes *boun'* to kill people, en lie en

11. For argument in detail on this question see Paul Baender, "Alias Macfarlane: A Revision of Mark Twain Biography," *American Literature* 38 (1966): 187–197.

steal en embellish, en den he take en jam him into de everlast'n fire en brimstone for it! . . . I'll resk it, dat any book dat's got any sich stuff as dat in it warn't ever writ by de Lawd. . . .[12]

In an 1887 notebook entry Mark Twain imagined a supernatural creature (Gahsh) with a gospel of his own, and his dimensions suggest that Gahsh was to be the "vast creature" whose veins man infested: "His foot-ball is suspended in front of his face, and every time he winks his eye, it is night on it. His speech is thunder and they run into their holes. His shoe-sole is 13 or 14,000 miles. So is his face."[13] Later, after putting aside "The Character of Man," Mark Twain rephrased several of its accusations in "Letters from a Dog" (1889?), in which the philosophic Newfoundland Smith tells another dog about human vices. Verbal parallels show that this manuscript led in turn to the doctrinal part of "Macfarlane," with only the change of spokesmen. Still other such vehicles were Hank Morgan in A Connecticut Yankee, Philip Traum in the "Chronicle of Young Satan" version of "The Mysterious Stranger," the slave Jerry in "Corn-Pone Opinions" (1901), Sol Bailey in "Which Was It?" and the Old Man in What Is Man? In 1898 his notes show that he even thought of using an ant as spokesman: "Visit to and talks with politicians and professors, soldiers and slaves among the ants. One had written a book on human beings—proves Selfishness, No Merit, &c."[14]

Disguise of his own opinions was not Mark Twain's only motive for inventing spokesmen. He used his Negroes and other outsiders to remind middle-class readers that different perspectives could be wiser than their own, and often he used nonhuman or antihuman spokesmen to support condemnations of human nature. If man, the only creature with the Moral Sense, was selfish, cruel, bigoted, and slavish, and yet given to fantastic conceit, it would take an extrahuman morality to comprehend his viciousness. Thus he needed figures like Newfoundland Smith, the ant-

12. Notebook 16, TS p. 42.   13. Notebook 22, TS p. 5.
14. Notebook 32, TS p. 52; the "book on human beings" was What Is Man?, begun in the same year.

author of *What Is Man?*, and the discursive Satan of "The
Mysterious Stranger" and "Letters from the Earth"—characters
widely spaced on the scale of species but equal in their moral
superiority to man. The rare human spokesmen who were com-
parably disengaged had weird manners and at times spectral appearances, like Macfarlane, "The Corpse" in the fragmentary "A
Human Bloodhound," and Orrin Lloyd Godkin in another fragment, "Indiantown."

[Godkin] always spoke in light and airy disparagement of the human
race; and also as if it were a species in which he had no personal concern; in fact he isolated himself from the human race by a pregnant
phrase, and complacently spoke of its members collectively as "those
foreigners." Invited to explain this attitude, he said he had a super-
human strain. . . . Asked how he could condescend to associate with
the human race, he said it was very simple: to him, men were the same
as the other animals.[15]

The use of such characters was also a way of reducing man to a
trivial place in the range of existence. From "Captain Stormfield's Visit to Heaven" through "Three Thousand Years Among
the Microbes," Mark Twain invented myths and figures to shock
human egoism with the spectacle of a universe inhabited at its
telescopic, microscopic, and generic reaches by moral beings un-
concerned about mankind.

After the 1880s the chief development in Mark Twain's religious opinions was that they became systematically contemptuous. In passages deleted from "The Character of Man" he had conceived religious motivation no less bitterly than he did in later
years, but in the 1880s such conceptions required special impetus—
in 1885, for example, his fury against Hartford Republicans who
had opposed the Mugwumps. Otherwise his attacks were comparatively restrained. Even a work so heated by dislike as "Letter from
the Recording Angel" (1887) did not become a diatribe on religion; it was at most a charge that there were self-righteous hypo-

15. WWD, p. 165.

crites among conventional believers, a charge that the most fervent Christian would not have denied. Similarly, his criticisms in "Bible Teaching and Religious Practice" (1890) admitted a progress of civilization beyond the ages of intolerance, superstition, and slavery; he was only reminding lay Christians that the clergy had opposed every advance and that the former sanctions of barbarity were still in the Bible. But as the 1890s wore on, he settled upon motives of conformism and selfishness to characterize believers. They were Christians or Muhammadans, Catholics or Baptists, chiefly because of training, and the personal forces that led to conversion or devoutness were all self-interested though in respectable disguise. In his last decade he ridiculed these motives through many examples—the biased reading of historical events by the light of supposed prophecy ("As Concerns Interpreting the Deity," 1905); the acceptance of moral imperatives that ran counter to human nature ("In the Animal's Court," 1905); the glorification of God for His creation though no one altogether admired it ("God," 1905).

The severity of Mark Twain's views on religious motivation was part of the increasing cynicism of his last twenty years. He lost Hank Morgan's belief in "that one microscopic atom . . . that is truly *me*," insofar as this meant a freedom from the determinisms of temperament and environment, and he added another and more sinister force, the Moral Sense. The Moral Sense became, for Mark Twain, a source of man's incorrigible depravity: it enabled man to distinguish right from wrong so as to choose the wrong, which he chose from a vicious disposition. In keeping with these traits, Mark Twain devised a dynamics and pattern of history. Men were moved by prospects of power and dominance, with the result that among individuals, classes, and nations the typical relation was a tyranny of the strong over the weak. Even fortunate countries like the United States, whose institutions provided a certain equilibrium and restraint, would degenerate into this condition. Those already in power would entrench themselves or, with a change of circumstances, the victims would become the

masters. Mark Twain often projected the second alternative. As
early as the eighties he imagined "Negro supremacy—the whites
underfoot" in a hundred years,[16] and later he predicted shifts of
religious power: "The Catholics are moving steadily and surely
toward dominion";[17] by 1940 the Christian Scientists would become "the governing power in the Republic—to remain that, permanently."[18] Self-interested and therefore easily led, the masses
would fall into line no matter how drastic the upheavals. From a
need to seem rational and independent they would supply reasoned conviction for the beliefs imposed upon them, and with all
the more zeal if the beliefs were absurd.

Mark Twain's conceptions of God changed accordingly. In
"Three Statements of the Eighties" he could still say without
irony that "the goodness, the justice, and the mercy of God [were]
manifested in His works," for he believed the nature and condition of man were on the whole benign. But when he came to
believe otherwise, he characterized God as the "Source of all inconsistency."[19] The creator of man was responsible for man—for
his physical and mental agonies, for his vices and misfortunes. If
He damned sinners, He was cruel. If He did not mean to train
them to righteousness, "it proves one thing conclusively: if our
Maker *is* all-powerful for good or evil, He is not in His right
mind."[20] On the other hand, God would be petty to care about
a creature so trivial as man. A truly superior being might create
our world with all its tortures, but after the creation He should
"turn His attention elsewhere and trouble Himself no further
about the matter."[21] Through these conceptions Mark Twain
offered more specific attacks on Christianity than he might have
through the general denials of atheism. For his target was not so

16. Notebook 18, TS p. 19.
17. Late marginal note in *The Memoirs of the Duke of Saint-Simon*, trans. Bayle
St. John (London: Bickers and Son, n.d.), 3:3; MTP.
18. *Christian Science*; p. 251 of this volume.
19. "God," Supplement A4, p. 492.
20. "Things a Scotsman Wants to Know," p. 400.
21. "God," Supplement A4, p. 486.

much the Christian premises as their traditional conclusions; God was destructive rather than providential, contemptuous of man's sins rather than forgiving. Mark Twain's belief in these notions may be questioned because of their satiric convenience. But he claimed to believe in the God of his later views "with all [his] might,"[22] and if he really did not, the reason behind his claim was probably that he confused a private urgency with belief. For his later views were the revelation of a disaster he could express and tolerate only by giving it cosmic involvement. That man was a minor phase of evolution was true but not enough. He had to be trivial in the eyes of a God who created billions of worlds, and the pointlessness of his misery had to imply a God who began it pointlessly. With the imagination of these vast circumstances Mark Twain pictured the career of man as both a farce and a tragedy. Though a part of the action, he kept an onlooker's distance sufficient to preserve his sensibilities of astonishment, disgust, and protest.

What Is Man?

Mark Twain wrote the first draft of *What Is Man?* between April and July 1898 in Vienna and the nearby resort of Kaltenleutgeben.[23] Much of it appeared without revision in the published book; it was a first draft in the sense that it covered only slightly more than half of the final text. As was typical of his writing, the draft shows few extensive changes made during original composition, and in this case the author was working with a form and an argument so familiar to him that composition was unusually congenial. He had experimented with the dialogue form as early as 1882, in the Negro fragment mentioned earlier, and as late as

22. "God," p. 477.
23. So dated and placed in Mark Twain's hand on the cover of the earliest typescript. Because the writing of *What Is Man?* was extremely complicated, a more detailed account, with table, is provided in the Textual Notes.

1897, in a draft of "The Moral Sense." He tended toward this form when his material was controversial, for he liked to envision a masterfulness in speakers who represented his views, and sophistry and humiliation in their antagonists. In works like "Facts Concerning the Recent Carnival of Crime in Connecticut," "Which Was It?" and "The Mysterious Stranger," he inserted dialogues whose formal difference from *What Is Man?* consisted in little more than their narrative context.

All the controlling ideas appeared in the 1898 draft. Man is a machine in that his behavior is determined by heredity and temperament, environment and training. Thus he deserves no praise for good acts or blame for bad; every act is beyond his control, and he always seeks to please himself. One should not attempt to deny these facts by the conventional distinctions between men and animals. The superiority of human intelligence is a matter of degree rather than quality, and the Moral Sense does not raise man above the other creatures. In a chapter later deleted, Mark Twain argued that it placed man beneath them because it enabled him to do wrong. In two other deleted chapters he turned to considerations of God.[24] Traditional accounts of heaven tell us, he contended, that only the devout and righteous are admitted, thus showing that God does not prize intellectual achievement. From experience and the Bible it is also obvious that He loathes mankind. He inflicts miseries as a matter of course and punishes man for sins He made him able to commit. But man deserves hardly more than God's indifference because man, like God, is cruel, vindictive, and tyrannical. Thus it seems absurd to believe that heaven is God's reward for righteousness, particularly if the "lower animals"—morally superior to man—are not admitted. And besides, the miseries of this life suggest that God furnishes greater ones in the hereafter.

Mark Twain did not add substantially to the 1898 draft until

24. "The Quality of Man," Supplement A3, and "God," Supplement A4. The latter was called a continuation on the cover of its typescript, as though Mark Twain also considered it a sequel to the first draft.

late 1901 or early 1902, more than a year after his return to America in the fall of 1900. Other projects may have been more urgent, such as "The Man That Corrupted Hadleyburg," probably begun in August 1898, or his first sustained commentary on Christian Science, begun in the fall of that year. But it is likely that he put the draft aside because he considered it done; indeed had he published it upon composition, he might never have touched it again. From 1898 through 1905, however, he regarded his "gospel" as a private interest to be shared only with his household and chosen acquaintances, too dangerous to his reputation for public knowledge. And so as time passed the manuscript became subject to elaborations and afterthoughts, which is all that the later additions contributed. The first were the segment "Instances in Point" (but not "Further Instances") and another containing the "Admonition." "Instances in Point" was chiefly a long example of self-interest based upon a novel Mark Twain happened to read. The "Admonition" segment has been judged contradictory, in that it appears to grant the possibility of deliberate moral action.[25] But Mark Twain intended no compromise of his deterministic principles. He argued that even if a man could improve his character, he could not do so through resolution and could not transcend self-contentment as the motive for his action. He could at most follow the inevitable forces of training and pleasure to his moral advantage.

Mark Twain later said he completed *What Is Man?* in 1902.[26] This was a typical misrecollection. In 1902 he had his daughter Jean prepare a typescript that incorporated the parts just mentioned, but he continued adding and revising at least through September 1905. Earlier that year he had Jean prepare a fresh typescript, which eventually became printer's copy. Among the additions was "After an Interval of Days," the first half probably

25. For instance, in John Adams, "Mark Twain as Psychologist," *Bookman* (London) 39, no. 234 (March 1911): 271. The standard modern analysis of this problem, and of the dialogue as a whole, is Alexander E. Jones, "Mark Twain and the Determinism of *What Is Man?*," *American Literature* 29 (1957): 1–17.
26. MTE, p. 242.

written between 1902 and 1904 but not typed until 1905, the second half written and typed in 1905. "Free Will," "A Difficult Question," and the "Conclusion" were written and typed in 1905. "Further Instances," "Not Two Values, but only One," and "The Master Passion" were holograph insertions in the printer's copy. Another important change in the printer's copy was a reversal in the original order of chapters 1 and 2. The last revision of consequence, possibly made as late as 1906, was a systematic change in what had become chapter 2 of language relating to motivation. From the 1898 draft through the typing of the printer's copy, Mark Twain had used "selfishness" and allied terms to characterize the personal force behind all actions; indeed "Selfishness" was a provisional title in 1898.[27] Over these terms he now inscribed "spiritual comfort" and similar expressions. Thus "Hamilton's act was thoroughly selfish" became "Hamilton's act was compelled by the inborn necessity of contenting his own spirit"; and "[Love, Hate, Charity, etc.] are all forms of Selfishness" became "They are all forms of self-contentment, self-gratification." Such changes made the tone less opprobrious, and he may have thought of them only when editing the text for publication, as a way of appeasing his readers. Yet the revisions also affected meaning. Many passages in the original version implied selfishness in the ordinary sense, that is, as a deliberate choice of self-interest which one was free to refuse. The revisions expressed what Mark Twain meant all along: men were selfish in the sense that they had to satisfy their consciences and temperaments, regardless of consequences.

In March or April 1906 he decided to have *What Is Man?* printed privately.[28] The book was set, corrected, and finally revised during May and June, and the manufacture completed by mid-August of a limited edition of 250 copies.[29] The publication

27. For instance, in Notebook 32, TS p. 29.
28. On 20 March Mark Twain had to cancel a luncheon engagement with the Doubledays, to whom he planned to read the dialogue (Isabel Lyon typescript diary, 20 March [1906]), and by 16 May Doubleday had received proof for galley no. 19 (Frank N. Doubleday to SLC, 16 May 1906).
29. *MTB*, p. 1321; *BAL*, p. 216; Frank N. Doubleday to SLC, 24 August 1906.

was anonymous, and he took care to conceal his authorship from most people. He had his friend Frank N. Doubleday, of Doubleday, Page & Co., serve as liaison with the printer, the DeVinne Press of New York. The printer's copy went from Clemens through Doubleday to DeVinne, and Doubleday returned proofs to the author. Proof revisions and printer's queries went through the same channels.[30] Beneath the preface in printer's copy his daughter Jean had typed "Mark Twain," which her father cut out of the page realizing that even heavy cancellation lines could allow the compositor to discover his identity from impressions on the back. In proof he deleted an obsession and a recurrent dream which, though attributed to the Young Man, would probably have suggested Mark Twain to knowledgeable readers.[31] He had Doubleday copyright the book in the name of J. W. Bothwell, DeVinne's superintendent,[32] and drafted a statement to be sent out over Bothwell's signature: "By an early mail I am venturing to send you a copy of a small book entitled 'What Is Man?' 250 copies of which have been printed, for private circulation only. I am doing this by request of the author, who wishes to remain unknown."[33] The following year Clemens recalled presenting only four copies on his own—to "discreet persons"—but ten or twelve by Doubleday through Bothwell.[34]

The printing of *What Is Man?* was merely a convenience to the author. From the 1898 draft through 1905 he had tried the dialogue on many people, sometimes on those disposed to admire,

30. For instance, as evident in J. W. Bothwell to Frank N. Doubleday, 29 May and 20 July 1906; Frank N. Doubleday to SLC, 28 May 1906.

31. An obsession with the "Punch, brothers, punch" jingle and the dream of being snowbound in the Humboldt Mountains; see the Textual Notes for the text and place of these passages.

32. As correctly identified in *MTB*, p. 1321, and the Autobiographical Dictation of 2 November 1908 (though Mark Twain misrecalls his name and other details); see also letters cited in note 30, above. Merle Johnson incorrectly identified him as a clerk in the law offices that handled Clemens' account: *A Bibliography of the Works of Mark Twain*, rev. ed. (New York: Harper & Brothers, 1935), p. 83. The source of this error is unknown.

33. Isabel Lyon secretarial notebook, 4 August 1906.

34. *MTE*, p. 242.

man, and is about equally sure to waste-basket a philosophy which comes to him untagged with a name commanding attention; the other was, that no man, howsoever sane and intelligent can read a new philosophy understandingly.[43]

Personal confrontation had been the wiser course: "whenever I read the small book myself to a person of good intelligence . . . I always captured a disciple. Generally against the disciple's will. . . ."

Mark Twain's opinions, as well as his authorship, remained unknown to the general public until he died. Two days after his death, as though awaiting the occasion, the New York *Tribune* broke the secret in a feature article replete with long quotations, and the news was picked up by other papers and journals.[44] Though the *Tribune* reporter apparently had seen the book, he described the argument as bearing particularly on "religious beliefs." Probably from an informant, whose source may have been Mark Twain, he heard what became a common explanation of the secrecy: "the author, discouraged because the world always wanted to make a joke of whatever he wrote or spoke, took the anonymous method of putting his thoughts before them. . . ." Popular reaction to the disclosure was mixed but seldom warm. The *Dial* thought the meditations on necessity and free will "failed to produce any results of significance," especially because they lacked "novelty."[45] *Current Literature* indulged in pathos: "It is surely one of the ironies of fate that Mark Twain, greatest of American humorists, should have been a sad-hearted man, a fatalist and a pessimist. He did not often reveal his philosophy. He almost seemed ashamed of it."[46] The journal included two late photos, one showing Clemens in bed, pen in hand, looking up sadly, with

43. Autobiographical Dictation of 2 November 1908, for this and the following quotation.
44. New York *Tribune*, 23 April 1910, p. 7.
45. *Dial* 48, no. 574 (16 May 1910): 345.
46. "Mark Twain's Pessimistic Philosophy," *Current Literature* 48, no. 6 (June 1910): 643–647.

a caption that read: "THE MOST DESPAIRING OF HUMORISTS | By an irony of fate, Mark Twain, who made the whole world laugh, was at heart pessimistic and melancholy." The other showed him regarding the landscape from his veranda at Redding, Connecticut with a caption that began: "HIS LAST LOOK AT THE SKY." This sentimentality did not accompany an endorsement of *What Is Man?* By fashioning Mark Twain as a romantic clown—humorous on the outside, somber on the inside—the journal suggested the refutation which later critics would make explicit, that his pessimism was a function of his personal griefs and disappointments.

The book did not altogether lack supporters. In 1910 the Rationalist Press Association, whose honorary members included Ernst Haeckel, Paul Carus, and Lester Frank Ward, sponsored the first English edition.[47] In 1919 the British journal *Athenaeum*, though quite unfavorable, reported that the work had been "hailed with jubilation by the rebels. . . ."[48] But by 1920 formulas of disapproval were set that have not much changed to the present day. Reviewing *What Is Man? and Other Essays*, the first American trade edition and the first edition to reach a wide audience, the New York *Times* complained:

It would be difficult to find anything more dreary, cynical, pessimistic than the view of life here revealed. One refuses to believe that it voices the settled, mature convictions held by Mr. CLEMENS—at least one does not wish to believe it. . . . What gain is there in being told that man is merely a machine, and that there is practically nothing real in his idealism, no basis for his brave dreams, his aspirations toward a life of spiritual beauty and achievement? There is nothing new in pessimism of this kind.[49]

The United States had just entered World War I when this edition came out in May 1917, and Mark Twain's arguments were

47. For bibliographical data see Description of Texts, under the Textual Notes. Paine's statement that the edition was published in the absence of an English copyright implies that it was unauthorized; see 26Z:xi.

48. *Athenaeum* no. 4675 (5 December 1919): 1289.

49. *New York Times Review of Books*, 3 June 1917, p. 216.

scarcely suited to the temper of the time. Yet objections after the war were equally intense and were based upon a similar preference for hopeful views. One critic, discounting Mark Twain's pessimism by his "intense sensitiveness to suffering and evil," advised listening "to the real Mark Twain—the man who testifies to his thorough and unceasing happiness. . . ."[50] Another critic, much like Brooks and DeVoto later, thought *What Is Man?* "the profane utterance of a defeated soul."[51] Although more recent critics have not openly been disturbed by Mark Twain's somberness, they have continued to dismiss the work because of its personal motives and its lack of novelty. The work refers us chiefly to his "private sorrows and apprehensions," and "the kind of determinism Mark Twain was presenting had been presented many times before. . . ."[52]

CHRISTIAN SCIENCE

Mark Twain wrote *Christian Science* in two stints, fall 1898 to May 1899 in Vienna, and summer or fall 1902 through February 1903 in the United States. If he began it only after completing "The Man That Corrupted Hadleyburg," the earliest possible month was October 1898.[53] In the first period he wrote what became book 1, chapters 1 through 8, originally planned as a series of articles. In America he completed book 1 in summer or fall 1902; and in January and February 1903 (at Riverdale, New York) he completed all of book 2—far more, and in much less time, than the initial phase. The manuscript and structure of the initial phase

50. Horace James Bridges, *As I Was Saying* (Boston: Marshall Jones Co., 1923), pp. 38, 50; from "The Pessimism of Mark Twain," an essay first published in the *Standard* (Cooperstown, New York) in July 1919.

51. Waldo Frank, *Our America* (New York: Boni and Liveright, 1919), p. 43.

52. Warner Berthoff, *The Ferment of Realism* (New York: Free Press, 1965), p. 75; James M. Cox, *Mark Twain: The Fate of Humor* (Princeton: Princeton University Press, 1966), p. 290.

53. The last leaf of the "Hadleyburg" manuscript (Morgan Library) is dated October 1898.

suggest sporadic composition, with pauses after chapters 4 and 6. But there were several reasons for swift completion in 1903. He then had a book in mind, to consist of the earlier portion and the work in progress, which Harper & Brothers wanted to publish at once. In December 1902 he began communications with W. D. McCrackan and Frederick W. Peabody—the first a partisan, the other an enemy of Christian Science—which helped inspire his anger and zest during the next two months. Throughout that winter Livy was bedridden with heart disease and nervous prostration, and on Christmas Eve Jean contracted pneumonia.[54] Clemens' resulting confinement was particularly suited to the lengthy disputations of book 2.

The publication of *Christian Science* was a more complicated matter than the writing. What became book 1, chapters 1 through 4, was published as "Christian Science and the Book of Mrs. Eddy," in *Cosmopolitan* for October 1899. The article was a popular success, for which the author received $200 as a bonus,[55] yet he did not carry out his plan of a series. He may have changed his mind as soon as Henry Mills Alden, editor of *Harper's Magazine*, proposed a new collection of his short works to be issued by Harper, for on Alden's letter he jotted "Xn Science" as a possible item under the heading "Articles for new book of sketches."[56] Harper issued *The Man That Corrupted Hadleyburg and Other Stories and Essays* the next year, but the Christian Science material appeared only in the English and German versions, *The Man That Corrupted Hadleyburg and Other Stories and Sketches*. In this, besides the original "Christian Science and the Book of Mrs. Eddy," Mark Twain included what became book 1, chapters 5 through 8, under the same title, dated 1 May 1899. He then apparently dropped the subject of further publication until summer

54. LLMT, pp. 338–339, 341.
55. MTB, p. 1068; MTHL, p. 709.
56. Henry Mills Alden to SLC, 14 [24?] September 1899, and SLC to Henry Mills Alden, 30 October 1899. Mark Twain had thought of publication in a book even before the *Cosmopolitan* article appeared: SLC to Frank E. Bliss, 31 March 1899, TS in MTP.

1902, when he considered running a series in *Cosmopolitan* which Collier would later issue as a book.[57] These ideas came to nothing, and in September he tried to place unspecified Christian Science material with *Harper's Weekly*.[58] The items were probably those he succeeded in placing with the *North American Review* the following month[59] and which appeared in December 1902 and January 1903 as "Christian Science" and "Christian Science—II." These installments were slightly revised versions of what became book 1, chapters 5 through 8, already published in the English and German editions of *Hadleyburg*. "Christian Science—III," in the February number, and "Mrs. Eddy in Error," published in April, were excerpts from the work in progress. Minus the "Later Still" section, the former became book 1, chapter 9.

In early December 1902 Mark Twain was planning to use his old and new writings on Christian Science only as part, though a large part, of another miscellaneous volume.[60] But by late January he had stipulated with Harper a book entirely on the subject. At this point the story becomes ironic. On 28 January Frederick A. Duneka, the Harper editor, wrote him that Harper wished to issue the book in the spring, and on 11 February he wrote again, pressing Mark Twain to finish the book for publication by the end of April.[61] The author did as urged, despite a siege of bronchitis in February,[62] and the book was set in type and proofread by the middle of March. Yet after all this rush the publishers suddenly changed their minds. In *Publishers' Weekly* for 21 March their advertisement included *Christian Science* in the spring list, but in the number for 11 April they announced that "Neither Harper & Brothers nor the *North American Review* will publish in book form Mark Twain's papers on 'Christian Science.' All orders for

57. Notebook 35, TS p. 24.
58. *Ibid.*, p. 26.
59. *Ibid.*, p. 32.
60. SLC to W. D. McCrackan, 5 December 1902.
61. F. A. Duneka to SLC, 28 January and 11 February 1903.
62. *LLMT*, p. 342.

the book now on file will be cancelled."[63] Mark Twain's explanation for this reversal was that Harper did not dare antagonize the Christian Scientists.[64] There is reason to believe him. Harper had been the only publisher of three to omit "Christian Science and the Book of Mrs. Eddy" from the *Hadleyburg* volume. In his letter of 28 January, immediately after urging the author to finish his book, Duneka called it "mighty strong meat"—and presumably he had seen none of book 2. Yet without known pressure from Mark Twain, who claimed indifference, Harper renewed interest as early as 1905 and finally issued the book in February 1907.[65] They chose a propitious time: Christian Science and Mary Baker Eddy were once again under strong attack in newspapers and periodicals, as they had not been in 1903.[66] Harper apparently scrupled at offending the Christian Scientists only while the popular temper was calm.

The eccentric structure of the book was due mainly to these vagaries of composition and publication. While his articles ran in the *North American Review*, Mark Twain received corrections of factual errors from W. D. McCrackan and other correspondents. He corrected some in the main text; others he corrected in footnotes, as if supplements were appropriate for material written four years earlier. Thus the statement on the original title page—"With Notes Containing Corrections to Date"—referred only to the footnotes in book 1. A greater oddity was the location of the appendixes before the last two chapters. The reason for it was his decision to include "Mrs. Eddy in Error." Originally this was part

63. *Publisher's Weekly* 63, no. 1625 (21 March 1903): 772; *ibid.*, no. 1628 (11 April 1903): 984.

64. For instance, in SLC to Dr. Powell, 27 May 1907.

65. Mark Twain claimed indifference in his letter to Dr. Powell of 27 May 1907 (cited above), but in 1906 he was clearly irked at Harper's continued failure to issue the book: SLC to H. H. Rogers, 18 May and 13 June 1906, MTHHR, pp. 607, 610. Harper's renewal of interest is discussed in F. A. Duneka to SLC, 7 April 1905.

66. Ernest Sutherland Bates and John V. Dittemore, *Mary Baker Eddy, The Truth and the Tradition* (New York: A. A. Knopf, 1932), pp. 378, 402.

of book 2, chapter 8, following "The Sanctum Sanctorum and the Sacred Chair"; later he had it follow chapter 9. After taking it out for the April *North American Review*, he apparently could not with ease insert it in either place, perhaps because that section was already set in type. But location after the appendixes gave "Mrs. Eddy in Error" the status of a conclusion, for which it was obviously unsuited, and so Mark Twain wrote another chapter to follow. The division into books 1 and 2 accommodated his shift in focus between 1899 and 1903. In the first part he treated Christian Science as a recent socio-religious development. Thus he covered its peculiarities of tenet and language, with humorous stress upon an outsider's difficulties in understanding them; the basis of its special attraction, with testimonials from believers; its prospects as a trust and an established church in view of its shrewd appeal to human needs. In 1903 his chief target was Mrs. Eddy. Though he had more to say about church tenets and organization, he regarded them as evidence of her rare gifts for gaining and consolidating power. He transposed to book 2 his charge in *Cosmopolitan* that she did not write *Science and Health*, and all his humor and ridicule in book 2 were at her expense.

Because of its diffuseness and its complexities of attitude *Christian Science* often confused early readers, not just believers and skeptics but moderate critics who wanted the author to take a clear-cut stand based on familiar points. His disfavor was qualified, and some of his arguments were uncommon. Though he might satirize the extravagances of faith-healing, he regarded it as legitimate treatment for certain ailments and on occasion recommended it to his family. Yet he despised Christian Science as a religious movement, with its prophet and disciples, its sacred texts, idols, and cultist vocabulary. He believed it was an exploitation, for the founder's own ends, of man's ability to cause and cure illness through acts of mind. The movement, he predicted, would expand until it became an established church, with full control over politics and culture in America, because it directed human credulity toward two most important goals, physical and spiritual well-being. Euphoria as a treatment for dysphoria might confirm men in a cycle of illusion, but it was known to work, and when given a religious character it too well flattered their cosmic status for them to give it up. No other modern religion so appealed to this credulity as Christian Science, and thus the movement would prove irresistible. As early as December 1902, writing to Frederick W. Peabody, Mark Twain disowned all hope of persuasion:

Have I given you the impression that I was combating Xn Science? or that I am caring how the Xn Scientists "hail" my articles? Relieve yourself of those errors. I wrote the articles to please MYSELF. . . . I am not combating Xn Science—I haven't a thing in the world against it. Making fun of that shameless old swindler, Mother Eddy, is the only thing about it I take any interest in. At bottom I suppose I take a private delight in seeing the human race making an ass of itself again —which it has always done whenever it had a chance. That's its affair— it has the right—and it will sweat blood for it a century hence, and for many centuries thereafter. . . .

See them get down and worship that old creature. A century hence, they'll all be at it. Sanity—in the human race! This is really fulsome.[67]

Extremist reviewers on both sides did not like Mark Twain's articles or his book. Spokesmen for Christian Science disputed his facts and arguments but took greatest offense at his tone. One of them believed it "impossible to read Mark Twain's book . . . without coming to the conclusion that not only Christian Science but every other religious belief appeals to his sense of humor . . . and this gives rise to the question . . . whether the comic point of view is a valuable or even a reliable point of view in the consideration

67. SLC to Frederick W. Peabody, 5 December 1902, quoted in Frederick W. Peabody, *The Religio-Medical Masquerade*, 2nd ed. (New York: F. H. Revell Co., 1915), p. 28. In a draft of a letter to "Dear Sir" (probably Peabody), 11 December [1902], Mark Twain violently objected to unauthorized use of his correspondence; Peabody did not publish the letter of 5 December until after Mark Twain's death.

of religious topics."[68] From Clemens' "pernicious habit" of "license or intemperance in expression" B. O. Flower inferred that his "sense of moral proportion at times seems seriously impaired."[69] The most violent review came earlier, and from the other side. In January 1903, considering only the first *North American Review* article, the *Philadelphia Medical Journal* contended that

[Mark Twain showed] his weakness, both as a prophet and a critic, in what he says about the claims of Mrs. Eddy's religion to be the real thing. 'Its great offer,' he says, 'is to rid the race of pain and disease.' . . . In other words, Mr. Clemens himself comes so near being a follower of Mrs. Eddy that he has not critical insight enough left to see that her claim to be able to abolish disease is the gist of the whole humbug. He already says that Christian Science can abolish *four-fifths* of the disease that afflicts mankind! Clearly, Mark Twain is already four-fifths Eddyite, and of all the blatherskite he has ever written his latest is a little the most senile.[70]

The controversy over Christian Science was too severe and its parties too exclusive for either to take comfort in a marginal allegiance.

Reviewers with more composure were troubled by Mark Twain's irresolution. In December 1902 *Harper's Weekly* suspected that the reader of his recent *North American Review* article would "wonder where Mark Twain has left him; whether Mark approves Christian Science or not."[71] In 1907 the *Dial*, calling the book "curiously tempered," traced the problem to a "mingling of caricature and sober attack" that made it difficult "to determine under which mask the part is going forward."[72] Similarly, the

---

68. Charles Klein, "Mark Twain and Christian Science," *North American Review* 184, no. 611 (15 March 1907): 636.

69. B. O. Flower, "Mark Twain's Attack on Christian Science," *Arena* 38, no. 216 (November 1907): 567.

70. *Philadelphia Medical Journal* 11, no. 1 (3 January 1903): 5.

71. *Harper's Weekly* 46, no. 2401 (27 December 1902): 2022.

72. *Dial* 42, no. 498 (16 March 1907): 190.

Nation judged the work a "skimble-skamble" that could not "be regarded as either a serious or a humorous contribution to the discussion."[73] The mixture of modes, especially the addition of humor, was a common objection among moderate reviewers. The *Spectator* also believed readers would be "bewildered by the confused method,"[74] and the *Catholic World* protested that the "national humorist" so often "had recourse to irreverence towards religious subjects . . . that no person of any religious belief could consider him a suitable candidate for the office of pronouncing a verdict on any cult or creed, even though it be one so grotesque and extravagant as Christian Science."[75] In view of this reaction Mark Twain was wise to suppress other humorous touches. Reminded of Mrs. Eddy's resemblance to Lydia Pinkham, he once planned to include portraits of Mrs. Pinkham in book 1 and Mrs. Eddy in book 2, with no name under either.[76] He had also planned to include several satiric illustrations—his own drawings, crude as ever. One shows Mrs. Eddy as the Statue of Liberty, raising *Science and Health* in her right hand and a dollar in her left, with the faith-healer J. A. Dowie climbing up her side on a ladder. Another shows a stick figure holding *Science and Health*, from which three smaller volumes looking like butterflies are escaping. He labeled them Greek, Hebrew, and Latin in reference to Mrs. Eddy's claim of a youthful proficiency at languages.[77]

Some reviews were favorable. The New York *Times* found the author "vigorous" and "uncompromising," and the *Athenaeum* believed it was "not easy to see how the subject itself could be more fairly dealt with."[78] But these were estimates of his position at least as much as of his performance. No one without animus toward Christian Science or Mrs. Eddy thought highly of

73. *Nation* 84, no. 2172 (14 February 1907): 154.
74. *Spectator* (London) 98, no. 4110 (6 April 1907): 536.
75. *Catholic World* 86, no. 512 (November 1907): 244.
76. Adaline Wheelock Sterling to SLC, 6 April 1903, and manuscript note in Paine 42.
77. Paine 42; for Mrs. Eddy's claim see *Christian Science*, book 2, chapter 1.
78. *New York Times Saturday Review of Books*, 15 June 1907, p. 386; *Athenaeum*, no. 4147 (20 April 1907): 467.

Mark Twain's book, and it has been generally ignored since these subjects ceased to be controversial. There is little evidence of Clemens' feelings about the reception. Drafts of answers to un-favorable letters indicate testiness, which can be explained by his belief that the correspondents had not read the book.[79] Though he had professed not to care whether Harper issued it, he never re-gretted the publication. And whether or not he expected to per-suade anyone, he must have been pleased at the responses of Christian Scientists. Their outrage merely confirmed his long-standing conviction that people who believed they had found the truth looked no further. For the same reason he could enjoy the dissatisfaction of those who thought his criticisms did not go far enough. He had roused in these people prejudices no less absurd than the illusions of Christian Science.

"LETTERS FROM THE EARTH"

Mark Twain wrote "Letters from the Earth" in October and November 1909 at "Stormfield," his home near Redding, Con-necticut. It was his last writing of such length, almost the last of all his works. He may have left the manuscript incomplete—there is no contemporary typescript of it—but he clearly regarded the work as a major statement of his opinions. Like *What Is Man?* it warranted declamation among friends but was too dangerous for publication. "I've been writing 'Letters from the Earth,'" he in-formed his young friend Elizabeth Wallace, "and if you will come here and see us, I'll read passages to you. This book will never be published. Paine likes it, but then, Paine is going to be damned anyhow."[80] Owing much to patterns adapted from Mark Twain's lectures and his Autobiographical Dictation, "Letters from the Earth" was a loose commentary on several of his favorite themes,

79. For instance, in a draft of SLC to J. C. Tebbetts, 7 February [1907], Isabel Lyon secretarial notebook.

80. SLC to Elizabeth Wallace, 13 November 1909, cited in Elizabeth Wallace, *Mark Twain and the Happy Island* (Chicago: A. C. McClurg & Co., 1913), p. 134.

brought up during a running attack on Christian myths and interpretations.

Satan, the voice of the commentary, had fascinated Mark Twain for years.[81] He was attracted by the image of a character rebelling against God, seeing energy and independence in this action, rather than evil. To indicate his liberation from traditional fears, he cast Satan in several works as a figure innocent and glamorous, at times indeed a supernatural Hank Morgan indulging his "circus side" in prodigies of creation and destruction ("The Mysterious Stranger"). For a number of reasons Satan was necessary in the countermyth of Mark Twain's late period. When Satan pitied mankind (for example, "That Day in Eden"), he expressed an awareness of man's original innocence and God's responsibility for man's degradation, a knowledge that could not be trusted if expounded by a merely human character. On the other hand, Satan loathed mankind for offenses that neither God nor man rightly appreciated: sins not against God but against man's best qualities. Mark Twain's Satan was a paragon of those qualities. He possessed the freedom, intelligence, and humor which men claimed for themselves yet denied in their actions and codes. And since he also represented the best in a deity—compassion and disdain where merited—Satan was a measure for the shortcomings of both God and man. By picking for this standard the evil figure in Christian myth, Mark Twain might show how far Western man's habituation in biblical morality had corrupted his moral judgment.

There were important differences between the Satans of "The Mysterious Stranger" and "Letters from the Earth." In the earlier work he was an actor as well as a voice for arguments. Despite his air of unconcern, he interceded on behalf of the good characters and severely punished the bad. Though his wisdom was beyond human comprehension, he addressed the boy narrator with urgency, as if an effort at instruction was worthwhile. If Mark

81. The standard discussion is Coleman O. Parsons, "The Devil and Samuel Clemens," *Virginia Quarterly Review* 23, no. 4 (Autumn 1947): 582–606.

Twain's notion of the character led to his choice of literary form, the Satan of "Letters from the Earth" showed a significant change in conception. The moral and philosophic paragon no longer acted or spoke with a human representative because there could be no profitable relations with mankind. Satan had nothing to do, whether for man or against God, and so his proper role was that of an observer, alien to all except members of his select species. Hence Mark Twain resorted to epistolary fantasy, a form he had used so long ago as 1889 when he wrote his "Letters from a Dog." But the earlier work, spare and august, was a conventional rendering of the genre that tried to avoid the tone of human personality in the speaker. In "Letters from the Earth" the speaker's style, indeed many of his interests and examples, were obviously typical of the author. He no longer cared to aggrandize his opinions through the eloquence and marvels of a Philip Traum. His own style was fit for the arguments, and the arguments only needed expression.

Mark Twain's statement that the work would never be published was apparently only a way of classifying it among those manuscripts too shocking for general knowledge. He did not prohibit publication, and as early as 1912 Albert Bigelow Paine could include a passage in his biography of the author without making it seem a remarkable disclosure.[82] But publication of the whole work was not contemplated until Bernard DeVoto became executor of the Mark Twain Papers following Paine's death in 1937.[83] One of DeVoto's first projects was a miscellaneous volume with "Letters from the Earth" as its feature. He got his typescripts ready for the printer, only to have Clemens' daughter Clara protest the inclusion of certain items. The publication was postponed for more than twenty years, until she withdrew her objections. DeVoto's texts were issued posthumously by Harper & Row in September 1962, through the agency of Henry Nash Smith, then Literary Editor of the Mark Twain Papers. The publication was

82. *MTB*, pp. 1532–1533.
83. For information regarding this publication the editor is indebted to Henry Nash Smith's preface, *LE*, pp. vii–ix.

greeted as an important event, for by the 1960s Mark Twain was counted among the classic American writers—and was one of the few with popular appeal. *Life* magazine printed several selections.[84] The book was on best-seller lists for many weeks and soon gained wide circulation as an inexpensive paperback. Major newspapers and journals issued long reviews, some of them by eminent literary scholars.

"Letters from the Earth," the title piece, received particular attention, and most of it was favorable. Reviewers liked the brilliance of the prose, characterizing it in such phrases as "compressed and savage" and "the real Twain effervescence."[85] But though enough time had passed for a later generation to enjoy the author's style, too much had passed for a serious concern with his opinions. One reviewer thought they would shock only "someone's Victorian aunt" and readers unacquainted with similar products of Mark Twain's late years.[86] After describing Mark Twain's contempt for Christianity as "less likely to shock the modern reader than he imagined," *Time* said that Mark Twain's "bleak outlook in his old age was shaped partly by personal tragedy" and that he was "a 19th century American romantic with a romantic's aversion . . . to organized religion."[87] His arguments had become so dated that the magazine could dismiss them with biographical and historical truisms. The most specific objection to the arguments was that they were too literal. As another reviewer put it, "Biblical scholarship has so radically altered the literalness Twain read into the Scriptures, his satire is likely to seem naive."[88] Noting the same characteristic, *Time* thought it a stratagem to make "the worst possible case for [the Bible] by interpreting it as literally as

84. *Life*, 28 September 1962, pp. 109–121.

85. Howard Mumford Jones, "The Other Face of the Humorist," *New York Times Book Review*, 23 September 1962, p. 7; Willard Thorp, "A Posthumous Treasury of Bittersweet Twain," *New York Herald-Tribune Books*, 30 September 1962, p. 4.

86. Walter Harding, "A Heterogeneous Collection from Twain's Last Writings," *Chicago Sunday Tribune Magazine of Books*, 23 September 1962, p. 2.

87. *Time*, 21 September 1962, p. 91.

88. Jones, p. 53.

possible." The objection also appeared in a religious periodical. In the guise of "Luciferino" writing to Satan, a reviewer decided that "this isn't really the diabolical book we have been waiting for. If it had only come out in Bob Ingersoll's day I could have made fine tinder with it. Nowadays, about the only place to use it is with some naïve, rebelling kid brought up in literalism."[89] But this charge ignored an at least equal literalism in the Christianity Mark Twain was attacking, and thus indicated how foreign his issues had become in fifty-three years. He was trying to demonstrate the incompatibility of Christian faith with the earthly desires of men, the discrepancy between the Christian image of a benign God and the God of the Bible; and in the long run, a tendency in men to construct religions that flattered and abased them. Reviewers probably did not mean to avoid these issues. Their causal explanations and the charge of literalism suggest rather that they did not believe an individual could legitimately argue his convictions. The reviewers were living in an era when the literate public considered the religious disputes of individuals vulgar and pointless, in part because it doubted the claims of individuals to religious certitude, even a certitude of doubt.

But to Mark Twain, although there were prudential reasons for hiding his opinions, there was no arrogance in holding them, no naïveté in thinking they counted, and no futility in repeating them in the manuscripts he suppressed. In his age it was imperative to have religious convictions or, among unbelievers, convictions about religion. Church membership was not only a social convention and career advantage but a gauge of one's place in the culture, for distinctions among denominations followed ethnic and class lines. If one could not accept such distinctions, or if one became an agnostic, one laid claim to a higher wisdom that demanded at least a private formulation of principles. A man might hope to support his claim because in that transitional period he still trusted his own religious insights though he considered other

89. Robert Root, "A Devil's Lament," *Christian Century* 79, no. 47 (21 November 1962): 1423.

men's to be shaped by circumstance. For religious deviates like Mark Twain the negativity of their insights was an important test of truth. Believing that the general optimism represented a weakness for pleasant fancies, such men could respond to the concept of an inhospitable and destructive universe with somber jubilation because it seemed the hard-won object of a courageous understanding. Few men dared, like Ingersoll and Francis Newman, to be iconoclasts in public, but though there is relevance in the familiar charge of hypocrisy against secret skeptics, they thought they were honorable in maintaining their private beliefs while submitting to the compromise of an outer decorum. Far from being eccentric, Mark Twain's concern with his philosophical ideas was crucial to his dignity.

A Note on the Text

This volume includes Mark Twain's previously published philosophical writings. Fictional pieces (even some which develop arguments contained here) are ordinarily excluded, as are other works appropriate to different volumes in this edition. However "Letter from the Recording Angel," "The Five Boons of Life," and "Letters from the Earth," although they are in a strict sense fictional, have been judged more relevant to the present volume than to the volumes of short fiction. "Things a Scotsman Wants to Know," previously unpublished, is included by agreement with the editor of The Mark Twain Papers, as being especially relevant to themes of this volume. Other unpublished items appear as supplements because of their close relation to *What Is Man?*, *Christian Science*, and " 'The Turning Point of My Life.' "

The two works that break off with unfinished sentences, "Bible Teaching and Religious Practice" and the introductory section of "Letters from the Earth," were abandoned by the author or else their endings have been lost. The order of works in this volume is according to date of publication or, for those unpublished during the author's lifetime, date of composition. For works published during his lifetime, dates of first publication appear in roman type below titles; for works first published after his death, dates are in italics and indicate time of composition.

THE TEXTS

THE TEXTS

1   *Sabbath Reflections*

[1866]

T HIS is the Sabbath to-day. This is the day set apart by a benig-
nant Creator for rest—for repose from the wearying toils of
the week, and for calm and serious [Brown's dog has commenced
to howl again—I wonder why Brown persists in keeping that dog
chained up?] meditation upon those tremendous subjects pertaining to our future existence. How thankful we ought to be
[There goes that rooster, now.] for this sweet respite; how fervently we ought to lift up our voice and [Confound that old hen—
lays an egg every forty minutes, and then cackles until she lays the
next one.] testify our gratitude. How sadly, how soothingly the
music of that deep-toned bell floats up from the distant church!
How gratefully we murmur [Scat!—that old gray tom-cat is always
bully-ragging that other one—got him down, now, and digging the
hair out of him by the handfull.] thanksgiving for these Sabbath
blessings. How lovely the day is! ["Buy a broom! buy a broom!"]
How mild and beautiful the ["*Golden Era* 'n' *Sund'* Mercry, two
for a bit apiece!"] sun smites upon the tranquil ["*Alta, Mon' Call,*
an' *Merican Flag!*"] city! ["Po—ta-to-o-o-es, ten pounds for two
bits—po—ta-to-o-o-es, ten pounds for quart-va-dollar!"]

However, never mind these Sunday reflections—there are too
many distracting influences abroad. This people have forgotten
that San Francisco is not a ranch—or rather, that it ought not properly to be a ranch. It has got all the disagreeable features of a

ranch, though. Every citizen keeps from ten to five hundred chickens, and these crow and cackle all day and all night; they stand watches, and the watch on duty makes a racket while the off-watch sleeps. Let a stranger get outside of Montgomery and Kearney from Pacific to Second, and close his eyes, and he can imagine himself on a well-stocked farm, without an effort, for his ears will be assailed by such a vile din of gobbling of turkeys, and crowing of hoarse-voiced roosters, and cackling of hens, and howling of cows, and whinnying of horses, and braying of jackasses, and yowling of cats, that he will be driven to frenzy, and may look to perform prodigies of blasphemy such as he never knew himself capable of before.

Sunday reflections! A man might as well try to reflect in Bedlam as in San Francisco when her millions of live-stock are in tune. Being calm, now, I will call down no curse upon these dumb brutes (as they are called by courtesy), but I will go so far as to say I wish they may all die without issue, and that a sudden and violent death may overtake any person who afterwards attempts to reinstate the fowl and brute nuisance.

2   *Reflections on the Sabbath*

[1866]

THE day of rest comes but once a week, and sorry I am that it does not come oftener. Man is so constituted that he can stand more rest than this. I often think regretfully that it would have been so easy to have two Sundays in a week, and yet it was not so ordained. The omnipotent Creator could have made the world in three days just as easily as he made it in six, and this would have doubled the Sundays. Still it is not our place to criticise the wisdom of the Creator. When we feel a depraved inclination to question the judgment of Providence in stacking up double eagles in the coffers of Michael Reese and leaving better men to dig for a livelihood, we ought to stop and consider that we are not expected to help order things, and so drop the subject. If all-powerful Providence grew weary after six days' labor, such worms as we are might reasonably expect to break down in three, and so require two Sundays—but as I said before, it ill becomes us to hunt up flaws in matters which are so far out of our jurisdiction. I hold that no man can meddle with the exclusive affairs of Providence and offer suggestions for their improvement, without making himself in a manner conspicuous. Let us take things as we find them— though, I am free to confess, it goes against the grain to do it, sometimes.

What put me into this religious train of mind, was attending church at Dr. Wadsworth's this morning. I had not been to church before for many months, because I never could get a pew, and therefore had to sit in the gallery, among the sinners. I stopped that because my proper place was down among the elect, inasmuch as I was brought up a Presbyterian, and consider myself a brevet member of Dr. Wadsworth's church. I always was a brevet. I was sprinkled in infancy, and look upon that as conferring the rank of Brevet Presbyterian. It affords none of the emoluments of the Regular Church—simply confers honorable rank upon the recipient and the right to be punished as a Presbyterian hereafter; that is, the substantial Presbyterian punishment of fire and brimstone instead of this heterodox hell of remorse of conscience of these blamed wildcat religions. The heaven and hell of the wildcat religions are vague and ill defined but there is nothing mixed about the Presbyterian heaven and hell. The Presbyterian hell is all misery; the heaven all happiness—nothing to do. But when a man dies on a wildcat basis, he will never rightly know hereafter which department he is in—but he will think he is in hell anyhow, no matter which place he goes to; because in the good place they progress, pro-gress, pro-gress—study, study, study, all the time—and if this isn't hell I don't know what is; and in the bad place he will be worried by remorse of conscience. Their bad place is preferable, though, because eternity is long, and before a man got half through it he would forget what it was he had been so sorry about. Naturally he would then become cheerful again; but the party who went to heaven would go on progressing and progressing, and studying and studying until he would finally get discouraged and wish he were in hell, where he wouldn't require such a splendid education.

Dr. Wadsworth never fails to preach an able sermon; but every now and then, with an admirable assumption of not being aware of it, he will get off a firstrate joke and then frown severely at any one who is surprised into smiling at it. This is not fair. It is like throwing a bone to a dog and then arresting him with a look just as he is going to seize it. Several people there on Sunday suddenly laughed and as suddenly stopped again, when he gravely gave the Sunday school books a blast and spoke of "the good little boys in them who always went to Heaven, and the bad little boys who infallibly got drowned on Sunday," and then swept a savage frown around the house and blighted every smile in the congregation.

3   *Mr. Beecher and the Clergy*

[1869]

The Ministerial Union of Elmira, N. Y., at a recent meeting, passed resolutions disapproving the teachings of Rev. T. K. Beecher, declining to cooperate with him in his Sunday evening services at the Opera House, and requesting him to withdraw from their Monday morning meeting. This has resulted in his withdrawal, and thus the pastors are relieved from further responsibility as to his action.—*N. Y. Evangelist.*

POOR BEECHER! All this time he could do whatever he pleased that was wrong, and then be perfectly serene and comfortable over it, because the Ministerial Union of Elmira was responsible to GOD for it. He could lie, if he wanted to, and those ministers had to answer for it; he could promote discord in the church of CHRIST, and those parties had to make it all right with the Deity as best they could; he could teach false doctrines to empty Opera Houses, and those sorrowing lambs of the Ministerial Union had to get out their sackcloth and ashes and stand responsible for it. He had *such* a comfortable thing of it! But he went too far. In an evil hour he slaughtered the simple geese that laid the golden egg of responsibility for him,—and now they will uncover their customary production and view it with their customary complacency, and lift up their customary cackle in his behalf no more. And so, at last, he finds himself in the novel position of being responsible to GOD for his acts instead of to the Ministerial Union of Elmira. To say that this is appalling, is to state it with a degree of mildness which amounts to insipidity.

We cannot justly estimate this calamity, without first reviewing certain facts that conspired to bring it about. Mr. BEECHER was and is in the habit of preaching to a full congregation in the Independent Congregational Church in this city. The meeting house was not large enough to accommodate all the people who desired admittance. Mr. BEECHER regularly attended the meetings of the Ministerial Union of Elmira every Monday morning, and they received him into their fellowship and never objected to the doctrines which he taught in his church. So, in an unfortunate moment, he conceived the strange idea that they would connive at the teaching of the same doctrines in the same way in a larger house. Therefore he secured the Opera House and proceeded to preach there every Sunday evening to assemblages comprising from a thousand to fifteen hundred persons. He felt warranted in this course by a passage of Scripture which says: "Go ye into all the world and preach the gospel unto every creature." Opera Houses were not ruled out specifically in this passage, and so he considered it proper to regard Opera Houses as a part of "all the world." He looked upon the people who assembled there as coming under the head of "every creature." These ideas were as absurd as they were far-fetched, but still they were the honest ebullitions of a diseased mind. His great mistake was in supposing that when he had the Savior's endorsement of his conduct, he had all that was necessary. He overlooked the fact that there might possibly be a conflict of opinion between the Savior and the Ministerial Union of Elmira. And there *was*. Wherefore, blind and foolish, Mr. BEECHER went to his destruction. The Ministerial Union withdrew their approbation, and left him dangling in the air with no other support than the countenance and approval of the gospel of Christ.

Mr. BEECHER invited his brother ministers to join forces with him and help him conduct the Opera House meetings. They declined with great unanimity. In this they were wrong. Since they did not approve of those meetings, it was a duty they owed to their consciences and their God to contrive their discontinuance. They knew this. They felt it. Yet they turned coldly away and refused to help at those meetings, when they well knew that their help, earnestly and persistently given, was able to kill any great religious enterprise that ever was conceived of.

The ministers refused, and the calamitous meetings at the Opera House continued—and not only continued but grew in interest and importance and sapped of their congregations churches where the gospel was preached with that sweet monotonous tranquility and that impenetrable profundity which stir up such consternation in the strongholds of sin. It is a pity to have to record here that one clergyman refused to preach at the Opera House at Mr. BEECHER's request, even when that incendiary was sick and disabled—and if that man's conscience justifies him in that refusal, I do not. Under the plea of charity for a sick brother, he could have preached to that Opera House multitude a sermon that would have done incalculable damage to the Opera House experiment. And he need not have been particular about the sermon he chose, either. He could have relied on any he had in his barrel.

The Opera House meetings went on.—Other congregations were thin, and grew thinner, but the Opera House assemblages were vast. Every Sunday night, in spite of sense and reason, multitudes passed by the churches where they might have been saved, and marched deliberately to the Opera House to be damned. The community talked, talked, talked. Everybody discussed the fact that the Ministerial Union disapproved of the Opera House meetings; also the fact that they disapproved of the teachings put forth there. And everybody wondered *how* the Ministerial Union could tell whether to approve or disapprove of those teachings, seeing that those clergymen had *never attended an Opera House meeting,* and therefore didn't know *what* was taught there. Everybody wondered over that curious question—and they had to take it out in wondering.

Mr. BEECHER asked the Ministerial Union to state their objections to the Opera House matter. They could not—at least they did not. He said to them that if they would come squarely out and tell him that they desired the discontinuance of those meetings, he would discontinue them. They declined to do that. Why should they have declined? They had no *right* to decline, and no *excuse* to decline, if they honestly believed that those meetings interfered in the slightest degree with the best interests of religion. [That is a proposition which the profoundest head among them cannot get around]

But the Opera House meetings *went on*. That was the mischief of it. And so, one Monday morning, when Mr. B. appeared at the usual Ministers' meeting, his brother clergymen desired him to come there no more. He asked why. They gave no reason. They simply declined to have his company longer. Mr. B. said he could not accept of this execution without a trial, and since he loved them and had nothing against them, he must insist upon meeting with them in future just the same as ever. And so after that, they met in secret, and thus got rid of this man's importunate affection.

The Ministerial Union had ruled out BEECHER—a point gained. He would get up an excitement about it in public. But that was a miscalculation. He never mentioned it. They waited and waited for the grand crash, but it never came. After all their labor pains, their ministerial mountain had brought forth only a mouse, —and a still-born one at that. BEECHER had not told on them— BEECHER malignantly persisted in not telling on them. The opportunity was slipping away. Alas for the humiliation of it, they had to come out and tell it themselves! And after all, their bombshell did not hurt anybody, when they did explode it. They had ceased to be responsible to God for BEECHER, and yet nobody seemed paralyzed about it. Somehow, it was not even of sufficient importance, apparently, to get into the papers—though even the poor little facts that SMITH has bought a trotting team and Alderman JONES' child has the measles, are chronicled there with avidity. Something *must* be done. As the Ministerial Union had *told* about their desolating action when nobody else considered it of enough impor-

tance to tell, they would also *publish* it, now that the reporters
failed to see anything in it important enough to print. And so they
startled the entire religious world, no doubt, by solemnly printing
in the *Evangelist* the paragraph which heads this article. They
have got their excommunication-bull started at last. It is going
along quite lively, now, and making considerable stir, let us hope.
They even know it in Podunk, wherever that may be. It excited a
two line paragraph there. Happy, happy world, that knows at last
that a little Congress of congregationless clergymen of whom it
had never heard before, have crushed a famous BEECHER and reduced his audiences from fifteen hundred down to fourteen hundred and seventy-five at one fell blow! Happy, happy world, that
knows at last that these obscure innocents are no longer responsible for the blemishless teachings, the power, the pathos, the logic,
and the other and manifold intellectual pyrotechnics that seduce
but to damn the Opera House assemblages every Sunday night in
Elmira! And miserable, O thrice miserable BEECHER!—for the
Ministerial Union of Elmira will never, no never more be responsible to God for his shortcomings. [Excuse these tears]

[For the protection of a man who is uniformly charged with
all the newspaper deviltry that sees the light in Elmira journals, I
take this opportunity of stating, under oath, duly subscribed before a magistrate, that Mr. BEECHER did not write this article. And
further, that he did not inspire it. And further still, the Ministerial
Union of Elmira did not write it. And finally, the Ministerial
Union did not ask me to write it. No—I have taken up this cudgel
in defence of the Ministerial Union of Elmira solely from a love
of justice. Without solicitation, I have constituted myself the
champion of the Ministerial Union of Elmira, and it shall be a
labor of love with me to conduct their side of a quarrel in print for
them whenever they desire me to do it—or if they are busy and
have not time to ask me, I will cheerfully do it anyhow. In closing
this, I must remark that if any question the right of the clergymen
of Elmira to turn Mr. BEECHER out of the Ministerial Union, to
such I answer that Mr. BEECHER re-created that institution after it

had been dead for many years and invited those gentlemen to come into it—which they did, and so of course they have a right to turn him out if they want to. The difference between BEECHER and the man who put an adder in his bosom, is, that BEECHER put in more adders than he did, and consequently had a proportionately livelier time of it when they got warmed up]

Cheerfully,   S'CAT.

4 *About Smells*

[1870]

IN a recent issue of the "Independent," the Rev. T. De Witt Talmage, of Brooklyn, has the following utterance on the subject of "Smells":

I have a good Christian friend who, if he sat in the front pew in church, and a working man should enter the door at the other end, would smell him instantly. My friend is not to blame for the sensitiveness of his nose, any more than you would flog a pointer for being keener on the scent than a stupid watch-dog. The fact is, if you had all the churches free, by reason of the mixing up of the common people with the uncommon, you would keep one-half of Christendom sick at their stomach. If you are going to kill the church thus with bad smells, I will have nothing to do with this work of evangelization.

We have reason to believe that there will be laboring men in heaven; and also a number of negroes, and Esquimaux, and Tierra del Fuegans, and Arabs, and a few Indians, and possibly even some Spaniards and Portuguese. All things are possible with God. We shall have all these sorts of people in heaven; but, alas! in getting them we shall lose the society of Dr. Talmage. Which is to say, we shall lose the company of one who could give more real "tone" to celestial society than any other contribution Brooklyn could furnish. And what would eternal happiness be without the Doctor? Blissful, unquestionably—we know that well enough—

but would it be *distingué*, would it be *recherché* without him? St. Matthew without stockings or sandals; St. Jerome bareheaded, and with a coarse brown blanket robe dragging the ground; St. Sebastian with scarcely any raiment at all—these we should see, and should enjoy seeing them; but would we not miss a spike-tailed coat and kids, and turn away regretfully, and say to parties from the Orient: "These are well enough, but you ought to see Talmage of Brooklyn." I fear me that in the better world we shall not even have Dr. Talmage's "good Christian friend." For if he were sitting under the glory of the Throne, and the keeper of the keys admitted a Benjamin Franklin or other laboring man, that "friend," with his fine natural powers infinitely augmented by emancipation from hampering flesh, would detect him with a single sniff, and immediately take his hat and ask to be excused.

To all outward seeming, the Rev. T. De Witt Talmage is of the same material as that used in the construction of his early predecessors in the ministry; and yet one feels that there must be a difference somewhere between him and the Savior's first disciples. It may be because here, in the nineteenth century, Dr. T. has had advantages which Paul and Peter and the others could not and did not have. There was a lack of polish about them, and a looseness of etiquette, and a want of exclusiveness, which one cannot help noticing. They healed the very beggars, and held intercourse with people of a villainous odor every day. If the subject of these remarks had been chosen among the original Twelve Apostles, he would not have associated with the rest, because he could not have stood the fishy smell of some of his comrades who came from around the Sea of Galilee. He would have resigned his commission with some such remark as he makes in the extract quoted above: "Master, if thou art going to kill the church thus with bad smells, I will have nothing to do with this work of evangelization." He is a disciple, and makes that remark to the Master; the only difference is, that he makes it in the nineteenth instead of the first century.

Is there a choir in Mr. T.'s church? And does it ever occur

that they have no better manners than to sing that hymn which is
so suggestive of laborers and mechanics:

> "Son of the Carpenter! receive
> This humble work of mine?"

Now, can it be possible that in a handful of centuries the
Christian character has fallen away from an imposing heroism that
scorned even the stake, the cross, and the axe, to a poor little
effeminacy that withers and wilts under an unsavory smell? We are
not prepared to believe so, the reverend Doctor and his friend to
the contrary notwithstanding.

5 The Indignity Put upon the Remains of George Holland by the Rev. Mr. Sabine

[1871]

WHAT a ludicrous satire it was upon Christian charity!—
even upon the vague, theoretical idea of it which doubtless this small saint mouths from his own pulpit every Sunday.
Contemplate this freak of Nature, and think what a Cardiff giant
of self-righteousness is crowded into his pigmy skin. If we probe,
and dissect, and lay open this diseased, this cancerous piety of his,
we are forced to the conviction that it is the production of an impression on his part that his guild do about all the good that is done
in the earth, and hence are better than comman clay—hence are
competent to say to such as George Holland, "You are unworthy;
you are a play-actor, and consequently a sinner; I cannot take the
responsibility of recommending you to the mercy of Heaven." It
must have had its origin in that impression, else he would have
thought, "We are all instruments for the carrying out of God's
purposes; it is not for me to pass judgment upon your appointed
share of the work, or to praise or to revile it; I have divine authority
for it that we are *all* sinners, and therefore it is not for me to discriminate and say we will supplicate for this sinner, for he was a
merchant prince or a banker, but we will beseech no forgiveness
for this other one, for he was a play-actor." It surely requires the
furthest possible reach of self-righteousness to enable a man to

lift his scornful nose in the air and turn his back upon so poor and pitiable a thing as a dead stranger come to beg the last kindness that humanity can do in its behalf. This creature has violated the letter of the gospel and judged George Holland—not George Holland either, but his *profession* through him. Then it is in a measure fair that we judge this creature's guild through *him*. In effect he has said, "We are the salt of the earth; we do all the good work that is done; to learn how to be good and do good, men must come to us; actors and such are obstacles to moral progress."* Pray look at the thing reasonably for a moment, laying aside all biasses of education and custom. If a common public impression is fair evidence of a thing, then this minister's legitimate, recognized, and acceptable business is to *tell* people calmly, coldly, and in stiff, written sentences, from the pulpit, to go and do right, be just, be merciful, be charitable. And his congregation forget it all between church and home. But for fifty years it was George Holland's business, on the stage, to *make* his audience go and do right, and be just, merciful, and charitable—because by his living, breathing, feeling pictures, he showed them what it *was* to do these things, and *how* to do them, and how instant and ample was the reward! Is it not a singular teacher of men, this reverend gentleman who is so poorly informed himself as to put the whole stage under ban, and say, "I do not think it teaches moral lessons"?

Where was ever a sermon preached that could make filial ingratitude so hateful to men as the sinful play of "King Lear"? Or where was there ever a sermon that could so convince men of the wrong and the cruelty of harboring a pampered and unana-

---

* Reporter—What answer did you make, Mr. Sabine?

Mr. Sabine—I said that I had a distaste for officiating at such a funeral, and that I did not care to be mixed up in it. I said to the gentleman that I was willing to bury the deceased from his house, but that I objected to having the funeral solemnized at a church.

Reporter—Is it one of the laws of the Protestant Episcopal Church that a deceased theatrical performer shall not be buried from the church?

Mr. Sabine—It is not; but I have always warned the professing members of my congregation to keep away from theatres and not to have anything to do with them. I don't think that they teach moral lessons.—*New York Times.*

lyzed jealousy as the sinful play of "Othello"? And where are there ten preachers who can stand in the pulpit teaching heroism, unselfish devotion, and lofty patriotism, and hold their own against any one of five hundred William Tells that can be raised up upon five hundred stages in the land at a day's notice? It is almost fair and just to aver (although it is profanity) that nine-tenths of all the kindness and forbearance and Christian charity and generosity in the hearts of the American people to-day, got there by being filtered down from their fountain-head, the gospel of Christ, *through dramas and tragedies and comedies on the stage, and through the despised novel and the Christmas story, and through the thousand and one lessons, suggestions, and narratives of generous deeds that stir the pulses, and exalt and augment the nobility of the nation day by day from the teeming columns of ten thousand newspapers,* and NOT from the drowsy pulpit!

All that is great and good in our particular civilization came straight from the hand of Jesus Christ, and many creatures, and of divers sorts, were doubtless appointed to disseminate it; and let us believe that *this seed and the result* are the main thing, and not the cut of the sower's garment; and that whosoever, in his way and according to his opportunity, sows the one and produces the other, has done high service and worthy. And further, let us try with all our strength to believe that whenever old simple-hearted George Holland sowed this seed, and reared his crop of broader charities and better impulses in men's hearts, it was just as acceptable before the Throne as if the seed had been scattered in vapid platitudes from the pulpit of the ineffable Sabine himself.

Am I saying that the pulpit does not do its share toward disseminating the marrow, the *meat* of the gospel of Christ? (For we are not talking of ceremonies and wire-drawn creeds now, but the living heart and soul of what is pretty often only a spectre.)

No, I am not saying that. The pulpit teaches assemblages of people twice a week—nearly two hours, altogether—and does what it can in that time. The theatre teaches large audiences seven times a week—28 or 30 hours altogether; and the novels and newspapers plead, and argue, and illustrate, stir, move, thrill, thunder, urge, persuade, and supplicate, at the feet of millions and millions of people every single day, and all day long, and far into the night; and so these vast agencies till *nine-tenths* of the vineyard, and the pulpit tills the other tenth. Yet now and then some complacent blind idiot says, "You unanointed are coarse clay and useless; you are not as we, the regenerators of the world; go, bury yourselves elsewhere, for we cannot take the responsibility of recommending idlers and sinners to the yearning mercy of Heaven." How *does* a soul like that stay in a carcass without getting mixed with the secretions and sweated out through the pores? Think of this insect condemning the whole theatrical service as a disseminator of bad morals because it has Black Crooks in it; forgetting that if that were sufficient ground, people would condemn the pulpit because it had Cooks, and Kallochs, and Sabines in it.

No, I am not trying to rob the pulpit of any atom of its full share and credit in the work of disseminating the meat and marrow of the gospel of Christ; but I am trying to get a moment's hearing for worthy agencies in the same work, that with overwrought modesty seldom or never claim a recognition of their great services. I am aware that the pulpit does its excellent one-tenth (and credits itself with it now and then, though most of the time a press of business causes it to forget it); I am aware that in its honest and well-meaning way it bores the people with uninflammable truisms about doing good; bores them with correct compositions on charity; bores them, chloroforms them, stupefies them with argumentative mercy without a flaw in the grammar, or an emotion which the minister could put in in the right place if he turned his back and took his finger off the manuscript. And in doing these things the pulpit is doing its duty, and let us believe that it is likewise doing its best, and doing it in the most harmless and respectable way. And so I have said, and shall keep on saying, let us give the pulpit its full share of credit in elevating and ennobling the people; but when a pulpit takes to itself authority to pass judgment upon the work and the worth of just as legitimate an instrument of God as itself, who spent a long life preaching from the stage the self-same gospel without the alteration of a single sentiment or a single axiom of right, it is fair and just that somebody who believes that actors were made for a high and good purpose, and that they *accomplish the object of their creation* and accomplish it well, should protest. And having protested, it is also fair and just—being driven to it, as it were—to whisper to the Sabine pattern of clergyman, under the breath, a simple, instructive truth, and say, "Ministers are not the only servants of God upon earth, nor His most efficient ones either, by a very, very long distance!" Sensible ministers already know this, and it may do the other kind good to find it out.

But to cease teaching and go back to the beginning again, was it not pitiable, that spectacle? Honored and honorable old George Holland, whose theatrical ministry had for fifty years softened hard hearts, bred generosity in cold ones, kindled emotion in dead ones, uplifted base ones, broadened bigoted ones, and made many and many a stricken one glad and filled it brim full of gratitude, figuratively spit upon in his unoffending coffin by this crawling, slimy, sanctimonious, self-righteous reptile!

6 [*Three Statements of the Eighties*]

[*1880–1885?*]

[I]

I BELIEVE in God the Almighty.

I do not believe He has ever sent a message to man by anybody, or delivered one to him by word of mouth, or made Himself visible to mortal eyes at any time or in any place.

I believe that the Old and New Testaments were imagined and written by man, and that no line in them was authorized by God, much less inspired by Him.

I think the goodness, the justice, and the mercy of God are manifested in His works; I perceive that they are manifested toward me in this life; the logical conclusion is that they will be manifested toward me in the life to come, if there should be one.

I do not believe in special providences. I believe that the universe is governed by strict and immutable laws. If one man's family is swept away by a pestilence and another man's spared, it is only the law working: God is not interfering in that small matter, either against the one man or in favor of the other.

I cannot see how eternal punishment hereafter could accomplish any good end, therefore I am not able to believe in it. To chasten a man in order to perfect him might be reasonable enough; to annihilate him when he shall have proved himself incapable of reaching perfection might be reasonable enough: but to roast him forever for the mere satisfaction of seeing him roast would not be reasonable—even the atrocious God imagined by the Jews would tire of the spectacle eventually.

There may be a hereafter, and there may *not* be. I am wholly indifferent about it. If I am appointed to live again, I feel sure it will be for some more sane and useful purpose than to flounder about for ages in a lake of fire and brimstone for having violated a confusion of ill-defined and contradictory rules said (but not evidenced,) to be of divine institution. If annihilation is to follow death, I shall not be *aware* of the annihilation, and therefore shall not care a straw about it.

I believe that the world's moral laws are the outcome of the world's experience. It needed no God to come down out of heaven to tell men that murder and theft and the other immoralities were bad, both for the individual who commits them and for society which suffers from them.

If I break all these moral laws, I cannot see how I injure God by it, for He is beyond the reach of injury from me—I could as easily injure a planet by throwing mud at it. It seems to me that my mis-conduct could only injure me and other men. I cannot *benefit* God by obeying these moral laws—I could as reasonably benefit the planet by withholding my mud. [Let these sentences be read in the light of the fact that I believe I have received moral laws *only* from man—none whatever from God.] Consequently I do not see why I should either be punished or rewarded hereafter for the deeds I do here.

[II]

I would not interfere with any one's religion, either to strengthen it or weaken it. I am not able to believe one's religion can affect his hereafter one way or the other, no matter what that religion may be. But it may easily be a great comfort to him in this life—hence it is a valuable possession to him.

Latter-day Protestantism, by selecting the humaner passages of the Bible, and teaching them to the world, whilst allowing those of a different sort to lie dormant, has produced the highest and purest and best individuals which modern society has known. Thus used, the Bible is the most valuable of books. But the strongly-worded authority for all the religious atrocities of the Middle Ages is still in it, and some day or other it may again become as heavy a curse to the world as it formerly was. The devastating powers of the Book are only suspended, not extinguished. An Expurgated Bible would not be an unuseful thing.

[III]

If the very greatest and wisest and most experienced man the earth could produce should write a book, it would be instinct with common sense—it would not totally lack this quality in any clause or sentence. If it made a statement, it would be a statement possible of belief. If it made a requirement, it would be one possible to be obeyed.

If the Bible had been written by God, it also would have possessed these virtues. But it conspicuously lacks them in places. Therefore I think that it not only was not written by God, but was not even written by remarkably capable *men*.

God could have said "Thou shalt not commit adultery;" but He would not have followed it up in the same book by plainly violating His own law with Mary the betrothed bride of Joseph. The lamest of modern book-makers would hardly be guilty of so egregious a blunder as that.

To become a right Christian, one must *hate* his brother, his sister, his wife, etc. The laws of God and nature being stronger than those of men, this one must always remain a dead-letter. It was not worth while to cumber the Book with this one, since no single individual of all the earth's myriads would ever be able to obey it.

"Straight is the gate and narrow is the way, and *few there be*," etc. This is the utterance of the same authority which commands man to "multiply and replenish the earth." What! meekly and obediently proceed to beget children, with the distinct understanding that *nearly all* of them must become fuel for the fires of hell? The person who could obey such a command, under such an understanding, would be simply a monster—no gentler term would describe him. How easily men are self-duped. Many *think* they believe they are begetting fuel for hell, but down in their hearts they believe nothing of the kind.

7   *The Character of Man*

[1885]

CONCERNING Man—he is too large a subject to be treated as a whole; so I will merely discuss a detail or two of him at this time. I desire to contemplate him from this point of view —this premiss: that he was not made for any useful purpose, for the reason that he hasn't served any; that he was most likely not even made *intentionally*; and that his working himself up out of the oyster bed to his present position was probably matter of surprise and regret to the Creator. . . . For his history, in all climes, all ages and all circumstances, furnishes oceans and continents of proof that of all the creatures that were made he is the most detestable. Of the entire brood he is the only one—the solitary one— that possesses malice. That is the basest of all instincts, passions, vices—the most hateful. That one thing puts him below the rats, the grubs, the trichinæ. He is the only creature that inflicts pain for sport, knowing it to *be* pain. But if the cat knows she is inflicting pain when she plays with the frightened mouse, then we must make an exception here; we must grant that in one detail man is the moral peer of the cat. *All* creatures kill—there seems to be no exception; but of the whole list, man is the only one that kills for fun; he is the only one that kills in malice, the only one that kills for revenge. Also—in all the list he is the only creature that has a nasty mind.

Shall he be extolled for his noble qualities, for his gentleness, his sweetness, his amiability, his lovingness, his courage, his devotion, his patience, his fortitude, his prudence, the various charms and graces of his spirit? The other animals share *all* these with him, yet are free from the blacknesses and rottennesses of his character.

. . . . There are certain sweet-smelling sugar-coated lies current in the world which all politic men have apparently tacitly conspired together to support and perpetuate. One of these is, that there is such a thing in the world as independence: independence of thought, independence of opinion, independence of action. Another is, that the world loves to *see* independence—admires it, applauds it. Another is, that there is such a thing in the world as toleration—in religion, in politics, and such matters; and with it trains that already mentioned auxiliary lie that toleration is admired, and applauded. Out of these trunk-lies spring many branch ones: to-wit, the lie that not all men are slaves; the lie that men are glad when other men succeed; glad when they prosper; glad to see them reach lofty heights; sorry to see them fall again. And yet other branch-lies: to-wit, that there is heroism in man; that he is not mainly made up of malice and treachery; that he is sometimes not a coward; that there is something about him that ought to be perpetuated—in heaven, or hell, or somewhere. And these other branch-lies, to-wit: that conscience, man's moral medicine chest, is not only created by the Creator, but is put into man ready-charged with the right and only true and authentic correctives of conduct—and the duplicate chest, with the self-same correctives, unchanged, unmodified, distributed to all nations and all epochs. And yet one other branch-lie, to-wit, that I am I, and you are you; that we are units, individuals, and have natures of our own, instead of being the tail-end of a tape-worm eternity of ancestors extending in linked procession back—and back—and back—to our source in the monkeys, with this so-called individuality of ours a decayed and rancid mush of inherited instincts and teachings derived, atom by atom, stench by stench, from the entire line of that sorry column, and not so much new and original matter in it as you

could balance on a needle point and examine under a microscope.
This makes well nigh fantastic the suggestion that there can be
such a thing as a personal, original and responsible nature in a
man, separable from that in him which is not original, and findable
in such quantity as to enable the observer to say, This is a man,
not a procession.

. . . . Consider that first mentioned lie: that there is such a thing
in the world as independence; that it exists in individuals, that it
exists in bodies of men. Surely if anything *is* proven, by whole
oceans and continents of evidence, it is that the quality of independence was almost wholly left out of the human race. The scattering exceptions to the rule only emphasize it, light it up, make it
glare. The whole population of New England meekly took their
turns, for years, in standing up in the railway trains, without so
much as a complaint above their breath, till at last these un-
counted millions were able to produce exactly one single independent man, who stood to his rights and made the railroad give
him a seat. Statistics and the law of probabilities warrant the
assumption that it will take New England forty years to breed his
fellow. There is a law, with a penalty attached, forbidding trains
to occupy the Asylum street crossing more than five minutes at a
time. For years people and carriages used to wait there nightly as
much as twenty minutes on a stretch while New England trains
monopolized that crossing. I used to hear men use vigorous language about that insolent wrong—but they waited, just the same.

We are discreet sheep; we wait to see how the drove is going,
and then go with the drove. We have two opinions: one private,
which we are afraid to express; and another one—the one we use—
which we force ourselves to wear to please Mrs. Grundy, until
habit makes us comfortable in it, and the custom of defending it
presently makes us love it, adore it, and forget how pitifully we
came by it. Look at it in politics. Look at the candidates whom
we loathe, one year, and are afraid to vote against the next; whom
we cover with unimaginable filth, one year, and fall down on the
public platform and worship, the next—and keep on doing it until

the habitual shutting of our eyes to last year's evidences brings us presently to a sincere and stupid belief in this year's.* Look at the tyranny of party—at what is called party allegiance, party loyalty —a snare invented by designing men for selfish purposes—and which turns voters into chattels, slaves, rabbits; and all the while, their masters, and they themselves are shouting rubbish about liberty, independence, freedom of opinion, freedom of speech, honestly unconscious of the fantastic contradiction; and forgetting or ignoring that their fathers and the churches shouted the same blasphemies a generation earlier when they were closing their doors against the hunted slave, beating his handful of humane defenders with Bible-texts and billies, and pocketing the insults and licking the shoes of his Southern master.

If we would learn what the human race really *is*, at bottom, we need only observe it in election times. A Hartford clergyman met me in the street, and spoke of a new nominee—denounced the nomination, in strong, earnest words—words that were refreshing for their independence, their manliness.** He said, "I ought to be proud, perhaps, for this nominee is a relative of mine; on the contrary I am humiliated and disgusted; for I know him intimately— familiarly—and I know that he is an unscrupulous scoundrel, and always has been." You should have seen this clergyman preside at a political meeting forty days later; and urge, and plead, and gush—and you should have heard him paint the character of this same nominee. You would have supposed he was describing the Cid, and Great-heart, and Sir Galahad, and Bayard the Spotless all rolled into one. Was he sincere? Yes—by that time; and therein lies the pathos of it all, the hopelessness of it all. It shows at what trivial cost of effort a man can teach himself a lie, and learn to believe it, when he perceives, by the general drift, that that is the popular thing to do. Does he believe his lie *yet*? Oh, probably not;

* Jan. 11/o6. It is long ago, but it plainly means Blaine. M.T.
** *Jan. 11*, 'o6. I can't remember his name. It began with K, I think. He was one of the American revisers of the New Testament, and was nearly as great a scholar as Hammond Trumbull.

he has no further use for it. It was but a passing incident; he spared to it the moment that was its due, then hastened back to the serious business of his life.

And what a paltry poor lie is that one which teaches that independence of action and opinion is prized in men, admired, honored, rewarded. When a man leaves a political party, he is treated as if the party owned him—as if he were its bond slave, as most party men plainly are—and had stolen himself, gone off with what was not his own. And he is traduced, derided, despised, held up to public obloquy and loathing. His character is remorselessly assassinated; no means, however vile, are spared to injure his property and his business.

The preacher who casts a vote for conscience' sake, runs the risk of starving. And is rightly served; for he has been teaching a falsity—that men respect and honor independence of thought and action.

Mr. Beecher may be charged with a *crime*, and his whole following will rise as one man, and stand by him to the bitter end; but who so poor to be his friend when he is charged with casting a vote for conscience' sake? Take the editor so charged—take—take anybody.

All the talk about tolerance, in anything or anywhere, is plainly a gentle lie. It does not exist. It is in no man's heart; but it unconsciously and by moss-grown inherited habit, drivels and slabbers from all men's lips. Intolerance is everything for one's self, and nothing for the other person. The main-spring of man's nature is just that—selfishness.

Let us skip the other lies, for brevity's sake. To consider them would prove nothing, except that man is what he is—loving, toward his own, lovable, to his own,—his family, his friends—and otherwise the buzzing, busy, trivial, enemy of his race—who tarries his little day, does his little dirt, commends himself to God, and then goes out into the darkness, to return no more, and send no messages back—selfish even in death.

8   [*Letter from the Recording Angel*]

[1887]

Office of the Recording Angel,
Dept. of Petitions, Jan. 20.

Andrew Langdon,
   Coal Dealer, Buffalo, N. Y.

I have the honor, as per command, to inform you that your recent act of benevolence and self-sacrifice has been recorded upon a page by itself of the Book called Golden Deeds of Men; a distinction, I am permitted to remark, which is not merely extraordinary, it is unique.

As regards your prayers, for the week ending the 19th, I have the honor to report as follows:

1. For weather to advance hard coal 15 cents per ton. Granted.

2. For influx of laborers to reduce wages 10 per cent. Granted.

3. For a break in rival soft-coal prices. Granted.

4. For a visitation upon the man, or upon the family of the man, who has set up a competing retail coal-yard in Rochester. Granted, as follows: diphtheria, 2, 1 fatal; scarlet fever, 1, to result in deafness and imbecility. NOTE. This prayer should have been directed against this subordinate's principals, the N. Y. Central RR Co.

5. For deportation to Sheol, of annoying swarms of persons

who apply daily for work, or for favors of one sort or another. Taken under advisement for later decision and compromise, this petition appearing to conflict with another one of same date, which will be cited further along.

6. For application of some form of violent death to neighbor who threw brick at family cat, whilst the which was serenading. Reserved for consideration and compromise, because of conflict with a prayer of even date to be cited further along.

7. To "damn the missionary cause." Reserved also—as above.

8. To increase December profits of $22,230 to $45,000 for January, and perpetuate a proportionate monthly increase thereafter—"which will satisfy you." The prayer granted; the added remark accepted with reservations.

9. For cyclone, to destroy the works and fill up the mine of the North Pennsylvania Co. NOTE: Cyclones are not kept in stock in the winter season. A reliable article of fire-damp can be furnished upon application.

Especial note is made of the above list, they being of particular moment. The 298 remaining supplications classifiable under the head of Special Providences, Schedule A, for week ending 19th, are granted in a body, except that 3 of the 32 cases requiring immediate death have been modified to incurable disease.

This completes the week's invoice of petitions known to this office under the technical designation of Secret Supplications of the Heart, and which for a reason which may suggest itself, always receive our first and especial attention.

The remainder of the week's invoice falls under the head of what we term Public Prayers, in which classification we place prayers uttered in Prayer Meeting, Sunday School, Class Meeting, Family Worship, etc. These kinds of prayers have value according to classification of Christian uttering them. By rule of this office, Christians are divided into two grand classes, to-wit: 1, Professing Christians; 2, Professional Christians. These, in turn, are minutely subdivided and classified by Size, Species, and Family; and finally, Standing is determined by carats, the minimum being 1, the maximum 1,000.

As per balance-sheet for quarter ending Dec. 31st, 1847, you stood classified as follows:

Grand Classification, Professing Christian.

Size, one-fourth of maximum.

Species, Human-Spiritual.

Family, A of the Elect, Division 16.

Standing, 322 carats fine.

As per balance-sheet for quarter just ended,—that is to say, forty years later,—you stand classified as follows:

Grand Classification, Professional Christian.

Size, six one-hundredths of maximum.

Species, Human-Animal.

Family, W of the Elect, Division 1547.

Standing, 3 carats fine.

I have the honor to call your attention to the fact that you seem to have deteriorated.

To resume report upon your Public Prayers—with the side remark that in order to encourage Christians of your grade and of approximate grades, it is the custom of this office to grant many things to them which would not be granted to Christians of a higher grade—partly because they would not be asked for:

Prayer for weather mercifully tempered to the needs of the poor and the naked. Denied. This was a Prayer-Meeting prayer. It conflicts with Item 1 of this Report, which was a Secret Supplication of the Heart. By a rigid rule of this office, certain sorts of Public Prayers of Professional Christians are forbidden to take precedence of Secret Supplications of the Heart.

Prayer for better times and plentier food "for the hard handed son of toil whose patient and exhausting labors make comfortable the homes, and pleasant the ways, of the more fortunate, and entitle him to our vigilant and effective protection from the wrongs and injustices which grasping avarice would do him, and to the tenderest offices of our grateful hearts." Prayer-Meeting Prayer. Refused. Conflicts with Secret Supplication of the Heart No. 2.

Prayer "that such as in any way obstruct our preferences may be generously blessed, both themselves and their families, we here calling our hearts to witness that in their worldly prosperity we are spiritually blessed, and our joys made perfect." Prayer-Meeting Prayer. Refused. Conflicts with Secret Supplications of the Heart Nos. 3 and 4.

"Oh, let none fall heir to the pains of perdition through words or acts of ours." Family Worship. Received fifteen minutes in advance of Secret Supplication of the Heart No. 5, with which it distinctly conflicts. It is suggested that one or the other of these prayers be withdrawn, or both of them modified.

"Be mercifully inclined toward all who would do us offence in our persons or our property." Includes man who threw brick at cat. Family Prayer. Received some minutes in advance of No. 6, Secret Supplications of the Heart. Modification suggested, to reconcile discrepancy.

"Grant that the noble missionary cause, the most precious labor entrusted to the hands of men, may spread and prosper without let or limit in all heathen lands that do as yet reproach us with their spiritual darkness." Uninvited prayer shoved in at meeting of American Board. Received nearly half a day in advance of No. 7, Secret Supplications of the Heart. This office takes no stock in missionaries, and is not connected in any way with the American Board. We should like to grant one of these prayers, but cannot grant both. It is suggested that the American Board one be withdrawn.

This office desires for the twentieth time to call urgent attention to your remark appended to No. 8. It is a chestnut.

Of the 464 specifications contained in your Public Prayers for the week, and not previously noted in this report, we grant 2, and deny the rest. To-wit: Granted, (1), "that the clouds may continue to perform their office; (2), and the sun his." It was the divine purpose anyhow; it will gratify you to know that you have not disturbed it. Of the 462 details refused, 61 were uttered in Sunday School. In this connection I must once more remind you that we grant no Sunday School Prayers of Professional Christians of the classification technically known in this office as the John Wanamaker grade. We merely enter them as "words," and they count to his credit according to number uttered within certain limits of time, 3,000 per quarter-minute required, or no score; 4,200 in a possible 5,000 is a quite common Sunday School score, among experts, and counts the same as two hymns and a bouquet furnished by young ladies in the assassin's cell, execution-morning. Your remaining 401 details count for wind only. We bunch them and use them for head-winds in retarding the ships of improper people, but it takes so many of them to make an impression that we cannot allow anything for their use.

I desire to add a word of my own to this report. When certain sorts of people do a sizeable good deed, we credit them up a thousand-fold more for it than we would in the case of a better man—on account of the strain. You stand far away above your classification-record here, because of certain self-sacrifices of yours which greatly exceed what could have been expected of you. Years ago, when you were worth only $100,000, and sent $2 to your impoverished cousin the widow, when she appealed to you for help, there were many in heaven who were not able to believe it, and many more who believed that the money was counterfeit. Your character went up many degrees when it was shown that these suspicions were unfounded. A year or two later, when you sent the poor girl $4 in answer to another appeal, everybody believed it, and you were all the talk here for days together. Two years later you sent $6, upon supplication, when the widow's youngest child died, and that act made perfect your good fame. Everybody in heaven said, "Have you heard about Andrew?"—for you are now affectionately called Andrew here. Your increasing donation, every two or three years, has kept your name on all lips, and warm in all hearts. All heaven watches you Sundays, as you drive to church in your handsome carriage; and when your hand retires from the contribution plate, the glad shout is heard even to the ruddy walls of remote Sheol, "Another nickel from Andrew!" But the climax came a few days ago, when the widow wrote and said she could get a school in a far village to teach if she had $50 to get herself and her two surviving children over the long journey; and you counted up last month's clear profit from your three coal mines—$22,230—and added to it the certain profit for the current month—$45,000 and a possible fifty—and then got down your pen and your check-book and mailed her *fifteen whole dollars!* Ah, Heaven bless and keep you forever and ever, generous heart! There was not a dry eye in the realms of bliss; and amidst the hand-shakings, and embracings, and praisings, the decree was thundered forth from the shining mount, that this deed should out-honor all the historic self-sacrifices of men and angels, and be recorded by itself upon a page of its own, for that the strain of it upon you had been heavier and bitterer than the strain it costs ten thousand martyrs to yield up their lives at the fiery stake; and all said, "What is the giving up of life, to a noble soul, or to ten thousand noble souls, compared with the giving up of fifteen dollars out of the greedy grip of the meanest white man that ever lived on the face of the earth?"

And it was a true word. And Abraham, weeping, shook out the contents of his bosom and pasted the eloquent label there, "Reserved;" and Peter, weeping, said, "He shall be received with a torchlight procession when he comes;" and then all heaven boomed, and was glad you were going there. And so was hell.

[Signed]

The Recording Angel. [seal.]

By command.

9 [Bible Teaching and Religious Practice]

[1890]

RELIGION had its share in the changes of civilization and national character, of course. What share? The lion's. In the history of the human race this has always been the case, will always be the case, to the end of time, no doubt; or at least until man by the slow processes of evolution shall develop into something really fine and high—some billions of years hence, say.

The Christian's Bible is a drug-store. Its contents remain the same; but the medical practice changes. For eighteen hundred years these changes were slight—scarcely noticeable. The practice was allopathic—allopathic in its rudest and crudest form. The dull and ignorant physician day and night, and all the days and all the nights, drenched his patient with vast and hideous doses of the most repulsive drugs to be found in the store's stock; he bled him, cupped him, purged him, puked him, salivated him, never gave his system a chance to rally, nor nature a chance to help. He kept him religion-sick for eighteen centuries, and allowed him not a well day during all that time. The stock in the store was made up of about equal portions of baleful and debilitating poisons, and healing and comforting medicines; but the practice of the time confined the physician to the use of the former; by consequence, he could only damage his patient, and that is what he did.

Not until far within our century was any considerable change in the practice introduced; and then mainly, or in effect only, in

Great Britain and the United States. In the other countries to-day, the patient either still takes the ancient treatment or does not call the physician at all. In the English-speaking countries the changes observable in our century were forced by that very thing just referred to—the revolt of the patient against the system; they were not projected by the physician. The patient fell to doctoring himself, and the physician's practice began to fall off. He modified his methods to get back his trade. He did it gradually, reluctantly; and never yielded more at a time than the pressure compelled. At first he relinquished the daily dose of hell and damnation, and administered it every other day only; next he allowed another day to pass; then another and presently another; when he had restricted it at last to Sundays, and imagined that now there would surely be a truce, the homeopath arrived on the field and made him abandon hell and damnation altogether, and administer Christ's love, and comfort, and charity and compassion in its stead. These had been in the drug-store all the time, gold-labeled and conspicuous among the long shelf-loads of repulsive purges and vomits and poisons, and so the practice was to blame that they had remained unused, not the pharmacy. To the ecclesiastical physician of fifty years ago, his predecessor for eighteen centuries was a quack; to the ecclesiastical physician of to-day, his predecessor of fifty years ago was a quack. To the every-man-his-own-ecclesiastical-doctor of—when?—what will the ecclesiastical physician of to-day be? Unless evolution, which has been a truth ever since the globed suns and planets of the solar systems were but wandering films of meteor-dust, shall reach a limit and become a lie, there is but one fate in store for him.

The methods of the priest and the parson have been very curious, their history is very entertaining. In all the ages the Roman Church has owned slaves, bought and sold slaves, authorized and encouraged her children to trade in them. Long after some Christian peoples had freed their slaves, the Church still held on to hers. If any could know, to absolute certainty, that all this was right, and according to God's will and desire, surely it was she, since she was God's specially appointed representative in the earth and sole authorized and infallible expounder of His Bible. There were the texts; there was no mistaking their meaning; she was right; she was doing, in this thing, what the Bible had mapped out for her to do. So unassailable was her position that in all the centuries she had no word to say against human slavery. Yet now at last, in our immediate day, we hear a pope saying slave-trading is wrong, and we see him sending an expedition to Africa to stop it. The texts remain: it is the practice that has changed. Why? Because the world has corrected the Bible. The Church never corrects it; and also never fails to drop in at the tail of the procession—and take the credit of the correction. As she will presently do in this instance.

Christian England supported slavery and encouraged it for two hundred and fifty years, and her Church's consecrated ministers looked on, sometimes taking an active hand, the rest of the time indifferent. England's interest in the business may be called a Christian interest, a Christian industry. She had her full share in its revival after a long period of inactivity, and this revival was a Christian monopoly; that is to say, it was in the hands of Christian countries exclusively. English parliaments aided the slave traffic and protected it; two English kings held stock in slave-catching companies. The first regular English slave-hunter—John Hawkins, of still revered memory—made such successful havoc, on his second voyage, in the matter of surprising and burning villages, and maiming, slaughtering, capturing and selling their unoffending inhabitants, that his delighted queen conferred the chivalric honor of knighthood on him—a rank which had acquired its chief esteem and distinction in other and earlier fields of Christian effort. The new knight, with characteristic English frankness and brusque simplicity, chose as his device the figure of a negro slave, kneeling and in chains. Sir John's work was the invention of Christians, was to remain a bloody and awful monopoly in the hands of Christians for a quarter of a millenium, was to destroy homes, separate families, enslave friendless men and women, and break a myriad of human hearts, to the end that Christian nations might be prosperous and comfortable, Christian churches be built, and the gospel of the meek and merciful Redeemer be spread abroad in the earth; and so in the name of his ship, unsuspected but eloquent and clear, lay hidden prophecy: she was called "The Jesus."

But at last, in England, an illegitimate Christian rose against slavery. It is curious that when a Christian rises against a rooted wrong at all, he is usually an illegitimate Christian, member of some despised and bastard sect. There was a bitter struggle, but in the end the slave trade had to go—and went. The Biblical authorizations remained, but the practice changed.

Then—the usual thing happened: the visiting English critic among us began straightway to hold up his pious hands in horror at our slavery. His distress was unappeasable, his words full of bitterness and contempt. It is true we had not so many as fifteen hundred thousand slaves for him to worry about, while his England still owned twelve millions, in her foreign possessions; but that fact did not modify his wail any, or stay his tears, or soften his censure. The fact that every time we had tried to get rid of our slavery in previous generations but had always been obstructed, balked and defeated by England, was a matter of no consequence to him; it was ancient history, and not worth the telling.

Our own conversion came at last. We began to stir against slavery. Hearts grew soft, here, there, and yonder. There was no place in the land where the seeker could not find some small budding sign of pity for the slave. No place in all the land but one —the pulpit. It yielded at last; it always does. It fought a strong and stubborn fight, and then did what it always does, joined the procession—at the tail end. Slavery fell. The slavery-texts remained; the practice changed, that was all.

During many ages, there were witches. The Bible said so. The Bible commanded that they should not be allowed to live. Therefore the Church, after doing its duty in but a lazy and indolent way for eight hundred years, gathered up its halters, thumb-screws and firebrands, and set about its holy work in earnest. She worked hard at it night and day during nine centuries and imprisoned, tortured, hanged and burned whole hordes and armies of witches, and washed the Christian world clean with their foul blood.

⎾Then it was discovered that there was no such thing as witches, and never had been. One does not know whether to laugh or to cry. Who discovered that there was no such a thing as a witch—the priest, the parson? No, these never discover anything. At Salem, the parson clung pathetically to his witch-text after the laity had abandoned it in remorse and tears for the crimes and cruelties it had persuaded them to do. The parson wanted more blood, more shame, more brutalities; it was the unconsecrated laity that stayed his hand. In Scotland the parson killed the witch after the magistrate had pronounced her innocent; and when the merciful legislature proposed to sweep the hideous laws against witches from the statute book, it was the parson who came imploring, with tears and imprecations, that they be suffered to stand.⏌

⎾There are no witches. The witch-text remains; only the practice has changed. Hell-fire is gone, but the text remains. Infant damnation is gone, but the text remains. More than two hundred death penalties are gone from the law books, but the texts that authorized them remain.⏌

Is it not well worthy of note that of all the multitude of texts through which man has driven his annihilating pen he has never once made the mistake of obliterating a good and useful one? It does certainly seem to suggest that if man

10 [Macfarlane]

[1894?]

WHEN I was just turned twenty I wandered to Cincinnati, and was there several months. Our boarding house crew was made of commonplace people of various ages and both sexes. They were full of bustle, frivolity, chatter, and the joy of life, and were good-natured, clean-minded, and well meaning; but they were oppressively uninteresting, for all that—with one exception. This was Macfarlane, a Scotchman. He was forty years old—just double my age—but we were opposites in most ways, and comrades from the start. I always spent my evenings by the wood fire in his room, listening in comfort to his tireless talk and to the dulled complainings of the winter storms, until the clock struck ten. At that hour he grilled a smoked herring, after the fashion of my earlier friend in Philadelphia, the Englishman Sumner. His herring was his nightcap and my signal to go.

He was six feet high and rather lank, a serious and sincere man. He had no humor, nor any comprehension of it. He had a sort of smile, whose office was to express his good nature, but if I ever heard him laugh the memory of it is gone from me. He was intimate with no one in the house but me, though he was courteous and pleasant with all. He had two or three dozen weighty books—philosophies, histories and scientific works—and at the head of this procession was his Bible and his dictionary. After his herring he always read two or three hours in bed.

Diligent talker as he was, he seldom said anything about himself. To ask him a personal question gave him no offence—nor the asker any information; he merely turned the matter aside and flowed placidly on about other things. He told me once that he had had hardly any schooling, and that such learning as he had, he had picked up for himself. That was his sole biographical revelation, I believe. Whether he was bachelor, widower, or grass-widower, remained his own secret. His clothes were cheap, but neat and care-takingly preserved; ours was a cheap boarding house; he left the house at six, mornings, and returned to it toward six, evenings; his hands were not soft: so I reasoned that he worked at some mechanical calling ten hours a day, for humble wages—but I never knew. As a rule, technicalities of a man's vocation, and figures and metaphors drawn from it, slip out in his talk and reveal his trade; but if this ever happened in Macfarlane's case I was none the wiser, although I was constantly on the watch during half a year for those very betrayals. It was mere curiosity, for I didn't care what his trade was, but I wanted to detect it in true detective fashion and was annoyed because I couldn't do it. I think he was a remarkable man, to be able to keep the shop out of his talk all that time.

There was another noteworthy feature about him: he seemed to know his dictionary from beginning to end. He claimed that he did. He was frankly proud of this accomplishment and said I would not find it possible to challenge him with an English word which he could not promptly spell and define. I lost much time trying to hunt up a word which would beat him, but those weeks were spent in vain and I finally gave it up; which made him so proud and happy that I wished I had surrendered earlier.

He seemed to be as familiar with his Bible as he was with his dictionary. It was easy to see that he considered himself a philosopher and a thinker. His talk always ran upon grave and large questions; and I must do him the justice to say that his heart and conscience were in his talk and that there was no appearance of reasoning and arguing for the vain pleasure of hearing himself do it.

Of course his thinkings and reasonings and philosophizings were those of a but partly taught and wholly untrained mind, yet he hit by accident upon some curious and striking things. For instance. The time was the early part of 1856—fourteen or fifteen years before Mr. Darwin's "Descent of Man" startled the world— yet here was Macfarlane talking the same idea to me, there in the boarding house in Cincinnati.

The same general idea, but with a difference. Macfarlane considered that the animal life in the world was developed in the course of æons of time from a few microscopic seed-germs, or perhaps *one* microscopic seed-germ deposited upon the globe by the Creator in the dawn of time; and that this development was progressive upon an ascending scale toward ultimate perfection until *man* was reached; and that then the progressive scheme broke pitifully down and went to wreck and ruin!

He said that man's heart was the only bad heart in the animal kingdom; that man was the only animal capable of feeling malice, envy, vindictiveness, vengefulness, hatred, selfishness, the only animal that loved drunkenness, almost the only animal that could endure personal uncleanliness and a filthy habitation, the sole animal in whom was fully developed the base instinct called *patriotism*, the sole animal that robs, persecutes, oppresses, and kills members of his own immediate tribe, the sole animal that steals and enslaves the members of *any* tribe.

He claimed that man's intellect was a brutal addition to him and degraded him to a rank far below the plane of the other animals, and that there was never a man who did not use his intellect daily all his life to advantage himself at other people's expense. The divinest divine reduced his domestics to humble servitude under him by advantage of his superior intellect, and those servants in turn were above a still lower grade of people by force of brains that were still a little better than theirs.

11 Contract with Mrs. T. K. Beecher

[1895]

I

If you prove right and I prove wrong
A million years from now,
In language plain and frank and strong
My error I'll avow
To your dear mocking face.

II

If I prove right, by God His grace,
Full sorry I shall be,
For in that solitude no trace
There'll be of you and me,
Nor of our vanished race.

III

A million years, O patient stone,
You've waited for this message.
Deliver it a million hence!
[Survivor pays expressage.]

MARK TWAIN

12 [Man's Place in the Animal World]

[1896]

In August, 1572, similar things were occurring in Paris and else-where in France. In this case it was Christian against Christian. The Roman Catholics, by previous concert, sprung a surprise upon the unprepared and unsuspecting protestants, and butchered them by thousands—both sexes and all ages. This was the memorable St. Bartholomew's Day. At Rome the Pope and the Church gave public thanks to God when the happy news came.

During several centuries hundreds of heretics were burned at the stake every year because their religious opinions were not satisfactory to the Roman Church.

In all ages the savages of all lands have made the slaughtering of their neighboring brothers and the enslaving of their women and children the common business of their lives.

Hypocrisy, envy, malice, cruelty, vengefulness, seduction, rape, robbery, swindling, arson, bigamy, adultery, and the oppression and humiliation of the poor and the helpless in all ways, have been and still are more or less common among both the civilized and uncivilized peoples of the earth.

For many centuries "the common brotherhood of man" has been urged—on Sundays—and "patriotism" on Sundays and week-days both. Yet patriotism *contemplates the opposite of a common brotherhood.*

Woman's equality with man has never been conceded by any people, ancient or modern, civilized or savage.

I HAVE been scientifically studying the traits and dispositions of the "lower animals" (so-called,) and contrasting them with the traits and dispositions of man. I find the result profoundly humiliating to me. For it obliges me to renounce my allegiance to the Darwinian theory of the Ascent of Man from the Lower Animals; since it now seems plain to me that that theory ought to be vacated in favor of a new and truer one, this new and truer one to be named the *Descent* of Man from the Higher Animals.

In proceeding toward this unpleasant conclusion I have not guessed or speculated or conjectured, but have used what is commonly called the scientific method. That is to say, I have subjected every postulate that presented itself, to the crucial test of actual experiment, and have adopted it or rejected it according to the result. Thus I verified and established each step of my course in its turn before advancing to the next. These experiments were made in the London Zöological Gardens, and covered many months of pains-taking and fatiguing work.

Before particularizing any of the experiments, I wish to state one or two things which seem to more properly belong in this place than further along. This in the interest of clearness. The massed experiments established to my satisfaction certain generalizations, to-wit:

1. That the human race is of one distinct species. It exhibits slight variations—in color, stature, mental calibre, and so on—due to climate, environment, and so forth; but it is a species by itself, and not to be confounded with any other.

2. That the quadrupeds are a distinct family, also. This family exhibits variations—in color, size, food-preferences and so on; but it is a family by itself.

3. That the other families—the birds, the fishes, the insects, the reptiles, etc., are more or less distinct, also. They are in the procession. They are links in the chain which stretches down from the higher animals to man at the bottom.

Some of my experiments were quite curious. In the course of

my reading I had come across a case where, many years ago, some hunters on our Great Plains organized a buffalo hunt for the entertainment of an English earl—that, and to provide some fresh meat for his larder. They had charming sport. They killed seventy-two of those great animals; and ate part of one of them and left the seventy-one to rot. In order to determine the difference between an anaconda and an earl—if any—I caused seven young calves to be turned into the anaconda's cage. The grateful reptile immediately crushed one of them and swallowed it, then lay back satisfied. It showed no further interest in the calves, and no disposition to harm them. I tried this experiment with other anacondas; always with the same result. The fact stood proven that the difference between an earl and an anaconda is, that the earl is cruel and the anaconda isn't; and that the earl wantonly destroys what he has no use for, but the anaconda doesn't. This seemed to suggest that the anaconda was not descended from the earl. It also seemed to suggest that the earl was descended from the anaconda, and had lost a good deal in the transition.

I was aware that many men who have accumulated more millions of money than they can ever use, have shown a rabid hunger for more, and have not scrupled to cheat the ignorant and the helpless out of their poor savings in order to partially appease that appetite. I furnished a hundred different kinds of wild and tame animals the opportunity to accumulate vast stores of food, but none of them would do it. The squirrels and bees and certain birds made accumulations, but stopped when they had gathered a winter's supply, and could not be persuaded to add to it either honestly or by chicane. In order to bolster up a tottering reputation the ant pretended to store up supplies, but I was not deceived. I know the ant. These experiments convinced me that there is this difference between man and the higher animals: he is avaricious and miserly, they are not.

In the course of my experiments I convinced myself that among the animals man is the only one that harbors insults and injuries, broods over them, waits till a chance offers, then takes revenge. The passion of revenge is unknown to the higher animals.

Roosters keep harems, but it is by consent of their concubines; therefore no wrong is done. Men keep harems, but it is by brute force, privileged by atrocious laws which the other sex were allowed no hand in making. In this matter man occupies a far lower place than the rooster.

Cats are loose in their morals, but not consciously so. Man, in his descent from the cat, has brought the cat's looseness with him but has left the unconsciousness behind—the saving grace which excuses the cat. The cat is innocent, man is not.

Indecency, vulgarity, obscenity—these are strictly confined to man; he invented them. Among the higher animals there is no trace of them. They hide nothing; they are not ashamed. Man, with his soiled mind, covers himself. He will not even enter a drawing room with his breast and back naked, so alive is he and his mates to indecent suggestion. Man is "the Animal that Laughs." But so does the monkey, as Mr. Darwin pointed out; and so does the Australian bird that is called the laughing jackass. No—man is the Animal that Blushes. He is the only one that does it—or has occasion to.

At the head of this article we see how "three monks were burnt to death" a few days ago, and a prior "put to death with atrocious cruelty." Do we inquire into the details? No; or we should find out that the prior was subjected to unprintable mutilations. Man—when he is a North American Indian—gouges out his prisoner's eyes; when he is King John, with a nephew to render untroublesome, he uses a red-hot iron; when he is a religious zealot dealing with heretics in the Middle Ages, he skins his capture alive and scatters salt on his back; in the first Richard's time he shuts up a multitude of Jew families in a tower and sets fire to it; in Columbus's time he captures a family of Spanish Jews and—but *that* is not printable; in our day in England a man is fined ten shillings for beating his mother nearly to death with a chair, and another man is fined forty shillings for having four pheasant eggs in his possession without being able to satisfactorily explain how he got them. Of all the animals, man is the only one that is cruel. He is the only one that inflicts pain for the pleasure of doing it. It is a trait that is not known to the higher animals. The cat plays with the frightened mouse; but she has this excuse, that she does not know that the mouse is suffering. The cat is moderate—unhumanly moderate: she only scares the mouse, she does not hurt it; she doesn't dig out its eyes, or tear off its skin, or drive splinters under its nails—man-fashion; when she is done playing with it she makes a sudden meal of it and puts it out of its trouble. Man is the Cruel Animal. He is alone in that distinction.

The higher animals engage in individual fights, but never in organized masses. Man is the only animal that deals in that atrocity of atrocities, War. He is the only one that gathers his brethren about him and goes forth in cold blood and with calm pulse to exterminate his kind. He is the only animal that for sordid wages will march out, as the Hessians did in our Revolution, and as the boyish Prince Napoleon did in the Zulu war, and help to slaughter strangers of his own species who have done him no harm and with whom he has no quarrel.

Man is the only animal that robs his helpless fellow of his country—takes possession of it and drives him out of it or destroys him. Man has done this in all the ages. There is not an acre of ground on the globe that is in possession of its rightful owner, or that has not been taken away from owner after owner, cycle after cycle, by force and bloodshed.

Man is the only Slave. And he is the only animal who enslaves. He has always been a slave in one form or another, and has always held other slaves in bondage under him in one way or another. In our day he is always some man's slave for wages, and does that man's work; and this slave has other slaves under him for minor wages, and they do *his* work. The higher animals are the only ones who exclusively do their own work and provide their own living.

Man is the only Patriot. He sets himself apart in his own country, under his own flag, and sneers at the other nations, and keeps multitudinous uniformed assassins on hand at heavy expense to grab slices of other people's countries, and keep *them* from grabbing slices of *his*. And in the intervals between campaigns he washes the blood off his hands and works for "the universal brotherhood of man"—with his mouth.

Man is the Religious Animal. He is the only Religious Animal. He is the only animal that has the True Religion—several of them. He is the only animal that loves his neighbor as himself, and cuts his throat if his theology isn't straight. He has made a graveyard of the globe in trying his honest best to smooth his brother's path to happiness and heaven. He was at it in the time of the Caesars, he was at it in Mahomet's time, he was at it in the time of the Inquisition, he was at it in France a couple of centuries, he was at it in England in Mary's day, he has been at it ever since he first saw the light, he is at it to-day in Crete—as per the telegrams quoted above—he will be at it somewhere else to-morrow. The higher animals have no religion. And we are told that they are going to be left out, in the Hereafter. I wonder why? It seems questionable taste.

Man is the Reasoning Animal. Such is the claim. I think it is open to dispute. Indeed, my experiments have proven to me that he is the Unreasoning Animal. Note his history, as sketched above. It seems plain to me that whatever he is he is *not* a reasoning animal. His record is the fantastic record of a maniac. I consider that the strongest count against his intelligence is the fact that with that record back of him he blandly sets himself up as the head animal of the lot; whereas by his own standards he is the bottom one.

In truth, man is incurably foolish. Simple things which the other animals easily learn, he is incapable of learning. Among my experiments was this. In an hour I taught a cat and a dog to be friends. I put them in a cage. In another hour I taught them to be friends with a rabbit. In the course of two days I was able to add a fox, a goose, a squirrel and some doves. Finally a monkey. They lived together in peace; even affectionately.

Next, in another cage I confined an Irish Catholic from Tipperary, and as soon as he seemed tame I added a Scotch Presbyterian from Aberdeen. Next a Turk from Constantinople; a Greek Christian from Crete; an Armenian; a Methodist from the wilds of Arkansaw; a Bhuddist from China; a Brahmin from Benares. Finally, a Salvation Army Colonel from Wapping. Then I stayed away two whole days. When I came back to note results, the cage of Higher Animals was all right, but in the other there was but a chaos of gory odds and ends of turbans and fezzes and plaids and bones and flesh—not a specimen left alive. These Reasoning Animals had disagreed on a theological detail and carried the matter to a Higher Court.

One is obliged to concede that in true loftiness of character, Man cannot claim to approach even the meanest of the Higher Animals. It is plain that he is constitutionally incapable of approaching that altitude; that he is constitutionally afflicted with a Defect which must make such approach forever impossible, for it is manifest that this Defect is permanent in him, indestructible, ineradicable.

I find this Defect to be THE MORAL SENSE. He is the only animal that has it. It is the secret of his degradation. It is the quality *which enables him to do wrong*. It has no other office. It is incapable of performing any other function. It could never have been intended to perform any other. Without it, man could do no wrong. He would rise at once to the level of the Higher Animals.

Since the Moral Sense has but the one office, the one capacity —to enable man to do wrong—it is plainly without value to him. It is as valueless to him as is disease. In fact it manifestly *is* a disease. *Rabies* is bad, but it is not so bad as this disease. Rabies enables a man to do a thing which he could not do when in a healthy state: kill his neighbor with a poisonous bite. No one is the better man for having rabies. The Moral Sense enables a man to do wrong. It enables him to do wrong in a thousand ways. Rabies is an innocent disease, compared to the Moral Sense. No one, then, can be the better man for having the Moral Sense. What, now, do we find the Primal Curse to have been? Plainly what it was in the beginning: the infliction upon man of the Moral Sense; the ability to distinguish good from evil; and with it, necessarily, the ability to *do* evil; for there can be no evil act without the presence of consciousness of it in the doer of it.

And so I find that we have descended and degenerated, from some far ancestor,—some microscopic atom wandering at its pleasure between the mighty horizons of a drop of water perchance,— insect by insect, animal by animal, reptile by reptile, down the long highway of smirchless innocence, till we have reached the bottom stage of development—nameable as the Human Being. Below us —nothing. Nothing but the Frenchman.

There is only one possible stage below the Moral Sense; that is the Immoral Sense. The Frenchman has it. Man is but little lower than the angels. This definitely locates him. He is between the angels and the French.

Man seems to be a rickety poor sort of a thing, any way you take him; a kind of British Museum of infirmities and inferiorities. He is always undergoing repairs. A machine that was as unreliable as he is would have no market. On top of his specialty—the Moral Sense—are piled a multitude of minor infirmities; such a multitude, indeed, that one may broadly call them countless. The higher animals get their teeth without pain or inconvenience. Man gets his through months and months of cruel torture; and at a time of life when he is but ill able to bear it. As soon as he has got them they must all be pulled out again, for they were of no value in the first place, not worth the loss of a night's rest. The second set will answer for a while, by being reinforced occasionally with rubber or plugged up with gold; but he will never get a set which can really be depended on till a dentist makes him one. This set will be called "false" teeth—as if he had ever worn any other kind.

In a wild state—a natural state—the Higher Animals have a few diseases; diseases of little consequence; the main one is old age. But man starts in as a child and lives on diseases till the end, as a regular diet. He has mumps, measles, whooping cough, croup, tonsilitis, diphtheria, scarlet fever, almost as a matter of course. Afterward, as he goes along, his life continues to be threatened at every turn: by colds, coughs, asthma, bronchitis, itch, cholera, cancer, consumption, yellow fever, bilious fever, typhus fevers, hay fever, ague, chilblains, piles, inflammation of the entrails, indigestion, toothache, earache, deafness, dumbness, blindness, influenza, chicken pox, cow pox, small pox, liver complaint, constipation, bloody flux, warts, pimples, boils, carbuncles, abscesses, bunions, corns, tumors, fistulas, pneumonia, softening of the brain, melancholia and fifteen other kinds of insanity; dysentery, jaundice, diseases of the heart, the bones, the skin, the scalp, the spleen, the kidneys, the nerves, the brain, the blood; scrofula, paralysis, leprosy, neuralgia, palsy, fits, headache, thirteen kinds of rheumatism, forty-six of gout, and a formidable supply of gross and unprintable disorders of one sort and another. Also—but why continue the list. The mere names of the agents appointed to keep this shackly machine out of repair would hide him from sight if printed on his body in the smallest type known to the founder's art. He is but a basket of festering offal provided for the support and entertainment of swarming armies of bacilli,—armies commissioned to rot him and destroy him, and each army equipped with a special detail of the work. The process of waylaying him, persecuting him, rotting him, killing him, begins with his first breath, and there is no mercy, no pity, no truce till he draws his last one.

Look at the workmanship of him, in certain of its particulars. What are his tonsils for? They perform no useful function; they have no value. They have no business there. They are but a trap. They have but the one office, the one industry: to provide tonsilitis and quinzy and such things for the possessor of them. And what is the vermiform appendix for? It has no value; it cannot perform any useful service. It is but an ambuscaded enemy whose sole interest in life is to lie in wait for stray grape seeds and employ them to breed strangulated hernia. And what are the male's mammals for? For business, they are out of the question; as an ornament, they

are a mistake. What is his beard for? It performs no useful function; it is a nuisance and a discomfort; all nations hate it; all nations persecute it with the razor. And because it is a nuisance and
a discomfort, Nature never allows the supply of it to fall short, in
any man's case, between puberty and the grave. You never see a
man bald-headed on his chin. But his hair! It is a graceful ornament, it is a comfort, it is the best of all protections against certain
perilous ailments, man prizes it above emeralds and rubies. And
because of these things Nature puts it on, half the time, so that it
won't stay. Man's sight, smell, hearing, sense of locality—how
inferior they are. The condor sees a corpse at five miles; man has
no telescope that can do it. The bloodhound follows a scent that
is two days old. The robin hears the earth-worm burrowing his
course under the ground. The cat, deported in a closed basket,
finds its way home again through twenty miles of country which it
has never seen.

For style, look at the Bengal tiger—that ideal of grace, beauty,
physical perfection, majesty. And then look at Man—that poor
thing. He is the Animal of the Wig, the Trepanned Skull, the Ear
Trumpet, the Glass Eye, the Pasteboard Nose, the Porcelain
Teeth, the Silver Windpipe, the Wooden Leg—a creature that is
mended and patched all over, from top to bottom. If he can't
get renewals of his brickabrac in the next world, what will he
look like?

He has just one stupendous superiority. In his intellect he is
supreme. The Higher Animals cannot touch him there. It is curious, it is noteworthy, that no heaven has ever been offered him
wherein his one sole superiority was provided with a chance to
enjoy itself. Even when he himself has imagined a heaven, he has
never made provision in it for intellectual joys. It is a striking
omission. It seems a tacit confession that heavens are provided for
the Higher Animals alone. This is matter for thought; and for
serious thought. And it is full of a grim suggestion: that we are not
as important, perhaps, as we had all along supposed we were.

13 [Something about Repentance]

[1898]

IT is curious—the mis-association of certain words. For instance, the word Repentance. Through want of reflection, we associate it exclusively with Sin. We get the notion early, and keep it always, that we repent of bad deeds only; whereas we do a formidably large business in repenting of good deeds which we have done. Often when we repent of a sin, we do it perfunctorily, from principle, coldly and from the head; but when we repent of a good deed the repentance comes hot and bitter, and straight from the heart. Often, when we repent of a sin, we can forgive ourselves and drop the matter out of our minds; but when we repent of a good deed we seldom get peace—we go on repenting, to the end. And the repentance is so perennially young and strong and vivid and vigorous! A great benefaction, conferred with your whole heart upon an ungrateful man—with what immortal persistence and never-cooling energy do you repent of that! Repentance of a sin is a pale poor perishable thing compared to it. I am quite sure that the average man is built just as I am; otherwise I should not be making this revelation of my inside. I say the average man, and stop there; for I am quite certain that there are people who do not repent of their good deeds when the return they get for them is treachery and ingratitude. I think that these few ought to be in heaven; they are in the way here. In my time I have committed several millions of sins. Many of them I probably repented of—I do not remember, now; others I was partly minded to repent of, but it did not seem worth while; all of them but the recent ones and a few scattering former ones I have forgotten. In my time I have done eleven good deeds. I remember all of them; four of them with crystal clearness. These four I repent of whenever I think of them—and that is not seldomer than fifty-two times a year. I repent of them in the same old original furious way, undiminished, always. If I wake up, away in the night, they are there, waiting and ready; and they keep me company till the morning. I have not committed any sin that has lasted me like this, save one; and I have not repented of any sin with the unmodifying earnestness and sincerity with which I have repented of these four gracious and beautiful good deeds.

Possibly you who are reading these paragraphs are of those few who have got mislaid and ought to be in heaven. In that case you will not understand what I have been saying, and will have no sympathy with it; but your neighbor will, if he is fifty years old.

14   *Corn-Pone Opinions*

[1901]

FIFTY years ago, when I was a boy of fifteen and helping to in-habit a Missourian village on the banks of the Mississippi, I had a friend whose society was very dear to me because I was for-bidden by my mother to partake of it. He was a gay and impudent and satirical and delightful young black man—a slave—who daily preached sermons from the top of his master's woodpile, with me for sole audience. He imitated the pulpit style of the several clergy-men of the village, and did it well, and with fine passion and energy. To me he was a wonder. I believed he was the greatest orator in the United States, and would some day be heard from. But it did not happen; in the distribution of rewards he was over-looked. It is the way, in this world.

He interrupted his preaching, now and then, to saw a stick of wood; but the sawing was a pretence—he did it with his mouth; exactly imitating the sound the buck-saw makes in shrieking its way through the wood. But it served its purpose: it kept his master from coming out to see how the work was getting along. I listened to the sermons from the open window of a lumber-room at the back of our house. One of his texts was this:

"You tell me whar a man gits his corn-pone, en I'll tell you what his 'pinions is."

I can never forget it. It was deeply impressed upon me. By my mother. Not upon my memory, but elsewhere. She had slipped in

upon me while I was absorbed and not watching. The black philosopher's idea was, that a man is not independent, and cannot
afford views which might interfere with his bread and butter. If he
would prosper, he must train with the majority; in matters of large
moment, like politics and religion, he must think and feel with the
bulk of his neighbors, or suffer damage in his social standing and in
his business prosperities. He must restrict himself to corn-pone
opinions—at least on the surface. He must get his opinions from
other people; he must reason out none for himself; he must have
no first-hand views.

I think Jerry was right, in the main, but I think he did not
go far enough.

1. It was his idea that a man conforms to the majority-view
of his locality by calculation and intention. This happens, but I
think it is not the rule.

2. It was his idea that there is such a thing as a first-hand
opinion; an original opinion; an opinion which is coldly reasoned-
out in a man's head, by a searching analysis of the facts involved,
with the heart unconsulted, and the jury-room closed against
outside influences. It may be that such an opinion has been born
somewhere, at some time or other, but I suppose it got away before they could catch it and stuff it and put it in the museum.

I am persuaded that a coldly thought-out and independent
verdict upon a fashion in clothes, or manners, or literature, or
politics, or religion, or any other matter that is projected into the
field of our notice and interest, is a most rare thing—if it has indeed
ever existed.

A new thing in costume appears—the flaring hoop-skirt, for
example—and the passers-by are shocked, and the irreverent laugh.
Six months later everybody is reconciled; the fashion has established itself; it is admired, now, and no one laughs. Public opinion
resented it before, public opinion accepts it now, and is happy in
it. Why? Was the resentment reasoned out? Was the acceptance
reasoned out? No. The instinct that moves to conformity did the
work. It is our nature to conform; it is a force which not many can

successfully resist. What is its seat? The inborn requirement of Self-Approval. We all have to bow to that; there are no exceptions. Even the woman who refuses from first to last to wear the hoop-skirt comes under that law and is its slave; she could not wear the skirt and have her own approval; and that she *must* have, she cannot help herself. But as a rule our self-approval has its source in but one place and not elsewhere—the approval of other people. A person of vast consequence can introduce any kind of novelty in dress and the general world will presently adopt it—moved to do it, in the first place, by the natural instinct to passively yield to that vague something recognized as authority, and in the second place by the human instinct to train with the multitude and have its approval. An Empress introduced the hoop-skirt, and we know the result. A nobody introduced the Bloomer, and we know the result. If Eve should come again, in her ripe renown, and reintroduce her quaint styles—well, we know what would happen. And we should be cruelly embarrassed, along at first.

The hoop-skirt runs its course, and disappears. Nobody reasons about it. One woman abandons the fashion; her neighbor notices this and follows her lead; this influences the next woman; and so on and so on, and presently the skirt has vanished out of the world, no one knows how nor why; nor cares, for that matter. It will come again, by and by; and in due course will go again.

Twenty-five years ago, in England, six or eight wine glasses stood grouped by each person's plate at a dinner party, and they were used, not left idle and empty; to-day there are but three or four in the group, and the average guest sparingly uses about two of them. We have not adopted this new fashion yet, but we shall do it presently. We shall not think it out, we shall merely conform, and let it go at that. We get our notions and habits and opinions from outside influences, we do not have to study them out.

Our table manners, and company manners, and street manners change from time to time, but the changes are not reasoned out; we merely notice and conform. We are creatures of outside influences; as a rule we do not think, we only imitate. We cannot invent standards that will stick; what we mistake for standards are only fashions, and perishable. We may continue to admire them, but we drop the use of them. We notice this in literature. Shakspeare is a standard, and fifty years ago we used to write tragedies which he couldn't tell from—from somebody else's; but we don't do it any more, now. Our prose standard, three-quarters of a century ago, was ornate and diffuse; some authority or other changed it in the direction of compactness and simplicity, and conformity followed, without argument. The historical novel starts up suddenly, and sweeps the land. Everybody writes one, and the nation is glad. We had historical novels before; but nobody read them, and the rest of us conformed—without reasoning it out. We are conforming in the other way, now, because it is another case of everybody.

The outside influences are always pouring in upon us, and we are always obeying their orders and accepting their verdicts. The Smiths like the new play; the Joneses go to see it, and they copy the Smith verdict. Morals, religions, politics, get their following from surrounding influences and atmospheres, almost entirely; not from study, not from thinking. A man must and will have his own approval first of all, in each and every moment and circumstance of his life—even if he must repent of a self-approved act the moment after its commission, in order to get his self-approval *again*; but, speaking in general terms, a man's self-approval, in the large concerns of life, has its source in the approval of the people about him, and not in a searching personal examination of the matter. Mohammedans are Mohammedans because they are born and reared among that sect, not because they have thought it out and can furnish sound reasons for being Mohammedans; we know why Catholics are Catholics; why Presbyterians are Presbyterians; why Baptists are Baptists; why Mormons are Mormons; why thieves are thieves; why monarchists are monarchists; why republicans are republicans, and democrats democrats. We know it is a matter of association and sympathy, not reasoning and examination; that hardly a man in the world has an opinion upon morals, politics or

religion which he got otherwise than through his associations and
sympathies. Broadly speaking, there are none but corn-pone opinions. And broadly speaking, Corn-Pone stands for Self-Approval.
Self-approval is acquired mainly from the approval of other people. The result is Conformity. Sometimes Conformity has a sordid
business interest—the bread-and-butter interest—but not in most
cases, I think. I think that in the majority of cases it is unconscious
and not calculated; that it is born of the human being's natural
yearning to stand well with his fellows, and have their inspiring
approval and praise—a yearning which is commonly so strong and
so insistent that it cannot be effectually resisted, and must have
its way.

A political emergency brings out the corn-pone opinion in
fine force in its two chief varieties—the pocket-book variety, which
has its origin in self-interest, and the bigger variety, the sentimental variety—the one which can't bear to be outside the pale;
can't bear to be in disfavor; can't endure the averted face and the
cold shoulder; wants to stand well with the friends, wants to be
smiled upon, wants to be welcome, wants to hear the precious
words *"he's* on the right track!" Uttered, perhaps, by an ass, but
still an ass of high degree, an ass whose approval is gold and diamonds to a smaller ass, and confers glory, and honor and happiness, and membership in the herd. For these gauds many a man
will dump his life-long principles into the street, and his conscience along with them. We have seen it happen. In some millions of instances.

Men think they think upon great political questions, and
they do; but they think with their party, not independently; they
read its literature, but not that of the other side; they arrive at convictions, but they are drawn from a partial view of the matter in
hand and are of no particular value. They swarm with their party,
they feel with their party, they are happy in their party's approval;
and where the party leads they will follow, whether for right and
honor, or through blood and dirt and a mush of mutilated morals.

In our late canvas half of the nation passionately believed

that in silver lay salvation, the other half as passionately believed that that way lay destruction. Do you believe that a tenth part of the people, on either side, had any rational excuse for having an opinion about the matter at all? I studied that mighty question to the bottom—and came out empty. Half of our people passionately believe in high tariff, the other half believe otherwise. Does this mean study and examination, or only feeling? The latter, I think. I have deeply studied that question, too—and didn't arrive. We all do no end of feeling, and we mistake it for thinking. And out of it we get an aggregation which we consider a Boon. Its name is Public Opinion. It is held in reverence. It settles everything. Some think it the Voice of God. Pr'aps.

I suppose that in more cases than we should like to admit, we have two sets of opinions: one private, the other public; one secret and sincere, the other corn-pone, and more or less tainted.

15   *The Five Boons of Life*

[1902]

I

IN the morning of life came the good fairy with her basket, and said:

"Here are gifts. Take one, leave the others. And be wary, choose wisely; oh, choose wisely! for only one of them is valuable."

The gifts were five: Fame, Love, Riches, Pleasure, Death. The youth said eagerly:

"There is no need to consider;" and he chose Pleasure.

He went out into the world and sought out the pleasures that youth delights in. But each in its turn was short-lived and disappointing, vain and empty; and each, departing, mocked him. In the end he said: "These years I have wasted. If I could but choose again, I would choose wisely."

II

The fairy appeared, and said:

"Four of the gifts remain. Choose once more; and oh, remember—time is flying, and only one of them is precious."

The man considered long, then chose Love; and did not mark the tears that rose in the fairy's eyes.

After many, many years the man sat by a coffin, in an empty home. And he communed with himself, saying: "One by one they

have gone away and left me; and now she lies here, the dearest and
the last. Desolation after desolation has swept over me; for each
hour of happiness the treacherous trader, Love, has sold me I have
paid a thousand hours of grief. Out of my heart of hearts I
curse him."

III

"Choose again." It was the fairy speaking. "The years have
taught you wisdom—surely it must be so. Three gifts remain. Only
one of them has any worth—remember it, and choose warily."

The man reflected long, then chose Fame; and the fairy,
sighing, went her way.

Years went by and she came again, and stood behind the man
where he sat solitary in the fading day, thinking. And she knew
his thought:

"My name filled the world, and its praises were on every
tongue, and it seemed well with me for a little while. How little a
while it was! Then came envy; then detraction; then calumny;
then hate; then persecution. Then derision, which is the beginning
of the end. And last of all came pity, which is the funeral of fame.
Oh, the bitterness and misery of renown! target for mud in its
prime, for contempt and compassion in its decay."

IV

"Choose yet again." It was the fairy's voice. "Two gifts remain. And do not despair. In the beginning there was but one that
was precious, and it is still here."

"Wealth—which is power! How blind I was!" said the man.
"Now, at last, life will be worth the living. I will spend, squander,
dazzle. These mockers and despisers will crawl in the dirt before
me, and I will feed my hungry heart with their envy. I will have all
luxuries, all joys, all enchantments of the spirit, all contentments
of the body that man holds dear. I will buy, buy, buy! deference,
respect, esteem, worship—every pinchbeck grace of life the market
of a trivial world can furnish forth. I have lost much time, and

chosen badly heretofore, but let that pass; I was ignorant then, and could but take for best what seemed so."

Three short years went by, and a day came when the man sat shivering in a mean garret; and he was gaunt and wan and hollow-eyed, and clothed in rags; and he was gnawing a dry crust and mumbling:

"Curse all the world's gifts, for mockeries and gilded lies! And miscalled, every one. They are not gifts, but merely lendings. Pleasure, Love, Fame, Riches: they are but temporary disguises for lasting realities—Pain, Grief, Shame, Poverty. The fairy said true; in all her store there was but one gift which was precious, only one that was not valueless. How poor and cheap and mean I know those others now to be, compared with that inestimable one, that dear and sweet and kindly one, that steeps in dreamless and enduring sleep the pains that persecute the body, and the shames and griefs that eat the mind and heart. Bring it! I am weary, I would rest."

V

The fairy came, bringing again four of the gifts, but Death was wanting. She said:

"I gave it to a mother's pet, a little child. It was ignorant, but trusted me, asking me to choose for it. You did not ask me to choose."

"Oh, miserable me! What is there left for me?"

"What not even you have deserved: the wanton insult of Old Age."

16 "Was the World made for Man?"

[1903]

"Alfred Russell Wallace's revival of the theory that this earth is at the centre of the stellar universe, and is the only habitable globe, has aroused great interest in the world."—*Literary Digest.*

"For ourselves we do thoroughly believe that man, as he lives just here on this tiny earth, is in essence and possibilities the most sublime existence in all the range of non-divine being—the chief love and delight of God."—*Chicago "Interior,"* (Presb.)

I SEEM to be the only scientist and theologian still remaining to be heard from on this important matter of whether the world was made for man or not. I feel that it is time for me to speak.

I stand almost with the others. They believe the world was made for man, I believe it likely that it was made for man; they think there is proof, astronomical mainly, that it was made for man, I think there is evidence only, not proof, that it was made for him. It is too early, yet, to arrange the verdict, the returns are not all in. When they are all in, I think they will show that the world was made for man; but we must not hurry, we must patiently wait till they are all in.

Now as far as we have got, astronomy is on our side. Mr. Wallace has clearly shown this. He has clearly shown two things: that the world was made for man, and that the universe was made for the world—to stiddy it, you know. The astronomy part is settled, and cannot be challenged.

We come now to the geological part. This is the one where the evidence is not all in, yet. It is coming in, hourly, daily, coming in all the time, but naturally it comes with geological carefulness and deliberation, and we must not be impatient, we must not get excited, we must be calm, and wait. To lose our tranquillity will not hurry geology; nothing hurries geology.

It takes a long time to prepare a world for man, such a thing is not done in a day. Some of the great scientists, carefully ciphering the evidences furnished by geology, have arrived at the conviction that our world is prodigiously old, and they may be right, but Lord Kelvin is not of their opinion. He takes a cautious, conservative view, in order to be on the safe side, and feels sure it is not so old as they think. As Lord Kelvin is the highest authority in science now living, I think we must yield to him and accept his view. He does not concede that the world is more than a hundred million years old. He believes it is that old, but not older. Lyell believed that our race was introduced into the world 31,000 years ago, Herbert Spencer makes it 32,000. Lord Kelvin agrees with Spencer.

Very well. According to these figures it took 99,968,000 years to prepare the world for man, impatient as the Creator doubtless was to see him and admire him. But a large enterprise like this has to be conducted warily, painstakingly, logically. It was foreseen that man would have to have the oyster. Therefore the first preparation was made for the oyster. Very well, you cannot make an oyster out of whole cloth, you must make the oyster's ancestor first. This is not done in a day. You must make a vast variety of invertebrates, to start with—belemnites, trilobites, jebusites, amalekites, and that sort of fry, and put them to soak in a primary sea, and wait and see what will happen. Some will be a disappointment —the belemnites, the ammonites and such; they will be failures, they will die out and become extinct, in the course of the 19,000,000 years covered by the experiment, but all is not lost, for the amalekites will fetch the home-stake; they will develop gradually into encrinites, and stalactites, and blatherskites, and one thing and another as the mighty ages creep on and the Archaean and the Cambrian Periods pile their lofty crags in the primordial seas, and at last the first grand stage in the preparation of the world for man stands completed, the Oyster is done. An oyster has hardly any more reasoning power than a scientist has; and so it is reasonably certain that this one jumped to the conclusion that the nineteen-million years was a preparation for *him*; but that would be just like an oyster, which is the most conceited animal there is, except man. And anyway, this one could not know, at that early date, that he was only an incident in a scheme, and that there was some more to the scheme, yet.

The oyster being achieved, the next thing to be arranged for in the preparation of the world for man, was fish. Fish, and coal—to fry it with. So the Old Silurian seas were opened up to breed the fish in, and at the same time the great work of building Old Red Sandstone mountains 80,000 feet high to cold-storage their fossils in was begun. This latter was quite indispensable, for there would be no end of failures again, no end of extinctions—millions of them—and it would be cheaper and less trouble to can them in the rocks than keep tally of them in a book. One does not build the coal beds and 80,000 feet of perpendicular Old Red Sandstone in a brief time—no, it took twenty million years. In the first place, a coal bed is a slow and troublesome and tiresome thing to construct. You have to grow prodigious forests of tree-ferns and reeds and calamites and such things in a marshy region; then you have to sink them under out of sight and let them rot; then you have to turn the streams on them, so as to bury them under several feet of sediment, and the sediment must have time to harden and turn to rock; next you must grow another forest on top, then sink it and put on another layer of sediment and harden it; then more forest and more rock, layer upon layer, three miles deep—ah, indeed it is a sickening slow job to build a coal-measure and do it right!

So the millions of years drag on; and meantime the fish-culture is lazying along and frazzling out in a way to make a person tired. You have developed ten thousand kinds of fishes from the oyster; and come to look, you have raised nothing but fossils, nothing but extinctions. There is nothing left alive and progressive but a ganoid or two and perhaps half a dozen asteroids. Even the cat wouldn't eat such.

Still, it is no great matter; there is plenty of time, yet, and they will develop into something tasty before man is ready for them. Even a ganoid can be depended on for that, when he is not going to be called on for sixty million years.

The Palaeozoic time-limit having now been reached, it was necessary to begin the next stage in the preparation of the world for man, by opening up the Mesozoic Age and instituting some reptiles. For man would need reptiles. Not to eat, but to develop himself from. This being the most important detail of the scheme, a spacious liberality of time was set apart for it—thirty million years. What wonders followed! From the remaining ganoids and asteroids and alkaloids were developed by slow and steady and pains-taking culture those stupendous saurians that used to prowl about the steamy world in those remote ages, with their snaky heads reared forty feet in the air and sixty feet of body and tail racing and thrashing after. All gone, now, alas—all extinct, except the little handful of Arkansawrians left stranded and lonely with us here upon this far-flung verge and fringe of time.

Yes, it took thirty million years and twenty million reptiles to get one that would stick long enough to develop into something else and let the scheme proceed to the next step.

Then the Pterodactyl burst upon the world in all his impressive solemnity and grandeur, and all Nature recognized that the Cainozoic threshold was crossed and a new Period open for business, a new stage begun in the preparation of the globe for man. It may be that the Pterodactyl thought the thirty million years had been intended as a preparation for himself, for there was nothing too foolish for a Pterodactyl to imagine, but he was in error, the preparation was for man. Without doubt the Pterodactyl attracted great attention, for even the least observant could see that there was the making of a bird in him. And so it turned out. Also the makings of a mammal, in time. One thing we have to say to his credit, that in the matter of picturesqueness he was the triumph of his Period; he wore wings and had teeth, and was a starchy and wonderful mixture altogether, a kind of long-distance premonitory symptom of Kipling's marine:

> 'E isn't one o' the reg'lar Line, nor 'e isn't one of the crew,
> 'E's a kind of a giddy harumfrodite—soldier an' sailor too!

From this time onward for nearly another thirty million years the preparation moved briskly. From the Pterodactyl was developed the bird; from the bird the kangaroo, from the kangaroo the other marsupials; from these the mastodon, the megatherium, the giant sloth, the Irish elk, and all that crowd that you make useful and instructive fossils out of—then came the first great Ice Sheet, and they all retreated before it and crossed over the bridge at Behring's strait and wandered around over Europe and Asia and died. All except a few, to carry on the preparation with. Six Glacial Periods with two million years between Periods chased these poor orphans up and down and about the earth, from weather to weather—from tropic swelter at the poles to Arctic frost at the equator and back again and to and fro, they never knowing what kind of weather was going to turn up next; and if ever they settled down anywhere the whole continent suddenly sank under them without the least notice and they had to trade places with the fishes and scramble off to where the seas had been, and scarcely a dry rag on them; and when there was nothing else doing a volcano would let go and fire them out from wherever they had located. They led this unsettled and irritating life for twenty-five million years, half the time afloat, half the time aground, and always wondering what it was all for, they never suspecting, of course, that it was a preparation for man and had to be done just so or it wouldn't be any proper and harmonious place for him when he arrived.

And at last came the monkey, and anybody could see that man wasn't far off, now. And in truth that was so. The monkey went on developing for close upon 5,000,000 years, and then turned into a man—to all appearances.

Such is the history of it. Man has been here 32,000 years. That it took a hundred million years to prepare the world for him is proof that that is what it was done for. I suppose it is. I dunno. If the Eiffel tower were now representing the world's age, the skin of paint on the pinnacle-knob at its summit would represent man's share of that age; and anybody would perceive that that skin was what the tower was built for. I reckon they would, I dunno.

17 *God*

[1905]

H E made all things. There is not in the universe a thing, great
or small, which He did not make. He pronounced His work
"good." The word covers the whole of it; it puts the seal of His
approval upon each detail of it, it praises each detail of it. We also
approve and praise—with our mouths. With our mouths we praise
and approve the whole work. We do it loudly, we do it fervently
—also judiciously. Judiciously. For we do not enter into particulars.
Daily we pour out freshets of disapproval, dispraise, censure, passionate resentment, upon a considerable portion of the work—but
not with our mouths. No it is our acts that betray us, not our words.
Our words are all compliments, and they deceive Him. Without
a doubt they do. They make Him think we approve of all of
His works.

That is the way we argue. For ages we have taught ourselves to
believe that when we hide a disapproving fact, burying it under a
mountain of complimentary lies, He is not aware of it, does not
notice it, perceives only the compliments, and is deceived. But is
it really so? Among ourselves we concede that acts speak louder
than words, but we have persuaded ourselves that in His case it is
different; we imagine that all He cares for is words—noise; that if
we make the words pretty enough they will blind Him to the acts
that give them the lie.

But seriously, does any one really believe that? Is it not a daring affront to the Supreme Intelligence to believe such a thing? Does any of us inordinately praise a mother's whole family to her face, indiscriminately, and in that same moment slap one of her children? Would not that act turn our inflamed eulogy into nonsense? Would the mother be deceived? Would she not be offended—and properly?

But see what we do in His case. We approve all His works, we praise all His works, with a fervent enthusiasm—of words; and in the same moment we kill a fly, which is as much one of His works as is any other, and has been included and complimented in our sweeping eulogy. We not only kill the fly, but we do it in a spirit of measureless disapproval—even a spirit of hatred, exasperation, vindictiveness; and we regard that creature with disgust and loathing—which is the essence of contempt—and yet we have just been praising it, approving it, glorifying it. We have been praising it to its Maker, and now our act insults its Maker. The praise was dishonest, the act is honest; the one was wordy hypocrisy, the other is compact candor.

We hunt the fly remorselessly; also the flea, the rat, the snake, the disease-germ and a thousand other creatures which He pronounced good, and was satisfied with, and which we loudly praise and approve—with our mouths—and then harry and chase and malignantly destroy, by wholesale.

Manifestly this is not well, not wise, not right. It breeds falsehood and sham. Would He be offended if we should change it and appear before Him with the truth in our mouths as well as in our acts? May we not, trustingly and without fear, change our words and say—

"O Source of Truth, we have lied, and we repent. Hear us confess that which we have felt from the beginning of time, but have weakly tried to conceal from Thee: humbly we praise and glorify many of Thy works, and are grateful for their presence in our earth, Thy footstool, but not all of them."

That would be sufficient. It would not be necessary to name the exceptions.

18 *As Concerns Interpreting the Deity*

[1905]

THIS line of hieroglyphs was for fourteen years the despair of all the scholars who labored over the mysteries of the Rosetta stone:

After five years of study Champollion translated it thus:

Therefore let the worship of Epiphanes be maintained in all the temples; this upon pain of death.

That was the twenty-fourth translation that had been furnished by scholars. For a time, it stood. But only for a time. Then doubts began to assail it and undermine it, and the scholars resumed their labors. Three years of patient work produced eleven new translations; among them, this, by Grünfeldt, was received with considerable favor:

The horse of Epiphanes shall be maintained at the public expense; this upon pain of death.

But the following rendering, by Gospodin, was received by the learned world with yet greater favor:

The priest shall explain the wisdom of Epiphanes to all the people, and these shall listen with reverence, upon pain of death.

Seven years followed, in which twenty-one fresh and widely varying renderings were scored—none of them quite convincing. But now, at last, came Rawlinson, the youngest of all the scholars, with a translation which was immediately and universally recognised as being the correct version, and his name became famous in a day. So famous, indeed, that even the children were familiar with it; and such a noise did the achievement itself make that not even the noise of the monumental political event of that same year—the Flight from Elba—was able to smother it to silence. Rawlinson's version reads as follows:

Therefore, walk not away from the wisdom of Epiphanes, but turn and follow it; so shall it conduct thee to the temple's peace, and soften for thee the sorrows of life and the pains of death.

Here is another difficult text:

It is demotic—a style of Egyptian writing and a phase of the language which had perished from the knowledge of all men 2500 years before the Christian era. But the scholars of our day have penetrated its secret. The above text baffled them, however, for twenty-two years, and in that time they framed forty-six versions of it before they hit upon the right one—which is this:

It is forbidden the unconsecrated to utter foolish and irreverent speeches concerning sacred things: this privilege, by decree of the Holy Synod, being restricted to the clergy.

Our red Indians have left many records, in the form of pictures, upon our crags and boulders. It has taken our most gifted and pains-taking students two centuries to get at the meanings hidden in these pictures; yet there are still two little lines of hieroglyphs among the figures grouped upon the Dighton Rocks which they have not succeeded in interpreting to their satisfaction. These:

The suggested solutions of this riddle are practically innumerable; they would fill a book.

Thus we have infinite trouble in solving man-made mysteries; it is only when we set out to discover the secrets of God that our difficulties disappear. It was always so. In antique Roman times it was the custom of the Deity to try to conceal His intentions in the entrails of birds, and this was patiently and hopefully continued century after century, although the attempted concealment never succeeded, in a single recorded instance. The augurs could read entrails as easily as a modern child can read coarse print. Roman history is full of the marvels of interpretation which these extraordinary men performed. These strange and wonderful achievements move our awe and compel our admiration. Those men could pierce to the marrow of a mystery instantly. If the Rosetta-stone idea had been introduced it would have defeated them, but entrails had no embarrassments for them. But entrails have gone out, now—entrails and dreams. It was at last found out that as hiding-places for the divine intentions they were inadequate.

A part of the wall of Velletri having in former times been struck with thunder, the response of the soothsayers was, that a native of that town would some time or other arrive at supreme power. *Bohn's Suetonius,* p. 138.

"Some time or other." It looks indefinite, but no matter, it happened, all the same; one needed only to wait, and be patient, and keep watch, then he would find out that the thunder-stroke had Caesar Augustus in mind, and had come to give notice.

There were other advance-advertisements. One of them appeared just before Caesar Augustus was born, and was most poetic and touching and romantic in its feelings and aspects. It was a dream. It was dreamed by Caesar Augustus's mother, and interpreted at the usual rates:

Atia, before her delivery, dreamed that her bowels stretched to the stars, and expanded through the whole circuit of heaven and earth. *Suetonius,* p. 139.

That was in the augur's line, and furnished him no difficulties, but it would have taken Rawlinson and Champollion fourteen years to make sure of what it meant, because they would have been surprised and dizzy. It would have been too late to be valuable, then, and the bill for service would have been barred by the statute of limitations.

In those old Roman days a gentleman's education was not complete until he had taken a theological course at the seminary and learned how to translate entrails. Caesar Augustus's education received this final polish. All through his life, whenever he had poultry on the menu he saved the interiors and kept himself informed of the Deity's plans by exercising upon those interiors the arts of augury.

In his first consulship, while he was observing the auguries, twelve vultures presented themselves, as they had done to Romulus. And when he offered sacrifice, the livers of all the victims were folded inward in the lower part; a circumstance which was regarded by those present who had skill in things of that nature, as an indubitable prognostic of great and wonderful fortune. *Suetonius,* p. 141.

"Indubitable" is a strong word, but no doubt it was justified, if the livers were really turned that way. In those days chicken livers were strangely and delicately sensitive to coming events, no matter how far off they might be; and they could never keep still, but would curl and squirm like that, particularly when vultures came, and showed interest in that approaching great event and in breakfast.

II

We may now skip eleven hundred and thirty or forty years, which brings us down to enlightened Christian times and the troubled days of King Stephen of England. The augur has had his day and has been long ago forgotten; the priest has fallen heir to his trade.

King Henry is dead; Stephen, that bold and outrageous person, comes flying over from Normandy to steal the throne from Henry's daughter. He accomplished his crime, and Henry of Huntingdon, a priest of high degree, mourns over it in his Chronicle. The Archbishop of Canterbury consecrated Stephen: "wherefore the Lord visited the Archbishop with the same judgment which he had inflicted upon him who struck Jeremiah the great priest: he died within a year."

Stephen's was the greater offence, but Stephen could wait; not so the Archbishop, apparently.

The kingdom was a prey to intestine wars; slaughter, fire and rapine spread ruin throughout the land; cries of distress, horror and woe rose in every quarter.

That was the result of Stephen's crime. These unspeakable conditions continued during nineteen years. Then Stephen died as comfortably as any man ever did, and was honorably buried. It makes one pity the poor Archbishop, and wish that he, too, could have been let off as leniently. How did Henry of Huntingdon know that the Archbishop was sent to his grave by judgment of God for consecrating Stephen? He does not explain. Neither does he explain why Stephen was awarded a pleasanter death than he was entitled to, while the aged King Henry his predecessor, who had ruled England thirty-five years to H. H.'s and the people's strongly-worded satisfaction was condemned to close his life in circumstances most distinctly unpleasant, inconvenient, and disagreeable:

Meantime, the remains of King Henry lay still unburied in Normandy. His corpse was carried to Rouen, where his bowels, with his brain and eyes, were deposited. The body being slashed by knives, and copiously sprinkled with salt, was sewn up in ox hides to prevent the ill effluvia, which so tainted the air as to be pestilential to the by-standers. Even the man who was hired by a large reward to sever the head with an axe and extract the brain, which was very offensive, died in consequence, although he wore a thick linen veil; so that *he was the last of that great multitude King Henry slew.** The corpse being then carried to Caen, was deposited in the church where his father was interred; but notwithstanding the quantity of salt which had been used, and the folds of skins in which it was wrapped, so much foul matter continually exuded that it was caught in vessels placed under the bier, in emptying which the attendants were affected with horror and faintings. *Bohn's Henry of Huntingdon*, p. 262.

This is probably the most uninspiring funeral that is set down in history. There is not a detail about it that is attractive. It is difficult to believe that we are reading about a king, there is something so humble, so unpretending, so unregal, about the whole spectacle, something so simply human and unconventional. We hear nothing of tears, of regret, of a sense of loss, of a reluctance to say farewell, we have only a picture of cold and perfunctory persons who are there by invitation, not by intrusion, and who have no wish to remain longer than courtesy requires. It is one of the saddest funerals there is any account of. There does not appear to have been any music; yet music would have tempered it, music would have made it beautiful, if they could have thought of anything appropriate to play. But I suppose there was no old music

* The reader will please skip what now follows.—M. T.

that would quite do, none that would be harmonious, and no time
to think out any new music and compose it. It would be difficult,
of course, and could take a good while, no doubt, on account of
the conditions. It seems to have been just the funeral for Stephen,
and even at this far distant day it is matter of just regret that by an
indiscretion the wrong man got it.

Whenever God punishes a man, Henry of Huntingdon
knows why it was done, and tells us; and his pen is eloquent with
admiration; but when a man has earned punishment and escapes,
he does not explain. He is evidently puzzled, but he does not say
anything. I think it is often apparent that he is pained by these
discrepancies, but loyally tries his best not to show it. When he
cannot praise, he delivers himself of a silence so marked that a
suspicious person could mistake it for suppressed criticism. However, he has plenty of opportunities to feel contented with the way
things go—his book is full of them.

King David of Scotland . . . under color of religion caused his
followers to deal most barbarously with the English. They ripped open
pregnant women, tossed children on the points of their spears, butchered priests at the altars, and, cutting off the heads from the images on
crucifixes, placed them on the bodies of the slain, while in exchange
they fixed on the crucifixes the heads of their victims. Wherever the
Scots came, there was the same scene of horror and cruelty: women
shrieking, old men lamenting, amid the groans of the dying and the
despair of the living.

But the English got the victory.

Then the chief of the men of Lothian fell, pierced by an arrow,
and all his followers were put to flight. For the Almighty was offended
at them, and their strength was rent like a cobweb.

Offended at them for what? For committing those fearful
butcheries? No, for that was the common custom on both sides,
and not open to criticism. Then, was it for doing the butcheries

"under cover of religion?" No, that was not it; religious feeling was often expressed in that fervent way all through those old centuries. The truth is, He was not offended at "them" at all; He was only offended at their King, who had been false to an oath. Then why did not He put the punishment upon the King instead of upon "them?" It is a difficult question. One can see by the Chronicle that the "judgments" fell rather customarily upon the wrong person, but Henry of Huntingdon does not explain why. Here is one that went true; the chronicler's satisfaction in it is not hidden:

In the month of August Providence displayed its justice in a remarkable manner; for two of the nobles who had converted monasteries into fortifications, expelling the monks, their sin being the same, met with a similar punishment. Robert Marmion was one, Godfrey de Mandeville the other. Robert Marmion issuing forth against the enemy was slain under the walls of the monastery, being the only one who fell, though he was surrounded by his troops. Dying excommunicated, he became subject to death everlasting. In like manner earl Godfrey was singled out among his followers, and shot with an arrow by a common foot-soldier. He made light of the wound, but he died of it in a few days, under excommunication. See here the like just judgment of God, memorable through all ages!

This exultation jars upon me; not because of the death of the men, for they deserved that, but because it is death eternal, in white-hot fire and flame. It makes my flesh crawl. I have not known more than three men, or perhaps four, in my whole lifetime, whom I would rejoice to see writhing in those fires for even a year, let alone forever. I believe I would relent before the year was up, and get them out if I could. I could sit and watch a dog that I didn't like, several years, but not forever. I often put a dog on the fire and hold him down with the tongs, and enjoy his yelps and moans and strugglings and supplications, but with a man it would be different, I think. I think that in the long run, if his wife and babies, who had not harmed me, should come crying and pleading, I couldn't stand it; I know I should forgive him and let

him go, even if he had violated a monastery. Henry of Huntingdon
has been watching Godfrey and Marmion fry, nearly seven hundred and fifty years, now, but I couldn't do it, I know I couldn't.
I am soft and gentle in my nature, and I should have forgiven them
seventy and seven times, long ago. And I think God has; but this is
only an opinion, and not authoritative, like Henry of Huntingdon's interpretations. I could learn to interpret, but I have never
tried, I get so little time.

All through his book Henry exhibits his familiarity with the
intentions of God, and with the reasons for the intentions. Sometimes—very often, in fact—the act follows the intention after such
a wide interval of time, that one wonders how Henry could fit one
act out of a hundred to one intention out of a hundred and get the
thing right, every time, when there was such abundant choice
among acts and intentions. Sometimes a man offends the Deity
with a crime, and is punished for it thirty years later; meantime he
has committed a million other crimes: no matter, Henry can pick
out the one that brought the worms. Worms were generally used
in those days for the slaying of particularly wicked people. This
has gone out, now, but in old times it was a favorite. It always indicated a case of "wrath." For instance,

> . . . the just God avenging Robert Fitzhildebrand's perfidy, a
> worm grew in his vitals, which, gradually gnawing its way through his
> intestines, fattened on the abandoned man till, tortured with excru-
> ciating sufferings and venting himself in bitter moans, he was by a
> fitting punishment brought to his end; (p. 400).

It was probably an alligator, but we cannot tell; we only know
it was a particular breed, and only used to convey wrath. Some
authorities think it was an ichthiosaurus, but there is much doubt.
Anyway, it has gone out, now, thanks be.

However, one thing we do know; and that is, that that worm
had been due, years and years. Robert F. had violated a monastery
once; he had committed unprintable crimes since, and they had
been permitted—under disapproval—but the ravishment of the

monastery had not been forgotten nor forgiven, and the worm came at last.

Why were these reforms put off in this strange way? What was to be gained by it? Did Henry of Huntingdon really know his facts, or was he only guessing? Sometimes I am half persuaded that he is only a guesser, and not a good one. The divine wisdom must surely be of a better quality than he makes it out to be.

Five hundred years before Henry's time some forecasts of the Lord's purposes were furnished by a pope, who perceived, by certain perfectly trustworthy signs furnished by the Deity for the information of His familiars, that the end of the world was

. . . about to come. But as this end of the world draws near, many things are at hand which have not before happened, as changes in the air, terrible signs in the heavens, tempests out of the common order of the seasons, wars, famines, pestilences, earthquakes in various places; all which will not happen in our days, but after our days all will come to pass.

Still, the end was so near that these signs were "sent before in order that we may be careful for our souls and be found prepared to meet the impending judgment."

That was thirteen hundred years ago. This is really no improvement upon the work of the Roman augurs. Has the trade of interpreting the Lord's matters gone out, discouraged by the time-worn fact that nobody succeeds at it? No, it still flourishes; there was never a century nor a country that was short of experts who knew the Deity's mind and were willing to reveal it. Whenever there has been an opportunity to attribute to Him reasonings and conduct which would make a half-witted human being ridiculous, there has always been an expert ready and glad to take advantage of it. Quotation from newspaper several months old:

GOD BEHIND THIS WAR.
It Is His Way of Destroying Tyranny,
Dr. Hillis Says.

Preaching yesterday morning in Plymouth Church, Brooklyn, on "Christ at Once the Ideal Radical and the Ideal Conservative," the Rev. Dr. Newell Dwight Hillis referred to Russia as an example of the false conservative in politics, and declared that God, who as a radical only destroyed for the sake of safety, was destroying the idea of tyranny through war.

"Look to the Far East," said Dr. Hillis. "God's ploughshare of war is running through the nations and the old and false idea of tyranny is being turned up and under. Yet, when the thunderstorm has passed, does any man doubt that the air will be sweeter and purer? You say all the East is filled with destruction. It is because God's army is on the march. You do not hear the trumpet call, but God is the guide. Peace is to be the future of the people, oppression is to be destroyed, and government is to be for and by all the people."

So God's ploughshare has got started at last. But is there any occasion to fly into ecstasies of admiration over it? The villainies, the slaughters and the tyrannies which have so suddenly dawned upon the Deity and excited His Brooklyn interpreter to such an indecorous degree have been known to the very cats for three hundred years. If these villainies are wrong, they were wrong three centuries ago; if they are worth the Deity's attention now, they were worth it three centuries ago; if they are legitimate matter to rouse the divine wrath now, they were not otherwise three centuries ago; if it is fine and great to stamp out these tyrannies now, it would have been infinitely finer and greater to do it three centuries ago; if it is matter for high Brooklyn commendation that the deep miseries of the hungry and oppressed Russian millions have awakened pity at last, it should be matter for high Brooklyn regret that it was not awakened at the start, instead of away down at this late day, after more than 400,000,000,000 of those poor creatures have been oppressed into their graves.

Brooklyn praise is half slander. No, it is more than that, it is whole slander. To charge upon a man—and not a smart man at that—such a devastating record of immortal stupidities as this, would subject the utterer of the charge to a criminal libel suit, and quite properly, but any one can slander the Deity who has been lawfully consecrated to that work. But not you, and not me. We should be accused of irreverence.

God's army is on the march. You do not hear the trumpet-call, but God is the guide. . . . oppression is to be destroyed.

All this noise about an army and a plow,—belated—all this inflamed jubilation over a mixed military and agricultural expedition which is only just now getting started when it is already three centuries overdue. It would not do for a person to praise me for being three centuries late at a fire with my hook and ladder company; I should not like it.

In view of the fact that it takes the Rawlinsons, the Champollions and the Indian experts years and years to dig the meaning out of the modestest little batch of hieroglyphs; and that in interpreting the intentions of God the Roman augurs never scored a single demonstrable success; and that from their day to ours all attempts by men to lay bare to us the mind of the Deity have as signally failed, it seems to me that now is a good time for the interpreting-trade to take a rest. If it goes on trying (in *its* way) to magnify the wisdom of God, there will come a time by and by when there will not be any left to magnify.

19   *In the Animal's Court*

[1905]

THE RABBIT. The testimony showed, (1), that the Rabbit, having declined to volunteer, was enlisted by compulsion, and (2) deserted in the face of the enemy on the eve of battle. Being asked if he had anything to say for himself before sentence of death should be passed upon him for violating the military law forbidding cowardice and desertion, he said he had not desired to violate that law, but had been obliged to obey a higher law which took precedence of it and set it aside. Being asked what law that was, he answered, "the law of God, which denies courage to the rabbit."

Verdict of the Court. To be disgraced in the presence of the army; stripped of his uniform; marched to the scaffold, bearing a placard marked "Coward," and hanged.

II

THE LION. The testimony showed that the Lion, by his splendid courage and matchless strength and endurance, saved the battle.

Verdict of the Court. To be given a dukedom, his statue to be set up, his name to be writ in letters of gold at the top of the roll in the Temple of Fame.

III

THE FOX. The testimony showed that he had broken the divine law, "Thou shalt not steal." Being asked for his defence, he pleaded that he had been obliged to obey the divine law, "The Fox shall steal."

Verdict of the Court. Imprisonment for life.

IV

THE HORSE. The evidence showed that he had spent many days and nights, unwatched, in the paddock with the poultry, yet had triumphed over temptation.

Verdict of the Court. Let his name be honored; let his deed be praised throughout the land by public proclamation.

V

THE WOLF. The evidence showed that he had transgressed the law "Thou shalt not kill." In arrest of judgment, he pleaded the law of his nature.

Verdict of the Court. Death.

VI

THE SHEEP. The evidence showed that he had had manifold temptations to commit murder and massacre, yet had not yielded.

Verdict of the Court. Let his virtue be remembered forever.

VII

THE MACHINE. *The Court*: Prisoner, it is charged and proven that you are poorly contrived and badly constructed. What have you to say to this?

Answer. I did not contrive myself, I did not construct myself.

The Court. It is charged and proven that you have moved when you should not have moved; that you have turned out of your course when you should have gone straight; that you have moved swiftly through crowds when the law and the public weal forbade a speed like that; that you leave a stench behind you wherever you go, and you persist in this, although you know it is improper and that other machines refrain from doing it. What have you to say to these things?

Answer. I am a machine. I am slave to the law of my make, I have to obey it, under all conditions. I do nothing, of myself. My forces are set in motion by outside influences, I never set them in motion myself.

The Court. You are discharged. Your plea is sufficient. You are a pretty poor thing, with some good qualities and some bad ones; but to attach personal merit to conduct emanating from the one set, and personal demerit to conduct emanating from the other set would be unfair and unjust. To a machine, that is—to a machine.

20   *What Is Man?*

[1906]

F EBRUARY, 1905. The studies for these papers were begun twenty-five or twenty-seven years ago. The papers were written seven years ago. I have examined them once or twice per year since and found them satisfactory. I have just examined them again, and am still satisfied that they speak the truth.

Every thought in them has been thought (and accepted as unassailable truth) by millions upon millions of men—and concealed, kept private. Why did they not speak out? Because they dreaded (*and could not bear*) the disapproval of the people around them. Why have not I published? The same reason has restrained me, I think. I can find no other.

1

a. *Man the Machine*   b. *Personal Merit*

[The Old Man and the Young Man had been conversing. The Old Man had asserted that the human being is merely a machine, and nothing more. The Young Man objected, and asked him to go into particulars and furnish his reasons for his position.]

OLD MAN.   What are the materials of which a steam-engine is made?

YOUNG MAN.   Iron, steel, brass, white-metal, and so on.

O. M.   Where are these found?

Y. M.   In the rocks.

O. M.   In a pure state?

Y. M.   No—in ores.

O. M.   Are the metals suddenly deposited in the ores?

Y. M.   No—it is the patient work of countless ages.

O. M.   You could make the engine out of the rocks themselves?

Y. M.   Yes, a brittle one and not valuable.

O. M.   You would not require much, of such an engine as that?

Y. M.   No—substantially nothing.

O. M.   To make a fine and capable engine, how would you proceed?

Y. M.   Drive tunnels and shafts into the hills; blast out the iron ore; crush it, smelt it, reduce it to pig-iron; put some of it through the Bessemer process and make steel of it. Mine and treat and combine the several metals of which brass is made.

O. M.   Then?

Y. M.   Out of the perfected result, build the fine engine.

O. M.   You would require much, of this one?

Y. M.   Oh, indeed yes.

o. m.   It could drive lathes, drills, planers, punches, polishers, in a word all the cunning machines of a great factory?

y. m.   It could.

o. m.   What could the stone engine do?

y. m.   Drive a sewing-machine, possibly—nothing more, perhaps.

o. m.   Men would admire the other engine and rapturously praise it?

y. m.   Yes.

o. m.   But not the stone one?

y. m.   No.

o. m.   The merits of the metal machine would be far above those of the stone one?

y. m.   Of course.

o. m.   Personal merits?

y. m.   *Personal* merits? How do you mean?

o. m.   It would be personally entitled to the credit of its own performance?

y. m.   The engine? Certainly not.

o. m.   Why not?

y. m.   Because its performance is not personal. It is a result of the law of its construction. It is not a *merit* that it does the things which it is set to do—it can't *help* doing them.

o. m.   And it is not a personal demerit in the stone machine that it does so little?

y. m.   Certainly not. It does no more and no less than the law of its make permits and compels it to do. There is nothing *personal* about it; it cannot choose. In this process of "working up to the matter" is it your idea to work up to the proposition that a man and a machine are about the same thing, and that there is no personal merit in the performance of either?

o. m.   Yes—but do not be offended; I am meaning no offence. What makes the grand difference between the stone engine and the steel one? Shall we call it training, education? Shall we call the stone engine a savage and the steel one a civilized man?

The original rock contained the stuff of which the steel one was built—but along with it a lot of sulphur and stone and other obstructing inborn heredities, brought down from the old geologic ages—prejudices, let us call them. Prejudices which nothing within the rock itself had either *power* to remove or any *desire* to remove. Will you take note of that phrase?

Y. M. Yes. I have written it down: "Prejudices which nothing within the rock itself had either power to remove or any desire to remove." Go on.

O. M. Prejudices which must be removed by *outside influences* or not at all. Put that down.

Y. M. Very well: "Must be removed by outside influences or not at all." Go on.

O. M. The iron's prejudice against ridding itself of the cumbering rock. To make it more exact, the iron's absolute *indifference* as to whether the rock be removed or not. Then comes the *outside influence* and grinds the rock to powder and sets the ore free. The *iron* in the ore is still captive. An *outside influence* smelts it free of the clogging ore. The iron is emancipated iron, now, but indifferent to further progress. An *outside influence* beguiles it into the Bessemer furnace and refines it into steel of the first quality. It is educated, now—its training is complete. And it has reached its limit. By no possible process can it be educated into *gold*. Will you set that down?

Y. M. Yes: "Everything has its limit—iron ore cannot be educated into gold."

O. M. There are gold men, and tin men, and copper men, and leaden men, and steel men, and so on—and each has the limitations of his nature, his heredities, his training and his environment. You can build engines out of each of those metals, and they will all perform, but you must not require the weak ones to do equal work with the stronger ones. In each case, to get the best results, you must free the metal from its obstructing prejudicial ores by education—smelting, refining, and so forth.

Y. M. You have arrived at man, now?

o. m.   Yes. Man the machine—man, the impersonal engine. Whatsoever a man is, is due to his *make*, and to the *influences* brought to bear upon it by his heredities, his habitat, his associations. He is moved, directed, COMMANDED, by *exterior* influences —*solely*. He *originates* nothing, himself—not even an opinion, not even a thought.

y. m.   Oh, come! Where did I get my opinion that this which you are talking is all foolishness?

o. m.   It is a quite natural opinion—indeed an inevitable opinion—but *you* did not create the materials out of which it is formed. They are odds and ends of thoughts, impressions, feelings, gathered unconsciously from a thousand books, a thousand conversations, and from streams of thought and feeling which have flowed down into your heart and brain out of the hearts and brains of ten centuries of ancestors. *Personally* you did not create even the smallest microscopic fragment of the materials out of which your opinion is made; and personally you cannot claim even the slender merit of *putting the borrowed materials together*. That was done—*automatically*—by your mental machinery, in strict accordance with the law of that machinery's construction. And you not only did not make that machinery yourself, but you have *not even any command over it*.

y. m.   This is too much. You think I could have formed no opinion but that one?

o. m.   Spontaneously? No. And *you did not form that one*; your machinery did it for you—automatically and instantly, without reflection or the need of it.

y. m.   Suppose I had reflected? How then?

o. m.   Suppose you try.

y. m.   (*After a quarter of an hour.*) I have reflected.

o. m.   You mean you have tried to change your opinion—as an experiment?

y. m.   Yes.

o. m.   With success?

y. m.   No. It remains the same; it is impossible to change it.

o. m.   I am sorry, but you see, yourself, that your mind is merely a machine, nothing more. You have no command over it, it has no command over itself—it is worked *solely from the outside*. That is the law of its make; it is the law of all machines.

y. m.   Can't I *ever* change one of these automatic opinions?

o. m.   No. You can't, yourself, but *exterior influences* can do it.

y. m.   And exterior ones *only*?

o. m.   Yes—exterior ones only.

y. m.   That position is untenable—I may say ludicrously untenable.

o. m.   What makes you think so?

y. m.   I don't merely think it, I know it. Suppose I resolve to enter upon a course of thought, and study, and reading, with the deliberate purpose of changing that opinion; and suppose I succeed. *That* is not the work of an exterior impulse, the whole of it is mine and personal; for I originated the project.

o. m.   Not a shred of it. *It grew out of this talk with me.* But for that it would never have occurred to you. No man ever originates anything. All his thoughts, all his impulses, come *from the outside*.

y. m.   It's an exasperating subject. The *first* man had original thoughts, anyway; there was nobody to draw from.

o. m.   It is a mistake. Adam's thoughts came to him from the outside. *You* have a fear of death. You did not invent that—you got it from outside, from talk and teaching. Adam had no fear of death—none in the world.

y. m.   Yes he had.

o. m.   When he was created?

y. m.   No.

o. m.   When, then?

y. m.   When he was threatened with it.

o. m.   Then it came from the *outside*. Adam is quite big enough; let us not try to make a god of him. *None but gods have ever had a thought which did not come from the outside.* Adam probably had a good head, but it was of no sort of use to him until it was filled up *from the outside*. He was not able to invent the triflingest little thing with it. He had not a shadow of a notion of the difference between good and evil—he had to get the idea *from the outside*. Neither he nor Eve was able to originate the idea that it was immodest to go naked: the knowledge came in with the apple *from the outside*. A man's brain is so constructed that *it can originate nothing whatever*. It can only use material obtained *outside*. It is merely a machine; and it works automatically, not by will power. *It has no command over itself, its owner has no command over it.*

Y. M.   Well, never mind Adam; but certainly Shakspeare's creations—

O. M.   No, you mean Shakspeare's *imitations*. Shakspeare created nothing. He correctly observed, and he marvelously painted. He exactly portrayed people whom *God* had created, but he created none himself. Let us spare him the slander of charging him with trying. Shakspeare could not create. *He was a machine, and machines do not create.*

Y. M.   Where *was* his excellence, then?

O. M.   In this. He was not a sewing-machine, like you and me, he was a Gobelin loom. The threads and the colors came into him *from the outside*; outside influences, suggestions, *experiences*, (reading, seeing plays, playing plays, borrowing ideas, and so on), framed the patterns in his mind and started up its complex and admirable machinery, and *it automatically* turned out that pictured and gorgeous fabric which still compels the astonishment of the world. If Shakspeare had been born and bred on a barren and unvisited rock in the ocean his mighty intellect would have had no *outside material* to work with, and could have invented none; and *no outside influences*, teachings, mouldings, persuasions, inspirations, of a valuable sort, and could have invented none; and so, Shakspeare would have produced nothing. In Turkey he would have produced something—something up to the highest limit of

Turkish influences, associations and training. In France he would have produced something better—something up to the highest limit of the French influences and training. In England he rose to the highest limit attainable through the *outside helps afforded by that land's ideals, influences and training.* You and I are but sewing-machines. We must turn out what we can; we must do our endeavor, and care nothing at all when the unthinking reproach us for not turning out Gobelins.

Y. M.   And so we are mere machines! And machines may not boast, nor feel proud of their performance, nor claim personal merit for it, nor applause and praise. It is an infamous doctrine.

O. M.   It isn't a doctrine, it is merely a fact.

Y. M.   I suppose, then, there is no more merit in being brave than in being a coward?

O. M.   *Personal* merit? No. A brave man does not *create* his bravery. He is entitled to no personal credit for possessing it. It is born to him. A baby born with a billion dollars—where is the personal merit in that? A baby born with nothing—where is the personal demerit in that? The one is fawned upon, admired, worshiped, by sycophants, the other is neglected and despised—where is the sense in it?

Y. M.   Sometimes a timid man sets himself the task of conquering his cowardice and becoming brave—and succeeds. What do you say to that?

O. M.   That it shows the value of *training in right directions over training in wrong ones.* Inestimably valuable is training, influence, education, in right directions—*training one's self-approbation to elevate its ideals.*

Y. M.   But as to merit—the personal merit of the victorious coward's project and achievement?

O. M.   There isn't any. In the world's view he is a worthier man than he was before, but *he* didn't achieve the change—the merit of it is not his.

Y. M.   Whose, then?

o. m.   His *make*, and the influences which wrought upon it from the outside.

y. m.   His make?

o. m.   Yes. To start with, he was *not* utterly and completely a coward, or the influences would have had nothing to work upon. He was not afraid of a cow, though perhaps of a bull; not afraid of a woman, but afraid of a man. There was something to build upon. There was a *seed.* No seed, no plant. Did he make that seed himself, or was it born in him? It was no merit of *his* that the seed was there.

y. m.   Well, anyway, the idea of *cultivating* it, the resolution to cultivate it, was meritorious, and he originated that.

o. m.   He did nothing of the kind. It came whence *all* impulses, good or bad, come—from *outside.* If that timid man had lived all his life in a community of human rabbits; had never read of brave deeds; had never heard speech of them; had never heard any one praise them nor express envy of the heroes that had done them, he would have had no more idea of bravery than Adam had of modesty, and it could never by any possibility have occurred to him to *resolve* to become brave. He *could not originate the idea—* it had to come to him from the *outside.* And so, when he heard bravery extolled and cowardice derided, it woke him up. He was ashamed. Perhaps his sweetheart turned up her nose and said "I am told that you are a coward!" It was not *he* that turned over the new leaf—she did it for him. *He* must not strut around in the merit of it—it is not his.

y. m.   But anyway he reared the plant after she watered the seed.

o. m.   No. *Outside influences* reared it. At the command— and trembling—he marched out into the field—with other soldiers and in the daytime, not alone and in the dark. He had the *influence of example,* he drew courage from his comrades' courage; he was afraid, and wanted to run, but he did not dare; he was *afraid* to run, with all those soldiers looking on. He was progressing, you see—the moral fear of shame had risen superior to the physical fear of harm. By the end of the campaign experience will have taught him that not *all* who go into battle get hurt—an outside influence which will be helpful to him; and he will also have learned how sweet it is to be praised for courage and be huzza'd at with tear-choked voices as the war-worn regiment marches past the worshiping multitude with the flags flying and the drums beating. After that he will be as securely brave as any veteran in the army —and there will not be a shade nor suggestion of *personal merit* in it anywhere; it will all have come from the *outside*. The Victoria Cross breeds more heroes than—

Y. M.   Hang it, where is the sense in his becoming brave if he is to get no credit for it?

O. M.   Your question will answer itself presently. It involves an important detail of man's make which we have not yet touched upon.

Y. M.   What detail is that?

O. M.   The impulse which moves a person to do things—the only impulse that ever moves a person to do a thing.

Y. M.   The *only* one! Is there but one?

O. M.   That is all. There is only one.

Y. M.   Well, certainly that is a strange enough doctrine. What is the sole impulse that ever moves a person to do a thing?

O. M.   The impulse to *content his own spirit*—the *necessity* of contenting his own spirit and *winning its approval*.

Y. M.   Oh, come, that won't do!

O. M.   Why won't it?

Y. M.   Because it puts him in the attitude of always looking out for his own comfort and advantage; whereas an unselfish man often does a thing solely for another person's good when it is a positive disadvantage to himself.

O. M.   It is a mistake. The act must do *him* good, FIRST; otherwise he will not do it. He may *think* he is doing it solely for the other person's sake, but it is not so; he is contenting his own spirit *first*—the other person's benefit has to always take *second* place.

    Y. M.   What a fantastic idea! What becomes of self-sacrifice? Please answer me that.

    O. M.   What is self-sacrifice?

    Y. M.   The doing good to another person where no shadow nor suggestion of benefit to one's self can result from it.

Man's Sole Impulse—The Securing of His Own Approval

o. m. There have been instances of it—you think?

y. m. *Instances?* Millions of them!

o. m. You have not jumped to conclusions? You have examined them—critically?

y. m. They don't need it; the acts themselves reveal the golden impulse back of them.

o. m. For instance?

y. m. Well, then, for instance. Take the case in the book here. The man lives three miles up town. It is bitter cold, blowing hard, snowing hard, midnight. He is about to enter the horse-car when a gray and ragged old woman, a touching picture of misery, puts out her lean hand and begs for rescue from hunger and death. The man finds that he has but a quarter in his pocket, but he does not hesitate; he gives it her and trudges home through the storm. There—it is noble, it is beautiful; its grace is marred by no fleck or blemish or suggestion of self-interest.

o. m. What makes you think that?

y. m. Pray what else could I think? Do you imagine that there is some other way of looking at it?

o. m. Can you put yourself in the man's place and tell me what he felt and what he thought?

y. m. Easily. The sight of that suffering old face pierced his generous heart with a sharp pain. He could not bear it. He could endure the three-mile walk in the storm, but he could not endure the tortures his conscience would suffer if he turned his back and left that poor old creature to perish. He would not have been able to sleep, for thinking of it.

o. m. What was his state of mind on his way home?

Y. M.   It was a state of joy which only the self-sacrificer knows. His heart sang, he was unconscious of the storm.

O. M.   He slept well?

Y. M.   One cannot doubt it.

O. M.   Very well. Now let us add up the details and see how much he got for his twenty-five cents. Let us try to find out the *real* why of his making the investment. In the first place *he* couldn't bear the pain which the suffering old face gave him. So he was thinking of *his* pain—this good man. He must buy a salve for it. If he did not succor the old woman *his* conscience would torture him all the way home. Thinking of *his* pain again. He must buy relief from that. If he didn't relieve the old woman *he* would not get any sleep. He must buy some sleep—still thinking of *himself*, you see. Thus, to sum up, he bought himself free of a sharp pain in his heart, he bought himself free of the tortures of a waiting conscience, he bought a whole night's sleep—all for twenty-five cents! This able trader got a hundred dollars' worth of clean profit out of an investment of twenty-five cents. It should make Wall street ashamed of itself. On his way home his heart was joyful, and it sang—profit on top of profit! The impulse which moved the man to succor the old woman was—*first*—to *content his own spirit*; secondly, to relieve *her* sufferings. Is it your opinion that men's acts proceed from one central and unchanging and inalterable impulse, or from a variety of impulses?

Y. M.   From a variety, of course—some high and fine and noble, others not. What is your opinion?

O. M.   That there is but *one* law, one source.

Y. M.   That both the noblest impulses and the basest proceed from that one source?

O. M.   Yes.

Y. M.   Will you put that law into words?

O. M.   Yes. This is the law. Keep it in your mind. *From his cradle to his grave a man never does a single thing which has any* FIRST AND FOREMOST *object but one—to secure peace of mind, spiritual comfort, for* HIMSELF.

Y. M.   Come! He never does anything for any one else's comfort, spiritual or physical?

O. M.   No. *Except on those distinct terms*—that it shall *first* secure *his own* spiritual comfort. Otherwise, he will not do it.

Y. M.   It will be easy to expose the falsity of that proposition.

O. M.   For instance?

Y. M.   Take that noble passion, love of country, patriotism. A man who loves peace and dreads pain, leaves his pleasant home and his weeping family and marches out to manfully expose himself to hunger, cold, wounds and death. Is that seeking spiritual comfort?

O. M.   He loves peace and dreads pain?

Y. M.   Yes.

O. M.   Then perhaps there is something that he loves *more* than he loves peace—*the approval of his neighbors and the public.* And perhaps there is something which he dreads more than he dreads pain—the *disapproval* of his neighbors and the public. If he is sensitive to shame he will go to the field—not because his spirit will be *entirely* comfortable there, but because it will be more comfortable there than it would be if he remained at home. He will always do the thing which will bring him the *most* mental comfort—for that is *the sole law of his life.* He leaves the weeping family behind; he is sorry to make them uncomfortable, but not sorry enough to sacrifice his *own* comfort to secure theirs.

Y. M.   Do you really believe that mere public opinion could force a timid and peaceful man to—

O. M.   Go to the wars? Yes—public opinion can force some men to do *anything*.

Y. M.   *Anything?*

O. M.   Yes—anything.

Y. M.   I don't believe that. Can it force a right-principled man to do a wrong thing?

O. M.   Yes.

Y. M.   Can it force a kind man to do a cruel thing?

O. M.   Yes.

Y. M.   Give an instance.

O. M.   Alexander Hamilton was a conspicuously high-principled man. He regarded dueling as wrong, and as opposed to the teachings of religion—but in deference to *public opinion* he fought a duel. He deeply loved his family, but to buy public approval he treacherously deserted them and threw his life away, ungenerously leaving them to life-long sorrow in order that he might stand well with a foolish world. In the then condition of the public standards of honor he could not have been comfortable with the stigma upon him of having refused to fight. The teachings of religion, his devotion to his family, his kindness of heart, his high principles, all went for nothing when they stood in the way of his spiritual comfort. A man will do *anything*, no matter what it is, *to secure his spiritual comfort*; and he can neither be forced nor persuaded to any act which has not that goal for its object. Hamilton's act was compelled by the inborn necessity of contenting his own spirit; in this it was like all the other acts of his life, and like all the acts of all men's lives. Do you see where the kernel of the matter lies? A man cannot be comfortable without *his own* approval. He will secure the largest share possible of that, at all costs, all sacrifices.

Y. M.   A minute ago you said Hamilton fought the duel to get the *public* approval.

O. M.   I did. By refusing to fight the duel he could have secured his family's approval and a large share of his own; but the public approval was more valuable in his eyes than all other approvals put together—in the earth or above it; to secure that would furnish him the *most* comfort of mind, the most *self*-approval; so he sacrificed all other values to get it.

Y. M.   Some noble souls have refused to fight duels, and have manfully braved the public contempt.

O. M.   They acted *according to their make*. They valued their principles and the approval of their families *above* the public approval. They took the thing they valued *most* and let the rest go. They took what would give them the *largest* share of *personal con-*

tentment and approval—a man *always* does. Public opinion cannot force that kind of men to go to the wars. When they go, it is for other reasons. Other spirit-contenting reasons.

Y. M.   Always spirit-contenting reasons?

O. M.   There are no others.

Y. M.   When a man sacrifices his life in trying to save a little child from a burning building, what do you call that?

O. M.   When he does it, it is the law of *his* make. *He* can't bear to see the child in that peril, (a man of a different make *could*), and so he tries to save the child, and loses his life. But he has got what he was after—*his own approval.*

Y. M.   What do you call Love, Hate, Charity, Revenge, Humanity, Magnanimity, Forgiveness?

O. M.   Different results of the one Master Impulse: the necessity of securing one's self-approval. They wear diverse clothes and are subject to diverse moods, but in whatsoever ways they masquerade they are the *same person* all the time. To change the figure, the *compulsion* that moves a man—and there is but the one —is the necessity of securing the contentment of his own spirit. When it stops, the man is dead.

Y. M.   This is foolishness. Love—

O. M.   Why, love is that impulse, that law, in its most uncompromising form. It will squander life and everything else on its object. Not *primarily* for the object's sake, but for *its own.* When its object is happy *it* is happy—and that is what it is unconsciously after.

Y. M.   You do not even except the lofty and gracious passion of mother-love?

O. M.   No, *it* is the absolute slave of that law. The mother will go naked to clothe her child; she will starve that it may have food; suffer torture to save it from pain; die that it may live. She takes a living *pleasure* in making these sacrifices. *She does it for that reward*—that self-approval, that contentment, that peace, that comfort. *She would do it for your child* IF SHE COULD GET THE SAME PAY.

Y. M.   This is an infernal philosophy of yours.

O. M.   It isn't a philosophy, it is a fact.

Y. M.   Of course you must admit that there are some acts which—

O. M.   No. There is *no* act, large or small, fine or mean, which springs from any motive but the one—the necessity of appeasing and contenting one's own spirit.

Y. M.   The world's philanthropists—

O. M.   I honor them, I uncover my head to them—from habit and training; but *they* could not know comfort or happiness or self-approval if they did not work and spend for the unfortunate. It makes *them* happy to see others happy; and so with money and labor they buy what they are after—*happiness, self-approval*. Why don't misers do the same thing? Because they can get a thousand-fold more happiness by *not* doing it. There is no other reason. They follow the law of their make.

Y. M.   What do you say of duty for duty's sake?

O. M.   That *it does not exist*. Duties are not performed for duty's *sake*, but because their *neglect* would make the man *uncomfortable*. A man performs but *one* duty—the duty of contenting his spirit, the duty of making himself agreeable to himself. If he can most satisfyingly perform this sole and only duty by *helping* his neighbor, he will do it; if he can most satisfyingly perform it by *swindling* his neighbor, he will do that. But always he looks out for Number One—*first*; the effects upon others are a *secondary* matter. Men pretend to self-sacrifices, but this is a thing which, in the ordinary value of the phrase, *does not exist and has not existed*. A man often honestly *thinks* he is sacrificing himself merely and solely for some one else, but he is deceived: his bottom impulse is to content a requirement of his nature and training, and thus acquire peace for his soul.

Y. M.   Apparently, then, all men, both good and bad ones, devote their lives to contenting their consciences?

O. M.   Yes. That is a good enough name for it: Conscience—that independent Sovereign, that insolent absolute Monarch inside of a man who is the man's Master. There are all kinds of consciences, because there are all kinds of men. You satisfy an assassin's conscience in one way, a philanthropist's in another, a miser's in another, a burglar's in still another. As a *guide* or *incentive* to any authoritatively prescribed line of morals or conduct, (leaving *training* out of the account), a man's conscience is totally valueless. I knew a kind-hearted Kentuckian whose self-approval was lacking—whose conscience was troubling him, to phrase it with exactness—*because he had neglected to kill a certain man*—a man whom he had never seen. The stranger had killed this man's friend in a fight, this man's Kentucky training made it his duty to kill the stranger for it. He neglected this duty—kept dodging it, shirking it, putting it off, and his unrelenting conscience kept persecuting him for this conduct. At last, to get ease of mind, comfort, self-approval, he hunted up the stranger and took his life. It was an immense act of *self-sacrifice*, (as per the usual definition), for he did not want to do it, and he never would have done it if he could have bought a contented spirit and an unworried mind at smaller cost. But we are so made that we will pay *anything* for that contentment—even another man's life.

Y. M. You spoke a moment ago of *trained* consciences. You mean that we are not *born* with consciences competent to guide us aright?

O. M. If we were, children and savages would know right from wrong, and not have to be taught it.

Y. M. But consciences can be *trained*?

O. M. Yes.

Y. M. Of course by parents, teachers, the pulpit, and books.

O. M. Yes—they do their share; they do what they can.

Y. M. And the rest is done by—

O. M. Oh, a million unnoticed influences—for good or bad; influences which work without rest during every waking moment of a man's life, from cradle to grave.

Y. M. You have tabulated these?

O. M. Many of them—yes.

Y. M.   Will you read me the result?

O. M.   Another time, yes. It would take an hour.

Y. M.   A conscience can be trained to shun evil and prefer good?

O. M.   Yes.

Y. M.   But will prefer it for spirit-contenting reasons only?

O. M.   It *can't* be trained to do a thing for any *other* reason. The thing is impossible.

Y. M.   There *must* be a genuinely and utterly self-sacrificing act recorded in human history somewhere.

O. M.   You are young. You have many years before you. Search one out.

Y. M.   It does seem to me that when a man sees a fellow-being struggling in the water and jumps in at the risk of his life to save him—

O. M.   Wait. Describe the *man*. Describe the *fellow-being*. State if there is an *audience* present; or if they are *alone*.

Y. M.   What have these things to do with the splendid act?

O. M.   Very much. Shall we suppose, as a beginning, that the two are alone, in a solitary place, at midnight?

Y. M.   If you choose.

O. M.   And that the fellow-being is the man's daughter?

Y. M.   Well, n-no—make it some one else.

O. M.   A filthy, drunken ruffian, then?

Y. M.   I see. Circumstances alter cases. I suppose that if there was no audience to observe the act, the man wouldn't perform it.

O. M.   But there is here and there a man who *would*. People, for instance, like the man who lost his life trying to save the child from the fire; and like the man who gave the needy old woman his 25 cents and walked home in the storm—there are here and there men like that who would do it. And why? Because they couldn't *bear* to see a fellow-being struggling in the water and not jump in and help. It would give *them* pain. They would save the fellow-being on that account. *They wouldn't do it otherwise.* They strictly obey the law which I have been insisting upon. You must remember and always distinguish the people who *can't bear* things from the people who *can*. It will throw light upon a number of apparently "self-sacrificing" cases.

Y. M.   Oh, dear, it's all so disgusting.

O. M.   Yes. And so true.

Y. M.   Come—take the good boy who does things which he doesn't want to do, in order to gratify his mother.

O. M.   He does seven-tenths of the act because it gratifies *him* to gratify his mother. Throw the bulk of advantage the other way and the good boy would not do the act. He *must* obey the iron law. None can escape it.

Y. M.   Well, take the case of a bad boy who—

O. M.   You needn't mention it, it is a waste of time. It is no matter about the bad boy's act. Whatever it was, he had a spirit-contenting reason for it. Otherwise you have been misinformed, and he didn't do it.

Y. M.   It is very exasperating. A while ago you said that a man's conscience is not a born judge of morals and conduct, but has to be taught and trained. Now I think a conscience can get drowsy and lazy, but I don't think it can go wrong; and if you wake it up—

A LITTLE STORY

O. M.   I will tell you a little story:

Once upon a time an Infidel was a guest in the house of a Christian widow whose little boy was ill and near to death. The Infidel often watched by the bedside and entertained the boy with talk, and he used these opportunities to satisfy a strong longing of his nature—that desire which is in us all to better other people's condition by having them think as we think. He was successful. But the dying boy, in his last moments, reproached him and said—

"*I believed, and was happy in it; you have taken my belief away, and my comfort. Now I have nothing left, and I die miserable; for the things which you have told me do not take the place of that which I have lost.*"

And the mother, also, reproached the Infidel, and said—

"My child is forever lost, and my heart is broken. How could you do this cruel thing? We had done you no harm, but only kindness; we made our house your home, you were welcome to all we had, and this is our reward."

The heart of the Infidel was filled with remorse for what he had done, and he said—

"It was wrong—I see it now; but I was only trying to do him good. In my view he was in error; it seemed my duty to teach him the truth."

Then the mother said—

"I had taught him, all his little life, what I believed to be the truth, and in his believing faith both of us were happy. Now he is dead—and lost; and I am miserable. Our faith came down to us through centuries of believing ancestors; what right had you, or any one, to disturb it? Where was your honor, where was your shame?"

Y. M.   He was a miscreant, and deserved death!

O. M.   He thought so himself, and said so.

Y. M.   Ah—you see, *his conscience was awakened!*

O. M.   Yes—his Self-Disapproval was. It *pained* him to see the mother suffer. He was sorry he had done a thing which brought *him* pain. It did not occur to him to think of the mother when he was mis-teaching the boy, for he was absorbed in providing *pleasure* for himself, then. Providing it by satisfying what he believed to be a call of duty.

Y. M.   Call it what you please, it is to me a case of *awakened conscience*. That awakened conscience could never get itself into that species of trouble again. A cure like that is a *permanent* cure.

O. M.   Pardon—I had not finished the story. We are creatures of *outside influences*—we originate *nothing* within. Whenever we take a new line of thought and drift into a new line of belief and action, the impulse is *always* suggested from the *outside*. Remorse so preyed upon the Infidel that it dissolved his harshness toward the boy's religion and made him come to regard it with tolerance, next with kindness, and presently with tenderness, for the boy's sake and the mother's. Finally he found himself examining it. From that moment his progress in his new trend was steady and rapid. He became a believing Christian. And now his remorse for having robbed the dying boy of his faith and his salvation was bitterer than ever. It gave him no rest, no peace. He *must* have rest and peace—it is the law of our nature. There seemed but one way to get it; he must devote himself to saving imperiled souls. He became a missionary. He landed in a pagan country ill and helpless. A native widow took him into her humble home and nursed him back to convalescence. Then her young boy was taken hopelessly ill, and the grateful missionary helped her tend him. Here was his first opportunity to repair a part of the wrong done to the other boy by doing a precious service for this one by undermining his foolish faith in his false gods. He was successful. But the dying boy in his last moments reproached him, and said—

"*I believed, and was happy in it; you have taken my belief away, and my comfort. Now I have nothing left, and I die miserable; for the things which you have told me do not take the place of that which I have lost.*"

And the mother, also, reproached the missionary, and said—

"*My child is forever lost, and my heart is broken. How could you do this cruel thing? We had done you no harm, but only kindness; we made our house your home, you were welcome to all we had, and this is our reward.*"

The heart of the missionary was filled with remorse for what he had done, and he said—

"*It was wrong—I see it now; but I was only trying to do him good. In my view he was in error; it seemed my duty to teach him the truth.*"

Then the mother said—

"*I had taught him, all his little life, what I believed to be the truth, and in his believing faith both of us were happy. Now he is dead—and lost; and I am miserable. Our faith came down to us through centuries of believing ancestors; what right had you, or any one, to disturb it? Where was your honor, where was your shame?"*

The missionary's anguish of remorse and sense of treachery were as bitter and persecuting and unappeasable, now, as they had been in the former case. The story is finished. What is your comment?

Y. M.   The man's conscience was a fool! It was morbid. It didn't know right from wrong.

O. M.   I am not sorry to hear you say that. If you grant that *one* man's conscience doesn't know right from wrong, it is an admission that there are others like it. This single admission pulls down the whole doctrine of infallibility of judgment in consciences. Meantime there is one thing which I ask you to notice.

Y. M.   What is that?

O. M.   That in both cases the man's *act* gave him no spiritual discomfort, and that he was quite satisfied with it and got pleasure out of it. But afterward when it resulted in *pain* to *him,* he was sorry. Sorry it had inflicted pain upon the others, *but for no reason under the sun except that their pain gave* HIM *pain.* Our consciences take *no* notice of pain inflicted upon others until it reaches a point where it gives pain to *us.* In *all* cases without exception we are absolutely indifferent to another person's pain until his sufferings make us uncomfortable. Many an infidel would not have been troubled by that Christian mother's distress. Don't you believe that?

Y. M.   Yes. You might almost say it of the *average* infidel, I think.

O. M.   And many a missionary, sternly fortified by his sense of duty, would not have been troubled by the pagan mother's distress—Jesuit missionaries in Canada in the early French times, for instance; see episodes quoted by Parkman.

Y. M.   Well, let us adjourn. Where have we arrived?

O. M.   At this. That we (mankind), have ticketed ourselves with a number of qualities to which we have given misleading names. Love, Hate, Charity, Compassion, Avarice, Benevolence, and so on. I mean, we attach misleading *meanings* to the names. They are all forms of self-contentment, self-gratification, but the names so disguise them that they distract our attention from the fact. Also, we have smuggled a word into the dictionary which ought not to be there at all—Self-Sacrifice. It describes a thing which does not exist. But worst of all, we ignore and never mention the Sole Impulse which dictates and compels a man's every act: the imperious necessity of securing his own approval, in every emergency and at all costs. To it we owe all that we are. It is our breath, our heart, our blood. It is our only spur, our whip, our goad, our only impelling power; we have no other. Without it we should be mere inert images, corpses; no one would do anything, there would be no progress, the world would stand still. We ought to stand reverently uncovered when the name of that stupendous power is uttered.

    Y. M.   I am not convinced.

    O. M.   You will be, when you think.

3

Instances in Point

o. m.   Have you given thought to the Gospel of Self-Approval since we talked?

y. m.   I have.

o. m.   It was I that moved you to it. That is to say, an *outside influence* moved you to it—not one that originated in your own head. Will you try to keep that in mind and not forget it?

y. m.   Yes. Why?

o. m.   Because by and by, in one of our talks, I wish to further impress upon you that neither you, nor I, nor any man ever originates a thought in his own head. *The utterer of a thought always utters a second-hand one.*

y. m.   Oh, now—

o. m.   Wait. Reserve your remark till we get to that part of our discussion—to-morrow or next day, say. Now, then, you have been considering the proposition that no act is ever born of any but a self-contenting impulse—(primarily). You have sought. What have you found?

y. m.   I have not been very fortunate. I have examined many fine and apparently self-sacrificing deeds in romances and biographies, but—

o. m.   Under searching analysis the ostensible self-sacrifice disappeared? It naturally would.

y. m.   But here in this novel is one which seems to promise. In the Adirondack woods is a wage-earner and lay preacher in the lumber-camps who is of noble character and deeply religious. An earnest and practical laborer in the New York slums comes up there on vacation—he is leader of a section of the University Settlement. Holme, the lumberman, is fired with a desire to throw away his excellent worldly prospects and go down and save souls on the East Side. He counts it happiness to make this sacrifice for the glory of God and for the cause of Christ. He resigns his place, makes the sacrifice cheerfully, and goes to the East Side and preaches Christ and Him crucified every day and every night to little groups of half-civilized foreign paupers who scoff at him. But he rejoices in the scoffings, since he is suffering them in the great cause of Christ. You have so filled my mind with suspicions that I was constantly expecting to find a hidden questionable impulse back of all this, but I am thankful to say I have failed. This man saw his duty, and for *duty's sake* he sacrificed self and assumed the burden it imposed.

o. m.   Is that as far as you have read?

y. m.   Yes.

o. m.   Let us read further, presently. Meantime, in sacrificing himself—*not* for the glory of God, *primarily*, as *he* imagined, but *first* to content that exacting and inflexible master within him —*did he sacrifice anybody else?*

y. m.   How do you mean?

o. m.   He relinquished a lucrative post and got mere food and lodging in place of it. Had he dependants?

y. m.   Well—yes.

o. m.   In what way and to what extent did his self-sacrifice affect *them*?

y. m.   He was the support of a superannuated father. He had a young sister with a remarkable voice—he was giving her a musical education, so that her longing to be self-supporting might be gratified. He was furnishing the money to put a young brother through a polytechnic school and satisfy his desire to become a civil engineer.

o. m.   The old father's comforts were now curtailed?

y. m.   Quite seriously. Yes.

o. m.   The sister's music-lessons had to stop?

y. m.   Yes.

o. m.   The young brother's education—well, an extinguishing blight fell upon that happy dream, and he had to go to sawing wood to support the old father, or something like that?

Y. M.   It is about what happened. Yes.

O. M.   What a handsome job of self-sacrificing he did do! It seems to me that he sacrificed everybody *except* himself. Haven't I told you that no man *ever* sacrifices himself; that there is no instance of it upon record anywhere; and that when a man's Interior Monarch requires a thing of its slave for either its *momentary* or its *permanent* contentment, that thing must and will be furnished and that command obeyed, no matter who may stand in the way and suffer disaster by it? That man *ruined his family* to please and content his Interior Monarch—

Y. M.   And help Christ's cause.

O. M.   Yes—*secondly*. Not firstly. *He* thought it was firstly.

Y. M.   Very well, have it so, if you will. But it could be that he argued that if he saved a hundred souls in New York—

O. M.   The sacrifice of the *family* would be justified by that great profit upon the—the—what shall we call it?

Y. M.   Investment?

O. M.   Hardly. How would *speculation* do? how would *gamble* do? Not a solitary soul-capture was sure. He played for a possible thirty-three hundred per cent profit. It was *gambling*—with his family for "chips." However, let us see how the game came out. Maybe we can get on the track of the secret original impulse, the *real* impulse, that moved him to so nobly self-sacrifice his family in the Savior's cause under the superstition that he was sacrificing himself. I will read a chapter or so. . . . . Here we have it! it was bound to expose itself sooner or later. He preached to the East-Side rabble a season, then went back to his old dull and obscure life in the lumber camps *"hurt to the heart, his pride humbled."* Why? Were not his efforts acceptable to the Savior, for Whom alone they were made? Dear me, that detail is *lost sight of*, is not even referred to, the fact that it started out as a motive is entirely forgotten! Then what is the trouble? The authoress quite innocently and unconsciously gives the whole business away. The trouble was this: this man merely *preached* to the poor; that is not the University Settlement's way; it deals in larger and better things than that, and it did not enthuse over that crude Salvation-Army eloquence. It was courteous to Holme—but cool. It did not pet him, did not take him to its bosom. *"Perished were all his dreams of distinction, the praise and grateful approval of—"* Of whom? The Savior? No; the Savior is not mentioned. Of whom, then? Of "his *fellow-workers.*" Why did he want that? Because the Master inside of him wanted it, and would not be content without it. That emphasized sentence quoted above, reveals the secret we have been seeking, the original impulse, the *real* impulse, which moved the obscure and unappreciated Adirondack lumberman to sacrifice his family and go on that crusade to the East Side—which said original impulse was this, to-wit: without knowing it *he went there to show a neglectful world the large talent that was in him, and rise to distinction.* As I have warned you before, *no* act springs from any but the one law, the one motive. But I pray you, do not accept this law upon my say-so, but diligently examine for yourself. Whenever you read of a self-sacrificing act or hear of one, or of a duty done for *duty's sake,* take it to pieces and look for the *real* motive. It is always there.

Y. M. I do it every day. I cannot help it, now that I have gotten started upon the degrading and exasperating quest. For it is hatefully interesting!—in fact, fascinating is the word. As soon as I come across a golden deed in a book I have to stop and take it apart and examine it, I cannot help myself.

O. M. Have you ever found one that defeated the rule?

Y. M. No—at least, not yet. But take the case of servant-tipping in Europe. You pay the *hotel* for service; you owe the servants *nothing,* yet you pay them, besides. Doesn't that defeat it?

O. M. In what way?

Y. M. You are not *obliged* to do it, therefore its source is compassion for their ill-paid condition, and—

O. M. Has that custom ever vexed you, annoyed you, irritated you?

Y. M. Well—yes.

o. m.   Still you succumbed to it?

y. m.   Of course.

o. m.   Why of course?

y. m.   Well, custom is law, in a way, and laws must be submitted to—everybody recognizes it as a *duty*.

o. m.   Then you pay the irritating tax for *duty's* sake?

y. m.   I suppose it amounts to that.

o. m.   Then the impulse which moves you to submit to the tax is not *all* compassion, charity, benevolence?

y. m.   Well—perhaps not.

o. m.   Is *any* of it?

y. m.   I—perhaps I was too hasty in locating its source.

o. m.   Perhaps so. In case you ignored the custom would you get prompt and effective service from the servants?

y. m.   Oh, hear yourself talk! Those European servants? Why, you wouldn't get any at all, to speak of.

o. m.   Couldn't *that* work as an impulse to move you to pay the tax?

y. m.   I am not denying it.

o. m.   Apparently, then, it is a case of for-duty's-sake with a little self-interest added?

y. m.   Yes, it has the look of it. But here is a point: we pay that tax knowing it to be unjust and an extortion; yet we go away with a pain at the heart if we think we have been stingy with the poor fellows; and we heartily wish we were back again, so that we could do the right thing, and *more* than the right thing, the *generous* thing. I think it will be difficult for you to find any thought of self in that impulse.

o. m.   I wonder why you should think so. When you find service charged in the *hotel* bill does it annoy you?

y. m.   No.

o. m.   Do you ever complain of the amount of it?

y. m.   No, it would not occur to me.

o. m.   The *expense*, then, is not the annoying detail. It is a fixed charge, and you pay it cheerfully, you pay it without a murmur. When you came to pay the servants, how would you like it if each of the men and maids had a fixed charge?

Y. M.   Like it? I should rejoice!

O. M.   Even if the fixed tax were a shade *more* than you had been in the habit of paying in the form of tips?

Y. M.   Indeed, yes!

O. M.   Very well, then. As I understand it, it isn't really compassion nor yet duty that moves you to pay the tax, and it isn't the *amount* of the tax that annoys you. Yet *something* annoys you. What is it?

Y. M.   Well, the trouble is, you never know *what* to pay, the tax varies so, all over Europe.

O. M.   So you have to guess?

Y. M.   There is no other way. So you go on thinking and thinking, and calculating and guessing, and consulting with other people and getting their views; and it spoils your sleep, nights, and makes you distraught in the day-time, and while you are pretending to look at the sights you are only guessing and guessing and guessing all the time, and being worried and miserable.

O. M.   And all about a debt which you don't owe and don't have to pay unless you want to! Strange. What is the purpose of the guessing?

Y. M.   To guess out what is right to give them, and not be unfair to any of them.

O. M.   It has a quite noble look—taking so much pains and using up so much valuable time in order to be just and fair to a poor servant to whom you owe nothing, but who needs money and is ill paid.

Y. M.   I think, myself, that if there is any ungracious motive back of it it will be hard to find.

O. M.   How do you know when you have not paid a servant fairly?

Y. M.   Why, he is silent; does not thank you. Sometimes he gives you a look that makes you ashamed. You are too proud to rectify your mistake there, with people looking, but afterward you keep on wishing and wishing you *had* done it. My, the shame and the pain of it! Sometimes you see, by the signs, that you have hit it *just right,* and you go away mightily satisfied. Sometimes the man is so effusively thankful that you know you have given him a good deal *more* than was necessary.

o. m.   *Necessary?* Necessary for what?

y. m.   To content him.

o. m.   How do you feel *then?*

y. m.   Repentant.

o. m.   It is my belief that you have *not* been concerning yourself in guessing out his just dues, but only in ciphering out what would *content* him. And I think you had a self-deluding reason for that.

y. m.   What was it?

o. m.   If you fell short of what he was expecting and wanting, you would get a look which would *shame you before folk.* That would give you *pain.* You—for you are only working for yourself, not *him.* If you gave him too much you would be *ashamed of yourself* for it, and that would give *you* pain—another case of thinking of *yourself,* protecting yourself, *saving yourself from discomfort.* You never think of the servant once—except to guess out how to secure *his approval.* If you get that, you get your *own* approval, and that is the sole and only thing you are after. The Master inside of you is then satisfied, contented, comfortable; there was *no other* thing at stake, as a matter of *first* interest, anywhere in the transaction.

FURTHER INSTANCES

y. m.   Well, to think of it: Self-Sacrifice for others, the grandest thing in man, ruled out! non-existent!

o. m.   Are you accusing me of saying that?

y. m.   Why, certainly.

o. m.   I haven't said it.

y. m.   What did you say, then?

o. m.   That no man has ever sacrificed himself in the common meaning of that phrase—which is, self-sacrifice for another *alone*. Men make daily sacrifices for others, but it is for their own sake *first*. The act must content their own spirit *first*. The other beneficiaries come second.

Y. M.   And the same with duty for duty's sake?

O. M.   Yes. No man performs a duty for mere duty's sake; the act must content his spirit *first*. He must feel better for *doing* the duty than he would for shirking it. Otherwise he will not do it.

Y. M.   Take the case of the *Berkeley Castle*.

O. M.   It was a noble duty, greatly performed. Take it to pieces and examine it, if you like.

Y. M.   A British troop-ship crowded with soldiers and their wives and children. She struck a rock and began to sink. There was room in the boats for the women and children only. The colonel lined-up his regiment on the deck and said "it is our duty to die, that they may be saved." There was no murmur, no protest. The boats carried away the women and children. When the death-moment was come, the colonel and his officers took their several posts, the men stood at shoulder-arms, and so, as on dress-parade, with their flag flying and the drums beating, they went down, a sacrifice to duty for duty's sake. Can you view it as other than that?

O. M.   It was something as fine as that, as exalted as that. Could you have remained in those ranks and gone down to your death in that unflinching way?

Y. M.   Could I? No, I could not.

O. M.   Think. Imagine yourself there, with that watery doom creeping higher and higher around you.

Y. M.   I can imagine it. I feel all the horror of it. I could not have endured it, I could not have remained in my place. I know it.

O. M.   Why?

Y. M.   There is no why about it: I know myself, and I know I couldn't *do* it.

O. M.   But it would be your *duty* to do it.

Y. M.   Yes, I know—but I couldn't.

O. M.   It was more than a thousand men, yet not one of them flinched. Some of them must have been born with your temperament; if they could do that great duty for duty's *sake*, why not you? Don't you know that you could go out and gather together a thousand clerks and mechanics and put them on that deck and ask them to die for duty's sake, and not two dozen of them would stay in the ranks to the end?

Y. M.   Yes, I know that.

O. M.   But you *train* them, and put them through a campaign or two; then they would be soldiers; soldiers, with a soldier's pride, a soldier's self-respect, a soldier's ideals. They would have to content a *soldier's* spirit then, not a clerk's, not a mechanic's. They could not content that spirit by shirking a soldier's duty, could they?

Y. M.   I suppose not.

O. M.   Then they would do the duty not for the *duty's* sake, but for their *own* sake—primarily. The *duty* was *just the same*, and just as imperative, when they were clerks, mechanics, raw recruits, but they wouldn't perform it for that. As clerks and mechanics they had other ideals, another spirit to satisfy, and they satisfied it. They *had* to; it is the law. *Training* is potent. Training toward higher, and higher, and ever higher ideals is worth any man's thought and labor and diligence.

Y. M.   Consider the man who stands by his duty and goes to the stake rather than be recreant to it.

O. M.   It is his make and his training. He has to content the spirit that is in him, though it cost him his life. Another man, just as sincerely religious, but of different temperament, will fail of that duty, though recognizing it as a duty, and grieving to be unequal to it; but he must content the spirit that is in him—he cannot help it. He could not perform that duty for duty's *sake*, for that would not content his spirit, and the contenting of his spirit must be looked to *first*. It takes precedence of all other duties.

Y. M.   Take the case of a clergyman of stainless private morals who votes for a thief for public office, on his own party's ticket, and against an honest man on the other ticket.

o. m. He has to content his spirit. He has no public morals; he has no private ones, where his party's prosperity is at stake. He will always be true to his make and training.

TRAINING

4

Training

Y. M. You keep using that word—training. By it do you particularly mean—

O. M. Study, instruction, lectures, sermons? That is a part of it—but not a large part. I mean *all* the outside influences. There are a million of them. From the cradle to the grave, during all his waking hours, the human being is under training. In the very first rank of his trainers stands *association*. It is his human environment which influences his mind and his feelings, furnishes him his ideals, and sets him on his road and keeps him in it. If he leave that road he will find himself shunned by the people whom he most loves and esteems, and whose approval he most values. He is a chameleon; by a law of his nature he takes the color of his place of resort. The influences about him create his preferences, his aversions, his politics, his tastes, his morals, his religion. He creates none of these things for himself. He *thinks* he does, but that is because he has not examined into the matter. You have seen Presbyterians?

Y. M. Many.

O. M. How did they happen to be Presbyterians and not Congregationalists? And why were the Congregationalists not Baptists, and the Baptists Roman Catholics, and the Roman Catholics Buddhists, and the Buddhists Quakers, and the Quakers Episcopalians, and the Episcopalians Millerites, and the Millerites Hindoos, and the Hindoos Atheists, and the Atheists Spiritualists, and the Spiritualists Agnostics, and the Agnostics Methodists, and the Methodists Confucians, and the Confucians Unitarians, and the Unitarians Mohammedans, and the Mohammedans Salvation Warriors, and the Salvation Warriors Zoroastrians, and the Zoroastians Christian Scientists, and the Christian Scientists Mormons —and so on?

Y. M.   You may answer your question yourself.

O. M.   That list of sects is not a record of *studies*, searchings, seekings after light; it mainly (and sarcastically) indicates what *association* can do. If you know a man's nationality you can come within a split hair of guessing the complexion of his religion: English—Protestant; American—ditto; Spaniard, Frenchman, Irishman, Italian, South American, Austrian—Roman Catholic; Russian—Greek Catholic; Turk—Mohammedan; and so on. And when you know the man's religious complexion, you know what sort of religious books he reads when he wants some more light, and what sort of books he avoids, lest by accident he get more light than he wants. In America if you know which party-collar a voter wears, you know what his associations are, and how he came by his politics, and which breed of newspaper he reads to get light, and which breed he diligently avoids, and which breed of mass meetings he attends in order to broaden his political knowledge, and which breed of mass meetings he doesn't attend, except to refute its doctrines with brickbats. We are always hearing of people who are around *seeking after Truth*. I have never seen a (permanent) specimen. I think he has never lived. But I have seen several entirely sincere people who *thought* they were (permanent) Seekers after Truth. They sought diligently, persistently, carefully, cautiously, profoundly, with perfect honesty and a nicely adjusted judgment—until they believed that without doubt or question they had found the Truth. *That was the end of the search.* The man spent the rest of his life hunting up shingles wherewith to protect his Truth from the weather. If he was seeking after political Truth he found it in one or another of the hundred political gospels which govern men in the earth; if he was seeking after the Only True Religion he found it in one or another of the three thousand that are on the market. In any case, when he found his Truth *he sought no further*; but from that day forth, with his soldering iron in one hand and his bludgeon in the other he tinkered its leaks and reasoned with objectors. There have been innumerable Temporary Seekers after Truth—have you ever heard of a Permanent one? In the very nature of man such a person is impossible. However, to drop back to the text—training: all training is one form or another of *outside influence,* and *association* is the largest part of it. A man is never anything but what his outside influences have made him. They train him downwards or they train him upwards—but they *train* him; they are at work upon him all the time.

Y. M.   Then if he happen by the accidents of life to be evilly placed there is no help for him, according to your notions—he must train downwards.

O. M.   No help for him? No help for this chameleon? It is a mistake. It is in his chameleonship that his greatest good fortune lies. He has only to change his habitat—his *associations.* But the impulse to do it must come from the *outside*—he cannot originate it himself, with that purpose in view. Sometimes a very small and accidental thing can furnish him the initiatory impulse and start him on a new road, with a new ideal. The chance remark of a sweetheart, "I hear that you are a coward" may water a seed that shall sprout and bloom and flourish, and end in producing a surprising fruitage in the fields of war. The history of man is full of such accidents. The accident of a broken leg brought a profane and ribald soldier under religious influences and furnished him a new ideal. From that accident sprang the Order of the Jesuits, and it has been shaking thrones, changing policies, and doing other tremendous work for two hundred years—and will go on. The chance reading of a book, or of a paragraph in a newspaper can start a man on a new track and make him renounce his old associations and seek new ones that are *in sympathy with his new ideal;* and the result, for that man, can be an entire change of his way of life.

Y. M.   Are you hinting at a scheme of procedure?

O. M.   Not a new one—an old one. Old as mankind.

Y. M.   What is it?

O. M.   Merely the laying of traps for people. Traps baited with *Initiatory Impulses toward high ideals.* It is what the tract

distributor does. It is what the missionary does. It is what governments ought to do.

Y. M.   Don't they?

O. M.   In one way they do, in another way they don't. They
separate the small-pox patients from the healthy people, but in
dealing with crime they put the healthy into the pest-house along
with the sick. That is to say, they put the beginners in with the
confirmed criminals. This would be well if man were naturally
inclined to good, but he isn't, and so *association* makes the beginners worse than they were when they went into captivity. It is
putting a very severe punishment upon the comparatively innocent. However, all governments are hard on the innocent at times.
They hang a man—which is a trifling punishment; this breaks the
hearts of his family—which is a heavy one. They comfortably jail
and feed a wife-beater, and leave his innocent wife and children to
starve.

Y. M.   Do you believe in the doctrine that man is equipped
with an intuitive perception of good and evil?

O. M.   Adam hadn't it.

Y. M.   But has man acquired it since?

O. M.   No. I think he has no intuitions of any kind. He gets
all his ideas, all his impressions, all his opinions, from the outside.
I keep repeating this, in the hope that I may so impress it upon you
that you will be interested to observe and examine for yourself and
see whether it is true or false.

Y. M.   Where did you get your own aggravating notions?

O. M.   From the *outside*. I did not invent them. They are
gathered from a thousand unknown sources. Mainly *unconsciously* gathered.

Y. M.   Don't you believe that God could make an inherently
honest man?

O. M.   Yes, I know He could. I also know that He never did
make one.

Y. M.   A wiser observer than you has recorded the fact that
"an honest man's the noblest work of God."

o. m.   He didn't record a fact, he recorded a falsity. It is windy, and sounds well, but it is not true. God makes a man with honest and dishonest *possibilities* in him, and stops there. The man's *associations* develop the possibilities—the one set or the other. The result is accordingly an honest man or a dishonest one.

y. m.   And the honest one is not entitled to—

o. m.   Praise? No. How often must I tell you that? *He* is not the architect of his honesty.

y. m.   Now then, I will ask you to tell me where there is any sense in training people to lead virtuous lives. What is gained by it?

o. m.   The man himself gets large advantages out of it, and that is the main thing—to *him*. He is not a peril to his neighbors, he is not a damage to them—and so *they* get an advantage out of his virtues. That is the main thing to *them*. To train men to lead virtuous lives is an inestimably important thing. It can make this life comparatively comfortable to the parties concerned; the *neglect* of this training can make this life a constant peril and distress to the parties concerned.

y. m.   You have said that training is everything; that training is the man *himself*, for it makes him what he is.

o. m.   I said training and *another* thing. Let that other thing pass, for the moment. What were you going to say?

y. m.   We have an old servant. She has been with us twenty-two years. Her service used to be faultless, but now she has become very forgetful. We are all fond of her; we all recognize that she cannot help the infirmity which age has brought her; the rest of the family do not scold her for her remissnesses, but at times I do—I can't seem to control myself. Don't I try? I do try. Now, then, when I was ready to dress, this morning, no clean clothes had been put out. I lost my temper; I lose it easiest and quickest in the early morning. I rang; and immediately began to warn myself not to show temper, and to be careful and speak gently. I safeguarded myself most carefully. I even chose the very words I would use: "You've forgotten the clean clothes, Jane." When she appeared in the door I opened my mouth to say that phrase—and out

of it, moved by an instant surge of passion which I was not expecting and hadn't time to put under control, came the hot rebuke,
"You've forgotten them again!" You say a man always does the
thing which will best please his Interior Master. Whence came the
impulse to make careful preparation to save the girl the humiliation of a rebuke? Did that come from the Master, who is always
primarily concerned about *himself*?

    o. m.   Unquestionably. There is no other source for any im-
pulse. *Secondarily* you made preparation to save the girl, but
primarily its object was to save yourself, by contenting the Master.

    y. m.   How do you mean?

    o. m.   Has any member of the family ever implored you to
watch your temper and not fly out at the girl?

    y. m.   Yes. My mother.

    o. m.   You love her?

    y. m.   Oh, more than that!

    o. m.   You would always do anything in your power to
please her?

    y. m.   It is a delight to me to do anything to please her!

    o. m.   Why? *You would do it for pay, solely*—for *profit*.
What profit would you expect and certainly receive, from the
investment?

    y. m.   Personally? None. To please *her* is enough.

    o. m.   It appears, then, that your object, primarily, *wasn't*
to save the girl a humiliation, but to *please your mother*. It also
appears that to please your mother gives *you* a strong pleasure. Is
not that the profit which you get out of the investment? Isn't that
the *real* profit and *first* profit?

    y. m.   Oh, well? Go on.

    o. m.   In *all* transactions, the Interior Master looks to it that
you get the first profit. Otherwise there is no transaction.

    y. m.   Well, then, if I was so anxious to get that profit and
was so intent upon it, why did I throw it away by losing my
temper?

o. m. In order to get *another* profit which suddenly super-seded it in value.

y. m. Where was it?

o. m. Ambushed behind your born temperament, and wait-ing for a chance. Your native warm temper jumped suddenly to the front, and *for the moment* its influence was more powerful than your mother's, and abolished it. In that instant you were eager to flash out a hot rebuke and enjoy it. You did enjoy it, didn't you?

y. m. For—for a quarter of a second. Yes—I did.

o. m. Very well, it is as I have said: the thing which will give you the *most* pleasure, the most satisfaction, in any moment or *fraction* of a moment, is the thing you will always do. You must content the Master's *latest* whim, whatever it may be.

y. m. But when the tears came into the old servant's eyes I could have cut my hand off for what I had done.

o. m. Right. You had humiliated *yourself*, you see; you had given yourself *pain*. Nothing is of *first* importance to a man except results which damage *him* or profit him—all the rest is *secondary*. Your Master was displeased with you, although you had obeyed him. He required a prompt *repentance*; you obeyed again; you *had* to—there is never any escape from his commands. He is a hard master, and fickle; he changes his mind in the fraction of a second, but you must be ready to obey, and you will obey, *always*. If he requires repentance, to content him, you will always furnish it. He must be nursed, petted, coddled, and kept contented, let the terms be what they may.

y. m. Training! Oh, what is the use of it? Didn't I, and didn't my mother try to train me up to where I would no longer fly out at that girl?

o. m. Have you never managed to keep back a scolding?

y. m. Oh, certainly—many times.

o. m. More times this year than last?

y. m. Yes, a good many more.

o. m.   More times last year than the year before?

y. m.   Yes.

o. m.   There is a large improvement, then, in the two years?

y. m.   Yes, undoubtedly.

o. m.   Then your question is answered. You see there *is* use in training. Keep on. Keep faithfully on. You are doing well.

y. m.   Will my reform reach perfection?

o. m.   It will. Up to *your* limit.

y. m.   My limit? What do you mean by that?

o. m.   You remember you said that I said training was *everything*. I corrected you, and said "training and *another* thing." That other thing is *temperament*—that is, the disposition you were born with. *You can't eradicate your disposition nor any rag of it*—you can only put a pressure on it and keep it down and quiet. You have a warm temper?

y. m.   Yes.

o. m.   You will never get rid of it; but by watching it you can keep it down nearly all the time. *Its presence is your limit.* Your reform will never quite reach perfection, for your temper will beat you now and then, but you will come near enough. You have made valuable progress and can make more. There *is* use in training. Immense use. Presently you will reach a new stage of development, then your progress will be easier; will proceed on a simpler basis, anyway.

y. m.   Explain.

o. m.   You keep back your scoldings now, to please *yourself* by pleasing your *mother*; presently the mere triumphing over your temper will delight your vanity and confer a more delicious pleasure and satisfaction upon you than even the approbation of your *mother* confers upon you now. You will then labor for yourself directly and at *first hand*, not by the roundabout way through your mother. It simplifies the matter, and it also strengthens the impulse.

y. m.   Ah, dear! But I shan't ever reach the point where I will spare the girl for *her* sake *primarily*, not mine?

o. m. Why—yes. In heaven.

y. m. (*After a reflective pause.*) Temperament. Well, I see one must allow for temperament. It is a large factor, sure enough. My mother is thoughtful, and not hot-tempered. When I was dressed I went to her room; she was not there; I called, she answered from the bath-room. I heard the water running. I inquired. She answered, without temper, that Jane had forgotten her bath, and she was preparing it herself. I offered to ring, but she said, "No, don't do that; it would only distress her to be confronted with her lapse, and would be a rebuke; she doesn't deserve that— she is not to blame for the tricks her memory serves her." I say— has my mother an Interior Master?—and where was he?

o. m. He was there. There, and looking out for his own peace and pleasure and contentment. The girl's distress would have pained *your mother*. Otherwise the girl would have been rung up, distress and all. I know women who would have gotten a No. 1 *pleasure* out of ringing Jane up—and so they would infallibly have pushed the button and obeyed the law of their make and training, which are the servants of their Interior Masters. It is quite likely that a part of your mother's forbearance came from training. The *good* kind of training—whose best and highest function is to see to it that every time it confers a satisfaction upon its pupil a benefit shall fall at second hand upon others.

y. m. If you were going to condense into an admonition your plan for the general betterment of the race's condition, how would you word it?

ADMONITION

o. m. Diligently train your ideals *upward* and *still upward* toward a summit where you will find your chiefest pleasure in conduct which, while contenting you, will be sure to confer benefits upon your neighbor and the community.

y. m. Is that a new gospel?

o. m. No.

y. m. It has been taught before?

O. M.   For ten thousand years.

Y. M.   By whom?

O. M.   All the great religions—all the great gospels.

Y. M.   Then there is nothing new about it.

O. M.   Oh, yes there is. It is candidly stated, this time. That has not been done before.

Y. M.   How do you mean?

O. M.   Haven't I put *you* FIRST, and your neighbor and the community *afterward*?

Y. M.   Well, yes, that is a difference, it is true.

O. M.   The difference between straight speaking and crooked; the difference between frankness and shuffling.

Y. M.   Explain.

O. M.   The others offer you a hundred bribes to be good, thus conceding that the Master inside of you must be conciliated and contented first, and that you will do nothing at *first hand* but for his sake; then they turn square around and require you to do good for *others'* sake *chiefly*; and to do your duty for duty's *sake*, chiefly; and to do *unselfish* things; and to do acts of *self-sacrifice*. Thus at the outset we all stand upon the same ground—recognition of the supreme and absolute Monarch that resides in man, and we all grovel before him and appeal to him; then those others dodge and shuffle, and face around and unfrankly and inconsistently and illogically change the form of their appeal and direct its persuasions to man's *second-place* powers and to powers which have *no existence* in him, thus advancing them to *first* place; whereas in my Admonition I stick logically and consistently to the original position: I place the Interior Master's requirements *first*, and keep them there.

Y. M.   If we grant, for the sake of argument, that your scheme and the other schemes aim at and produce the same result —*right living*—has yours an advantage over the others?

O. M.   One, yes—a large one. It has no concealments, no deceptions. When a man leads a right and valuable life under it he is not deceived as to the *real* chief motive which impels him to it—in those other cases he is.

Y. M. Is that an advantage? Is it an advantage to live a lofty life for a mean reason? In the other cases he lives the lofty life under the *impression* that he is living it for a lofty reason. Is not that an advantage?

O. M. Perhaps so. The same advantage he might get out of thinking himself a duke, and living a duke's life, and parading in ducal fuss and feathers, when he wasn't a duke at all, and could find it out if he would only examine the herald's records.

Y. M. But anyway, he is obliged to do a duke's part; he puts his hand in his pocket and does his benevolences on as big a scale as he can stand, and that benefits the community.

O. M. He could do that without being a duke.

Y. M. But would he?

O. M. Don't you see where you are arriving?

Y. M. Where?

O. M. At the stand-point of the other schemes: That it is good morals to let an ignorant duke do showy benevolences for pride's sake, a pretty low motive, and go on doing them unwarned, lest if he were made acquainted with the actual motive which prompted them he might shut up his purse and cease to be good?

Y. M. But isn't it best to leave him in ignorance, as long as he *thinks* he is doing good for others' sake?

O. M. Perhaps so. It is the position of the other schemes. They think humbug is good enough morals when the dividend on it is good deeds and handsome conduct.

Y. M. It is my opinion that under your scheme of a man's doing a good deed for his *own* sake first-off, instead of first for the *good deed's* sake, no man would ever do one.

O. M. Have you committed a benevolence lately?

Y. M. Yes. This morning.

O. M. Give the particulars.

Y. M. The cabin of the old negro woman who nursed me

when I was a child and who saved my life once at risk of her own, was burned last night, and she came mourning this morning, and pleading for money to build another one.

o. m.   You furnished it?

y. m.   Certainly.

o. m.   You were glad you had the money?

y. m.   Money? I hadn't it. I sold my horse.

o. m.   You were glad you had the horse?

y. m.   Of course I was; for if I hadn't had the horse I should have been incapable, and my *mother* would have captured the chance to set old Sally up.

o. m.   You were cordially glad you were not caught out and incapable?

y. m.   Oh, I just was!

o. m.   Now then—

y. m.   Stop where you are! I know your whole catalogue of questions, and I could answer every one of them without your wasting the time to ask them; but I will summarize the whole thing in a single remark: I did the charity knowing it was because the act would give *me* a splendid pleasure, and because old Sally's moving gratitude and delight would give *me* another one; and because the reflection that she would be happy now and out of her trouble would fill *me* full of happiness. I did the whole thing with my eyes open and recognizing and realizing that I was looking out for *my* share of the profits *first*. Now then, I have confessed. Go on.

o. m.   I haven't anything to offer; you have covered the whole ground. Could you have been any *more* strongly moved to help Sally out of her trouble—could you have done the deed any more eagerly—if you had been under the delusion that you were doing it for *her* sake and profit only?

y. m.   No! Nothing in the world could have made the impulse which moved me more powerful, more masterful, more thoroughly irresistible. I played the limit!

o. m.   Very well. You begin to suspect—and I claim to *know*

—that when a man is a shade *more strongly moved* to do *one* of two things or of two dozen things than he is to do any one of the *others*, he will infallibly do that *one* thing, be it good or be it evil; and if it be good, not all the beguilements of all the casuistries can increase the strength of the impulse by a single shade or add a shade to the comfort and contentment he will get out of the act.

Y. M.   Then you believe that such tendency toward doing good as is in men's hearts would not be diminished by the removal of the delusion that good deeds are done primarily for the sake of No. 2 instead of for the sake of No. 1?

O. M.   That is what I fully believe.

Y. M.   Doesn't it somehow seem to take from the dignity of the deed?

O. M.   If there is dignity in falsity, it does. It removes that.

Y. M.   What is left for the moralist to do?

O. M.   Teach unreservedly what he already teaches with one side of his mouth and takes back with the other: Do right *for your own sake*, and be happy in knowing that your *neighbor* will certainly share in the benefits resulting.

Y. M.   Repeat your Admonition.

O. M.   *Diligently train your ideals upward and still upward toward a summit where you will find your chiefest pleasure in conduct which, while contenting you, will be sure to confer benefits upon your neighbor and the community.*

Y. M.   One's *every* act proceeds from *exterior influences*, you think?

O. M.   Yes.

Y. M.   If I conclude to rob a person, I am not the *originator* of the idea, but it came in from the *outside?* I see him handling money—for instance—and *that* moves me to the crime?

O. M.   That, by itself? O, certainly not. It is merely the *latest* outside influence of a procession of preparatory influences stretching back over a period of years. No *single* outside influence can make a man do a thing which is at war with his training. The most it can do is to start his mind on a new track and open it to the reception of *new* influences—as in the case of Ignatius Loyola. In time these influences can train him to a point where it will be consonant with his new character to yield to the *final* influence and do that thing. I will put the case in a form which will make my theory clear to you, I think. Here are two ingots of virgin gold. They shall represent a couple of characters which have been refined and perfected in the virtues by years of diligent right training. Suppose you wanted to break down these strong and well compacted characters—what influence would you bring to bear upon the ingots?

Y. M.   Work it out yourself. Proceed.

O. M.   Suppose I turn upon one of them a steam-jet during a long succession of hours. Will there be a result?

Y. M.   None that I know of.

O. M.   Why?

Y. M.   A steam-jet cannot break down such a substance.

O. M.   Very well. The steam is an *outside influence*, but it is ineffective, because the gold *takes no interest in it*. The ingot remains as it was. Suppose we add to the steam some quicksilver in a vaporized condition, and turn the jet upon the other ingot. Will there be an instantaneous result?

Y. M.   No.

O. M.   The *quicksilver* is an outside influence which gold (by its peculiar nature—say *temperament, disposition*), *cannot be indifferent to*. It stirs the interest of the gold, although we do not perceive it; but a *single* application of the influence works no damage. Let us continue the application in a steady stream, and call each minute a year. By the end of ten or twenty minutes—ten or twenty years—the little ingot is sodden with quicksilver, rotten with quicksilver, its virtues are gone, its character is degraded. At last it is ready to yield to a temptation which it would have taken no notice of, ten or twenty years ago. We will apply that temptation in the form of a pressure with my finger. You note the result?

Y. M.   Yes; the ingot has crumbled to sand. I understand, now. It is not the *single* outside influence that does the work, but only the *last* one of a long and disintegrating accumulation of them. I see, now, how my *single* impulse to rob the man is not the one that makes me do it, but only the *last* one of a preparatory series. You might illustrate it with a parable.

A PARABLE

o. m. I will. There was once a pair of New England boys—twins. They were alike in good dispositions, fleckless morals, and personal appearance. They were the models of the Sunday-school. At fifteen George had an opportunity to go as cabin-boy in a whale-ship, and sailed away for the Pacific. Henry remained at home in the village. At eighteen George was a sailor before the mast, and Henry was teacher of the advanced Bible class. At twenty-two George, through fighting-habits and drinking-habits acquired at sea and in the sailor boarding-houses of the European and Oriental ports, was a common rough in Hong Kong, and out of a job; and Henry was superintendent of the Sunday-school. At twenty-six George was a wanderer, a tramp, and Henry was pastor of the village church. Then George came home, and was Henry's guest. One evening a man passed by and turned down the lane, and Henry said, with a pathetic smile, "Without intending me a discomfort, that man is always keeping me reminded of my pinching poverty, for he carries heaps of money about him, and goes by here every evening of his life." That *outside influence*—that remark—was enough for George, but *it* was not the one that made him ambush the man and rob him, it merely represented the eleven years' accumulation of such influences, and gave birth to the act for which their long gestation had made preparation. It had never entered the head of Henry to rob the man—his ingot had been subjected to clean steam only; but George's had been subjected to vaporized quicksilver.

More About the Machine

NOTE.—When Mrs. W. asks how can a millionaire give a single dollar to colleges and museums while one human being is destitute of bread; she has answered her question herself. Her feeling for the poor shows that she has a standard of benevolence; therefore she has conceded the millionaire's privilege of having a standard; since she evidently requires him to adopt her standard she is by that act requiring herself to adopt his. The human being always looks down when he is examining another person's standard, he never finds one that he has to examine by looking up.

THE MAN-MACHINE AGAIN

Y. M.   You really think man is a mere machine?

O. M.   I do.

Y. M.   And that his mind works automatically and is independent of his control—carries on thought on its own hook?

O. M.   Yes. It is diligently at work, unceasingly at work, during every waking moment. Have you never tossed about all night, imploring, beseeching, commanding your mind to stop work and let you go to sleep?—you who perhaps imagine that your mind is your servant and must obey your orders, think what you tell it to think, and stop when you tell it to stop. When it chooses to work, there is no way to keep it still for an instant. The brightest man would not be able to supply it with subjects if he had to hunt them up. If it needed the man's help it would wait for him to give it work when he wakes in the morning.

Y. M.   Maybe it does.

O. M.   No, it begins right away, before the man gets wide enough awake to give it a suggestion. He may go to sleep saying, "The moment I wake I will think upon such and such a subject," but he will fail. His mind will be too quick for him; by the time he has become nearly enough awake to be half conscious, he will find that it is already at work on another subject. Make the experiment and see.

Y. M. At any rate he can make it stick to a subject if he wants to.

O. M. Not if it finds another that suits it better. As a rule it will listen to neither a dull speaker nor a bright one. It refuses all persuasion. The dull speaker wearies it and sends it far away in idle dreams; the bright speaker throws out stimulating ideas which it goes chasing after and is at once unconscious of him and his talk. You cannot keep your mind from wandering, if it wants to; it is master, not you.

After an Interval of Days

O. M. Now, dreams—but we will examine that later. Meantime, did you try commanding your mind to wait for orders from you, and not do any thinking on its own hook?

Y. M. Yes, I commanded it to stand ready to take orders when I should wake in the morning.

O. M. Did it obey?

Y. M. No. It went to thinking about something of its own initiation, without waiting for me. Also—as you suggested—at night I appointed a theme for it to begin on in the morning, and commanded it to begin on that one and no other.

O. M. Did it obey?

Y. M. No.

O. M. How many times did you try the experiment?

Y. M. Ten.

O. M. How many successes did you score?

Y. M. Not one.

O. M. It is as I have said: the mind is independent of the man. He has no control over it, it does as it pleases. It will take up a subject in spite of him; it will stick to it in spite of him; it will throw it aside in spite of him. It is entirely independent of him.

Y. M. Go on. Illustrate.

o. m.   Do you know chess?

y. m.   I learned it a week ago.

o. m.   Did your mind go on playing the game all night that first night?

y. m.   Don't mention it!

o. m.   It was eagerly, unsatisfiably interested; it rioted in the combinations; you implored it to drop the game and let you get some sleep?

y. m.   Yes. It wouldn't listen; it played right along. It wore me out and I got up haggard and wretched in the morning.

o. m.   At some time or other you have been captivated by a ridiculous rhyme-jingle?

y. m.   Indeed, yes!

> "I saw Esau kissing Kate,
> And she saw I saw Esau;
> I saw Esau, he saw Kate,
> And she saw —"

And so on. My mind went mad with joy over it. It repeated it all day and all night for a week in spite of all I could do to stop it, and it seemed to me that I must surely go crazy.

o. m.   And the new popular song?

y. m.   Oh, yes! "In the Swee-eet By and By;" etc. Yes, the new popular song with the taking melody sings thro' one's head day and night, asleep and awake, till one is a wreck. There is no getting the mind to let it alone.

o. m.   Yes, asleep as well as awake. The mind is quite independent. It is master. You have nothing to do with it. It is so apart from you that it can conduct its affairs, sing its songs, play its chess, weave its complex and ingeniously-constructed dreams, while you sleep. It has no use for your help, no use for your guidance, and never uses either, whether you be asleep or awake. You have imagined that you could originate a thought in your mind, and you have sincerely believed you could do it.

y. m.   Yes, I have had that idea.

o. m.   Yet you can't originate a dream-thought for it to work out, and get it accepted?

y. m.   No.

o. m.   And you can't dictate its procedure after it has originated a dream-thought for itself?

y. m.   No. No one can do it. Do you think the waking mind and the dream-mind are the same machine?

o. m.   There is argument for it. We have wild and fantastic day-thoughts? Things that are dream-like?

y. m.   Yes—like Mr. Wells's man who invented a drug that made him invisible; and like the Arabian tales of the Thousand Nights.

o. m.   And there are dreams that are rational, simple, consistent and unfantastic?

y. m.   Yes. I have dreams that are like that. Dreams which are just like real life; dreams in which there are several persons with distinctly differentiated characters—inventions of my mind and yet strangers to me: a vulgar person; a refined one; a wise person; a fool; a cruel person; a kind and compassionate one; a quarrelsome person; a peacemaker; old persons and young; beautiful girls and homely ones. They talk in character, each preserves his own characteristics. There are vivid fights, vivid and biting insults, vivid love-passages; there are tragedies and comedies, there are griefs that go to one's heart, there are sayings and doings that make you laugh: indeed the whole thing is exactly like real life.

o. m.   Your dreaming mind originates the scheme, consistently and artistically develops it, and carries the little drama creditably through—all without help or suggestion from you?

y. m.   Yes.

o. m.   It is argument that it could do the like awake without help or suggestion from you—and I think it does. It is argument that it is the same old mind in both cases, and never needs your help. I think the mind is purely a machine, a thoroughly independent machine, an automatic machine. Have you tried the other experiment which I suggested to you?

Y. M.   Which one?

O. M.   The one which was to determine how much influence you have over your mind—if any.

Y. M.   Yes, and got more or less entertainment out of it. I did as you ordered: I placed two texts before my eyes—one a dull one and barren of interest, the other one full of interest, inflamed with it, white-hot with it. I commanded my mind to busy itself solely with the dull one.

O. M.   Did it obey?

Y. M.   Well, no, it didn't. It busied itself with the other one.

O. M.   Did you try hard to make it obey?

Y. M.   Yes, I did my honest best.

O. M.   What was the text which it refused to be interested in or think about?

Y. M.   It was this question: if A owes B a dollar and a half, and B owes C two and three-quarters, and C owes A thirty-five cents, and D and A together owe E and B three-sixteenths of—of—I don't remember the rest, now, but anyway it was wholly uninteresting, and I could not force my mind to stick to it even half a minute at a time; it kept flying off to the other text.

O. M.   What was the other text?

Y. M.   It is no matter about that.

O. M.   But what was it?

Y. M.   A photograph.

O. M.   Your own?

Y. M.   No. It was hers.

O. M.   You really made an honest good test. Did you make a second trial?

Y. M.   Yes. I commanded my mind to interest itself in the morning paper's report of the pork market, and at the same time I reminded it of an experience of mine of sixteen years ago. It refused to consider the pork, and gave its whole blazing interest to that ancient incident.

O. M.   What was the incident?

Y. M.   An armed desperado slapped my face in the presence

of twenty spectators. It makes me wild and murderous every time
I think of it.

o. m. Good tests, both; very good tests. Did you try my
other suggestion?

y. m. The one which was to prove to me that if I would
leave my mind to its own devices it would find things to think
about without any of my help, and thus convince me that it was
a machine, an automatic machine, set in motion by exterior influences, and as independent of me as it could be if it were in
some one else's skull? Is that the one?

o. m. Yes.

y. m. I tried it. I was shaving. I had slept well, and my
mind was very lively, even gay and frisky. It was reveling in a fantastic and joyful episode of my remote boyhood which had suddenly
flashed up in my memory,—moved to this by the spectacle of a
yellow cat picking its way carefully along the top of the garden
wall. The color of this cat brought the bygone cat before me, and
I saw her walking along a side-step of the pulpit; saw her walk onto
a large sheet of sticky fly-paper and get all her feet involved; saw
her struggle and fall down, helpless and dissatisfied; saw her go
on struggling, on her back and getting more and more dissatisfied,
more and more urgent, more and more unreconciled, more and
more mutely profane; saw the silent congregation quivering like
jelly, and the tears running down their faces. I saw it all. The sight
of the tears whisked my mind to a far distant and a sadder scene—
in Tierra del Fuego—and with Darwin's eyes I saw a naked great
savage hurl his little boy against the rocks for a trifling fault; saw
the poor mother gather up her dying child and hug it to her breast
and weep, uttering no word. Did my mind stop to mourn with that
nude black sister of mine? No—it was far away from that scene
in an instant, and was busying itself with an ever-recurring and
disagreeable dream of mine. In this dream I always find myself,
stripped to my shirt, cringing and dodging about in the midst of
a great drawingroom throng of finely dressed ladies and gentlemen, and wondering how I got there. And so on and so on, picture

after picture, incident after incident, a drifting panorama of ever-changing, ever-dissolving views manufactured by my mind without any help from me—why, it would take me two hours to merely name the multitude of things my mind tallied off and photographed in fifteen minutes, let alone describe them to you.

o. m.   A man's mind, left free, has no use for his help. But there is one way whereby he can get its help when he desires it.

y. m.   What is that way?

o. m.   When your mind is racing along from subject to subject and strikes an inspiring one, open your mouth and begin to talk upon that matter—or take your pen and use that. It will interest your mind and concentrate it, and it will pursue the subject with satisfaction. It will take full charge, and furnish the words itself.

y. m.   But don't I tell it what to say?

o. m.   There are certainly occasions when you haven't time. The words leap out before you know what is coming.

y. m.   For instance?

o. m.   Well, take a "flash of wit"—repartee. Flash is the right word. It is out instantly. There is no time to arrange the words. There is no thinking, no reflecting. Where there is a wit-mechanism it is automatic in its action, and needs no help. Where the wit-mechanism is lacking, no amount of study and reflection can manufacture the product.

y. m.   You really think a man originates nothing, creates nothing.

THE THINKING-PROCESS

o. m.   I do. Men perceive, and their brain-machines automatically combine the things perceived. That is all.

y. m.   The steam-engine?

o. m.   It takes fifty men a hundred years to invent it. One meaning of invent is discover. I use the word in that sense. Little by little they discover and apply the multitude of details that go to make the perfect engine. Watt noticed that confined steam was strong enough to lift the lid of the teapot. He didn't create the idea, he merely discovered the fact; the cat had noticed it a hundred times. From the teapot he evolved the cylinder—from the displaced lid he evolved the piston-rod. To attach something to the piston-rod to be moved by it, was a simple matter—crank and wheel. And so there was a working engine.[1] One by one, improvements were discovered by men who used their eyes, not their creative powers—for they hadn't any—and now, after a hundred years the patient contributions of fifty or a hundred observers stand compacted in the wonderful machine which drives the ocean liner.

    Y. M.   A Shakspearean play?

    O. M.   The process is the same. The first actor was a savage. He reproduced in his theatrical war-dances, scalp-dances, and so on, incidents which he had seen in real life. A more advanced civilization produced more incidents, more episodes; the actor and the story-teller borrowed them. And so the drama grew, little by little, stage by stage. The elaborate Shakspearean play was the final outcome. It is made up of the facts of life, not creations. It took centuries to develop the Greek drama. It borrowed from preceding ages; it lent to the ages that came after. Men observe and combine, that is all. So does a rat.

    Y. M.   How?

    O. M.   He observes a smell, he infers a cheese, he seeks and finds. The astronomer observes this and that; adds his this and that to the this-and-thats of a hundred predecessors, infers an invisible planet, seeks it and finds it. The rat gets into a trap; gets out with trouble; infers that cheese in traps lacks value, and meddles with that trap no more. The astronomer is very proud of his achievement; the rat is proud of his. Yet both are machines, they have done machine-work, they have originated nothing, they have no right to be vain, the whole credit belongs to their Maker. They are entitled to no honors, no praises, no monuments when they die, no remembrance. One is a complex and elaborate machine, the

1. The Marquess of Worcester had done all of this more than a century earlier.

other a simple and limited machine, but they are alike in principle, function and process, and neither of them works otherwise than automatically, and neither of them may righteously claim a *personal* superiority or a personal dignity above the other.

Y. M.   In earned personal dignity, then, and in personal merit for what he does, it follows of necessity that he is on the same level as a rat?

O. M.   His brother the rat; yes, that is how it seems to me. Neither of them being entitled to any personal merit for what he does, it follows of necessity that neither of them has a right to arrogate to himself (personally-created) superiorities over his brother.

Y. M.   Are you determined to go on believing in these insanities? Would you go on believing in them in the face of able arguments backed by collated facts and instances?

O. M.   I have been a humble, earnest and sincere Truth Seeker.

Y. M.   Very well?

O. M.   The humble, earnest and sincere Truth Seeker is always convertible by such means.

Y. M.   I am thankful to God to hear you say this, for now I know that your conversion—

O. M.   Wait. You misunderstand. I said I have *been* a Truth Seeker.

Y. M.   Well?

O. M.   I am not that now. Have you forgotten? I told you that there are none but temporary Truth Seekers; that a permanent one is a human impossibility; that as soon as the Seeker finds what he is thoroughly convinced is the Truth, he seeks no further, but gives the rest of his days to hunting for junk to patch it and caulk it and prop it with, and make it weather-proof and keep it from caving in on him. Hence the Presbyterian remains a Presbyterian, the Mohammedan a Mohammedan, the Spiritualist a Spiritualist, the Democrat a Democrat, the Republican a Republican, the Monarchist a Monarchist; and if a humble, earnest and sincere Seeker after Truth should find it in the proposition that the moon is made of green cheese nothing could ever budge him from that position; for he is nothing but an automatic machine, and must obey the laws of his construction.

Y. M. And so—

O. M. Having found the Truth; perceiving that beyond question Man has but one moving impulse—the contenting of his own spirit—and is merely a Machine and entitled to no personal merit for anything he does, it is not humanly possible for me to seek further. The rest of my days will be spent in patching and painting and puttying and caulking my priceless possession, and in looking the other way when an imploring argument or a damaging fact approaches.

INSTINCT AND THOUGHT

Instinct and Thought

Y. M. It is odious. Those drunken theories of yours, advanced a while ago—concerning the rat and all that—strip Man bare of all his dignities, grandeurs, sublimities.

O. M. He hasn't any to strip—they are shams, stolen clothes. He claims credits which belong solely to his Maker.

Y. M. But you have no right to put him on a level with the rat.

O. M. I don't—morally. That would not be fair to the rat. The rat is well above him, there.

Y. M. Are you joking?

O. M. No, I am not.

Y. M. Then what do you mean?

O. M. That comes under the head of the Moral Sense. It is a large question. Let us finish with what we are about now, before we take it up.

Y. M. Very well. You have seemed to concede that you place Man and the rat on *a* level. What is it? The intellectual?

O. M. In form—not in degree.

Y. M. Explain.

O. M. I think that the rat's mind and the man's mind are the same machine, but of unequal capacities—like yours and Edison's; like the African pigmy's and Homer's; like the Bushman's and Bismarck's.

Y. M. How are you going to make that out, when the lower animals have no mental quality but instinct, while man possesses reason?

O. M. What is instinct?

Y. M. It is a merely unthinking and mechanical exercise of inherited habit.

O. M. What originated the habit?

Y. M. The first animal started it, its descendants have inherited it.

o. m.   How did the first one come to start it?

y. m.   I don't know; but it didn't *think* it out.

o. m.   How do you know it didn't?

y. m.   Well—I have a right to suppose it didn't, anyway.

o. m.   I don't believe you have. What is thought?

y. m.   I know what you call it: the mechanical and automatic putting together of impressions received from the outside, and drawing an inference from them.

o. m.   Very good. Now my idea of the meaningless term "instinct" is, that it is merely *petrified thought*; thought solidified and made inanimate by habit; thought which was once alive and awake, but is become unconscious—walks in its sleep, so to speak.

y. m.   Illustrate it.

o. m.   Take a herd of cows, feeding in a pasture. Their heads are all turned in one direction. They do that instinctively; they gain nothing by it, they have no reason for it, they don't know why they do it. It is an inherited habit which was originally thought—that is to say, observation of an exterior fact, and a valuable inference drawn from that observation and confirmed by experience. The original wild ox noticed that with the wind in his favor he could smell his enemy in time to escape; then he inferred that it was worth while to keep his nose to the wind. That is the process which man calls reasoning. Man's thought-machine works just like the other animals', but it is a better one and more Edisonian. Man, in the ox's place, would go further, reason wider: he would face a part of the herd the other way and protect both front and rear.

y. m.   Did you say the term instinct is meaningless?

o. m.   I think it is a bastard word. I think it confuses us; for as a rule it applies itself to habits and impulses which had a far-off origin in thought, and now and then breaks the rule and applies itself to habits which can hardly claim a thought-origin.

y. m.   Give an instance.

o. m.   Well, in putting on trousers a man always inserts the same old leg first—never the other one. There is no advantage in that, and no sense in it. All men do it, yet no man ever thought it out and adopted it of set purpose, I imagine. But it is a habit which is transmitted, no doubt, and will continue to be transmitted.

Y. M. Can you prove that the habit exists?

O. M. You can prove it, if you doubt. If you will take a man to a clothing store and watch him try on a dozen pairs of trousers, you will see.

Y. M. The cow-illustration is not—

O. M. Sufficient to show that a dumb animal's mental machine is just the same as a man's and its reasoning-processes the same? I will illustrate further. If you should hand Mr. Edison a box which you caused to fly open by some concealed device, he would infer a spring, and would hunt for it and find it. Now an uncle of mine had an old horse who used to get into the closed lot where the corn-crib was and dishonestly take the corn. I got the punishment myself, as it was supposed that I heedlessly failed to insert the wooden pin which kept the gate closed. These persistent punishments fatigued me; they also caused me to infer the existence of a culprit, somewhere; so I hid myself and watched the gate. Presently the horse came and pulled out the pin with his teeth and went in. Nobody taught him that; he had observed— then thought it out for himself. His process did not differ from Edison's; he put this and that together and drew an inference— and the peg, too; but I made him sweat for it.

Y. M. It has something of the seeming of thought about it. Still, it is not very elaborate. Enlarge.

O. M. Suppose that Edison has been enjoying some one's hospitalities. He comes again, by and by, and the house is vacant. He infers that his host has moved. A while afterward, in another town, he sees the man enter a house; he infers that that is the new home, and follows to inquire. Here, now, is the experience of a gull, as related by a naturalist. The scene is a Scotch fishing village where the gulls were kindly treated. This particular gull visited a cottage; was fed; came next day and was fed again; came into the house, next time, and ate with the family; kept on doing this almost daily, thereafter. But once the gull was away on a journey, for a few days, and when it returned the house was vacant. Its friends had removed to a village three miles distant. Several months later it saw the head of the family on the street there, followed him home, entered the house without excuse or apology, and became a daily guest again. Gulls do not rank high, mentally, but this one had memory and the reasoning faculty, you see, and applied them Edisonially.

Y. M.   Yet it was not an Edison and couldn't be developed into one.

O. M.   Perhaps not; could you?

Y. M.   That is neither here nor there. Go on.

O. M.   If Edison were in trouble and a stranger helped him out of it and next day he got into the same difficulty again, he would infer the wise thing to do in case he knew the stranger's address. Here is a case of a bird and a stranger as related by a naturalist. An English gentleman saw a bird flying around about his dog's head, down in the grounds, and uttering cries of distress. He went there to see about it. The dog had a young bird in his mouth—unhurt. The gentleman rescued it and put it on a bush and brought the dog away. Early the next morning the mother-bird came for the gentleman, who was sitting on his verandah, and by its maneuvers persuaded him to follow it to a distant part of the grounds—flying a little way in front of him and waiting for him to catch up, and so on; and keeping to the winding path, too, in-stead of flying the near way across lots. The distance covered was four hundred yards. The same dog was the culprit; he had the young bird again, and once more he had to give it up. Now the mother-bird had reasoned it all out: since the stranger had helped her once, she inferred that he would do it again; she knew where to find him, and she went upon her errand with confidence. Her mental processes were what Edison's would have been. She put this and that together—and that is all that thought *is*—and out of them built her logical arrangement of inferences. Edison couldn't have done it any better himself.

Y. M. Do you believe that many of the dumb animals can think?

O. M. Yes—the elephant, the monkey, the horse, the dog, the parrot, the macaw, the mocking-bird, and many others. The elephant whose mate fell into a pit, and who dumped dirt and rubbish into the pit till the bottom was raised high enough to enable the captive to step out, was equipped with the reasoning quality. I conceive that all animals that can learn things through teaching and drilling have to know how to observe, and put this and that together and draw an inference—the process of thinking. Could you teach an idiot the manual of arms, and to advance, retreat, and go through complex field-maneuvers at the word of command?

Y. M. Not if he were a thorough idiot.

O. M. Well, canary birds can learn all that; dogs and elephants learn all sorts of wonderful things. They must surely be able to notice, and to put things together, and say to themselves, "I get the idea, now: when I do so and so, as per order, I am praised and fed; when I do differently, I am punished." Fleas can be taught nearly anything that a Congressman can.

Y. M. Granting, then, that dumb creatures are able to think upon a low plane, is there any that can think upon a high one? Is there one that is well up toward man?

O. M. Yes. As a thinker and planner the ant is the equal of any savage race of men; as a self-educated specialist in several arts she is the superior of any savage race of men; and in one or two high mental qualities she is above the reach of any man, savage or civilized.

Y. M. O, come! you are abolishing the intellectual frontier which separates man and beast.

O. M. I beg your pardon. One cannot abolish what does not exist.

Y. M. You are not in earnest, I hope. You cannot mean to seriously say there is no such frontier.

O. M. I do say it seriously. The instances of the horse, the gull, the mother-bird and the elephant show that those creatures put their this's and that's together just as Edison would have done it and drew the same inferences that he would have drawn. Their mental machinery was just like his, also its manner of working. Their equipment was as inferior to his, in elaboration, as a Waterbury is inferior to the Strasburg clock, but that is the only difference—there is no frontier.

Y. M.   It looks exasperatingly true; and is distinctly offensive. It elevates the dumb beast to—to—

O. M.   Let us drop that lying phrase, and call them the Unrevealed Creatures; so far as we can know, there is no such thing as a dumb beast.

Y. M.   On what grounds do you make that assertion?

O. M.   On quite simple ones. "Dumb" beast suggests an animal that has no thought-machinery, no understanding, no speech, no way of communicating what is in its mind. We know that a hen *has* speech. We cannot understand everything she says, but we easily learn two or three of her phrases. We know when she is saying "I've laid an egg;" we know when she is saying to the chicks, "Run here, dears, I've found a worm;" we know what she is saying when she voices a warning: "Quick! hurry! gather yourselves under mamma, there's a hawk coming!" We understand the cat when she stretches herself out, purring with affection and contentment and lifts up a soft voice and says "Come, kitties, supper's ready;" we understand her when she goes mourning about and says "Where can they be?—they are lost—won't you help me hunt for them?" and we understand the disreputable Tom when he challenges at midnight from his shed: "You come over here, you product of immoral commerce, and I'll make your fur fly!" We understand a few of a dog's phrases, and we learn to understand a few of the remarks and gestures of any bird or other animal that we domesticate and observe. The clearness and exactness of the few of the hen's speeches which we understand is argument that she can communicate to her kind a hundred things which we cannot comprehend—in a word, that she can converse. And this argument is also applicable in the case of others of the great army of the Unrevealed. It is just like man's vanity and impertinence to call an animal dumb because it is dumb to his dull perceptions. Now as to the ant—

Y. M.   Yes, go back to the ant, the creature that—as you seem to think—sweeps away the last vestige of an intellectual frontier between man and the Unrevealed.

O. M.   That is what she surely does. In all his history the aboriginal Australian never thought out a house for himself and built it. The ant is an amazing architect. She is a wee little creature, but she builds a strong and enduring house eight feet high—a house which is as large in proportion to her size as is the largest capitol or cathedral in the world compared to man's size. No savage race has produced architects who could approach the ant in genius or culture. No civilized race has produced architects who could plan a house better for the uses proposed than can hers. Her house contains a throne room; nurseries for her young; granaries; apartments for her soldiers, her workers, etc.; and they and the multifarious halls and corridors which communicate with them are arranged and distributed with an educated and experienced eye for convenience and adaptibility.

Y. M.   That could all be mere instinct.

O. M.   It would elevate the savage much above what he is, if he had it. But let us look further before we decide. The ant has soldiers—battalions, regiments, armies; and they have their appointed captains and generals, who lead them to battle.

Y. M.   That could be instinct, too.

O. M.   We will look still further. The ant has a system of government; it is well planned, elaborate, and is well carried on.

Y. M.   Instinct again.

O. M.   She has crowds of slaves, and is a hard and unjust employer of forced labor.

Y. M.   Instinct.

o. m.   She has cows, and milks them.

y. m.   Instinct, of course.

o. m.   In Texas she lays out a farm twelve feet square, plants it, weeds it, cultivates it, gathers the crop and stores it away.

y. m.   Instinct, all the same.

o. m.   The ant discriminates between friend and stranger. Sir John Lubbock took ants from two different nests, made them drunk with whisky and laid them, unconscious, by one of the nests, near some water. Ants from this nest came and examined and discussed these disgraced creatures, then carried their friends home and threw the strangers overboard. Sir John repeated the experiment a number of times. For a while the sober ants did as they had done at first—carried their friends home and threw the strangers overboard. But finally they lost patience, seeing that their reformatory efforts went for nothing, and threw both friends and strangers overboard. Come—is this instinct, or is it thoughtful and intelligent discussion of a thing new—absolutely new—to their experience; with a verdict arrived at, sentence passed, and judgment executed? Is it instinct?—thought petrified by ages of habit —or isn't it brand-new thought, inspired by the new occasion, the new circumstances?

y. m.   I have to concede it. It was not a result of habit; it has all the look of reflection, thought, putting this and that together, as you phrase it. I believe it was thought.

o. m.   I will give you another instance of thought. Franklin had a cup of sugar on a table in his room. The ants got at it. He tried several preventives; the ants rose superior to them. Finally he contrived one which shut off access—probably set the table's legs in pans of water, or drew a circle of tar around the cup, I don't remember. At any rate he watched to see what they would do. They tried various schemes—failures, every one. The ants were badly puzzled. Finally they held a consultation, discussed the problem, arrived at a decision—and this time they beat that great philosopher. They formed in procession, crossed the floor, climbed the wall, marched across the ceiling to a point just over the cup, then one by one they let go and fell down into it! Was that instinct —thought petrified by ages of inherited habit?

Y. M. No, I don't believe it was. I believe it was a newly-reasoned scheme to meet a new emergency.

O. M. Very well. You have conceded the reasoning power in two instances. I come now to a mental detail wherein the ant is a long way the superior of any human being. Sir John Lubbock proved by many experiments that an ant knows a stranger-ant of her own species in a moment, even when the stranger is disguised —with paint. Also, he proved that an ant knows every individual in her hive of 500,000 souls. Also, that after a year's absence of one of the 500,000 she will straightway recognize the returned absentee and grace the recognition with an affectionate welcome. How were these recognitions made? Not by color, for painted ants were recognized. Not by smell, for ants that had been dipped in chloroform were recognized. Not by speech and not by antennæ-signs nor contacts, for the drunken and motionless ants were recognized and the friend discriminated from the stranger. The ants were all of the one species, therefore the friends had to be recognized by form and feature—friends who formed part of a hive of 500,000! Has any man a memory for form and feature approaching that?

Y. M. Certainly not.

O. M. Franklin's ants and Lubbock's ants show fine capacities for putting this and that together in new and untried emergencies and deducing smart conclusions from the combinations—a man's mental process exactly. With memory to help, man preserves his observations and reasonings, reflects upon them, adds to them, re-combines, and so proceeds, stage by stage, to far results— from the tea-kettle to the ocean greyhound's complex engine; from personal labor to slave labor; from wigwam to palace; from the capricious chase to agriculture and stored food; from nomadic life to stable government and concentrated authority; from incoherent hordes to massed armies. The ant has observation, the reasoning faculty, and the preserving adjunct of a prodigious memory; she has duplicated man's development and the essential features of his civilization, and you call it all instinct!

Y. M.   Perhaps I lacked the reasoning faculty myself.

O. M.   Well, don't tell anybody, and don't do it again.

Y. M.   We have come a good way. As a result—as I understand it—I am required to concede that there is absolutely no intellectual frontier separating Man and the Unrevealed Creatures?

O. M.   That is what you are required to concede. There is no
such frontier—there is no way to get around that. Man has a finer
and more capable machine in him than those others, but it is the
same machine and works in the same way. And neither he nor
those others can command the machine—it is strictly automatic,
independent of control, works when it pleases, and when it doesn't
please, can't be forced.

Y. M.   Then man and the other animals are all alike, as to
mental machinery, and there isn't any difference of any stupendous magnitude between them, except in quality, not in kind.

O. M.   That is about the state of it—intellectually. There are
pronounced limitations on both sides. We can't learn to understand much of their language, but the dog, the elephant, etc., learn
to understand a very great deal of ours. To that extent they are
our superiors. On the other hand they can't learn reading, writing,
etc., nor any of our fine and high things, and there we have a large
advantage over them.

Y. M.   Very well, let them have what they've got, and welcome; there is still a wall, and a lofty one. They haven't the Moral
Sense; we have it, and it lifts us immeasurably above them.

O. M.   What makes you think that?

Y. M.   Now look here—let us call a halt. I have stood the
other infamies and insanities and that is enough; I am not going to
have man and the other animals put on the same level morally.

O. M.   I wasn't going to hoist man up to that.

Y. M.   This is too much! I think it is not right to jest about
such things.

O. M.   I am not jesting, I am merely reflecting a plain and
simple truth—and without uncharitableness. The fact that man

knows right from wrong proves his *intellectual* superiority to the other creatures; but the fact that he can *do* wrong proves his *moral* inferiority to any creature that *cannot*. It is my belief that this position is not assailable.

FREE WILL

Y. M.   What is your opinion regarding Free Will?

O. M.   That there is no such thing. Did the man possess it who gave the old woman his last shilling and trudged home in the storm?

Y. M.   He had the choice between succoring the old woman and leaving her to suffer. Isn't it so?

O. M.   Yes, there was a choice to be made, between bodily comfort on the one hand and the comfort of the spirit on the other. The body made a strong appeal, of course—the body would be quite sure to do that; the spirit made a counter appeal. A choice had to be made between the two appeals, and was made. Who or what determined that choice?

Y. M.   Any one but you would say that the man determined it, and that in doing it he exercised Free Will.

O. M.   We are constantly assured that every man is endowed with Free Will, and that he can and must exercise it where he is offered a choice between good conduct and less-good conduct. Yet we clearly saw that in that man's case he really had no Free Will: his temperament, his training, and the daily influences which had moulded him and made him what he was, *compelled* him to rescue the old woman and thus save *himself*—save himself from spiritual pain, from unendurable wretchedness. He did not make the choice, it was made *for* him by forces which he could not control. Free Will has always existed in *words*, but it stops there, I think—stops short of *fact*. I would not use those words— Free Will—but others.

Y. M.   What others?

O. M.   Free Choice.

Y. M.   What is the difference?

O. M.   The one implies untrammeled power to *act* as you please, the other implies nothing beyond a mere *mental process*: the critical ability to determine which of two things is nearest right and just.

Y. M.   Make the difference clear, please.

O. M.   The mind can freely *select, choose, point out,* the right and just one—its function stops there. It can go no further in the matter. It has no authority to say that the right one shall be acted upon and the wrong one discarded. That authority is in other hands.

Y. M.   The man's?

O. M.   In the machine which stands for him. In his born disposition and the character which has been built around it by training and environment.

Y. M.   It will act upon the right one of the two?

O. M.   It will do as it pleases in the matter. George Washington's machine would act upon the right one; Pizarro's mind would know which was the right one and which the wrong, but the Master inside of Pizarro would act upon the wrong one.

Y. M.   Then as I understand it a bad man's mental machinery calmly and judicially points out which of two things is right and just—

O. M.   Yes, and his *moral* machinery will freely act upon the one or the other, according to its make, and be quite indifferent to the *mind's* feelings concerning the matter—that is, *would* be, if the mind had any feelings; which it hasn't. It is merely a thermometer: it registers the heat and the cold, and cares not a farthing about either.

Y. M.   Then we must not claim that if a man *knows* which of two things is right he is absolutely *bound* to do that thing?

O. M.   His temperament and training will decide what he shall do, and he will do it; he cannot help himself, he has no authority over the matter. Wasn't it right for David to go out and slay Goliah?

Y. M. Yes.

O. M. Then it would have been equally *right* for any one else to do it?

Y. M. Certainly.

O. M. Then it would have been *right* for a born coward to attempt it?

Y. M. It would—yes.

O. M. You know that no born coward ever would have attempted it, don't you?

Y. M. Yes.

O. M. You know that a born coward's make and temperament would be an absolute and insurmountable bar to his ever essaying such a thing, don't you?

Y. M. Yes, I know it.

O. M. He clearly perceives that it would be *right* to try it?

Y. M. Yes.

O. M. His mind has Free Choice in determining that it would be *right* to try it?

Y. M. Yes.

O. M. Then if by reason of his inborn cowardice he simply can *not* essay it, what becomes of his Free Will? where is his Free Will? why claim that he has Free Will when the plain facts show that he hasn't? why contend that because he and David *see* the right alike, both must *act* alike? why impose the same laws upon goat and lion?

Y. M. There is really no such thing as Free Will?

O. M. It is what I think. There is *Will*. But it has nothing to do with *intellectual perceptions of right and wrong,* and is not under their command. David's temperament and training had Will, and it was a compulsory force; David had to obey its decrees, he had no choice. The coward's temperament and training possess Will, and *it* is compulsory; it commands him to avoid danger, and he obeys, he has no choice. But neither the Davids nor the cowards possess Free Will—will that may do the right or do the wrong, as their *mental* verdict shall decide.

NOT TWO VALUES, BUT ONLY ONE

Y. M. There is one thing which bothers me: I can't tell where you draw the line between *material* covetousness and *spiritual* covetousness.

O. M. I don't draw any.

Y. M. How do you mean?

O. M. There is no such thing as *material* covetousness. All covetousness is spiritual.

Y. M. *All* longings, desires, ambitions *spiritual*, never material?

O. M. Yes. The Master in you requires that in *all* cases you shall content his *spirit*—that alone. He never requires anything else, he never interests himself in any other matter.

Y. M. Ah, come! When he covets somebody's money—isn't that rather distinctly material and gross?

O. M. No. The money is merely a symbol—it represents in visible and concrete form a *spiritual desire*. Any so-called material thing that you want is merely a symbol; you want it not for *itself*, but because it will content your spirit for the moment.

Y. M. Please particularize.

O. M. Very well. Maybe the thing longed for is a new hat. You get it and your vanity is pleased, your spirit contented. Suppose your friends deride the hat, make fun of it: at once it loses its value; you are ashamed of it, you put it out of your sight, you never want to see it again.

Y. M. I think I see. Go on.

O. M. It is the same hat, isn't it? It is in no way altered. But it wasn't the *hat* you wanted, but only what it stood for—a something to please and content your *spirit*. When it failed of that, the whole of its value was gone. There are no *material* values, there are only spiritual ones. You will hunt in vain for a material value that is *actual, real*—there is no such thing. The only value it possesses, for even a moment, is the spiritual value back of it: remove that and it is at once worthless—like the hat.

Y. M.   Can you extend that to money?

O. M.   Yes. It is merely a symbol, it has no *material* value; you think you desire it for its own sake, but it is not so. You desire it for the spiritual content it will bring; if it fail of that, you discover that its value is gone. There is that pathetic tale of the man who labored like a slave, unresting, unsatisfied, until he had accumulated a fortune, and was happy over it, jubilant about it; then in a single week a pestilence swept away all whom he held dear and left him desolate. His money's value was gone. He realized that his joy in it came not from the money itself, but from the spiritual contentment he got out of his family's enjoyment of the pleasures and delights it lavished upon them. Money has no *material* value; if you remove its spiritual value nothing is left but dross. It is so with all things, little or big, majestic or trivial—there are no exceptions. Crowns, sceptres, pennies, paste jewels, village notoriety, world-wide fame—they are all the same, they have no *material* value: while they content the *spirit* they are precious, when this fails they are worthless.

A DIFFICULT QUESTION

Y. M.   You keep me confused and perplexed all the time by your elusive terminology. Sometimes you divide a man up into two or three separate personalities, each with authorities, jurisdictions and responsibilities of its own, and when he is in that condition I can't grasp him. Now when *I* speak of a man, he is *the whole thing in one*, and easy to hold and contemplate.

O. M.   That is pleasant and convenient, if true. When you speak of "my body," who is the "my?"

Y. M.   It is the "me."

O. M.   The body is a property, then, and the Me owns it. Who is the Me?

Y. M.   The Me is *the whole thing*; it is a common property; an undivided ownership, vested in the whole entity.

O. M.   If the Me admires a rainbow, is it the whole Me that admires it, including the hair, hands, heels and all?

Y. M.   Certainly not. It is my *mind* that admires it.

O. M.   So *you* divide the Me yourself. Everybody does; everybody must. What, then, definitely, is the Me?

Y. M.   I think it must consist of just those two parts—the body and the mind.

O. M.   You think so? If you say "I believe the world is round," who is the "I" that is speaking?

Y. M.   The mind.

O. M.   If you say "I grieve for the loss of my father," who is the "I?"

Y. M.   The mind.

O. M.   Is the mind exercising an intellectual function when it examines and accepts the evidence that the world is round?

Y. M.   Yes.

O. M.   Is it exercising an intellectual function when it grieves for the loss of your father?

Y. M.   No. That is not cerebration, brain-work, it is a matter of *feeling*.

O. M.   Then its source is not in your mind, but in your *moral* territory?

Y. M.   I have to grant it.

O. M.   Is your mind a part of your *physical* equipment?

Y. M.   No. It is independent of it; it is spiritual.

O. M.   Being spiritual, it cannot be affected by physical influences?

Y. M.   No.

O. M.   Does the mind remain sober when the body is drunk?

Y. M.   Well—no.

O. M.   There *is* a physical effect present, then?

Y. M.   It looks like it.

O. M.   A cracked skull has resulted in a crazy mind. Why should that happen if the mind is spiritual, and *independent* of physical influences?

Y. M.   Well—I don't know.

o. m.   When you have a pain in your foot, how do you know it?

y. m.   I feel it.

o. m.   But you do not feel it until a nerve reports the hurt to the brain. Yet the brain is the seat of the mind, is it not?

y. m.   I think so.

o. m.   But isn't spiritual enough to learn what is happening in the outskirts without the help of the *physical* messenger? You perceive that the question of who or what the Me is, is not a simple one at all. You say "I admire the rainbow," and "I believe the world is round," and in these cases we find that the Me is not all speaking, but only the *mental* part. You say "I grieve," and again the Me is not all speaking, but only the *moral* part. You say the mind is wholly spiritual; then you say "I have a pain" and find that this time the Me is mental *and* spiritual combined. We all use the "I" in this indeterminate fashion, there is no help for it. We imagine a Master and King over what you call The Whole Thing, and we speak of him as "I," but when we try to define him we find we cannot do it. The intellect and the feelings can act quite *independently* of each other; we recognize that, and we look around for a Ruler who is master over both, and can serve as a *definite and indisputable "I,"* and enable us to know what we mean and who or what we are talking about when we use that pronoun, but we have to give it up and confess that we cannot find him. To me, Man is a machine, made up of many mechanisms; the moral and mental ones acting automatically in accordance with the impulses of an interior Master who is built out of born-temperament and an accumulation of multitudinous outside influences and trainings; a machine whose *one* function is to secure the spiritual contentment of the Master, be his desires good or be they evil; a machine whose Will is absolute and must be obeyed, and always *is* obeyed.

y. m.   Maybe the Me is the Soul?

o. m.   Maybe it is. What is the Soul?

Y. M.   I don't know.

O. M.   Neither does any one else.

THE MASTER-PASSION

Y. M.   What is the Master?—or, in common speech, the Conscience? Explain it.

O. M.   It is that mysterious autocrat, lodged in a man, which compels the man to content its desires. It may be called the Master Passion—the hunger for Self-Approval.

Y. M.   Where is its seat?

O. M.   In man's moral constitution.

Y. M.   Are its commands for the man's good?

O. M.   It is indifferent to the man's good; it never concerns itself about anything but the satisfying of its own desires. It can be *trained* to prefer things which will be for the man's good, but it will prefer them only because they will content *it* better than other things would.

Y. M.   Then even when it is trained to high ideals it is still looking out for its own contentment, and not for the man's good?

O. M.   True. Trained or untrained it cares nothing for the man's good, and never concerns itself about it.

Y. M.   It seems to be an *immoral* force seated in the man's moral constitution?

O. M.   It is a *colorless* force seated in the man's moral constitution. Let us call it an instinct—a blind, unreasoning instinct, which cannot and does not distinguish between good morals and bad ones, and cares nothing for results to the man provided its own contentment be secured; and it will *always* secure that.

Y. M.   It seeks money, and it probably considers that that is an advantage for the man?

O. M.   It is not always seeking money, it is not always seeking power, nor office, nor any other *material* advantage. In *all* cases it seeks a *spiritual* contentment, let the *means* be what they may. Its desires are determined by the man's temperament—and it is lord over that. Temperament, Conscience, Susceptibility, Spiritual

Appetite, are in fact the same thing. Have you ever heard of a person who cared nothing for money?

Y. M. Yes. A scholar who would not leave his garret and his books to take a place in a business house at a large salary.

O. M. He had to satisfy his master,—that is to say, his temperament, his Spiritual Appetite—and it preferred the books to money. Are there other cases?

Y. M. Yes, the hermit.

O. M. It is a good instance. The hermit endures solitude, hunger, cold, and manifold perils, to content his autocrat, who prefers these things, and prayer and contemplation, to money or to any show or luxury that money can buy. Are there others?

Y. M. Yes. The artist, the poet, the scientist.

O. M. Their autocrat prefers the deep pleasures of these occupations, either well paid or ill paid, to any others in the market, at any price. You *realize* that the Master Passion—the contentment of the spirit—concerns itself with many things besides so-called material advantage, material prosperity, cash, and all that?

Y. M. I think I must concede it.

O. M. I believe you must. There are perhaps as many Temperaments that would refuse the burdens and vexations and distinctions of public office as there are that hunger after them. The one set of Temperaments seek the contentment of the spirit, and that alone; and this is exactly the case with the other set. Neither set seeks anything *but* the contentment of the spirit. If the one is sordid, both are sordid; and equally so, since the end in view is precisely the same in both cases. And in both cases Temperament decides the preference—and Temperament is *born*, not made.

CONCLUSION

O. M. You have been taking a holiday?

Y. M. Yes; a mountain-tramp covering a week. Are you ready to talk?

O. M. Quite ready. What shall we begin with?

Y. M.   Well, lying abed resting-up, two days and nights, I have thought over all these talks, and passed them carefully in review. With this result: that . . . . that . . . . are you intending to publish your notions about Man some day?

O. M.   Now and then, in these past twenty years, the Master inside of me has half-intended to order me to set them to paper and publish them. Do I have to tell you why the order has remained unissued, or can you explain so simple a thing without my help?

Y. M.   By your doctrine, it is simplicity itself: outside influences moved your interior Master to give the order; stronger outside influences deterred him. Without the outside influences, neither of these impulses could ever have been born, since a person's brain is incapable of originating an idea within itself.

O. M.   Correct. Go on.

Y. M.   The matter of publishing or withholding is still in your Master's hands. If, some day, an outside influence shall determine him to publish, he will give the order, and it will be obeyed.

O. M.   That is correct. Well?

Y. M.   Upon reflection I have arrived at the conviction that the publication of your doctrines would be harmful. Do you pardon me?

O. M.   Pardon *you*? You have done nothing. You are an instrument—a speaking-trumpet. Speaking-trumpets are not responsible for what is said through them. Outside influences—in the form of life-long teachings, trainings, notions, prejudices, and other second-hand importations—have persuaded the Master within you that the publication of these doctrines would be harmful. Very well, this is quite natural, and was to be expected; in fact was inevitable. Go on; for the sake of ease and convenience, stick to habit: speak in the first person, and tell me what your Master thinks about it.

Y. M.   Well, to begin: it is a desolating doctrine; it is not inspiring, enthusing, uplifting. It takes the glory out of man, it takes the pride out of him, it takes the heroism out of him, it denies him all personal credit, all applause; it not only degrades him to a machine, but allows him no control over the machine; makes a mere coffee-mill of him, and neither permits him to supply the coffee nor turn the crank; his sole and piteously humble function being to grind coarse or fine, according to his make, outside impulses doing all the rest.

o. m. It is correctly stated. Tell me—what do men admire most in each other?

y. m. Intellect, courage, majesty of build, beauty of countenance, charity, benevolence, magnanimity, kindliness, heroism, and—and—

o. m. I would not go any further. These are *elementals*. Virtue, fortitude, holiness, truthfulness, loyalty, high ideals—these, and all the related qualities that are named in the dictionary, are *made out of the elementals*, by blendings, combinations, and shadings of the elementals, just as one makes green by blending blue and yellow, and makes several shades and tints of red by modifying the elemental red. There are seven elemental colors, they are all in the rainbow; out of them we manufacture and name fifty shades of them. You have named the elementals of the human rainbow, and also one *blend*—heroism, which is made out of courage and magnanimity. Very well, then; which of these elements does the possessor of it manufacture for himself? Is it intellect?

y. m. No.

o. m. Why?

y. m. He is born with it.

o. m. Is it courage?

y. m. No. He is born with it.

o. m. Is it majesty of build, beauty of countenance?

y. m. No. They are birthrights.

o. m. Take those others—the elemental moral qualities—charity, benevolence, magnanimity, kindliness; fruitful seeds, out of which spring, through cultivation by outside influences, all the

manifold blends and combinations of virtues named in the dictionaries: does man manufacture any one of those seeds, or are
they all born in him?

Y. M.   Born in him.

O. M.   Who manufactures them, then?

Y. M.   God.

O. M.   Where does the credit of it belong?

Y. M.   To God.

O. M.   And the glory of which you spoke, and the applause?

Y. M.   To God.

O. M.   Then it is *you* who degrade man. You make him claim
glory, praise, flattery, for every valuable thing he possesses—*borrowed* finery, the whole of it; no rag of it earned by himself, not a
detail of it produced by his own labor. *You* make man a humbug;
have I done worse by him?

Y. M.   You have made a machine of him.

O. M.   Who devised that cunning and beautiful mechanism,
a man's hand?

Y. M.   God.

O. M.   Who devised the law by which it automatically ham-
mers out of a piano an elaborate piece of music, without error,
while the man is thinking about something else, or talking to a
friend?

Y. M.   God.

O. M.   Who devised the blood? Who devised the wonderful
machinery which automatically drives its renewing and refreshing
streams through the body, day and night, without assistance or
advice from the man? Who devised the man's mind, whose machinery works automatically, interests itself in what it pleases, regardless of his will or desire, labors all night when it likes, deaf to
his appeals for mercy? God devised all these things. *I* have not
made man a machine, God made him a machine. I am merely
calling attention to the fact, nothing more. Is it wrong to call attention to a fact? Is it a crime?

Y. M.   I think it is wrong to *expose* a fact when harm can come of it.

O. M.   Go on.

Y. M.   Look at the matter as it stands now. Man has been taught that he is the supreme marvel of the Creation; he believes it; in all the ages he has never doubted it, whether he was a naked savage, or clothed in purple and fine linen, and civilized. This has made his heart buoyant, his life cheery. His pride in himself, his sincere admiration of himself, his joy in what he supposed were his own and unassisted achievements, and his exultation over the praise and applause which they evoked—these have exalted him, enthused him, ambitioned him to higher and higher flights; in a word, made his life worth the living. But by your scheme, all this is abolished: he is degraded to a machine, he is a nobody, his noble prides wither to mere vanities; let him strive as he may, he can never be any better than his humblest and stupidest neighbor; he would never be cheerful again, his life would not be worth the living.

O. M.   You really think that?

Y. M.   I certainly do.

O. M.   Have you ever seen me uncheerful, unhappy?

Y. M.   No.

O. M.   Well, *I* believe these things. Why have they not made me unhappy?

Y. M.   Oh, well—temperament, of course! You never let *that* escape from your scheme.

O. M.   That is correct. If a man is born with an unhappy temperament, nothing can make him happy; if he is born with a happy temperament, nothing can make him unhappy.

Y. M.   What—not even a degrading and heart-chilling system of beliefs?

O. M.   Beliefs? Mere beliefs? Mere convictions? They are powerless. They strive in vain against inborn temperament.

Y. M.   I can't believe that, and I don't.

o. m.   Now you are speaking hastily. It shows that you have
not studiously examined the facts. Of all your intimates, which
one is the happiest? Isn't it Burgess?

y. m.   Easily.

o. m.   And which one is the unhappiest? Henry Adams?

y. m.   Without a question!

o. m.   I know them well. They are extremes, abnormals;
their temperaments are as opposite as the poles. Their life-histories
are about alike—but look at the results! Their ages are about the
same—around about fifty. Burgess has always been buoyant, hopeful, happy; Adams has always been cheerless, hopeless, despon-
dent. As young fellows, both tried country journalism—and failed.
Burgess didn't seem to mind it; Adams couldn't smile, he could
only mourn and groan over what had happened, and torture himself with vain regrets for not having done so-and-so instead of
so-and-so—*then* he would have succeeded. They tried the law—
and failed. Burgess remained happy—because he couldn't help it,
Adams was wretched—because he couldn't help it. From that day
to this, those two men have gone on trying things and failing:
Burgess has come out happy and cheerful every time, Adams the
reverse. Now we do absolutely know that these men's inborn
temperaments have remained unchanged through all the vicissi-
tudes of their material affairs. Let us see how it is with their im-
materialities. Both have been zealous democrats; both have been
zealous republicans; both have been zealous mugwumps. Burgess
has always found happiness and Adams unhappiness, in these
several political beliefs and in their migrations out of them. Both
of these men have been Presbyterians, Universalists, Methodists,
Catholics,—then Presbyterians again, then Methodists again. Burgess has always found rest in these excursions, and Adams unrest;
they are trying Christian Science, now, with the customary result,
the inevitable result. No political or religious belief can make
Burgess unhappy or the other man happy. I assure you it is purely
a matter of temperament. Beliefs are *acquirements*, temperaments

are *born*; beliefs are subject to change, nothing whatever can change temperament.

Y. M.   You have instanced extreme temperaments.

O. M.   Yes. The half dozen others are modifications of the extremes. But the law is the same. Where the temperament is two-thirds happy, or two-thirds unhappy, no political or religious beliefs can change the proportions. The vast majority of temperaments are pretty equally balanced; the intensities are absent, and this enables a nation to learn to accommodate itself to its political and religious circumstances and like them, be satisfied with them, at last prefer them. Nations do not *think*, they only *feel*. They get their feelings at second-hand—through their temperaments, not their brains. A nation can be brought—by force of circumstances, not argument—to reconcile itself to *any kind of government or religion that can be devised*; in time it will fit itself to the required conditions; later, it will prefer them; and will fiercely fight for them. As instances, you have all history: the Greeks, the Romans, the Persians, the Egyptians, the Russians, the Germans, the French, the English, the Spaniards, the Americans, the South Americans, the Japanese, the Chinese, the Hindoos, the Turks— a thousand wild and tame religions, every kind of government that can be thought of, from tiger to housecat, each nation *knowing* it has the only true religion and the only sane system of government, each despising all the others, each an ass and not suspecting it, each proud of its fancied supremacy, each perfectly sure it is the pet of God, each with undoubting confidence summoning Him to take command in time of war, each surprised when He goes over to the enemy, but by habit able to excuse it and resume compliments—in a word, the whole human race content, always content, persistently content, indestructibly content, happy, thankful, proud, *no matter what its religion is, nor whether its master be tiger or housecat*. Am I stating facts? You know I am. Is the human race cheerful? You know it is. Considering what it can stand, and be happy, you do me too much honor when you think that *I* can place before it a system of plain cold facts that can take the cheerfulness out of it. Nothing can do that. Everything has been tried. Without success. I beg you not to be troubled.

21   *Christian Science*

[1907]

PREFACE

BOOK I of this volume occupies a quarter or a third of the volume, and consists of matter written about four years ago, but not hitherto published in book form. It contained errors of judgment and of fact. I have now corrected these, to the best of my ability and later knowledge.

Book II was written at the beginning of 1903, and has not until now appeared in any form. In it my purpose has been to present a character-portrait of Mrs. Eddy, drawn from her own acts and words solely, not from hearsay and rumor; and to explain the nature and scope of her Monarchy, as revealed in the Laws by which she governs it, and which she wrote herself.

MARK TWAIN.

NEW YORK, *January, 1907.*

BOOK I

"It is the first time since the dawn-days of Creation that a Voice has gone crashing through space with such placid and complacent confidence and command."

CHAPTER 1

Vienna, 1899.

This last summer, when I was on my way back to Vienna from the Appetite-Cure in the mountains, I fell over a cliff in the twilight and broke some arms and legs and one thing or another, and by good luck was found by some peasants who had lost an ass and they carried me to the nearest habitation, which was one of those large, low, thatch-roofed farm-houses, with apartments in the garret for the family, and a cunning little porch under the deep gable decorated with boxes of bright-colored flowers and cats; and on the ground floor a large and light sitting-room, separated from the milch-cattle apartment by a partition; and in the front yard rose stately and fine the wealth and pride of the house, the manure-pile. That sentence is Germanic, and shows that I am acquiring that sort of mastery of the art and spirit of the language which enables a man to travel all day in one sentence without changing cars.

There was a village a mile away, and a horse-doctor lived there, but there was no surgeon. It seemed a bad outlook; mine was distinctly a surgery case. Then it was remembered that a lady from Boston was summering in that village, and she was a Christian Science doctor and could cure anything. So she was sent for. It was night by this time, and she could not conveniently come, but sent word that it was no matter, there was no hurry, she would give me "absent treatment" now, and come in the morning; meantime she begged me to make myself tranquil and comfortable and remember that there was nothing the matter with me. I thought there must be some mistake.

"Did you tell her I walked off a cliff seventy-five feet high?"

"Yes."

"And struck a boulder at the bottom and bounced?"

"Yes."

"And struck another one and bounced again?"

"Yes."

"And struck another one and bounced yet again?"

"Yes."

"And broke the boulders?"

"Yes."

"That accounts for it; she is thinking of the boulders. Why didn't you tell her I got hurt, too?"

"I did. I told her what you told me to tell her: that you were now but an incoherent series of compound fractures extending from your scalplock to your heels, and that the comminuted projections caused you to look like a hat-rack."

"And it was after this that she wished me to remember that there was nothing the matter with me?"

"Those were her words."

"I do not understand it. I believe she has not diagnosed the case with sufficient care. Did she look like a person who was theorizing, or did she look like one who has fallen off of precipices herself and brings to the aid of abstract science the confirmations of personal experience?"

"*Bitte?*"

It was too large a contract for the Stubenmädchen's vocabulary; she couldn't call the hand. I allowed the subject to rest there, and asked for something to eat and smoke, and something hot to drink, and a basket to pile my legs in; but I could not have any of these things.

"Why?"

"She said you would need nothing at all."

"But I am hungry, and thirsty, and in desperate pain."

"She said you would have these delusions, but must pay no attention to them. She wants you to particularly remember that there are no such things as hunger and thirst and pain."

"She does, does she?"

"It is what she said."

"Does she seem to be in full and functionable possession of her intellectual plant, such as it is?"

"*Bitte?*"

"Do they let her run at large, or do they tie her up?"

"Tie her up?"

"There, good-night, run along; you are a good girl, but your mental Geschirr is not arranged for light and airy conversation. Leave me to my delusions."

CHAPTER 2

It was a night of anguish, of course—at least I supposed it was, for it had all the symptoms of it—but it passed at last, and the Christian Scientist came, and I was glad. She was middle-aged, and large and bony, and erect, and had an austere face and a resolute jaw and a Roman beak and was a widow in the third degree, and her name was Fuller. I was eager to get to business and find relief, but she was distressingly deliberate. She unpinned and unhooked and uncoupled her upholsteries one by one, abolished the wrinkles with a flirt of her hand and hung the articles up; peeled off her gloves and disposed of them, got a book out of her handbag, then drew a chair to the bedside, descended into it without hurry, and I hung out my tongue. She said, with pity but without passion:

"Return it to its receptacle. We deal with the mind only, not with its dumb servants."

I could not offer my pulse, because the connection was broken; but she detected the apology before I could word it, and indicated by a negative tilt of her head that the pulse was another dumb servant that she had no use for. Then I thought I would tell her my symptoms and how I felt, so that she would understand the case; but that was another inconsequence, she did not need to know those things; moreover my remark about how I felt was an abuse of language, a misapplication of terms—

"One does not *feel*," she explained, "there is no such thing as feeling; therefore, to speak of a non-existent thing as existent is a contradiction. Matter has no existence; nothing exists but mind; the mind cannot feel pain, it can only imagine it."

"But if it hurts, just the same—"

"It doesn't. A thing which is unreal cannot exercise the functions of reality. Pain is unreal; hence, pain cannot hurt." In making a sweeping gesture to indicate the act of shooing the illusion of pain out of the mind she raked her hand on a pin in her dress, said "Ouch!" and went tranquilly on with her talk. "You should never allow yourself to speak of how you feel, nor permit others to ask you how you are feeling; you should never concede that you are ill, nor permit others to talk about disease or pain or death or similar non-existences in your presence. Such talk only encourages the mind to continue its empty imaginings." Just at that point the Stubenmädchen trod on the cat's tail, and the cat let fly a frenzy of cat-profanity. I asked with caution:

"Is a cat's opinion about pain valuable?"

"A cat has no opinion; opinions proceed from mind only; the lower animals, being eternally perishable have not been granted mind; without mind, opinion is impossible."

"She merely *imagined* she felt a pain—the cat?"

"She cannot imagine a pain, for imagination is an effect of mind; without mind, there is no imagination. A cat has no imagination."

"Then she had a *real* pain?"

"I have already told you there is no such *thing* as real pain."

"It is strange and interesting. I do wonder what was the matter with the cat. Because, there being no such thing as a real pain, and she not being able to imagine an imaginary one, it would seem that God in His pity has compensated the cat with some kind of a mysterious emotion usable when her tail is trodden on which for the moment joins cat and Christian in one common brotherhood of—"

She broke in with an irritated—

"Peace! The cat feels nothing, the Christian feels nothing. Your empty and foolish imaginings are profanation and blasphemy and can do you an injury. It is wiser and better and holier to recognize and confess that there is no such thing as disease or pain or death."

"I am full of imaginary tortures," I said, "but I do not think I could be any more uncomfortable if they were real ones. What must I do to get rid of them?"

"There is no occasion to get rid of them, since they do not exist. They are illusions propagated by matter, and matter has no existence; there is no such thing as matter."

"It sounds right and clear, but yet it seems in a degree elusive; it seems to slip through, just when you think you are getting a grip on it."

"Explain."

"Well, for instance: if there is no such thing as matter, how can matter propagate things?"

In her compassion she almost smiled. She would have smiled if there was any such thing as a smile.

"It is quite simple," she said, "the fundamental propositions of Christian Science explain it, and they are summarized in the four following self-evident propositions. 1. God is All in all. 2. God is good. Good is Mind. 3. God, Spirit, being all, nothing is matter. 4. Life, God, omnipotent Good, deny death, evil, sin, disease. There—now you see."

It seemed nebulous. It did not seem to say anything about the difficulty in hand—how non-existent matter can propagate illusions. I said, with some hesitancy:

"Does—does it explain?"

"*Doesn't* it? Even if read backward it will do it."

With a budding hope I asked her to do it backward.

"Very well. Disease sin evil death deny Good omnipotent God life matter is nothing all being Spirit God Mind is Good good is God all in All is God. There—do you understand now?"

"It—it—well, it is plainer than it was before; still—"

"Well?"

"Could you try it some more ways?"

"As many as you like; it always means the same. Interchanged in any way you please it cannot be made to mean anything different from what it means when put in any other way. Because it is perfect. You can jumble it all up, and it makes no difference: it always comes out the way it was before. It was a marvelous mind that produced it. As a mental *tour de force* it is without a mate; it defies alike the simple, the concrete and the occult."

"It seems to be a corker."

I blushed for the word, but it was out before I could stop it.

"A what?"

"A—a wonderful structure—combination, so to speak, of profound thoughts—unthinkable ones—un—"

"It is true. Read backwards, or forwards, or perpendicularly, or at any given angle, these four propositions will always be found to agree in statement and proof."

"Ah—proof. Now we are coming at it. The *statements* agree; they agree with—with—anyway, they agree; I noticed that; but what is it they prove—I mean, in particular?"

"Why, nothing could be clearer. They prove: 1. GOD—Principle, Life, Truth, Love, Soul, Spirit, Mind. Do you get that?"

"I—well, I seem to. Go on, please."

"2. MAN—God's universal idea, individual, perfect, eternal. Is it clear?"

"It—I think so. Continue."

"3. IDEA—An image in Mind; the immediate object of understanding. There it is—the whole sublime Arcana of Christian Science in a nutshell. Do you find a weak place in it anywhere?"

"Well—no; it seems strong."

"Very well. There is more. Those three constitute the Scien-

tific Definition of Immortal Mind. Next, we have the Scientific
Definition of Mortal Mind. Thus. First Degree: *Depravity*.
1. Physical—Passions and appetites, fear, depraved will, pride,
envy, deceit, hatred, revenge, sin, disease, death."

"Phantasms, madam—unrealities, as I understand it."

"Every one. Second Degree: *Evil Disappearing*. 1. Moral—
Honesty, affection, compassion, hope, faith, meekness, temper-
ance. Is it clear?"

"Crystal."

"Third Degree: *Spiritual Salvation*. 1. Spiritual—Faith,
wisdom, power, purity, understanding, health, love. You see how
searchingly and coördinately interdependent and anthropomorphous it all is. In this Third Degree, as we know by the revelations
of Christian Science, mortal mind disappears."

"Not earlier?"

"No, not until the teaching and preparation for the Third
Degree are completed."

"It is not until then that one is enabled to take hold of
Christian Science effectively, and with the right sense of sympathy
and kinship, as I understand you. That is to say, it could not succeed during the processes of the Second Degree, because there
would still be remains of mind left; and therefore—but I interrupted you. You were about to further explain the good results
proceeding from the erosions and disintegrations effected by the
Third Degree. It is very interesting; go on, please."

"Yes, as I was saying, in this Third Degree mortal mind disappears. Science so reverses the evidence before the corporeal
human senses as to make this Scriptural testimony true in our
hearts, 'the last shall be first and the first shall be last,' that God
and His idea may be to us—what divinity really is, and must of
necessity be—all-inclusive."

"It is beautiful. And with what exhaustive exactness your
choice and arrangement of words confirm and establish what you
have claimed for the powers and functions of the Third Degree.
The Second could probably produce only temporary absence of

mind, it is reserved to the Third to make it permanent. A sentence framed under the auspices of the Second could have a kind of meaning—a sort of deceptive semblance of it—whereas it is only under the magic of the Third that that defect would disappear. Also, without doubt, it is the Third Degree that contributes another remarkable specialty to Christian Science: viz., ease and flow and lavishness of words, and rhythm and swing and smoothness. There must be a special reason for this?"

"Yes—God-all, all-God, good God, non-Matter, Matteration, Spirit, Bones, Truth."

"That explains it."

"There is nothing in Christian Science that is not explicable; for God is one, Time is one, Individuality is one, and may be one of a series, one of many, as an individual man, individual horse; whereas God is one, not one of a series, but one alone and without an equal."

"These are noble thoughts. They make one burn to know more. How does Christian Science explain the spiritual relation of systematic duality to incidental deflection?"

"Christian Science reverses the seeming relation of Soul and body—as astronomy reverses the human perception of the movement of the solar system—and makes body tributary to Mind. As it is the earth which is in motion, while the sun is at rest, though in viewing the sunrise one finds it impossible to believe the sun not to be really rising, so the body is but the humble servant of the restful Mind, though it seems otherwise to finite sense; but we shall never understand this while we admit that soul is in body, or mind in matter, and that man is included in non-intelligence. Soul is God, unchangeable and eternal; and man co-exists with and reflects Soul, for the All-in-all is the Altogether, and the Altogether embraces the All-one, Soul-Mind, Mind-Soul, Love, Spirit, Bones, Liver, one of a series, alone and without an equal."

"What is the origin of Christian Science? Is it a gift of God, or did it just happen?"

"In a sense, it is a gift of God. That is to say, its powers are from Him, but the credit of the discovery of the powers and what they are for, is due to an American lady."

"Indeed? When did this occur?"

"In 1866. That is the immortal date when pain and disease and death disappeared from the earth to return no more forever. That is, the fancies for which those terms stand, disappeared. The things themselves had never existed; therefore as soon as it was perceived that there were no such things, they were easily banished. The history and nature of the great discovery are set down in the book here, and—"

"Did the lady write the book?"

"Yes, she wrote it all, herself. The title is *Science and Health, with Key to the Scriptures*—for she explains the Scriptures; they were not understood before. Not even by the twelve Disciples. She begins thus—I will read it to you."

But she had forgotten to bring her glasses.

"Well, it is no matter," she said, "I remember the words— indeed all Christian Scientists know the book by heart; it is necessary in our practice. We should otherwise make mistakes and do harm. She begins thus: 'In the year 1866 I discovered the Science of Metaphysical Healing, and named it Christian Science.' And she says—quite beautifully, I think—'Through Christian Science, religion and medicine are inspired with a diviner nature and essence, fresh pinions are given to faith and understanding, and thoughts acquaint themselves intelligently with God.' Her very words."

"It is elegant. And it is a fine thought, too—marrying religion to medicine, instead of medicine to the undertaker in the old way; for religion and medicine properly belong together, they being the basis of all spiritual and physical health. What kind of medicine do you give for the ordinary diseases, such as—"

"We never give medicine in *any* circumstances whatever! We—"

"But madam, it *says*—"

"I don't care what it says, and I don't wish to talk about it."

"I am sorry if I have offended, but you see the mention seemed in some way inconsistent, and—"

"There *are* no inconsistencies in Christian Science. The thing is impossible, for the Science is absolute. It cannot be otherwise, since it proceeds directly from the All-in-all and the Everything-in-which, also Soul, Bones, Truth, one of a series, alone and without equal. It is mathematics purified from material dross and made spiritual."

"I can see that, but—"

"It rests upon the immovable basis of an Apodictical Principle."

The word flattened itself against my mind in trying to get in, and disordered me a little, and before I could inquire into its pertinency, she was already throwing the needed light:

"This Apodictical Principle is the absolute Principle of Scientific Mind-healing, the sovereign Omnipotence which delivers the children of men from pain, disease, decay, and every ill that flesh is heir to."

"Surely not every ill, every decay?"

"Every one; there are no exceptions; there is no such thing as decay—it is an unreality, it has no existence."

"But without your glasses your failing eyesight does not permit you to—"

"My eyesight cannot fail; nothing can fail; the Mind is master, and the Mind permits no retrogression."

She was under the inspiration of the Third Degree, therefore there could be no profit in continuing this part of the subject. I shifted to other ground and inquired further concerning the Discoverer of the Science.

"Did the discovery come suddenly, like Klondyke, or after long study and calculation, like America?"

"The comparisons are not respectful, since they refer to trivialities—but let it pass. I will answer in the Discoverer's own

words: 'God had been graciously fitting me, during many years, for
the reception of a final revelation of the absolute Principle of
Scientific Mind-healing.' "

"Many years. How many?"

"Eighteen centuries!"

"All-God, God-good, good-God, Truth, Bones, Liver, one of
a series, alone and without equal—it is amazing!"

"You may well say it, sir. Yet it is but the truth. This American lady, our revered and sacred Founder, is distinctly referred to
and her coming prophesied, in the twelfth chapter of the Apocalypse; she could not have been more plainly indicated by St. John
without actually mentioning her name."

"How strange, how wonderful!"

"I will quote her own words, from her Key to the Scriptures:
'The twelfth chapter of the Apocalypse *has a special suggestive-
ness in connection with this nineteenth century.*' There—do you
note that? Think—note it well."

"But—what does it mean?"

"Listen, and you will know. I quote her inspired words again:
'In the opening of the Sixth Seal, typical of six thousand years
since Adam, there is one distinctive feature *which has special
reference to the present age.* Thus:

" 'Revelation xii. 1. And there appeared a great wonder in
Heaven—a *woman* clothed with the sun, and the moon under her
feet, and upon her head a crown of twelve stars.'

"That is our Head, our Chief, our Discoverer of Christian
Science—nothing can be plainer, nothing surer. And note this:

" 'Revelation xii. 6. And the woman fled into the wilderness,
where she hath a place prepared of God.'

"That is Boston."

"I recognize it, madam. These are sublime things, and impressive; I never understood those passages before; please go on
with the—with the—proofs."

"Very well. Listen:

" 'And I saw another mighty angel come down from heaven, clothed with a cloud; and a rainbow was upon his head, and his face was as it were the sun, and his feet as pillars of fire. And he had in his hand *a little book*.'

"A little book, merely a little book—could words be modester? Yet how stupendous its importance! Do you know what book that was?"

"Was it—"

"I hold it in my hand—Christian Science!"

"Love, Livers, Lights, Bones, Truth, Kidneys, one of a series, alone and without equal—it is beyond imagination for wonder!"

"Hear our Founder's eloquent words: 'Then will a voice from harmony cry, "Go and take the little book. . . . take it and eat it up, and it shall make thy belly bitter; but it shall be in thy mouth sweet as honey." Mortal, obey the heavenly evangel. Take up Divine Science. Read it from beginning to end. Study it, ponder it. It will be indeed sweet at its first taste, when it heals you; but murmur not over Truth, if you find its digestion bitter.' You now know the history of our dear and holy Science, sir, and that its *origin* is not of this earth, but only its *discovery*. I will leave the book with you and will go, now; but give yourself no uneasiness— I will give you absent treatment from now till I go to bed."

CHAPTER 3

Under the powerful influences of the near treatment and the absent treatment together, my bones were gradually retreating inwards and disappearing from view. The good work took a brisk start, now, and went on quite swiftly. My body was diligently straining and stretching, this way and that, to accommodate the processes of restoration, and every minute or two I heard a dull click inside and knew that the two ends of a fracture had been successfully joined. This muffled clicking and gritting and grinding and rasping continued during the next three hours, and then stopped—the connections had all been made. All excepting dislocations; there were only seven of these: hips, shoulders, knees, neck; so that was soon over; one after another they slipped into their sockets with a sound like pulling a distant cork, and I jumped up as good as new, as to framework, and sent for the horse-doctor.

I was obliged to do this because I had a stomach ache and a cold in the head, and I was not willing to trust these things any longer in the hands of a woman whom I did not know, and in whose ability to successfully treat mere disease I had lost all confidence. My position was justified by the fact that the cold and the ache had been in her charge from the first, along with the fractures, but had experienced not a shade of relief; and indeed the ache was even growing worse and worse, and more and more bitter, now, probably on account of the protracted abstention from food and drink.

The horse-doctor came, a pleasant man and full of hope and professional interest in the case. In the matter of smell he was pretty aromatic, in fact quite horsy, and I tried to arrange with him for absent treatment, but it was not in his line, so out of delicacy I did not press it. He looked at my teeth and examined my hock, and said my age and general condition were favorable to energetic measures; therefore he would give me something to turn the stomach ache into the botts and the cold in the head into the blind staggers; then he should be on his own beat and would know what to do. He made up a bucket of bran mash, and said a dipperful of it every two hours, alternated with a drench with turpentine and axle-grease in it would either knock my ailments out of me in twenty-four hours or so interest me in other ways as to make me forget they were on the premises. He administered my first dose himself, then took his leave, saying I was free to eat and drink anything I pleased and in any quantity I liked. But I was not hungry any more, and did not care for food.

I took up the Christian Science book and read half of it, then took a dipperful of drench and read the other half. The resulting experiences were full of interest and adventure. All through the rumblings and grindings and quakings and effervescings accompanying the evolution of the ache into the botts and the cold into the blind staggers I could note the generous struggle for mastery going on between the mash and the drench and the literature; and often I could tell which was ahead, and could easily distinguish the literature from the others when the others were separate, though not when they were mixed; for when a bran mash and an eclectic drench are mixed together they look just like the Apodictical Principle out on a lark, and no one can tell it from that. The finish was reached at last, the evolutions were complete and a fine success; but I think that this result could have been achieved with fewer materials. I believe the mash was necessary to the conversion of the stomach ache into the botts, but I think one could develop the blind staggers out of the literature by itself; also, that blind staggers produced in this way would be of a better quality and more lasting than any produced by the artificial processes of a horse-doctor.

For of all the strange, and frantic, and incomprehensible, and uninterpretable books which the imagination of man has created, surely this one is the prize sample. It is written with a limitless confidence and complacency, and with a dash and stir and earnestness which often compel the effects of eloquence, even when the words do not seem to have any traceable meaning. There are plenty of people who imagine they understand the book; I know this, for I have talked with them; but in all cases they were people who also imagined that there were no such things as pain, sickness and death, and no realities in the world; nothing actually existent but Mind. It seems to me to modify the value of their testimony. When these people talk about Christian Science they do as Mrs. Fuller did: they do not use their own language, but the book's; they pour out the book's showy incoherencies, and leave you to find out later that they were not originating, but merely quoting; they seem to know the volume by heart, and to revere it as they would a Bible—another Bible, perhaps I ought to say. Plainly the book was written under the mental desolations of the Third Degree, and I feel sure that none but the membership of that Degree can discover meanings in it. When you read it you seem to be listening to a lively and aggressive and oracular speech delivered in an unknown tongue, a speech whose spirit you get but not the particulars; or, to change the figure, you seem to be listening to a vigorous instrument which is making a noise which it thinks is a tune, but which to persons not members of the band is only the martial tooting of a trombone, and merely stirs the soul through the noise but does not convey a meaning.

The book's serenities of self-satisfaction do almost seem to smack of a heavenly origin—they have no blood-kin in the earth. It is more than human to be so placidly certain about things, and so finely superior, and so airily content with one's performance. Without ever presenting anything which may rightfully be called by the strong name of Evidence, and sometimes without even *mentioning* a reason for a deduction at all, it thunders out the startling words, "I have *Proved*" so and so. It takes the Pope and all the great guns of his Church in battery assembled to authoritatively settle and establish the meaning of a sole and single unclarified passage of Scripture, and this at vast cost of time and study and reflection, but the author of this work is superior to all that: she finds the whole Bible in an unclarified condition, and at small expense of time and no expense of mental effort she clarifies it from lid to lid, reorganizes and improves the meanings, then authoritatively settles and establishes them with formulæ which you cannot tell from "Let there be light!" and "Here you have it!" It is the first time since the dawn-days of Creation that a Voice has gone crashing through space with such placid and complacent confidence and command.[1]

1. *January*, 1903. The first reading of any book whose terminology is new and strange is nearly sure to leave the reader in a bewildered and sarcastic state of mind.

CHAPTER 4

No one doubts—certainly not I—that the mind exercises a powerful influence over the body. From the beginning of time the sorcerer, the interpreter of dreams, the fortune-teller, the charlatan, the quack, the wild medicine-man, the educated physician, the mesmerist, and the hypnotist, have made use of the

But now that during the past two months I have by diligence gained a fair acquaintanceship with *Science and Health* technicalities, I no longer find the bulk of that work hard to understand.—M. T.

P. S. The wisdom harvested from the foregoing thoughts, has already done me a service, and saved me a sorrow. Nearly a month ago there came to me from one of the universities a tract by Dr. Edward Anthony Spitzka on the "Encephalic Anatomy of the Races." I judged that my opinion was desired by the university, and I was greatly pleased with this attention and wrote and said I would furnish it as soon as I could. That night I put my plodding and disheartening Christian Science mining aside, and took hold of the matter. I wrote an eager chapter, and was expecting to finish my opinion the next day, but was called away for a week, and my mind was soon charged with other interests. It was not until to-day, after the lapse of nearly a month, that I happened upon my Encephalic chapter again. Meantime the new wisdom had come to me, and I read it with shame. I recognized that I had entered upon that work in far from the right temper, far from the respectful and judicial spirit which was its due of reverence. I had begun on it with the following paragraph for fuel:

"FISSURES OF THE PARIETAL AND OCCIPITAL LOBES (LATERAL SURFACE).—*The Postcentral Fissural Complex.*—In this hemicerebrum, the postcentral and subcentral are combined to form a continuous fissure, attaining a length of 8.5 cm. Dorsally, the fissure bifurcates, embracing the gyre indented by the caudal limb of the paracentral. The caudal limb of the postcentral is joined by a transparietal piece. In all, five additional rami spring from the combined fissure. A vadum separates it from the parietal; another from the central."

It humiliates me, now, to see how angry I got over that, and how scornful. I said that the style was disgraceful; that it was labored and tumultuous, and in places violent; that the treatment was involved and erratic, and almost as a rule bewildering; that to lack of simplicity was added a lack of vocabulary; that there was quite too much feeling shown; that if I had a dog that would get so excited and incoherent over a tranquil subject like Encephalic Anatomy I would not pay his tax; and at that point I got excited myself and spoke bitterly of these mongrel insanities, and said a person might as well try to understand *Science and Health*.

I know, now, where the trouble was, and am glad of the interruption that saved me from sending my verdict to the university. It makes me cold to think what those people might have thought of me.—M. T.

client's *imagination* to help them in their work. They have all recognized the potency and availability of that force. Physicians cure many patients with a bread pill; they know that where the disease is only a fancy, the patient's confidence in the doctor will make the bread pill effective.

Faith in the doctor. Perhaps that is the entire thing. It seems to look like it. In old times the King cured the King's evil by the touch of the royal hand. He frequently made extraordinary cures. Could his footman have done it? No—not in his own clothes. Disguised as the King could he have done it? I think we may not doubt it. I think we may feel sure that it was not the King's touch that made the cure in any instance, but the patient's faith in the efficacy of a King's touch. Genuine and remarkable cures have been achieved through contact with the relics of a saint. Is it not likely that any other bones would have done as well if the substitution had been concealed from the patient? When I was a boy a farmer's wife who lived five miles from our village had great fame as a faith-doctor—that was what she called herself. Sufferers came to her from all around, and she laid her hand upon them and said "Have faith—it is all that is necessary," and they went away well of their ailments. She was not a religious woman, and pretended to no occult powers. She said that the patient's faith in her did the work. Several times I saw her make immediate cures of severe tooth-aches. My mother was the patient. In Austria there is a peasant who drives a great trade in this sort of industry and has both the high and the low for patients. He gets into prison every now and then for practising without a diploma, but his business is as brisk as ever when he gets out, for his work is unquestionably successful and keeps his reputation high. In Bavaria there is a man who performed so many great cures that he had to retire from his profession of stage carpentering in order to meet the demands of his constantly increasing body of customers. He goes on from year to year doing his miracles, and has become very rich. He pretends to no religious helps, no supernatural aids, but thinks there is something in his make-up which inspires the confidence of his patients, and that it is this confidence which does the work and not some mysterious power issuing from himself.[1]

Within the past quarter of a century, in America, several sects of curers have appeared under various names and have done notable things in the way of healing ailments without the use of medicines. There is the Mind-Cure, the Faith Cure, the Prayer-Cure, the Mental Science Cure and the Christian Science Cure; and apparently they all do their miracles with the same old powerful instrument—*the patient's imagination*. Differing names, but no difference in the process. But they do not give that instrument the credit; each sect claims that its way differs from the ways of the others.

They all achieve some cures, there is no question about it, and the Faith Cure and the Prayer-Cure probably do no harm when they do no good, since they do not forbid the patient to help out the cure with medicines if he wants to; but the others bar medicines, and claim ability to cure every conceivable human ailment through the application of their mental forces alone. There would seem to be an element of danger here. It has the look of claiming too much, I think. Public confidence would probably be increased if less were claimed.[2]

The Christian Scientist was not able to cure my stomach ache and my cold; but the horse-doctor did it. This convinces me that Christian Science claims too much. In my opinion it ought to let diseases alone and confine itself strictly to surgery. There it would have everything its own way.

1. *January*, 1903. I have personal and intimate knowledge of the "miraculous" cure of a case of paralysis which had kept the patient helpless in bed during two years, in spite of all that the best medical science of New York could do. The traveling "quack" (that is what they called him), came on two successive mornings and lifted the patient out of bed and said "Walk!" and the patient walked. That was the end of it. It was forty-one years ago. The patient has walked ever since. —M. T.

2. *February*, 1903. I find that Christian Science claims that the healing-force which it employs is radically different from the force used by any other party in the healing business. I shall talk about this toward the end of this work.—M. T.

The horse-doctor charged me thirty Kreutzers, and I paid
him; in fact I doubled it and gave him a shilling. Mrs. Fuller
brought in an itemised bill for a crate of broken bones mended in
234 places—one dollar per fracture.

"Nothing exists but Mind?"

"Nothing," she answered. "All else is substanceless, all else
is imaginary."

I gave her an imaginary check, and now she is suing me for
substantial dollars. It looks inconsistent.

NOTE.—The foregoing chapters appeared originally in the *Cosmopolitan
Magazine,* about three years ago.—M. T.

CHAPTER 5

Let us consider that we are all partially insane. It will explain
us to each other; it will unriddle many riddles; it will make clear
and simple many things which are involved in haunting and
harassing difficulties and obscurities now.

Those of us who are not in the asylum, and not demonstrably due there, are nevertheless no doubt insane in one or two
particulars—I think we must admit this; but I think that we are
otherwise healthy-minded. I think that when we all see one thing
alike, it is evidence that as regards that one thing our minds are
perfectly sound. Now there are really several things which we do
all see alike; things which we all accept, and about which we do
not dispute. For instance, we who are outside of the asylum all
agree that water seeks its level; that the sun gives light and heat;
that fire consumes; that fog is damp; that 6 times 6 are thirty-six;
that 2 from 10 leaves eight; that 8 and 7 are fifteen. These are
perhaps the only things we are agreed about; but although they
are so few, they are of inestimable value, because they make an
infallible standard of sanity. Whosoever accepts them we know
to be substantially sane; sufficiently sane; in the working essentials,
sane. Whoever disputes a single one of them we know to be wholly
insane, and qualified for the asylum.

Very well, the man who disputes none of them we concede to be entitled to go at large—but that is concession enough; we cannot go any further than that; for we know that in all matters of mere *opinion*, that same man is insane—just as insane as we are; just as insane as Shakespeare was, just as insane as the Pope is. We know exactly where to put our finger upon his insanity: *it is where his opinion differs from ours.*

That is a simple rule, and easy to remember. When I, a thoughtful and unbiased Presbyterian, examine the Kuran, I know that beyond any question every Mohammedan is insane; not in all things, but in religious matters. When a thoughtful and unbiased Mohammedan examines the Westminster Catechism, he knows that beyond any question I am spiritually insane. I cannot prove to him that he is insane, because you never can prove anything to a lunatic—for that is a part of his insanity and the evidence of it. He cannot prove to me that I am insane, for my mind has the same defect that afflicts his. All democrats are insane, but not one of them knows it; none but the republicans and mugwumps know it. All the republicans are insane, but only the democrats and mugwumps can perceive it. The rule is perfect: *in all matters of opinion our adversaries are insane.* When I look around me I am often troubled to see how many people are mad. To mention only a few:

The Atheist,

The Infidel,

The Agnostic,

The Baptist,

The Methodist,

The Christian Scientist,

The Catholic, and the other 115 Christian sects,

the Presbyterian excepted,

The 72 Mohammedan sects,

The Buddhist,

The Blavatsky-Buddhist,

The Nationalist,

The Confucian,
The Spiritualist,
The 2,000 East Indian sects,
The Peculiar People,
The Theosophists,
The Swedenborgians,
The Shakers,
The Millerites,
The Mormons,
The Laurence Oliphant Harrisites,
The Grand Lama's people,
The Monarchists,
The Imperialists,
The Democrats,
The Republicans (but not the Mugwumps),
The Mind-Curists,
The Faith-Curists,
The Mental Scientists,
The Allopaths,
The Homeopaths,
The Electropaths,

The—but there's no end to the list; there are millions of them! And all insane; each in his own way; insane as to his pet fad or opinion, but otherwise sane and rational.

This should move us to be charitable toward each other's lunacies. I recognize that in his special belief the Christian Scientist is insane, because he does not believe as I do; but I hail him as my mate and fellow because I am as insane as he—insane from his point of view, and his point of view is as authoritative as mine and worth as much. That is to say, worth a brass farthing. Upon a great religious or political question the opinion of the dullest head in the world is worth the same as the opinion of the brightest head in the world—a brass farthing. How do we arrive at this? It is simple: The affirmative opinion of a stupid man is neutralized by the negative opinion of his stupid neighbor—no decision is reached;

the affirmative opinion of the intellectual giant Gladstone is neutralized by the negative opinion of the intellectual giant Newman—no decision is reached. Opinions that prove nothing are of course without value—any but a dead person knows that much. This obliges us to admit the truth of the unpalatable proposition just mentioned above—that in disputed matters political and religious, one man's opinion is worth no more than his peer's, and hence it follows that no man's opinion possesses any real value. It is a humbling thought, but there is no way to get around it: *all* opinions upon these great subjects are brass-farthing opinions.

It is a mere plain simple fact—as clear and as certain as that 8 and 7 make fifteen. And by it we recognize that we are all insane, as concerns those matters. If we were sane we should all see a political or religious doctrine alike; there would be no dispute; it would be a case of 8 and 7—just as it is in heaven, where all are sane and none insane. There, there is but one religion, one belief; the harmony is perfect; there is never a discordant note.

Under protection of these preliminaries I suppose I may now repeat without offence, that the Christian Scientist is insane. I mean him no discourtesy, and I am not charging—nor even imagining—that he is insaner than the rest of the human race. I think he is more picturesquely insane than some of us. At the same time I am quite sure that in one important and splendid particular he is much saner than is the vast bulk of the race.

Why is he insane? I told you before: it is because his opinions are not ours. I know of no other reason, and I do not need any other; it is the only way we *have* of discovering insanity when it is not violent. It is merely the picturesqueness of his insanity that makes it more interesting than my kind or yours. For instance, consider his "little book;" the "little book" exposed in the sky eighteen centuries ago by the flaming angel of the Apocalypse and handed down in our day to Mrs. Mary Baker G. Eddy of New Hampshire and translated by her, word for word, into English (with help of a polisher), and now published and distributed in hundreds of editions by her at a clear profit per volume, above cost, of 700 per cent![1]—a profit which distinctly belongs to the angel of the Apocalypse, and let him collect it if he can; a "little book" which the C. S. very frequently calls by just that name, and always enclosed in quotation-marks to keep its high origin exultantly in mind; a "little book" which "explains" and reconstructs and new-paints and decorates the Bible and puts a mansard roof on it and a lightning rod and all the other modern improvements; a little book which for the present affects to travel in yoke with the Bible and be friendly to it, and within half a century will hitch it in the rear and thenceforth travel tandem, itself in the lead, in the coming great march of Christian Scientism through the Protestant dominions of the planet.

CHAPTER 6

"Hungry ones throng to hear the Bible read in connection with the text-book of Christian Science, *Science and Health, with Key to the Scriptures,* by Mary Baker G. Eddy. *These* are our only preachers. *They* are the word of God."— *Christian Science Journal, October,* 1898.

Is that picturesque? A lady has told me that in a chapel of the Mosque in Boston there is a picture or image of Mrs. Eddy, and that before it burns a never-extinguished light.[2] Is that picturesque? How long do you think it will be before the Christian Scientist will be worshiping that image and praying to it? How long do you think it will be before it is claimed that Mrs. Eddy is a Redeemer, a Christ, and Christ's equal?[3] Already her army of

1. *February,* 1903. This has been disputed by novices. It is not possible that the copy possessed by me could have cost above 37½ cents. I have been a printer and book-maker myself. I shall go into some particulars concerning this matter in a later chapter.—M. T.

2. *February,* 1903. There is a dispute about that picture. I will render justice concerning it in the new half of this book.—M. T.

3. This suggestion has been scorned. I will examine the matter in the new half of the book.—M. T.

disciples speak of her reverently as "Our Mother." How long will it be before they place her on the steps of the Throne beside the Virgin—and later a step higher? First, Mary the Virgin and Mary the Matron; later, with a change of precedence, Mary the Matron and Mary the Virgin. Let the artist get ready with his canvas and his brushes; the new Renaissance is on its way, and there will be money in altar-canvases—a thousand times as much as the Popes and their Church ever spent on the Old Masters; for their riches were poverty as compared with what is going to pour into the treasure-chest of the Christian Scientist Papacy by and by, let us not doubt it. We will examine the financial outlook presently and see what it promises. A favorite subject of the new Old Master will be the first verse of the twelfth chapter of Revelation,—a verse which Mrs. Eddy says (in her Annex to the Scriptures) has "one distinctive feature which has special reference to the present age" —and to *her*, as is rather pointedly indicated:

"And there appeared a great wonder in heaven—a *woman* clothed with the sun, and the moon under her feet," etc.

The woman clothed with the sun will be a portrait of Mrs. Eddy.

Is it insanity to believe that Christian Scientism is destined to make the most formidable show that any new religion has made in the world since the birth and spread of Mohammedanism, and that within a century from now it may stand second to Rome only in numbers and power in Christendom?

If this is a wild dream it will not be easy to prove it so just yet, I think. There seems argument that it may come true. The Christian Science "boom," proper, is not yet five years old; yet already it has 250 churches.[1]

It has its start, you see, and it is a phenomenally good one. Moreover, it is latterly spreading with a constantly accelerating swiftness. It has a better chance to grow and prosper and achieve permanency than any other existing "ism;" for it has *more to offer*

1. *February*, 1903. Through misinformation I doubled those figures when I wrote this chapter four years ago.—M. T.

than any other. The past teaches us that in order to succeed, a movement like this must not be a mere philosophy, it must be a religion; also, that it must not claim entire originality but content itself with passing for an improvement on an *existing* religion, and show its hand later, when strong and prosperous—like Mohammedanism.

Next, there must be money—and plenty of it.

Next, the power and authority and capital must be concentrated in the grip of a small and irresponsible clique, with nobody outside privileged to ask questions or find fault.

Next, as before remarked, it must bait its hook with some new and attractive advantages over the baits offered by its competitors.

A new movement equipped with some of these endowments —like Spiritualism, for instance—may count upon a considerable success; a new movement equipped with the bulk of them—like Mohammedanism, for instance—may count upon a widely extended conquest. Mormonism had all the requisites but one—it had nothing new and nothing valuable to bait with. Spiritualism lacked the important detail of concentration of money and authority in the hands of an irresponsible clique.

The above equipment is excellent, admirable, powerful, but not perfect. There is yet another detail which is worth the whole of it put together—and more; a detail which has never been joined (in the *beginning* of a religious movement) to a supremely good working equipment since the world began, until now: *a new personage to worship.*[1] Christianity had the Savior, but at first and for generations it lacked money and concentrated power. In Mrs. Eddy, Christian Science possesses the new personage for worship, and in addition—here in the very beginning—a working equipment that has not a flaw in it. In the beginning, Mohammedanism had no money; and it has never had anything to offer its client but heaven—nothing here below that was valuable. In addition to

1. *That* has been disputed by a Christian Science friend. This surprises me. I will examine this detail in the new half of the book.—M. T.

heaven hereafter, Christian Science has *present health and a cheer-ful spirit* to offer; and in comparison with this bribe all other this-world bribes are poor and cheap. You recognize that this estimate is admissible, do you not?

To whom does Bellamy's "Nationalism" appeal? Necessarily to the few: people who read, and dream, and are compassionate, and troubled for the poor and the hard-driven. To whom does Spiritualism appeal? Necessarily to the few; its "boom" has lasted for half a century and I believe it claims short of four millions of adherents in America. Who are attracted by Swedenborgianism and some of the other fine and delicate "isms?" The few again: educated people, sensitively organized, with superior mental en-dowments, who seek lofty planes of thought and find their con-tentment there. And who are attracted by Christian Science? There is no limit; its field is horizonless; its appeal is as universal as is the appeal of Christianity itself. It appeals to the rich, the poor, the high, the low, the cultured, the ignorant, the gifted, the stupid, the modest, the vain, the wise, the silly, the soldier, the civilian, the hero, the coward, the idler, the worker, the godly, the godless, the freeman, the slave, the adult, the child: *they who are ailing in body or mind, they who have friends that are ailing in body or mind.* To mass it in a phrase, its *clientèle* is the Human Race. Will it march? I think so.

Remember its principal great offer: *to rid the Race of pain and disease.* Can it do it? In large measure, yes. How much of the pain and disease in the world are created by the imaginations of the sufferers, and then kept alive by those same imaginations? Four-fifths? Not anything short of that, I should think. Can Chris-tian Science banish that four-fifths? I think so. Can any other (or-ganized) force do it? None that I know of. Would this be a new world when that was accomplished? And a pleasanter one—for us well people, as well as for those fussy and fretting sick ones? Would it seem as if there was not as much gloomy weather as there used to be? I think so.

In the meantime would the Scientist kill off a good many

patients? I think so. More than get killed off now by the legalized methods? I will take up that question presently.

At present I wish to ask you to examine some of the Scientist's performances, as registered in his magazine, the *Christian Science Journal*—October number, 1898. First, a Baptist clergyman gives us this true picture of "the average orthodox Christian" —and he could have added that it is a true picture of the average (civilized) human being:

"He is a worried and fretted and fearful man; afraid of himself and his propensities, afraid of colds and fevers, afraid of treading on serpents or drinking deadly things."

Then he gives us this contrast:

"The average Christian Scientist has put all anxiety and fretting under his feet. He does have a victory over fear and care that is not achieved by the average orthodox Christian."

He has put all anxiety and fretting under his feet. What proportion of your earnings or income would you be willing to pay for that frame of mind, year in and year out? It really outvalues any price that can be put upon it. Where can you purchase it, at any outlay of any sort, in any Church or out of it, except the Scientist's?

Well, it is the anxiety and fretting about colds, and fevers, and draughts, and getting our feet wet, and about forbidden food eaten in terror of indigestion, that brings on the cold and the fever and the indigestion and the most of our other ailments; and so, if the Science can banish that anxiety from the world I think it can reduce the world's disease and pain about four-fifths.[1]

In this October number many of the redeemed testify and give thanks; and not coldly, but with passionate gratitude. As a rule they seem drunk with health, and with the surprise of it, the wonder of it, the unspeakable glory and splendor of it, after a long sober spell spent in inventing imaginary diseases and concreting

1. *February*, 1903. In a letter to me a distinguished New York physician finds fault with this notion. If four-fifths of our pains and diseases are not the result of unwholesome fears and imaginings, the Science has a smaller field than I was guessing; but I still think four-fifths is a sound guess.—M. T.

them with doctor-stuff. The first witness testifies that when "this most beautiful Truth first dawned on him" he had "nearly all the ills that flesh is heir to;" that those he did not have he thought he had—and thus made the tale about complete. What was the natural result? Why, he was a dump-pit "for all the doctors, druggists and patent medicines of the country." Christian Science came to his help, and "the old sick conditions passed away" and along with them the "dismal forebodings" which he had been accustomed to employ in conjuring up ailments. And so he was a healthy and cheerful man, now, and astonished.

But I am not astonished, for from other sources I know what must have been his method of applying Christian Science. If I am in the right, he watchfully and diligently *diverted his mind from unhealthy channels and compelled it to travel in healthy ones.* Nothing contrivable by human invention could be more formidably effective than that, in banishing imaginary ailments and in closing the entrances against subsequent applicants of their breed. I think his method was, to keep saying "I am well! I am sound!— sound and well! well and sound! perfectly sound, perfectly well! I have no pain, there's no such thing as pain! I have no disease, there's no such thing as disease! nothing is real but Mind, all is Mind, All-Good, Good-Good, Life, Soul, Liver, Bones, one of a series, ante and pass the buck!"

I do not mean that that was exactly the formula used, but that it doubtless contains the spirit of it. The Scientist would attach value to the *exact* formula, no doubt, and to the religious spirit in which it was used. I should think that *any* formula that would divert the mind from unwholesome channels and force it into healthy ones would answer every purpose with some people, though not with all. I think it most likely that a very religious man would find the addition of the religious spirit a powerful reinforcement in his case.

The second witness testifies that the Science banished "an old organic trouble" which the doctor and the surgeon had been nursing with drugs and the knife for seven years.

He calls it his "claim." A surface-miner would think it was not *his* claim at all, but the property of the doctor and his pal the surgeon—for he would be misled by that word, which is Christian Science slang for "ailment." The Christian Scientist *has* no ailment; to him there is no such thing, and he will not use the hateful word. All that happens to him is, that upon his attention an imaginary disturbance sometimes obtrudes itself which *claims* to be an ailment, but isn't.

This witness offers testimony for a clergyman seventy years old who had preached forty years in a Christian church, and has now gone over to the new sect. He was "almost blind and deaf." He was treated by the C. S. method, and "when he heard the voice of Truth he saw spiritually." Saw spiritually? It is a little indefinite; they had better treat him again. Indefinite testimonies might properly be waste-basketed, since there is evidently no lack of definite ones procurable, but this C. S. magazine is poorly edited, and so mistakes of this kind must be expected.

The next witness is a soldier of the Civil War. When Christian Science found him, he had in stock the following claims:

Indigestion,
Rheumatism,
Catarrh,
Chalky deposits in
  Shoulder joints, ⎫
  Arm joints, ⎬
  Hand joints, ⎭
Atrophy of the muscles
  of
  Arms, ⎫
  Shoulders, ⎭
Stiffness of all those joints,
Insomnia,
Excruciating pains most of the time.

These claims have a very substantial sound. They came of exposure in the campaigns. The doctors did all they could, but it was little. Prayers were tried, but "I never realized any physical relief from that source." After thirty years of torture he went to a Christian Scientist and took an hour's treatment and went home painless. Two days later he "began to eat like a well man." Then "the claims vanished—some at once, others more gradually;" finally, "they have almost entirely disappeared." And—a thing which is of still greater value—he is now *contented and happy*. That is a detail which, as earlier remarked, is a Scientist-Church specialty. And, indeed, one may go farther and assert with little or no exaggeration that it is a Christian Science monopoly. With thirty-one years' effort the Methodist Church had not succeeded in furnishing it to this harassed soldier.

And so the tale goes on. Witness after witness bulletins his claims, declares their prompt abolishment, and gives Mrs. Eddy's Discovery the praise. Milk-leg is cured; nervous prostration is cured; consumption is cured; and St. Vitus's dance made a pastime. Even without a fiddle. And now and then an interesting new addition to the Science-slang appears on the page. We have "demonstrations over" chilblains and such things. It seems to be a curtailed way of saying "demonstrations of the power of Christian Science Truth over the fiction which masquerades under the name of chilblains." The children, as well as the adults, share in the blessings of the Science. "Through the study of the 'little book' they are learning how to be healthful, peaceful and wise." Sometimes they are cured of their little claims by the professional healer, and sometimes more advanced children say over the formula and cure themselves.

A little Far Western girl of nine, equipped with an adult vocabulary, states her age and says, "I thought I would write a demonstration to you." She had a claim, derived from getting flung over a pony's head and landed on a rock-pile. She saved herself from disaster by remembering to say "God is All" while she was in the air. I couldn't have done it. I shouldn't even have thought of it. I should have been too excited. Nothing but Christian Science could have enabled that child to do that calm and thoughtful and judicious thing in those circumstances. She came down on her head, and by all the rules she should have broken it; but the intervention of the formula prevented that, so the only claim resulting was a blackened eye. Monday morning it was still swollen and shut. At school "it hurt pretty badly—that is, it *seemed* to." So, "I was excused, and went down in the basement and said, 'Now I am depending on mamma instead of God, and I *shall* depend on God instead of mamma.' " No doubt this would have answered; but to make sure, she added Mrs. Eddy to the team and recited "the Scientific Statement of Being," which is one of the principal incantations, I judge. Then "I felt my eye opening." Why, dear, it would have opened an oyster. I think it is one of the touchingest things in child-history, that pious little rat down cellar pumping away at the Scientific Statement of Being.

There is a page about another good child—little Gordon. Little Gordon "came into the world without the assistance of surgery or anæsthetics." He was a "demonstration." A painless one; therefore his coming evoked "joy and thankfulness to God and the Discoverer of Christian Science." It is a noticeable feature of this literature—the so frequent linking together of the Two Beings in an equal bond; also of Their Two Bibles. When little Gordon was two years old, "he was playing horse on the bed, where I had left my 'little book.' I noticed him stop in his play, take the book carefully in his little hands, kiss it softly, then look about for the highest place of safety his arms could reach, and put it there." This pious act filled the mother "with such a train of thought as I had never experienced before. I thought of the sweet mother of long ago who kept things in her heart," etc. It is a bold comparison; however, unconscious profanations are about as common in the mouths of the lay membership of the new Church as are frank and open ones in the mouths of its consecrated chiefs.

Some days later, the family library—Christian Science books —was lying in a deep-seated window. It was another chance for the holy child to show off. He left his play and went there and pushed all the books to one side except the Annex. "*It* he took in both hands, slowly raised it to his lips, then removed it carefully, and seated himself in the window." It had seemed to the mother too wonderful to be true, that first time, but now she was convinced that "neither imagination nor accident had anything to do with it." Later, little Gordon let the author of his being see him do it. After that he did it frequently; probably every time anybody was looking. I would rather have that child than a chromo. If this tale has any object, it is to intimate that the inspired book was supernaturally able to convey a sense of its sacred and awful character to this innocent little creature without the intervention of outside aids. The magazine is not edited with high-priced discretion. The editor has a claim, and he ought to get it treated.

Among other witnesses there is one who had a "jumping tooth-ache" which several times tempted her to "believe that there was sensation in matter, but each time it was overcome by the power of Truth." She would not allow the dentist to use cocaine, but sat there and let him punch and drill and split and crush the tooth, and tear and slash its ulcerations, and pull out the nerve, and dig out fragments of bone; and she wouldn't once confess that it hurt. And to this day she thinks it didn't, and I have not a doubt that she is nine-tenths right, and that her Christian Science faith did her better service than she could have gotten out of cocaine.

There is an account of a boy who got broken all up into small bits by an accident, but said over the Scientific Statement of Being or some of the other incantations and got well and sound without having suffered any real pain and without the intrusion of a surgeon.

Also there is an account of the restoration to perfect health, in a single night, of a fatally injured *horse*, by the application of Christian Science. I can stand a good deal, but I recognize that the ice is getting thin, here. That horse had as many as fifty claims; how could *he* demonstrate over them? Could he do the All-Good, Good-Good, Good-Gracious, Liver, Bones, Truth, All down but Nine, Set them up on the Other Alley? Could he intone the Scien-

tific Statement of Being? Now could he? Wouldn't it give him a
relapse? Let us draw the line at horses. Horses and furniture.

There is a plenty of other testimonies in the magazine, but
these quoted samples will answer. They show the kind of trade the
Science is driving. Now we come back to the question, does it kill
a patient here and there and now and then? We must concede it.
Does it compensate for this? I am persuaded that it can make a
plausible showing in that direction. For instance: when it lays its
hand upon a soldier who has suffered thirty years of helpless torture and makes him whole in body and mind, what is the actual
sum of that achievement? This, I think: that it has restored to life
a subject who had essentially died ten deaths a year for thirty
years, and each of them a long and painful one. But for its interference that man would have essentially died thirty times more,
in the three years which have since elapsed. There are thousands
of young people in the land who are now ready to enter upon a life-
long death similar to that man's. Every time that the Science
captures one of these and secures to him life-long immunity from
imagination-manufactured disease, it may plausibly claim that in
his person it has saved 300 lives. Meantime it will kill a man every
now and then, but no matter, it will still be far ahead on the
credit side.

NOTE.—I have received several letters (two from educated and ostensibly intelligent persons), which contained, in substance, this protest: "I don't object to men
and women chancing their lives with these people, but it is a burning shame that
the law should allow them to trust their helpless little children in their deadly
hands." Isn't it touching? isn't it deep? isn't it modest? It is as if the person said,
"I know that to a parent his child is the core of his heart, the apple of his eye, a
possession so dear, so precious that he will trust its life in no hands but those which
he believes with all his soul to be the very best and the very safest, but it is a burning
shame that the law does not require him to come to *me* to ask what kind of healer
I will allow him to call." The public is merely a multiplied "me."—M. T.

CHAPTER 7[1]

"We consciously declare that *Science and Health, with
Key to the Scriptures*, was foretold, *as well as its author,*

1. Written in Europe in 1899 but not hitherto published in book form.—M. T.

Mary Baker Eddy, in Revelation x. She is the 'mighty angel,' or God's highest thought to this age (verse 1), giving us the spiritual interpretation of the Bible in the 'little book *open*' (verse 2). Thus we prove that Christian Science is the second coming of Christ—Truth—Spirit."—*Lecture by Dr. George Tomkins, D.D. C.S.*

There you have it in plain speech. She is the mighty angel; she is the divinely and officially sent bearer of God's highest thought. For the present, she *brings* the Second Advent. We must expect that before she has been in her grave fifty years she will be regarded by her following as having been *herself* the Second Advent. She is already worshiped, and we must expect this feeling to spread, territorially, and also to deepen in intensity.[1]

Particularly after her death; for then, as any one can foresee, Eddy-worship will be taught in the Sunday-schools and pulpits of the cult. Already whatever she puts her trade-mark on, though it be only a memorial-spoon, is holy and is eagerly and gratefully bought by the disciple, and becomes a fetish in his house. I say bought, for the Boston Christian Science Trust gives nothing away; everything it has is for sale. And the terms are cash; and not only cash, but cash in advance. Its god is Mrs. Eddy first, then the Dollar. Not a spiritual Dollar, but a real one. From end to end of the Christian Science literature not a single (material) thing in the world is conceded to be real, except the Dollar. But all through and through its advertisements that reality is eagerly and persistently recognized.

The Dollar is hunted down in all sorts of ways; the Christian Science Mother Church and Bargain-Counter in Boston peddles all kinds of spiritual wares to the faithful, and always on the one condition—*cash*, cash in advance. The Angel of the Apocalypse

1. After *raising a dead child to life*, the disciple who did it writes an account of her performance to Mrs. Eddy, and closes it thus: "My prayer daily is to be more spiritual, that I may do more as you would have me do. . . . and may we all love you more, and so live it that the world may know that the Christ is come."—*Printed in the Concord, N. H., Independent Statesman, March* 9, 1899. If this is not worship, it is a good imitation of it.—M. T.

could not go there and get a copy of his own pirated book on credit. Many, many precious Christian Science things are to be had there —for cash: Bible Lessons; Church Manual; C. S. Hymnal; History of the building of the Mother Church; lot of Sermons; Communion Hymn, "Saw Ye My Savior," by Mrs. Eddy, half a dollar a copy, "words used by special permission of Mrs. Eddy." Also we have Mrs. Eddy's and the Angel's little Bible-Annex in eight styles of binding at eight kinds of war-prices; among these a sweet thing in "levant, divinity circuit, leather lined to edge, round corners, gold edge, silk sewed, each, *prepaid*, $6," and if you take a million you get them a shilling cheaper—that is to say, "prepaid, $5.75." Also we have Mrs. Eddy's *Miscellaneous Writings*, at 'andsome big prices, the divinity-circuit style heading the extortions, shilling discount where you take an edition. Next comes *Christ and Christmas*, by the fertile Mrs. Eddy—a *poem*—would God I could see it!—price $3, cash in advance. Then follow five more books by Mrs. Eddy, at highwayman's rates, some of them in "leatherette covers," some of them in "pebbled cloth," with divinity circuit, compensation balance, twin screw, and the other modern improvements; and at the same bargain-counter can be had the *Christian Science Journal*.

Christian Science literary discharges are a monopoly of the Mother Church Headquarters Factory in Boston; none genuine without the trade-mark of the Trust. You must apply there, and not elsewhere.[1]

The Trust has still other sources of income. Mrs. Eddy is president (and proprietor) of the Trust's Metaphysical College in Boston, where the student of C. S. healing learns the game by a three weeks' course, and pays *one hundred dollars* for it.[2] And I

1. *February*, 1903. I applied last month, but they returned my money, and wouldn't play. We are not on speaking terms now.—M. T.

2. An error. For one hundred, read *three* hundred. That was for 12 brief lessons. But this cheapness only lasted until the end of 1888—fourteen years ago. [I am making this note in December, 1902.] Mrs. Eddy—over her own signature—then made a change; the new terms were three hundred dollars for *seven* lessons. See *Christian Science Journal* for December, 1888.—M. T.

have a case among my statistics where the student had a three weeks' course and paid *three* hundred for it.

The Trust does love the Dollar, when it isn't a spiritual one.

In order to force the sale of Mrs. Eddy's Bible-Annex, no healer, Metaphysical-College-bred or other, is allowed to practise the game unless he possess a copy of that book. That means a large and constantly augmenting income for the Trust. No C. S. family would consider itself loyal or pious or pain-proof without an Annex or two in the house. That means an income for the Trust —in the near future—of millions; not thousands—millions a year.

No member, young or old, of a branch Christian Scientist church can acquire and retain membership in the Mother Church unless he pay "capitation-tax" (of "not less than a dollar," say the By-Laws) to the Boston Trust every year. That means an income for the Trust—in the near future—of—let us venture to say— millions more per year.

It is a reasonably safe guess that in America in 1920 there will be 10,000,000[1] Christian Scientists, and 3,000,000 in Great Britain; that these figures will be trebled by 1930; that in America in 1920 the Christian Scientists will be a political force, in 1930 politically formidable, and in 1940 the governing power in the Republic—to remain that, permanently. And I think it a reasonable guess that the Trust (which is already in our day pretty brusque in its ways) will then be the most insolent and unscrupulous and tyrannical politico-religious master that has dominated a people since the palmy days of the Inquisition. And a stronger master than the strongest of bygone times, because this one will have a financial strength not dreamed of by any predecessor; as effective a concentration of irresponsible power as any predecessor has had;[2] in the railway, the telegraph, and the subsidized newspaper, better facilities for watching and managing his empire than any prede-

1. Written in 1899. It is intended to include men, women and children. Although the calculation was based upon inflated statistics, I believe to-day that it is not far out.—M. T.

2. It can be put stronger than that and still be true.—M. T.

cessor has had; and after a generation or two he will probably divide Christendom with the Catholic Church.

The Roman Church has a perfect organization, and it has an effective centralization of power—but not of its cash. Its multitude of Bishops are rich, but their riches remain in large measure in their own hands. They collect from 200,000,000 of people, but they keep the bulk of the result at home. The Boston Pope of by and by will draw his dollar-a-head capitation-tax from 300,000,000 of the human race,[1] and the Annex and the rest of his book-shop stock will fetch in as much more; and his Metaphysical Colleges, the annual pilgrimage to Mrs. Eddy's tomb, from all over the world—admission, the Christian Science Dollar (payable in advance)—purchases of consecrated glass beads, candles, memorial-spoons, aureoled chromo-portraits and bogus autographs of Mrs. Eddy, cash offerings at her shrine—no crutches of cured cripples received, and no imitations of miraculously restored broken legs and necks allowed to be hung up except when made out of the Holy Metal and proved by fire-assay; cash for miracles worked at the tomb: these money-sources, with a thousand to be yet invented and ambushed upon the devotee, will bring the annual increment well up above a billion. And nobody but the Trust will have the handling of it. In that day the Trust will monopolize the manufacture and sale of the Old and New Testaments as well as the Annex, and raise their price to Annex rates, and compel the devotee to buy (for even to-day a healer has to have the Annex *and* the Scriptures or he is not allowed to work the game), and that will bring several hundred million dollars more. In those days the Trust will have an income approaching $5,000,000 a day, and no expenses to be taken out of it; no taxes to pay, and *no charities to support*. That last detail should not be lightly passed over by the reader; it is well entitled to attention.

1. In that day by force; it is voluntary, now. In the new half of this book the reader will perceive that all imaginable compulsions are possible under the Mother Church's body of Laws. To-day more is expected than the one dollar. This is indicated in the wording of the By-Law. Much more comes, from many members.—M. T.

No charities to support. No, nor even to contribute to. One searches in vain the Trust's advertisements and the utterances of its organs for any suggestion that it spends a penny on orphans, widows, discharged prisoners, hospitals, ragged schools, night-missions, city missions, libraries, old people's homes, or any other object that appeals to a human being's purse through his heart.[1]

I have hunted, hunted, and hunted, by correspondence and otherwise, and have not yet got upon the track of a farthing that the Trust has spent upon any worthy object. Nothing makes a Scientist so uncomfortable as to ask him if he knows of a case where Christian Science has spent money on a benevolence, either among its own adherents or elsewhere. He is obliged to say no. And then one discovers that the person questioned has been asked the question many times before, and that it is getting to be a sore subject with him. Why a sore subject? Because he has written his chiefs and asked with high confidence for an answer that will confound these questioners—and the chiefs did not reply. He has written again—and then again—not with confidence, but humbly, now, and has begged for defensive ammunition in the voice of supplication. A reply does at last come—to this effect: "We must have faith in Our Mother, and rest content in the conviction that whatever She[2] does with the money it is in accordance with orders from heaven, for She does no act of any kind without first 'demonstrating over' it."

That settles it—as far as the disciple is concerned. His Mind is satisfied with that answer; he gets down his Annex and does an incantation or two, and that mesmerizes his spirit and puts *that* to sleep—brings it peace. Peace and comfort and joy, until some inquirer punctures the old sore again.

Through friends in America I asked some questions, and in some cases got definite and informing answers; in other cases the answers were not definite and not valuable. To the question,

1. In two years (1898–99) the membership of the Established Church in England gave voluntary contributions amounting to $73,000,000 to the Church's benevolent enterprises. Churches that give have nothing to hide.—M. T.

2. I may be introducing the capital S a little early—still, it is on its way.—M. T.

"Does any of the money go to charities?" the answer from an authoritative source was: "No, *not in the sense usually conveyed by this word.*" (The italics are mine.) That answer is cautious. But definite, I think—utterly and unassailably definite—although quite Christian-scientifically foggy in its phrasing. Christian Science testimony is generally foggy, generally diffuse, generally garrulous. The writer was aware that the first word in his phrase answered the question which I was asking, but he could not help adding nine dark words. Meaningless ones, unless explained by him. It is quite likely—as intimated by him—that Christian Science has invented a new class of objects to apply the word charity to, but without an explanation we cannot know what they are. We quite easily and naturally and confidently guess that they are in all cases objects which will return five hundred per cent on the Trust's investment in them, but guessing is not knowledge; it is merely, in this case, a sort of nine-tenths certainty deducible from what we think we know of the Trust's trade principles and its sly and furtive and shifty ways.[1]

Sly? Deep? Judicious? The Trust understands business. The Trust does not give itself away. It defeats all the attempts of us impertinents to get at its trade secrets. To this day, after all our diligence, we have not been able to get it to confess what it does with the money. It does not even let its own disciples find out. All it says is, that the matter has been "demonstrated over." Now and then a lay Scientist says, with a grateful exultation, that Mrs. Eddy is enormously rich, but he stops there; as to whether any of the money goes to other charities or not, he is obliged to admit that he does not know. However, the Trust is composed of human beings; and this justifies the conjecture that if it had a charity on its list which it was proud of, we should soon hear of it.

"Without money and without price." Those used to be the

1. *February*, 1903. A letter has come to me, this month, from a lady who says that while she was living in Boston a few years ago, she visited the Mother Church and offices and had speech with Judge Septimus J. Hanna, the "first reader," who "stated positively that the Church, as a body, does no philanthropic work whatever."—M. T.

terms. Mrs. Eddy's Annex cancels them. The motto of Christian Science is, "The laborer is worthy of his hire." And now that it has been "demonstrated over," we find its spiritual meaning to be, "Do anything and everything your hand may find to do; and charge cash for it, and collect the money in advance." The Scientist has on his tongue's end a cut-and-dried, Boston-supplied set of rather lean arguments whose function is to show that it is a heaven-commanded *duty* to do this, and that the croupiers of the game have no choice but to obey.[1]

The Trust seems to be a reincarnation. Exodus xxxii. 4.

1. *February*, 1903. If I seem to be charging any one outside of the Trust with an exaggerated appetite for money, I have not meant to do it. The exactions of the ordinary C. S. "healer" are not exorbitant. If I have prejudices against the Trust—and I do feel that I have—they do not extend to the lay membership.

"The laborer is worthy of his hire." And is entitled to receive it, too, and charge his own price (when he is laboring in a lawful calling). The great surgeon charges a thousand dollars, and no one is justified in objecting to it. The great preacher and teacher in religion receives a large salary and is entitled to it; Henry Ward Beecher's was $20,000. Mrs. Eddy's Metaphysical College was chartered by the State, and she had a legal right to charge amazing prices, and she did it. She allows only a few persons to *teach* Christian Science. The calling of these teachers is not illegal. Mrs. Eddy appoints the sum their students must pay, and it is a round one; but that is no matter, since they need not come unless they want to.

But when we come to the C. S. "healer," the *practitioner*, that is another thing. He exists by the hundred; his services are prized by his C. S. patient, they are preferred above all other human help, and are thankfully paid for. As I have just remarked, his prices are not large. But there is hardly a State wherein he can lawfully practise his profession. In the name of religion, of morals, and of Christ—represented on the earth by Mrs. Eddy—he enters upon his trade a commissioned lawbreaker.

A law-breaker. It is curious, but if the Second Advent should happen now, Jesus could not heal the sick in the State of New York. He could not do it lawfully; therefore He could not do it morally; therefore He could not do it at all.—M. T.

March 12, 1903. While I am reading the final proofs of this book, the following letter has come to me. It is not marked private, therefore I suppose I may without impropriety insert it here, if I suppress the signature:

"Dear Sir,—In the *North American Review* for January is the statement, in effect, that Christian Scientists give nothing to charities. It has had wide reading and is doubtless credited. To produce a true impression, it seems as if other facts should have been stated in connection.

"With regret for adding anything to the burden of letters from strangers, I am impelled to write what I know from a limited acquaintance in the sect. I am not connected with it myself.

"The charity freely given by individual practitioners, so far as I know it, is at

I have no reverence for the Trust, but I am not lacking in reverence for the sincerities of the lay membership of the new Church. There is every evidence that the lay members are entirely sincere in their faith, and I think sincerity is always entitled to honor and respect, let the inspiration of the sincerity be what it may. Zeal and sincerity can carry a new religion further than any other missionary except fire and sword, and I believe that the new religion will conquer the half of Christendom in a hundred years. I am not intending this as a compliment to the human race, I am merely stating an opinion. And yet I think that perhaps it *is* a compliment to the race. I keep in mind that saying of an orthodox preacher—quoted further back. He conceded that this new Christianity frees its possessor's life from *frets, fears, vexations, bitterness, and all sorts of imagination-propagated maladies and pains, and fills his world with sunshine and his heart with gladness.* If Christian Science, with this stupendous equipment—and final

---

least equal to that of regular physicians. Charges are made with much more than equal consideration of the means of the patient. Of course druggists' bills and the enormous expenses involved in the employment of a trained nurse, exist in small degree or not at all.

"As to organized charities: It is hard to find one where the most intelligent laborers in it feel that they are reaching the root of an evil. They are putting a few plasters on a body of disease. Complaint is made, too, that the machinery, by which of necessity systematic charity must be administered, prevents the personal friendliness and sympathy which should pervade it throughout.

"Christian Science claims to be able to abolish the need for charity. The results of drunkenness make great demands upon the charitable. But the principle of Christian Science takes away the desire for strong drink. If sexual propensities were dominated, not only by reason, but by Christian love for both the living and the unborn—Christian Science is emphatic on this subject—many existing charitable societies would have no reason to be. So far as Christian Science prevents disease, the need for hospitals is lessened. Not only illness, but poverty, is a subject for the practice of Christian Science. If this evil were prevented there would be no occasion to alleviate its results.

"The faith, hope, and love which the few Christian Scientists I have known have lived and radiated, made conditions needing organized charity vanish before them.

"With renewed apology for intrusion upon one whose own 'Uncle Silas' was 'loved back' to sanity,

"I am, etc., etc.

"WOBURN, MASS.,
"*March* 10, 1903."

salvation added—cannot win half the Christian globe, I must be badly mistaken in the make-up of the human race.

I think the Trust will be handed down like the other papacy, and will always know how to handle its limitless cash. It will press the button; the zeal, the energy, the sincerity, the enthusiasm of its countless vassals will do the rest.

CHAPTER 8

The power which a man's imagination has over his body to heal it or make it sick is a force which none of us is born without. The first man had it, the last one will possess it. If left to himself a man is most likely to use only the mischievous half of the force —the half which invents imaginary ailments for him and cultivates them; and if he is one of these very wise people he is quite likely to scoff at the beneficent half of the force and deny its existence. And so, to heal or help that man, *two* imaginations are required: his own and some outsider's. The outsider, B, must imagine that *his* incantations are the healing-power that is curing A, and A must imagine that this is so. I think it is not so, at all; but no matter, the cure is effected, and that is the main thing. The outsider's work is unquestionably valuable; so valuable that it may fairly be likened to the essential work performed by the engineer when he handles the throttle and turns on the steam: the actual power is lodged exclusively in the engine, but if the engine were left alone it would never start of itself. Whether the engineer be named Jim, or Bob, or Tom, it is all one—his services are necessary, and he is entitled to such wage as he can get you to pay. Whether he be named Christian Scientist, or Mental Scientist, or Mind-Curist, or Lourdes Miracle-Worker, or King's-Evil Expert, or Hypnotist, it is all one, he is merely the Engineer, he simply turns on the same old steam and the engine does the whole work.

The Christian Scientist engineer drives exactly the same trade as the other engineers, yet he out-prospers the whole of them put together.[1] Is it because he has captured the takingest name? I think that that is only a small part of it. I think that the secret of his high prosperity lies elsewhere.

The Christian Scientist has *organized* the business. Now that was certainly a gigantic idea. Electricity, in limitless volume, has existed in the air and the rocks and the earth and everywhere since time began—and was going to waste all the while. In our time we have *organized* that scattered and wandering force and set it to work, and backed the business with capital, and concentrated it in few and competent hands, and the results are as we see.

The Christian Scientist has taken a force which has been lying idle in every member of the human race since time began, and has organized it, and backed the business with capital, and concentrated it at Boston headquarters in the hands of a small and very competent Trust, and there are results.

Therein lies the promise that this monopoly is going to extend its commerce wide in the earth. I think that if the business were conducted in the loose and disconnected fashion customary with such things, it would achieve but little more than the modest prosperity usually secured by unorganized great moral and commercial ventures; but I believe that so long as this one remains compactly organized and closely concentrated in a Trust, the spread of its dominion will continue.

CHAPTER 9

Four years ago I wrote the preceding chapters.[2] I was assured by the wise that Christian Science was a fleeting craze and would soon perish. This prompt and all-competent stripe of prophet is always to be had in the market at ground-floor rates. He does not stop to load, or consider, or take aim, but lets fly just as he stands.

1. *February*, 1903. As I have already remarked in a footnote, the Scientist claims that he uses a force not used by any of the others.—M. T.
2. That is to say, in 1898.—M. T.

Facts are nothing to him, he has no use for such things, he works wholly by inspiration. And so, when he is asked why he considers a new movement a passing fad and quickly perishable, he finds himself unprepared with a reason and is more or less embarrassed. For a moment. Only for a moment. Then he waylays the first spectre of a reason that goes flitting through the desert places of his mind, and is at once serene again, and ready for conflict. Serene and confident. Yet he should not be so, since he has had no chance to examine his catch, and cannot know whether it is going to help his contention or damage it.

The impromptu reason furnished by the early prophets of whom I have spoken was this:

"There is nothing *to* Christian Science; there is nothing about it that appeals to the intellect; its market will be restricted to the unintelligent, the mentally inferior, the people who do not think."

They called that a reason why the cult would not flourish and endure. Its seems the equivalent of saying—

"There is no money in tinware; there is nothing about it that appeals to the rich; its market will be restricted to the poor."

It is like bringing forward the best reason in the world why Christian Science should flourish and live, and then blandly offering it as a reason why it should sicken and die.

That reason was furnished me by the complacent and unfrightened prophets four years ago, and it has been furnished me again to-day. If conversions to new religions or to old ones were in any considerable degree achieved through the intellect, the aforesaid reason would be sound and sufficient, no doubt; the inquirer into Christian Science might go away unconvinced and unconverted. But we all know that conversions are seldom made in that way; that such a thing as a serious and pains-taking and fairly-competent inquiry into the claims of a religion or of a political dogma is a rare occurrence; and that the vast mass of men and women are far from being capable of making such an examination. They are not capable, for the reason that their minds, howsoever good they may be, are not trained for such examinations. The mind not trained for that work is no more competent to do it than are lawyers and farmers competent to make successful clothes without learning the tailor's trade. There are 75,000,000 men and women among us who do not know how to cut out and make a dress-suit, and they would not think of trying; yet they all think they can competently think out a political or religious scheme without any apprenticeship to the business, and many of them believe they have actually worked that miracle. But indeed the truth is, almost all the men and women of our nation or of any other get their religion and their politics where they get their astronomy— entirely at second hand. Being untrained, they are no more able to intelligently examine a dogma or a policy than they are to calculate an eclipse.

Men are usually competent thinkers along the lines of their specialized training only. Within those limits alone are their opinions and judgments valuable; outside of them they grope and are lost—usually without knowing it. In a church assemblage of five hundred persons there will be a man or two whose trained minds can seize upon each detail of a great manufacturing scheme and recognize its value or its lack of it promptly; and can pass the details in intelligent review, section by section, and finally as a whole, and then deliver a verdict upon the scheme which cannot be flippantly set aside nor easily answered. And there will be one or two other men there who can do the same thing with a great and complicated educational project; and one or two others who can do the like with a large scheme for applying electricity in a new and unheard-of way; and one or two others who can do it with a showy scheme for revolutionizing the scientific world's accepted notions regarding geology. And so on, and so on. But the manufacturing experts will not be competent to examine the educational scheme intelligently, and their opinion about it would not be valuable; neither of these groups will be able to understand and pass upon the electrical scheme; none of the three batches of experts will be able to understand and pass upon the geological revolution—and probably not one man in the entire lot will be competent to examine, capably, the intricacies of a political or religious scheme, new or old, and deliver a judgment upon it which any one need regard as precious.

There you have the top crust. There will be four hundred and seventy-five men and women present who can draw upon their training and deliver incontrovertible judgments concerning cheese, and leather, and cattle, and hardware, and soap, and tar, and candles, and patent medicines, and dreams, and apparitions, and garden truck, and cats, and baby food, and warts, and hymns, and time-tables, and freight-rates, and summer resorts, and whisky, and law, and surgery, and dentistry, and blacksmithing, and shoemaking, and dancing, and Huyler's candy, and mathematics, and dog fights, and obstetrics, and music, and sausage, and dry goods, and molasses, and railroad stocks, and horses, and literature, and labor unions, and vegetables, and morals, and lamb's fries, and etiquette, and agriculture. And not ten among the five hundred—let their minds be ever so good and bright—will be competent, by grace of the requisite specialized mental training, to take hold of a complex abstraction of any kind and make head or tail of it.

The whole five hundred are thinkers, and they are all capable thinkers—but only within the narrow limits of their specialized trainings. Four hundred and ninety of them cannot competently examine either a religious plant or a political one. A scattering few of them do examine both—that is, they think they do. With results as precious as when I examine the nebular theory and explain it to myself.

If the four hundred and ninety got their religion through their minds, and by weighed and measured detail, Christian Science would not be a scary apparition. But they don't; they get a little of it through their minds, more of it through their feelings, and the overwhelming bulk of it through their environment.

Environment is the chief thing to be considered when one is proposing to predict the future of Christian Science. It is not the ability to reason that makes the Presbyterian, or the Baptist or the Methodist or the Catholic or the Mohammedan or the Buddhist or the Mormon, it is *environment*. If religions were got by reasoning, we should have the extraordinary spectacle of an American family with a Presbyterian in it, and a Baptist, a Methodist, a Catholic, a Mohammedan, a Buddhist, and a Mormon. A Presbyterian family does not produce Catholic families or other religious brands, it produces its own kind; and not by intellectual processes, but by association. And so also with Mohammedanism, that cult which in our day is spreading with the sweep of a world-conflagration through the Orient, that native home of profound thought and of subtle intellectual fence, that fertile womb whence has sprung every great religion that exists. Including our own; for with all our brains we cannot invent a religion and market it.

The language of my quoted prophets recurs to us now, and we wonder to think how small a space in the world the mighty Mohammedan Church would be occupying now, if a successful trade in its line of goods had been conditioned upon an exhibit that would "appeal to the intellect" instead of to "the unintelligent, the mentally inferior, the people who do not think."

The Christian Science Church, like the Mohammedan Church, makes no embarrassing appeal to the intellect, has no occasion to do it, and can get along quite well without it.

Provided. Provided, what? That it can secure that thing which is worth two or three hundred thousand times more than an "appeal to the intellect"—an *environment*. Can it get it? Will it be a menace to regular Christianity if it gets it? Is it time for regular Christianity to begin to get alarmed? Or shall regular Christianity smile a smile and turn over and take another nap? Won't it be wise and proper for regular Christianity to do the old way, the customary way, the historical way—lock the stable door after the horse is gone? Just as Protestantism has smiled and nodded this long time (while the alert and diligent Catholic was slipping in and capturing the public schools), and is now beginning to hunt around for the key when it is too late?

Will Christian Science get a chance to show its wares? It has *already* secured it. Will it flourish and spread and prosper if it shall create for itself the one thing essential to those conditions— an environment? It has *already* created it. There are families of Christian Scientists in every community in America, and each family is a factory; each family turns out a Christian Science product at the customary intervals, and contributes it to the Cause in the only way in which contributions of recruits to Churches are ever made on a large scale—by the puissant forces of personal contact and association. Each family is an agency for the Cause, and makes converts among the neighbors, and starts some more factories.

Four years ago there were six Christian Scientists in a certain town that I am acquainted with; a year ago there were 250 there; they have built a church, and its membership numbers 400 now. This has all been quietly done; done without frenzied revivals, without uniforms, brass bands, street parades, corner-oratory, or any of the other customary persuasions to a godly life. Christian Science, like Mohammedanism, is "restricted" to the "unintelligent, the people who do not think." Therein lies the danger. It makes it formidable. It is "restricted" to ninety-nine one-hundredths of the human race, and must be reckoned with by regular Christianity. And will be, as soon as it is too late.

BOOK II

"There were remarkable things about the stranger called the Man-Mystery—things so very extraordinary that they monopolized attention and made *all* of him seem extraordinary; but this was not so, the most of his qualities being of the common everyday size and like anybody else's. It was curious. He was of the ordinary stature, and had the ordinary aspects; yet in him were hidden such strange contradictions and disproportions! He was majestically fearless and heroic; he had the strength of thirty men and the daring of thirty thousand; handling armies, organizing states, administering governments—these were pastimes to him; he publicly and ostentatiously accepted the human race at its own valuation—as demigods—and privately and successfully dealt with it at quite another and juster valuation—as children and slaves; his ambitions were stupendous, and his dreams had no commerce with the humble plain, but moved with the cloud-rack among the snow-summits. These features of him were indeed extraordinary, but the rest of him was ordinary and usual. He was so meanminded, in the matter of jealousy, that it was thought he was descended from a god; he was vain in little ways, and had a pride in trivialities; he doted on ballads about moonshine and bruised hearts; in education he was deficient, he was indifferent to literature, and knew nothing of art; he was dumb upon all subjects but one, indifferent to all except that one—the Nebular Theory. Upon that one his flow of words was full and free, he was a geyser. The official astronomers disputed his facts and derided his views, and said that he had invented both, they not being findable in any of the books. But many of the laity who wanted their nebulosities fresh, admired his doctrine and adopted it, and it attained to great prosperity in spite of the hostility of the experts."—*The Legend of the Man-Mystery, Ch. I.*

CHAPTER 1

January, 1903. When we do not know a public man personally, we guess him out by the facts of his career. When it is Washington, we all arrive at about one and the same result. We agree
that his words and his acts clearly interpret his character to us, and
that they never leave us in doubt as to the motives whence the
words and acts proceeded. It is the same with Joan of Arc, it is the
same with two or three or five or six others among the immortals.
But in the matter of motives and of a few details of character we
agree to disagree upon Napoleon, Cromwell, and all the rest; and
to this list we must add Mrs. Eddy. I think we can peacefully agree
as to two or three extraordinary features of her make-up, but not
upon the other features of it. We cannot peacefully agree as to her
motives, therefore her character must remain crooked to some of
us and straight to the others.

No matter, she is interesting enough without an amicable
agreement. In several ways she is the most interesting woman that
ever lived, and the most extraordinary. The same may be said of
her career, and the same may be said of its chief result. She started
from nothing. Her enemies charge that she surreptitiously took
from Quimby a peculiar system of healing which was mind-cure
with a Biblical basis. She and her friends deny that she took anything from him. This is a matter which we can discuss by and by.
Whether she took it or invented it, it was—materially—a sawdust
mine when she got it, and she has turned it into a Klondyke; its
spiritual dock had next to no custom, if any at all: from it she has
launched a world-religion which has now six hundred and sixty-
three churches, and she charters a new one every four days. When
we do not know a person—also when we do—we have to judge his
size by the size and nature of his achievements, as compared with
the achievements of others in his special line of business—there is
no other way. Measured by this standard, it is thirteen hundred

years since the world has produced any one who could reach up
to Mrs. Eddy's waistbelt.

Figuratively speaking, Mrs. Eddy is already as tall as the Eiffel
tower. She is adding surprisingly to her stature every day. It is
quite within the probabilities that a century hence she will be the
most imposing figure that has cast its shadow across the globe since
the inauguration of our era. I grant that after saying these strong
things, it is necessary that I offer some details calculated to satisfactorily demonstrate the proportions which I have claimed for
her. I will do that presently; but before exhibiting the matured
sequoia gigantea, I believe it will be best to exhibit the sprout from
which it sprang. It may save the reader from making miscalcula-
tions. The person who imagines that a Big Tree sprout is bigger
than other kinds of sprouts is quite mistaken. It is the ordinary
thing; it makes no show, it compels no notice, it hasn't a detectible
quality in it that entitles it to attention, or suggests the future
giant its sap is suckling. That is the kind of sprout Mrs. Eddy was.
From her childhood days up to where she was running a half century a close race and gaining on it, she was most humanly
commonplace.

She is the witness I am drawing this from. She has revealed it
in her autobiography. Not intentionally, of course—I am not
claiming that. An autobiography is the most treacherous thing
there is. It lets out every secret its author is trying to keep; it lets
the truth shine unobstructed through every harmless little decep-
tion he tries to play; it pitilessly exposes him as a tin hero worshiping himself as Big Metal every time he tries to do the modest-
unconsciousness act before the reader. This is not guessing; I am
speaking from autobiographical personal experience; I was never
able to refrain from mentioning, with a studied casualness that
could deceive none but the most incautious reader, that an ancestor of mine was sent ambassador to Spain by Charles I, nor that
in a remote branch of my family there exists a claimant to an earldom, nor that an uncle of mine used to own a dog that was descended from the dog that was in the Ark; and at the same time I

was never able to persuade myself to call a gibbet by its right name
when accounting for other ancestors of mine, but always spoke of
it as the "platform"—puerilely intimating that they were out lecturing when it happened.

It is Mrs. Eddy over again. As regards her minor half, she is
as commonplace as the rest of us. Vain of trivial things all the first
half of her life, and still vain of them at seventy and recording them
with naïve satisfaction—even rescuing some early rhymes of hers
of the sort that we all scribble in the innocent days of our youth—
rescuing them and printing them without pity or apology, just as
the weakest and commonest of us do in our gray age. More—she
still frankly admires them; and in her introduction of them pro-
fanely confers upon them the holy name of "poetry." Sample:

> "And laud the land whose talents rock
>   The cradle of her power,
> And wreathes are twined round Plymouth Rock
>   From erudition's bower."

> "Minerva's silver sandals still
>   Are loosed and not effete."

You note that it is not a shade above the thing which all human beings churn out in their youth.

You would not think that in a little wee primer—for that is
what the autobiography is—a person with a tumultuous career of
seventy years behind her could find room for two or three pages of
padding of this kind, but such is the case. She evidently puts narrative together with difficulty and is not at home in it, and is glad to
have something ready-made to fill in with. Another sample:

> "Here fame-honored Hickory rears his bold form,
>   And bears[1] a brave breast to the lightning and storm,
> While Palm, Bay, and Laurel in classical glee,
>   Chase Tulip, Magnolia, and fragrant Fringe-tree."

---

1. Meaning *bares?* I think so.—M. T.

Vivid? you can fairly see those trees galloping around. That she could still treasure up, and print, and manifestly admire those Poems, indicates that the most daring and masculine and masterful woman that has appeared in the earth in centuries has the same soft girly-girly places in her that the rest of us have.

When it comes to selecting her ancestors she is still human, natural, vain, commonplace—as commonplace as I am myself when I am sorting ancestors for my autobiography. She combs out some creditable Scots, and labels them and sets them aside for use, not overlooking the one to whom Sir William Wallace gave "a heavy sword encased in a brass scabbard," and naïvely explaining *which* Sir William Wallace it was, lest we get the wrong one by the hassock:[1] this is the one "from whose patriotism and bravery comes that heart-stirring air, 'Scots wha hae wi' Wallace bled.' " Hannah More was related to her ancestors. She explains who Hannah More was.

Whenever a person informs us who Sir William Wallace was, or who wrote *Hamlet,* or where the Declaration of Independence was fought, it fills us with a suspicion well-nigh amounting to conviction, that that person would not suspect us of being so empty of knowledge if he wasn't suffering from the same "claim" himself. Then we turn to page 20 of the autobiography and happen upon this passage, and that hasty suspicion stands rebuked:

"I gained book-knowledge with far less labor than is usually requisite. At ten years of age I was as familiar with Lindley Murray's Grammar as with the Westminster Catechism; and the latter I had to repeat every Sunday. My favorite studies were Natural Philosophy, Logic, and Moral Science. From my brother Albert I received lessons in the ancient tongues, Hebrew, Greek, and Latin."

You catch your breath in astonishment, and feel again and still again the pang of that rebuke. But then your eye falls upon

1. I am in some doubt as to what a hassock is, but anyway it sounds good. —M. T.

the next sentence but one, and the pain passes away and you set up the suspicion again with evil satisfaction:

"After my discovery of Christian Science, most of the knowledge I had gleaned from schoolbooks vanished like a dream."

That disappearance accounts for much in her miscellaneous writings. As I was saying, she handles her "ancestral shadows" as she calls them, just as I do mine. It is remarkable. When she runs across "a relative of my Grandfather Baker, General Henry Knox, of Revolutionary fame," she sets him down; when she finds another good one, "the late Sir John Macneill, in the line of my Grandmother Baker's family," she sets him down, and remembers that he "was prominent in British politics, and at one time held the position of ambassador to Persia;" when she discovers that her grandparents "were likewise connected with Captain John Lovewell, whose gallant leadership and death in the Indian troubles of 1722–25 caused that prolonged contest to be known historically as Lovewell's War," she sets the Captain down; when it turns out that a cousin of her grandmother "was John Macneil the New Hampshire general who fought at Lundy's Lane and won distinction in 1814 at the battle of Chippewa," she catalogues the General. [And tells where Chippewa was.] And then she skips *all* her platform-people, never mentions one of them. It shows that she is just as human as any of us.

Yet after all, there is something very touching in her pride in these worthy small-fry, and something large and fine in her modesty in not caring to remember that their kinship to her can confer no distinction upon her, whereas her mere mention of their names has conferred upon them a fadeless earthly immortality.

CHAPTER 2

When she wrote this little biography her great life-work had already been achieved, she was become renowned, to multitudes of reverent disciples she was a sacred personage, a familiar of God, and His inspired channel of communication with the human race. Also, to them these following things were facts, and not doubted:

She had written a Bible, in middle age, and had published it; she had recast it, enlarged it, and published it again; she had not stopped there, but had enlarged it further, polished its phrasing, improved its form, and published it yet again. It was at last become a compact, grammatical, dignified, and workmanlike body of literature. This was good training, persistent training; and in all arts it is training that brings the art to perfection. We are now confronted with one of the most teasing and baffling riddles of Mrs. Eddy's history—a riddle which may be formulated thus:

How is it that a primitive literary gun which began as a hundred-yard flint-lock smooth-bore muzzle-loader, and in the course of forty years has acquired one notable improvement after another—percussion cap; fixed cartridge; rifled barrel; efficiency at half a mile—how is it that such a gun, sufficiently good on an elephant-hunt (Christian Science) from the beginning, and growing better and better all the time during forty years, has *always* collapsed back to its original flint-lock estate the moment the huntress trained it on any other creature than an elephant?

Something more than a generation ago Mrs. Eddy went out with her flint-lock on the rabbit-range, and this was a part of the result:

"After his decease, and a severe casualty deemed fatal by skilful physicians, we discovered that the Principle of all healing and the law that governs it is God, a divine Principle, and a spiritual not material law, and regained health."—Preface to *Science and Health*, first revision, 1883.

N. B., not from the book *itself*; from the *Preface*.

You will notice the awkwardness of that English. If you should carry that paragraph up to the Supreme Court of the United States in order to find out for good and all whether the fatal casualty happened to the dead man—as the paragraph almost asserts—or to some person or persons not even hinted at in the paragraph, the Supreme Court would be obliged to say that the evidence established nothing with certainty except that *there had been a casualty*—victim not known.

The context thinks it explains who the victim was, but it does nothing of the kind. It furnishes some guessing-material of a sort which enables you to infer that it was "we" that suffered the mentioned injury, but if you should carry the language to a court you would not be able to prove that it necessarily meant that.

"We" are Mrs. Eddy; a funny little affectation. She replaced it later with the more dignified third person.

The quoted paragraph is from Mrs. Eddy's preface to the first revision of *Science and Health* (1883). Sixty-four pages further along—in the body of the book, (the elephant-range), she went out with that same flint-lock, and got this following result. Its English is very nearly as straight and clean and competent as is the English of the latest revision of *Science and Health* after the gun has been improved from smooth-bore musket up to globe-sighted long-distance rifle:

"Man controlled by his Maker has no physical suffering. His body is harmonious, his days are multiplying instead of diminishing, he is journeying toward Life instead of death, and bringing out the new man and crucifying the old affections, cutting them off in every material direction until he learns the utter supremacy of Spirit and yields obedience thereto."

In the latest revision of *Science and Health* (1902), the perfected gun furnishes the following. The English is clean, compact, dignified, almost perfect. But it is observable that it is not prominently better than it is in the above paragraph, which was a product of the primitive flint-lock:

"How unreasonable is the belief that we are wearing out life and hastening to death, and that at the same time we are communing with Immortality? If the departed are in rapport with mortality, or matter, they are not spiritual, but must still be mortal, sinful, suffering, and dying. Then wherefore look to them— even were communication possible—for proofs of immortality, and accept them as oracles?"—*Edition of* 1902, *p.* 78.

With the above paragraphs compare these that follow. It is
Mrs. Eddy writing—after a good long twenty years of pen-practice.
Compare also with the alleged Poems already quoted. The prominent characteristic of the Poems is affectation, artificiality; their
make-up is a complacent and pretentious outpour of false figures
and fine-writing, in the sophomoric style. The same qualities and
the same style will be found, unchanged, unbettered, in these
following paragraphs—after a lapse of more than fifty years, and
after—as aforesaid—long literary training. The italics are mine:

1. "What plague spot, or bacilli were [*sic*] gnawing [*sic*] at
the heart of this metropolis . . . and bringing it [the heart] on
bended knee? Why, it was an *institute* that had entered its *vitals*—
that, among other things, taught games," et cetera.—*C. S. Journal*,
p. 670, article entitled "A Narrative—by Mary Baker G. Eddy."

2. "Parks sprang up [*sic*] . . . electric street cars run [*sic*]
merrily through several streets, concrete sidewalks and macadamized roads dotted [*sic*] the place," et cetera. (*Ibid.*)

3. "Shorn [*sic*] of its suburbs it had indeed little left to admire, save to [*sic*] such as fancy a skeleton above ground *breathing*
[*sic*] slowly through a barren [*sic*] breast." (*Ibid.*)

This is not English—I mean, grown-up English. But it is
fifteen-year-old English, and has not grown a month since the
same mind produced the Poems. The standard of the Poems and
of the plague-spot-and-bacilli effort is exactly the same. It is most
strange that the same intellect that worded the simple and self-
contained and clean-cut paragraph beginning with "How unreasonable is the belief," should in the very same lustrum discharge
upon the world such a verbal chaos as the utterance concerning
that plague-spot or bacilli which were gnawing at the insides of
the metropolis and bringing its heart on bended knee, thus exposing to the eye the rest of the skeleton breathing slowly through a
barren breast.

The immense contrast between the legitimate English of
Science and Health and the bastard English of Mrs. Eddy's miscellaneous work, and between the maturity of the one diction and

the juvenility of the other, suggests—compels—the question, Are there *two* guns? It would seem so. Is there a poor foolish old scattering flint-lock for rabbit, and a long-range, center-driving up-to-date Mauser-magazine for elephant? It looks like it. For it is observable that in *Science and Health* (the elephant-ground), the practice was good at the start and has remained so, and that the practice in the miscellaneous outside small-game field was very bad at the start and was never less bad at any later time.

I wish to say, that of Mrs. Eddy I am not requiring perfect English, but only good English. No one can write perfect English and keep it up through a stretch of ten chapters. It has never been done. It was approached in the "well of English undefiled;" it has been approached in Mrs. Eddy's Annex to that Book, it has been approached in several English grammars, I have even approached it myself; but none of us has made port.

Now, the English of *Science and Health* is good. In passages to be found in Mrs. Eddy's autobiography (on pages 53, 57, 101 and 113) and on page 6 of her squalid preface to *Science and Health*, first revision, she seems to me to claim the whole and sole authorship of the book.

That she wrote the autobiography, and *that preface,*[1] and the Poems, and the Plague-spot-Bacilli, we are not permitted to doubt. Indeed, we know she wrote them. But the very certainty that she wrote these things compels a doubt that she wrote *Science and Health*. She is guilty of little awkwardnesses of expression in the autobiography which a practised pen would hardly allow to go uncorrected in even a hasty private letter, and could not dream of passing by uncorrected in passages intended for print. But she passes them placidly by; as placidly as if she did not suspect that they were offences against third-class English. I think that that placidity was born of that very unawareness, so to speak. I will cite a few instances from the autobiography. The italics are mine:

"I remember reading in my childhood certain manuscripts

1. See Appendix A for it.—M. T.

containing Scriptural Sonnets, besides *other* verses and enigmas,"
etc. Page 7.

On page 27: "Many pale cripples went into the Church leaning on crutches who went out carrying them on their shoulders."

It is awkward, because at the first glance it seems to say that
the cripples went in leaning on crutches which went out carrying
the cripples on their shoulders. It would have cost her no trouble
to put her "who" after her "cripples." I blame her, a little; I think
her proof-reader should have been shot. We may let her capital C
pass, but it is another awkwardness, for she is talking about a
building, not about a religious society.

"Marriage and Parentage" (Chapter-heading). Page 30.

You imagine that she is going to begin a talk about her marriage and finish with some account of her father and mother. And
so you will be deceived. "Marriage" was right, but "Parentage"
was not the best word for the rest of the record. It refers to the
birth of her own child. After a certain period of time "my babe was
born." Marriage and Motherhood—Marriage and Maternity—
Marriage and Product—Marriage and Dividend—either of these
would have fitted the facts and made the matter clear.

"Without my knowledge he was appointed a guardian."
Page 32.

She is speaking of her child. She means that a guardian *for*
her child was appointed, but that isn't what she says.

"If spiritual conclusions are separated from their premises,
the nexus is lost, and the argument, with its rightful conclusions,
becomes correspondingly obscure." Page 34.

We shall never know why she put the word "correspondingly" in there. Any fine large word would have answered just as
well: psychosuperintangibly—electroincandescently—oligarcheo-
logically—sanchrosynchrostereoptically—any of these would have
answered, any of these would have filled the void.

"His spiritual noumenon and phenomenon, silenced portraiture." Page 34.

Yet she says she forgot everything she knew, when she discovered Christian Science. I realize that noumenon is a daisy; and I will not deny that I shall use it whenever I am in a company which I think I can embarrass with it; but at the same time I think it is out of place among friends in an autobiography. There, I think a person ought not to have anything up his sleeve. It undermines confidence. But my dissatisfaction with the quoted passage is not on account of noumenon; it is on account of the misuse of the word "silenced." You cannot silence portraiture with a noumenon; if portraiture should make a noise, a way could be found to silence it, but even then it could not be done with a noumenon. Not even with a brick, some authorities think.

"It may be that the mortal life-battle still wages," etc. Page 35.

That is clumsy. Battles do not wage, battles are waged. Mrs. Eddy has one very curious and interesting peculiarity: whenever she notices that she is chortling along without saying anything, she pulls up with a sudden "God is over us all," or some other sounding irrelevancy, and for the moment it seems to light up the whole district; then, before you can recover from the shock, she goes flitting pleasantly and meaninglessly along again, and you hurry hopefully after her, thinking you are going to get something this time; but as soon as she has led you far enough away from her turkeylet she takes to a tree. Whenever she discovers that she is getting pretty disconnected, she couples-up with an ostentatious "*But*" which has nothing to do with anything that went before or is to come after, then she hitches some empties to the train—unrelated verses from the Bible, usually—and steams out of sight and leaves you wondering how she did that clever thing. For striking instances, see bottom paragraph on page 34 and the paragraph on page 35 of her autobiography. She has a purpose—a deep and dark and artful purpose—in what she is saying in the first paragraph, and you guess what it is, but that is due to your own talent, not hers; she has made it as obscure as language could do it. The other paragraph has no meaning, and no discoverable intention. It is merely one of her God-over-alls. I cannot spare room for it, in this place.[1]

"I beheld with ineffable awe our great Master's marvelous skill in demanding neither obedience to hygienic laws nor," etc. Page 41.

The word is loosely chosen—skill. She probably meant judgment, intuition, penetration, or wisdom.

"Naturally, my first jottings were but efforts to express in feeble diction Truth's ultimate." Page 43.

One understands what she means, but she should have been able to say what she meant—at any time before she discovered Christian Science and forgot everything she knew—and after it, too. If she had put "feeble" in front of "efforts" and then left out "in" and "diction," she would have scored.

". . . its written expression increases in . . . perfection under the guidance of the great Master." Page 43.

It is an error. Not even in those advantageous circumstances can increase be added to perfection.

"Evil is not mastered by evil; it can only be overcome with Good. This brings out the nothingness of evil; and the eternal Somethingness, vindicates the Divine Principle, and improves the race of Adam." Page 76.

This is too extraneous for me. That is the trouble with Mrs. Eddy when she sets out to explain an over-large exhibit; the minute you think the light is bursting upon you the candle goes out and your mind begins to wander.

"No one else can drain the cup which I have drunk to the dregs, as the discoverer and teacher of Christian Science." Page 47.

That is saying one cannot empty an empty cup. We knew it before; and we know she meant to tell us that that particular cup is going to remain empty. That is, we think that that was the idea, but we cannot be sure. She has a perfectly astonishing talent for

1. See Appendix B.—M. T.

putting words together in such a way as to make successful inquiry into their intention impossible.

She generally makes me uneasy when she begins to tune up on her fine-writing timbrel. It carries me back to her Plague-Spot and Poetry days, and I just dread those:

"Into mortal mind's material obliquity I gazed, and stood abashed. Blanched was the cheek of pride. My heart bent low before the omnipotence of Spirit, and a tint of humility, soft as the heart of a moonbeam, mantled the earth. Bethlehem and Bethany, Gethsemane and Calvary, spoke to my chastened sense as by the tearful lips of a babe." Page 48.

The heart of a moonbeam is a pretty enough Friendship's Album expression—let it pass, though I do think the figure a little strained; but humility has no tint, humility has no complexion, and if it had it it could not mantle the earth. A moonbeam might —I do not know—but she did not say it was the moonbeam. But let it go, I cannot decide it, she mixes me up so. A babe hasn't "tearful lips," it's its eyes. You find none of Mrs. Eddy's kind of English in *Science and Health*—not a line of it.

CHAPTER 3

Setting aside title-page, index, etc., the little autobiography begins on page 7 and ends on page 130. My quotations are from the first forty pages. They seem to me to prove the presence of the 'prentice hand. The style of the forty pages is loose and feeble and 'prentice-like. The movement of the narrative is not orderly and sequential, but rambles around, and skips forward and back and here and there and yonder, 'prentice-fashion. Many a journeyman has broken up his narrative and skipped about and rambled around, but he did it for a purpose, for an advantage; there was art in it, and points to be scored by it; the observant reader perceived the game, and enjoyed it and respected it, if it was well played. But Mrs. Eddy's performance was without intention, and destitute of art. She could score no points by it on those terms, and almost any reader can see that her work was the uncalculated puttering of a novice.

In the above paragraph I have described the first third of the booklet. That third being completed, Mrs. Eddy leaves the rabbit-range, crosses the frontier, and steps out upon her far-spreading big-game territory—Christian Science—and there is an instant change! The style smartly improves, and the clumsy little technical offences disappear. In those two-thirds of the booklet I find only one such offence, and it has the look of being a printer's error.

I leave the riddle with the reader. Perhaps he can explain how it is that a person—trained or untrained—who, on the one day, can write nothing better than Plague-Spot-Bacilli and feeble and stumbling and wandering personal history littered with false figures and obscurities and technical blunders, can on the next day sit down and write fluently, smoothly, compactly, capably and confidently on a great big thundering subject, and do it as easily and comfortably as a whale paddles around the globe.

As for me, I have scribbled so much in fifty years that I have become saturated with convictions of one sort and another concerning a scribbler's limitations; and these are so strong that when I am familiar with a literary person's work I feel perfectly sure that I know enough about his limitations to know what he can *not* do. If Mr. Howells should pretend to me that he wrote the Plague-Spot-Bacilli rhapsody I should receive the statement courteously but I should know it for a—well, for a perversion. If the late Josh Billings should rise up and tell me that he wrote Herbert Spencer's philosophies, I should answer and say that the spelling casts a doubt upon his claim. If the late Jonathan Edwards should rise up and tell me he wrote Mr. Dooley's books, I should answer and say that the marked difference between his style and Dooley's is argument against the soundness of his statement. You see how much I think of *circumstantial evidence*. In literary matters—in my belief—it is often better than any person's word, better than any shady character's oath. It is difficult for me to believe that the same hand that wrote the Plague-Spot-Bacilli and the first third of the little Eddy biography wrote also *Science and Health*. Indeed it is more than difficult, it is impossible.

Largely speaking, I have read acres of what purported to be Mrs. Eddy's writings, in the past two months. I cannot know, but I am convinced, that the circumstantial evidences show that her actual share in the work of composing and phrasing these things was so slight as to be inconsequential. Where she puts her literary foot down her trail across her paid polisher's page is as plain as the elephant's in a Sunday-school procession. Her verbal output, when left undoctored by her clerks, is quite unmistakeable. It always exhibits the strongly distinctive features observable in the virgin passages from her pen already quoted by me:

Desert vacancy, as regards thought.

Self-complacency.

Puerility.

Sentimentality.

Affectations of scholarly learning.

Lust after eloquent and flowery expression.

Repetition of pet poetic picturesquenesses.

Confused and wandering statement.

Metaphor gone insane.

Meaningless words, used because they are pretty, or showy, or unusual.

Sorrowful attempts at the epigrammatic.

Destitution of originality.

The fat volume called *Miscellaneous Writings of Mrs. Eddy* contains several hundred pages. Of the 554 pages of prose in it I find 10 lines on page 319 to be Mrs. Eddy's; also about a page of the Preface or "Prospectus;" also about 15 pages scattered along through the book. If she wrote any of the rest of the prose, it was re-written after her by another hand. Here I will insert two-thirds of her page of the Prospectus. It is evident that whenever, under the inspiration of the Deity, she turns out a book, she is always

allowed to do some of the Preface. I wonder why that is? It always
mars the work. I think it is done in humorous malice. I think the
clerks like to see her give herself away. They know she will, her
stock of usable materials being limited and her procedure in employing them always the same, substantially. They know that
when the initiated come upon her first erudite allusion, or upon
any one of her other stage-properties, they can shut their eyes and
tell what will follow. She usually throws off an easy remark all sodden with Greek or Hebrew or Latin learning; she usually has a
person watching for a star—she can seldom get away from that
poetic idea—sometimes it is a Chaldee, sometimes a Walking
Delegate, sometimes an entire stranger, but be he what he may, he
is generally there when the train is ready to move, and has his pass
in his hat-band; she generally has a Being with a Dome on him, or
some other cover that is unusual and out of the fashion; she likes
to fire off a Scripture-verse where it will make the handsomest
noise and come nearest to breaking the connection; she often
throws out a Forefelt, or a Foresplendor, or a Foreslander where
it will have a fine nautical foretogallant sound and make the sentence sing; after which she is nearly sure to throw discretion away
and take to her deadly passion, Intoxicated Metaphor. At such a
time the Mrs. Eddy that does not hesitate is lost:

"The ancient Greek looked longingly for the Olympiad. The
Chaldee watched the appearing of a star; to him, no higher destiny
dawned on the dome of being than that foreshadowed by signs in
the heavens. The meek Nazarene, the scoffed of all scoffers, said,
'Ye can discern the face of the sky; but can ye not discern the signs
of the times?'—for he forefelt and foresaw the ordeal of a perfect
Christianity, hated by sinners.

"To kindle all minds with a gleam of gratitude, the new idea
that comes welling up from infinite Truth needs to be understood.
The seer of this age should be a sage.

"Humility is the stepping-stone to a higher recognition of
Deity. The mounting sense gathers fresh forms and strange fire
from the ashes of dissolving self, and drops the world. Meekness

heightens immortal attributes, only by removing the dust that dims them. Goodness reveals another scene and another self seemingly rolled up in shades, but brought to light by the evolutions of advancing thought, whereby we discern the power of Truth and Love to heal the sick.

"Pride is ignorance; those assume most who have the least wisdom or experience; and they steal from their neighbor, because they have so little of their own." (*Miscellaneous Writings*, page 1, and 6 lines at top of page 2.)

It is not believable that the hand that wrote those clumsy and affected sentences wrote the smooth English of *Science and Health*.

CHAPTER 4

It is often said in print that Mrs. Eddy claims that God was the Author of *Science and Health*. Mr. Peabody states in his pamphlet that "she says not she but God was the Author." I cannot find that in her autobiography she makes this transference of the authorship, but I think that in it she definitely claims that she did her work under His inspiration—definitely for her; for as a rule she is not a very definite person, even when she seems to be trying her best to be clear and positive. Speaking of the early days when her Science was beginning to unfold itself and gather form in her mind, she says (autobiography, p. 43):

"The divine hand led me into a new world of light and Life, a fresh universe—old to God, but new to His 'little one.' "

She being His little one, as I understand it.

The divine hand led her. It seems to mean "God inspired me;" but when a person uses metaphors in place of statistics—and that is Mrs. Eddy's common fashion—one cannot always feel sure about the intention.

Page 56:

"Even the Scripture gave no direct interpretation of the Sci-

entific basis for demonstrating the spiritual Principle of healing, until our Heavenly Father saw fit, through the Key to the
Scriptures, in *Science and Health*, to unlock this 'mystery of
godliness.' "

Another baffling metaphor. If she had used plain forecastle
English, and said "God wrote the Key and I put it in my book;" or
if she had said "God furnished me the solution of the mystery and
I put it on paper;" or if she had said "God did it all," then we
should understand; but her phrase is open to any and all of those
translations, and is a Key which unlocks nothing—for us. However,
it seems to at least mean "God inspired me," if nothing more.

There was personal and intimate communion, at any rate—
we get that much out of the riddles. The connection extended to
business, after the establishment of the teaching and healing
industry:

Page 71. "When God impelled me to set a price on my instruction," etc. Further down: "God has since shown me, in multitudinous ways, the wisdom of this decision."

She was not able to think of a "financial equivalent"—meaning a pecuniary equivalent—for her "instruction in Christian Science Mind-healing." In this emergency she was "led" to charge
three hundred dollars for a term of "twelve half-days." She does
not say who led her, she only says that the amount greatly troubled
her. I think it means that the price was suggested from above,
"led" being a theological term identical with our commercial
phrase "personally conducted." She "shrank from asking it, but
was finally led, by a strange providence, to accept this fee." "Providence" is another theological term. Two leds and a providence,
taken together, make a strong argument for inspiration. I think
that these statistics make it clear that the price was arranged
above. This view is constructively supported by the fact, already
quoted, that God afterward approved, "in multitudinous ways"
her wisdom in accepting the mentioned fee. "Multitudinous ways"
—multitudinous encoring—suggests enthusiasm. Business enthusi-

asm. And it suggests nearness. God's nearness to His "little one." Nearness, and a watchful personal interest. A warm, palpitating Standard Oil interest, so to speak. All this indicates inspiration. We may assume, then, two inspirations: one for the book, the other for the business.

The evidence for inspiration is further augmented by the testimony of Rev. George Tomkins, D.D., already quoted, that Mrs. Eddy and her book were foretold in Revelation, and that Mrs. Eddy "*is* God's highest thought to this age, giving us the spiritual interpretation of the Bible in the 'little book'" of the Angel.

I am aware that it is not Mr. Tomkins that is speaking, but Mrs. Eddy. The commissioned lecturers of the C. S. Church have to be members of the Board of Lectureship. (By-Laws, Sec. 2, p. 70.) The Board of Lectureship is selected by the Board of Directors of the Church. (By-Laws, Sec. 3, p. 70.) The Board of Directors of the Church is the property of Mrs. Eddy. (By-Laws, p. 22.) Mr. Tomkins did not make that statement without authorization from headquarters. He necessarily got it from the Board of Directors, the Board of Directors from Mrs. Eddy, Mrs. Eddy from the Deity. Mr. Tomkins would have been turned down by that procession if his remarks had been unsatisfactory to it.

It may be that there is evidence somewhere—as has been claimed—that Mrs. Eddy has charged upon the Deity the verbal authorship of *Science and Health*. But if she ever made the charge, she has withdrawn it (as it seems to me), and in the most formal and unqualified of all ways. See autobiography, page 57:

"When the demand for this book increased . . . the copyright was infringed. I entered a suit at Law, and my copyright was protected."

Thus it is plain that she did not plead that the Deity was the (verbal) Author; for if she had done that, she would have lost her case—and with rude promptness. It was in the old days before the Berne Convention and before the passage of our amended law of

284   CHRISTIAN SCIENCE

1891, and the Court would have quoted the following stern clause from the existing statute and frowned her out of the place:

"No Foreigner can acquire copyright in the United States."

To sum up. The evidence before me indicates three things:

1. That Mrs. Eddy claims the verbal authorship for herself;

2. That she denies it to the Deity;

3. That—in her belief—she wrote the book under the inspiration of the Deity, but furnished the language herself.

In one place in the autobiography she claims both the language and the *ideas*; but when this witness is testifying, one must draw the line somewhere, or she will prove both sides of her case—nine sides, if desired.

It is too true. Much too true. Many, many times too true. She is a most trying witness—*the* most trying witness that ever kissed the Book, I am sure. There is no keeping up with her erratic testimony. As soon as you have got her share of the authorship nailed where you half hope and half believe it will stay and cannot be joggled loose any more, she joggles it loose again—or seems to; you cannot be sure, for her habit of dealing in meaningless metaphors instead of in plain straightforward statistics, makes it nearly always impossible to tell just what it is she is trying to say. She was definite when she claimed both the language and the ideas of the book. That seemed to settle the matter. It seemed to distribute the percentages of credit with precision between the collaborators: 92 per cent to Mrs. Eddy, who did all the work, and 8 per cent to the Deity, who furnished the inspiration—not enough of it to damage the copyright in a country closed against Foreigners, and yet plenty to advertise the book and market it at famine rates. Then Mrs. Eddy does not keep still, but fetches around and comes forward and testifies again. It is most injudicious. For she resorts to metaphor this time, and it makes trouble, for she seems to reverse the percentages and claim only the 8 per cent for herself. I quote from Mr. Peabody's book (*Eddyism, or Christian Science*; Boston: 15 Court Square, price 25 cents):

"Speaking of this book, Mrs. Eddy, in January last (1901), said, 'I should blush to write of *Science and Health, with Key to the Scriptures* as I have, were it of human origin, and I, apart from God, its author; but as I was only a scribe echoing the harmonies of Heaven in divine metaphysics, I cannot be supermodest of the Christian Science text-book.' "

Mr. Peabody's comment:

"Nothing could be plainer than that. Here is a distinct avowal that the book entitled *Science and Health* was the work of Almighty God."

It does seem to amount to that. She was only a "scribe." Confound the word, it is just a confusion, it has no determinable meaning there, it leaves us in the air. A scribe is merely a person who writes. He may be a copyist, he may be an amanuensis, he may be a writer of originals, and furnish both the language and the ideas. As usual with Mrs. Eddy, the connection affords no help— "echoing" throws no light upon "scribe." A rock can reflect an echo, a wall can do it, a mountain can do it, many things can do it, but a scribe can't. A scribe that could reflect an echo could get over thirty dollars a week in a side-show. Many impresarios would rather have him than a cow with four tails. If we allow that this present scribe was *setting down* the "harmonies of Heaven"—and certainly that seems to have been the case—then there was only one way to do it that I can think of: listen to the music and put down the notes one after another as they fell. In that case Mrs. Eddy did not invent the tune, she only entered it on paper. Therefore—dropping the metaphor—she was merely an amanuensis, and furnished neither the language of *Science and Health*, nor the ideas. It reduces her to 8 per cent (and the dividends on that and the rest).

Is that it? We shall never know. For Mrs. Eddy is liable to testify again at any time. But until she does it, I think we must conclude that the Deity was Author of the whole book, and Mrs. Eddy merely His telephone and stenographer. Granting this, her claim as the Voice of God stands—for the present—justified and established.

POSTSCRIPT

I overlooked something. It appears that there was more of that utterance than Mr. Peabody has quoted in the above paragraph. It will be found in Mrs. Eddy's organ, the *Christian Science Journal* (January, 1901), and reads as follows:

"It was not myself . . . which dictated *Science and Health, with Key to the Scriptures.*"

That is certainly clear enough. The words which I have removed from that important sentence explain Who it was that did the dictating. It was done by

"the divine power of Truth and Love, infinitely above me."

Certainly that is definite. At last, through her personal testimony, we have a sure grip upon the following vital facts, and they settle the authorship of *Science and Health* beyond peradventure:

1. Mrs. Eddy furnished "the ideas and the language."
2. God furnished the ideas and the language.

It is a great comfort to have the matter authoritatively settled.

CHAPTER 5

It is hard to locate her, she shifts about so much. She is a shining drop of quicksilver which you put your finger on and it isn't there. There is a paragraph in the autobiography (p. 96) which places in seemingly darkly-significant procession, three Personages:

1. The Virgin Mary.
2. Jesus of Nazareth.
3. Mrs. Eddy.

This is the paragraph referred to:

"No person can take the individual place of the Virgin Mary.

No person can compass or fulfill the individual mission of Jesus of Nazareth. No person can take the place of the author of *Science and Health*, the discoverer and founder of Christian Science. Each individual must fill his own niche in time and eternity."

I have read it many times, but I still cannot be sure that I rightly understand it. If the Savior's name had been placed first and the Virgin Mary's second and Mrs. Eddy's third, I should draw the inference that a descending scale from First Importance to Second Importance and then to Small Importance was indicated; but to place the Virgin first, the Savior second and Mrs. Eddy third, seems to turn the scale the other way and make it an ascending scale of Importances, with Mrs. Eddy ranking the other two and holding first place.

I think that that was perhaps the intention, but none but a seasoned Christian Scientist can examine a literary animal of Mrs. Eddy's creation and tell which end of it the tail is on. She is easily the most baffling and bewildering writer in the literary trade.

EDDY is a commonplace name, and would have an unimpressive aspect in the list of the reformed Holy Family. She has thought of that. In the book of By-Laws written by her—"impelled by a power not one's own"—there is a paragraph which explains how and when her disciples came to confer a title upon her; and this explanation is followed by a warning as to what will happen to any female Scientist who shall desecrate it:

"*The Title of Mother.* Therefore if a student of Christian Science shall apply this title, either to herself or to others, except as the term for kinship according to the flesh, it shall be regarded by the Church as an indication of disrespect for their Pastor Emeritus, and unfitness to be a member of the Mother Church."

She is the pastor emeritus.

While the quoted paragraph about the Procession seems to indicate that Mrs. Eddy is expecting to occupy the First Place in it, that expectation is not definitely avowed. In an earlier utterance of hers she is clearer—clearer, and does not claim the First

Place all to herself, but only the half of it. I quote from Mr. Peabody's book again:

"In the *Christian Science Journal* for April, 1889, when it
was her property, and published by her, it was claimed for her, and
with her sanction, that she was equal with Jesus, and elaborate
effort was made to establish the claim.

"Mrs. Eddy has distinctly *authorized* the claim in her behalf
that she herself was the chosen successor to and equal of Jesus."

In her *Miscellaneous Writings* (using her once favorite
"We" for "I") she says that "While we entertain decided views
. . . and shall express them as duty demands, we shall claim no
especial gift from our divine origin," etc.

Our divine origin. It suggests Equal again. It is inferable,
then, that in the near by and by the new Church will officially rank
the Holy Family in the following order:

1. Jesus of Nazareth.   1. Our Mother.
2. The Virgin Mary.

SUMMARY

I am not playing with Christian Science and its founder, I
am examining them; and I am doing it because of the interest I
find in the inquiry. My results may seem inadequate to the reader,
but they have (for me) clarified a muddle and brought a sort of
order out of a chaos, and so I value them. My readings of Mrs.
Eddy's uninspired miscellaneous literary efforts have convinced
me of several things:

1. That She did not write *Science and Health*;
2. That the Deity did (or did not) write it;
3. That She thinks She wrote it;
4. That She believes She wrote it under the Deity's inspiration;
5. That She believes She is a Member of the Holy Family;
6. That She believes She is the equal of the Head of it.

Finally, I think She is now entitled to the capital S—on her
own evidence.

CHAPTER 6

Thus far we have a part of Mrs. Eddy's portrait. Not made of fictions, surmises, reports, rumors, innuendoes, dropped by her enemies; no, she has furnished all of the materials herself, and laid them on the canvas, under my general superintendence and direction. As far as she has gone with it, it is the presentation of a complacent, commonplace, illiterate New England woman who "forgot everything she knew" when she discovered her discovery, then wrote a Bible in good English under the inspiration of God, and climbed up it to the supremest summit of earthly grandeur attainable by man—where she sits serene to-day, beloved and worshiped by a multitude of human beings of as good average intelligence as is possessed by those that march under the banner of any competing cult. This is not intended to flatter the competing cults, it is merely a statement of cold fact.

That a commonplace person should go climbing aloft and become a god or a half-god or a quarter-god and be worshiped by men and women of average intelligence, is nothing. It has happened a million times, it will happen a hundred million more. It has been millions of years since the first of these supernaturals appeared, and by the time the last one—in that inconceivably remote future—shall have performed his solemn little high-jinks on the stage and closed the business, there will be enough of them accumulated in the museum on the Other Side to start a heaven of their own—and jam it.

Each in his turn those little supernaturals of our bygone ages and æons joined the monster procession of his predecessors and marched horizonward, disappeared, and was forgotten. They changed nothing, they built nothing, they left nothing behind to remember them by, nothing to hold their disciples together, nothing to solidify their work and enable it to defy the assaults of time and the weather. They passed, and left a vacancy. They made one fatal mistake; they all made it, each in his turn: they failed to *organize* their forces, they failed to *centralize* their strength, they failed to provide a fresh Bible and a sure and perpetual cash income for business, and often they failed to provide a new and accepted Divine Personage to worship.

Mrs. Eddy is not of that small fry. The materials that go to the making of the rest of her portrait will prove it. She will furnish them herself:

She published her book. She copyrighted it. She copyrights everything. If she should say "Good morning, how do you do?" she would copyright it; for she is a careful person, and knows the value of small things.

She began to teach her Science, she began to heal, she began to gather converts to her new religion—fervent, sincere, devoted, grateful people. A year or two later she organized her first Christian Science "Association," with six of her disciples on the roster.

She continued to teach and heal. She was charging nothing, she says, although she was very poor. She taught and healed gratis four years altogether, she says.

Then, in 1879–81, she was become strong enough, and well enough established, to venture a couple of impressively important moves. The first of these moves was to aggrandize the "Association" to a "*Church*." Brave? It is the right name for it, I think. The former name suggested nothing, invited no remark, no criticism, no inquiry, no hostility; the new name invited them all. She must have made this intrepid venture on her own motion. She could have had no important advisers at that early day. If we accept it as her own idea and her own act—and I think we *must*—we have one key to her character. And it will explain subsequent acts of hers that would merely stun us and stupefy us without it. Shall we call it courage? Or shall we call it recklessness? Courage observes; reflects; calculates; surveys the whole situation; counts the cost, estimates the odds, makes up its mind; then goes at the enterprise resolute to win or perish. Recklessness does not reflect, it plunges fearlessly in with a hurrah, and takes the risks, whatever they may be, regardless of expense. Recklessness often fails, Mrs. Eddy has never failed—from the point of view of her followers. The point of view of other people is naturally not a matter of weighty importance to her.

The new Church was not born loose-jointed and featureless, but had a defined plan, a definite character, definite aims, and a name which was a challenge, and defied all comers. It was "a Mind-healing Church." It was *without a creed.* Its name, "The Church of Christ, Scientist."

Mrs. Eddy could not copyright her Church, but she chartered it, which was the same thing and relieved the pain. It had twenty-six charter members. Mrs. Eddy was at once installed as its pastor.

The other venture, above referred to, was Mrs. Eddy's Massachusetts Metaphysical College, in which was taught "the pathology of spiritual power." She could not copyright it, but she got it chartered. For faculty it had herself, her husband of the period (Dr. Eddy), and her adopted son, Dr. Foster-Eddy. The college term was "barely three weeks," she says. Again she was bold, brave, rash, reckless—choose for yourself—for she not only began to charge the student, but charged him *a hundred dollars a week* for the college's enlightenments. And got it? some may ask. Easily. Pupils flocked from far and near. They came by the hundred. Presently the term was cut down nearly half, but the price remained as before. To be exact, the term-cut was to 7 lessons— price, $300. The college "yielded a large income." This is believable. In seven years Mrs. Eddy taught, as she avers, over 4,000 students in it. (Preface to 1902 edition of *Science and Health.*) Three hundred times four thousand is—but perhaps you can cipher it yourself. I could do it, ordinarily, but I fell down yesterday and hurt my leg. Cipher it; you will see that it is a grand sum for a woman to earn in seven years. Yet that was not all she got out of her college in the seven.

At the time that she was charging the primary student $300 for 12 lessons she was not content with this tidy assessment, but had other ways of plundering him. By advertisement she offered

him privileges whereby he could add 18 lessons to his store for five
hundred dollars more. That is to say, he could get a total of 30
lessons in her College for $800.

Four thousand times 800 is—but it is a difficult sum for a
cripple who has not been "demonstrated over" to cipher; let it go.
She taught "over" 4,000 students in seven years. "Over" is not
definite, but it probably represents a non-paying surplus of learners over and above the paying 4,000. Charity students, doubtless.
I think that as interesting an advertisement as has been printed
since the romantic old days of the other buccaneers, is this one
from the *Christian Science Journal* for September, 1886:

"MASSACHUSETTS METAPHYSICAL COLLEGE

"REV. MARY BAKER G. EDDY, PRESIDENT

"571 Columbus Ave., Boston

"The collegiate course in Christian Science metaphysical healing
includes 12 lessons. Tuition, $300.

"Course in Metaphysical Obstetrics includes 6 daily lectures, and
is open only to students from this College. Tuition, $100.

"Class in Theology, open (like the above) to graduates, receives
6 additional lectures on the Scriptures, and summary of the principle
and practice of Christian Science, $200.

"Normal class is open to those who have taken the first course at
this College; 6 daily lectures complete the Normal Course. Tuition, $200.

"No invalids, and only persons of good moral character, are
accepted as students. All students are subject to examination and
rejection; and they are liable to leave the class if found unfit to
remain in it.

"A limited number of clergymen received free of charge.

"Largest discount to indigent students, $100 on the first course.

"No reduction on the others.

"Husband and wife, entered together, $300.

"Tuition for all strictly in advance."

There it is—the horse-leech's daughter alive again, after a three-century vacation. Fifty or sixty hours' lecturing for $800.

I was in error, as to one matter: there are no charity students. Gratis-taught clergymen must not be placed under that head; they are merely an advertisement. Pauper students can get into the infant class on a two-third rate (cash in advance), but not even an archangel can get into the rest of the game at anything short of par, cash down. For it is "in the spirit of Christ's charity, as one who is joyful to bear healing to the sick"[1] that Mrs. Eddy is working the game. She sends the healing to them outside. She cannot bear it to them inside the college, for the reason that she does not allow a sick candidate to get in. It is true that this smells of inconsistency,[2] but that is nothing; Mrs. Eddy would not be Mrs. Eddy if she should ever chance to be consistent about anything two days running.

Except in the matter of the Dollar. The Dollar, and appetite for power and notoriety. English must also be added; she is always consistent, she is always Mrs. Eddy, in her English: it is always and consistently confused and crippled and poor. She wrote the Advertisement; her literary trade-marks are there. When she says all "students" are subject to examination, she does not mean students, she means candidates for that lofty place. When she says students are "liable" to leave the class if found unfit to remain in it, she does not mean that if they find themselves unfit, or be found unfit by others, they will be likely to ask permission to leave the class, she means that if *she* finds them unfit she will be "liable" to fire them out. When she nobly offers "tuition for all strictly in advance," she does not mean "*instruction* for all in advance— payment for it later." No, that is only what she says, it is not what she means. If she had written Science and Health, the oldest man in the world would not be able to tell with certainty what any passage in it was intended to mean.

1. Mrs. Eddy's Introduction to Science and Health.—M. T.
2. "There is no disease;" "sickness is a belief only."—Science and Health, vol. II, page 173, edition of 1884.—M. T.

CHAPTER 7

Her Church was on its legs.

She was its pastor. It was prospering.

She was appointed one of a committee to draft By-Laws for its government. It may be observed without overplus of irreverence, that this was larks for her. *She did all of the drafting herself.* From the very beginning she was always in the front seat when there was business to be done; in the front seat, with both eyes open, and looking sharply out for Number One; in the front seat, working Mortal Mind with fine effectiveness and giving Immortal Mind a rest for Sunday. When her Church was reorganized, by and by, the By-Laws were retained. She saw to that. In these Laws for the government of her Church, her empire, her despotism, Mrs. Eddy's character is embalmed for good and all. I think a particularized examination of these Church-Laws will be found interesting. And not the less so if we keep in mind that they were "impelled by a power not one's own," as she says—*Anglice,* the inspiration of God.

It is a Church "without a creed." Still, it has one. Mrs. Eddy drafted it—and copyrighted it. In her own name. You cannot become a member of the Mother Church (nor of any C. S. Church) without signing it. It forms the first chapter of the By-Laws, and is called "Tenets." "Tenets of The Mother Church, The First Church of Christ, Scientist." It has no hell in it—it throws it overboard.

THE PASTOR EMERITUS

About the time of the reorganization, Mrs. Eddy retired from her position of pastor of her Church, abolished the office of pastor in all branch Churches, and appointed her *book, Science and Health,* to be *pastor-universal.* Mrs. Eddy did not disconnect herself from office entirely, when she retired, but appointed herself Pastor Emeritus. It is a misleading title, and belongs to the family of that phrase "without a creed." It advertises her as being a merely honorary official, with nothing to do, and no authority. The Czar of Russia is Emperor Emeritus on the same terms. Mrs. Eddy was Autocrat of the Church before, with limitless authority, and she kept her grip on that limitless authority when she took that fictitious title.

It is curious and interesting to note with what an unerring instinct the Pastor Emeritus has thought out and forecast all possible encroachments upon her planned autocracy, and barred the way against them, in the By-Laws which she framed and copyrighted—under the guidance of the Supreme Being.

THE BOARD OF DIRECTORS

For instance, when Article I speaks of a President and Board of Directors, you think you have discovered a formidable check upon the powers and ambitions of the honorary pastor, the ornamental pastor, the functionless pastor, the Pastor Emeritus, but it is a mistake. These great officials are of the phrase-family of the Church-Without-a-Creed and the Pastor-With-Nothing-to-Do; that is to say, of the family of Large Names Which Mean Nothing. The Board is of so little consequence that the By-Laws do not state how it is chosen, nor who does it; but they do state, most definitely, that the Board cannot fill a vacancy in its number *"except the candidate is approved by the Pastor Emeritus."*

The *"candidate."* The Board cannot even proceed to an election until the Pastor Emeritus has examined the list and squelched such candidates as are not satisfactory to her.

Whether the original first Board began as the personal property of Mrs. Eddy or not, it was foreseeable that in time, under this By-Law, she would own it. Such a first Board might chafe under such a rule as that, and try to legislate it out of existence some day. But Mrs. Eddy was awake. She foresaw that danger, and added this ingenious and effective clause:

"This By-Law can neither be amended nor annulled, except by consent of Mrs. Eddy, the Pastor Emeritus."

The Board of Directors, or Serfs, or Ciphers, elects the President.

On these clearly-worded terms: *"Subject to the approval of the Pastor Emeritus."*

Therefore *She* elects him.

A long term can invest a high official with influence and power, and make him dangerous. Mrs. Eddy reflected upon that; so she limits the President's term to *a year*. She has a capable commercial head, an organizing head, a head for government.

There is a Treasurer and a Clerk. They are elected by the Board of Directors. That is to say, *by Mrs. Eddy*.

Their terms of office expire on the first Tuesday in June of each year, *"or upon the election of their successors."* They must be watchfully obedient and satisfactory to her, or she will elect and instal their successors with a suddenness that can be unpleasant to them. It goes without saying that the Treasurer manages the Treasury to suit Mrs. Eddy, and is in fact merely Temporary Deputy Treasurer.

Apparently the Clerk has but two duties to perform: to read messages from Mrs. Eddy to First Members assembled in solemn Council, and provide lists of candidates for Church membership. The select body entitled First Members are the aristocracy of the Mother Church, the Charter Members, the Aborigines, a sort of stylish but unsalaried little college of cardinals, good for show, but not indispensable. *Nobody* is indispensable in Mrs. Eddy's empire; she sees to that.

When the Pastor Emeritus sends a letter or message to that little Sanhedrin, it is the Clerk's "imperative duty" to read it "at the place and time specified." Otherwise, the world might come to an end. These are fine large frills, and remind us of the ways of Emperors and such. Such do not use the penny post, they send a gilded and painted special messenger, and he strides into the Parliament, and business comes to a sudden and solemn and awful stop; and in the impressive hush that follows, the Chief Clerk reads the document. It is his "imperative duty." If he should neglect it, his official life would end. It is the same with this Mother Church Clerk; "if he fail to perform this important function of his office," certain majestic and unshirkable solemnities *must* follow: a special meeting "shall" be called; a member of the Church "shall" make formal complaint; then the Clerk "shall" be "removed from office." Complaint is sufficient, no trial is necessary.

There is something very sweet and juvenile and innocent and pretty about these little tinsel vanities, these grave apings of monarchical fuss and feathers and ceremony, here on our ostentatiously democratic soil. She is the same lady that we found in the autobiography, who was so naïvely vain of all that little ancestral military riff-raff that she had dug up and annexed. A person's nature never changes. What it is in childhood, it remains. Under pressure, or a change of interest, it can partially or wholly disappear from sight, and for considerable stretches of time, but nothing can ever permanently modify it, nothing can ever remove it.

BOARD OF TRUSTEES

There isn't any—now. But with power and money piling up higher and higher every day and the Church's dominion spreading daily wider and further, a time could come when the envious and the ambitious could start the idea that it would be wise and well to put a watch upon these mighty assets—a watch equipped with properly large authority. By custom, a Board of Trustees. Mrs. Eddy has foreseen that probability—for she is a woman with a long, long look ahead, the longest look ahead that ever a woman had—and she has provided for that emergency. In Art. I, Sec. 5 she has decreed that no Board of Trustees shall ever exist in the Mother Church *"except it be constituted by the Pastor Emeritus."*

The magnificence of it, the daring of it! Thus far, she is
The Massachusetts Metaphysical College;
Pastor Emeritus;
President;
Board of Directors;
Treasurer;
Clerk; and future
Board of Trustees;
and is still moving onward, ever onward. When I contemplate her
from a commercial point of view, there are no words that can
convey my admiration of her.

READERS

These are a feature of *first* importance in the church-
machinery of Christian Science. For they occupy the pulpit. They
hold the place that the preacher holds in the other Christian
Churches. They hold that place, but *they do not preach.* Two of
them are on duty at a time—a man and a woman. One reads a
passage from the Bible, the other reads the explanation of it from
Science and Health—and so they go on alternating. This consti-
tutes the service—this, with choir-music. *They utter no word of
their own.* Art. IV, Sec. 6, closes their mouths with this uncompromising gag:

*"They shall make no remarks explanatory of the Lesson-
Sermon at any time during the service."*

It seems a simple little thing. One is not startled by it at a first
reading of it; nor at the second, nor the third. One may have to
read it a dozen times before the whole magnitude of it rises before
the mind. It far and away oversizes and outclasses the best
business-idea yet invented for the safeguarding and perpetuating
of a religion. If it had been thought of and put in force eighteen
hundred and seventy years ago, there would be but one Christian
sect in the world now, instead of ten dozens of them.

There are many varieties of men in the world, consequently
there are many varieties of minds in its pulpits. This insures many

differing interpretations of important Scripture-texts, and this in turn insures the splitting up of a religion into many sects. It is what has happened; it was sure to happen.

Mrs. Eddy has noted this disastrous result of preaching, and has put up the bars. She will have no preaching in her Church. *She* has explained all essential Scriptures, and set the explanations down in her book. In her belief her underlings cannot improve upon those explanations, and in that stern sentence *"they shall make no explanatory remarks"* she has barred them for all time from trying. She will be obeyed; there is no question about that.

In arranging her government she has borrowed ideas from various sources—not poor ones, but the best in the governmental market—but this one is new, this one came out of no ordinary business-head, this one must have come out of her own, there has been no other commercial skull in a thousand centuries that was equal to it. She has borrowed freely and wisely, but I am sure that this idea is many times larger than all her borrowings bulked together. One must respect the business-brain that produced it—the splendid pluck and impudence that ventured to promulgate it, anyway.

ELECTION OF READERS

Readers are not taken at hap-hazard, any more than preachers are taken at hap-hazard for the pulpits of other sects. No, Readers are elected by the Board of Directors. *But—*

"Section 3. The Board shall inform the Pastor Emeritus of the names of *candidates* for readers before they are elected, and *if she objects to the nomination, said candidates shall not be chosen."*

Is *that* an election?—by the *Board?* Thus far I have not been able to find out what that Board of Spectres is for. It certainly has no real function, no duty which the hired girl could not perform, no office beyond the mere recording of the autocrat's decrees.

There are no dangerously long office-terms in Mrs. Eddy's

government. The Readers are elected for but a year. This insures their subserviency to their proprietor.

Readers are not allowed to copy out passages and read them from the *manuscript* in the pulpit; they must read from *Mrs. Eddy's book* itself. She is right. Slight changes could be slyly made, repeated, and in time get acceptance with congregations. Branch sects could grow out of these practices. Mrs. Eddy knows the human race, and how far to trust it. Her limit is not over a quarter of an inch. It is all that a wise person will risk.

Mrs. Eddy's inborn disposition to copyright everything, charter everything, secure the rightful and proper credit to herself for everything she does, and everything she thinks she does, and everything she thinks, and everything she thinks she thinks or has thought or intends to think, is illustrated in section 5 of Article IV, defining the duties of official Readers—in church:

"*Naming Book and Author.* The Reader of *Science and Health, with Key to the Scriptures,* before commencing to read from this book, shall *distinctly announce its full title and give the author's name.*"

Otherwise the congregation might get the habit of forgetting who (ostensibly) wrote the book.

THE ARISTOCRACY

This consists of First Members and their apostolic succession. It is a close corporation, and its membership-limit is 100. Forty will answer, but if the number fall below that, there must be an election, to fill the grand quorum.

This Sanhedrin can't *do* anything of the slightest importance, but it can *talk.* It can "discuss." That is, it can discuss "important questions relative to Church members;" evidently persons who are already Church members. This affords it amusement, and does no harm.

It can "fix the salaries of the Readers."

Twice a year it "votes on" admitting candidates. That is, candidates for Church membership. But its work is cut out for it be-forehand, by Sec. 2, Article IX:

Every recommendation for membership in the Church "shall be countersigned by a loyal student of Mrs. Eddy's, by a Director of this Church, or by a First Member."

All these three classes of beings are the personal property of Mrs. Eddy. She has absolute control of the elections.

Also it must "transact any Church business that may properly come before it."

"Properly" is a thoughtful word. No important business can come before it. The By-Laws have attended to that. No important business goes before *any* one for the final word except Mrs. Eddy. She has looked to that.

The Sanhedrin "votes on" candidates for admission to its own body. But is its vote worth any more than mine would be? No, it isn't. Section 4, of Article V—Election of First Members —makes this quite plain:

"Before being elected, the candidates for First Members *shall be approved by the Pastor Emeritus over her own signature.*"

Thus the Sanhedrin is the personal property of Mrs. Eddy. She owns it. It has no functions, no authority, no real existence. It is another Board of Shadows. Mrs. Eddy is the Sanhedrin herself.

But it is time to foot up again and "see where we are at." Thus far, Mrs. Eddy is

The Massachusetts Metaphysical College;

Pastor Emeritus;

President;

Board of Directors;

Treasurer;

Clerk;

Future Board of Trustees;

Proprietor of the Priesthood;

Dictator of the Services;

Proprietor of the Sanhedrin.

She has come far; and is still on her way.

CHURCH MEMBERSHIP

In this Article there is another exhibition of a couple of the
large features of Mrs. Eddy's remarkable make-up: her business-
talent and her knowledge of human nature.

She does not beseech and implore people to join her Church.
She knows the human race better than that. She gravely goes
through the motions of reluctantly granting admission to the applicant as a favor to him. The idea is worth untold shekels. She
does not stand at the gate of the fold with welcoming arms spread,
and receive the lost sheep with glad emotion and set up the fatted
calf and invite the neighbors and have a time. No, she looks upon
him coldly, she snubs him, she says, "Who are you? who is your
sponsor? who asked you to come here? go away, and don't come
again until you are invited."

It is calculated to strikingly impress a person accustomed to
Moody and Sankey and Sam Jones revivals; accustomed to brain-
turning appeals to the unknown and unendorsed sinner to come
forward and enter into the joy, etc.,—"just as he is;" accustomed to
seeing him do it; accustomed to seeing him pass up the aisle
through sobbing seas of welcome, and love, and congratulation,
and arrive at the mourner's bench and be received like a long-lost
government bond.

No, there is nothing of that kind in Mrs. Eddy's system. She
knows that if you wish to confer upon a human being something
which he is not sure he wants, the best way is, to make it apparently
difficult for him to get it—then he is no son of Adam if that apple
does not assume an interest in his eyes which it lacked before. In
time this interest can grow into desire. Mrs. Eddy knows that when
you cannot get a man to try—free of cost—a new and effective
remedy for a disease he is afflicted with, you can generally sell it
to him if you will put a price upon it which he cannot afford.[1]

1. I offered to cure of his passion—gratis—a victim of the drinking habit, by a
simple and (as it seemed to me) not difficult intellectual method which I had
successfully tried upon the tobacco habit. I failed to get him interested. I think my

When, in the beginning, she taught Christian Science gratis, (for good reasons), pupils were few and reluctant, and required persuasion; it was when she raised the limit to three hundred dollars for a dollar's worth that she could not find standing room for the invasion of pupils that followed.

With fine astuteness she goes through the motions of making it difficult to get membership in her Church. There is a two-fold value in this system: it gives membership a high value in the eyes of the applicant; and at the same time the requirements exacted enable Mrs. Eddy to keep him out if she has doubts about his value to her. A word further as to applications for membership:

Applications of students of the Metaphysical College must be signed by the *Board of Directors.*

That is safe. Mrs. Eddy is proprietor of that Board.

Children of twelve may be admitted if invited by "one of Mrs. Eddy's loyal students, or by a First Member, or by a Director."

These sponsors are the property of Mrs. Eddy, therefore her Church is safeguarded from the intrusion of undesirable children.

Other Students. Applicants who have not studied with Mrs. Eddy can get in only "by invitation and recommendation from students of Mrs. Eddy . . . or from members of the Mother Church."

Other paragraphs explain how two or three other varieties of applicants are to be challenged and obstructed, and tell us who is authorized to invite them, recommend them, endorse them, and all that.

The safeguards are definite, and would seem to be sufficiently strenuous—to Mr. Sam Jones, at any rate. Not for Mrs. Eddy. She adds this clincher:

"The candidates shall be elected by a majority vote of the First Members present."

---

proposition couldn't rouse him, couldn't strongly appeal to him, could not electrify him, because it offered a thing so easy to get, and which could be had for nothing. Within a month afterward a famous Drink-Cure opened, and at my suggestion he willingly went there, at once, and got himself (temporarily) cured of his habit. Because he had to pay $150. One values a thing when one can't afford it.—M. T.

That is the aristocracy, the aborigines, the Sanhedrin. It is
Mrs. Eddy's property. She is *herself* the Sanhedrin. No one can
get into the Church if she wishes to keep him out.

This veto power could some time or other have a large value
for her, therefore she was wise to reserve it.

It is likely that it is not frequently used. It is also probable
that the difficulties attendant upon getting admission to membership have been instituted more to invite than to deter, more to
enhance the value of membership and make people long for it than
to make it really difficult to get. I think so because the Mother
Church has many thousands of members more than its building
can accommodate.

'ANDSOME ENGLISH REQUIRED

Mrs. Eddy is very particular as regards one detail—curiously
so, for her, all things considered. The Church Readers must
be "good English scholars;" they must be "thorough English
scholars."

She is thus sensitive about the English of her subordinates for
cause, possibly. In her chapter defining the duties of the Clerk
there is an indication that she harbors resentful memories of an
occasion when the hazy quality of her own English made unforeseen and mortifying trouble:

"*Understanding Communications. Sec. 2.* If the Clerk of this
Church shall receive a communication from the Pastor Emeritus
which he does not fully understand, he shall inform her of this
fact before presenting it to the Church, and obtain a clear understanding of the matter,—then act in accordance therewith." She
should have waited to calm down, then, but instead she added this,
which lacks sugar: "Failing to adhere to this By-Law, the Clerk
must *resign*."

I wish I could see that communication that broke the camel's
back. It was probably the one beginning, "What plague-spot or
bacilli were gnawing at the heart of this metropolis and bringing it
on bended knee?" and I think it likely that the kindly-disposed

Clerk tried to translate it into English and lost his mind and had to go to the hospital. That By-Law was not the offspring of a forecast, an intuition, it was certainly born of a sorrowful experience. Its temper gives the fact away.

The little book of By-Laws has manifestly been tinkered by one of Mrs. Eddy's "thorough English scholars," for in the majority of cases its meanings are clear. The book is not even marred by Mrs. Eddy's peculiar specialty—lumbering clumsinesses of speech. I believe the salaried polisher has weeded them all out but one. In one place, after referring to *Science and Health*, Mrs. Eddy goes on to say "the Bible and the above-named book, with other works by the same author," etc.

It is an unfortunate sentence, for it could mislead a hasty or careless reader for a moment. Mrs. Eddy framed it—it is her very own—it bears her trade-mark. "The Bible and *Science and Health*, with other works by the same author" could have come from no literary vacuum but the one which produced the remark (in the autobiography), "I remember reading in my childhood, certain manuscripts containing Scriptural Sonnets, besides other verses and enigmas."

We know what she means, in both instances, but a low-priced Clerk would not necessarily know, and on a salary like his he could quite excusably aver that the Pastor Emeritus had commanded him to come and make proclamation that she was author of the Bible, and that she was thinking of discharging some Scriptural sonnets and other enigmas upon the congregation. It could lose him his place, but it would not be fair, if it happened before the edict about "Understanding Communications" was promulgated.

"READERS" AGAIN

The By-Law book makes a showy pretence of orderliness and system, but it is only a pretence. I will not go so far as to say it is a harum-scarum jumble, for it is not that, but I think it fair to say it is at least jumbulacious in places. For instance, Articles III and IV set forth in much detail the qualifications and duties of Readers, she then skips some thirty pages and takes up the subject again. It looks like slovenliness, but it may be only art. The belated By-Law has a sufficiently quiet look, but it has a ton of dynamite in it. *It makes all the Christian Science Church-Readers on the globe the personal chattels of Mrs. Eddy.* Whenever she chooses, she can stretch her long arm around the world's fat belly and flirt a Reader out of his pulpit, though he be tucked away in seeming safety and obscurity in a lost village in the middle of China:

"*In Any Church. Sec. 2.* The Pastor Emeritus of the Mother Church shall have the right (through a *letter* addressed to the individual and Church of which he is the reader) to remove a reader from this office in any Church of Christ, Scientist, both in America and in foreign nations; or to appoint the reader to fill any office belonging to the Christian Science denomination."

She does not have to prefer charges against him, she does not have to find him lazy, careless, incompetent, untidy, ill-mannered, unholy, dishonest, she does not have to discover a fault of any kind in him, she does not have to tell him nor his congregation why she dismisses and disgraces him and insults his meek flock, she does not have to explain to his family why she takes the bread out of their mouths and turns them out of doors homeless and ashamed in a strange land; she does not have to do anything but send a *letter* and say, "Pack!—and ask no questions!"

Has the Pope this power?—the other Pope—the one in Rome. Has he anything approaching it? Can he turn a priest out of his pulpit and strip him of his office and his livelihood just upon a whim, a caprice, and meanwhile furnishing no reasons to the parish? Not in America. And not elsewhere, we may believe.

It is odd and strange, to see intelligent and educated people among us worshiping this self-seeking and remorseless tyrant as a God. This worship is denied—by persons who are themselves worshipers of Mrs. Eddy. I feel quite sure that it is a worship which will continue during ages.

That Mrs. Eddy wrote that amazing By-Law with her own hand we have much better evidence than her word. We have her

English. It is there. It cannot be imitated. She ought never to go to the expense of copyrighting her verbal discharges. When any one tries to claim them she should call me; I can always tell them from any other literary apprentice's at a glance. It was like her to call America a "nation;" she would call a sand-bar a nation if it should fall into a sentence in which she was speaking of peoples, for she would not know how to untangle it and get it out and classify it by itself. And the closing arrangement of that By-Law is in true Eddysonian form, too. In it she reserves authority to make a Reader fill any office connected with a Science church—sexton, grave-digger, advertising-agent, Annex-polisher, leader of the choir, President, Director, Treasurer, Clerk, etc. She did not mean that. She already possessed that authority. She meant to clothe herself with power, despotic and unchallengeable, to appoint all Science Readers to their office, both at home and abroad. The phrase "or to appoint" is another miscarriage of intention; she did not mean "or," she meant "and."

That By-Law puts into Mrs. Eddy's hands *absolute command* over the most formidable force and influence existent in the Christian Science kingdom outside of herself, and it does this *unconditionally* and (by auxiliary force of Laws already quoted) *irrevocably*. Still, she is not quite satisfied. Something might happen, she doesn't know what. Therefore she drives in one more nail, to make sure, and drives it deep:

"*This By-Law can neither be amended nor annulled, except by consent of the Pastor Emeritus.*"

Let some one with a wild and delirious fancy try and see if he can imagine her furnishing that consent.

MONOPOLY OF SPIRITUAL BREAD

Very properly, the first qualification for membership in the Mother Church is belief in the doctrines of Christian Science.

But these doctrines must not be gathered from secondary sources. There is but *one* recognized source. The candidate must be a believer in the doctrines of Christian Science *"according to the platform and teaching contained in the Christian Science text-book, 'Science and Health, with Key to the Scriptures,' by Rev. Mary Baker G. Eddy."*

That is definite, and is final. There are to be no Commentaries, no labored volumes of exposition and explanation by anybody except Mrs. Eddy. Because such things could sow error, create warring opinions, split the religion into sects, and disastrously cripple its power. Mrs. Eddy will do the *whole* of the explaining, herself—has done it, in fact. She has written several books. They are to be had, (for cash in advance), they are all sacred; additions to them, improvements upon them, can never be needed and will never be permitted. They tell the candidate how to instruct himself, how to teach others, how to do all things comprised in the business—and they close the door against all would-be competitors, and monopolize the trade:

"The Bible and the above-named book [*Science and Health*], with other works by the same author," must be his *only* text-books for the commerce—he cannot forage outside.

Mrs. Eddy's words are to be the *sole* elucidators of the Bible and *Science and Health*—forever. Throughout the ages, whenever there is doubt as to the meaning of a passage in either of these books the inquirer will not dream of trying to explain it to himself; he would shudder at the thought of such temerity, such profanity; he would be haled to the Inquisition and thence to the public square and the stake if he should be caught studying into text-meanings on his own hook; he will be prudent and seek the meanings at the only permitted source, *Mrs. Eddy's commentaries.*

Value of this Strait-jacket. One must not underrate the magnificence of this long-headed idea, one must not underestimate its giant possibilities in the matter of hooping the Church solidly together and keeping it so. It squelches independent inquiry, and makes such a thing impossible, profane, criminal, it authoritatively settles every dispute that can arise. It *starts* with *finality*—a point which the Roman Church has traveled toward during fifteen or sixteen centuries, stage by stage, and has not yet reached. The matter of the Immaculate Conception of the Virgin Mary was not authoritatively settled until the days of Pius IX—yesterday, so to speak.

As already noticed, the Protestants are broken up into a long array of sects, a result of disputes about the meanings of texts, disputes made unavoidable by the absence of an infallible authority to submit doubtful passages to. A week or two ago (I am writing in the middle of January, 1903), the clergy and others hereabouts had a warm dispute in the papers over this question: Did Jesus anywhere claim to be God? It seemed an easy question, but it turned out to be a hard one. It was ably and elaborately discussed, by learned men of several denominations, but in the end it remained unsettled.

A week ago, another discussion broke out. It was over this text:

"Sell all that thou hast and distribute unto the poor."

One verdict was worded as follows:

"When Christ answered the rich young man and said for him to give to the poor all he possessed or he could not gain everlasting life, he did not mean it in the literal sense. My interpretation of His words is that we should part with what comes between us and Christ.

"There is no doubt that Jesus believed that the rich young man thought more of his wealth than he did of his soul, and, such being the case, it was his duty to give up the wealth.

"Every one of us knows that there is something we should give up for Christ. Those who are true believers and followers know what they have given up, and those who are not yet followers know down in their hearts what they must give up."

Ten clergymen of various denominations were interviewed, and nine of them agreed with that verdict. That did not settle the matter, because the tenth said the language of Jesus was so strait and definite that it explained *itself*: "Sell *all*," not a percentage.

There is a most unusual feature about that dispute: the nine

persons who decided alike, quoted not a single authority in support of their position. I do not know when I have seen trained dis-
putants do the like of that before. The nine merely furnished their
own opinions, founded upon—nothing at all. In the other dispute
("Did Jesus anywhere claim to be God?") the same kind of men—
trained and learned clergymen—backed up their arguments with
chapter and verse. On both sides. Plenty of verses. Were no rein-
forcing verses to be found in the present case? It looks that way.

The opinion of the nine seems strange to me, for it is unsupported by authority, while there was at least constructive authority
for the opposite view.

It is hair-splitting differences of opinion over disputed text-
meanings that have divided into many sects a once united Church.
One may infer from some of the names in the following list, that
some of the differences are very slight—so slight as to be not distinctly important, perhaps—yet they have moved groups to withdraw from communions to which they belonged and set up a sect
of their own. The list—accompanied by various Church-statistics
for 1902 compiled by Rev. Dr. H. K. Carroll—was published, January 8, 1903, in the New York *Christian Advocate*:

Adventists (6 bodies)
Baptists (13 bodies)
Brethren (River) (3 bodies)
Brethren (Plymouth) (4 bodies)
Catholics (8 bodies)
Catholic Apostolic
Christadelphians
Christian Connection
Christian Catholics (Dowie)
Christian Missionary Association
Christian Scientists
Church of God (Winebrennarian)
Church of the New Jerusalem
Congregationalists
Disciples of Christ

Dunkards (4 bodies)
Evangelical (2 bodies)
Friends (4 bodies)
Friends of the Temple
German Evangelical Protestant
German Evangelical Synod
Jews (2 bodies)
Latter-Day Saints (2 bodies)
Lutherans (22 bodies)
Swedish Evangelical Miss. Covenant (Waldenstromians)
Mennonites (12 bodies)
Methodists (17 bodies)
Moravians
Presbyterians (12 bodies)
Protestant Episcopal (2 bodies)
Reformed (3 bodies)
Schwenkfeldians
Social Brethren
Spiritualists
United Brethren (2 bodies)
Unitarians
Universalists
Independent congregations.
Total of sects and splits—139.

In the present month (February), Mr. E. I. Lindh, A. M., has communicated to the Boston *Transcript* a hopeful article on the solution of the problem of the "divided church." Divided is not too violent a term. Subdivided could have been permitted if he had thought of it. He came near thinking of it, for he mentions some of the subdivisions himself: "the 12 kinds of Presbyterians, the 17 kinds of Methodists, the 13 kinds of Baptists, etc." He overlooked the 12 kinds of Mennonites and the 22 kinds of Lutherans, but they are in Rev. Mr. Carroll's list. Altogether, 76 splits under 5 flags. The *Literary Digest* (February 14th), is pleased with Mr. Lindh's optimistic article, and also with the signs of the times, and perceives that "the idea of Church unity is in the air."

Now, then, is not Mrs. Eddy profoundly wise in forbidding, for all time, all explanations of her religion except such as she shall let on to be her own?

I think so. I think there can be no doubt of it. In a way, they will be her own; for, no matter which member of her clerical staff shall furnish the explanations, not a line of them will she ever allow to be printed until she shall have approved it, accepted it, copyrighted it, cabbaged it. We may depend on that with a four-ace confidence.

THE NEW INFALLIBILITY

All in proper time Mrs. Eddy's factory will take hold of that Commandment, and explain it for good and all. It may be that one member of the shift will vote that the word "all" means *all*; it may be that ten members of the shift will vote that "all" means only a percentage; but it is *Mrs. Eddy*, not the eleven, who will do the *deciding*. And if she says it is percentage, then percentage it is, forevermore—and that is what I am expecting, for she doesn't sell all herself, nor any considerable part of it, and as regards the poor she doesn't declare any dividend; but if she says "all" means all, then all it is, to the end of time, and no follower of hers will ever be allowed to reconstruct that text, or shrink it, or inflate it, or meddle with it in any way at all. Even to-day—right here in the beginning—she is the sole person who, in the matter of Christian Science exegesis, is privileged to exploit the Spiral Twist.[1] The Christian world has *two* Infallibles now.

Of equal power? For the present only. When Leo XIII passes to his rest another Infallible will ascend his throne;[2] others, and yet

---

1. That is a technicality—that phrase. I got it of an uncle of mine. He had once studied in a theological cemetery, he said, and he called the Department of Biblical Exegesis the Spiral Twist "for short." He said it was always difficult to drive a straight text through an unaccommodating cork, but that if you twisted it it would go. He had kept bar in his less poetical days.—M. T.

2. It has since happened.—M. T.

others, and still others will follow him, and be as infallible as he, and decide questions of doctrine as long as they may come up, all down the far future; but Mary Baker G. Eddy is the *only* Infallible that will ever occupy the Science throne. Many a Science Pope will succeed her, but she has closed their mouths; they will repeat and reverently praise and adore her infallibilities, but venture none themselves. In her grave she will still outrank all other Popes, be they of what Church they may. She will hold the supremest of earthly titles, The Infallible—with a capital T.

Many in the world's history have had a hunger for such nuggets and slices of power as they might reasonably hope to grab out of an empire's or a religion's assets, but Mrs. Eddy is the only person alive or dead who has ever struck for the *whole* of them. For small things she has the eye of a microscope, for large ones the eye of a telescope, and whatever she sees, she wants. Wants it all.

THE SACRED POEMS

When Mrs. Eddy's "sacred revelations" (that is the language of the By-Laws), are read in public, their authorship must be named. The By-Laws twice command this, therefore we mention it twice, to be fair.

But it is also commanded that when a member publicly quotes "from the poems of our Pastor Emeritus" the authorship shall be named. For these are sacred, too. There are kindly people who may suspect a hidden generosity in that By-Law; they may think it is there to protect the Official Reader from the suspicion of having written the poems himself. Such do not know Mrs. Eddy. She does an inordinate deal of protecting, but in no distinctly named and specified case in her history has No. 2 been the object of it. Instances have been claimed, but they have failed of proof, and even of plausibility.

"Members shall also instruct their students" to look out and advertise the authorship when they read those poems and things. Not on Mrs. Eddy's account, but "for the good of our Cause."

THE CHURCH EDIFICE

1. Mrs. Eddy gave the land. It was not of much value at the time, but it is very valuable now.

2. Her people built the Mother Church edifice on it, at a cost of $250,000.

3. Then they gave the whole property to her.

4. Then she gave it to the Board of Directors. *She* is the Board of Directors. She took it out of one pocket and put it in the other.

5. *Sec. 10 (of the deed).* "Whenever said Directors shall determine that it is inexpedient to maintain preaching, reading or speaking in said church in accordance with the terms of this deed, they are authorized and *required* to reconvey *forthwith* said lot of land with the building thereon to Mary Baker G. Eddy, her heirs and assigns forever, by a proper deed of conveyance."

She is never careless, never slip-shod, about a matter of business. Owning the property through her Board of Waxworks was safe enough, still it was sound business to set another grip on it to cover accidents, and she did it.

Her barkers (what a curious name; I wonder if it is copyrighted); her barkers persistently advertise to the public her generosity in giving away a piece of land which cost her a trifle, and a two-hundred-and-fifty-thousand-dollar church which cost her nothing; and they can hardly speak of the unselfishness of it without breaking down and crying; yet they know she gave nothing away, and never intended to. However, such is the human race. Often it does seem such a pity that Noah and his party did not miss the boat.

Some of the hostiles think that Mrs. Eddy's idea in protecting this property in the interest of her heirs, and in accumulating a great money-fortune, is, that she may leave her natural heirs well provided for when she goes. I think it is a mistake. I think she is of late years giving herself large concern about only one interest—her power and glory, and the perpetuation and worship of her Name—

with a capital N. Her Church is her pet heir, and I think it will get her wealth. It is the torch which is to light the world and the ages with her glory.

I think she once prized money for the ease and comfort it could bring, the showy vanities it could furnish, and the social promotion it could command; for we have seen that she was born into the world with little ways and instincts and aspirations and affectations that are duplicates of our own. I do not think her money-passion has ever diminished in ferocity, I do not think she has ever allowed a dollar that had no friends to get by her alive, but I think her reason for wanting it has changed. I think she wants it now to increase and establish and perpetuate her power and glory with, not to add to her comforts and luxuries, not to furnish paint and fuss and feathers for vain display. I think her ambitions have soared away above the fuss-and-feather stage. She still likes the little shows and vanities—a fact which she exposed in a public utterance two or three days ago when she was not noticing[1]—but I think she does not place a large value upon them now. She could build a mighty and far-shining brass-mounted palace if she wanted to, but she does not do it. She would have had that kind of an ambition in the early scrabbling times. She could go to England to-day and be worshiped by earls, and get a comet's attention from the million, if she cared for such things. She would have gone in the early scrabbling days for much less than an earl, and been vain of it, and glad to show off before the remains of the Scotch kin. But those things are very small to her now—next to invisible, observed through the cloud-rack from the dizzy summit where she perches in these great days. She does not want that church property for herself. It is worth but a quarter of a million—a sum she could call in from her far-spread flocks to-morrow with a lift of her hand. Not a squeeze of it, just a lift. It would come without a murmur; come gratefully, come gladly. And if her glory stood in more need of the money in Boston than it does where her flocks are propagating it, she would lift the hand, I think.

1. This is a reference to her public note of January 17th. See Appendix.—M. T.

She is still reaching for the Dollar, she will continue to reach for it; but not that she may spend it upon herself; not that she may spend it upon charities; not that she may indemnify an early deprivation and clothe herself in a blaze of North Adams gauds; not that she may have nine breeds of pie for breakfast, as only the rich New Englander can; not that she may indulge any petty material vanity or appetite that once was hers and prized and nursed, but that she may apply that Dollar to statelier uses, and place it where it may cast the metallic sheen of her glory furthest across the receding expanses of the globe.

PRAYER

A brief and good one is furnished in the book of By-Laws. The Scientist is required to pray it every day.

THE LORD'S PRAYER—AMENDED

This is not in the By-Laws, it is in the first chapter of *Science and Health*, edition of 1902. I do not find it in the edition of 1884. It is probable that it had not at that time been handed down. *Science and Health*'s (latest) rendering of its "spiritual sense" is as follows:

"Our Father-Mother God, all-harmonious, Adorable One. Thy kingdom is within us, Thou art ever-present. Enable us to know,—as in heaven, so on earth,—God is supreme. Give us grace for to-day; feed the famished affections; And infinite Love is reflected in love; And Love leadeth us not into temptation, but delivereth us from sin, disease and death. For God is now and forever all Life, Truth, and Love."[1]

If I thought my opinion was desired and would be properly revered, I should say that in my judgment that is as good a piece of carpentering as any of those eleven Commandment-experts could do with the material, after all their practice. I notice only one doubtful place. "Lead us not into temptation" seems to me

1. For the latest version, see Appendix.—M. T.

to be a very definite request, and that the new rendering turns the definite request into a definite assertion. I shall be glad to have that turned back to the old way and the marks of the Spiral Twist removed, or varnished over; then I shall be satisfied, and will do the best I can with what is left. At the same time, I do feel that the shrinkage in our spiritual assets is getting serious. First the Commandments, now the Prayer. I never expected to see these steady old reliable securities watered down to this. And this is not the whole of it. Last summer the Presbyterians extended the Calling and Election suffrage to nearly everybody entitled to salvation. They did not even stop there, but let out all the unbaptised American infants we had been accumulating for two hundred years and more. There are some that believe they would have let the Scotch ones out, too, if they could have done it. Everything is going to ruin; in no long time we shall have nothing left but the love of God.

THE NEW UNPARDONABLE SIN

"*Working Against the Cause. Sec. 2.* If a member of this Church shall work against the accomplishment *of what the Discoverer and Founder of Christian Science understands is advantageous* to the individual, to this Church and to the Cause of Christian Science"—out he goes. *Forever.*

The member may *think* that what he is doing will advance the Cause, but he is not invited to do any thinking. More than that, he is not *permitted* to do any—as he will clearly gather from this By-Law. When a person joins Mrs. Eddy's Church he must leave his thinker at home. Leave it permanently. To make sure that it will not go off some time or other when he is not watching, it will be safest for him to spike it. If he should forget himself and think just *once*, the By-Law provides that he shall be fired out—instantly—forever—no return.

"It shall be the duty of this Church immediately to call a meeting, and *drop forever the name of this member from its records.*"

My, but it breathes a towering indignation!

There are forgivable offences, but this is not one of them; there are admonitions, probations, suspensions, in several minor cases; mercy is shown the derelict, in those cases, he is gently used, and in time he can get back into the fold—even when he has repeated his offence. But let him *think*, just *once*, without getting his thinker set to Eddy time, and that is enough; his head comes off. There is no second offence, and there is no gate open to that lost sheep, ever again.

"*This rule cannot be changed, amended, or annulled, except by unanimous vote of all the First Members.*"

The same being *Mrs. Eddy.* It is naïvely sly and pretty to see her keep putting forward First Members, and Boards of This and That, and other broideries and ruffles of her raiment, as if they were independent entities, instead of a part of her clothes, and could do things all by themselves when she was outside of them.

Mrs. Eddy did not need to copyright the sentence just quoted, its English would protect it. None but she would have shoveled that comically superfluous word "all" in there.

The former Unpardonable Sin has gone out of service. We may frame the new Christian Science one thus:

"Whatsoever Member shall think, and without Our Mother's permission act upon his think, the same shall be cut off from the Church forever."

It has been said that I make many mistakes about Christian Science through being ignorant of the spiritual meanings of its terminology. I believe it is true. I have been misled all this time by that word, Member, because there was no one to tell me that its spiritual meaning was Slave.

AXE AND BLOCK

There is a By-Law which forbids Members to practise hypnotism; the penalty is excommunication.

1. If a member is found to be a mental practitioner—
2. Complaint is to be entered against him—

3. By the Pastor Emeritus, and by *none else*;

4. No member is allowed to make complaint to *her* in the matter;

5. *Upon* MRS. EDDY's *mere "complaint"— unbacked by evidence or proof, and without giving the accused a chance to be heard*—"his name shall be dropped from this Church."

Mrs. Eddy has only to *say* a member is guilty—that is all. That ends it. It is not a case of he "may" be cut off from Christian Science salvation, it is a case of he *"shall"* be. Her serfs must see to it, and say not a word.

Does the other Pope possess this prodigious and irresponsible power? Certainly not in our day.

Some may be curious to know how Mrs. Eddy *finds out* that a member is practising hypnotism, since no one is allowed to come before her throne and accuse him. She has explained this in *Christian Science History*, first and second editions, page 16:

"I possess *a spiritual sense of what the malicious mental practitioner is mentally arguing* which cannot be deceived. I can discern in the human mind thoughts, motives, and purpose; and neither mental arguments nor psychic power can affect this spiritual insight."

A marvelous woman; with a hunger for power such as has never been seen in the world before. No thing, little or big, that contains any seed or suggestion of power escapes her avaricious eye; and when once she gets that eye on it, her remorseless grip follows. There isn't a Christian Scientist who isn't ecclesiastically as much her property as if she had bought him and paid for him, and copyrighted him and got a charter. She cannot be satisfied when she has handcuffed a member, and put a leg-chain and ball on him and plugged his ears and removed his thinker, she goes on wrapping needless chains round and round him, just as a spider would. For she trusts no one, believes in no one's honesty, judges every one by herself. Although we have seen that she has absolute and irresponsible command over her spectral Boards and over every official and servant of her Church, at home and abroad, over every minute detail of her Church's government, *present and future*, and can purge her membership of guilty or suspected persons by various plausible formalities and whenever she will, she is still not content, but must set her queer mind to work and invent a way by which she can take a member—any member—by neck and crop and fling him out without anything resembling a formality at all.

She is sole accuser and sole witness, and her testimony is final and carries uncompromising and irremediable doom with it.

The Sole-Witness Court! It should make the Council of Ten and the Council of Three turn in their graves for shame, to see how little they knew about satanic concentrations of irresponsible power. Here we have one Accuser, one Witness, one Judge, one Headsman—and all four bunched together in Mrs. Eddy, the Inspired of God, His Latest Thought to His People, New Member of the Holy Family, the Equal of Jesus.

When a Member is not satisfactory to Mrs. Eddy, and yet is blameless in his life and faultless in his membership and in his Christian Science walk and conversation, shall he hold up his head and tilt his hat over one ear and imagine himself safe because of these perfections? Why, in that very moment Mrs. Eddy will cast that spiritual X-ray of hers through his dungarees and say: "I see his hypnotism working, amongst his insides—remove him to the block!"

What shall it profit him to know it isn't so? Nothing. His testimony is of no value. No one wants it, no one will ask for it. He is not present to offer it (he does not know he has been accused), and if he were there to offer it it would not be listened to.

It was out of powers approaching Mrs. Eddy's—though not equaling them—that the Inquisition and the devastations of the Interdict grew. She will transmit hers. The man born two centuries from now will think he has arrived in hell; and all in good time he will think he knows it. Vast concentrations of irresponsible power have never in any age been used mercifully, and there is nothing to suggest that the Christian Science Papacy is going to spend money on novelties.

Several Christian Scientists have asked me to refrain from prophecy. There *is* no prophecy in our day but history. But history is a trustworthy prophet. History is always repeating itself, because *conditions* are always repeating themselves. Out of duplicated conditions history always gets a duplicate product.

READING LETTERS AT MEETINGS

I wonder if there is anything a Member *can* do that will not raise Mrs. Eddy's jealousy? The By-Laws seem to hunt him from pillar to post all the time, and turn all his thoughts and acts and words into sins against the meek and lowly new deity of his worship. Apparently her jealousy never sleeps. Apparently any trifle can offend it, and but one penalty appease it—excommunication. The By-Laws might properly and reasonably be entitled Laws for the Coddling and Comforting of Our Mother's Petty Jealousies. The By-Law named at the head of this paragraph reads its transgressor out of the Church if he shall carry a letter from Mrs. Eddy to the congregation and forget to read it or fail to read the whole of it.

HONESTY REQUISITE

Dishonest members are to be admonished; if they continue in dishonest practices, excommunication follows. Considering who it is that drafted this law, there is a certain amount of humor in it.

FURTHER APPLICATIONS OF THE AXE

Here follow the titles of some more By-Laws whose infringement is punishable by excommunication:
Silence Enjoined.
Misteaching.
Departure from Tenets.

Violation of Christian Fellowship.
Moral Offences.
Illegal Adoption.
Broken By-Laws.
Violation of By-Laws. (What is the difference?)
Formulas Forbidden.
Official Advice. (Forbids Tom, Dick and Harry's clack.)
Unworthy of Membership.
Final Excommunication.
Organizing Churches.

This looks as if Mrs. Eddy had devoted a large share of her time and talent to inventing ways to get rid of her Church members. Yet in another place she seems to invite membership. Not in any urgent way, it is true, still she throws out a bait to such as like notice and distinction (in other words, the Human Race). Page 82:

"It is important that these seemingly strict conditions be complied with, as *the names of the Members of the Mother Church will be recorded in the history* of the Church and become a part thereof."

We all want to be historical.

MORE SELF-PROTECTIONS

The Hymnal. There is a Christian Science Hymnal. Entrance to it was closed in 1898. Christian Science students who make hymns nowadays may possibly get them sung in the Mother Church, *"but not unless approved by the Pastor Emeritus."* Art. XXVII, Sec. 2.

Solo Singers. Mrs. Eddy has contributed the words of three of the hymns in the Hymnal. Two of them appear in it six times, altogether, each of them being set to three original forms of musical anguish. Mrs. Eddy, always thoughtful, has promulgated a By-Law requiring the singing of one of her three hymns in the Mother Church "as often as once each month." It is a good idea. A congregation could get tired of even Mrs. Eddy's muse in the course of time, without the cordializing incentive of compulsion. We all know how wearisome the sweetest and touchingest things can become, through rep-rep-repetition, and still rep-rep-repetition, and more rep-rep-repetition—like "the sweet byanby, *in* the sweet byanby," for instance, and "Tah-rah-rah boom-de-aye;" and surely it is not likely that Mrs. Eddy's machine has turned out goods that could outwear those great heart-stirrers, without the assistance of the lash. "O'er Waiting Harpstrings of the Mind" is pretty good—quite fair to middling—the whole seven of the stanzas—but repetition would be certain to take the excitement out of it in the course of time, even if there were fourteen, and then it would sound like the multiplication table, and would cease to save. The congregation would be perfectly sure to get tired; in fact, *did* get tired—hence the compulsory By-Law. It is a measure born of experience, not foresight.

The By-Law says that "if a solo singer shall neglect or refuse to sing alone" one of those three hymns as often as once a month, and oftener if so directed by the Board of Directors—which is Mrs. Eddy—the singer's salary shall be stopped. It is circumstantial evidence that some soloists neglected this sacrament and others refused it. At least that is the charitable view to take of it. There is only one other view to take: that Mrs. Eddy did really foresee that there would be singers who would some day get tired of doing her hymns and proclaiming the authorship, unless persuaded by a By-Law, with a penalty attached. The idea could of course occur to her wise head, for she would know that a seven-stanza break might well be a calamitous strain upon a soloist, and that he might therefore avoid it if unwatched. He could not curtail it, for the whole of anything that Mrs. Eddy does is sacred, and cannot be cut.

BOARD OF EDUCATION

It consists of four members, one of whom is President of it. Its members are elected annually. *Subject to Mrs. Eddy's approval.* Art. XXX, Sec. 2.

She owns the Board—*is* the Board.

Mrs. Eddy is President of the Metaphysical College. If at any time she shall vacate that office, the Directors of the College (that is to say, Mrs. Eddy), *"shall"* elect to the vacancy the President of the Board of Education (which is merely re-electing herself).

It is another case of pastor "emeritus." She gives up the shadow of authority, but keeps a good firm hold on the substance.

PUBLIC TEACHERS

Applicants for admission to this industry must pass a thorough three-days' examination before the Board of Education "in *Science and Health*, chapter on 'Recapitulation;' the Platform of Christian Science; page 403 of *Christian Science Practice*, from line second to the second paragraph of page 405; and page 488, second and third paragraphs."

BOARD OF LECTURESHIP

The lecturers are exceedingly important servants of Mrs. Eddy, and she chooses them with great care. Each of them has an appointed territory in which to perform his duties—in the North, the South, the East, the West, in Canada, in Great Britain, and so on—and each must stick to his own territory and not forage beyond its boundaries. I think it goes without saying—from what we have seen of Mrs. Eddy—that no lecture is delivered until she has examined and approved it, and that the lecturer is not allowed to change it afterward.

The members of the Board of Lectureship are elected annually—

"Subject to the approval of Rev. Mary Baker G. Eddy."

MISSIONARIES

There are but four. They are elected—like the rest of the domestics—annually. So far as I can discover, not a single servant of the Sacred Household has a steady job except Mrs. Eddy. It is plain that she trusts no human being but herself.

THE BY-LAWS

The branch Churches are strictly forbidden to use them.

So far as I can see, they could not do it if they wanted to. The By-Laws are merely the voice of the master issuing commands to the servants. There is nothing and nobody for the servants to re-utter them to.

That useless edict is repeated in the little book, a few pages further on. There are several other repetitions of prohibitions in the book that could be spared—they only take up room for nothing.

THE CREED

It is copyrighted. I do not know why, but I suppose it is to keep adventurers from some day claiming that they invented it, and not Mrs. Eddy and that "strange Providence" that has suggested so many clever things to her.

No Change. It is forbidden to change the Creed. That is important, at any rate.

COPYRIGHT

I can understand why Mrs. Eddy copyrighted the early editions and revisions of *Science and Health,* and why she had a mania for copyrighting every scrap of every sort that came from her pen in those jejune days when to be in print probably seemed a wonderful distinction to her in her provincial obscurity, but why she should continue this delirium in these days of her godship and her far-spread fame, I cannot explain to myself. And particularly as regards *Science and Health.* She knows, now, that that Annex is going to live for many centuries; and so, what good is a fleeting forty-two-year copyright going to do it?

Now a *perpetual* copyright would be quite another matter. I would like to give her a hint. Let her strike for a perpetual copyright on that book. There is precedent for it. There is one book

in the world which bears the charmed life of perpetual copyright
(a fact not known to twenty people in the world). By a hardy perversion of privilege on the part of the law-making power the Bible
has perpetual copyright in Great Britain. There is no justification
for it in fairness, and no explanation of it except that the Church
is strong enough there to have its way, right or wrong. The recent
Revised Version enjoys perpetual copyright, too—a stronger precedent, even, than the other one.

Now, then, what is the Annex but a Revised Version itself?
Which of course it is—Lord's Prayer and all. With that pair of
formidable British precedents to proceed upon, what Congress
of ours—

But how short-sighted I am. Mrs. Eddy has thought of it long
ago. She thinks of everything. She knows she has only to keep her
copyright of 1902 alive through its first stage of twenty-eight years,
and perpetuity is assured. A Christian Science Congress will reign
in the Capitol then. She probably attaches small value to the first
edition (1875). Although it was a Revelation from on high, it was
slim, lank, incomplete, padded with bales of refuse rags, and
puffs from lassoed celebrities to fill it out, an uncreditable book,
a book easily spareable, a book not to be mentioned in the same
year with the sleek, fat, concise, compact, compressed and competent Annex of to-day, in its dainty flexible covers, gilt-edged,
rounded corners, twin screw, spiral twist, compensation balance,
Testament-counterfeit, and all that; a book just born to curl up
on the hymn-book-shelf in church and look just too sweet and
holy for anything. Yes, I see now what she was copyrighting that
child for.

C. S. PUBLISHING ASSOCIATION

It is true—in matters of business Mrs. Eddy thinks of everything. She thought of an organ, to disseminate the Truth as it was
in Mrs. Eddy. Straightway she started one—the *Christian Science
Journal*.

It is true—in matters of business Mrs. Eddy thinks of everything. As soon as she had got the *Christian Science Journal* sufficiently in debt to make its presence on the premises disagreeable to her, it occurred to her to make somebody a present of it. Which she did, along with its debts. It was in the summer of 1889. The victim selected was her Church—called, in those days, The National Christian Scientist Association.

She delivered this sorrow to those lambs as a "gift" in consideration of their "loyalty to our great cause."

Also—still thinking of everything—she told them to retain Mr. Bailey in the editorship and make Mr. Nixon publisher. We do not know what it was she had against those men; neither do we know whether she scored on Bailey or not, we only know that God protected Nixon, and for that I am sincerely glad, although I do not know Nixon and have never even seen him.

Nixon took the *Journal* and the rest of the Publishing Society's liabilities, and demonstrated over them during three years, then brought in his report:

"On assuming my duties as publisher, there was not a dollar in the treasury; but on the contrary the Society owed unpaid printing and paper bills to the amount of several hundred dollars, not to mention a contingent liability of many more hundreds"—represented by advance-subscriptions paid for the *Journal* and the "Series," the which goods Mrs. Eddy had not delivered. And couldn't, very well, perhaps, on a Metaphysical College income of but a few thousand dollars a day, or a week, or whatever it was in those magnificently flourishing times. The struggling *Journal* had swallowed up those advance-payments, but its "claim" was a severe one and they had failed to cure it. But Nixon cured it in his diligent three years, and joyously reported the news that he had cleared off all the debts and now had a fat $6,000 in the bank.

It made Mrs. Eddy's mouth water.

At the time that Mrs. Eddy had unloaded that dismal gift onto her National Association, she had followed her inveterate custom: she had tied a string to its hind leg, and kept one end of it hitched to her belt. We have seen her do that in the case of her

Boston Mosque. When she deeds property, she puts in that string-
clause. It provides that under certain conditions she can pull the
string and land the property in the cherished home of its happy
youth. In the present case she believed she had made provision
that if at any time the National C. S. Association should dissolve
itself by a formal vote, she could pull.

A year after Nixon's handsome report, she writes the Association that she has a "unique request to lay before it." It has dissolved, and she is not quite sure that the *Christian Science Journal*
has "already fallen into her hands" by that act, though it "seems"
to her to have met with that accident; so she would like to have the
matter decided by a formal vote. But whether there is a doubt or
not, "I see the wisdom," she says, "of again owning this Christian
Science waif."

I think that that is unassailable evidence that the waif was
making money, hands down.

She pulled her gift in. A few years later she donated the Publishing Society, along with its real estate, its buildings, its plant, its
publications and its money—the whole worth $22,000, and free of
debt—to—

Well, *to the Mother Church!*

That is to say, to herself. There is an account of it in the
Christian Science Journal, and of how she had already made some
other handsome gifts—to her Church—and others to—to her
Cause—besides "an almost countless number of private charities"
of cloudy amount and otherwise indefinite. This landslide of generosities overwhelmed one of her literary domestics. While he was
in that condition he tried to express what he felt:

"Let us endeavor to lift up our hearts in thankfulness to . . .
our Mother in Israel for these evidences of a generosity and self-
sacrifice that appeal to our deepest sense of gratitude, even while
surpassing our comprehension."

A year or two later, Mrs. Eddy promulgated some By-Laws
of a self-sacrificing sort which assuaged him, perhaps, and perhaps

enabled his surpassed comprehension to make a sprint and catch up. These are to be found in Article XII, entitled

THE C. S. PUBLISHING SOCIETY

This Article puts the whole publishing business into the hands of a publishing Board—special. *Mrs. Eddy appoints to its vacancies.*

The profits go semi-annually to the Treasurer of the Mother Church. *Mrs. Eddy owns the Treasurer.*

Editors and publishers of the *Christian Science Journal cannot be elected or removed without Mrs. Eddy's knowledge and consent.*

Every candidate for employment in a high capacity or a low one, on the other periodicals or in the publishing house, *must first be "accepted by Mrs. Eddy as suitable."* And "by the Board of Directors"—which is surplusage, since Mrs. Eddy owns the Board.

If at any time a weekly shall be started, *"it shall be owned by The First Church of Christ, Scientist"*—which is Mrs. Eddy.

CHAPTER 8

I think that any one who will carefully examine the By-Laws (I have placed all of the important ones before the reader), will arrive at the conclusion that of late years the master passion in Mrs. Eddy's heart is a hunger for power and glory; and that while her hunger for money still remains, she wants it now for the expansion and extension it can furnish to that power and glory, rather than for what it can do for her toward satisfying minor and meaner ambitions.

I wish to enlarge a little upon this matter. I think it is quite clear that the reason why Mrs. Eddy has concentrated in herself all powers, all distinctions, all revenues that are within the command of the Christian Science Church Universal, is that she desires and intends to devote them to the purpose just suggested—the upbuilding of her personal glory—hers, and no one else's; that, and the continuing of her name's glory after she shall have passed away. *If she has overlooked a single power, howsoever minute, I cannot discover it. If she has found one, large or small, which she has not seized and made her own, there is no record of it, no trace of it.* In her foragings and depredations she usually puts forward the Mother Church—a lay figure—and hides behind it. Whereas, she is in manifest reality the Mother Church, herself. It has an impressive array of officials, and committees, and Boards of Direction, of Education, of Lectureship, and so on—geldings, every one, shadows, spectres, apparitions, wax-figures: she is supreme over them all, she is autocrat over them all, she can abolish them when she will; blow them out as she would a candle. She is herself the Mother Church. Now there is one By-Law which says that the Mother Church

"shall be officially controlled by no other church."

That does not surprise us—we know by the rest of the By-Laws that that is a quite irrelevant remark. Yet we do vaguely and hazily wonder why she takes the trouble to say it; why she wastes the words; what her object can be—seeing that that emergency has been in so many, many ways, and so effectively and drastically barred off and made impossible. Then presently the object begins to dawn upon us. That is, it does after we have read the rest of the By-Law three or four times, wondering and admiring to see Mrs. Eddy—Mrs. Eddy—Mrs. Eddy, of all persons—throwing away power!—making a fair exchange—doing a fair thing for once—more, an almost generous thing! Then we look it through yet once more—unsatisfied, a little suspicious—and find that it is nothing but a sly, thin make-believe, and that even the very title of it is a sarcasm and embodies a falsehood—"self"-government:

"Local Self-Government. The First Church of Christ, Scientist, in Boston, Mass., shall assume no official control of other churches of this denomination; it shall be officially controlled by no other church."

It has a most pious and deceptive give-and-take air of perfect fairness, unselfishness, magnanimity—almost godliness, indeed. But it is all art.

In the By-Law, Mrs. Eddy, speaking by the mouth of her other self the Mother Church, proclaims that she will assume no official control of other Churches—branch Churches. We examine the other By-Laws, and they answer some important questions for us:

1. What *is* a branch Church? It is a body of Christian Scientists, organized in the one and only permissible way—by a member, in good standing, of the Mother Church, and who is also a pupil of one of Mrs. Eddy's accredited students. That is to say, one of her properties. *No other can do it.* There are other indispensable requisites; what are they?

2. The new Church cannot enter upon its functions until its members have individually signed, and pledged allegiance to, a *Creed furnished by Mrs. Eddy.*

3. *They are obliged to study her books, and order their lives by them.* And they must read *no outside religious works.*

4. *They must sing the hymns and pray the prayers provided by her*, and use no others in the services, except by her permission.

5. They cannot have preachers and pastors. *Her law.*

6. In their Church they must have two Readers—a man and a woman.

7. They must read the services framed and appointed by *her.*

8. *She*—not the branch Church—*appoints* those Readers.

9. *She*—not the branch Church—*dismisses* them and *fills the vacancies.*

10. She can do this *without consulting the branch Church, and without explaining.*

11. The branch Church can have a religious lecture from time to time. *By applying to Mrs. Eddy.* There is no other way.

12. But the branch Church cannot select the lecturer. *Mrs. Eddy does it.*

13. The branch Church pays his fee.

14. The harnessing of all C. S. wedding-teams, members of

the branch Church, must be done by duly authorized and conse-crated C. S. functionaries. *Her factory is the only one that makes and licenses them.*

[15. Nothing is said about christenings. It is inferable from this that a C. S. child is born a C. S. and requires no tinkering.

[16. Nothing is said about funerals. It is inferable, then, that a branch Church is privileged to do in that matter as it may choose.]

To sum up. Are *any* important Church-functions absent from the list? I cannot call any to mind. Are there any lacking ones whose exercise could make the branch in any noticeable way in-dependent of the Mother Church?—even in any trifling degree? I can think of none. If the named functions were abolished would there still be a Church left? Would there be even a shadow of a Church left? Would there be anything at all left?—even the bare *name?*

Manifestly not. There isn't a single vital and essential Church-function of any kind, that is not named in the list. And over every one of them the Mother Church has permanent and unchallengeable control, upon every one of them Mrs. Eddy has set her irremovable grip. *She holds, in perpetuity, autocratic and indisputable sovereignty and control over every branch Church in the earth;* and yet says, in that sugary, naïve, angel-beguiling way of hers, that the Mother Church

"shall assume no official control of other churches of this denomination."

Whereas in truth the unmeddled-with liberties of a branch Christian Science Church are but very, very few in number, and are these:

1. It can appoint its own furnace-stoker, winters.

2. It can appoint its own fan-distributors, summers.

3. It can, in accordance with its own choice in the matter, burn, bury or preserve members who are pretending to be dead—whereas there is no such thing as death.

4. It can take up a collection.

The branch Churches have *no* important liberties, none that give them an important voice in their own affairs. Those are all locked up, and Mrs. Eddy has the key. "Local Self-Government" is a large name and sounds well; but the branch Churches have no more of it than have the privates in the King of Dahomey's army.

"MOTHER CHURCH UNIQUE"

Mrs. Eddy, with an envious and admiring eye upon the solitary and rivalless and world-shadowing majesty of St. Peter's, reveals in her By-Laws her purpose to set the Mother Church apart by itself in a stately seclusion and make it duplicate that lone sublimity under the Western sky. The By-Law headed "Mother Church Unique" says—

"In its relation to other Christian Science churches, the Mother Church stands alone.

"It occupies a position that no other church can fill;

"Then for a branch church to assume such position would be disastrous to Christian Science.

"Therefore—"

Therefore no branch Church is allowed to have branches. There shall be no Christian Science St. Peter's in the earth but just the one—the Mother Church in Boston.

"NO FIRST MEMBERS"

But for the thoughtful By-Law thus entitled, every Science branch in the earth would imitate the Mother Church and set up an aristocracy. Every little group of ground-floor Smiths and Fergusons and Shadwells and Simpsons that organized a branch would assume that great title, of "First Members," along with its vast privileges of "discussing" the weather and casting blank ballots, and soon there would be such a locust-plague of them burdening the globe that the title would lose its value and have to be abolished.

But where business and glory are concerned, Mrs. Eddy thinks of everything, and so she did not fail to take care of her

Aborigines, her stately and exclusive One Hundred, her college of functionless cardinals, her Sanhedrin of Privileged Talkers (Limited). After taking away *all* the liberties of the branch Churches, and in the same breath disclaiming all official control over their affairs, she smites them on the mouth with this—the very mouth that was watering for those nobby ground-floor honors—

"*No First Members*. Branch churches shall not organize with First Members, that special method of organization being adapted to the Mother Church alone."

And so, first members being prohibited, we pierce through the cloud of Mrs. Eddy's English and perceive that they must then necessarily organize with Subsequent Members. There is no other way. It will occur to them by and by to found an aristocracy of Early Subsequent Members. There is no By-Law against it.

"THE"

I uncover to that imperial word. And to the mind, too, that conceived the idea of seizing and monopolizing it as a title. I believe it is Mrs. Eddy's dazzlingest invention. For show, and style, and grandeur, and thunder and lightning and fireworks it outclasses all the previous inventions of man, and raises the limit on the Pope. He can never put his avid hand on that word of words— it is preëmpted. And copyrighted, of course. It lifts the Mother Church away up in the sky, and fellowships it with the rare and select and exclusive little company of the THE's of deathless glory —persons and things whereof history and the ages could furnish only single examples, not two: *the* Savior, *the* Virgin, *the* Milky Way, *the* Bible, *the* Earth, *the* Equator, *the* Devil, *the* Missing Link—and now *The* First Church, Scientist. And by clamor of edict and By-Law Mrs. Eddy gives personal notice to all branch Scientist Churches on this planet to leave that THE alone.

She has demonstrated over it and made it sacred to the Mother Church:

"*The article 'The' must not be used before the titles of branch churches—*

"Nor written on applications for membership in naming such churches."

Those are the terms. There can and will be a million First Churches of Christ, Scientist, scattered over the world, in a million towns and villages and hamlets and cities, and each may call itself (suppressing the article), "First Church of Christ, Scientist"—it is permissible, and no harm; but there is only one *The* Church of Christ, Scientist, and there will never be another. And whether that great word fall in the middle of a sentence or at the beginning of it, it must always have its capital T.

I do not suppose that a juvenile passion for fussy little worldly shows and vanities can furnish a match to this, anywhere in the history of the nursery. Mrs. Eddy does seem to be a shade fonder of little special distinctions and pomps than is usual with human beings.

She instituted that immodest "The" with her own hand; she did not wait for somebody else to think of it.

A LIFE-TERM MONOPOLY

There is but *one* human Pastor in the whole Christian Science world; she reserves that exalted place to herself.

A PERPETUAL ONE

There is but *one other* object in the whole Christian Science world honored with that title and holding that office: it is her book, the Annex—*permanent Pastor of The First Church and of all branch Churches.*

With her own hand she drafted the By-Laws which make her the only really absolute sovereign that lives to-day in Christendom.[1]

---

1. Even that ideal representative of irresponsible power, the General of the Jesuits, is not in the running, with Mrs. Eddy. He is authentically described as follows:

"The Society of Jesus has really but one head, the General. He must be a professed Jesuit of the four vows, and it is the professed Jesuits of the four vows only who take part in his election, which is by secret ballot. He has four 'assistants' to

She does not allow any objectionable pictures to be exhibited in the room where her book is sold, nor any indulgence in idle gossip there; and from the general look of that By-Law I judge that a lightsome and improper person can be as uncomfortable in that place as he could be in heaven.

THE SANCTUM SANCTORUM AND SACRED CHAIR

In a room in The First Church of Christ, Scientist, there is a museum of objects which have attained to holiness through contact with Mrs. Eddy—among them an electrically-lighted oil picture of a *chair* which she used to sit in—and disciples from all about the world go softly in there, in restricted groups, under proper guard, and reverently gaze upon those relics. It is worship. Mrs. Eddy could stop it if she was not fond of it, for her sovereignty over that temple is supreme.

The fitting up of that place as a shrine is not an accident, not a casual unweighed idea; it is imitated from age-old religious custom. In Treves the pilgrim reverently gazes upon the Seamless Robe, and humbly worships; and does the same in that other continental church where they keep a duplicate; and does likewise in the Church of the Holy Sepulchre, in Jerusalem, where memorials of the Crucifixion are preserved; and now, by good fortune we have our Holy Chair and things, and a market for our adorations nearer home.

But is there not a detail that is new, fresh, original? Yes, whatever old thing Mrs. Eddy touches gets something new by the contact—something not thought of before by any one—something original, all her own, and copyrightable. The new feature is *self-worship*—exhibited in permitting this shrine to be installed during her lifetime, and winking her sacred eye at it.

A prominent Christian Scientist has assured me that the Scientists do not worship Mrs. Eddy, and I think it likely that

---

help him, and an 'admonisher,' elected in the same way as himself, to keep him in, or, if need be, to bring him back to the right path. The electors of the General have the right of *deposing* him if he is guilty of a serious fault."

there really may be five or six of the cult in the world who do not worship her; but she herself is certainly not of that company. Any healthy-minded person who will examine Mrs. Eddy's little autobiography and the Manual of By-Laws written by her will be convinced that she worships herself; and that she brings to this service a fervor of devotion surpassing even that which she formerly laid at the feet of the Dollar, and equaling that which rises to the Throne of Grace from any quarter.

I think this is as good a place as any to salve a hurt which I was the means of inflicting upon a Christian Scientist lately. The first third of this book was written in 1899 in Vienna. Until last summer I had supposed that that third had been printed in a book which I published about a year later—a hap which had not happened. I then sent the chapters composing it to the *North American Review*, but failed, in one instance, to date them. And so, in an undated chapter I said a lady told me "last night" so and so. There was nothing to indicate to the reader that that "last night" was several years old, therefore the phrase seemed to refer to a night of very recent date. What the lady had told me was, that in a part of the Mother Church in Boston she had seen Scientists worshiping a portrait of Mrs. Eddy before which a light was kept constantly burning.

A Scientist came to me and wished me to retract that "untruth." He said there was no such portrait, and that if I wanted to be sure of it I could go to Boston and see for myself. I explained that my "last night" meant a good while ago; that I did not doubt his assertion that there was no such portrait there now, but that I should continue to believe it had been there at the time of the lady's visit until she should retract her statement herself. I was at no time vouching for the truth of the remark, nevertheless I considered it worth par.

And yet I am sorry the lady told me, since a wound which brings me no happiness has resulted. I am most willing to apply such salve as I can. The best way to set the matter right and make everything pleasant and agreeable all around will be to print in this place a description of the shrine as it appeared to a recent visitor, Mr. Frederick W. Peabody, of Boston. I will copy his newspaper account, and the reader will see that Mrs. Eddy's portrait is not there now:

"We lately stood at the threshold of the Holy of Holies of the Mother Church, and with a crowd of worshipers patiently waited for admittance to the hallowed precincts of the 'Mother's Room.' Over the doorway was a sign informing us that but four persons at a time would be admitted; that they would be permitted to remain but five minutes only, and would please retire from the 'Mother's Room' at the ringing of the bell. Entering with three of the faithful, we looked with profane eyes upon the consecrated furnishings. A show-woman in attendance monotonously announced the character of the different appointments. Set in a recess of the wall and illumined with electric light was an oil painting the show-woman seriously declared to be a lifelike and realistic picture of the Chair in which the Mother sat when she composed her 'inspired' work. It was a picture of an old-fashioned, country, hair-cloth rocking-chair, and an exceedingly commonplace-looking table with a pile of manuscript, an ink-bottle and pen conspicuously upon it. On the floor were sheets of manuscript. 'The mantelpiece is of pure onyx,' continued the show-woman, 'and the beehive upon the window sill is made from one solid block of onyx; the rug is made of a hundred breasts of eider-down ducks, and the toilet room you see in the corner is of the latest design, with gold-plated drainpipes; the painted windows are from the Mother's poem, *Christ and Christmas,* and that case contains complete copies of all the Mother's books.' The chairs upon which the sacred person of the Mother had reposed were protected from sacrilegious touch by a broad band of satin ribbon. My companions expressed their admiration in subdued and reverent tones, and at the tinkling of the bell we reverently tip-toed out of the room to admit another delegation of the patient waiters at the door."

Now then, I hope the wound is healed. I am willing to relinquish the portrait, and compromise on the Chair. At the same time, if I were going to worship either, I should not choose the Chair.

As a picturesquely and persistently interesting personage, there is no mate to Mrs. Eddy, the accepted Equal of the Savior. But some of her tastes are so different from His! I find it quite impossible to imagine Him, in life, standing sponsor for that museum there, and taking pleasure in its sumptuous shows. I believe He would put that Chair in the fire, and the bell along with it; and I think He would make the show-woman go away. I think He would break those electric bulbs, and the "mantelpiece of pure onyx," and say reproachful things about the golden drain-pipes of the lavatory, and give the costly rug of duck-breasts to the poor, and sever the satin ribbon and invite the weary to rest and ease their aches in the consecrated chairs. What He would do with the painted windows we can better conjecture when we come presently to examine their peculiarities.

THE C. S. PASTOR-UNIVERSAL

When Mrs. Eddy turned the pastors out of all the C. S. churches and abolished the office for all time—as far as human occupancy is concerned—she appointed the Holy Ghost to fill their place. If this language be blasphemous, I did not invent the blasphemy, I am merely stating a fact. I will quote from page 227 of *Science and Health* (ed. 1899), as a first step toward an explanation of this startling matter—a passage which sets forth and classifies the Christian Science Trinity:

"Life, Truth, and Love constitute the triune God, or triply divine Principle. They represent a trinity in unity, three in one, —the same in essence, though multiform in office: God the Father; Christ the type of Sonship; Divine Science, or the Holy Comforter. . . .

"The *Holy Ghost*, or Spirit, *reveals* this triune Principle, and [*the Holy Ghost*] is expressed in *Divine Science*, which is *the Comforter*, leading into all Truth, and revealing the divine Principle of the universe,—universal and perpetual harmony."

I will cite another passage. Speaking of Jesus—

"His students then *received the Holy Ghost.* By this is meant, that by all they had witnessed and suffered they were roused to an enlarged *understanding of Divine Science,* even to the *spiritual interpretation . . . of his teachings,*" etc.

Also, page 579, in the chapter called the Glossary:

"HOLY GHOST. *Divine Science;* the developments of eternal Life, Truth, and Love."

The Holy Ghost *reveals* the massed spirit of the fused trinity; this massed spirit is *expressed* in Divine Science, and is the *Comforter;* Divine Science *conveys* to men the "*spiritual interpretation*" of the Savior's teachings. That seems to be the meaning of the quoted passages.

Divine Science is Christian Science; the book *Science and Health* is a "*revelation*" of the whole spirit of the Trinity, and is therefore "*The Holy Ghost;*" it conveys to men the "*spiritual interpretation*" of the Bible's teachings, and therefore is "the Comforter."

I do not find this analyzing-work easy, I would rather saw wood; and a person can never tell whether he has added up a *Science and Health* sum right or not, anyway, after all his trouble. Neither can he easily find out whether the texts are still on the market or have been discarded from the Book; for 258 editions of it have been issued, and no two editions seem to be alike. The annual changes—in technical terminology; in matter and wording; in transpositions of chapters and verses; in leaving out old chapters and verses and putting in new ones—seem to be next to innumerable, and as there is no index, there is no way to find a thing one wants without reading the book through. If ever I inspire a Bible-Annex I will not rush at it in a half-digested helter-skelter way and have to put in thirty-eight years trying to get some of it the way I want it, I will sit down and think it out and know what it is I want to say before I begin. An inspirer cannot inspire for Mrs. Eddy and keep his reputation. I have never seen such slipshod work, bar the ten that interpreted for the home market the "sell all thou hast."

I have quoted one "spiritual" rendering of the Lord's Prayer, I have seen one other one, and am told there are five more.[1] Yet the inspirer of Mrs. Eddy the new Infallible casts a complacent critical stone at the other Infallible for being unable to make up its mind about such things. *Science and Health,* ed. 1899, p. 33:

"The decisions, by vote of Church Councils, as to what should and should not be considered Holy Writ, the manifest mistakes in the ancient versions; the thirty thousand different readings in the Old Testament and the three hundred thousand in the New—these facts show how a mortal and material sense stole into the divine record, darkening, to some extent, the inspired pages with its own hue."

To some extent, yes—speaking cautiously. But it is nothing, really nothing; Mrs. Eddy is only a little way behind, and if her inspirer lives to get her Annex to suit him that Catholic record will have to "go 'way back and set down," as the ballad says. Listen to the boastful song of Mrs. Eddy's organ, the *Christian Science Journal* for March, 1902, about that year's revamping and half-soling of *Science and Health,* whose official name is the Holy Ghost, the Comforter, and who is now the Official Pastor and Infallible and Unerring Guide of every Christian Science church in the two hemispheres; hear Simple Simon that met the pieman brag of the Infallible's fallibility:

"Throughout the entire book the verbal changes are so numerous as to indicate the vast amount of time and labor Mrs. Eddy has devoted to this revision. The time and labor thus bestowed is relatively as great as that of the committee who revised the Bible. ... Thus we have additional evidence of the herculean efforts our beloved Leader has made and is constantly making for the promulgation of Truth and the furtherance of her divinely bestowed mission," etc.

It is a steady job. I could help inspire if desired, I am not doing much now, and would work for half price, and should not object to the country.

1. See a second rendering in Appendix. (Lord's Prayer.)—M. T.

PRICE OF THE PASTOR-UNIVERSAL

The price of the Pastor-Universal, *Science and Health*, called in Science literature the Comforter—and by that other sacred Name—is three dollars in cloth, as heretofore, six when it is finely bound, and shaped to imitate the Testament, and is broken into verses. Margin of profit above cost of manufacture, from 500 to 700 per cent, as already noted. In the profane subscription-trade, it costs the publisher heavily to canvass a three-dollar book; he must pay the general agent *sixty per cent* commission—that is to say, $1.80. Mrs. Eddy escapes this blistering tax, because she owns the C. S. canvasser, and can compel him to work for nothing. Read the following *command*—not request—fulminated by Mrs. Eddy, over her signature, in the *Christian Science Journal* for March, 1897, and quoted by Mr. Peabody in his book. The book referred to is *Science and Health*:

"It shall be the duty of all Christian Scientists to circulate and to sell as many of these books as they can."

That is flung at all the elect, everywhere that the sun shines, but no penalty is shaken over their heads to scare them. The same command was issued to the members (numbering to-day 25,000) of the Mother Church, also, but with it went a *threat*, of the infliction, in case of disobedience, of the most dreaded punishment that has a place in the Church's list of penalties for transgressions of Mrs. Eddy's edicts—excommunication:

"If a member of The First Church of Christ, Scientist, shall fail to obey this injunction, it will render him liable to lose his membership in this Church. MARY BAKER EDDY."

It is the spirit of the Spanish Inquisition.

None but accepted and well established *gods* can venture an affront like that and do it with confidence. But the human race will take anything from that class. Mrs. Eddy knows the human race; knows it better than any mere human being has known it in a thousand centuries. My confidence in her human-beingship is getting shaken, my confidence in her godship is stiffening.

SEVEN HUNDRED PER CENT

A Scientist out West has visited a book-seller—with intent to find fault with me—and has brought away the information that the price at which Mrs. Eddy sells *Science and Health* is not an unusually high one for the size and make of the book. That is true. But in the book-trade—that profit-devourer unknown to Mrs. Eddy's book—a three-dollar book that is made for 35 or 40 cents in large editions is put at three dollars because the publisher has to pay author, middle-man and advertising, and if the price were much below three the profit accruing would not pay him fairly for his time and labor. At the same time if he could get ten dollars for the book he would take it, and his morals would not fall under criticism.

But if he were an inspired person commissioned by the Deity to receive and print and spread broadcast among sorrowing and suffering and poor men a precious message of healing and cheer and salvation, he would have to do as Bible Societies do—sell the book at a pinched margin above cost to such as could pay, and give it free to all that couldn't; and his name would be praised. But if he sold it at 700 per cent profit and put the money in his pocket, his name would be mocked and derided. Just as Mrs. Eddy's is. And most justifiably, as it seems to me.

The complete Bible contains 1,000,000 words. The New Testament by itself contains 240,000 words.

My '84 edition of *Science and Health* contains 120,000 words —just half as many as the New Testament.

Science and Health has since been so inflated by later inspirations that the 1902 edition contains 180,000 words—not counting the 30,000 at the back, devoted by Mrs. Eddy to advertising the book's healing-abilities—and the inspiring continues right along.

If you have a book whose market is so sure and so great that you can give a printer an everlasting order for thirty or forty or fifty thousand copies a year he will furnish them at a cheap rate, because whenever there is a slack time in his press-room and bind-ery he can fill the idle intervals on your book and be making some-thing instead of losing. That is the kind of contract that can be let on *Science and Health* every year. I am obliged to doubt that the three-dollar *Science and Health* costs Mrs. Eddy above 15 cents, or that the six-dollar copy costs her above 80 cents. I feel quite sure that the average profit to her on these books, above cost of manu-facture, is all of 700 per cent.

Every proper Christian Scientist has to buy and own (and canvass for) *Science and Health* (180,000 words), and he must also own a Bible (1,000,000 words). He can buy the one for from $3 to $6, and the other for 15 cents. Or, if $3 is all the money he has, he can get his Bible for *nothing*. When the Supreme Being disseminates a saving Message through uninspired agents—the New Testament, for instance—it can be done for 5 cents a copy; but when He sends one containing only two-thirds as many words through the shop of a Divine Personage it costs *sixty times as much*. I think that in matters of such importance it is bad economy to employ a wildcat agency.

Here are some figures which are perfectly authentic, and which seem to justify my opinion:

"These [Bible] societies, inspired only by a sense of religious duty, are issuing the Bible at a price so small that they have made it *the cheapest book printed*. For example, the American Bible Society offers an edition of *the whole Bible as low as 15 cents* and the *New Testament at 5 cents*, and the British Society at *sixpence and one penny, respectively*. These low prices, made possible by their policy of selling the books *at cost or below cost*," etc.—New York *Sun*, February 25, 1903.

CHAPTER 9

We may now make a final footing-up of Mrs. Eddy, and see what she is, in the fulness of her powers. She is

The Massachusetts Metaphysical College;

Pastor Emeritus;

President;

Board of Directors;

Board of Education;

Board of Lectureships;

Future Board of Trustees;

Proprietor of the Publishing House and Periodicals;

Treasurer;

Clerk;

Proprietor of the Teachers;

Proprietor of the Lecturers;

Proprietor of the Missionaries;

Proprietor of the Readers; Dictator of the Services: sole Voice of the Pulpit;

Proprietor of the Sanhedrin;

Sole Proprietor of the Creed. (Copyrighted.)

Indisputable Autocrat of the Branch Churches, with their life and death in her hands;

Sole Thinker for The First Church (and the others?);

Sole and Infallible Expounder of Doctrine, in life and in death;

Sole permissible Discoverer, Denouncer, Judge and Executioner of Ostensible Hypnotists;

Fifty-handed God of Excommunication—with a thunderbolt in every hand;

Appointer and Installer of the Pastor of all the Churches—the Perpetual Pastor-Universal, *Science and Health*, "the Comforter."

CHAPTER 10

There she stands—painted by herself. No witness but herself has been allowed to testify. She stands there painted by her *acts*, and decorated by her words. When she talks, she has only a decorative value as a witness, either for or against herself, for she deals mainly in unsupported assertion; and in the rare cases where she puts forward a verifiable fact, she gets out of it a meaning which it refuses to furnish to anybody else. Also, when she talks, she is unstable; she wanders, she is incurably inconsistent; what she says to-day, she contradicts to-morrow.

But her *acts* are consistent. They are always faithful to her, they never misinterpret her, they are a mirror which always reflects her exactly, precisely, minutely, unerringly, and always the same, to date, with only those progressive little natural changes in stature, dress, complexion, mood and carriage that mark—exteriorly—the march of the years and record the accumulations of experience, while—interiorly—through all this steady drift of evolution the one essential detail, the commanding detail, the master-detail of the make-up, remains as it was in the beginning, suffers no change and *can* suffer none: the *basis* of the character; the temperament, the disposition, that indestructible iron framework upon which the character is *built*, and whose shape it must take, and keep, throughout life. We call it a person's *nature*.

The man who is born stingy can be taught to give liberally—with his hands; but not with his heart. The man born kind and compassionate can have that disposition crushed down out of sight by embittering experience, but if it were an organ the post mortem would find it still in his corpse. The man born ambitious of power and glory may live long without finding it out, but when the opportunity comes he will know, will strike for the largest thing within the limit of his chances at the time—constable, perhaps—and will be glad and proud when he gets it, and will write home about it. But he will not stop with that start; his appetite will come again; and by and by again, and yet again; and when he has climbed to police commissioner it will at last begin to dawn upon him that what his Napoleon soul wants and was born for, is something away higher up—he does not quite know what, but Circumstance and

Opportunity will indicate the direction and he will cut a road through and find out.

I think Mrs. Eddy was born with a far-seeing business-eye, but did not know it; and with a great organizing and executive talent, and did not know it; and with a large appetite for power and distinction, and did not know it. I think the reason that her make did not show up until middle life was, that she had General Grant's luck—Circumstance and Opportunity did not come her way when she was younger. The qualities that were born in her had to wait for circumstance and opportunity—but they were there; they were there to stay, whether they ever got a chance to fructify or not. If they had come early, they would have found her ready and competent. And they—not she—would have determined what they would set her at and what they would make of her. If they had elected to commission her as second-assistant cook in a bankrupt boarding house, I know the rest of it—I know what would have happened. She would have owned the boarding house within six months; she would have had the late proprietor on salary and humping himself, as the worldly say; she would have had that boarding house spewing money like a mint; she would have worked the servants and the late landlord up to the limit, she would have squeezed the boarders till they wailed, and by some mysterious quality born in her she would have kept the affections of certain of the lot whose love and esteem she valued, and flung the others down the back area; in two years she would own all the boarding houses in the town, in five all the boarding houses in the State, in twenty all the hotels in America, in forty all the hotels on the planet, and would sit at home with her finger on a button and govern the whole combination as easily as a bench-manager governs a dog-show.

It would be a grand thing to see, and I feel a kind of disappointment—but never mind, a religion is better and larger; and there is more *to* it. And I have not been steeping myself in Christian Science all these weeks without finding out that the one sensible thing to do with a disappointment is to put it out of your mind and think of something cheerfuler.

We outsiders cannot conceive of Mrs. Eddy's Christian Science Religion as being a sudden and miraculous birth, but only as a growth from a seed planted by circumstances, and developed stage by stage by command and compulsion of the same force. What the stages were we cannot know, but are privileged to guess. She may have gotten the mental-healing idea from Quimby—it had been experimented with for ages, and was no one's special property. [For the present, for convenience' sake, let us proceed upon the hypothesis that that was *all* she got of him, and that she put up the rest of the assets herself. This will strain us, but let us try it.] In each and all its forms, and under all its many names, mental-healing had had limits, always, and they were rather narrow ones—Mrs. Eddy, let us imagine, removed the fence, abolished the frontiers. Not by expanding mental-healing, but by absorbing its small bulk into the vaster bulk of Christian Science—Divine Science, The Holy Ghost, the Comforter—which was a quite different and sublimer force, and one which had long lain dormant and unemployed.

The Christian Scientist believes that the Spirit of God (life and love) pervades the universe like an atmosphere; that whoso will study *Science and Health* can get from it the secret of how to inhale that transforming air; that to breathe it is to be made new; that from the new man all sorrow, all care, all miseries of the mind vanish away, for that only peace, contentment and measureless joy can live in that divine fluid; that it purifies the body from disease, which is a vicious creation of the gross human mind, and cannot continue to exist in the presence of the Immortal Mind, the renewing Spirit of God.

The Scientist finds this reasonable, natural, and not harder to believe than that the disease-germ, a creature of darkness, perishes when exposed to the light of the great sun—a new revelation of profane science which no one doubts. He reminds us that the actinic ray, shining upon lupus, cures it—a horrible disease which was incurable fifteen years ago, and had been incurable for ten million years before; that this wonder, unbelievable by the physicians at first, is believed by them now; and so he is tranquilly confident that the time is coming when the world will be educated up to a point where it will comprehend and grant that the light of the Spirit of God, shining unobstructed upon the soul, is an actinic ray which can purge both mind and body from disease and set them free and make them whole.

It is apparent, then, that in Christian Science it is not one man's mind acting upon another man's mind that heals; that it is solely the Spirit of God that heals; that the healer's mind performs no office but to convey that force to the patient; that it is merely the wire which carries the electric fluid, so to speak, and delivers the message. Therefore, if these things be true, mental-healing and Science-healing are separate and distinct processes, and no kinship exists between them.

To heal the body of its ills and pains is a mighty benefaction, but in our day our physicians and surgeons work a thousand miracles—prodigies which would have ranked as miracles fifty years ago—and they have so greatly extended their dominion over disease that we feel so well protected that we are able to look with a good deal of composure, and absence of hysterics, upon the claims of new competitors in that field.

But there is a mightier benefaction than the healing of the body, and that is the healing of the spirit—which is Christian Science's other claim. So far as I know, so far as I can find out, it makes it good. Personally I have not known a Scientist who did not seem to be serene, contented, unharassed. I have not found an outsider whose observation of Scientists furnished him a view that differed from my own. Buoyant spirits, comfort of mind, freedom from care—these happinesses we all have, at intervals; but in the spaces between, dear me, the black hours! They have put a curse upon the life of every human being I have ever known, young or old. I concede not a single exception. Unless it might be those Scientists just referred to. They may have been playing a part with me; I hope they were not, and I believe they were not.

Time will test the Science's claim. If time shall make it good; if time shall prove that the Science can heal the persecuted spirit of man and banish its troubles and keep it serene and sunny and content—why, then Mrs. Eddy will have a monument that will reach above the clouds. For if she did not hit upon that imperial idea and evolve it and deliver it, its discoverer can never be identified with certainty, now, I think. It is the giant feature, it is the sun that rides in the zenith of Christian Science, the auxiliary features are of minor consequence. [Let us still leave the large "if" aside, for the present, and proceed as if it had no existence.]

It is not supposable that Mrs. Eddy realized, at first, the size of her plunder. (No, *find*—that is the word; she did not realize the size of her find, at first.) It had to grow upon her, by degrees, in accordance with the inalterable custom of Circumstance which works by stages, and by stages only, and never furnishes any mind with all the materials for a large idea at one time.

In the beginning, Mrs. Eddy was probably interested merely in the mental-healing detail. And perhaps mainly interested in it pecuniarily, for she was poor.

She would succeed in anything she undertook. She would attract pupils, and her commerce would grow. She would inspire in patient and pupil confidence in her earnestness; her history is evidence that she would not fail of that.

There probably came a time, in due course, when her students began to think there was something deeper in her teachings than they had been suspecting—a mystery beyond mental-healing, and higher. It is conceivable that by consequence their manner toward her changed little by little, and from respectful became reverent. It is conceivable that this would have an influence upon her; that it would incline her to wonder if their secret thought— that she was inspired—might not be a well grounded guess. It is conceivable that as time went on, the thought in their minds and its reflection in hers might solidify into conviction.

She would remember, then, that as a child, she had been

called, more than once, by a mysterious voice—just as had happened to little Samuel. (Mentioned in her autobiography.) She would be impressed by that ancient reminiscence, now, and it could have a prophetic meaning for her.

It is conceivable that the persuasive influences around her and within her would give a new and powerful impulse to her philosophizings, and that from this, in time, would result that great birth, the healing of body and mind by the inpouring of the Spirit of God—the central and dominant idea of Christian Science—and that when this idea came, she would not doubt that it was an inspiration direct from heaven.

CHAPTER 11

[I must rest a little, now. To sit here and painstakingly spin out a scheme which imagines Mrs. Eddy, of all people, working her mind on a plane above commercialism; imagines her thinking, philosophizing, discovering majestic things; and even imagines her dealing in sincerities—to be frank, I find it a large contract. But I have begun it, and I will go through with it.]

CHAPTER 12

It is evident that she made disciples fast, and that their belief in her and in the authenticity of her heavenly ambassadorship was not of the lukewarm and halfway sort, but was profoundly earnest and sincere. Her book was issued from the press in 1875, it began its work of convert-making, and within six years she had successfully launched a new Religion and a new system of healing, and was teaching them to crowds of eager students in a College of her own, at prices so extraordinary that we are almost compelled to accept her statement (no, her guarded intimation) that the rates were arranged on high, since a mere human being unacquainted with commerce and accustomed to think in pennies, could hardly put up such a hand as that without supernatural help.

From this stage onward—Mrs. Eddy being what she was—the rest of the development-stages would follow naturally and inevitably. But if she had been anybody else there would have been a different arrangement of them, with different results. Being the extraordinary person she was, she realized her position and its possibilities; realized the possibilities, and had the daring to use them for all they were worth.

We have seen what her methods were after she passed the stage where her divine ambassadorship was granted its exequatur in the hearts and minds of her followers; we have seen how steady, and fearless, and calculated, and orderly was her march thenceforth from conquest to conquest; we have seen her strike dead, without hesitancy, any hostile or questionable force that rose in her path: first, the horde of pretenders that sprang up and tried to take her Science and its market away from her—she crushed them, she obliterated them; when her own National Christian Science Association became great in numbers and influence, and loosely and dangerously garrulous, and began to expound the doctrines according to its own uninspired notions, she took up her sponge without a tremor of fear and wiped that Association out; when she perceived that the preachers in her pulpits were becoming afflicted with doctrine-tinkering, she recognized the danger of it, and did not hesitate nor temporize, but promptly dismissed the whole of them in a day, and abolished their office permanently; we have seen that as fast as her power grew, she was competent to take the measure of it, and that as fast as its expansion suggested to her gradually-awakening native ambition a higher step she took it; and so, by this evolutionary process we have seen the gross money-lust relegated to second place, and the lust of empire and glory rise above it. A splendid dream; and by force of the qualities born in her she is making it come true.

These qualities—and the capacities growing out of them by the nurturing influences of training, observation and experience—

seem to be clearly indicated by the character of her career and its achievements. They seem to be:

A clear head for business, and a phenomenally long one;
Clear understanding of business situations;
Accuracy in estimating the opportunities they offer;
Intelligence in planning a business move;
Firmness in sticking to it after it has been decided upon;
Extraordinary daring;
Indestructible persistency;
Devouring ambition;
Limitless selfishness;

A knowledge of the weaknesses and poverties and docilities of human nature and how to turn them to account which has never been surpassed, if ever equaled;

And—necessarily—the foundation-stone of Mrs. Eddy's character is, a never-wavering confidence in herself.

It is a granite character. And—quite naturally—a measure of the talc of smallnesses common to human nature is mixed up in it and distributed through it. When Mrs. Eddy is not dictating servilities from her throne in the clouds to her official domestics in Boston or to her far-spread subjects round about the planet, but is down on the ground, she is kin to us and one of us: sentimental as a girl, garrulous, ungrammatical, incomprehensible, affected, vain of her little human ancestry, unstable, inconsistent, unreliable in statement and naïvely and everlastingly self-contradictory —oh, trivial and common and commonplace as the commonest of us! just a Napoleon, as Madame de Rémusat saw him, a brass god with clay legs.

CHAPTER 13

In drawing Mrs. Eddy's portrait it has been my purpose to restrict myself to materials furnished by *herself*, and I believe I have done that. If I have misinterpreted any of her acts, it was not done intentionally.

It will be noticed that in skeletonizing a list of the qualities which have carried her to the dizzy summit which she occupies, I have not mentioned the power which was the commanding force employed in achieving that lofty flight. It did not belong in that list; it was a force that was not a detail of her character, but was an outside one. It was the power which proceeded from her people's recognition of her as a supernatural personage, conveyer of the Latest Word, and divinely commissioned to deliver it to the world. The form which such a recognition takes, consciously or unconsciously, is *worship*; and worship does not question nor criticise, it obeys. The object of it does not need to coddle it, bribe it, beguile it, reason with it, convince it,—it commands it; that is sufficient; the obedience rendered is not reluctant, but prompt and whole-hearted. Admiration for a Napoleon, confidence in him, pride in him, affection for him, can lift him high and carry him far; and these are forms of worship, and are strong forces, but they are worship of a mere human being after all, and are infinitely feeble, as compared with those that are generated by that other worship, the worship of a divine personage. Mrs. Eddy has this efficient worship, this massed and centralized force, this force which is indifferent to opposition, untroubled by fear, and goes to battle singing, like Cromwell's soldiers; and while she has it she can command and it will obey, and maintain her on her throne, and extend her empire.

She will have it until she dies; and then we shall see a curious and interesting further development of her revolutionary work begin.

CHAPTER 14

The President and Board of Directors will succeed her, and the government will go on without a hitch. The By-Laws will bear that interpretation. All the Mother Church's vast powers are concentrated in that Board. Mrs. Eddy's unlimited personal reservations make the Board's ostensible supremacy, during her life, a sham, and the Board itself a shadow. But Mrs. Eddy has not made those reservations for any one but herself—they are distinctly personal, they bear her name, they are not usable by another individual. When she dies her reservations die, and the Board's shadow-powers become real powers, without the change of any important By-Law, and the Board sits in her place as absolute and irresponsible a sovereign as she was.

It consists of but five persons, a much more manageable Cardinalate than the Roman Pope's. I think it will elect its Pope from its own body, and that it will fill its own vacancies. An elective Papacy is a safe and wise system, and a long-liver.

CHAPTER 15

We may take that up, now.

It is not a single if, but a several-jointed one; not an oyster, but a vertebrate.

1. Did Mrs. Eddy borrow from Quimby the Great Idea, or only the little one, the old-timer, the ordinary mental-healing—healing by "mortal" mind?

2. If she borrowed the Great Idea, did she carry it away in her head, or in manuscript?

3. Did she hit upon the Great Idea herself?

By the Great Idea I mean, of course, the conviction that the Force involved was still existent, and could be applied now just as it was applied by Christ's Disciples and their converts, and as successfully.

4. Did she philosophize it, systematize it, and write it down in a book?

5. Was it she, and not another, that built a new Religion upon the book and organized it?

I think No. 5 can be answered with a Yes, and dismissed from the controversy. And I think that the Great Idea, great as it was, would have enjoyed but a brief activity and would then have gone to sleep again for some more centuries, but for the perpetuating impulse it got from that organized and tremendous force.

As for Numbers 1, 2 and 4, the hostiles contend that Mrs. Eddy got the Great Idea from Quimby and carried it off in manuscript. But their testimony, while of consequence, lacks the most important detail: so far as my information goes, the Quimby manuscript has not been produced. I think we cannot discuss No. 1 and No. 2 profitably. Let them go.

For me, No. 3 has a mild interest, and No. 4 a violent one.

As regards No. 3. Mrs. Eddy was brought up, from the cradle, an old-time, boiler-iron, Westminster-Catechism Christian, and knew her Bible as well as Captain Kydd knew his, "when he sailed, when he sailed," and perhaps as sympathetically. The Great Idea had struck a million Bible readers before her as being possible of resurrection and application—it must have struck as many as that, and been cogitated, indolently, doubtingly, then dropped and forgotten—and it could have struck *her,* in due course. But how it could *interest* her, how it could appeal to her—with her make—is a thing that is difficult to understand.

For the thing back of it is wholly gracious and beautiful: the power, through loving mercifulness and compassion, to heal all fleshly ills and pains and griefs—*all*—with a word, with a touch of the hand! This power was given by the Savior to the Disciples, and to *all* the converted. All—every one. It was *exercised* for generations afterward. Any Christian who was in earnest and not a make-believe, not a policy-Christian, not a Christian for revenue only, had that healing power, and could cure with it *any disease or any hurt or damage possible to human flesh and bone.* These things are true, or they are not. If they were true seventeen and eighteen and nineteen centuries ago it would be difficult to satisfactorily explain why or how or by what argument that power should be non-existent in Christians now.[1]

1. See Appendix.—M. T.

To wish to exercise it could occur to Mrs. Eddy—but would it?

Grasping, sordid, penurious, famishing for everything she sees—money, power, glory—vain, untruthful, jealous, despotic, arrogant, insolent, pitiless where thinkers and hypnotists are concerned, illiterate, shallow, incapable of reasoning outside of commercial lines, immeasurably selfish—

Of course the Great Idea *could* strike her, we have to grant that, but why it should *interest* her, is a question which can easily overstrain the imagination and bring on nervous prostration, or something like that, and is better left alone by the judicious, it seems to me—

Unless we call to our help the alleged other side of Mrs. Eddy's make and character—the side which her multitude of followers see, and sincerely believe in. Fairness requires that their view be stated here. It is the opposite of the one which I have drawn from Mrs. Eddy's history and from her By-Laws. To her followers she is this:

Patient, gentle, loving, compassionate, noble-hearted, unselfish, sinless, widely cultured, splendidly equipped mentally, a profound thinker, an able writer, a divine personage, an inspired messenger whose acts are dictated from the Throne, and whose every utterance is the Voice of God.

She has delivered to them a religion which has revolutionized their lives, banished the glooms that shadowed them, and filled them and flooded them with sunshine and gladness and peace; a religion which has no hell; a religion whose heaven is not put off to another time, with a break and a gulf between, but begins here and now, and melts into eternity as fancies of the waking day melt into the dreams of sleep.

They believe it is a Christianity that is in the New Testament; that it has always been there; that in the drift of the ages it was lost through disuse and neglect, and that this benefactor has found it and given it back to men, turning the night of life into

day, its terrors into myths, its lamentations into songs of emancipation and rejoicing.[1]

There we have Mrs. Eddy as her followers see her. She has
lifted them out of grief and care and doubt and fear, and made
their lives beautiful: she found them wandering forlorn in a wintry
wilderness, and has led them to a tropic paradise like that of which
the poet sings:

"O, islands there are on the face of the deep
    Where the leaves never fade and the skies never weep."

To ask them to examine with a microscope the character of
such a benefactor; to ask them to examine it at all; to ask them to
look at a blemish which another person believes he has found in
it—well, in their place could you do it? Would you do it? Wouldn't
you be ashamed to do it? If a tramp had rescued your child from
fire and death, and saved its mother's heart from breaking, could
you see his rags? could you smell his breath? Mrs. Eddy has done
more than that for these people.

They are prejudiced witnesses. To the credit of human nature
it is not possible that they should be otherwise. They sincerely
believe that Mrs. Eddy's character is pure and perfect and beautiful, and her history without stain or blot or blemish. But that does
not settle it. They sincerely believe she did not borrow the Great
Idea from Quimby, but hit upon it herself. It may be so, and it
could be so. Let it go—there is no way to settle it. They believe she
carried away no Quimby manuscripts. Let that go, too—there is
no way to settle it. They believe that she, and not another, built
the Religion upon the book, and organized it. I believe it, too.

Finally, they believe that she philosophized Christian Science, explained it, systematized it, and wrote it all out with her
own hand in the book, *Science and Health*.

I am not able to believe that. Let us draw the line there. The
known and undisputed products of her pen are a formidable witness against her. They do seem to me to prove, quite clearly and

1. For a clear understanding of the two claims of Christian Science, read the
novel, *The Life Within*, published by Lothrops, Boston.—M. T.

conclusively, that writing, upon even simple subjects, is a difficult labor for her; that she has never been able to write anything above third-rate English; that she is weak in the matter of grammar; that she has but a rude and dull sense of the values of words; that she so lacks in the matter of literary precision that she can seldom put a thought into words that express it lucidly to the reader and leave no doubts in his mind as to whether he has rightly understood or not; that she cannot even draft a Preface that a person can fully comprehend, nor one which can by any art be translated *into* a fully understandable form; that she can seldom inject into a Preface even single sentences whose meaning is uncompromisingly clear—yet Prefaces are her specialty if she has one.

Mrs. Eddy's known and undisputed writings are very limited in bulk; they exhibit no depth, no analytical quality, no thought above school-composition size, and but juvenile ability in handling thoughts of even that modest magnitude. She has a fine commercial ability, and could govern a vast railway system in great style; she could draft a set of rules that Satan himself would say could not be improved on—for devilish effectiveness—by his staff; but we know, by our excursions among the Mother Church's By-Laws, that their English would discredit the deputy baggage-smasher. I am quite sure that Mrs. Eddy cannot write well upon any subject, even a commercial one.

In the very first revision of *Science and Health*, (1883), Mrs. Eddy wrote a Preface which is an unimpeachable witness that the rest of the book was written by somebody else. I have put it in the Appendix[1] along with a page or two taken from the body of the book,[2] and will ask the reader to compare the labored and lumbering and confused gropings of this Preface with the easy and flowing and direct English of the other exhibit, and see if he can believe that the one hand and brain produced both.

And let him take the Preface apart, sentence by sentence, and searchingly examine each sentence word by word, and see if he

1. See Appendix A.—M. T.
2. Appendix B.—M. T.

can find half a dozen sentences whose meanings he is so sure of that he can re-phrase them—in words of his own—and reproduce what he takes to be those meanings. Money can be lost on this game. I know, for I am the one that lost it.

Now let the reader turn to the excerpt which I have made from the chapter on "Prayer"[1] (last year's edition of *Science and Health*) and compare that wise and sane and elevated and lucid and compact piece of work with the aforesaid Preface, and with Mrs. Eddy's poetry concerning the gymnastic trees, and Minerva's not yet effete sandals, and the wreaths imported from erudition's bower for the decoration of Plymouth Rock, and the Plague-spot and Bacilli, and my other exhibits (turn back to my chapters i and ii) from the autobiography, and finally with the late Communication concerning me,[2] and see if he thinks anybody's affirmation, or anybody's sworn testimony, or any other testimony of any imaginable kind, would ever be likely to convince him that Mrs. Eddy wrote that chapter on Prayer.

I do not wish to impose my opinion upon any one who will not permit it, but such as it is I offer it here for what it is worth. I cannot believe, and I do not believe, that Mrs. Eddy originated any of the thoughts and reasonings out of which the book *Science and Health* is constructed; and I cannot believe, and do not believe, that she ever wrote any part of that book.

I think that if anything in the world stands proven, and well and solidly proven, by unimpeachable testimony—the treacherous testimony of her own pen in her known and undisputed literary productions—it is that Mrs. Eddy is not capable of thinking upon high planes, nor of reasoning clearly nor writing intelligently upon low ones.

Inasmuch as—in my belief—the very first editions of the book *Science and Health* were far above the reach of Mrs. Eddy's mental and literary abilities, I think she has from the very beginning been

1. See Appendix.—M. T.
2. See Appendix. This reference is to the article "Mrs. Eddy in Error," in the *North American Review* for April, 1903.—M. T.

claiming as her own another person's book, and wearing as her own property laurels rightfully belonging to that person—the *real* author of *Science and Health*. And I think the reason—and the only reason—that he has not protested, is because his work was not exposed to print until after he was safely dead.

That with an eye to business, and by grace of her business talent, she has restored to the world neglected and abandoned features of the Christian religion which her thousands of followers find gracious and blessed and contenting, I recognize and confess; but I am convinced that every single detail of the work except just that one—the delivery of the product to the world—was conceived and performed by another.

APPPENDIX A

Original First Preface to *Science and Health*

There seems a Christian necessity of learning God's power and purpose to heal both mind and body. This thought grew out of our early seeking Him in all our ways, and a hopeless as singular invalidism that drugs increased instead of diminished, and hygiene benefited only for a season. By degrees we have drifted into more spiritual latitudes of thought, and experimented as we advanced until demonstrating fully the power of mind over the body. About the year 1862, having heard of a mesmerist in Portland who was treating the sick by manipulation, we visited him; he helped us for a time, then we relapsed somewhat. After his decease, and a severe casualty deemed fatal by skilful physicians, we discovered that the Principle of all healing and the law that governs it is God, a divine Principle, and a spiritual not material law, and regained health.

It was not an individual or mortal mind acting upon another so-called mind that healed us. It was the glorious truths of Christian Science that we discovered as we neared that verge of so-called material life named death; yea, it was the great Shekinah, the spirit of Life, Truth, and Love illuminating our understanding of the action and might of Omnipotence! The old gentleman to whom we have referred had some very advanced views on healing, but he was not avowedly religious neither scholarly. We interchanged thoughts on the subject of healing the sick. I restored some patients of his that he failed to heal, and left in his possession some manuscripts of mine containing corrections of his desultory pennings, which I am informed at his decease passed into the hands of a patient of his, now residing in Scotland. He died in 1865 and left no published works. The only manuscript that we ever held of his, longer than to correct it, was one of perhaps a dozen pages, most of which we had composed. He manipulated the sick; hence his ostensible method of healing was physical instead of *mental*.

We helped him in the esteem of the public by our writings, but never knew of his stating orally or in writing that he treated his patients *mentally*; never heard him give any directions to that effect; and have it from one of his patients, who now asserts that he was the founder of mental healing, that he never revealed to any one his method. We refer to these facts simply to refute the calumnies and false claims of our enemies, that we are preferring dishonest claims to the discovery and founding at this period of Metaphysical Healing or Christian Science.

The Science and laws of a purely mental healing and their method of application through spiritual power alone, else a mental argument against disease, are our own discovery at this date. True, the Principle is divine and eternal; but the application of it to heal the sick had been lost sight of, and required to be again spiritually discerned and its science discovered, that man might retain it through the understanding. Since our discovery in 1866 of the divine science of Christian Healing, we have labored with tongue and pen to found this system. In this endeavor every obstacle has been thrown in our path that the envy and revenge of a few disaffected students could devise. The superstition and ignorance of even this period have not failed to contribute their mite towards misjudging us, while its Christian advancement and scientific research have helped sustain our feeble efforts.

Since our first Edition of *Science and Health*, published in 1875, two of the aforesaid students have plagiarized and pirated our works. In the issues of E. J. A., almost exclusively ours, were thirteen paragraphs, without credit, taken verbatim from our books.

Not one of our printed works was ever copied or abstracted from the published or from the unpublished writings of any one. Throughout our publications of metaphysical healing or Christian Science, when writing or dictating them, we have given ourselves to contemplation wholly apart from the observation of the material senses: to look upon a copy would have distracted our thoughts from the subject before us. We were seldom able to copy our own compositions, and have employed an amanuensis for the last six years. Every work that we have had published has been extemporaneously written; and out of fifty lectures and sermons that we have delivered the past year, forty-four have been extemporaneous. We have distributed many of our unpublished manuscripts; loaned to one of our youngest students, R. K————y, between three and four hundred pages, of which we were sole author —giving him liberty to copy but not to publish them.

Leaning on the sustaining Infinite with loving trust, the trials of to-day grow brief, and to-morrow is big with blessings.

The wakeful shepherd, tending his flocks, beholds from the mountain's top the first faint morning beam ere cometh the risen day. So from Soul's loftier summits shines the pale star to prophet-shepherd, and it traverses night, over to where the young child lies, in cradled obscurity, that shall waken a world. Over the night of error dawn the morning beams and guiding star of Truth, and "the wise men" are led by it to Science, which repeats the eternal harmony that is reproduced, in proof of immortality. The time for thinkers has come; and the time for revolutions, ecclesiastical and civil, must come. Truth, independent of doctrines or time-honored systems, stands at the threshold of history. Contentment with the past, or the cold conventionality of custom, may no longer shut the door on science; though empires fall, "He whose right it is shall reign." Ignorance of God should no longer be the stepping-stone to faith; understanding Him, "whom to know aright is Life eternal," is the only guaranty of obedience.

This volume may not open a new thought, and make it at once familiar. It has the sturdy task of a pioneer, to hack away at the tall oaks and cut the rough granite, leaving future ages to declare what it has done. We made our first discovery of the adaptation of metaphysics to the treatment of disease in the winter of 1866; since then we have tested the Principle on ourselves and others, and never found it to fail to prove the statements herein made of it. We must learn the science of Life, to reach the perfection of man. To understand God as the Principle of all being, and to live in accordance with this Principle, is the Science of Life. But to reproduce this harmony of being, the error of personal sense must yield to science, even as the science of music corrects tones caught from the ear, and gives the sweet concord of sound. There are many theories of physic and theology, and many calls in each of their directions for the right way; but we propose to settle the question of "What is Truth?" on the ground of proof, and let that method of healing the sick and establishing Christianity be adopted that is found to give the most health and to make the best Christians; science will then have a fair field, in which case we are assured of its triumph over all opinions and beliefs. Sickness and sin have ever had their doctors; but the question is, Have they become less because of them? The longevity of our antediluvians would say, No! and the criminal records of to-day utter their voices little in favor of such a conclusion. Not that we would deny to Cesar the things that are his, but that we ask for the things that belong to Truth; and safely affirm, from the demonstrations we have been able to make, that the science of man understood would have eradicated sin, sickness, and death, in a less period than six thousand years. We find great difficulties in starting this work right. Some shockingly false claims are already made to a metaphysical practice; mesmerism, its very antipodes, is one of them. Hitherto we have never, in a single instance of our discovery, found the slightest resemblance between mesmerism and metaphysics. No especial idiosyncrasy is requisite to acquire a knowledge of metaphysical healing; spiritual sense is more important to its discernment than the intellect; and those who would learn this science without a high moral standard of thought and action, will fail to understand it until they go up higher. Owing to our explanations constantly vibrating between the same points, an irksome repetition of words must occur; also the use of capital letters, genders, and technicalities peculiar to the science. Variety of language, or beauty of diction, must give place to close analysis and unembellished thought. "Hoping all things, enduring all things," to do good to our enemies, to bless them that curse us, and to bear to the sorrowing and the sick consolation and healing, we commit these pages to posterity.

MARY BAKER G. EDDY.

The Gospel narratives bear brief testimony even to the life of our great Master. His spiritual noumenon and phenomenon, silenced portraiture. Writers, less wise than the Apostles, essayed in the Apocryphal New Testament, a legendary and traditional history of the early life of Jesus. But Saint Paul summarized the character of Jesus as the model of Christianity, in these words: "Consider him who endured such contradictions of sinners against himself. Who for the joy that was set before him, endured the cross, despising the shame, and is set down at the right hand of the throne of God."

It may be that the mortal life-battle still wages, and must continue till its involved errors are vanquished by victory-bringing Science; but this triumph will come! God is over all. He alone is our origin, aim, and Being. The real man is not of the dust, nor is he ever created through the flesh; for his father and mother are the one Spirit, and his brethren are all the children of one parent, the eternal Good.

Any kind of literary composition was excessively difficult for Mrs. Eddy. She found it grinding hard work to dig out anything to say. She realized, at the above stage in her life, that with all her trouble she had not been able to scratch together even material enough for a child's Autobiography, and also that what she had secured was in the main not valuable, not important, considering the age and the fame of the person she was writing about; and so it occurred to her to attempt, in that paragraph, to excuse the meagreness and poor quality of the feast she was spreading, by letting on that she could do ever so much better if she wanted to, but was under constraint of Divine etiquette: to feed with more than a few indifferent crumbs a plebeian appetite for personal details about Personages in her class, was not the correct thing; and she blandly points out that there is Precedent for this reserve. When Mrs. Eddy tries to be artful—in literature—it is generally after the manner of the ostrich; and with the ostrich's luck. Please try to find the connection between the two paragraphs.—M. T.

APPENDIX C

The following is the spiritual signification of the Lord's Prayer:

Principle, eternal and harmonious,
Nameless and adorable Intelligence,
Thou art ever present and supreme.
And when this supremacy of Spirit shall appear, the dream of matter will disappear.
Give us the understanding of Truth and Love.
And loving we shall learn God, and Truth will destroy all error.
And lead us unto the Life that is Soul, and deliver us from the errors of sense, sin, sickness, and death,
For God is Life, Truth, and Love for ever.
—*Science and Health, edition of 1881.*

It seems to me that this one is distinctly superior to the one that was inspired for last year's edition. It is strange, but to my mind plain, that inspiring is an art which does not improve with practice.—M. T.

For verily I say unto you, That whosoever shall say unto this mountain, Be thou removed, and be thou cast into the sea; and shall not doubt in his heart, but shall believe that those things which he saith shall come to pass; he shall have whatsoever he saith. Therefore I say unto you, What things soever ye desire when ye pray, believe that ye receive them, and ye shall have them.

Your Father knoweth what things ye have need of, before ye ask Him.—CHRIST JESUS.

The prayer that reclaims the sinner and heals the sick, is an absolute faith that all things are possible to God,—a spiritual understanding of Him,—an unselfed love. Regardless of what another may say or think on this subject, I speak from experience. This prayer, combined with self-sacrifice and toil, is the means whereby God has enabled me to do what I have done for the religion and health of mankind.

Thoughts unspoken are not unknown to the divine Mind. Desire is prayer; and no loss can occur from trusting God with our desires, that they may be moulded and exalted before they take form in audible word, and in deeds.

What are the motives for prayer? Do we pray to make ourselves better, or to benefit those who hear us; to enlighten the Infinite, or to be heard of men? Are we benefited by praying? Yes, the desire which goes forth hungering after righteousness is blessed of our Father, and it does not return unto us void.

God is not moved by the breath of praise to do more than He has already done; nor can the Infinite do less than bestow all good, since He is unchanging Wisdom and Love. We can do more for ourselves by humble fervent petitions; but the All-loving does not grant them simply on the ground of lip-service, for He already knows all.

Prayer cannot change the Science of Being, but it does bring us into harmony with it. Goodness reaches the demonstration of Truth. A request that another may work for us never does our work. The habit of pleading with the divine Mind, as one pleads with a human being, perpetuates the belief in God as humanly circumscribed,—an error which impedes spiritual growth.

God is Love. Can we ask Him to be more? God is Intelligence. Can we inform the infinite Mind, or tell Him anything He does not already comprehend? Do we hope to change perfection? Shall we plead for more at the open fount, which always pours forth more than we receive? The unspoken prayer does bring us nearer the Source of all existence and blessedness.

Asking God to *be* God is a "vain repetition." God is "the same yesterday, and to-day, and forever;" and He who is immutably right will do right, without being reminded of His province. The wisdom of man is not sufficient to warrant him in advising God.

Who would stand before a blackboard, and pray the principle of mathematics to work out the problem? The rule is already established, and it is our task to work out the solution. Shall we ask the divine Principle of all goodness to do His own work? His work is done; and we have only to avail ourselves of God's rule, in order to receive the blessing thereof.

The divine Being must be reflected by man,—else man is not the image and likeness of the patient, tender, and true, the one "altogether lovely;" but to understand God is the work of eternity, and demands absolute concentration of thought and energy.

How empty are our conceptions of Deity! We admit theoretically that God is good, omnipotent, omnipresent, infinite, and then we try to give information to this infinite Mind; and plead for unmerited pardon, and a liberal outpouring of benefactions. Are we really grateful for the good already received? Then we shall avail ourselves of the blessings we have, and thus be fitted to receive more. Gratitude is much more than a verbal expression of thanks. Action expresses more gratitude than speech.

If we are ungrateful for Life, Truth, and Love, and yet return thanks to God for all blessings, we are insincere; and incur the sharp censure our Master pronounces on hypocrites. In such a case the only acceptable prayer is to put the finger on the lips and remember our blessings. While the heart is far from divine Truth and Love, we cannot conceal the ingratitude of barren lives, for God knoweth all things.

What we most need is the prayer of fervent desire for growth in grace, expressed in patience, meekness, love, and good deeds. To keep the commandments of our Master and follow his example, is our proper debt to him, and the only worthy evidence of our gratitude for all he has done. Outward worship is not of itself sufficient to express loyal and heartfelt gratitude, since he has said: "If ye love me, keep my commandments."

The habitual struggle to be always good, is unceasing prayer. Its motives are made manifest in the blessings they bring,—which, if not acknowledged in audible words, attest our worthiness to be made partakers of Love.

Simply asking that we may love God will never make us love Him; but the longing to be better and holier,—expressed in daily watchfulness, and in striving to assimilate more of the divine character,—this will mould and fashion us anew, until we awake in His likeness. We reach the Science of Christianity through demonstration of the divine nature; but in this wicked world goodness will "be evil spoken of," and patience must work experience.

Audible prayer can never do the works of spiritual understanding, which regenerates; but silent prayer, watchfulness, and devout obedience, enable us to follow Jesus' example. Long prayers, ecclesiasticism, and creeds, have clipped the divine pinions of Love, and clad religion in human robes. They materialize worship, hinder the Spirit, and keep man from demonstrating his power over error.

Sorrow for wrong-doing is but one step towards reform, and the very easiest step. The next and great step required by Wisdom is the test of our sincerity,—namely, reformation. To this end we are placed under the stress of circumstances. Temptation bids us repeat the offence, and woe comes in return for what is done. So it will ever be, till we learn that there is no discount in the law of justice, and that we must pay "the uttermost farthing." The measure ye mete "shall be measured to you again," and it will be full "and running over."

Saints and sinners get their full award, but not always in this world. The followers of Christ drank his cup. Ingratitude and persecution filled it to the brim; but God pours the riches of His love into the understanding and affections, giving us strength according to our day. Sinners flourish "like a green bay-tree;" but, looking farther, the Psalmist could see their end,—namely, the destruction of sin through suffering.

Prayer is sometimes used, as a confessional, to cancel sin. This error impedes true religion. Sin is forgiven, only as it is destroyed by Christ,—Truth and Life. If prayer nourishes the belief that sin is cancelled, and that man is made better by merely praying, it is an evil. He grows worse who continues in sin because he thinks himself forgiven.

An apostle says that the Son of God [Christ] came to "destroy the works of the devil." We should follow our divine Exemplar, and seek the destruction of all evil works, error and disease included. We cannot escape the penalty due for sin. The Scriptures say, that if we deny Christ, "he also will deny us."

The divine Love corrects and governs man. Men may pardon, but this divine Principle alone reforms the sinner. God is not separate from the wisdom He bestows. The talents He gives we must improve. Calling on Him to forgive our work, badly done or left undone, implies the vain supposition that we have nothing to do but to ask pardon, and that afterwards we shall be free to repeat the offence.

To cause suffering, as the result of sin, is the means of destroying sin. Every supposed pleasure in sin will furnish more than its equivalent of pain, until belief in material life and sin is destroyed.

To reach heaven, the harmony of Being, we must understand the divine Principle of Being.

"God is Love." More than this we cannot ask; higher we cannot look; farther we cannot go. To suppose that God forgives or punishes sin, according as His mercy is sought or unsought, is to misunderstand Love and make prayer the safety-valve for wrongdoing.

Jesus uncovered and rebuked sin before he cast it out. Of a sick woman he said that Satan had bound her; and to Peter he said, "Thou art an offence unto me." He came teaching and showing men how to destroy sin, sickness, and death. He said of the fruitless tree, "It is hewn down."

It is believed by many that a certain magistrate, who lived in the time of Jesus, left this record: "His rebuke is fearful." The strong language of our Master confirms this description.

The only civil sentence which he had for error was, "Get thee behind me, Satan." Still stronger evidence that Jesus' reproof was pointed and pungent is in his own words,—showing the necessity for such forcible utterance, when he cast out devils and healed the sick and sinful. The relinquishment of error deprives material sense of its false claims.

Audible prayer is impressive; it gives momentary solemnity and elevation to thought; but does it produce any lasting benefit? Looking deeply into these things, we find that "a zeal . . . not according to knowledge," gives occasion for reaction unfavorable to spiritual growth, sober resolve, and wholesome perception of God's requirements. The motives for verbal prayer may embrace too much love of applause to induce or encourage Christian sentiment.

Physical sensation, not Soul, produces material ecstasy, and emotions. If spiritual sense always guided men at such times, there would grow out of those ecstatic moments a higher experience and a better life, with more devout self-abnegation, and purity. A self-satisfied ventilation of fervent sentiments never makes a Christian. God is not influenced by man. The "divine ear" is not an auditorial nerve. It is the all-hearing and all-knowing Mind, to whom each want of man is always known, and by whom it will be supplied.

The danger from audible prayer is, that it may lead us into temptation. By it we may become involuntary hypocrites, uttering desires which are not real, and consoling ourselves in the midst of sin, with the recollection that we have prayed over it,—or mean to ask forgiveness at some later day. Hypocrisy is fatal to religion.

A wordy prayer may afford a quiet sense of self-justification, though it makes the sinner a hypocrite. We never need despair of an honest heart; but there is little hope for those who only come spasmodically face to face with their wickedness, and then seek to hide it. Their prayers are indexes which do not correspond with their character. They hold secret fellowship with sin; and such externals are spoken of by Jesus as "like unto whited sepulchres . . . full of all uncleanness."

If a man, though apparently fervent and prayerful, is impure, and therefore insincere, what must be the comment upon him? If he had reached the loftiness of his prayer, there would be no occasion for such comment. If we feel the aspiration, humility, gratitude, and love which our words express,—this God accepts; and it is wise not to try to deceive ourselves or others, for "there is nothing covered that shall not be revealed." Professions and audible prayers are like charity in one respect,—they "cover a multitude of sins." Praying for humility, with whatever fervency of expression, does not always mean a desire for it. If we turn away from the poor, we are not ready to receive the reward of Him who blesses the poor. We confess to having a very wicked heart, and ask that it may be laid bare before us; but do we not already know more of this heart than we are willing to have our neighbor see?

We ought to examine ourselves, and learn what is the affection and purpose of the heart; for this alone can show us what we honestly are. If a friend informs us of a fault, do we listen to the rebuke patiently, and credit what is said? Do we not rather give thanks that we are "not as other men"? During many years the author has been most grateful for merited rebuke. The sting lies in unmerited censure,—in the falsehood which does no one any good.

The test of all prayer lies in the answer to these questions: Do we love our neighbor better because of this asking? Do we pursue the old selfishness, satisfied with having prayed for something better, though we give no evidence of the sincerity of our requests by living consistently with our prayer? If selfishness has given place to kindness, we shall regard our neighbor unselfishly, and bless them that curse us; but we shall never meet this great duty by simply asking that it may be done. There is a cross to be taken up, before we can enjoy the fruition of our hope and faith.

Dost thou "love the Lord thy God with all thy heart, and with all thy soul, and with all thy mind"? This command includes much,—even the surrender of all merely material sensation, affection and worship. This is the El Dorado of Christianity. It involves the Science of Life, and recognizes only the divine control of Spirit, wherein Soul is our master, and material sense and human will have no place.

Are you willing to leave all for Christ, for Truth, and so be counted among sinners? No! Do you really desire to attain this point? No! Then why make long prayers about it, and ask to be Christians, since you care not to tread in the footsteps of our dear Master? If unwilling to follow his example, wherefore pray with the lips that you may be partakers of his nature? Consistent prayer is the desire to do right. Prayer means that we desire to, and will, walk in the light so far as we receive it, even though with bleeding footsteps, and waiting patiently on the Lord, will leave our real desires to be rewarded by Him.

The world must grow to the spiritual understanding of prayer. If good enough to profit by Jesus' cup of earthly sorrows, God will sustain us under these sorrows. Until we are thus divinely qualified, and willing to drink his cup, millions of vain repetitions will never pour into prayer the unction of Spirit, in demonstration of power, and "with signs following." Christian Science reveals a necessity for overcoming the world, the flesh and evil, and thus destroying all error.

Seeking is not sufficient. It is striving which enables us to enter. Spiritual attainments open the door to a higher understanding of the divine Life.

One of the forms of worship in Thibet is to carry a praying-machine through the streets, and stop at the doors to earn a penny by grinding out a prayer; whereas civilization pays for clerical prayers, in lofty edifices. Is the difference very great, after all?

Experience teaches us that we do not always receive the blessings we ask for in prayer. There is some misapprehension of the source and means of all goodness and blessedness, or we should certainly receive what we ask for. The Scriptures say: "Ye ask, and receive not, because ye ask amiss, that ye may consume it upon your lusts." What we desire and ask for, it is not always best for us to receive. In this case infinite Love will not grant the request. Do you ask Wisdom to be merciful, and not punish sin? Then "ye ask amiss." Without punishment, sin would multiply. Jesus' prayer, "forgive us our debts," specified also the terms of forgiveness. When forgiving the adulterous woman he said, "Go, and sin no more."

A magistrate sometimes remits the penalty, but this may be no moral benefit to the criminal; and at best, it only saves him from one form of punishment. The moral law, which has the right to acquit or condemn, always demands restitution, before mortals can "go up higher." Broken law brings penalty, in order to compel this progress.

Mere legal pardon (and there is no other, for divine Principle never pardons our sins or mistakes till they are corrected) leaves the offender free to repeat the offence; if, indeed, he has not already suffered sufficiently from vice to make him turn from it with loathing. Truth bestows no pardon upon error, but wipes it out in the most effectual manner. Jesus suffered for our sins, not to annul the divine sentence against an individual's sin, but to show that sin must bring inevitable suffering.

Petitions only bring to mortals the results of their own faith. We know that a desire for holiness is requisite in order to gain it; but if we desire holiness above all else, we shall sacrifice everything for it. We must be willing to do this, that we may walk securely in the only practical road to holiness. Prayer alone cannot change the unalterable Truth, or give us an understanding of it; but prayer coupled with a fervent habitual desire to know and do the will of God will bring us into all Truth. Such a desire has little need of audible expression. It is best expressed in thought and life.

APPENDIX E

Reverend Heber Newton on Christian Science

To begin, then, at the beginning, Christian Science accepts the work of healing sickness as an integral part of the discipleship of Jesus Christ. In Christ it finds, what the Church has always recognized, theoretically, though it has practically ignored the fact—the Great Physician. That Christ healed the sick, we none of us question. It stands plainly upon the record. This ministry of healing was too large a part of his work to be left out from any picture of that life. Such service was not an incident of his career— it was an essential element of that career. It was an integral factor in his mission. The Evangelists leave us no possibility of confusion on this point. Co-equal with his work of instruction and inspiration was his work of healing.

The records make it equally clear that the Master laid his charge upon his disciples to do as he had done. "When he had called unto him his twelve disciples, he gave them power over unclean spirits, to cast them out, and to heal all manner of sickness and all manner of disease."[1] In sending them forth, "he commanded them, saying, . . . As ye go, preach, saying, The kingdom of heaven is at hand. Heal the sick, cleanse the lepers, raise the dead, cast out demons."[2]

1. Matt. x., 11. 2. Ib., x., 5, 7, 8.

That the twelve disciples undertook to do the Master's work of healing, and that they, in their measure, succeeded, seems beyond question. They found in themselves the same power that the Master found in himself, and they used it as he had used his power. The record of The Acts of the Apostles, if at all trustworthy history, shows that they, too, healed the sick.

Beyond the circle of the original twelve, it is equally clear that the early disciples believed themselves charged with the same mission, and that they sought to fulfil it. The records of the early Church make it indisputable that powers of healing were recognized as among the gifts of the Spirit. St. Paul's letters render it certain that these gifts were not a privilege of the original twelve, merely, but that they were the heritage into which all the disciples entered.

Beyond the era of the primitive Church, through several generations, the early Christians felt themselves called to the same ministry of healing, and enabled with the same secret of power. Through wellnigh three centuries, the gifts of healing appear to have been, more or less, recognized and exercised in the Church. Through those generations, however, there was a gradual disuse of this power, following upon a failing recognition of its possession. That which was originally the rule became the exception. By degrees, the sense of authority and power to heal passed out from the consciousness of the Church. It ceased to be a sign of the indwelling Spirit. For fifteen centuries, the recognition of this authority and power has been altogether exceptional. Here and there, through the history of these centuries, there have been those who have entered into this belief of their own privilege and duty, and have used the gift which they recognized. The Church has never been left without a line of witnesses to this aspect of the discipleship of Christ. But she has come to accept it as the normal order of things that what was once the rule in the Christian Church should be now only the exception. Orthodoxy has framed a theory of the words of Jesus to account for this strange departure of his Church from them. It teaches us to believe that his example was not meant to be followed, in this respect, by all his disciples. The power of healing which was in him was a purely exceptional power. It was used as an evidence of his divine mission. It was a miraculous gift. The gift of working miracles was not bestowed upon his Church at large. His original disciples, the twelve apostles, received this gift, as a necessity of the critical epoch of Christianity— the founding of the Church. Traces of the power lingered on, in weakening activity, until they gradually ceased, and the normal condition of the Church was entered upon, in which miracles are no longer possible.

We accept this, unconsciously, as the true state of things in Christianity. But it is a conception which will not bear a moment's examination. There is not the slightest suggestion upon record that Christ set any limit to this charge which he gave his disciples. On the contrary, there are not lacking hints that he looked for the possession and exercise of this power wherever his spirit breathed in men.

Even if the concluding paragraph of St. Mark's Gospel were a later appendix, it may none the less have been a faithful echo of words of the Master, as it certainly is a trustworthy record of the belief of the early Christians as to the thought of Jesus concerning his followers. In that interesting passage, Jesus, after his death, appeared to the eleven, and formally commissioned them, again, to take up his work in the world; bidding them, "Go ye into all the world and preach the gospel to every creature." "And these signs," he tells them, "shall follow them that believe"—not the apostles only, but "them that believe," without limit of time; "in my name they shall cast out devils . . . they shall lay hands on the sick and they shall recover."[1] The concluding discourse to the disciples, recorded in the Gospel according to St. John, affirms the same expectation on the part of Jesus; emphasizing it in his solemn way: "Verily, verily, I say unto you, He that believeth on me, the works that I do shall he do also; and greater works than these shall he do."[2]

1. Mark xvi., 15, 17, 18.   2. John xiv., 12.

Few will deny that an intelligence apart from man formed and governs the spiritual universe and man: and this intelligence is the eternal Mind, and neither matter nor man created this intelligence and divine Principle; nor can this Principle produce aught unlike itself. All that we term sin, sickness, and death is comprised in the belief of matter. The realm of the real is spiritual; the opposite of Spirit is matter; and the opposite of the real is unreal or material. Matter is an error of statement, for there is no matter. This error of premises leads to error of conclusion in every statement of matter as a basis. Nothing we can say or believe regarding matter is true, except that matter is unreal, simply a belief that has its beginning and ending.

The conservative firm called matter and mind God never formed. The unerring and eternal Mind destroys this imaginary copartnership, formed only to be dissolved in a manner and at a period unknown. This copartnership is obsolete. Placed under the microscope of metaphysics matter disappears. Only by understanding there are not two, matter and mind, is a logical and correct conclusion obtained of either one. Science gathers not grapes of thorns or figs of thistles. Intelligence never produced non-intelligence, such as matter: the immortal never produced mortality, good never resulted in evil. The science of Mind shows conclusively that matter is a myth. Metaphysics are above physics, and drag not matter, or what is termed that, into one of its premises or conclusions. Metaphysics resolves things into thoughts, and exchanges the objects of sense for the ideas of Soul. These ideas are perfectly tangible and real to consciousness, and they have this advantage,—they are eternal. Mind and its thoughts comprise the whole of God, the universe, and of man. Reason and revelation coincide with this statement, and support its proof every hour, for nothing is harmonious or eternal that is not spiritual:

the realization of this will bring out objects from a higher source of thought; hence more beautiful and immortal.

The fact of spiritualization produces results in striking contrast to the farce of materialization: the one produces the results of chastity and purity, the other the downward tendencies and earthward gravitation of sensualism and impurity.

The exalting and healing effects of metaphysics show their fountain. Nothing in pathology has exceeded the application of metaphysics. Through mind alone we have prevented disease and preserved health. In cases of chronic and acute diseases, in their severest forms, we have changed the secretions, renewed structure, and restored health; have elongated shortened limbs, relaxed rigid muscles, made cicatrized joints supple; restored carious bones to healthy conditions, renewed that which is termed the lost substance of the lungs; and restored healthy organizations where disease was organic instead of functional.

MRS. EDDY IN ERROR

I feel almost sure that Mrs. Eddy's inspiration-works are getting out of repair. I think so because they made some errors in a statement which she uttered through the press on the 17th of January. Not large ones, perhaps, still it is a friend's duty to straighten such things out and get them right when he can, therefore I will put my other duties aside for a moment and undertake this helpful service. She said as follows:

"In view of the circulation of certain criticisms from the pen of Mark Twain, I submit the following statement:

"It is a fact, well understood, that I begged the students who first gave me the endearing appellative 'mother' not to name me thus. But, without my consent, that word spread like wildfire. I still must think the name is not applicable to me. I stand in relation to this century as a Christian discoverer, founder and leader. I regard self-deification as blasphemous; I may be more loved, but I am less lauded, pampered, provided for and cheered than others before me—and wherefore? Because Christian Science is not yet popular, and I refuse adulation.

"My visit to the Mother Church after it was built and dedicated pleased me, and the situation was satisfactory. The dear members wanted to greet me with escort and the ringing of bells, but I declined, and went alone in my carriage to the church, entered it and knelt in thanks upon the steps of its altar. There the foresplendor of the beginnings of truth fell mysteriously upon my spirit. I believe in one Christ, teach one Christ, know of but one Christ. I believe in but one incarnation, one Mother Mary, and know I am not that one, and never claimed to be. It suffices me to learn the Science of the Scriptures relative to this subject.

"Christian Scientists have no quarrel with Protestants,

Catholics or any other sect. They need to be understood as following the divine Principle—God, Love—and not imagined to be unscientific worshippers of a human being.

"In the aforesaid article, of which I have seen only extracts, Mark Twain's wit was not wasted in certain directions. Christian Science eschews divine rights in human beings. If the individual governed human consciousness, my statement of Christian Science would be disproved, but to understand the spiritual idea is essential to demonstrate Science and its pure monotheism—one God, one Christ, no idolatry, no human propaganda. Jesus taught and proved that what feeds a few feeds all. His life work subordinated the material to the spiritual, and he left this legacy of truth to mankind. His metaphysics is not the sport of philosophy, religion or Science; rather is it the pith and finale of them all.

"I have not the inspiration or aspiration to be a first or second Virgin-Mother—her duplicate, antecedent or subsequent. What I am remains to be proved by the good I do. We need much humility, wisdom and love to perform the functions of foreshadowing and foretasting heaven within us. This glory is molten in the furnace of affliction."

She still thinks the name of Our Mother not applicable to her; and she is also able to remember that it distressed her when it was conferred upon her, and that she begged to have it suppressed. Her memory is at fault here. If she will take her By-Laws, and refer to Section 1 of Article XXII,—written with her own hand—she will find that she has reserved that title to herself, and is so pleased with it and so—may we say jealous?—about it that she threatens with excommunication any sister Scientist who shall call herself by it. This is that Section 1:

"*The Title of Mother.* In the year 1895 loyal Christian Scientists had given to the author of their text-book, the Founder of Christian Science, the individual, endearing term of Mother. Therefore if a student of Christian Science shall apply this title, either to herself or to others, except as the term for kinship according to the flesh, it shall be regarded by the Church as an indication of disrespect for their Pastor Emeritus, and unfitness to be a member of the Mother Church."

Mrs. Eddy is herself the Mother Church—its powers and authorities are in her possession solely—and she can abolish that title whenever it may please her to do so. She has only to command her people, wherever they may be in the earth, to use it no more, and it will never be uttered again. She is aware of this.

It may be that she "refuses adulation" when she is not awake, but when she is awake she encourages it and propagates it in that museum called "Our Mother's Room," in her Church in Boston. She could abolish that institution with a word, if she wanted to. She is aware of that. I will say a further word about the museum presently.

Further down the column her memory is unfaithful again:

"I believe in . . . but one Mother Mary, and know I am not that one, and never claimed to be."

At a session of the National Christian Science Association held in the city of New York on the 27th of May, 1890, the secretary was "instructed to send to our Mother greetings and words of affection from her assembled children." [Page 24, Official Report.]

Her telegraphic response was read to the Association at next day's meeting:

"All hail! He hath filled the hungry with good things and the sick hath He not sent empty away.—MOTHER MARY." [Page 24, Official Report.]

Which Mother Mary is this one? Are there two? If so, she is both of them; for when she signed this telegram in this satisfied and unprotesting way, the Mother-title which she was going to so strenuously object to, and put from her with humility, and seize with both hands, and reserve as her sole property, and protect her monopoly of it with a stern By-Law, while recognizing with diffidence that it was "not applicable" to her (then and to-day),—*that* Mother-title was not yet born, and would not be offered to her until five years later. The date of the above "Mother Mary" is

1890; the "individual, endearing title of Mother" was given her "in 1895"—according to her own testimony. See her By-Law, quoted above.

In his opening Address to that Convention of 1890 the President recognized this Mary—our Mary—and abolished all previous ones. He said:

"There was but one Moses, one Jesus; and there is but one Mary." [Page 13, Official Report.]

The confusions being now dispersed, we have this clarified result:

There had *been* a Moses at one time, and only one; there had *been* a Jesus at one time, and only one; there *is* a Mary and "only one." She is not a Has Been, she is an Is—the "Author of *Science and Health*; and we cannot ignore her." [Page 13, Official Report.]

1. In 1890 there was but one Mother Mary. The President said so.

2. Mrs. Eddy was that one—she said so, in signing the telegram.

3. Mrs. Eddy was not that one—for she says so, in her Associated Press utterance of January 17th.

4. And has "never claimed to be" that one—unless the signature to the telegram is a claim.

Thus it stands proven and established that she is that Mary and isn't, and thought she was and knows she wasn't. That much is clear.

She is also "The Mother," by the election of 1895, and did not want the title, and thinks it is not applicable to her, and will excommunicate any one that tries to take it away from her. So that is clear.

I think that the only really troublesome confusion connected with these particular matters has arisen from the name—Mary. Much vexation, much misunderstanding, could have been avoided if Mrs. Eddy had used some of her other names in place of that one. "Mother Mary" was certain to stir up discussion. It would have been much better if she had signed the telegram

"Mother Baker;" then there would have been no Biblical competition, and of course that is a thing to avoid. But it is not too
late, yet.

I wish to break in here with a parenthesis, and then take up
this examination of Mrs. Eddy's Claim[1] of January 17th again.

The history of her "Mother Mary" telegram—as told to me
by one who ought to be a very good authority—is curious and interesting. The telegram ostensibly quotes verse 53 from the "Magnificat," but really makes some pretty formidable changes in it.
This is St. Luke's version:

"He hath filled the hungry with good things; and the *rich*
He hath sent empty away."

This is "Mother Mary's" telegraphed version:

"He hath filled the hungry with good things, and the *sick*
hath He *not* sent empty away." [Page 24, Official Report.]

To judge by the Official Report, the bursting of this bombshell in that massed convention of trained Christians created no
astonishment, since it caused no remark, and the business of the
convention went tranquilly on, thereafter, as if nothing had
happened.

Did those people detect those changes? We cannot know. I
think they must have noticed them, the wording of St. Luke's
verse being as familiar to all Christians as is the wording of the
Beatitudes; and I think that the reason the new version provoked
no surprise and no comment was, that the assemblage took it for a
"Key"—a spiritualized explanation of verse 53, newly sent down
from heaven through Mrs. Eddy. For all Scientists study their
Bibles diligently, and they know their Magnificat. I believe that
their confidence in the authenticity of Mrs. Eddy's inspirations is
so limitless and so firmly established that no change, however
violent, which she might make in a Bible text could disturb their
composure or provoke from them a protest.

Her improved rendition of verse 53 went into the conven-

1. "*Claim.*" In Christian Science terminology, "Claims" are errors of mortal
mind, fictions of the imagination.—M. T.

tion's report and appeared in a New York paper the next day. The (at-that-time) Scientist whom I mentioned a minute ago, and who had not been present at the convention, saw it and marveled; marveled and was indignant—indignant with the printer or the telegrapher, for making so careless and so dreadful an error. And greatly distressed, too, for of course the newspaper people would fall foul of it, and be sarcastic, and make fun of it and have a blithe time over it, and be properly thankful for the chance. It shows how innocent he was; it shows that he did not know the limitations of newspaper men in the matter of Biblical knowledge. The new verse 53 raised no insurrection in the press; in fact it was not even remarked upon; I could have told him the boys would not know there was anything the matter with it. I have been a newspaper man myself, and in those days I had my limitations like the others.

The Scientist hastened to Concord and told Mrs. Eddy what a disastrous mistake had been made, but he found to his bewilderment that she was tranquil about it and was not proposing to correct it. He was not able to get her to promise to make a correction. He asked her secretary if he had heard aright when the telegram was dictated to him; he said he had, and took his filed copy of it and verified its authenticity by comparing it with his stenographic notes.

Mrs. Eddy did make the correction, two months later, in her official organ. It attracted no attention among the Scientists; and naturally none elsewhere, for that periodical's circulation was practically confined to disciples of the cult.

That is the tale as it was told to me by an ex-Scientist. Verse 53—renovated and spiritualized—had a narrow escape from a tremendous celebrity. The newspaper men would have made it as famous as the assassination of Caesar, but for their limitations.

To return to the Claim. I find myself greatly embarrassed by Mrs. Eddy's remark: "I regard self-deification as blasphemous." If she is right about that, I have written a half-ream of manuscript this past week which I must not print, either in the book which I am writing, or elsewhere: for it goes into that very matter with extensive elaboration, citing, in detail, words and acts of Mrs. Eddy's which seem to me to prove that she is a faithful and untiring worshiper of herself, and has carried self-deification to a length which has not before been ventured in ages. If ever. There is not room enough in this chapter for that Survey, but I can epitomise a portion of it here.

With her own untaught and untrained mind, and without outside help, she has erected upon a firm and lasting foundation the most minutely perfect and wonderful and smoothly and exactly-working and best safe-guarded system of government that has yet been devised in the world, as I believe, and as I am sure I could prove if I had room for my documentary evidences here.

It is a despotism (on this democratic soil); a sovereignty more absolute than the Roman Papacy, more absolute than the Russian Czarship; it has not a single power, not a shred of authority, legislative or executive, which is not lodged solely in the sovereign; all its dreams, its functions, its energies, have a single object, a single reason for existing, and only the one—to build to the sky the glory of the sovereign, and keep it bright to the end of time.

Mrs. Eddy is the sovereign; she devised that great place for herself, she occupies that throne.

In 1895 she wrote a little primer, a little body of autocratic laws, called the *Manual of The First Church of Christ, Scientist*, and put those laws in force, in permanence. Her government is all there; all in that deceptively-innocent-looking little book, that cunning little devilish book, that slumbering little brown volcano, with hell in its bowels. In that book she has planned out her system, and classified and defined its purposes and powers.

MAIN PARTS OF THE MACHINE

A Supreme Church. At Boston.

Branch Churches. All over the world.

One Pastor for the whole of them: to-wit, her *book, Science and Health.* Term of the book's office—*forever.*

In every C. S. pulpit, two "Readers," a man and a woman.

No talkers, no preachers, in any Church—readers only. *Readers of the Bible and her books*—no others. No commentators allowed to write or print.

A *Church Service.* She has framed it,—for all the C. S. Churches—selected its readings, its prayers, and the hymns to be used, and has appointed the order of procedure. No changes permitted.

A *Creed.* She wrote it. All C. S. Churches must subscribe to it. No other permitted.

A *Treasury.* At Boston. She carries the key.

A *C. S. Book-Publishing House.* For books approved by her. No others permitted.

Journals and Magazines. These are organs of hers, and are controlled by her.

A *College.* For teaching C. S.

DISTRIBUTION OF THE MACHINE'S POWERS AND DIGNITIES

Supreme Church:
Pastor Emeritus—Mrs. Eddy.
Board of Directors.
Board of Education.
Board of Finance.
College Faculty.
Various Committees.
Treasurer.
Clerk.
First Members (of the Supreme Church).
Members of the Supreme Church.

It looks fair, it looks real, but it is all a fiction. Even the title "Pastor Emeritus" is a fiction. Instead of being merely an honorary and ornamental official, Mrs. Eddy is the only official in the entire body that has the slightest power. In her Manual she has provided a prodigality of ways and forms whereby she can rid herself of any functionary in the government whenever she wants to. The officials are all shadows, save herself; she is the only reality.

She allows no one to hold office more than a year—no one gets a chance to become over-popular or over-useful, and dangerous. "Excommunication" is the favorite penalty—it is threatened at every turn. It is evidently the pet dread and terror of the Church's membership.

The member who *thinks,* without getting his thought from Mrs. Eddy before uttering it, is banished *permanently.* One or two kinds of sinners can plead their way back into the fold, but this one, never. To *think*—in the Supreme Church—is the New Unpardonable Sin.

To nearly every severe and fierce rule, Mrs. Eddy adds this rivet: "*This By-Law shall not be changed without the consent of the Pastor Emeritus.*"

Mrs. Eddy is the entire Supreme Church, in her own person, in the matter of powers and authorities.

Although she has provided so many ways of getting rid of unsatisfactory members and officials, she was still afraid she might have left a life-preserver lying around somewhere, therefore she devised a rule to cover that defect. By applying it she can excommunicate (and *this* is perpetual again), every functionary connected with the Supreme Church, and every one of the 25,000 members of that Church, at an hour's notice—and *do it all by herself without anybody's help.*

By authority of this astonishing By-Law she has only to *say* a person connected with that Church is secretly practising hypnotism or mesmerism: whereupon, immediate excommunication, without a hearing, is his portion! She does not have to order a trial and produce evidence—her *accusation* is all that is necessary.

Where is the Pope? and where the Czar? As the ballad says:
"Ask of the winds that far away
With fragments strewed the sea!"

The Branch Church's pulpit is occupied by two "Readers." Without them the Branch Church is as dead as if its throat had been cut. To have control, then, of the Readers, is to have control of the Branch Churches. Mrs. Eddy has that control—a control wholly without limit, a control shared with no one.

1. No Reader can be appointed to any Church in the Christian Science world without her *express* approval.

2. She can summarily expel from his or her place any Reader, at home or abroad, by a mere *letter* of dismissal, over her signature, and without furnishing any reason for it, to either the congregation or the Reader.

Thus she has as absolute control over all Branch Churches as she has over the Supreme Church. This power exceeds the Pope's.

In simple truth, *she is the only absolute sovereign in all Christendom.* The authority of the other sovereigns has limits, hers has none. None whatever. And her yoke does not fret, does not offend. Many of the subjects of the other monarchs feel their yoke, and are restive under it; their loyalty is insincere. It is not so with this one's human property; their loyalty is genuine, earnest, sincere, enthusiastic. The sentiment which they feel for her is one which goes out in sheer perfection to no other occupant of a throne; for it is love, pure from doubt, envy, exaction, fault-seeking, a love whose sun has no spot—that form of love, strong, great, uplifting, limitless, whose vast proportions are compassable by no word but one, the prodigious word, *Worship.* And it is not as a human being that her subjects worship her, but as a supernatural one, a divine one, one who has comradeship with God, and speaks by His voice.

Mrs. Eddy has herself created all these personal grandeurs and autocracies—with others which I have not (in this chapter) mentioned. They place her upon an Alpine solitude and supremacy of power and spectacular show not hitherto attained by any other self-seeking enslaver disguised in the Christian name, and they persuade me that although she may regard "self-deification as blasphemous," she is as fond of it as I am of pie.

She knows about "Our Mother's Room" in the Supreme Church in Boston,—above referred to—for she has been in it. In a recently published *North American Review* article,[1] I quoted a lady as saying Mrs. Eddy's portrait could be seen there in a shrine,

1. 1902.—M. T.

lit by always-burning lights, and that C. S. disciples came there and worshiped it. That remark hurt the feelings of more than one Scientist. They said it was not true, and asked me to correct it. I comply with pleasure. Whether the portrait was there four years ago or not, it is not there now, for I have inquired. The object in the shrine now, and lit by electrics,—and worshiped,—is an oil portrait of the horse-hair *chair* Mrs. Eddy used to sit in when she was writing *Science and Health*! It does seem to me that adulation has struck bottom, here.

Mrs. Eddy knows about that. She has been there, she has seen it, she has seen the worshipers. She could abolish that sarcasm with a word. She withholds the word. Once more I seem to recognize in her exactly the same appetite for self-deification that I have for pie. We seem to be curiously alike; for the love of self-deification is really only the spiritual form of the material appetite for pie, and nothing could be more strikingly Christian-Scientifically "harmonious."

I note this phrase:

"Christian Science eschews divine rights in human beings."

"Rights" is vague; I do not know what it means there. Mrs. Eddy is not well acquainted with the English language, and she is seldom able to say in it what she is trying to say. She has no ear for the exact word, and does not often get it. "Rights." Does she mean honors? attributes?

"Eschews." It is another umbrella where there should be a torch; it does not illumine the sentence, it only deepens the shadows. Does she mean denies? refuses? forbids?—or something in that line? Does she mean—

Christian Science denies divine honors to human beings? Or:

Christian Science refuses to recognize divine attributes in human beings? Or:

Christian Science forbids the worship of human beings?

The bulk of the succeeding sentence is to me a tunnel, but when I emerge at this end of it I seem to come into daylight. Then

I seem to understand both sentences—with this result:

Christian Science recognizes but one God, forbids the worship of human beings, and refuses to recognize the possession of divine attributes by any member of the race.

I am subject to correction, but I think that that is about what Mrs. Eddy was intending to convey. Has her English—which is always difficult to me—beguiled me into misunderstanding the following remark, which she makes (calling herself "we," after an old regal fashion of hers), in her preface to her *Miscellaneous Writings*? Page 3:

"While we entertain decided views as to the best method for elevating the race physically, morally, and spiritually, and shall express these views as duty demands, we shall claim no especial gift from our divine origin, no supernatural power."

Was she meaning to say—

"Although I am of divine origin and gifted with supernatural power, I shall not draw upon these resources in determining the best method of elevating the race?"

If she had left out the word "our" she might then seem to say—

"I claim no especial or unusual degree of divine origin—."

Which is awkward—most awkward—for one has either *a* divine origin or hasn't; shares in it, degrees of it, are surely impossible. The idea of crossed breeds in cattle is a thing we can entertain, for we are used to it and know it is possible, but the idea of a divine mongrel is unthinkable.

Well, then, what does she mean? I am sure I do not know, for certain. It is the word "our" that makes all the trouble. With the "our" in, she is plainly saying "*my* divine origin." The word "from" seems to be intended to mean "on account of." It has to mean that or nothing, if "our" is allowed to stay. The clause then says:

"I shall claim no especial gift on account of my divine origin."

And I think that the full sentence was intended to mean what I have already suggested:

"Although I am of divine origin, and gifted with supernatural power, I shall not draw upon these resources in determining the best method of elevating the race."

When Mrs. Eddy copyrighted that Preface seven years ago, she had long been used to regarding herself as a divine personage. I quote from Mr. F. W. Peabody's book:[1]

"In the *Christian Science Journal* for April, 1889, when it was her property, and published by her, it was claimed for her, and *with her sanction*, that she was equal with Jesus, and elaborate effort was made to establish the claim.

"Mrs. Eddy has distinctly *authorized* the claim in her behalf that she herself was the chosen successor to and equal of Jesus."

The following remark, in that April number, indicates that the claim had been previously made, and had excited "horror" among some "good people!" (Quoted by Mr. Peabody):

"Now, a word about the horror many good people have of our making the Author of *Science and Health* 'equal with Jesus.'"

Surely if it had excited horror in Mrs. Eddy also, she would have published a disclaimer. She owned the paper; she could say what she pleased in its columns. Instead of rebuking her editor, she lets him rebuke those "good people" for objecting to the claim.

These things seem to throw light upon those words, "our [my] divine origin."

It may be true that "Christian Science eschews divine rights in human beings," and forbids worship of any but "one God, one Christ," but if that is the case it looks as if Mrs. Eddy is a very unsound Christian Scientist, and needs disciplining. I believe she has a serious malady—"self-deification"—and that it will be well to have one of the experts demonstrate over it.

Meantime, let her go on living—for my sake. Closely examined, painstakingly studied, she is easily the most interesting person on the planet, and, in several ways, as easily the most extraordinary woman that was ever born upon it.

P. S.—Since I wrote the foregoing, Mr. McCrackan's article

1. Boston: 15 Court Square.—M. T.

appeared (in the March number of the *North American Review*). Before his article appeared—that is to say, during December, January and February—I had written a new book, a character-portrait of Mrs. Eddy, drawn from her own acts and words, and it was then—together with the three brief articles previously published in the *North American Review*—ready to be delivered to the printer for issue in book form. In that book, by accident and good luck, I have answered the objections made by Mr. McCrackan to my views, and therefore do not need to add an answer here. Also, in it I have corrected certain misstatements of mine which he has noticed, and several others which he has not referred to. There are one or two important matters of opinion upon which he and I are not in disagreement; but there are others upon which we must continue to disagree, I suppose, indeed I know we must; for instance he believes Mrs. Eddy wrote *Science and Health*, whereas I am quite sure I can convince a person unhampered by predilections that she did not.

As concerns one considerable matter I hope to convert him. He believes Mrs. Eddy's word; in his article he cites her as a witness, and takes her testimony at par; but if he will make an excursion through my book when it comes out, and will dispassionately examine her testimonies as there accumulated, I think he will in candor concede that she is by a large percentage the most erratic and contradictory and untrustworthy witness that has occupied the stand since the days of the lamented Ananias.

CONCLUSION

Broadly speaking, the hostiles reject and repudiate all the pretensions of Christian Science Christianity. They affirm that it has added nothing new to Christianity; that it can do nothing that Christianity could not do and was not doing before Christian Science was born.

In that case is there no field for the new Christianity, no opportunity for usefulness, precious usefulness, great and distinguished usefulness? I think there is. I am far from being confident that it can fill it, but I will indicate that unoccupied field—without charge—and if it can conquer it it will deserve the praise and gratitude of the Christian world, and will get it, I am sure.

The present Christianity makes an excellent private Christian, but its endeavors to make an excellent public one go for nothing, substantially.

This is an honest nation—in private life. The American Christian is a straight and clean and honest man, and in his private commerce with his fellows can be trusted to stand faithfully by the principles of honor and honesty imposed upon him by his religion. But the moment he comes forward to exercise a public trust he can be confidently counted upon to betray that trust in nine cases out of ten, if "party loyalty" shall require it.

If there are two tickets in the field in his city, one composed of honest men and the other of notorious blatherskites and criminals, he will not hesitate to lay his private Christian honor aside and vote for the blatherskites if his "party honor" shall exact it. His Christianity is of no use to him and has no influence upon him when he is acting in a public capacity. He has sound and sturdy private morals, but he has no public ones. In the last great municipal election in New York almost a complete one-half of the votes representing 3,500,000 Christians were cast for a ticket that had hardly a man on it whose earned and proper place was outside of a jail. But that vote was present at Church next Sunday the same as ever, and as unconscious of its perfidy as if nothing had happened.

Our Congresses consist of Christians. In their private life they are true to every obligation of honor; yet in every session they violate them all, and do it without shame. Because honor to party is above honor to themselves. It is an accepted law of public life that in it a man may soil his honor in the interest of party expediency—*must* do it when party expediency requires it. In private life those men would bitterly resent—and justly—any insinuation that it would not be safe to leave unwatched money within their reach; yet you could not wound their feelings by reminding them that every time they vote ten dollars to the pension appropriation nine of it is stolen money and they the marauders. They have filched the money to take care of the party, they believe it was right to do it, they do not see how their private honor is affected, therefore their consciences are clear and at rest. By vote they do wrongful things every day, in the party interest, which they could not be persuaded to do in private life. In the interest of party expediency they give solemn pledges, they make solemn compacts; in the interest of party expediency they repudiate them without a blush. They would not dream of committing these strange crimes in private life.

Now then, can Christian Science introduce the Congressional Blush? There are Christian Private Morals, but there are no Christian Public Morals, at the polls, or in Congress or anywhere else—except here and there and scattered around, like lost comets in the solar system. Can Christian Science persuade the nation and Congress to throw away their public morals and use none but their private ones henceforth in all their activities, both public and private?

I do not think so; but no matter about me: there is the field— a grand one, a splendid one, a sublime one; and absolutely unoccupied: has Christian Science confidence enough in itself to undertake to enter in and try to possess it? Make the effort, Christian Science; it is a most noble cause, and it might succeed. It could succeed. Then we should have a new literature, with romances entitled How To Be an Honest Congressman Though a Christian; How To Be a Creditable Citizen Though a Christian.

THE END

22 *Things a Scotsman Wants to Know*

[1909]

Augusta, Maine, Aug. 31.

To the Editor of Harper's Weekly.

My fellow-townsman, Kaufman, has tried to help the Scotsman. If I may try also, I will do the best I can.

Is God personal, or impersonal?

Nobody knows; but we can all join the pulpit, and guess. My guess is, that He is personal; that He is supreme, that He is limitlessly powerful, that He is all-knowing, and that He is the Creator of the universe and everything in it.

Is God the author of evil?

Necessarily, since He is the author of the conditions which produce it and make it unavoidable. And inasmuch as He created man—without man's consent or desire—He is responsible for everything man does and says between the cradle and the grave. He has no moral right to dictate to man what his conduct shall be. He has furnished man a large equipment of instincts, partialities, prejudices, magnanimities, generosities, and malignities, and it is man's moral right to do what he pleases with this equipment. As far as God is concerned. He cannot sin against God, he owes Him no allegiance, no obedience. God can compel him, yes, just as a strong man can compel a weak one to do things he is under no contract to do. But He cannot exercise this compulsion without descending a long way below the moral grade of the average civilized human being.

Evil? There is a plenty of it here below—invented in heaven and sent down day and night by the giant cargo and prodigally distributed over an utterly innocent and unoffending world. For what purpose? That bright darling, the pulpit, says, to discipline man, and incline him to love his Maker. What a splendid idea! I doubt if there is a cow in the country that is intellectual enough to invent the match to it.

Every day the cargo comes down, with presents for us all—Christmas all the year round, as it were: cholera, mumps, chills, the Indian Black Death, diphtheria, small pox, scarlet fever, consumption, epilepsy, measles, whooping cough, pneumonia, blindness, lameness, deafness, dumbness, heart failure, apoplexy, hydrophobia, idiocy, insanity, palsy, lockjaw, boils, ulcers, cancers, lumbago, St. Vitus's dance, gout, yellow fever, sleeping sickness, nervous prostration, religion, catalepsy, dropsy, typhoid, malaria, the house-fly, the mosquito, the flea, the louse, appendicitis, meningitis, hunger, cold, poverty, grief, misery in a million forms, and thirty-eight billion hostile microbes in every man's lower intestine waiting to take a chance if the other inducements to holy living fail to catch the student out and hale him to the grave.

Christmas every day, as you see, and something for everybody. Isn't it a wonderful grab-bag? Invented in heaven, too, not in the other place. Have you ever been acquainted with a mere man who would consent to provide any one of these things for the instruction and improvement of his family and friends? Have you ever been acquainted with a mere man who would not be ashamed if you charged him with inflicting any one of them either openly or secretly upon his enemy? If you charged him with it and proved it, and he explained that he did it to make the beneficiary love him, would you let him continue to run at large? The pulpit says God's ways are not our ways. Thanks. Let us try to get along with our own the best we can; we can't improve on them by experimenting with His.

All these horrors are emptied upon man, woman, and helpless child indiscriminately, to discipline them and make them
good, and incline them to love their Maker. So the pulpit says.
But the like are emptied upon the reptile, the bird, the quadruped
and the insect, in the same lavish way. They torture each other,
they mutilate each other, they rob each other, they kill each other,
they eat each other, they live in the hourly fear of death all their
days. Is the idea to train *them* to righteousness, and make them
pious, and fit them for heaven?

If it isn't, then what is it for? Why is it done? There is certainly no sense in it, either in their case or man's. Even the cow,
with all her intellectual prejudices, will think twice before she
disputes that. Then what is it for? Why is it done? It seems to me
that it proves one thing conclusively: if our Maker *is* all-powerful
for good or evil, He is not in His right mind.

BERUTH A. W. KENNEDY.

23   *Letters from the Earth*

[1909]

I

THE Creator sat upon the throne, thinking. Behind Him stretched the illimitable continent of heaven, steeped in a glory of light and color; before Him rose the black night of Space, like a wall. His mighty bulk towered rugged and mountain-like into the zenith, and His divine head blazed there like a distant sun. At His feet stood three colossal figures, diminished to extinction, almost, by contrast—archangels—their heads level with His ancle-bone.

When the Creator had finished thinking, He said,

"I have thought. Behold!"

He lifted His hand, and from it burst a fountain-spray of fire, a million stupendous suns, which clove the blackness and soared, away and away and away, diminishing in magnitude and intensity as they pierced the far frontiers of Space, until at last they were but as diamond nail-heads sparkling under the domed vast roof of the universe.

At the end of an hour the Grand Council was dismissed.

II

They left the Presence impressed and thoughtful, and retired to a private place, where they might talk with freedom. None of the three seemed to want to begin, though all wanted somebody to do it. Each was burning to discuss the great event, but would prefer not to commit himself till he should know how the others regarded it. So there was some aimless and halting conversation about matters of no consequence, and this dragged tediously along, arriving nowhere, until at last the archangel Satan gathered his courage together—of which he had a very good supply—and broke ground. He said—

"We know what we are here to talk about, my lords, and we may as well put pretence aside, and begin. If this is the opinion of the Council—"

"It is, it is!" said Gabriel and Michael, gratefully interrupting.

"Very well, then, let us proceed. We have witnessed a wonderful thing; as to that, we are necessarily agreed. As to the value of it—if it has any—that is a matter which does not personally concern us. We can have as many opinions about it as we like, but that is our limit. We have no vote. I think Space was well enough, just as it was, and useful, too. Cold and dark—a restful place, now and then, after a season of the over-delicate climate and trying splendors of heaven. But these are details of no considerable moment; the new feature, the immense feature, is—what, gentlemen?"

"The invention and introduction of automatic, unsupervised, self-regulating *law* for the government of those myriads of whirling and racing suns and worlds!"

"That is it!" said Satan. "You perceive that it is a stupendous idea. Nothing approaching it has been evolved from the Master Intellect before. Law—*automatic* Law—exact and unvarying Law—requiring no watching, no correcting, no readjusting while the eternities endure! He said those countless vast bodies would plunge through the wastes of Space ages and ages, at unimaginable speed, around stupendous orbits, yet never collide, and never lengthen nor shorten their orbital periods by so much as the hundredth part of a second in two thousand years! That is the new miracle, and the greatest of all—*Automatic Law!* And He gave it a name—the LAW OF NATURE—and said Natural Law is the LAW OF

GOD—interchangeable names for one and the same thing."

"Yes," said Michael, "and He said He would establish Natural Law—the Law of God—throughout His dominions, and its authority should be supreme and inviolable."

"Also," said Gabriel, "He said He would by and by create animals, and place them, likewise, under the authority of that Law."

"Yes," said Satan, "I heard Him, but did not understand. What *is* animals, Gabriel?"

"Ah, how should I know? How should any of us know? It is a new word."

[*Interval of three centuries, celestial time—the equivalent of a hundred million years, earthly time. Enter a messenger-Angel.*]

"My lords, He is making animals. Will it please you to come and see?"

They went, they saw, and were perplexed. Deeply perplexed —and the Creator noticed it, and said—

"Ask. I will answer."

"Divine One," said Satan, making obeisance, "what are they for?"

"They are an experiment in Morals and Conduct. Observe them, and be instructed."

There were thousands of them. They were full of activities. Busy, all busy—mainly in persecuting each other. Satan remarked —after examining one of them through a powerful microscope—

"This large beast is killing weaker animals, Divine One."

"The tiger—yes. The law of his nature is ferocity. The law of his nature is the law of God. He cannot disobey it."

"Then in obeying it he commits no offence, Divine One?"

"No, he is blameless."

"This other creature here, is timid, Divine One, and suffers death without resisting."

"The rabbit—yes. He is without courage. It is the law of his nature—the law of God. He must obey it."

"Then he cannot honorably be required to go counter to his nature and resist, Divine One?"

"No. No creature can be honorably required to go counter to the law of his nature—the law of God."

After a long time and many questions, Satan said—

"The spider kills the fly, and eats it; the bird kills the spider and eats it; the wildcat kills the goose; the—well, they all kill each other. It is murder all along the line. Here are countless multitudes of creatures, and they all kill, kill, kill, they are all murderers. And they are not to blame, Divine One?"

"They are not to blame. It is the law of their nature. And always the law of nature is the law of God. Now—observe—behold! A new creature—and the masterpiece—*Man!*"

Men, women, children, they came swarming in flocks, in droves, in millions.

"What shall you do with them, Divine One?"

"Put into each individual, in differing shades and degrees, all the various Moral Qualities, in mass, that have been distributed, a single distinguishing characteristic at a time, among the non-speaking animal world—courage, cowardice, ferocity, gentleness, fairness, justice, cunning, treachery, magnanimity, cruelty, malice, malignity, lust, mercy, pity, purity, selfishness, sweetness, honor, love, hate, baseness, nobility, loyalty, falsity, veracity, untruthfulness—each human being shall have *all* of these in him, and they will constitute his nature. In some, there will be high and fine characteristics which will submerge the evil ones, and those will be called good men; in others the evil characteristics will have dominion, and those will be called bad men. Observe—behold—they vanish!"

"Whither are they gone, Divine One?"

"To the earth—they and all their fellow-animals."

"What is the earth?"

"A small globe I made, a time, two times and half a time ago. You saw it, but did not notice it in the explosion of worlds and suns that sprayed from my hand. Man is an experiment, the other animals are another experiment. Time will show whether they were worth the trouble. The exhibition is over; you may take your leave, my lords."

III

Several days passed by.

This stands for a long stretch of (our) time, since in heaven a day is as a thousand years.

Satan had been making admiring remarks about certain of the Creator's sparkling industries—remarks which, being read between the lines, were sarcasms. He had made them confidentially to his safe friends the other archangels, but they had been overheard by some ordinary angels and reported at Headquarters.

He was ordered into banishment for a day—the celestial day. It was a punishment he was used to, on account of his too flexible tongue. Formerly he had been deported into Space, there being nowhither else to send him, and had flapped tediously around, there, in the eternal night and the arctic chill; but now it occurred to him to push on and hunt up the Earth and see how the Human-Race experiment was coming along.

By and by he wrote home—very privately—to St. Michael and St. Gabriel about it.

Satan's Letter.

This is a strange place, an extraordinary place, and interesting. There is nothing resembling it at home. The people are all insane, the other animals are all insane, the Earth is insane, Nature itself is insane. Man is a marvelous curiosity. When he is at his very very best he is a sort of low grade nickel-plated angel; at his worst he is unspeakable, unimaginable; and first and last and all the time he is a sarcasm. Yet he blandly and in all sincerity calls himself the "noblest work of God." This is the truth I am telling you. And this is not a new idea with him, he has talked it through all the ages, and believed it. Believed it, and found nobody among all his race to laugh at it.

Moreover—if I may put another strain upon you—he thinks he is the Creator's pet. He believes the Creator is proud of him; he even believes the Creator loves him; has a passion for him; sits up nights to admire him; yes, and watch over him and keep him out of trouble. He prays to Him, and thinks He listens. Isn't it a quaint idea? Fills his prayers with crude and bald and florid flatteries of Him, and thinks He sits and purrs over these extravagancies and enjoys them. He prays for help, and favor, and protection, every day; and does it with hopefulness and confidence, too, although no prayer of his has ever been answered. The daily affront, the daily defeat, do not discourage him, he goes on praying just the same. There is something almost fine about this perseverance. I must put one more strain upon you: he thinks he is going to heaven!

He has salaried teachers who tell him that. They also tell him there is a hell, of everlasting fire, and that he will go to it if he doesn't keep the Commandments. What are the Commandments? They are a curiosity. I will tell you about them by and by.

The salaried teacher tells them God is good. Good, and merciful, and kind, and just, and generous, and patient, and loving. To whom? His "children." And who are His children? Why, these misbegotten creatures! They use that expression themselves. Speaking by and large, man is made up of ninety-

Letters from the Earth

Letter IV

I have told you nothing about man that is not true. You must pardon me if I repeat that remark now and then in these letters; I want you to take seriously the things I am telling you, and I feel that if I were in your place and you in mine, I should need that reminder from time to time, to keep my credulity from flagging.

For there is nothing about Man that is not strange to an Immortal. He looks at nothing as we look at it, his sense of proportion is quite different from ours, and his sense of values is so widely divergent from ours, that with all our large intellectual powers it is not likely that even the most gifted among us would ever be quite able to understand it.

For instance, take this sample: he has imagined a heaven, and has left entirely out of it the supremest of all his delights, the one ecstasy that stands first and foremost in the heart of every individual of his race—and of ours—sexual intercourse!

It is as if a lost and perishing person in a roasting desert should be told by a rescuer he might choose and have all longed-for things but one, and he should elect to leave out water!

His heaven is like himself: strange, interesting, astonishing, grotesque. I give you my word, it has not a single feature in it that he *actually values*. It consists—utterly and entirely—of diversions which he cares next to nothing about, here in the earth, yet is quite sure he will like in heaven. Isn't it curious? Isn't it interesting? You must not think I am exaggerating, for it is not so. I will give you details.

Most men do not sing, most men cannot sing, most men will not stay where others are singing if it be continued more than two hours. Note that.

Only about two men in a hundred can play upon a musical instrument, and not four in a hundred have any wish to learn how. Set that down.

Many men pray, not many of them like to do it. A few pray long, the others make a short cut.

More men go to church than want to.

To forty-nine men in fifty the Sabbath Day is a dreary, dreary bore.

Of all the men in a church on a Sunday, two-thirds are tired when the service is half over, and the rest before it is finished.

The gladdest moment for all of them is when the preacher uplifts his hands for the benediction. You can hear the soft rustle of relief that sweeps the house, and you recognize that it is eloquent with gratitude.

All nations look down upon all other nations.

All nations dislike all other nations.

All white nations despise all colored nations, of whatever hue, and oppress them when they can.

White men will not associate with "niggers," nor marry them. They will not allow them in their schools and churches.

All the world hates the Jew, and will not endure him except when he is rich.

I ask you to note all those particulars.

Further. All sane people detest noise.

All sane people, sane or insane, like to have variety in their life. Monotony quickly wearies them.

Every man, according to the mental equipment that has fallen to his share, exercises his intellect constantly, ceaselessly, and this exercise makes up a vast and valued and essential part of his life. The lowest intellect, like the highest, possesses a skill of some kind and takes a keen pleasure in testing it, proving it, perfecting it. The urchin who is his comrade's superior in games is as diligent and as enthusiastic in his practice as are the sculptor, the painter, the pianist, the mathematician and the rest. Not one of them could be happy if his talent were put under an interdict.

Now then, you have the facts. You know what the human race enjoys, and what it doesn't enjoy. It has invented a heaven, out of its own head, all by itself: guess what it is like! In fifteen hundred eternities you couldn't do it. The ablest mind known to you or me in fifty million aeons couldn't do it. Very well, I will tell you about it.

II

1. First of all, I recall to your attention the extraordinary fact with which I began. To-wit, that the human being, like the immortals, naturally places sexual intercourse far and away above all other joys—yet he has left it out of his heaven! The very thought of it excites him; opportunity sets him wild; in this state he will risk life, reputation, everything—even his queer heaven itself—to

make good that opportunity and ride it to the overwhelming climax. From youth to middle age all men and all women prize copulation above all other pleasures combined, yet it is actually as I have said: it is not in their heaven, prayer takes its place.

They prize it thus highly; yet, like all their so-called "boons," it is a poor thing. At its very best and longest the act is brief beyond imagination—the imagination of an immortal, I mean. In the matter of repetition the man is limited—oh, quite beyond immortal conception. We who continue the act *and* its supremest ecstasies unbroken and without withdrawal for centuries, will never be able to understand or adequately pity the awful poverty of these people in that rich gift which, possessed as we possess it, makes all other possessions trivial and not worth the trouble of invoicing.

2. In man's heaven *everybody sings!* There are no exceptions. The man who did not sing on earth, sings there; the man who could not sing on earth is able to do it there. This universal singing is not casual, not occasional, not relieved by intervals of quiet, it goes on, all day long, and every day, during a stretch of twelve hours. And *everybody stays;* whereas in the earth the place would be empty in two hours. The singing is of hymns alone. Nay, it is of *one* hymn alone. The words are always the same, in number they are only about a dozen, there is no rhyme, there is no poetry: "Hosannah, hosannah, hosannah, Lord God of Sabaoth, 'rah! 'rah! 'rah!—ssht!—boom! . . . . . a-a-ah!"

3. Meantime, *every person* is playing on a harp—those millions and millions! whereas not more than twenty in the thousand of them could play an instrument in the earth, or ever *wanted* to.

Consider the deafening hurricane of sound—millions and millions of voices screaming at once, and millions and millions of harps gritting their teeth at the same time! I ask you—is it hideous, is it odious, is it horrible?

Consider further: it is a *praise* service; a service of compliment, of flattery, of adulation! Do you ask who it is that is willing to endure this strange compliment, this insane compliment; and who not only endures it but likes it, enjoys it, requires it, *commands* it? Hold your breath!

It is God! This race's God, I mean. He sits on his throne, attended by his four and twenty elders and some other dignitaries pertaining to his court, and looks out over his miles and miles of tempestuous worshippers, and smiles, and purrs, and nods his satisfaction northward, eastward, southward; as quaint and naif a spectacle as has yet been imagined in this universe, I take it.

It is easy to see that the inventor of the heaven did not originate the idea, but copied it from the show-ceremonies of some sorry little sovereign State up in the back settlements of the Orient somewhere.

All sane white people *hate noise*; yet they have tranquilly accepted this kind of a heaven—without thinking, without reflection, without examination—and they actually want to go to it! Profoundly devout old gray-headed men put in a large part of their time dreaming of the happy day when they will lay down the cares of this life and enter into the joys of that place. Yet you can see how unreal it is to them, and how little it takes a grip upon them as being *fact*, for they make no practical preparation for the great change: you never see one of them with a harp, you never hear one of them sing.

As you have seen, that singular show is a service of divine worship—a service of praise: praise by hymn, praise by instrumental ecstasies, praise by prostration. It takes the place of "church." Now then, in the earth these people cannot stand much church—an hour and a quarter is the limit, and they draw the line at once a week. That is to say, Sunday. One day in seven; and even then they do not look forward to it with longing. And so—consider what their heaven provides for them: "church" that lasts forever, and a *Sabbath that has no end!* They quickly weary of this brief hebdomadal Sabbath here, yet they long for that eternal one; they dream of it, they talk about it, they *think* they think they are going to enjoy it—with all their simple hearts they think they think they are going to be happy in it!

It is because they do not think *at all*; they only think they think. Whereas they can't think; not two human beings in ten thousand have anything to think with. And as to imagination— oh, well, look at their heaven! They accept it, they approve it, they admire it. That gives you their intellectual measure.

4. The inventor of their heaven empties into it all the nations of the earth, in one common jumble. All are on an equality absolute, no one of them ranking another; they have to be "brothers;" they have to mix together, pray together, harp together, hosannah together—whites, niggers, Jews, everybody—there's no distinction. Here in the earth all nations hate each other, every one of them hates the Jew. Yet every pious person adores that heaven and wants to get into it. He really does. And when he is in a holy rapture he thinks he thinks that if he were only there he would take all the populace to his heart, and hug, and hug, and hug!

He is a marvel—man is! I would I knew who invented him.

5. Every man in the earth possesses some share of intellect, large or small; and be it large or be it small he takes a pride in it. Also his heart swells at mention of the names of the majestic intellectual chiefs of his race, and he loves the tale of their splendid achievements. For he is of their blood, and in honoring themselves they have honored him. Lo, what the mind of man can do! he cries; and calls the roll of the illustrious of all the ages; and points to the imperishable literatures they have given to the world, and the mechanical wonders they have invented, and the glories wherewith they have clothed science and the arts; and to them he uncovers, as to kings, and gives to them the profoundest homage and the sincerest his exultant heart can furnish—thus exalting intellect above all things else in his world, and enthroning it there under the arching skies in a supremacy unapproachable. And then he contrives a heaven that hasn't a rag of intellectuality in it anywhere!

Is it odd, is it curious, is it puzzling? It is exactly as I have said, incredible as it may sound. This sincere adorer of intellect and prodigal rewarder of its mighty services here in the earth has invented a religion and a heaven which pay no compliments to intellect, offer it no distinctions, fling to it no largess: in fact, never even mention it.

By this time you will have noticed that the human being's heaven has been thought out and constructed upon an absolutely definite plan; and that this plan is, that it shall contain, in labored detail, each and every imaginable thing that is repulsive to a man, and not a single thing he likes!

Very well, the further we proceed the more will this curious fact be apparent.

Make a note of it: in man's heaven there are no exercises for the intellect, nothing for it to live upon. It would rot there in a year—rot and stink. Rot and stink—and at that stage become holy. A blessed thing; for only the holy can stand the joys of that bedlam.

Letter V

You have noticed that the human being is a curiosity. In times past he has had (and worn out and flung away) hundreds and hundreds of religions; to-day he has hundreds and hundreds of religions, and launches not fewer than three new ones every year. I could enlarge that number and still be within the facts.

One of his principal religions is called the Christian. A sketch of it will interest you. It is set forth in detail in a book containing 2,000,000 words, called the Old and New Testaments. Also it has another name—The Word of God. For the Christian thinks every word of it was dictated by God—the one I have been speaking of.

It is full of interest. It has noble poetry in it; and some clever fables; and some blood-drenched history; and some good morals; and some execrable morals; and a wealth of obscenity; and upwards of a thousand lies.

This Bible is built mainly out of the fragments of older Bibles that had their day and crumbled to ruin. So it noticeably lacks in originality, necessarily. Its three or four most imposing and impressive events all happened in earlier Bibles; all its best precepts and rules of conduct come also from those Bibles; there are only two new things in it: hell, for one, and that singular heaven I have told you about.

What shall we do? If we believe, with these people, that their God invented these cruel things, we slander him; if we believe that these people invented them themselves, we slander *them*. It is an unpleasant dilemma in either case, for neither of these parties has done *us* any harm.

For the sake of tranquillity, let us take a side. Let us join forces with the people and put the whole ungracious burden upon *him*—heaven, hell, Bible and all. It does not seem right, it does not seem fair; and yet when you consider that heaven, and how crushingly charged it is with everything that is repulsive to a human being, how *can* we believe a human being invented it? And when I come to tell you about hell, the strain will be greater still, and you will be likely to say *No*, a man would not provide *that* place, for either himself or anybody else; he simply *couldn't*.

That innocent Bible tells about the Creation. Of what—the universe? Yes, the universe. In *six days*!

God did it. He did not call it the universe—that name is modern. His whole attention was upon *this world*. He constructed it in five days—and then? It took him only *one* day to make *twenty million suns and eighty million planets*!

What were they for—according to his idea? To furnish light for this little toy-world. That was his whole purpose; he had no other. *One* of the 20,000,000 suns (the smallest one), was to light it in the day-time, the rest were to help *one* of the universe's countless moons modify the darkness of its nights.

It is quite manifest that he believed his fresh-made skies were diamond-sown with those myriads of twinkling stars the moment his first-day's sun sank below the horizon; whereas, in fact not a single star winked in that black vault until three years and a half after that memorable week's formidable industries had been completed.* Then one star appeared, all solitary and alone, and began to blink. Three years later another one appeared. The two blinked together for more than four years before a third joined them. At the end of the first hundred years there were not yet twenty-five stars twinkling in the wide wastes of those gloomy skies. At the end of a thousand years not enough stars were yet visible to make a show. At the end of a million years only half of the present array had sent their light over the telescopic frontiers, and it took another million for the rest to follow suit, as the vulgar phrase goes. There being at that time no telescope, their advent was not observed.

For three hundred years, now, the Christian astronomer has known that his Deity *didn't* make the stars in those tremendous six days; but the Christian astronomer does not enlarge upon that detail. Neither does the priest.

In his Book, God is eloquent in his praises of his mighty works, and calls them by the largest names he can find—thus indicating that he has a strong and just admiration of magnitudes; yet he made those millions of prodigious suns to light this wee little orb, instead of appointing this orb's little sun to dance attendance upon *them.* He mentions Arcturus in his Book—you remember Arcturus; we went there once. *It* is one of this earth's night-lamps!—that giant globe which is 50,000 times as large as this earth's sun, and compares with it as a melon compares with a cathedral.

However, the Sunday school still teaches the child that Arcturus was created to help light this earth, and the child grows up

---

* It takes the light of the nearest star (61 Cygni) three and a half years to come to the earth, traveling at the rate of 186,000 miles per second. Arcturus had been shining 200 years before it was visible from the earth. Remoter stars gradually became visible after thousands and thousands of years.—[*Editor.*

and continues to believe it long after he has found out that the
probabilities are against its being so.

According to the Book and its servants the universe is only
six thousand years old. It is only within the last hundred years that
studious, inquiring minds have found out that it is nearer a hundred million.

During the Six Days, God created man and the other animals.
He made a man and a woman and placed them in a pleasant
garden, along with the other creatures. They all lived together
there in harmony and contentment and blooming youth for some
time; then trouble came. God had warned the man and the woman
that they must not eat of the fruit of a certain tree. And he added
a most strange remark: he said that if they ate of it they should
surely *die*. Strange, for the reason that inasmuch as they had never
seen a sample of death they could not possibly know what he
meant. Neither would he nor any other god have been able to
make those ignorant children understand what was meant, without furnishing a sample. The mere *word* could have no meaning
for them, any more than it would have for an infant of days.

Presently a serpent sought them out privately, and came to
them walking upright, which was the way of serpents in those
days. The serpent said the forbidden fruit would store their vacant
minds with knowledge. So they ate it, which was quite natural,
for man is so made that he eagerly *wants to know*; whereas the
priest, like God, whose imitator and representative he is, has made
it his business from the beginning to keep him *from* knowing any
useful thing.

Adam and Eve ate the forbidden fruit, and at once a great
light streamed into their dim heads. They had acquired knowledge. What knowledge—useful knowledge? No—merely knowledge that there was such a thing as good, and such a thing as evil,
and how to *do* evil. They *couldn't* do it before, therefore all their

acts up to this time had been without stain, without blame, without offence.

But *now* they could do evil—and suffer for it; *now* they had acquired what the Church calls an invaluable possession, the Moral Sense; that sense which differentiates man from the beast and sets him *above* the beast. Instead of *below* the beast—where one would suppose his proper place would be, since he is always foul-minded and guilty and the beast always clean-minded and innocent. It is like valuing a watch that *must* go wrong, above a watch that *can't*.

The Church still prizes the Moral Sense as man's noblest asset to-day, although the Church knows God had a distinctly poor opinion of it and did what he could in his clumsy way to keep his happy Children of the Garden from acquiring it.

Very well, Adam and Eve now knew what evil was, and how to do it. They knew how to do various kinds of wrong things, and among them one principal one—the one God had his mind on principally. That one was, the art and mystery of sexual intercourse. To them it was a magnificent discovery, and they stopped idling around and turned their entire attention to it, poor exultant young things!

In the midst of one of these celebrations they heard God walking among the bushes, which was an afternoon custom of his, and they were smitten with fright. Why? Because they were naked. They had not known it before. They had not minded it before, neither had God.

In that memorable moment *immodesty* was born; and some people have valued it ever since, though it would certainly puzzle them to explain why.

Adam and Eve entered the world naked and unashamed—naked and pure-minded; and no descendant of theirs has ever entered it otherwise. All have entered it naked, unashamed, and clean in mind. They have entered it *modest*. They had to *acquire* immodesty and the soiled mind, there was no other way to get it. A Christian mother's first duty is to soil her child's mind, and she does not neglect it. Her lad grows up to be a missionary, and goes to the innocent savage and to the civilized Japanese, and soils their minds. Whereupon they adopt immodesty, they conceal their bodies, they stop bathing naked together.

The convention miscalled Modesty has no standard, and cannot have one, because it is opposed to nature and reason, and is therefore an artificiality and subject to anybody's whim, anybody's diseased caprice. And so, in India the refined lady covers her face and breasts and leaves her legs naked from the hips down, while the refined European lady covers her legs and exposes her face and her breasts. In lands inhabited by the innocent savage the refined European lady soon gets used to full-grown native stark-nakedness, and ceases to be offended by it. A highly cultivated French count and countess—unrelated to each other—who were marooned in their night clothes, by shipwreck, upon an uninhabited island in the eighteenth century, were soon naked. Also ashamed—for a week. After that their nakedness did not trouble them, and they soon ceased to think about it.

You have never seen a person with clothes on. Oh, well, you haven't lost anything.

To proceed with the Biblical curiosities. Naturally you will think the threat to punish Adam and Eve for disobeying was of course not carried out, since they did not create themselves, nor their natures nor their impulses nor their weaknesses, and hence were not properly subject to any one's commands, and not responsible to anybody for their acts. It will surprise you to know that the threat *was* carried out. Adam and Eve were punished, and that crime finds apologists unto this day. *The sentence of death was executed.*

As you perceive, the only person responsible for the couple's offence escaped; and not only escaped but became the executioner of the innocent.

In your country and mine we should have the privilege of making fun of this kind of morality, but it would be unkind to do it here. Many of these people have the reasoning faculty, but no one uses it in religious matters.

The best minds will tell you that when a man has begotten a child he is morally bound to tenderly care for it, protect it from hurt, shield it from disease, clothe it, feed it, bear with its way-wardness, lay no hand upon it save in kindness and for its own good, and never in any case inflict upon it a wanton cruelty. God's treatment of his earthly children, every day and every night, is the exact opposite of all that, yet those best minds warmly justify these crimes, condone them, excuse them, and indignantly refuse to regard them as crimes at all, when *he* commits them. Your country and mine is an interesting one, but there is nothing there that is half so interesting as the human mind.

Very well, God banished Adam and Eve from the Garden, and eventually assassinated them. All for disobeying a command which he had no right to utter. But he did not stop there, as you will see. He has one code of morals for himself, and quite another for his children. He requires his children to deal justly—and gently —with offenders, and forgive them seventy-and-seven times; whereas he deals neither justly nor gently with any one, and he did not forgive the ignorant and thoughtless first pair of juveniles even their first small offence and say "You may go free this time, I will give you another chance."

On the contrary! He elected to punish *their* children, all through the ages to the end of time, for a trifling offence com-mitted by others before they were born. He is punishing them yet. In mild ways? No, in atrocious ones.

You would not suppose that this kind of a Being gets many compliments. Undeceive yourself: the world calls him the All-Just, the All-Righteous, the All-Good, the All-Merciful, the All-Forgiving, the All-Truthful, the All-Loving, the Source of All Morality. These sarcasms are uttered daily, all over the world. But not as conscious sarcasms. No, they are meant seriously; they are uttered without a smile.

Letter . . .

So the First Pair went forth from the Garden under a curse—
a permanent one. They had lost every pleasure they had possessed
before "The Fall;" and yet they were rich, for they had gained one
worth all the rest: they knew the Supreme Art.

They practised it diligently, and were filled with contentment. The Deity *ordered* them to practise it. They obeyed, this
time. But it was just as well it was not forbidden, for they would
have practised it anyhow, if a thousand Deities had forbidden it.

Results followed. By the name of Cain and Abel. And these
had some sisters; and knew what to do with them. And so there
were some more results: Cain and Abel begot some nephews and
nieces. These, in their turn, begot some second-cousins. At this
point classification of relationships began to get difficult, and the
attempt to keep it up was abandoned.

The pleasant labor of populating the world went on from age
to age, and with prime efficiency; for in those happy days the sexes
were still competent for the Supreme Art when by rights they
ought to have been dead eight hundred years. The sweeter sex, the
dearer sex, the lovelier sex was manifestly at its very best, then, for
it was even able to attract gods. Real gods. They came down out
of heaven and had wonderful times with those hot young blos-
soms. The Bible tells about it.

By help of those visiting foreigners the population grew and
grew until it numbered several millions. But it was a disappointment to the Deity. He was dissatisfied with its morals; which in
some respects were not any better than his own. Indeed they were
an unflatteringly close imitation of his own. They were a very bad
people, and as he knew of no way to reform them, he wisely concluded to abolish them. This is the only really enlightened and
superior idea his Bible has credited him with, and it would have
made his reputation for all time if he could only have kept to it
and carried it out. But he was always unstable—except in his ad-

vertisements—and his good resolution broke down. He took a pride in man; man was his finest invention; man was his pet, after the housefly, and he could not bear to lose him wholly; so he finally decided to save a sample of him and drown the rest.

Nothing could be more characteristic of him. He created all those infamous people, and he alone was responsible for their conduct. Not one of them deserved death, yet it was certainly good policy to extinguish them; especially since in creating them the master crime had already been committed, and to allow them to go on procreating would be a distinct *addition* to the crime. But at the same time there could be no justice, no fairness, in any favoritism—*all* should be drowned or none.

No, he would not have it so; he would save half a dozen and try the race over again. He was not able to foresee that it would go rotten again, for he is only the Far-Sighted One in his advertisements.

He saved out Noah and his family, and arranged to exterminate the rest. He planned an Ark, and Noah built it. Neither of them had ever built an Ark before, nor knew anything about Arks; and so something out of the common was to be expected. It happened. Noah was a farmer, and although he knew what was required of the Ark he was quite incompetent to say whether this one would be large enough to meet the requirements or not (which it wasn't), so he ventured no advice. The Deity did not know it wasn't large enough, but took the chances and made no adequate measurements. In the end the ship fell far short of the necessities, and to this day the world still suffers for it.

Noah built the Ark. He built it the best he could, but left out most of the essentials. It had no rudder, it had no sails, it had no compass, it had no pumps, it had no charts, no lead-lines, no anchors, no log, no light, no ventilation; and as for cargo-room— which was the main thing—the less said about that the better. It was to be at sea eleven months, and would need fresh water enough to fill two Arks of its size—yet the additional Ark was not provided. Water from outside could not be utilized: half of it would be salt water, and men and land-animals could not drink it.

For not only was a sample of man to be saved, but business-samples of the other animals, too. You must understand that when Adam ate the apple in the Garden and learned how to multiply and replenish, the other animals learned the Art, too, by watching Adam. It was cunning of them, it was neat; for they got all that was worth having out of the apple without tasting it and afflicting themselves with the disastrous Moral Sense, the parent of all the immoralities.

Letter . . .

Noah began to collect animals. There was to be one couple of each and every sort of creature that walked or crawled, or swam or flew, in the world of animated nature. We have to guess at how long it took to collect the creatures and how much it cost, for there is no record of these details. When Symmachus made preparation to introduce his young son to grown-up life in imperial Rome, he sent men to Asia, Africa and everywhere to collect wild animals for the arena-fights. It took the men three years to accumulate the animals and fetch them to Rome. Merely quadrupeds and alligators, you understand—no birds, no snakes, no frogs, no worms, no lice, no rats, no fleas, no ticks, no caterpillars, no spiders, no houseflies, no mosquitoes,—nothing but just plain simple quadrupeds and alligators; and no quadrupeds except fighting ones. Yet it was as I have said: it took three years to collect them, and the cost of animals and transportation and the men's wages footed up $4,500,000.

How many animals? We do not know. But it was under 5,000, for that was the largest number *ever* gathered for those Roman shows, and it was Titus, not Symmachus, who made that collection. Those were mere baby-museums, compared to Noah's contract. Of birds and beasts and fresh-water creatures he had to collect 146,000 kinds; and of insects upwards of 2,000,000 species.

Thousands and thousands of those things are very difficult to catch, and if Noah had not given up and resigned, he would be on the job yet, as Leviticus used to say. However, I do not mean that he withdrew. No, he did not do that. He gathered as many creatures as he had room for, and then stopped.

If he had known all the requirements in the beginning, he would have been aware that what was needed was a fleet of Arks. But he did not know how many kinds of creatures there were, neither did his Chief. So he had no kangaroo, and no 'possum, and no Gila Monster, and no ornithorhynchus, and lacked a multitude of other indispensable blessings which a loving Creator had provided for man and forgotten about, they having long ago wandered to a side of his world which he had never seen and with whose affairs he was not acquainted. And so every one of them came within a hair of getting drowned.

They only escaped by an accident: there was not water enough to go around. Only enough was provided to flood one small corner of the globe—the rest of the globe was not then known, and was supposed to be non-existent.

However, the thing that really and finally and definitely determined Noah to stop with enough species for purely business purposes and let the rest become extinct, was an incident of the last days: an excited stranger arrived with some most alarming news. He said he had been camping among some mountains and valleys about six hundred miles away, and he had seen a wonderful thing there: he stood upon a precipice overlooking a wide valley, and up the valley he saw a billowy black sea of strange animal life coming. Presently the creatures passed by, struggling, fighting, scrambling, screeching, snorting—horrible vast masses of tumultuous flesh! Sloths as big as an elephant; frogs as big as a cow; a megatherium and his harem, huge beyond belief; saurians and saurians and saurians, group after group, family after family, species after species—a hundred feet long, thirty feet high, and twice as quarrelsome; one of them hit a perfectly blameless Durham bull a thump with its tail and sent it whizzing three hundred feet into the air and it fell at the man's feet with a sigh and was no more. The man said that these prodigious animals had heard about the Ark and were coming. Coming to get saved from the flood. And not coming in pairs, they were *all* coming: they did not know the passengers were restricted to pairs, the man said, and wouldn't care a rap for the regulations, anyway—they would sail in that Ark or know the reason why. The man said the Ark would not hold the half of them; and moreover they were coming hungry, and would eat up everything there was, including the menagerie and the family.

All these facts were suppressed, in the Biblical account. You find not a hint of them there. The whole thing is hushed up. Not even the names of those vast creatures are mentioned. It shows you that when people have left a reproachful vacancy in a contract they can be as shady about it in Bibles as elsewhere. Those powerful animals would be of inestimable value to man now, when transportation is so hard pressed and expensive, but they are all lost to him. All lost, and by Noah's fault. They all got drowned. Some of them as much as eight million years ago.

Very well, the stranger told his tale, and Noah saw that he must get away before the monsters arrived. He would have sailed at once, but the upholsterers and decorators of the housefly's drawing room still had some finishing touches to put on, and that lost him a day. Another day was lost in getting the flies aboard, there being sixty-eight billions of them and the Deity still afraid there might not be enough. Another day was lost in stowing 40 tons of selected filth for the fly's sustenance.

Then at last, Noah sailed; and none too soon, for the Ark was only just sinking out of sight on the horizon when the monsters arrived, and added their lamentations to those of the multitude of weeping fathers and mothers and frightened little children who were clinging to the wave-washed rocks in the pouring rain and lifting imploring prayers to an All-Just and All-Forgiving and All-Pitying Being who had never answered a prayer since those crags

were builded, grain by grain out of the sands, and would still not
have answered one when the ages should have crumbled them to
sand again.

Letter VII

On the third day, about noon, it was found that a fly had been
left behind. The return-voyage turned out to be long and difficult,
on account of the lack of chart and compass, and because of the
changed aspects of all coasts, the steadily rising water having submerged some of the lower landmarks and given to higher ones an
unfamiliar look; but after sixteen days of earnest and faithful
seeking, the fly was found at last, and received on board with
hymns of praise and gratitude, the Family standing meanwhile
uncovered, out of reverence for its divine origin. It was weary and
worn, and had suffered somewhat from the weather, but was otherwise in good estate. Men and their families had died of hunger
on barren mountain tops, but It had not lacked for food, the
multitudinous corpses furnishing it in rank and rotten richness.
Thus was the sacred bird providentially preserved.

Providentially. That is the word. For the fly had not been
left behind by accident. No, the hand of Providence was in it.
There are no accidents. All things that happen, happen for a purpose. They are foreseen from the beginning of time, they are ordained from the beginning of time. From the dawn of Creation
the Lord had foreseen that Noah, being alarmed and confused by
the invasion of the prodigious brevet Fossils, would prematurely
fly to sea unprovided with a certain invaluable disease. He would
have all the other diseases, and could distribute them among the
new races of men as they appeared in the world, but he would lack
one of the very best—typhoid fever; a malady which, when the
circumstances are especially favorable, is able to utterly wreck a
patient without killing him; for it can restore him to his feet with
a long life in him, and yet deaf, dumb, blind, crippled and idiotic.
The housefly is its main disseminator, and is more competent and
more calamitously effective than all the other distributors of the

dreaded scourge put together. And so, by foreordination from the beginning of time, this fly was left behind to seek out a typhoid corpse and feed upon its corruptions and gaum its legs with the germs and transmit them to the repeopled world for permanent business. From that one housefly, in the ages that have since elapsed, billions of sickbeds have been stocked, billions of wrecked bodies sent tottering about the earth, and billions of cemeteries recruited with the dead.

It is most difficult to understand the disposition of the Bible God, it is such a confusion of contradictions; of watery instabilities and iron firmnesses; of goody-goody abstract morals made out of words, and concreted hell-born ones made out of *acts*; of fleeting kindnesses repented of in permanent malignities.

However, when after much puzzling you get at the key to his disposition, you do at last arrive at a sort of understanding of it. With a most quaint and juvenile and astonishing frankness he has furnished that key himself. It is *jealousy*!

I expect that to take your breath away. You are aware—for I have already told you in an earlier letter—that among human beings jealousy ranks distinctly as a *weakness*; a trade-mark of small minds; a property of *all* small minds, yet a property which even the smallest is ashamed of; and when accused of its possession will lyingly deny it and resent the accusation as an insult.

Jealousy. Do not forget it, keep it in mind. It is the key. With it you will come to partly understand God as we go along; without it nobody can understand him. As I have said, he has openly held up this treasonous key himself, for all to see. He says, naïvely, outspokenly, and without suggestion of embarrassment,

"I the Lord thy God am a jealous God."

You see, it is only another way of saying,

"I the Lord thy God am a small God; a small God, and fretful about small things."

He was giving a warning: he could not bear the thought of any other God getting some of the Sunday compliments of this comical little human race—he wanted all of them for himself. He valued them. To him they were riches; just as tin money is to a Zulu.

But wait—I am not fair; I am misrepresenting him; prejudice is beguiling me into saying what is not true. He did not say he wanted all of the adulations; he said nothing about not being willing to share them with his fellow-gods; what he said was,

"Thou shalt have no other gods *before* me."

It is a quite different thing, and puts him in a much better light—I confess it. There was an abundance of gods, the woods were full of them, as the saying is, and all he demanded was, that he should be ranked as high as the others—not above any of them, but not below any of them. He was willing that they should fertilize earthly virgins, but not on any better terms than he could have for himself in his turn. He wanted to be held their equal. This he insisted upon, in the clearest language: he would have no other gods *before* him. They could march abreast with him, but none of them could head the procession, and he did not claim the right to head it himself.

Do you think he was able to stick to that upright and creditable position? No. He could keep to a bad resolution forever, but he couldn't keep to a good one a month. By and by he threw this one aside and calmly claimed to be the only God in the entire universe.

As I was saying, jealousy is the key; all through his history it is present and prominent. It is the blood and bone of his disposition, it is the basis of his character. How small a thing can wreck his composure and disorder his judgment if it touches the raw of his jealousy! And nothing warms up this trait so quickly and so surely and so exaggeratedly as a suspicion that some competition with the god-Trust is impending. The fear that if Adam and Eve ate of the fruit of the Tree of Knowledge they would "be as gods," so fired his jealousy that his reason was affected, and he could not treat those poor creatures either fairly or charitably, or even refrain from dealing cruelly and criminally with their blameless posterity.

To this day his reason has never recovered from that shock; a wild nightmare of vengefulness has possessed him ever since, and he has almost bankrupted his native ingenuities in inventing pains and miseries and humiliations and heartbreaks wherewith to embitter the brief lives of Adam's descendants. Think of the diseases he has contrived for them! They are multitudinous; no book can name them all. And each one is a trap, set for an innocent victim.

The human being is a machine. An automatic machine. It is composed of thousands of complex and delicate mechanisms, which perform their functions harmoniously and perfectly, in accordance with laws devised for their governance, and over which the man himself has no authority, no mastership, no control. For each one of these thousands of mechanisms the Creator has planned an enemy, whose office is to harass it, pester it, persecute it, damage it, afflict it with pains, and miseries, and ultimate destruction. Not one has been overlooked.

From cradle to grave these enemies are always at work, they know no rest, night nor day. They are an army; an organized army; a besieging army; an assaulting army; an army that is alert, watchful, eager, merciless; an army that never wearies, never relents, never grants a truce.

It moves by squad, by company, by battalion, by regiment, by brigade, by division, by army corps; upon occasion it masses its parts and moves upon mankind with its whole strength. It is the Creator's Grand Army, and he is the Commander in Chief. Along its battlefront its grisly banners wave their legends in the face of the sun: Disaster, Disease, and the rest.

Disease! that is the main force, the diligent force, the devastating force! It attacks the infant the moment it is born; it furnishes it one malady after another: croup, measles, mumps, bowel-troubles, teething-pains, scarlet fever, and other childhood specialties. It chases the child into youth and furnishes it some specialties for that time of life. It chases the youth into maturity; maturity into age, and age into the grave.

With these facts before you will you now try to guess man's chiefest pet name for this ferocious Commander in Chief? I will save you the trouble—but you must not laugh. It is Our Father in Heaven!

It is curious—the way the human mind works. The Christian begins with this straight proposition, this definite proposition, this inflexible and uncompromising proposition: *God is all-knowing, and all-powerful.*

This being the case, nothing can happen without his knowing beforehand that it is going to happen; nothing happens without his permission; nothing can happen that he chooses to prevent.

That is definite enough, isn't it? It makes the Creator distinctly responsible for everything that happens, doesn't it?

The Christian concedes it in that italicised sentence. Concedes it with feeling, with enthusiasm.

Then, having thus made the Creator responsible for all those pains and diseases and miseries above enumerated, and which he could have prevented, the gifted Christian blandly calls him Our Father!

It is as I tell you. He equips the Creator with every trait that goes to the making of a fiend, and then arrives at the conclusion that a fiend and a father are the same thing! Yet he would deny that a malevolent lunatic and a Sunday school superintendent are essentially the same. What do you think of the human mind? I mean, in case you think there is a human mind.

Letter . . .

Noah and his family were saved—if that could be called an advantage. I throw in the *if* for the reason that there has never been an intelligent person of the age of sixty who would consent to live his life over again. His or any one else's. The family were saved, yes, but they were not comfortable, for they were full of microbes. Full to the eyebrows; fat with them, obese with them; distended like balloons. It was a disagreeable condition, but it could not be helped, because enough microbes had to be saved to supply the future races of men with desolating diseases, and there were but eight persons on board to serve as hotels for them. The microbes were by far the most important part of the Ark's cargo, and the part the Creator was most anxious about and most infatuated with. They had to have good nourishment and pleasant accommodations. There were typhoid germs, and cholera germs, and hydrophobia germs, and lockjaw germs, and consumption germs, and black-plague germs, and some hundreds of other aristocrats, specially precious creations, golden bearers of God's love to man, blessed gifts of the infatuated Father to his children—all of which had to be sumptuously housed and richly entertained; these were located in the choicest places the interiors of the family could furnish: in the lungs, in the heart, in the brain, in the kidneys, in the blood, in the guts. In the guts particularly. The great intestine was the favorite resort. There they gathered, by countless billions, and worked, and fed, and squirmed, and sang hymns of praise and thanksgiving; and at night when it was quiet you could hear the soft murmur of it. The large intestine was in effect their heaven. They stuffed it solid; they made it as rigid as a coil of gaspipe. They took a pride in this. Their principal hymn made gratified reference to it:

> "Constipation, O constipation,
>   The joyful sound proclaim
> Till man's remotest entrail
>   Shall praise its makers' name."

The discomforts furnished by the Ark were many, and various. The family had to live right in the presence of the multitudinous animals, and breathe the distressing stench they made and be deafened day and night with the thunder-crash of noise their roarings and screechings produced; and in addition to these intolerable discomforts it was a peculiarly trying place for the ladies, for they could look in no direction without seeing some thousands of the creatures engaged in multiplying and replenishing. And then, there were the flies. They swarmed everywhere, and persecuted the family all day long. They were the first animals up, in the morning, and the last ones down, at night. But they must not be killed, they must not be injured, they were sacred, their origin was divine, they were the special pets of the Creator, his darlings.

By and by the other creatures would be distributed here and there about the earth—*scattered*: the tigers to India, the lion and the elephant to the vacant desert and the secret places of the jungle, the birds to the boundless regions of empty space, the insects to one or another climate, according to nature and requirement; but the fly? He is of no nationality; all the climates are his home, all the globe is his province, all creatures that breathe are his prey, and unto them all he is a scourge and a hell.

To man he is a divine ambassador, a minister plenipotentiary, the Creator's special representative. He infests him in his cradle; clings in bunches to his gummy eyelids; buzzes and bites and harries him, robbing him of his sleep and his weary mother of her strength in those long vigils which she devotes to protecting her child from this pest's persecutions. The fly harries the sick man in his home, in the hospital, even on his death-bed at his last gasp. Pesters him at his meals; previously hunts up patients suffering from loathsome and deadly diseases; wades in their sores, gaums its legs with a million death-dealing germs, then comes to that healthy man's table and wipes these things off on the butter and discharges a bowel-load of typhoid germs and excrement on his batter-cakes. The housefly wrecks more human constitutions and destroys more human lives than all God's multitude of misery-messengers and death-agents put together.

Shem was full of hookworms. It is wonderful, the thorough and comprehensive study which the Creator devoted to the great work of making man miserable. I have said he devised a special affliction-agent for each and every detail of man's structure, overlooking not a single one, and I said the truth. Many poor people have to go barefoot, because they cannot afford shoes. The Creator saw his opportunity. I will remark, in passing, that he always has his eye on the poor. Nine-tenths of his disease-inventions were intended for the poor, and they *get* them. The well-to-do get only what is left over. Do not suspect me of speaking unheedfully, for it is not so: the vast bulk of the Creator's affliction-inventions *are* specially designed for the persecution of the poor. You could guess this by the fact that one of the pulpit's finest and commonest names for the Creator is "The Friend of the Poor." Under no circumstances does the pulpit ever pay the Creator a compliment that has a vestige of truth in it. The poor's most implacable and unwearying enemy is their Father in Heaven. The poor's only real friend is their fellow man. He is sorry for them, he pities them, and he shows it by his deeds. He does much to relieve their distresses; and in every case their Father in Heaven gets the credit of it.

Just so with diseases. If science exterminates a disease which has been working for God, it is God that gets the credit, and all the pulpits break into grateful advertising-raptures and call attention to how good he is! Yes, *he* has done it. Perhaps he has waited a thousand years before doing it. That is nothing; the pulpit says he was thinking about it all the time. When exasperated men rise up and sweep away an age-long tyranny and set a nation free, the first thing the delighted pulpit does is to advertise it as God's work, and invite the people to get down on their knees and pour out their thanks to him for it. And the pulpit says with admiring emotion, "Let tyrants understand that the Eye that never sleeps is upon them; and let them remember that the Lord our God will not always be patient, but will loose the whirlwinds of his wrath upon them in his appointed day."

They forget to mention that he is the slowest mover in the universe; that his Eye that never sleeps, might as well, since it takes it a century to see what any other eye would see in a week; that in all history there is not an instance where he thought of a noble deed *first*, but always thought of it just a little after somebody else had thought of it and *done* it. He arrives then, and annexes the dividend.

Very well, six thousand years ago Shem was full of hookworms. Microscopic in size, invisible to the unaided eye. All of the Creator's specially-deadly disease-producers are invisible. It is an ingenious idea. For thousands of years it kept man from getting at the roots of his maladies, and defeated his attempts to master them. It is only very recently that science has succeeded in exposing some of these treacheries.

The very latest of these blessed triumphs of science is the discovery and identification of the ambuscaded assassin which goes by the name of the hookworm. Its special prey is the barefooted poor. It lies in wait in warm regions and sandy places and digs its way into their unprotected feet.

The hookworm was discovered two or three years ago by a physician, who had been patiently studying its victims for a long time. The disease induced by the hookworm had been doing its evil work here and there in the earth ever since Shem landed on Ararat, but it was never suspected to *be* a disease at all. The people who had it were merely supposed to be *lazy*, and were therefore despised and made fun of, when they should have been pitied. The hookworm is a peculiarly sneaking and underhand invention, and has done its surreptitious work unmolested for ages; but that physician and his helpers will exterminate it now.

God is back of this. He has been thinking about it for six thousand years, and making up his mind. The idea of exterminating the hookworm was his. He came very near doing it before Dr. Charles Wardell Stiles did. But he is in time to get the credit of it. He always is.

It is going to cost a million dollars. He was probably just in the act of contributing that sum when a man pushed in ahead of him—as usual. Mr. Rockefeller. He furnishes the million, but the credit will go elsewhere—as usual. This morning's journals tell us something about the hookworm's operations:

The hookworm parasites often so lower the vitality of those who are affected as to retard their physical and mental development, render them more susceptible to other diseases, make labor less efficient, and in the sections where the malady is most prevalent greatly increase the death rate from consumption, pneumonia, typhoid fever and malaria. It has been shown that the lowered vitality of multitudes, long attrib-

uted to malaria and climate and seriously affecting economic development, is in fact due in some districts to this parasite. The disease is by
no means confined to any one class; it takes its toll of suffering and
death from the highly intelligent and well to do as well as from the
less fortunate. It is a conservative estimate that two millions of our
people are affected by this parasite. The disease is more common and
more serious in children of school age than in other persons.

Widespread and serious as the infection is, there is still a most
encouraging outlook. The disease can be easily recognized, readily and
effectively treated and by simple and proper sanitary precautions successfully prevented, with God's help.

The poor little children are under the Eye that never sleeps,
you see. They have had that ill luck in all the ages. They and "the
Lord's poor"—as the sarcastic phrase goes—have never been able
to get away from that Eye's attentions.

Yes, the poor, the humble, the ignorant—they are the ones
that catch it. Take the "sleeping sickness," of Africa. This atrocious cruelty has for its victims a race of ignorant and unoffending
blacks whom God placed in a remote wilderness, and bent his
parental Eye upon them—the one that never sleeps when there is
a chance to breed sorrow for somebody. He arranged for these people before the Flood. The chosen agent was a fly, related to the
tzetze; the tzetze is a fly which has command of the Zambesi country and stings cattle and horses to death, thus rendering that region
uninhabitable by man. The tzetze's awful relative deposits a
microbe which produces the Sleeping Sickness. Ham was full of
these microbes, and when the voyage was over he discharged them
in Africa and the havoc began, never to find amelioration until six
thousand years should go by and science should pry into the mystery and hunt out the cause of the disease. The pious nations are
now thanking God, and praising him for coming to the rescue of
his poor blacks. The pulpit says the praise is due to him, for the
reason that the scientists got their inspiration from him. He is
surely a curious Being. He commits a fearful crime, continues that
crime unbroken for six thousand years, and is then entitled to

praise because he suggests to somebody else to modify its severities. He is called patient, and he certainly must be patient, or he would have sunk the pulpit in perdition ages ago for the ghastly compliments it pays him.

Science has this to say about the Sleeping Sickness, otherwise called the Negro Lethargy.

It is characterised by periods of sleep recurring at intervals. The disease lasts from four months to four years, and is always fatal. The victim appears at first languid, weak, pallid, and stupid. His eyelids become puffy, an eruption appears on his skin. He falls asleep while talking, eating, or working. As the disease progresses he is fed with difficulty and becomes much emaciated. The failure of nutrition and the appearance of bedsores are followed by convulsions and death. Some patients become insane.

It is he whom Church and people call Our Father in Heaven who has invented the fly and sent him to inflict this dreary long misery and melancholy and wretchedness, and decay of body and mind, upon a poor savage who has done the Great Criminal no harm. There isn't a man in the world who doesn't pity that poor black sufferer, and there isn't a man that wouldn't make him whole if he could. To find the one person who has no pity for him you must go to heaven; to find the one person who is able to heal him and couldn't be persuaded to do it, you must go to the same place. There is only one father cruel enough to afflict his child with that horrible disease—only one. Not all the eternities can produce another one. Do you like reproachful poetical indignations warmly expressed? Here is one, hot from the heart of a slave:

> "*Man's* inhumanity to man
> Makes countless thousands mourn!"

I will tell you a pleasant tale which has in it a touch of pathos. A man got religion, and asked the priest what he must do to be worthy of his new estate. The priest said, "Imitate our Father in

Heaven, learn to be like him." The man studied his Bible diligently and thoroughly and understandingly, and then with prayers
for heavenly guidance instituted his imitations. He tricked his wife
into falling down stairs, and she broke her back and became a
paralytic for life; he betrayed his brother into the hands of a
sharper, who robbed him of his all and landed him in the alms-
house; he inoculated one son with hookworms, another with the
sleeping sickness, another with the gonorrhea, he furnished one
daughter with scarlet fever and ushered her into her teens deaf
dumb and blind for life; and after helping a rascal seduce the remaining one, he closed his doors against her and she died in a
brothel cursing him. Then he reported to the priest, who said that
that was no way to imitate his Father in Heaven. The convert
asked wherein he had failed, but the priest changed the subject
and inquired what kind of weather he was having, up his way.

Letter . . .

Man is without any doubt the most interesting fool there is.
Also the most eccentric. He hasn't a single written law, in his
Bible or out of it, which has any but just one purpose and inten-
tion—to *limit or defeat a law of God.*

He can seldom take a plain fact and get any but a wrong
meaning out of it. He cannot help this; it is the way the confusion
he calls his mind is constructed. Consider the things he concedes,
and the curious conclusions he draws from them.

For instance, he concedes that God made man. Made him
without man's desire or privity.

This seems to plainly and indisputably make God, and God
alone, responsible for man's acts. But man denies this.

He concedes that God has made angels perfect, without
blemish, and immune from pain and death, and that he could have
been similarly kind to man if he had wanted to, but denies that
he was under any moral obligation to do it.

He concedes that man has no moral right to visit the child of
his begetting with wanton cruelties, painful diseases and death,

but refuses to limit God's privileges in this sort with the children of his begetting.

The Bible and man's statutes forbid murder, adultery, fornication, lying, treachery, robbery, oppression and other crimes, but contend that God is free of these laws and has a right to break them when he will.

He concedes that God gives to each man his temperament, his disposition, at birth; he concedes that man cannot by any process change this temperament, but must remain always under its dominion. Yet if it be full of dreadful passions, in one man's case, and barren of them in another man's, it is right and rational to punish the one for his crimes, and reward the other for abstaining from crime.

There—let us consider these curiosities.

Temperament (*disposition.*) Take two extremes of temperament—the goat and the tortoise.

Neither of these creatures makes its own temperament, but is born with it, like man, and can no more change it than can man.

Temperament is the *law of God*, written in the heart of every creature by God's own hand, and *must* be obeyed, and *will* be obeyed, in spite of all restricting or forbidding statutes, let them emanate whence they may.

Very well, lust is the dominant feature of the goat's temperament, the law of God in its heart, and it must obey it and *will* obey it the whole day long in the rutting season; without stopping to eat or drink. If the Bible said to the goat "Thou shalt not fornicate, thou shalt not commit adultery," even man—sapheaded man —would recognize the foolishness of the prohibition, and would grant that the goat ought not to be punished for obeying the law of his make. Yet he thinks it right and just that man should be put under the prohibition. *All* men. All alike.

On its face this is stupid, for, by temperament, which is the *real* law of God, many men are *goats* and can't *help* committing adultery when they get a chance; whereas there are numbers of men who, by temperament, can keep their purity and let an opportunity go by if the woman lacks in attractiveness. But the Bible doesn't allow adultery *at all*, whether a person can help it or not. It allows no distinction between goat and tortoise—the excitable goat, the emotional goat, that *has* to have some adultery every day or fade and die; and the tortoise, that cold calm puritan, that takes a treat only once in two years and then goes to sleep in the midst of it and doesn't wake up for sixty days. No lady goat is safe from criminal assault, even on the Sabbath Day, when there is a gentleman goat within three miles to leeward of her and nothing in the way but a fence fourteen feet high, whereas neither the gentleman tortoise nor the lady tortoise is ever hungry enough for the solemn joys of fornication to be willing to break the Sabbath to get them. Now according to man's curious reasoning, the goat has earned punishment, and the tortoise praise.

"Thou shalt not commit adultery" is a command which makes no distinction between the following persons. They are all required to obey it:

Children at birth.

Children in the cradle.

School children.

Youths and maidens.

Fresh adults.

Older ones.

Men and women of 40.

Of 50.

Of 60.

Of 70.

Of 80.

Of 90.

Of 100.

The command does not distribute its burden equally, and cannot.

It is not hard upon the three sets of children.

It is hard—harder—still harder upon the next three sets—cruelly hard.

It is blessedly softened to the next three sets.

It has now done all the damage it can, and might as well be put out of commission.

Yet with comical imbecility it is continued, and the four remaining estates are put under its crushing ban. Poor old wrecks, they couldn't disobey if they tried. And think—because they holily refrain from adulterating each other, they get praise for it! Which is nonsense; for even the Bible knows enough to know that if the oldest veteran there could get his lost hey-day back again for an hour he would cast that commandment to the winds and ruin the first woman he came across, even though she were an entire stranger.

It is as I have said: every statute in the Bible and in the law books is an attempt to defeat a law of God—in other words an unalterable and indestructible law of nature. These people's God has shown them by a million acts that he respects none of the Bible's statutes. He breaks every one of them himself, adultery and all.

The law of God, as quite plainly expressed in woman's *construction* is this:

There shall be *no limit* put upon your intercourse with the other sex sexually, at any time of life.

The law of God, as quite plainly expressed in *man's* construction is this:

During your entire life you shall be under inflexible *limits and restrictions*, sexually.

During 27 days in every month (in the absence of pregnancy) from the time a woman is seven years old till she dies of old age, she is ready for action, and *competent*. As competent as the candlestick is to receive the candle. Competent every day, competent every night. Also, she *wants* that candle—yearns for it, longs for it, hankers after it, as commanded by the law of God in her heart.

But man is only briefly competent; and only then in the moderate measure applicable to the word in *his* sex's case. He is competent from the age of sixteen or seventeen thenceforward for thirty-five years. After 50 his performance is of poor quality, the intervals between are wide, and its satisfactions of no great value to either party; whereas his great-grandmother is as good as new. There is nothing the matter with her plant. Her candlestick is as firm as ever, whereas his candle is increasingly softened and weakened by the weather of age, as the years go by, until at last it can no longer stand, and is mournfully laid to rest in the hope of a blessed resurrection which is never to come.

By the woman's make, her plant has to be out of service three days in the month and during a part of her pregnancy. These are times of discomfort, often of suffering. For fair and just compensation she has the high privilege of unlimited adultery all the other days of her life.

That is the law of God, as revealed in her make. What becomes of this high privilege? Does she live in the free enjoyment of it? No. Nowhere in the whole world. She is robbed of it everywhere. Who does this? Man. Man's statutes—ordained against her without allowing her a vote. Also God's statutes—if the Bible *is* the Word of God.

Now there you have a sample of man's "reasoning powers," as he calls them. He observes certain facts. For instance, that in all his life he never sees the day that he can satisfy *one* woman; also, that no woman ever sees the day that she can't overwork, and defeat, and put out of commission any *ten* masculine plants that can be put to bed to her.* He puts those strikingly-suggestive and

---

* In the Sandwich Islands in 1866 a buxom royal princess died. Occupying a place of distinguished honor at her funeral were 36 splendidly built young native men. In a laudatory song which celebrated the various merits, achievements and

luminous facts together, and from them draws this astonishing conclusion:

The Creator intended the woman to be restricted to one man.

So he concretes that singular conclusion into a *law*, for good and all.

And he does it without consulting the woman, although she has a thousand times more at stake in the matter than he has. His procreative competency is limited to an average of a hundred exercises per year for 50 years, hers is good for 3,000 a year for that whole time—and as many years longer as she may live. Thus his life-interest in the matter is 5,000 refreshments, while hers is 150,000; yet instead of fairly and honorably leaving the making of the law to the person who has an overwhelming interest at stake in it, this immeasurable hog, who has nothing at stake in it worth considering, makes it himself!

You have heretofore found out, by my teachings, that man is a fool; you are now aware that woman is a *damned* fool.

Now if you or any other really intelligent person were arranging the fairnesses and justices between man and woman, you would give the man a one-fiftieth interest in one woman, and the woman a *harem*. Now wouldn't you? Necessarily. I give you my word, this creature with the decrepit candle has arranged it exactly the other way. Solomon, who was one of the Deity's favorites, had a copulation-cabinet composed of 700 wives and 300 concubines. To save his life he could not have kept two of those young creatures satisfactorily refreshed, even if he had had fifteen experts to help him. Necessarily almost the entire thousand had to go hungry years and years on a stretch. Conceive of a man hard-hearted enough to look daily upon all that suffering and not be moved to mitigate it. He even wantonly *added* a sharp pang to that pathetic misery; for he kept within those women's sight, always, stalwart

---

accomplishments of the late princess those 36 stallions were called her *harem*, and the song said it had been her pride and her boast that she kept the whole of them busy, and that several times it had happened that more than one of them had been able to charge overtime.

watchmen whose splendid masculine forms made the poor lassies' mouths water but who hadn't anything to solace a candlestick with, these gentry being eunuchs. A eunuch is a person whose candle has been put out. By art.*

From time to time, as I go along, I will take up a Biblical statute and show you that it always violates a law of God, and then is imported into the law books of the nations, where it continues its violations. But those things will keep; there is no hurry.

Letter . . .

The Ark continued its voyage, drifting around here and there and yonder, compassless and uncontrolled, the sport of the random winds and the swirling currents. And the rain, the rain, the rain! it kept on falling, pouring, drenching, flooding. No such rain had ever been seen before. Sixteen inches a day had been heard of, but that was nothing to this. This was a hundred and twenty inches a day—ten feet! At this incredible rate it rained forty days and forty nights, and submerged every hill that was 400 feet high. Then the heavens and even the angels went dry; no more water was to be had.

As a Universal Flood it was a disappointment, but there had been heaps of Universal Floods before, as is witnessed by all the Bibles of all the nations, and this was as good as the best one.

At last the Ark soared aloft and came to a rest on the top of Mount Ararat, 17,000 feet above the valley, and its living freight got out and went down the mountain.

Noah planted a vineyard, and drank of the wine and was overcome.

This person had been selected from all the populations because he was the best sample there was. He was to start the human race on a new basis. This was the new basis. The promise was bad. To go further with the experiment was to run a great and most

* I purpose publishing these Letters here in the world before I return to you. Two editions. One, unedited, for Bible readers and their children; the other, expurgated, for persons of refinement.

unwise risk. Now was the time to do with these people what had been so judiciously done with the others—drown them. Anybody but the Creator would have seen this. But he didn't see it. That is, maybe he didn't.

It is claimed that from the beginning of time he foresaw everything that would happen in the world. If that is true, he foresaw that Adam and Eve would eat the apple; that their posterity would be unendurable and have to be drowned; that Noah's posterity would in their turn be unendurable, and that by and by he would have to leave his throne in heaven and come down and be crucified to save that same tiresome human race again. The whole of it? No! A part of it? Yes. How much of it? In each generation, for hundreds and hundreds of generations, a billion would die and all go to perdition except perhaps ten thousand out of the billion. The ten thousand would have to come from the little body of Christians, and only one in the hundred of that little body would stand any chance. None of them at all except such Roman Catholics as should have the luck to have a priest handy to sand-paper their souls at the last gasp, and here and there a Presbyterian. No others saveable. All the others damned. By the million.

Shall you grant that he foresaw all this? The pulpit grants it. It is the same as granting that in the matter of intellect the Deity is the Head Pauper of the Universe, and that in the matter of morals and character he is away down on the level of David.

Letter . . .

The two Testaments are interesting, each in its own way. The Old one gives us a picture of these people's Deity as he was before he got religion, the other one gives us a picture of him as he appeared afterward. The Old Testament is interested mainly in blood and sensuality, the New one in salvation. Salvation by fire.

The first time the Deity came down to earth he brought life and death; when he came the second time, he brought hell.

Life was not a valuable gift, but death was. Life was a fever-dream made up of joys embittered by sorrows, pleasure poisoned by pain; a dream that was a nightmare-confusion of spasmodic and fleeting delights, ecstasies, exultations, happinesses, interspersed with long-drawn miseries, griefs, perils, horrors, disappointments, defeats, humiliations and despairs—the heaviest curse devisable by divine ingenuity; but death was sweet, death was gentle, death was kind, death healed the bruised spirit and the broken heart, and gave them rest and forgetfulness; death was man's best friend, his only friend; when man could endure life no longer, death came, and set him free.

In time, the Deity perceived that death was a mistake; a mistake, in that it was insufficient; insufficient, for the reason that while it was an admirable agent for the inflicting of misery upon the survivor, it allowed the dead person himself to escape from all further persecution in the blessed refuge of the grave. This was not satisfactory. A way must be contrived to pursue the dead beyond the tomb.

The Deity pondered this matter during four thousand years unsuccessfully, but as soon as he came down to earth and became a Christian his mind cleared and he knew what to do. *He invented hell*, and proclaimed it.

Now here is a curious thing. It is believed by everybody that while he was in heaven he was stern, hard, resentful, jealous, and cruel; but that when he came down to earth and assumed the name Jesus Christ, he became the opposite of what he was before: that is to say, he became sweet, and gentle, merciful, forgiving, and all harshness disappeared from his nature and a deep and yearning love for his poor human children took its place. Whereas it was as Jesus Christ that he devised hell and proclaimed it!

Which is to say, that as the meek and gentle Savior he was a thousand billion times crueler than ever he was in the Old Testament—oh, incomparably more atrocious than ever he was when he was at his very worst in those old days!

Meek and gentle? By and by we will examine this popular sarcasm by the light of the hell which he invented.

Letter . . .

While it is true that the palm for malignity must be granted to Jesus, the inventor of hell, he was hard and ungentle enough for all godlike purposes even before he became a Christian. It does not appear that he ever stopped to reflect that *he* was to blame when a man went wrong, inasmuch as the man was merely acting in accordance with the disposition he had afflicted him with. No, he punished the man, instead of punishing himself. Moreover the punishment usually oversized the offence. Often, too, it fell, not upon the doer of a misdeed, but upon somebody else—a chief man, the head of a community, for instance.

And Israel abode in Shittim, and the people began to commit whoredom with the daughters of Moab.

And the Lord said unto Moses, Take *all the heads of the people*, and hang them up before the Lord against the sun, that the fierce anger of the Lord may be turned away from Israel.

Does that look fair to you? It does not appear that the "heads of the people" got any of the adultery, yet it is they that are hanged, instead of "the people."

If it was fair and right in that day it would be fair and right to-day, for the pulpit maintains that God's justice is eternal and unchangeable; also that he is the Fountain of Morals; and that his morals are eternal and unchangeable. Very well, then, we must believe that if the people of New York should begin to commit whoredom with the daughters of New Jersey, it would be fair and right to set up a gallows in front of the city hall and hang the mayor and the sheriff and the judges and the archbishop on it, although they did not get any of it. It does not look right to me.

Moreover, you may be quite sure of one thing: *it couldn't happen.* These people would not allow it. They are better than their Bible. *Nothing* would happen here, except some lawsuits, for damages, if the incident couldn't be hushed up; and even down

South they would not proceed against persons who did not get any of it; they would get a rope and hunt for the corespondents; and if they couldn't find them they would lynch a nigger.

Things have greatly improved since the Almighty's time, let the pulpit say what it may.

Will you examine the Deity's morals and disposition and conduct a little further? And will you remember that in the Sunday school the little children are urged to love the Almighty, and honor him, and praise him, and make him their model and try to be as like him as they can? Read:

1   And the LORD spake unto Moses, saying,

2   Avenge the children of Israel of the Midianites: afterward shalt thou be gathered unto thy people.

7   And they warred against the Midianites, as the LORD commanded Moses; and they slew all the males.

8   And they slew the kings of Midian, besides the rest of them that were slain; *namely*, Evi, and Rekem, and Zur, and Hur, and Reba, five kings of Midian: Balaam also the son of Beor they slew with the sword.

9   And the children of Israel took *all* the women of Midian captives, and their little ones, and took the spoil of all their cattle, and all their flocks, and all their goods.

10   And they burnt all their cities wherein they dwelt, and all their goodly castles, with fire.

11   And they took all the spoil, and all the prey, *both* of men and of beasts.

12   And they brought the captives, and the prey, and the spoil unto Moses and Eleazar the priest, and unto the congregation of the children of Israel, unto the camp at the plains of Moab, which *are* by Jordan *near* Jericho.

13   And Moses, and Eleazar the priest, and all the princes of the congregation, went forth to meet them without the camp.

14   And Moses was wroth with the officers of the host, *with* the captains over thousands, and captains over hundreds, which came from the battle.

15   And Moses said unto them, Have ye saved all the women alive?

16   Behold, these caused the children of Israel, through the counsel of Balaam, to commit trespass against the LORD in the matter of Peor, and there was a plague among the congregation of the LORD.

17   Now therefore kill every male among the little ones, and kill every woman that hath known man by lying with him.

18   But all the women-children, that have not known a man by lying with him, keep alive for yourselves.

19   And do ye abide without the camp seven days: whosoever hath killed any person, and whosoever hath touched any slain, purify *both* yourselves and your captives on the third day, and on the seventh day.

20   And purify all *your* raiment, and all that is made of skins, and all work of goats' *hair*, and all things made of wood.

21   And Eleazar the priest said unto the men of war which went to the battle, This *is* the ordinance of the law which the LORD commanded Moses.

25   And the LORD spake unto Moses, saying,

26   Take the sum of the prey that was taken, *both* of man and of beast, thou, and Eleazar the priest, and the chief fathers of the congregation:

27   And divide the prey into two parts; between them that took the war upon them, who went out to battle, and between all the congregation:

28   And levy a tribute unto the LORD of the men of war which went out to battle.

31   And Moses and Eleazar the priest did as the LORD commanded Moses.

32   And the booty, *being* the rest of the prey which the men of war had caught, was six hundred thousand, and seventy thousand, and five thousand sheep,

33   And threescore and twelve thousand beeves,

34   And threescore and one thousand asses,

35   And thirty and two thousand persons in all, of women that had not known man by lying with him.

40 And the persons *were* sixteen thousand, of which the LORD's tribute *was* thirty and two persons.

41 And Moses gave the tribute, *which was* the LORD's heave-offering, unto *Eleazar* the priest; as the LORD commanded Moses.

47 Even of the children of Israel's half, Moses took one portion of fifty, *both* of man and of beast, and gave them unto the Levites, which kept the charge of the tabernacle of the LORD; as the LORD commanded Moses.

10 When thou comest nigh unto a city to fight against it, then proclaim peace unto it.

13 And when the LORD thy God hath delivered it into thine hands, thou shalt smite every male thereof with the edge of the sword:

14 But the women, and the little ones, and the cattle, and all that is in the city, *even* all the spoil thereof, shalt thou take unto thyself: and thou shalt eat the spoil of thine enemies, which the LORD thy God hath given thee.

15 Thus shalt thou do unto all the cities *which* are very far off from thee, which are not of the cities of these nations.

16 But of the cities of these people, which the LORD thy God doth give thee for an inheritance, *thou shalt save alive* NOTHING THAT BREATHETH.

The Biblical law says:
"Thou shalt not kill."
The law of *God*, planted in the heart of man at his birth, says:
"Thou *shalt* kill."
The chapter I have quoted, shows you that the book-statute is once more a failure. It cannot set aside the more powerful law of nature.

According to the belief of these people, it was God himself who said:
"Thou shalt not kill."
Then it is plain that he cannot keep his own commandments.
He killed all those people—*every male.*
They had offended the Deity in some way. We know what

the offence was, without looking; that is to say, we know it was a trifle; some small thing that no one but a god would attach any importance to. It is more than likely that a Midianite had been duplicating the conduct of one Onan, who was commanded to "go in unto his brother's wife"—which he did; but instead of finishing, "he spilled it on the ground." The Lord slew Onan for that, for the Lord could never abide indelicacy. The Lord slew Onan, and to this day the Christian world cannot understand why he stopped with Onan, instead of slaying all the inhabitants for three hundred miles around—they being innocent of offence, and therefore the very ones he would usually slay. For that had always been his idea of fair dealing. If he had had a motto, it would have read, "Let no innocent person escape." You remember what he did in the time of the flood. There were multitudes and multitudes of tiny little children, and he knew they had never done him any harm; but their *relations* had, and that was enough for him: he saw the waters rise toward their screaming lips, he saw the wild terror in their eyes, he saw that agony of appeal in the mothers' faces which would have touched any heart but his, but he was after the guiltless particularly, and he drowned those poor little chaps.

And you will remember that in the case of Adam's posterity *all* the billions are innocent—*none* of them had a share in his offence, but the Deity holds them guilty to this day. None gets off, except by acknowledging that guilt—no cheaper lie will answer.

Some Midianite must have repeated Onan's act, and brought that dire disaster upon his nation. If that was not the indelicacy that outraged the feelings of the Deity, then I know what it was: some Midianite had been *pissing against the wall*. I am sure of it, for that was an impropriety which the Source of all Etiquette *never* could stand. A person could piss against a tree, he could piss on his mother, he could piss his own breeches, and get off, but he must not piss against the wall—that would be going quite too far. The origin of the divine prejudice against this humble crime is not stated; but we know that the prejudice was very strong—so strong that nothing but a wholesale massacre of the people inhabiting the region where the wall was defiled could satisfy the Deity.

Take the case of Jeroboam. "I will cut off from Jeroboam him that pisseth against the wall." It was done. And not only was the man that did it cut off, but everybody else.

The same with the house of Baasha: everybody was exterminated, kinsfolks, friends, and all, leaving "not one that pisseth against a wall."

In the case of Jeroboam you have a striking instance of the Deity's custom of not limiting his punishments to the guilty; the innocent are included. Even the "remnant" of that unhappy house was removed, even "as a man taketh away dung, till it be all gone." That includes the women, the young maids, and the little girls. All innocent, for *they* couldn't piss against a wall. Nobody of that sex can. None but members of the other sex can achieve that feat.

A curious prejudice. And it still exists. Protestant parents still keep the Bible handy in the house, so that the children can study it; and one of the first things the little boys and girls learn is to be righteous and holy and not piss against the wall. They study those passages more than they study any others, except those which incite to masturbation. *Those* they hunt out and study in private. No Protestant child exists who does not masturbate. That art is the earliest accomplishment his religion confers upon him. Also the earliest *her* religion confers upon *her*.

The Bible has this advantage over all other books that teach refinement and good manners: that it goes to the child: it goes to the mind at its most impressible and receptive age—the others have to wait.

"Thou shalt have a paddle upon thy weapon: and it shall be, when thou wilt ease thyself abroad, thou shalt dig therewith, and shalt turn back and cover that which cometh from thee."

That rule was made in the old days because

"The Lord thy God walketh in the midst of thy camp."

It is probably not worth while to try to find out, for certain, why the Midianites were exterminated. We can only be sure that it was for no large offence; for the cases of Adam, and the Flood, and the defilers of the wall, teach us that much. A Midianite may have left his paddle at home and thus brought on the trouble. However, it is no matter. The main thing is the trouble itself, and the morals of one kind and another that it offers for the instruction and elevation of the Christian of to-day.

God wrote upon the tables of stone—
"Thou shalt not kill."
Also—
"Thou shalt not commit adultery."

Paul, speaking by the divine voice, advised against sexual intercourse *altogether*. A great change from the divine view as it existed at the time of the Midianite incident.

Letter . . .

Human history in all ages, is red with blood, and bitter with hate, and stained with cruelties; but not since Biblical times have these features been without a limit of some kind. Even the Church, which is credited with having spilt more innocent blood, since the beginning of its supremacy, than all the political wars put together have spilt, has observed a limit. A sort of limit. But you notice that when the Lord God of Heaven and Earth, adored Father of Man, goes to war, there is no limit. He is totally without mercy—he, who is called the Fountain of Mercy. He slays, slays, slays! all the men, all the beasts, all the boys, all the babies; also all the women and all the girls, except those that have not been deflowered.

He makes no distinction between innocent and guilty. The babies were innocent, the beasts were innocent, many of the men, many of the women, many of the boys, many of the girls, were innocent, yet they had to suffer with the guilty. What the insane Father required was blood and misery; he was indifferent as to who furnished it.

The heaviest punishment of all was meted out to persons who could not by any possibility have deserved so horrible a fate—the 32,000 virgins. Their naked privacies were probed, to make sure that they still possessed the hymen unruptured; after this humiliation they were sent away from the land that had been their home, to be sold into slavery; the worst of slaveries and the shamefulest, the slavery of prostitution; bed-slavery, to excite lust, and satisfy it with their bodies; slavery to any buyer, be he gentleman or be he a coarse and filthy ruffian.

It was the Father that inflicted this ferocious and undeserved punishment upon those bereaved and friendless virgins, whose parents and kindred he had slaughtered before their eyes. And were they praying to him for pity and rescue, meantime? Without a doubt of it.

These virgins were "spoil," plunder, booty. He claimed his share and got it. What use had *he* for virgins? Examine his later history and you will know.

His priests got a share of the virgins, too. What use could priests make of virgins? The private history of the Roman Catholic confessional can answer that question for you. The confessional's chief amusement has been seduction—in all the ages of the Church. Père Hyacinth testifies that of 100 priests confessed by him, 99 had used the confessional effectively for the seduction of married women and young girls. One priest confessed that of 900 girls and women whom he had served as father confessor in his time, none had escaped his lecherous embrace but the elderly and the homely. The official list of questions which the priest is *required* to ask will overmasteringly excite any woman who is not a paralytic.

There is nothing in either savage or civilized history that is more utterly complete, more remorselessly sweeping than the

Father of Mercy's campaign among the Midianites. The official report does not furnish incidents, episodes, and minor details, it deals only in information in masses: *all* the virgins, *all* the men, *all* the babies, *all* "creatures *that breathe,*" *all* houses, *all* cities; it gives you just one vast picture, spread abroad here and there and yonder, as far as eye can reach, of charred ruin and storm-swept desolation; your imagination adds a brooding stillness, an aweful hush—the hush of death. But of course there *were* incidents. Where shall we get them?

Out of history of yesterday's date. Out of history made by the red Indian of America. He has duplicated God's work, and done it in the very spirit of God. In 1862 the Indians in Minnesota, having been deeply wronged and treacherously treated by the government of the United States, rose against the white settlers and massacred them; massacred all they could lay their hands upon, sparing neither age nor sex. Consider this incident:

Twelve Indians broke into a farm house at daybreak and captured the family. It consisted of the farmer and his wife and four daughters, the youngest aged fourteen and the eldest eighteen. They crucified the parents; that is to say, they stood them stark naked against the wall of the living room and nailed their hands to the wall. Then they stripped the daughters bare, stretched them upon the floor in front of their parents, and repeatedly ravished them. Finally they crucified the girls against the wall opposite the parents, and cut off their noses and their breasts. They also—but I will not go into that. There is a limit. There are indignities so atrocious that the pen cannot write them. One member of that poor crucified family—the father—was still alive when help came two days later.

Now you have *one* incident of the Minnesota massacre. I could give you fifty. They would cover all the different kinds of cruelty the brutal human talent has ever invented.

And now you know, by these sure indications, what happened under the personal direction of the Father of Mercies in his

Midianite campaign. The Minnesota campaign was merely a duplicate of the Midianite raid. Nothing happened in the one that did not happen in the other.

No, that is not strictly true. The Indian was more merciful than was the Father of Mercies. He sold no virgins into slavery to minister to the lusts of the murderers of their kindred while their sad lives might last; he raped them, then charitably made their subsequent sufferings brief, ending them with the precious gift of death. He burned some of the houses, but not all of them. He carried off innocent dumb brutes, but he took the lives of none.

Would you expect this same conscienceless God, this moral bankrupt, to become a *teacher* of morals; of gentleness; of meekness; of righteousness; of purity? It looks impossible, extravagant; but listen to him. These are his own words:

> Blessed are the poor in spirit, for theirs is the kingdom of heaven.
> Blessed are they that mourn, for they shall be comforted.
> Blessed are the meek, for they shall inherit the earth.
> Blessed are they which do hunger and thirst after righteousness, for they shall be filled.
> *Blessed are the merciful,* for they shall obtain mercy.
> Blessed are the pure in heart, for they shall see God.
> *Blessed are the peace-makers,* for they shall be called *the children of* God.
> Blessed are they which are persecuted for righteousness' sake, for theirs is the kingdom of heaven.
> Blessed are ye when men shall revile you and persecute you, and say all manner of evil against you falsely for my sake.

The mouth that uttered these immense sarcasms, these giant hypocrisies, is the very same that ordered the wholesale massacre of the Midianitish men and babies and cattle; the wholesale destruction of house and city; the wholesale banishment of the virgins into a filthy and unspeakable slavery. This is the same person who brought upon the Midianites the fiendish cruelties which were repeated by the red Indians, detail by detail, in Minnesota eighteen centuries later. The Midianite episode filled him with joy. So did the Minnesota one, or he would have prevented it.

The Beatitudes and the quoted chapters from Numbers and Deuteronomy ought always to be read from the pulpit *together*; then the congregation would get an all-around view of Our Father in Heaven. Yet not in a single instance have I ever known a clergyman to do this.

24 "The Turning Point of My Life"

[1910]

I

IF I understand the idea, the *Bazar* invites several of us to write upon the above text. It means the change in my life's course which introduced what must be regarded by me as the most *important* condition of my career. But it also implies—without intention, perhaps—that that turning point was *itself*, individually, the creator of the new condition. This gives it too much distinction, too much prominence, too much credit. It is only the *last* link in a very long chain of turning points commissioned to produce the weighty result; it is not any more important than the humblest of its ten thousand predecessors. Each of the ten thousand did its appointed share, on its appointed date, in forwarding the scheme, and they were all necessary; to have left out any one of them would have defeated the scheme and brought about *some other* result. I know we have a fashion of saying "such and such an event was *the* turning point in my life," but we shouldn't say it. We should merely grant that its place as *last* link in the chain makes it the most *conspicuous* link; in real importance it has no advantage over any one of its predecessors.

Perhaps the most celebrated turning point recorded in history was the crossing of the Rubicon. Suetonius says:

Coming up with his troops on the banks of the Rubicon, he halted for a while, and, revolving in his mind the importance of the step he was on the point of taking, he turned to those about him and said, "We may still retreat; but if we pass this little bridge, nothing is left for us but to fight it out in arms."

This was a stupendously important moment. And all the incidents, big and little, of Caesar's previous life had been leading up to it, stage by stage, link by link. This was the *last* link—merely the last one, and no bigger than the others; but as we gaze back at it through the inflating mists of our imagination, it looks as big as the orbit of Neptune.

You, the reader, have a *personal* interest in that link, and so have I; so has the rest of the human race. It was one of the links in your life-chain, and it was one of the links in mine. We may wait, now, with bated breath, while Caesar reflects. Your fate and mine are involved in his decision.

While he was thus hesitating, the following incident occurred. A person remarkable for his noble mien and graceful aspect, appeared close at hand, sitting and playing upon a pipe. When not only the shepherds, but a number of soldiers also, flocked to listen to him, and some trumpeters among them, he snatched a trumpet from one of them, ran to the river with it, and sounding the advance with a piercing blast, crossed to the other side. Upon this, Caesar exclaimed, "Let us go whither the omens of the gods and the iniquity of our enemies call us. *The die is cast.*"

So he crossed—and changed the future of the whole human race, for all time. But that stranger was a link in Caesar's life-chain, too; and a necessary one. We don't know his name, we never hear of him again, he was very casual, he acts like an accident; but he was no accident, he was there by compulsion of *his* life-chain, to blow the electrifying blast that was to make up Caesar's mind for him, and thence go piping down the aisles of history forever.

If the stranger hadn't been there! But he *was*. And Caesar crossed. With such results! Such vast events—each a link in the *human race's* life-chain; each event producing the next one, and that one the next one, and so on: the destruction of the republic; the founding of the empire; the breaking up of the empire; the rise of Christianity upon its ruins; the spread of the religion to other lands—and so on: link by link took its appointed place at its appointed time, the discovery of America being one of them; our Revolution another; the inflow of English and other immigrants another; their drift westward (my ancestors among them) another; the settlement of certain of them in Missouri—which resulted in *me*. For I was one of the unavoidable results of the crossing of the Rubicon. If the stranger, with his trumpet blast, had stayed away (which he *couldn't*, for he was an appointed link), Caesar would not have crossed. What would have happened, in that case, we can never guess. We only know that the things that did happen would not have happened. They might have been replaced by equally prodigious things, of course, but their nature and results are beyond our guessing. But the matter that interests me personally is, that I would not be *here*, now, but somewhere else; and probably black—there is no telling. Very well, I am glad he crossed. And very really and thankfully glad, too, though I never cared anything about it before.

II

To me, the most important feature of my life is its literary feature. I have been professionally literary something more than forty years. There have been many turning points in my life, but the one that was the last link in the chain appointed to conduct me to the literary guild is the most *conspicuous* link in that chain. *Because* it was the last one. It was not any more important than its predecessors. All the other links have an inconspicuous look, except the crossing of the Rubicon; but as factors in making me literary they are all of the one size, the crossing of the Rubicon included.

I know how I came to be literary, and I will tell the steps that led up to it and brought it about.

The crossing of the Rubicon was not the first one, it was hardly even a recent one; I should have to go back ages before Caesar's day to find the first one. To save space I will go back only a couple of generations, and start with an incident of my boyhood. When I was twelve and a half years old, my father died. It was in the spring. The summer came, and brought with it an epidemic of measles. For a time, a child died almost every day. The village was paralysed with fright, distress, despair. Children that were not smitten with the disease were imprisoned in their homes to save them from the infection. In the homes there were no cheerful faces, there was no music, there was no singing but of solemn hymns, no voice but of prayer, no romping was allowed, no noise, no laughter, the family moved spectrally about on tiptoe, in a ghostly hush. I was a prisoner. My soul was steeped in this awful dreariness—and in fear. At some time or other every day and every night a sudden shiver shook me to the marrow, and I said to my-self, "There, I've got it! and I shall die." Life on these miserable terms was not worth living, and at last I made up my mind to get the disease and have it over, one way or the other. I escaped from the house and went to the house of a neighbor where a playmate of mine was very ill with the malady. When the chance offered I crept into his room and got into bed with him. I was discovered by his mother and sent back into captivity. But I had the disease; they could not take that from me. I came near to dying. The whole village was interested, and anxious, and sent for news of me every day; and not only once a day, but several times. Everybody believed I would die; but on the fourteenth day a change came for the worse and they were disappointed.

This was a turning point of my life. (Link number one.) For when I got well my mother closed my school career and apprenticed me to a printer. She was tired of trying to keep me out of mischief, and the adventure of the measles decided her to put me into more masterful hands than hers.

I became a printer, and began to add one link after another to the chain which was to lead me into the literary profession. A long road, but I could not know that; and as I did not know what its goal was, or even that it had one, I was indifferent. Also contented.

A young printer wanders around a good deal, seeking and finding work; and seeking again, when necessity commands. N. B. Necessity is a *Circumstance*; Circumstance is man's master—and when Circumstance commands, he must obey; he may argue the matter—that is his privilege, just as it is the honorable privilege of a falling body to argue with the attraction of gravitation—but it won't do any good, he must *obey*. I wandered for ten years, under the guidance and dictatorship of Circumstance, and finally arrived in a city of Iowa, where I worked several months. Among the books that interested me in those days was one about the Amazon. The traveler told an alluring tale of his long voyage up the great river from Para to the sources of the Madeira, through the heart of an enchanted land, a land wastefully rich in tropical wonders, a romantic land where all the birds and flowers and animals were of the museum varieties, and where the alligator and the crocodile and the monkey seemed as much at home as if they were in the Zoo. Also, he told an astonishing tale about *coca*, a vegetable product of miraculous powers; asserting that it was so nourishing and so strength-giving that the native of the mountains of the Madeira region would tramp up-hill and down all day on a pinch of powdered coca and require no other sustenance.

I was fired with a longing to ascend the Amazon. Also with a longing to open up a trade in coca with all the world. During months I dreamed that dream, and tried to contrive ways to get to Para and spring that splendid enterprise upon an unsuspecting planet. But all in vain. A person may *plan* as much as he wants to, but nothing of consequence is likely to come of it until the magician *Circumstance* steps in and takes the matter off his hands. At last Circumstance came to my help. It was in this way. Circumstance, to help or hurt another man, made him lose a fifty-dollar bill in the street; and to help or hurt me, made me find it. I advertised the find, and left for the Amazon the same day. This was another turning point, another link.

Could Circumstance have ordered another dweller in that town to go to the Amazon and open up a world-trade in coca on a fifty-dollar basis and been obeyed? No, I was the only one. There were other fools there—shoals and shoals of them—but they were not of my kind. I was the only one of my kind.

Circumstance is powerful, but it cannot work alone, it has to have a partner. Its partner is man's *temperament*—his natural disposition. His temperament is not his invention, it is *born* in him, and he has no authority over it, neither is he responsible for its acts. He cannot change it, nothing can change it, nothing can modify it,—except temporarily. But it won't stay modified. It is permanent; like the color of the man's eyes and the shape of his ears. Blue eyes are gray, in certain unusual lights; but they resume their natural color when that stress is removed.

A Circumstance that will coerce one man, will have no effect upon a man of a different temperament. If Circumstance had thrown the bank note in Caesar's way, his temperament would not have made him start for the Amazon. His temperament would have compelled him to do something with the money, but not that. It might have made him advertise the note—and *wait*. We can't tell. Also, it might have made him go to New York and buy into the government; with results that would leave Tweed nothing to learn when it came his turn.

Very well, Circumstance furnished the capital, and my temperament told me what to do with it. Sometimes a temperament is an ass. When that is the case the owner of it is an ass, too, and is going to remain one. Training, experience, association, can temporarily so elevate him that people will think he is a mule, but they will be mistaken. Artificially he *is* a mule, for the time being, but at bottom he is an ass yet, and will remain one.

By temperament I was the kind of person that *does* things. Does them, and reflects afterwards. So I started for the Amazon, without reflecting, and without asking any questions. That was more than fifty years ago. In all that time my temperament has not changed, by even a shade. I have been punished many and many a time, and bitterly, for doing things first and reflecting afterward, but these tortures have been of no value to me; I still do the thing commanded by Circumstance and Temperament, and reflect afterward. Always violently. When I am reflecting, on those occasions, even deaf persons can hear me think.

I went by the way of Cincinnati, and down the Ohio and Mississippi. My idea was to take ship, at New Orleans, for Para. In New Orleans I inquired, and found there was no ship leaving for Para. Also, that there never had *been* one leaving for Para. I reflected. A policeman came and asked me what I was doing, and I told him. He made me move on; and said if he caught me reflecting in the public street again he would run me in.

After a few days I was out of money. Then Circumstance arrived, with another turning point of my life—a new link. On my way down, I had made the acquaintance of a pilot; I begged him to teach me the river, and he consented. I became a pilot.

By and by Circumstance came again—introducing the Civil War, this time, in order to push me ahead a stage or two toward the literary profession. The boats stopped running, my livelihood was gone.

Circumstance came to the rescue with a new turning point and a fresh link. My brother was appointed secretary to the new Territory of Nevada, and he invited me to go with him and help him in his office. I accepted.

In Nevada, Circumstance furnished me the silver fever and I went into the mines to make a fortune and enter the ministry. As I supposed; but that was not the idea. The idea was, to move me another step toward literature. For amusement I scribbled things for the Virginia City *Enterprise*. One isn't a printer ten years without setting up acres of good and bad literature, and learning—unconsciously at first, consciously later—to discriminate between the two, within his mental limitations; and meantime he is unconsciously acquiring what is called a "style." One of my efforts attracted attention, and the *Enterprise* sent for me, and put me on its staff.

And so I became a journalist—another link. By and by Circumstance and the Sacramento *Union* sent me to the Sandwich Islands for five or six months, to write up sugar. I did it; and threw in a good deal of extraneous matter that hadn't anything to do with sugar. But it was this extraneous matter that helped me to another link.

It made me notorious, and San Francisco invited me to lecture. Which I did. And profitably. I had long had a desire to travel and see the world, and now the platform had furnished me the means. So I joined the "Quaker City Excursion."

When I returned to America, Circumstance was waiting on the pier—with the *last* link: I was asked to *write a book*, and I did it, and called it *The Innocents Abroad*. Thus at last I became a member of the literary guild. That was forty-two years ago, and I have been a member ever since. Leaving the Rubicon incident away back where it belongs, I can say with truth that the reason I am in the literary profession is because I had the measles when I was twelve years old.

III

Now what interests me, as regards these details, is not the details themselves, but the fact that none of them was foreseen by me, none of them was planned by me, I was the author of none of them. Circumstance, working in harness with my temperament, created them all and compelled them all. I often offered help, and with the best intentions, but it was rejected: as a rule, uncourteously. I could never plan a thing and get it to come out the way I planned it. It came out some other way—some way I had not counted upon.

And so I do not admire the human being—as an intellectual marvel—as much as I did when I was young, and got him out of books, and did not know him personally. When I used to read that such and such a general did a certain brilliant thing, I believed it.

Whereas it was not so. Circumstance did it, by help of his temperament. The circumstances would have failed of effect with a general of another temperament: he might see the chance, but lose
the advantage by being by nature too slow or too quick or too
doubtful. Once General Grant was asked a question about a matter
which had been much debated by the public and the newspapers;
he answered the question without any hesitancy: "General, who
planned the march through Georgia?" "The enemy!" He added
that the enemy usually makes your plans for you. He meant that
the enemy, by neglect or through force of circumstances, leaves
an opening for you, and you see your chance and take advantage
of it.

Circumstances do the planning for us all, no doubt, by help
of our temperaments. I see no great difference between a man and
a watch, except that the man is conscious and the watch isn't, and
the man *tries* to plan things and the watch doesn't. The watch
doesn't wind itself, and doesn't regulate itself—these things are
done exteriorly. Outside influences, outside circumstances, wind
the *man* and regulate him. Left to himself he wouldn't get regu-
lated at all, and the sort of time he would keep would not be valuable. Some rare men are wonderful watches, with gold case,
compensation balance, and all those things, and some men are
only simple and sweet and humble Waterburys. I am a Waterbury. A Waterbury of that kind, some say.

A nation is only an individual, multiplied. It makes plans, and
Circumstance comes and upsets them—or enlarges them. A gang
of patriots throws the tea overboard; it destroys a Bastile. The
plans stop there; then Circumstance comes in, quite unexpectedly,
and turns these modest riots into a revolution.

And there was poor Columbus. He elaborated a deep plan to
find a new route to an old country. Circumstance revised his plan
for him, and he found a new *world*. And *he* gets the credit of it, to
this day. He hadn't anything to do with it.

Necessarily the scene of the real turning point of my life (and
of yours) was the Garden of Eden. It was there that the first link

was forged of the chain that was ultimately to lead to the emptying of me into the literary guild. Adam's *temperament* was the
first command the Deity ever issued to a human being on this
planet. And it was the only command Adam would *never* be able
to disobey. It said, "Be weak, be water, be characterless, be cheaply
persuadable." The later command, to let the fruit alone, was certain to be disobeyed. Not by Adam himself, but by his *temperament*—which he did not create and had no authority over. For the
temperament is the man; the thing tricked out with clothes and
named Man, is merely its Shadow, nothing more. The law of the
tiger's temperament is, Thou shalt kill; the law of the sheep's
temperament is, Thou shalt not kill. To issue later commands
requiring the tiger to let the 'fat stranger alone, and requiring the
sheep to imbue its hands in the blood of the lion is not worth
while, for those commands *can't* be obeyed. They would invite to
violations of the law of *temperament*, which is supreme, and takes
precedence of all other authorities. I cannot help feeling disappointed in Adam and Eve. That is, in their temperaments. Not in
them, poor helpless young creatures—afflicted with temperaments
made out of butter; which butter was commanded to get into contact with fire and *be melted*. What I cannot help wishing is, that
Adam and Eve had been postponed, and Martin Luther and Joan
of Arc put in their place—that splendid pair equipped with temperaments not made of butter, but of asbestos. By neither sugary
persuasions nor by hellfire could Satan have beguiled *them* to eat
the apple.

There would have been results! Indeed yes. The apple would
be intact to-day: there would be no human race; there would be
no *you*; there would be no *me*. And the old, old creation-dawn
scheme of ultimately launching me into the literary guild would
have been defeated.

Supplements

Unless otherwise stated, incorrect or inconsistent spellings and usages have not been emended when these present no problem for an understanding of the text. Errors which are troublesome have been corrected in square brackets. Empty brackets—[]—indicate editorial recognition that the preceding word or punctuation is redundant. The same use of brackets is followed in the Textual Notes.

SUPPLEMENT A

What Is Man? Fragments

THESE items were never part of the dialogue or were deleted by Mark Twain. They appear in known or conjectured order of composition.

A1.   [Draft of The Moral Sense]

MARK TWAIN probably wrote this prior to the main dialogue, inasmuch as he used numbers rather than "O.M.–Y.M." to designate the speakers. The paper is a double-ruled stationery of European make similar to paper he used for *What Is Man?* in 1898, except that this type is thick and soft in texture. Since he began using such paper in 1897, that year is the most likely date of composition. See the Textual Notes on *What Is Man?* for information concerning all manuscript paper noted here.

1.   What *are* the moral qualities?
       They are but two—love and hate. From each of these trees spring many branches, and the branches bear a variety of names: such as Charity, Pity, Forgiveness, Self-sacrifice, and so on, in the one case; and Greed, Envy, Revenge, and so on, in the other. Each tree has a hundred branches, and each branch has a name; but the sap that feeds them all and is the life of them all, is the same: Love, in the one case, Hate in the other.

These are the Trees of the Knowledge of Good and Evil.

Man has eaten of both, the beasts have eaten of neither.

This has given man the Moral Sense. The beast has not the Moral Sense. It is this that to a large degree determines what is man and what is beast.

What is the peculiar and sole function of the Moral Sense?

To enable us to do wrong.

2. No, it has a higher and nobler function—to enable us to do right (by teaching us what *is* right.)

1. You think so.

2. Certainly I do.

1. Can a beast do wrong?

2. No; for it is without consciousness.

1. Guilt cannot be attributed to a beast, then?

2. No.

1. Then whatever a beast does is right,—certainly not wrong.

2. Yes.

1. Then where the Moral Sense does not exist, only Right exists, —or its equivalent,—and there is no such thing as Wrong.

2. Evidently—yes.

1. Then it is as I said: the peculiar and sole function of the Moral Sense is to enable us to *do wrong*. It cannot *enable* us to do right, for without it we cannot do anything *but* right or its guiltless equivalent. I therefore repeat, and desire to burn into your memory and consciousness the simple truth that the only function the Moral Sense has or can exercise is to enable us to do wrong.

And so we arrive at this fact: that one of the two (claimed) moral superiorities which man possesses above the beast is that he can do wrong. Why is he proud of this defect? Can you explain it? Would it not be a strange thing to see a man who was filled with the germs of a hundred filthy diseases going around boasting about it among the healthy, with his nose in the air?

2. But his superiority does not consist merely in his ability to do wrong, but in this added quality: that to him is given the ability to *avoid* doing wrong, by taking thought and by watching himself.

1. Is that a valuable quality?

2. Certainly. And a lofty one.

1. Do you like a good watch?

2. Yes.

1. Do you prefer it to a poor one?

2. Certainly.

1. Which would you prefer? To be born with a sound body, or with a body cursed with the taint of hereditary leprosy?

2. With a sound body, of course?

1. Among created beings has man a moral superior?

2. Yes—one.

1. Who is that?

2. The angel.

1. Wherein lies his moral superiority?

2. He is born without sin, and—

1. And what? Without the ability to commit it?

2. Yes.

1. The beast and the angel, then, are moral twins?

2. Why—yes, it would seem so.

1. And yet, for one and the same reason the beast is man's moral inferior and the angel is his moral superior. Is this doubtful logic?

2. Proceed.

1. Has God distinctly testified that He holds in dearer affection and approval the animal that lacks the Moral Sense than the animal that has it?

2. I think not. How do you arrive at this?

1. Adam and Eve were without it. They were like the other animals—they could do right only, they did not know how to do wrong; for them, wrong had no existence. God tried to keep them pure and sinless, like the beasts and the angels, but he failed. Is not this true?

2. Yes.

1. What happened then?

2. They fell.

1. Fell from the estate of beasts and angels down to the estate of man?

2. "Fell" does not mean that they fell to a lower moral estate; it merely means that they fell from His grace and approval.

1. They went down, or they went up. Which was it?

2. They acquired the Moral Sense, and thus rose to an estate which was higher and better than their former one.

1.   They fell up, then; out of what He wanted them to be and into something superior to that. Still, He did not *want* them to fall up, but to remain as they were?

2.   Yes.

1.   He loved them?

2.   Unquestionably.

1.   He desired to do the best for them He could?

2.   Undoubtedly.

1.   He knew what was best for them better than they could know?

2.   Certainly.

1.   And He wanted them to remain without the Moral Sense—like the beasts and the angels—incapable of doing wrong.

2.   Why—it seems so.

1.   Couldn't you say it *is* so?

2.   I must grant it.

1.   I think you must; for when they rose by falling, He was so angered that He punished them calamitously—and their whole race after them. You are obliged to concede that it amply proves His stern disapproval of the Moral Sense—that quality whose peculiar and sole function is to enable its possessor to do wrong. Tell me, why do you have that phrase "the beasts that perish?"

2.   Because they do perish, forever.

1.   Why? Because they lack the Moral Sense?—that quality which God so strenuously disapproves of?

2.   Partly that, but also because they have no soul.

1.   What is the soul?

2.   It is that something in us which enables us to know God and adore Him.

1.   Adam had it?

2.   Yes. It was his great birthright.

1.   The angels had it?

2.   Yes.

1.   But they lacked the Moral Sense. Adam acquired that—by force. He is accounted a little lower than the angels—by that much, we may presume. It is demonstrably a pity that he acquired for himself and for us that taint, that disease, that grotesque incumbrance, that thing hated of God. It is like a sound dog interesting itself to acquire *rabies*,

so that it can destroy itself and its race; it is like a wise man interesting himself to become an idiot and transmit the taint; it is like a saint, secure of heaven, buying the privilege, transmissible to his heirs and assigns, of exchanging it for hell when so inclined. And when a man is proud of his Moral Sense, proud because he can do wrong and a beast cannot, surely he is a pathetic object. He is a watch that is vain because it is a poor thing and can go wrong; he is a man who is vain because there is leprosy in his blood.

A2.   THE MORAL SENSE

PROBABLY written in July 1898; chapter 4 in the original sequence. The paper is a white wove Mark Twain also used for the main dialogue in 1898. This section was in the first *What Is Man?* typescript but the pages were removed and destroyed. The text here is that of the second typescript, which incorporates revisions apparently made in the first, and it has been checked against the manuscript.

    O. M.   What is the Moral Sense, as you understand it?

    Y. M.   The knowledge of right and wrong; the ability to tell right from wrong.

    O. M.   Without it what would our condition be?

    Y. M.   For us there would be no right and no wrong; the terms would have no meaning; they would describe things which were nonexistent.

    O. M.   We couldn't do right?

    Y. M.   No; there being no such thing as right.

    O. M.   We couldn't do wrong?

    Y. M.   No; there being no such thing as wrong.

    O. M.   The Moral Sense, then, creates right for us?

    Y. M.   Yes.

    O. M.   Also enables us to perceive the right?

    Y. M.   Yes.

    O. M.   Also enables us to do right?

    Y. M.   Yes.

    O. M.   Without it we could not do right?

Y. M. Of course not.

O. M. That is a valuable office.

Y. M. Unspeakably precious.

O. M. It also creates wrong?

Y. M. Yes.

O. M. Also enables us to perceive the wrong?

Y. M. Yes.

O. M. Also enables us to *do* wrong?

Y. M. Y-yes.

O. M. Without it we could not do wrong?

Y. M. No—that is—well, no.

O. M. That is a valuable office?

Y. M. I—

O. M. I know what you are going to say: "it is an unspeakably precious office."

Y. M. I—well, I do not know that I was going to say that, for I had not thought of that side of it. But at any rate it must be valuable, it must be precious, or we shouldn't have it.

O. M. I see you have the reasoning faculty. You can put this and that together—like an Edison, like an ant, like an elephant.

Y. M. Stick to the subject! Go on.

O. M. You have been changing watches, I see.

Y. M. Yes; the other one didn't keep time.

O. M. This one is better?

Y. M. Oh, immensely better; perfect, in fact.

O. M. The other one gave you trouble?

Y. M. No end of it. I had to be forever fussing with it and tinkering at it to make it go right, or it would be always going wrong. This one doesn't know *how* to go wrong.

O. M. It's the other one that has the Moral Sense?

Y. M. I don't get your drift.

O. M. Never mind, it isn't important. I wonder if Adam was a good man. Do you think he was a good man?

Y. M. Adam? Why, he was not merely good, up to the Fall, he was perfect—absolutely perfect; and could have remained so if he and Eve had listened to God their friend instead of to Satan their enemy.

O. M. God wanted to have him remain as he was?—preferred him so?

Y. M. Infinitely. He loved him, He walked and talked with him; when he fell He drove him from the Garden and turned His back upon him.

O. M. It was because he ate the apple?

Y. M. Yes.

O. M. The apple revealed to him the knowledge of good and evil?

Y. M. Yes.

O. M. It gave him the Moral Sense?

Y. M. Y-yes.

O. M. It created good and evil in the world, and enabled him to do both?

Y. M. Yes.

O. M. He was wholly without the Moral Sense before?

Y. M. Wholly.

O. M. God infinitely preferred him without it?

Y. M. Why—yes.

O. M. To get it he didn't rise, but fell?

Y. M. Y-yes.

O. M. Only when *without* the Moral Sense was he perfect in the eyes of God?

Y. M. Yes—it is true.

O. M. Have the other animals the Moral Sense?

Y. M. No, they haven't.

O. M. A while ago you said "we have it and it lifts us immeasurably above them." What made you think that? Do you set up *your* estimate of the value of the Moral Sense as being *superior to God's?*

Y. M. Well, I—I didn't invent my estimate, it was taught me. I never looked at the thing in this way before.

O. M. You prefer a watch that doesn't know *how* to go wrong. I think you are right. Adam was perfect before he got the Moral Sense, imperfect as soon as he got it. In the one case he *couldn't* do wrong, in the other he could. Adam fell; the other animals have not fallen. By the supreme verdict of God they are *morally perfect.*

Y. M. You said you were not going to put man and the other animals on the same level morally.

O. M. I haven't. I have put man where he belongs—very much below the others.

Y. M.   Do you say that seriously?

O. M.   Yes, with entire seriousness and sincerity. I side with God. His estimate of the Moral Sense is sufficient for me. Whenever I look at the other animals and realize that whatever they do is blameless and that they can't do wrong, I envy them the dignity of their estate, its purity and its loftiness, and recognise that the Moral Sense is a thoroughly disastrous thing.

Y. M.   Why, without it there would be no dignity. It is man's ability to perceive wrong, and then to struggle with it, fight it day and night and all his life, and triumph over it, that gives him dignity.

O. M.   Yes; as much as tinkering at a tin watch.

A3.   THE QUALITY OF MAN

WRITTEN shortly after "The Moral Sense"; numbered chapter 5; paper as in "The Moral Sense." A notebook entry for August 1898, among other examples of the selfishness all actions have in common, contains a scarcely intelligible plan of continuation:

In "Quality of Man" [originally "Morals of Man"] turn Bruce and the Spider into a peasant persisting in a struggle to regain a pair of lost leather breeks—the cases alike and nothing sublime about either of them. (Notebook 32, TS p. 28.)

Y. M.   You have placed Man, the noblest work of God, in the same ship, intellectually—man in the first cabin and the brutes in the steerage; and morally you place the brutes far above man. It is shameful. What is your general opinion of man, anyway?

O. M.   That he is a very poor thing.

Y. M.   Where do you get that idea?

O. M.   Mainly from God, partly from observation.

Y. M.   How from God?

O. M.   Morally and in all other details but one—intellect—man is away below the other animals. God does not value intellect.

Y. M.   Where is your proof?

O. M.   In the accounts of heaven. There it is all harping, hymning, hosannahing, hurrahing, in a Rococo New Jerusalem—dissipations which feed merely the sentimental emotions. There are no intellectual employments there, no intellectual society. He has not praised any man for his intellect, he has not encouraged intellectual pursuits or ambitions in any way; he has offered no rewards for intellectual achievement; his promises are restricted to the meek, the righteous, the obedient, the truthful, the reverent, the pure, the God-fearing—moral specialties, all of them.

Y. M.   That does not prove that He does not value intellect.

O. M.   You are working your reasoning-machinery again. If He did not mention the moral qualities, nor encourage them nor reward them, what would you infer from that?

Y. M.   That is nothing, He *does* care for intellect.

O. M.   That settles it.

A4.   GOD

WRITTEN in 1898, paper as in "The Moral Sense." The dialogue has its own pagination, but Mark Twain planned it as a continuation of the main text. There is a contemporary typescript, stapled in a folder in the same way as the first typescript of *What Is Man?*, though typed on a different machine. The cover reads "Continuation" at the top, "15" beneath it, whereas the other typescript is "14." The numbers probably indicate an order of packing for one of the family's trips, perhaps from Austria to England or from England to America. At another time Mark Twain wrote "IV" on the cover, followed by a question mark, suggesting that he thought of replacing "The Moral Sense" with "God" as chapter 4. *What Is the Real Character of Conscience?*—an early title of *What Is Man?*—is typed on the cover. Much later, probably in 1905, Mark Twain printed "NOT TO BE USED" across the cover. The text is based on the manuscript, but it incorporates his holograph revisions in the typescript.

Young Man.   You mention God every now and then, and yet I take it that at bottom you are an Atheist.

Old Man.   How? You think I believe there is no God—Supreme Being—Creator and sole Lord of the Universe?

Y. M.   Yes.

O. M. It is a mistake. I do believe He exists. I do not claim to know it, but I believe it; and with all my might. I think He is not a bunch of laws, but a Personality.

Y. M. And that He is all-powerful?

O. M. Yes.

Y. M. And that he has revealed Himself to man?

O. M. By His deeds and works, yes—as we experience them in our persons and see them in Nature. But not in any other way, so far as I know.

Y. M. Not by His Book?

O. M. I think it may be *His* book, but I have no way of arriving at a certainty about it.

Y. M. The ablest minds in the earth have been certain that it was His book.

O. M. That is an argument, but that is all. It is not evidence.

Y. M. Gladstone, Bismarck, Washington, Lincoln, Shakspeare—

O. M. Henry VIII, Alexander VI, Philip II, Torquemada, Captain Kidd—there are thousands and thousands. It is nothing. It was their *training*, their *heredities*, their *environment* that enabled them to be convinced; and there is not one of them who would not have been as certain of the divine inspiration of the Koran if he had been a Turk by descent and surroundings. The fact that the greatest minds in the earth have been convinced, as you say, is merely *argument*, nothing more—and it is straining a compliment to dignify it to even that degree.

Y. M. It is an argument which has no weight at all with you?

O. M. None at all. A conviction of theirs drawn from established facts—like certain established facts of astronomy, chemistry and so on—would have weight with me—convincing weight. But here they have nothing solid, nothing substantial, nothing trustworthy to go upon.

Y. M. Are the internal evidences of the Book itself nothing?

O. M. Those "evidences," as you call them, have a good deal of weight with me. They go far toward persuading me that it *is* His book. His character, as portrayed in the Old Testament and in many passages of the New satisfactorily answers to His character as revealed in his conduct as exhibited to us daily.

Y. M. That is true! His goodness, his love, his compassion, his—

O. M. I was not thinking of those traits. He may have them. It is possible. One cannot tell.

Y. M. This is strange talk. He is *all* goodness, love, compassion.

O. M. Could you mention some instances?

Y. M. A million.

O. M. A couple will answer. Even one will do.

Y. M. He gave us our life. He—

O. M. Wait. We must not slur these benevolences over, and take them for granted. It is but fair that we examine them first. He made us. The day we are born he begins to persecute us. Even our littleness, our innocence, our helplessness cannot move him to any pity, any gentleness. Day after day, week after week, month after month, the wanton tortures go on. Pain, pain, pain—in the teeth, in the stomach, in the bowels; disease follows disease: measles, croup, whooping cough, mumps, colic, scarlet fever, ague, tonsilitis, dipththeria—there is no end to the list. Would *you* treat a little child so, that had done you no harm? How do you reconcile the infliction of these undeserved miseries with those traits which you have so confidently claimed for the inventor of them—goodness, love, compassion? What is the object of it? what is the explanation of it? what is the excuse for it? the pretext?

Y. M. We are not permitted to pry into these sacred mysteries. We must be satisfied with knowing that they are for our good—our discipline.

O. M. The pulpit itself could not furnish a more luminous answer. They are to discipline us? Would you discipline an offending or an unoffending child with dipththeria—*your* child?—or even your enemy's?

Y. M. Of course I wouldn't, but—

O. M. God the compassionate would? What is the discipline *for*?

Y. M. A preparation for the struggle of life.

O. M. Light, as from the pulpit again! The child dies. What becomes of that explanation now? Did God know beforehand that the child would die?

Y. M. From the beginning of time.

O. M. Then why did he discipline it for a struggle which was not to take place?

Y. M.   We cannot know.

O. M.   Hasn't it the aspect of entirely gratuitous cruelty? But let us go on. The child becomes a youth, the youth an adult, the adult old. Disease harries him all the way to the grave. He has diseases of his nails, of his bones, of his blood, of his skin, of his heart, his liver, his teeth, his lungs, his brain, his entrails. There is not a fibre in him anywhere which has not been especially and ingeniously designed to harbor a disease of its own and propagate pain and misery. He is the house and home of billions of germs and microbes whose sole office is to manufacture tortures for him. Is it not plain insanity to recognize in this exhibition the hand of goodness, love, compassion? How do you account for these horrors? Is it some more discipline?

Y. M.   Yes—partly; and partly the man brings them upon himself by transgressing the laws of nature.

O. M.   Who made the laws of nature?

Y. M.   God.

O. M.   And He made man?

Y. M.   Yes.

O. M.   Made him with the *ability* to transgress the laws?

Y. M.   Yes.

O. M.   And the *disposition* to do it?

Y. M.   Yes, he has the disposition.

O. M.   Designed the trap, then designed the victim with a disposition to go *into* it. When slave-hunters play such tricks upon their fellow men the pulpit calls them bitter hard names. Must you praise in a Deity what you execrate in a slave-hunter? It is not logic.

Y. M.   Man brings all his punishments upon himself through wilful and wicked transgression of the laws of nature.

O. M.   But he inherits *some* of his diseases from his forbears— the liquor habit, insanity, and such things, and cannot help himself.

Y. M.   Well, his forbears committed the transgressions.

O. M.   Am I to be hanged because my grandfather was a murderer?

Y. M.   It is written that the sins of the fathers shall be answered for by their posterity generations afterward.

O. M.   Is there some way to explain or justify this more-than-tigerish spirit, this age-long unappeasable appetite for the blood and misery of the innocent?

Y. M. I cannot explain it, I can only justify it.

O. M. How?

Y. M. By the knowledge that it is right and cannot be wrong, since it proceeds from the Source of all justice.

O. M. Is it from that Source that we get our own ideas of right and justice?

Y. M. Yes. From that Source, and from it alone, for there is no other.

O. M. We are but indifferent learners, then, for we do not pursue with our malice generation after generation of the innocent. Neither we nor the tigers. We seem to be better than our Teacher. Are the Savior and God one Person, or two?

Y. M. One. He is God.

O. M. Did he say we must forgive an offender seventy times seven times?

Y. M. He did.

O. M. And is it he, also, who pursues his offender down through generations of his innocent posterity?

Y. M. It is not to be denied. But His ways are not our ways. He may righteously do things which would be sin in us.

O. M. There must be something divine in us; for we, too, teach by example—when it is handy; and by precept when it isn't. You think we bring all our sufferings upon ourselves—except in infancy and in the matter of inherited disease—by transgressing the laws of nature. Sometimes an earthquake cripples a hundred people for life and breaks the hearts of a hundred more by killing their wives, parents, children, friends; cyclones and tidal waves do the same. Is there any transgression of the laws here?

Y. M. The killed and injured had transgressed certain laws, the bereft survivors also. All were punished.

O. M. Do the earthquakes and cyclones pick out the guilty and leave the innocent unharmed?

Y. M. Undoubtedly. Except in the case of innocent people whose ancestors had sinned.

O. M. The lightning kills people. Does the lightning discriminate, too?

Y. M. We may be sure of it.

O. M. Does it spare the holy?

Y. M. There can be no doubt of it.

O. M. It destroys churches with much frequency. And statues of saints—statues which have been spared three hundred years. The accounts of heaven seem to remain open a good while.

Y. M. A thousand years are to Him as a day.

O. M. That is unfortunate for us. Was it He that issued the command "Do unto others as you would like them to do unto you?"

Y. M. Yes.

O. M. And that we must forgive the transgressor seventy times seven?

Y. M. Yes.

O. M. And that persecutes little children with boils and colics and pains and miseries for transgressions committed by their great-grandfathers?

Y. M. His ways are not as our ways.

O. M. Let us be proud of it. It is He that requires us to forgive seventy times seven, and observe the Golden Rule. Is it He also who sends offenders into a lake of fire and brimstone to roast there throughout eternity?

Y. M. His ways are not as our ways.

O. M. For that let us rejoice. Did He create all things?

Y. M. All.

O. M. Including Satan?

Y. M. Yes.

O. M. And has condemned him to torment by fire forever?

Y. M. Yes. And justly; for Satan wrought evil in the earth and was disobedient.

O. M. Did He foresee that Satan would act so, and that He would burn him forever?

Y. M. He knew it when He created Satan.

O. M. Then necessarily He made *himself* responsible for Satan's crime. Why punish Satan for it instead of Himself, the guilty party?

Y. M. Satan could have obeyed, and did not do it.

O. M. And that was foreknown?

Y. M. Yes.

O. M. In that case we arrive where we were before: God was responsible for Satan's crime, just as He is unquestionably responsible for every foreknown or unforeknown crime committed by man, his creature. We poor worms and weevils do not claim to be very just and fair, yet if a man sees a blind child walking toward a precipice and does not save him—even by force, if necessary—we hold the man guilty of the child's death if it follow. Do you believe that God sends unbaptised children to eternal torture by fire?

Y. M.   I do not merely believe it, I know it. All Christians know it, and they solemnly state it when they enter upon Church membership.

O. M.   Have you friends who have children in hell?

Y. M.   Yes, several.

O. M.   How long have the children been there?

Y. M.   Some as many as thirty years.

O. M.   Have the parents gone mad?

Y. M.   No.

O. M.   What saves them from it?

Y. M.   I do not know. Doubtless, faith in His inexhaustible loving-kindness.

O. M.   As exhibited in burning the children. Do they still respect Him?

Y. M.   It is a blasphemous phrase. They more than respect Him, they adore Him, they worship Him.

O. M.   They are easily pleased. It is said that Lazarus looked down from heaven and saw Dives in hell. Will those parents look down and see their children burning?

Y. M.   Yes, without a doubt.

O. M.   Will it make heaven a hell for them?

Y. M.   No. It will increase the joys of heaven for them—as Baxter of the "Saint's Rest" has pointed out.

O. M.   For what reason?

Y. M.   Because it is by God's will and pleasure that they burn. To the right-hearted Christian whatever is in accordance with the will and pleasure of God, fills his own heart with joy and thanksgiving.

O. M.   What is the difference between a right-hearted Christian and a fiend—if any?

Y. M.   This is gross blasphemy, and I will not answer you.

O. M.   Perhaps it would trouble you to find an answer. Let us put it in another form. The right-hearted Christian sees his unoffending child broiling on the red-hot grates of hell, and proclaims from the housetops that the Author of this unspeakable atrocity is made up all of goodness, mercy and loving-kindness: what is the difference between a right-hearted Christian and an idiot—if any?

Y. M.   I will not answer such brutal questions.

O. M.   You would find it difficult, no doubt. If you should find an offending cat—or an unoffending cat—shut up in a hot stove and shrieking with pain, what would you do?

Y. M.   Release her, of course.

O. M.   By your own admission you are better than God. Better, kinder, gentler, more humane, more to be respected, honored, esteemed. And most men are like you; let us take credit to ourselves for it. Shall I tell you why the Christian parent can joyfully laugh in the daytime and peacefully sleep nights, during thirty years, while his unfriended child is wailing in the fires of hell all that time? It is because the Christian does not believe it—in his heart; but only with his head. The heart could not bear that burden. It would break.

Y. M.   He may not realize it, still it is so.

O. M.   I think you must be right. It reflects the remorseless character of God as betrayed in His daily deeds. For each small hour of happiness granted to us here he charges us two hours of unhappiness— usually collectable immediately; when we die we have paid the full bill, with usury; but that is nothing, He sends the most of us to hell anyway. He is a hard master.

Y. M.   He gives us many, many happinesses; and He never gives us pain except by our own fault or for our own good.

O. M.   The happinesses seem to be traps, and to have no other intent. He beguiles us into welding our heart to another heart—the heart of a child, perhaps—the years go by, and when at last that companionship has become utterly precious, utterly indispensable, He tears the hearts apart, He kills the child. Sleep comes upon us and in it we forget our disaster. In the morning we wake; we are confused; we seem to have had a bad dream. Then suddenly full consciousness comes, and we know! All the happiness that could be crowded into a lifetime could not compensate the bitterness of that one moment. And thenceforth the rest of our years are merely a burden. This is to discipline us? Is that your idea?

Y. M.   Yes. It is to draw us nearer to Him; it is to wean us from fleeting and foolish earthly loves and make us seek and cling to the only precious love, the divine love.

O. M.   It seems to betray a rare misapprehension of human nature and a large absence of tact and judgment. To my mind it is a cruel procedure.

Y. M.   It might be cruel if that were to be the end; but it is not. What we suffer here will be made up to us by an eternity of bliss in heaven—bliss perfect, bliss absolute.

O. M.   What is your idea about the lower animals? Are they going to heaven?

Y. M.   Certainly not. It is written that they perish.

O. M.   Upon each and every one of them God practices relentless cruelties. He appoints a parasite to attach itself to the eyes of certain fishes, cover them up and blind them. The fish cannot see its food, cannot find it; it goes about in the misery of hunger days and weeks, and is finally released from its cruel existence by starvation and death. The fish is not being educated for heaven, since it is not to go there. Why is it disciplined? What are the undeserved tortures for?

Y. M.   We cannot know, but God knows. They are for a good and loving purpose.

O. M.   We are privileged to doubt it. Each creature in the earth is commissioned to inflict pain and death upon some other creature; and another creature is commissioned to inflict pain and death upon *it*. There is not one creature, big or little, in the earth, that has not come into it specially commissioned to a career of persecution, mutilation and murder. Creatures detectible only under the most powerful microscopes are found to make their living by torturing and killing each other.

Y. M.   There is nothing unjust about it. It is their nature. They are made so.

O. M.   Who made them so?

Y. M.   God.

O. M.   Why?

Y. M.   It pleased Him to do it.

O. M.   Would it have pleased you to do it?

Y. M.   I am not God.

O. M.   In providing tortures for the animal world—that world denied the compensations of heaven—all the ingenuities of a malicious spirit have been exhausted. In New Zealand there is a harmless caterpillar whose creased back catches dust; the winds bring to this dust the seed of a certain weed appointed from on high to see that the caterpillar shall suffer long misery and final assassination; the roots of the seed strike down into his body, the weed grows and flourishes, sucking up the life-juices of the worm for its nourishment; in time the caterpillar is empty and dry, and death—the only really valuable boon vouchsafed to any of God's creatures—comes to its relief. To man has been appointed the fruits of the earth to live upon; and to each and every fruit of whatever kind, has been assigned a destroyer—insect, bug, locust, weevil or what not—to every plant a destroyer, an enemy to ruin the crop and rob the laborer. An all-powerful Being could have furnished these creatures with an appetite for sand. Why, do you suppose, did He not do it?

Y. M.   He had his reasons. It is not for us to criticise.

O. M.   They were founded in love, no doubt.

Y. M.   Our Father who art—

O. M.   Don't misuse that title. Leave that to the pulpit. Earthly fathers do not torture and harry and burn children—for discipline's sake or any other. Shall there be *no* honorable title among us sacred from the slanders of the pulpit? God is not a father in any kindly sense. The Book attributed to Him shows it, all Nature shouts it. Plainly if he cares for his creatures it is not in a spirit of love. It seems strange that he should care for them, or even think of them. Strangest of all that He should value men's flatteries. I cannot conceive of myself caring for the compliments of the wiggling cholera-germs concealed in a drop of putrid water. I cannot conceive of myself caring whether they appointed microbe-popes and priests to beslaver me with praises or didn't. I cannot conceive of myself being "jealous" about whether they mouthed and twaddled at me or didn't. I cannot conceive of myself reducing myself to invisibility and going down into the drop of water to beget myself on a microbe, and be re-born as a microbe, reared as a microbe, crucified as a microbe—suffering such small momentary pain as the evanescent microbe is capable of feeling—and all this foolishness to "save" the microbe species for the rest of time from the consequences of some inconsequential offence committed against me in the hoary antiquity of week before last—it is wholly impossible to conceive it. I should not care for the microbes nor their praise; I should not care for their sins, and should not trouble myself to keep an account of them; I should not care whether the microbes were saved or damned—particularly the former. As compared with such a prodigy as God, I am less than the billionth fraction of a microbe. Why should He interest Himself about me? Do you think he does?

    Y. M.   Not a sparrow falls to the ground without His notice. You have said, yourself, that He has invented a million tortures wherewith to make your life unhappy.

    O. M.   True. But he could invent the tortures and set in motion the laws and the machinery which should continue them through all time without his supervision, then turn His attention elsewhere and trouble Himself no further about the matter. I cannot imagine His being interested during even the half of one of his thousand-year days with the monotonous repetition, generation after generation, of man's trivial doings—his squabblings, his wars, his cheatings, swindlings, oppressions, his petty joys, his paltry heroisms, his griefs and pains and heart-breaks, his insulted hopes, his rickety old age, his longings for death, his despised worship, his affronted prayers, his foolish religions, his silly governments, his toy kings that made so great noise yesterday and will die to-day and stink to-morrow—*no* variety in the bill, never a new device to freshen up the inane monotony of it all—why, surely even God himself would die of the boredom of it and the threadbare poverty of it, if He did not at brief intervals leave the auditorium and hunt up some kind of rational amusement.

    Y. M.   Notwithstanding your opinion we are precious in His eyes, the proof of it is in His Book. He will gather to Himself at the Resurrection such as have deserved His forgiveness, and noble and satisfying will be their reward.

    O. M.   Why should He wish to make a collection of this riff-raff?

    Y. M.   Man is not riff-raff. Man—

    O. M.   We very well know what Man is. Man hides himself from himself during most hours of the day, and in books and sermons and speeches calls himself by fine names; but there is one hour in the twenty-four when he does not do that.

    Y. M.   What hour is that?

O. M.   It is when he wakes out of sleep, deep in the night. You know the bitterness of that hour; we all know it. The black thoughts come flocking through our brain, they show us our naked soul, our true soul, and we perceive and confess that we are despicable.

Y. M.   Those thoughts are messengers sent from Satan. We have only to pray; they cannot abide where prayer is.

O. M.   Why should Satan trouble himself about us? What reason has he to be interested in us?

Y. M.   Every reason. He is a malignant spirit, and spends all his days in devising ways to trick us into his hell, so that he may feast his appetite for misery by seeing us burn forever.

O. M.   In disposition he seems to be the twin of the Other One. Do you detect any difference?

Y. M.   God is always trying to save us from hell. But for Satan's machinations He would succeed.

O. M.   The fate of every man is foreknown to God before the man's birth? You said that?

Y. M.   Yes.

O. M.   Then how can Satan's interference affect the result?

Y. M.   Nevertheless we know that he is always trying.

O. M.   He cannot capture a soul which was foredoomed to heaven?

Y. M.   Indeed, no. It is impossible.

O. M.   And could not keep out a soul foredoomed to hell even if he tried?

Y. M.   Of course not.

O. M.   It seems to me that Satan's is the most unprofitable trade I have yet heard of. Nothing ever comes of his efforts. How do you suppose he has managed to get such a large reputation for capacity and efficiency?

Y. M.   It is not for me to say.

O. M.   It looks as if the pulpit gave it him. It is always advertising his business gratis, and making a great to-do over it, yet when you bring the pulpit to book its own testimony shows that he hasn't any trade to advertise. Plainly the pulpit itself has the easiest trade going. It can talk any insanities it pleases and get people like you to listen. Do you really believe that God is all-powerful?

Y. M.   I do.

O. M.   And do you believe that He would really like to see all men saved?

Y. M.   I know it.

O. M.   Then why doesn't He save them?

Y. M.   He cannot save the disobedient.

O. M.   Is His all-powerful power limited, then?

Y. M.   By principle, yes. He cannot break his own decrees.

O. M.   He could *annul* the decrees?

Y. M.   Of course.

O. M.   That would save the human race from a frightful fate. Why, do you suppose, doesn't He do it?

Y. M.   It would not be right.

O. M.   No, only cheaply charitable. I suppose you would do it if you could?

Y. M.   But I am not God.

O. M.   You paid yourself that compliment before. You have objected to the term "riff-raff" as applied to Man. I cannot see why. In the moral qualities he is infinitely inferior to the other animals, and—

Y. M.   Wait—how do you make that out?

O. M.   I told you a while ago. It is very simple. Man is cruel, malignant, vengeful. He inflicts pain for the mere love of it. Consider the strange and dreadful tortures which the North American Indians used to inflict upon their prisoners of war; consider how the Tartars used to seat a prisoner of war upon pointed stakes and hold him there hour after hour while the man's weight made the stake slowly penetrate the man's body and finally kill him; consider the rich variety of horrible and long-drawn-out tortures which the Christian priests of Spain—with the approval of the Pope—invented and applied to their victims in the shambles of their Holy Inquisition. The other animals kill, but only in sudden passion in the rutting season or for food—never in cold revenge. Have you anything to offer against that statement?

Y. M.   Go on.

O. M.   Man hunts down the other animals and slaughters them by hundreds, for mere pleasure—"sport" he calls it. The rich aristocracies of Europe turn great tracts of land into game preserves, and breed deer and birds to furnish this sport for them, and Parliaments protect their ghastly privileges with rigorous laws. A rich European noble has written with pride and satisfaction of how, in one day, on our Great Plains, he and his party of friends rode into a herd of buffaloes and killed seventy-one of them and left them on the ground to rot. Neither the tiger nor any other "beast" kills more than it needs for a single meal, nor ever kills for sport. Have you anything to offer against that statement?

Y. M.   Go on.

O. M.   Man is avaricious. He will grind his workmen to the bone till he has acquired millions more than he can spend, and will still go on grinding and oppressing to acquire more. Rich men have not scrupled to cheat the poor and the ignorant, the widow and the orphan in order to add to their riches. Misers have half starved themselves to save their savings. Among the beasts there are no misers, none that is avaricious.

Y. M.   Not *all* men are avaricious.

O. M.   No beast is.

Y. M.   Go on.

O. M.   Men keep harems, but it is by brute force privileged by odious laws which the other sex was allowed no hand in making. The rooster keeps a harem, but it is by consent of his concubines.

Y. M.   Proceed.

O. M.   Indecency, vulgarity, obscenity—these are strictly confined to Man. Among the other animals there is no trace of them. Like Adam when he had an unsoiled mind, they hide nothing and are not ashamed.

Y. M.   Go on.

O. M.   Man is the inventor and sole practicer of the atrocity of atrocities, War. He gathers his brethren about him and goes forth in cold blood and with calm pulse to exterminate his kind. He is the only animal that for sordid wages will march out, as the Hessians did in our Revolution, and as the boyish Prince Napoleon did in the Zulu war, and help to slaughter strangers of his own species who have done him no harm and with whom he has no quarrel. He is the only animal that robs his helpless fellow of his country—takes possession of it and drives him out of it or destroys him.

Y. M.   Continue.

O. M.   Man is the only animal that enslaves his own kind.

Y. M.   Except the ant.

O. M.   Except the ant. Man is the only religious animal. He has the Only True Religion—several thousand varieties of it, and all of them rich with "internal evidences" of having been conceived and worked out by Supreme Beings who had lost their minds. He is the only animal who loves his neighbor as himself and cuts his throat if his theology is not straight. He has made a grave-yard of the earth in trying to smooth his brother's path to happiness and heaven.

Y. M.   Not all religions have done this.

O. M.   I was thinking of the Christian religion particularly.

Y. M.   For shame! It is the very symbol of peace, the introducer and promoter of peace.

O. M.   The peace of God, perhaps, of which it has been justly remarked that it passeth understanding. Why, God himself said, at a time when topics like loving your enemies, and forgiving seventy times seven, and turning the other cheek were taking a rest, that He came into the world not to bring peace but a sword. However, to return to the subject: you think Man is not riff-raff. I cannot bring myself to agree with you. He has all the immoral qualities, the miscalled "lower" animals have none of them.

Y. M.   Man has no one to blame but himself. Adam was created morally perfect, as morally blemishless as the angels themselves. Before the Fall, which he brought upon himself and his posterity by disobedience, he was incapable of sin, for he was without the knowledge of good and evil—he did not know them apart.

O. M.   Then he was entirely satisfactory to God?

Y. M.   Entirely.

O. M.   And fit for heaven.

Y. M.   Yes, fit for heaven.

O. M.   Do the "lower" animals know good from evil?

Y. M.   No.

O. M.   And yet are ruled out of heaven?

Y. M.   Yes.

O. M.   Why?

Y. M.   It is by God's commandment.

O. M.   It seems unfair; and inconsistent. Being ignorant of good and evil and incapable of sin, they stand on a par with the angels. Why are they ruled out and the angels admitted?

Y. M.   It is by the command of God, whose wisdom is without bounds and whose justice is perfect.

O. M.   God did not wish Adam and Eve to eat of the fruit of the tree of knowledge and find out the difference between good and evil and how to commit sin?

Y. M.   He did not. He commanded them to refrain.

O. M.   He knew they would disobey?

Y. M.   Yes. He knew that they would be tempted by the serpent and that they would yield.

O. M.   He could have prevented the serpent from tempting them?

Y. M.   Certainly.

O. M.   He could have cut the tree down or removed it to a safe place in heaven?

Y. M.   All things are possible with God.

O. M.   Except square dealing, apparently. And common consistency. He knew beforehand that Adam would yield to temptation. Then where could have been the use in experimenting upon a sure thing? It looks as if he did not feel certain.

Y. M.   He *was* certain.

O. M.   He created a weak Adam when He could have created a strong one, then laid a trap for him which He foreknew he would fall into. Then He punished him when He was solely responsible for Adam's crime Himself. I think He did well to teach people to pray to Him not to lead them into temptation. Apparently He knows His own disposition. Isn't it a sorry business, this whole tangle of childish nonsense? Why was He so indiscreet as to reveal the fact that He knew everything that was going to happen in the world before He created it? It is a constantly recurring and insurmountable obstacle—it blocks His scheme at every turn. It makes prayer mere waste of breath; it is useless to pray against a foreknown and foreordained thing.

Y. M.   Contrite and sincere prayer *can* move Him to change it.

O. M.   Then it *isn't* a foreknown thing.

Y. M.   Yes it is; for it was foreknown that the prayer *would* change it.

O. M. Then it wasn't a foreordained thing.

Y. M. Yes it was. It was foreordained that the prayer should be made and the thing be thereby changed.

O. M. This forces upon us the fact that it was foreknown that for a million years the entire population of the earth would be without the Word; that without the knowledge of the Word not a man of them all would escape hell; that for 2,000 years after the Word was sent mighty populations in Asia and in the islands of the sea would still be without it and be pouring into hell year by year in countless multitudes. This colossal injustice and cruelty, which is in exact and striking harmony with the cruelties daily practiced upon all living creatures in the form of diseases, pains, hunger, cold, persecutions and mutilations, and upon man [in] the additional miseries of mental cares and distresses, and griefs of the heart, make a belief in hell—which is doubted by some who cannot reason from the myriad eloquent facts placed before their eyes—a thing entirely rational and worthy of adoption. The spirit that could invent such horrors, and without repenting continue them age after age, can be almost surely depended upon to furnish something as bad or worse in the hereafter, and can also be depended upon to furnish nothing that shall resemble a heaven—even the unendurable one pictured in the Book. That one offers nothing that could attract an intelligent person. In the Book no premium is anywhere placed upon intelligence, talent, mental superiority, is there?

Y. M. No. God cares nothing for those things, His heaven is for moral worth alone.

O. M. Yet He rules out the only creatures that are in any reasonable degree eligible—the so-called "lower" animals.

Y. M. They have not the Moral Sense.

O. M. When Adam was perfect he hadn't it. And only then was he satisfactory. It is doubtful if you have located the Source of all mercy, goodness and compassion aright, but there seems to be no real question as to where the Source of all inconsistency is to be found.

A5.   DISPOSITION

WRITTEN around 1901–1902; paper from one of the tablets (possibly "Par Value") Mark Twain often used after returning to America in 1900, but never before then. At top left of the first leaf he wrote "Character"; at the end of the manuscript he wrote "Read this" followed by "Aguinaldo" as a heading for a résumé or quotation but at that point abandoned the manuscript. In 1901–1902 he wrote or began several attacks on American policy in the Philippines, and he believed Emilio Aguinaldo, the Philippine guerrilla leader, was in a class with Joan of Arc. His marginal comments on Edwin Wildman's pro-American *Aguinaldo* (Boston: Lothrop, 1901—copy in MTP) are as violent as any he wrote.

O. M.   Please write down these two laws: 1. *The disposition that is born in a man determines what the man shall at bottom be*; and by no possibility can that disposition ever be actually altered, for either better or worse.

2. *Training and circumstances can* SEEM *to alter it by suppressing its expression and suspending its activities, but that is all.*

Y. M.   I have set them down.

O. M.   Do you clearly understand that in those two brief laws is compacted all the materials that go to the building of the character of a man? You think you do? Then prove it. Name, in two words, the sole materials out of which the character of a human being is built.

Y. M.   Disposition and Circumstances.

O. M.   That is correct. Into the word Circumstances is condensed everything called Training, Teaching, Education, etc.; for all these things are direct results of Circumstance—that is to say, *Accident* —for a man cannot create his circumstances, he is merely their slave and plaything. They cannot be ordered, they cannot be commanded.

Y. M.   Is Circumstance so powerful?

O. M.   It is *all*-powerful. The man's birth-place is an Accident; his sex is an Accident; his disposition is an Accident; his place in the social scale is an Accident; he is king by Accident, beggar by Accident; Chinaman by Accident, American by Accident; Pagan by Accident, Christian by Accident; Presbyterian, Baptist or Catholic by Accident; free by Accident, slave by Accident, royalist by Accident, democrat by Accident; honest by Accident, a thief by Accident; every circumstance of his life is an Accident and an educator, and is the child of a previous Accident and the father of a posterity of them. Life is one long linked tape-worm of Accidents.

Y. M. If it is all Accident and Circumstance, where does Disposition come in, and what office does it perform?

O. M. Its function is of formidable importance, for it *selects* from the flying myriad of Circumstances the ones which its appetite and tastes prefer, and out of these it builds its man's *character*.

Y. M. If it can select, that is *commanding*; then how is life merely Accident and a chain of Accidents?

O. M. Disposition does not *make* the Accident it selects, it only *chooses* between two or more Accidents.

Y. M. And then?

O. M. The Circumstance which it selects breeds other Circumstances immediately and infallibly; and the Disposition goes on selecting.

Y. M. For instance?

O. M. Given the Accident of a shipwrecked party flung ashore in a strange city. Disposition and previous training at once assert themselves. With a hundred kinds of environment to choose from, A selects the thieves' quarter and makes friends there—and a certain sort of Circumstances will certainly follow, one breeding another and that one in its turn breeding others; good influences will fall in A's way every day and every night, but his Disposition will be indifferent to them or antagonistic to them and they will have little effect or none; A goes straight on his preferential course through the flocking Circumstances, selecting as he goes—and by and by he will arrive at the grave, by way of jail, poor-house, and possibly gallows. On the other hand, with the same large variety of Circumstances to choose from, B's disposition and previous training will make him choose the higher and better sort, and he will move straight along this road, selecting as he goes, and his life will be vastly different from A's. But both lives will be based upon Disposition and moulded and ordered by Accident—that is to say, Circumstances. Read this:

A6.   MORAL COURAGE

PAINE dated the manuscript 1905, but the paper seems to be from a "Par Value" tablet, which Mark Twain is not known to have used after 1904. The placement of the lines across the short dimension of the leaves also argues against 1905, though no date more specific than 1901–1904 is possible.

Old Man. How would you define it?

Young Man. Moral courage is that great quality which enables a person to stand up for the right, at cost of popularity, caste, esteem,— sometimes at cost of fortune, liberty, or life.

O. M. Let us change it to "for the right *as he sees it.*" That will be better, I think. He can't always be sure he is right and everybody else wrong. Is moral courage a rare quality?

Y. M. Yes. So rare that its few possessors are always conspicuous.

O. M. You can name instances?

Y. M. The two or three men who began the anti-slavery crusade seventy years ago. Great moral courage was required for that. They lived in a storm of vituperation; they were hated, despised, shunned; the whole nation cursed them, not six pulpits in the Union ventured to defend them.

O. M. It is a good instance. Name another.

Y. M. Susan B. Anthony standing up for the rights of her sex against the contempt and slander and ribaldry of the entire nation, male and female.

O. M. Another good instance. Joshua Giddings and Susan B. Anthony would have championed any and all moral causes?

Y. M. Yes. I can conceive of none that they would have been afraid to do battle for. Their moral courage was limitless.

O. M. You are sure that moral courage is scarce. How scarce?

Y. M. I am convinced that not more than one person in half a million possesses it.

O. M. What is moral courage—a talent, or an acquisition?

Y. M. A talent, of course. It is born in a man, else he is without it.

O. M. Like a talent for mathematics, languages, billiards, poetry, and so on?

Y. M. Yes.

O. M. Can a man have a talent for mathematics and none for poetry, languages and billiards?

Y. M. Certainly.

O. M.   Can a man have a talent for poetry and none for mathematics, languages and billiards?

Y. M.   Of course.

O. M.   When a man has a considerable talent in one direction isn't it *usual* for him to be only ordinarily equipped with the other talents?

Y. M.   Yes, it is.

O. M.   Are all fine billiard players gifted in equal degree?

Y. M.   Oh, no. There are millions of fine players, but in talent they vary from each other by shades.

O. M.   Some are world-renowned?

Y. M.   Yes—five or six in a generation.

O. M.   We do not hear of the rest of the million?

Y. M.   The world doesn't. Their reputations are local. Some have a reputation in their city, some in their club, some in their village.

O. M.   The same with poets, mathematicians, linguists and the rest?

Y. M.   Yes.

O. M.   Then there are *degrees* in the several talents?

Y. M.   Certainly. It goes without saying.

O. M.   You say moral courage is a talent?

Y. M.   Yes, a talent.

O. M.   Yet you say only one person in half a million possesses it?

Y. M.   Well—it seems to be a talent apart; a most rare, most extraordinary talent. One can hardly subject it to the rules that govern the others.

O. M.   Let us leave the upper regions—let us leave the Giddingses and Anthonys and come to [] down to the common herd. You have spoken of an aunt of yours who was afraid of the dark, afraid of cows, afraid of the lightning, afraid to sleep in a room alone, afraid of ghosts—in fact was the joke of the village for her numberless timidities —yet was not afraid to face a mob of lynchers, all alone, and cry shame upon them, and denounce the leaders by name, although she knew she would be ostracised by the community for it. She did this brave thing on two occasions. Did she do battle for woman's rights also?

Y. M.   She? Oh, no.

O. M.   Did she believe in that movement?

Y. M. Privately—yes. But it was unpopular in the village, and she would not have been known in it for the world.

O. M. Did she favor other moral causes?

Y. M. Yes, she favored all moral causes, from principle, but not enough to work publicly for them unless they were popular.

O. M. She had a splendid and aggressive moral courage, but it was limited to lynchings?

Y. M. Yes, that is about it.

O. M. Take the cases of Smith, Jones, Brown, Robinson. You and I know them well. They are average men, obscure men, private men, altogether unknown to prominence—average men, that is the right phrase. They well represent the multitude. I think we may say that what they are the world is. These four are always to be found on the right side of every good cause—the right side according to their lights. They are always there, aren't they?

Y. M. Yes, it is true.

O. M. How do we know it?

Y. M. By talking with them.

O. M. Right. They are there privately. Not publicly, but privately. Isn't it so?

Y. M. Yes, it is.

O. M. Two of them are Republicans, privately, and democrats at the polls and in mixed company; in their circle they are afraid to be otherwise. The other two are democrats in private and republicans at the polls. They are all Christians in public and unbelievers in private. When President McKinley put the Declaration of Independence under his feet and sent General Merrit [Merritt] to the Phillipines with a pirate's commission in his pocket all four were indignant, along with the rest of the nation; eight months later—cowed by noise, nick-names and insult, they tucked their tails between their legs and became "patriots," along with the rest of the nation. I have suggested that these four tipify Christendom—I mean all Christendom. Have they moral courage?

Y. M. They are destitute of it.

O. M. No, they are not. Smith, a poor man and unknown, bought one share of H. H. railway stock twenty years ago, in order that he might be privileged to attend the annual meeting of the company and expose its legislature-bribings and the deliberate swindles whereby it cheats the State out of its constitutional share of the annual profits; and every year, for twenty years, he has stood up there, without hope or possibility of accomplishing anything, and read off his carefully prepared and unanswerable statistics, and endured the jeers and laughter of the stock-holders for an hour, and the derision, next day, of all the newspapers in the State. There isn't an upright man—editor or other—in Connecticut, but admires Smith's virtue and moral courage in private and makes cowardly fun of it in public. In one detail, then, Smith has this talent which you think is so rare, hasn't he?

Y. M.   He has. It is not to be denied.

O. M.   Take Jones. Forty-nine men in fifty have little or no respect for the missionary industry—privately; but they prudently contribute to it, Sundays, when the plate goes around. Jones publicly states his belief that the Golden Rule distinctly forbids the missionary to ply his trade in China or in any other country whose people he would be unwilling to allow to go to his American home and undermine the religious faith of his family. For this, Jones is disliked in his church and is often made to feel very uncomfortable. There are two thousand newspapers and other periodicals in the United States. Do you hear of any of them opposing or deriding the foreign missionary industry?

Y. M.   No.

O. M.   Do you hear speakers oppose or deride it in public gatherings, or talkers attack it in drawing-rooms.

Y. M.   Most certainly not.

O. M.   Yet it has but a small popularity, and even that little is only sentimental.

Y. M.   How—sentimental?

O. M.   The kind that approves with the mouth—and keeps its hand in its pocket. Three millions of persons, in two New England States, give 75 cents apiece a year to the foreign missionary cause, and seventy-three millions of people in forty-three States give 3½ cents apiece.

Y. M.   Are those the proportions?

O. M.   Yes. Yet my statistics are wrong, in one way. Broadly speaking, living people care nothing for the missionary cause, it is only the dead ones. It is a cause that lives on bequests—gets a friend's money after he is done with it. If it had to subsist on the money it gets from the living, it would starve to death in three months. It is a business which pretends to be of vast public importance and interest, whereas the nation cares nothing about it. No other trade in the world, flourishing on insincere sentiment and false appearances is so wide open to ridicule, yet no one dares to ridicule it. It is the chiefest of all the protected industries.

A7.   [SOLAR-LUNAR FRAGMENT]

THE script is across the long dimension of leaves from a "Pratt's Greater New York Tablet" or similar product the author used in the period 1905–1910. As John S. Tuckey has noted (*Mark Twain and Little Satan* [West Lafayette, Ind., 1963], p. 68), such placement was characteristic only of works written on such paper in 1905. Yet Mark Twain wrote the fragment before transposing the first two chapters in his printer's copy. At the head of the manuscript he wrote that it was to precede or follow the "first chapter," but the nature of the fragment shows he meant present chapter 2. He tore the leaves in half, but all of them survive and are easily assembled.

    Old Man.   You have at some time or other been in a cold storage vault?

    Young Man.   Yes.

    O. M.   You retain a strong impression of your first visit to such a place?

    Y. M.   Very strong, very vivid.

    O. M.   Just the mention of the words themselves—cold storage—revives that impression?

    Y. M.   Unquestionably. I feel the frosty chill again.

    O. M.   First visit to a Turkish bath. You had sensations, and remember them?

    Y. M.   Indeed yes. Nobody forgets them.

    O. M.   Those two words—Turkish bath—do they recal a sensation and produce an effect?

    Y. M.   Yes. When I hear them I am immediately swallowed up in a fog of white steam and I sit naked and gasping for breath while rivers of boiling perspiration pour down my back.

O. M. Valuable words!—turkish bath and cold storage. They carry no confusion to one's mind. How about the words Borrowing and Stealing: do they mean one thing, or two, to you.

Y. M. Two.

O. M. To say that a man borrowed a horse—does that lower the man in your estimation?

Y. M. Certainly not.

O. M. To say that he stole a horse—*that* lowers him?

Y. M. Decidedly, yes.

O. M. Valuable words!—borrow and steal. They carry no confusion to the mind. Is that true?

Y. M. Yes.

O. M. Not quite—no, not quite. There is a kind of stealing which is a disease of the mind, not a defect of morals, hence no guilt attaches to its practice.

Y. M. Ah, I remember. Kleptomania.

O. M. And so, to be fair, and avoid confusion, we give two definitions to the word thief. A Kleptomaniac is a thief, but we do not call him thief, because it would mislead. The hearer would despise him. But if we call him Kleptomaniac the hearer does not despise him, he only pities him. Is that true?

Y. M. Yes, and just.

O. M. Now we arrive at that troublesome word Selfishness.

Y. M. I believed I divined your drift.

O. M. All acts are selfish, but they are distinctly divisible into good selfishnesses and evil ones—selfishnesses which are innocent of harmful intent, and selfishnesses which can hurt. Yet we have but the one word; it makes no discrimination, and it *always* carries with it a reproach. It is as wrong as it would be to have but one word for theft, and include Kleptomania in it, thus putting a stain upon the Kleptomaniac which he does not deserve.

Y. M. I am far enough along, now, to realize that it certainly is an overloaded word—a word with *two* functions to perform, but shirks one of them entirely—a word which often conveys a slander where none is deserved. Cannot you throw it wholly out, and put something more light-throwing and discriminative in its place?

O. M. I have been thinking of that. When we examine the sole impulse which moves the human machinery we find that in all cases it has one function—one, and *only* one—to *content the spirit,* whether for a single moment or for a longer time. *Nothing* but self-approval can content the spirit and give it peace—peace for the moment or peace for a longer time. In most cases the source of this self-approval is the approval of *others*; in many cases a part of its source is the *disapproval* of others: as where a vicious man gets pleasure out of beating his wife and terrorizing his children, and gets an added pleasure out of the impotent disapproval of timid and outraged neighbors; and as where Tweed got joy and contentment out of robbing the city and an added pleasure out of the people's impotent cursings—which he answered with the jeering remark, "What are you going to do about it?" Do you follow?

Y. M.   Yes—go on.

O. M.   Now, then, no man invents his own impulses. They are the product wholly of his born-temperament, acted upon by his training and by the influences of his environment. Therefore, we do not want an *accusing* word, like Selfishness; we do not want a word which indicates *personal* initiative, there being no such thing; and finally we do not want a word implying merit or demerit in the *man,* or praise or blame, no such words being applicable to him, he being purely a machine and as destitute of initiative and of control over his movements as is any other machine. I think we want a word which will confine itself strictly to indicating the *quality* of a man's acts, and their *results,* upon himself and upon others, but attributing *neither praise nor blame to the man himself* for the acts and the results.

Y. M.   I see. You want a colorless word.

O. M.   Exactly. For instance: when we say the lunar influence affects the tides we are neither praising the moon nor censuring her; and we are neither praising nor blaming the sun when we say the solar influence affects the weather.

Y. M.   I get the idea. Why not abolish the word Selfishness and put Lunar and Solar in its place?

O. M.   They might answer.

Y. M.   The moon is lovely and beautiful, to all men, both savage and civilized. She gets pleasure out of shining—one always feels sure of that. Her shining gives pleasure and profit to all upon whom her beneficent light falls. There you have the *act,* also the double *result.* Then adopt the word. Say of a man "he has many lunar impulses; the acts proceeding from them have as a result that they bless and profit him and do the same for others." It describes the nature of the impulse but in no way claims that the *man* originated it; it merely mentions the acts proceeding from the impulse, without connecting him with the acts, but only connecting the acts with the *impulse*—which *he* did not originate; it describes the *result*, but imputes no merit to the *man* for it.

O. M.   I think Lunar will do.

Y. M.   So will Solar. The sun gets up infamous weather sometimes—hurricanes in summer, blizzards in winter. We can say of a man, "he has many solar impulses; he does not originate them, nor, consequently, the acts proceeding from them; the results of the acts are bad for him and for others, but he is not to blame for this, for he is merely a machine and is operated wholly by outside forces like any other machine.["]

O. M.   Solar will do. *The word Selfishness is now formally abolished from the vocabulary of this philosophy.* Let us try the new words. Here are a couple of paragraphs—one from the narrative of an American lady traveling in England, the other an occurrence in King Leopold's Congo State:

"The young Englishman, moved by the child's troubles, made advances, got its confidence, and was soon busy repairing the toy, the child looking on, grateful and happy, its tears gone, its eyes eloquent with interest and delight. I could have hugged that young fellow."

Do you see? He couldn't bear to see the child suffer, it gave him pain—gave *him* pain. He *had* to come to the rescue, to get peace of mind, freedom from pain, *contentment of spirit*. Contentment of spirit is derived from one source, and only one. What is it?

Y. M.   Self-approval.

O. M.   And self-approval is derived from—how many sources?

Y. M.   Two: results proceeding from lunar impulses and acts, and those that proceed from solar impulses and acts.

O. M.   Good! It goes very well. The young man was moved by—what?

Y. M.   A lunar impulse. The result of the consequent act was a satisfaction to him, *first*, and to the child *next*.

O. M.   True. This is the other passage:

"The prisoner's child cried, because of its broken wrist; this woke the soldier and enraged him, and he caught up the child and dashed its brains out against a tree and flung the corpse at the feet of its agonised mother."

The soldier was moved by a solar impulse. He was born with a cruel disposition; brutal companionships and a savage environment had trained him, and we have the result: he could get more satisfaction and self-approval out of giving rein to his bloody passions than he could have gotten out of restraining them, therefore he did as described. But he was not to blame for his impulse or his act; both were compulsions of his disposition and his training. The young Englishman is entitled to no praise for *his* impulse and its resulting act: they were compulsions of his temperament and training. Some day we will read over the chapter upon Selfishness, and use, in the place of that unfair word, *Self-Approval*; and use Lunar and Solar to describe the two kinds of impulse whereby self-approval is acquired. Maybe this will give the chapter a different and pleasanter aspect, and purge it of offence.

SUPPLEMENT B

CHRISTIAN SCIENCE FRAGMENTS

THE following items were deleted from or never became part of the *Christian Science* text. Several pages of reading notes are omitted, along with Mark Twain's illustrations and a few short fragments somewhere between outline and manuscript. The items are in the order they had or might have had in the book.

B1. [CHRISTIAN SCIENCE AND THE BOOK OF MRS. EDDY, SECTION IV]

MARK TWAIN'S first article on Christian Science, in *Cosmopolitan* for October 1899, contained a fourth section he deleted in printer's copy, preferring to question Mrs. Eddy's authorship in book 2. No manuscript survives; the text is that of the printer's copy setting.

IV

A word upon a question of authorship. Not that quite; but rather, a question of emendation and revision. We know that the Bible-Annex was not written by Mrs. Eddy, but was handed down to her eighteen hundred years ago by the Angel of the Apocalypse; but did she translate it alone, or did she have help? There seems to be evidence that she had help. For there are four several copyrights on it—1875, 1885, 1890, 1894. It did not come down in English, for in that language it could not have acquired copyright—there were no copyright laws eighteen centuries ago, and in my opinion no English language—at least up there. This makes it substantially certain that the Annex is a translation. Then, was not the first translation complete? If it was, on what grounds were the later copyrights granted?

I surmise that the first translation was poor; and that a friend or friends of Mrs. Eddy mended its English three times, and finally got it into its present shape, where the grammar is plenty good enough, and the sentences are smooth and plausible though they do not mean anything. I think I am right in this surmise, for Mrs. Eddy cannot write English to-day, and this is argument that she never could. I am not able to guess who did the mending, but I think it was not done by any member of the Eddy Trust, nor by the editors of the "C. S. Journal," for their English is not much better than Mrs. Eddy's.

However, as to the main point: it is certain that Mrs. Eddy did not doctor the Annex's English herself. Her original, spontaneous, undoctored English furnishes ample proof of this. Here are samples from recent articles from her unappeasable pen; double-columned with them are a couple of passages from the Annex. It will be seen that they throw light. The italics are mine:

1. "What plague spot, or bacilli were (*sic*) gnawing (*sic*) at the heart of this metropolis . . . and bringing it" (the heart) "on bended knee? Why, it was an *institute* that had entered its vitals—that, among other things, *taught games*," et cetera. (*P. 670, C. S. Journal, article entitled "A Narrative—by Mary Baker G. Eddy."*)

2. "Parks sprang up (*sic*) . . . electric street cars run (*sic*) merrily through several streets, concrete sidewalks and macadamized roads dotted (*sic*) the place," et cetera. (*Ibid.*)

3. "Shorn (*sic*) of its suburbs it had indeed little left to admire, save to (*sic*) such as fancy a skeleton above ground *breathing* (*sic*) slowly through a barren (*sic*) breast." (*Ibid.*)

"Therefore the efficient remedy is to destroy the patient's unfortunate belief, by both silently and audibly arguing the opposite facts in regard to harmonious being—representing man as healthful instead of diseased, and showing that it is impossible for matter to suffer, to feel pain or heat, to be thirsty or sick." (*P. 375, Annex.*)

"Man is never sick; for Mind is not sick, and matter cannot be. A false belief is both the tempter and the tempted, the sin and the sinner, the disease and its cause. It is well to be calm in sickness; to be hopeful is still better; but to understand that sickness is not real, and that Truth can destroy it, is best of all, for it is the universal and perfect remedy." (*Chapter xii, Annex.*)

You notice the contrast between the smooth, plausible, elegant, addled English of the doctored Annex and the lumbering, ragged, ignorant output of the translator's natural, spontaneous and unmedicated penwork. The English of the Annex has been slicked up by a very industrious and painstaking hand—but it was not Mrs. Eddy's.

If Mrs. Eddy really wrote or translated the Annex, her original draft was exactly in harmony with the English of her plague-spot or bacilli which were gnawing at the insides of the metropolis and bringing its heart on bended knee, thus exposing to the eye the rest of the skeleton breathing slowly through a barren breast. And it bore little or no resemblance to the book as we have it now—now that the salaried polisher has holystoned all of the genuine Eddyties out of it.

Will the plague-spot article go into a volume just as it stands? I think not. I think the polisher will take off his coat and vest and cravat and "demonstrate over" it a couple of weeks and sweat it into a shape something like the following—and then Mrs. Eddy will publish it and leave people to believe that she did the polishing herself:

1. What injurious influence was it that was affecting the city's morals? It was a social club which propagated an interest in idle amusements, disseminated a knowledge of games, et cetera.

2. By the magic of the new and nobler influences the sterile spaces were transformed into wooded parks, the merry electric car replaced the melancholy 'bus, smooth concrete the tempestuous plank sidewalk, the macadamized road the primitive corduroy, et cetera.

3. Its pleasant suburbs gone, there was little left to admire save the wrecked graveyard with its uncanny exposures.

The Annex contains one sole and solitary humorous remark. There is a most elaborate and voluminous Index, and it is preceded by this note:

"This Index will enable the student to find any thought or idea contained in the book."

B2.   [LATER STILL]

MARK TWAIN'S February article for the *North American Review* ("Christian Science—III") concluded with a portion of his "Eddypus" material (compare Paine 42a). The section came close to being book 1, chapter 10, for galley numbers indicate that he canceled it only after it was set. The manuscripts for this and the next four fragments consist of "Par Value" tablet leaves. The text is that of the *North American Review* pages used in printer's copy, as revised there by Mark Twain.

CHAPTER X
(LATER STILL.)—A THOUSAND YEARS AGO.[1]

Passages from the Introduction to the "Secret History of Eddypus, the World-Empire":

The First Part of this Introduction—which deals with Book I of my narrative—being now concluded and the outlines of that portion of the ancient world's history which preceded the rise of what was in time to be the sole Political and Religious Power in the earth—Christian Science—being clearly defined in the reader's mind, as I trust, I now arrive at the Second Part of my Introduction, which will tersely synopsize Book II of my History.

Accuracy is not claimed for Book I, as the reader will see when he comes to examine it. One of the first acts of the Christian Science (or Divine Science) Popes when they had attained to supreme power in the globe, was the destruction of all secular libraries, the suppression of all secular seats of learning, and the prohibition of all literature not issued by the papal press at Eddyflats (called by another name previously). This extinction of light was begun nearly nine hundred years ago, at the time that the Roman Catholic Church gave up the struggle and ceased to exist as an independent body, turning over what was left of its assets to the Christian Science Church on exceedingly good terms, and merging itself in that giant Trust, about the beginning of the reign of Her Divine Supremacy Pope Mary Baker G. Eddy IV, "Viceroy of God"—as the official formula of that remote age words it, a formula still used in our own day under Her Divine Supremacy Pope Mary Baker G. Eddy LXIX. Within a century after the beginning of this extinction of light all the ancient history-books had disappeared from the world. Within two centuries more the tale of the ancient world had ceased to be history, properly speaking, and had become legend. And mainly fantastic legend, too, as the reader will admit when he comes to study it.

1. Written A.D. 2902.

But my Book II deals not with legend, but with fact. Its materials are drawn from the great find of seven years ago, the inestimable Book which Mark Twain, the Father of History, wrote and sealed up in a special vault in an important city of his day, whose ruins were discovered under mounds in the desert wastes a hundred and fifty years ago, and in recent years have been clandestinely explored by one whose name I must not reveal, lest the Church learn it and bring the traitor to the rack and the stake.

This noble Book was written during the time of the Rise of Christian Science, and is the only authentic one in existence which treats of that extraordinary period, the Church histories being—what we know them to be, but do not speak it out except when we are writing as I am now, secretly and in the fear of consequences. The translation of the Book's quaint and mouldy English into the Language Universal, the English of our day, has been a slow and most difficult work—and withal dangerous—but it has been accomplished. The best reward of our handful of brave scholars is not publicity of their names!

What we know of the Father of History is gathered from modest chance admissions of his own, and will be found in the proper places in my succeeding volumes. We know that he was a statesman and moralist of world-wide authority, and a historian whose works were studied and revered by all the nations and colleges in his day. He has tacitly conceded this in chapter 4 of volume IX of his immortal Book. It is apparent that he had defects. This we learn by his attempts to conceal them. He often quotes things that have been said about him; and not always with good discretion, since they "give him away"—a curious phrase which he uses so frequently that we must suppose it was a common one in his time. In one place he quotes—with an evident pang, though he thinks he conceals the hurt—this remark from a book, by an unknown author, entitled the *St. Louis Globe-Democrat*: "He possesses every fine and great mental quality except the sense of humor." Nine-tenths of this verdict is nobly complimentary; yet instead of being satisfied with it and grateful for it, he devotes more than five pages to trying to prove that he *has* the sense of humor. And fails—though he is densely unaware of it. There is something pathetic about this. He has several other defects; the reader will find them noted in their proper places.

His Book is inestimably valuable, because of its transparent truthfulness, and because it covers the whole of that stupendous period, the birth and rise of Christian Science. He was born fifteen years after Our Mother, in the autumn of the year 15 of our era, which corresponds to the year 1835 of the so-called Christian Era, and was educated in five foreign and domestic Universities. He lived throughout Our Mother's earthly sojourn, and several years after her Translation in the Automobile of Fire. From him we learn that he was 246 years old when he finished his Book and buried it, but the date of his death is shrouded in obscurity. And the manner of it.

Briefly, then, let us outline the contents of my Book II.

In A.M. (year of Our Mother) 55, (A.D. 1875), Our Mother's Revelation was published. It bore the title "Science and Health, with Key to the Scriptures," and in the early days it was read by her disciples in connection with a volume, now long ago obsolete and forgotten, called the Old and New Testaments, as a translation of the meanings of that volume. A generation or two after her Ascension, she re-wrote "Science and Health," and discarded its previous contents, and also its title. She sent this perfected work down from on high by Revelation. From that day to ours her book has borne the simple title, "The Holy Bible, by Her Divine Supremacy Pope Mary Baker G. Eddy I." By command, left in her Will, the term "Christian Science" was changed to "Divine Science" as soon as her Church's universal dominion in the earth was secure. This happened at the time of the merger, when Her Divine Supremacy Pope Mary Baker G. Eddy IV ascended the throne. He was the first male Pope. By the terms of the Will all Popes must officially bear Our Mother's name and be called "She," regardless of sex. Our Popes have all been males since Our Mother's time.

The world's events are not ordered by gods nor by men, but solely by Circumstance—accidental, unplanned, and unforeseen. One Circumstance creates another, that one a third, and so on: just as a seed, falling in a barren place, creates a plant, the plant creates a forest, the forest condenses the humidity of the atmosphere and creates streams, the streams make the region fruitful, this invites men, a community results, a nation grows from it, a civilization develops, and with it its sure and inevitable crop of ambitions, jealousies, quarrels, wars, and squabbling little religions: the ages go on and on and on, and from century to century histories are written, wherein it is told how this and that and the other vast event was the work of such-and-such a king, or such-and-such a statesman, and not a word about *Accidental and Inevitable Circumstance*, which alone did those things, and would have done them anyhow, whether those kings and statesmen had existed or not. Meantime that small seed which fell in the desert in the beginning has been long ago forgotten and no man takes it into account; yet it was the Circumstance which produced all the other Circumstances, without knowing it or intending it; and without it the desert had remained a desert and there had been no nation, no kings, and no history.

Out of a Circumstance of ten million years ago grew the world's entire history—every minute detail of it; and there was never at any time a possibility of changing or preventing any Circumstance in the whole crop, nor of postponing it a fraction of a second nor of hastening it a fraction of a second by the ingenuity of any man or body of men. That pregnant Circumstance was the very first act or motion of the very first microscopic living germ that Nature produced. From that wee Circumstance proceeded all history of the past, and from it will proceed all happenings of the future, to the end of time.

Nothing could have prevented it, ten million years ago, from producing, in its due and far distant season, the discovery of America, the colonization of it, the Rebellion against the crown, the creation of the Republic, the birth and flowering of its sordid and mighty civilization, the advent of the unsuccessful Quimby, the fertilizing of his idea by Our Mother, the inflating of that idea into a religion, the unforeseen and unexpected expansion of that religion by the accident of Circumstances which no man could control nor direct nor delay, the growth abreast of it of the giant forces of Labor and Capital, their destruction of the Republic, the erection of the Absolute Monarchy, the swallowing up of the civil Monarchy in the colossal religious Autocracy of the World-Empire of Eddypus, the exalting of the Founder of Divine Science to the Second Place in the Holy Family, the extinction of the world's civilizations, and the closing down of the Black Night through whose sombre and melancholy shadows the human race has now been groping hopeless and forlorn these eight hundred years.

About the year 1870 of the so-called Christian era (A.M. 50), ingenious men massed together a multitude of small and unprofitable oil-industries under the control of a restricted body of able managers—

and that was the first Trust. Circumstances had compelled this. These Circumstances were railways and telegraphs. Businesses which had been wide apart before, could live upon their local markets; but the new Circumstances compelled them to send their products from their widely separated sources to the great centres of commerce, and meet the resulting competition with a new device—concentration of the streams, and control of them. Thus, Circumstances furnished the Opportunity and created the first Trust.

The first Trust created the second, the second the third, and so on. In the course of a generation they created hundreds. Little by little, steadily and inevitably, the movement grew. It forced each industry to band its capital and its companies together, whether it wanted to or not; for Circumstances are arbitrary and are not affected by any man's opinions or principles or desires.

Meantime Circumstances had been doing some other notable work. For many, many ages, in the world, the masters of each old-time industry had formed themselves into close corporations—guilds—for their protection: to control trade and regulate competition. But each guild concerned itself with its own interests only; the ironmongers did not combine with the silk mercers nor with the furriers (skinners), nor did any two or more unrelated industries pool their affairs and thus secure each other's protection. Also, for ages, the wage-earning servants of each guild had compacted themselves into close unions, for protection against intruding and alien practisers of their trades, and to limit the number of apprentices, prevent the making of too many journeymen, and keep up the wages. But the subordinates of no two or more, or of all the trades, thought of banding together and commanding the situation. This formidable idea was not born until the world was old and gray.

Circumstances gave it birth. A Circumstance—what it was is centuries ago forgotten—compelled a pair of unrelated unions to join together; this bred another and another combination; the movement grew and spread, according to the law of Circumstance, and by ten or fifteen years after the formation of the Oil Trust, the Knights of Labor were in business. It was smiled at by the wise and the sarcastic, but the smile was premature. It had its ups and downs, but it grew in strength nevertheless, and prospered. In time it discarded its fantastic title and adopted a sober and dignified one.

It was itself a Trust, of course, and by the end of its birth-century was become the mightiest and the most merciless and remorseless of all; yet with the dearest and sweetest and most engaging dulness and innocence it preached a lofty and immaculate holy war against all other Trusts!

It marched side by side with the commercial Trusts for a good while, then it marched ahead of them. It was the first Trust that bound all its vast machinery, all its multitudinous unrelated parts, in one bond of iron—accomplishing this extraordinary thing years before Circumstances did the same with the nation's commercial Trusts.

Side by side with the Labor Trust and the Commercial Trusts was moving the Christian Science Trust—quite unheeded, except to be despised by the wise and smiled at by the sarcastic. Prematurely. All attention was upon the other two—those busy servants that were opening and smoothing the road for their and the world's future master without suspecting it.

The years drifted on. Labor whipped Capital, Capital whipped Labor—turn about. All the railways, ships, telegraphs, telephones, manufactures, newspapers—all the industries of the nation, in a word —became combined in one prodigious Trust, and in its home office its Board directed all the affairs of the country.

Its chairman uttered his command, and next day every newspaper in the land spoke his views with one voice; he touched a button and delivered his orders, and the Conventions nominated his candidate for President, and on election day the people elected that candidate; he dictated the President's policy and was obeyed; he dictated the laws, and the Congress passed them; he officered the army and the navy to suit the Board, he made war when he pleased and peace when he chose.

In its regular and recurrent turn the Labor Trust swept him and his Board away, and took over the government and continued it on the same lordly plan until Capital got the upper hand once more.

In the course of one of its innings Capital abolished the spectre Republic and erected a herditary Monarchy on its ruins, with dukes and earls and the other ornaments; and later, Labor rose and seized the whole outfit and turned out the Billionaire Royal Family and set up a Walking Delegate and his household in their place.

Meantime the Science was growing, relentlessly growing, ceaselessly growing. When it numbered 10,000,000 its presence began to be privately felt; when it numbered 30,000,000 its presence began to be publicly felt; when it numbered 60,000,000 it began to take a hand— quietly; when it numbered half the country's population, it lifted up its chin and began to dictate.

It was time for the intellect of the land to realize where power and profit were to be had, and it went over to the Science, solid—just as had happened in all times with all successful vast movements of all kinds.

The game was made. Four-fifths of the nation skurried to the Church, the rest were *lashed* into it. The Church was master, supreme and undisputed, all other powers were dead and buried, the Empire was an established perpetuity, its authority spread to the ends of the earth, its revenues were estimable in astronomical terms only, they went to but one place in the earth—the Treasury at Eddyflats, called "Boston" in ancient times; the Church's dominion covered every land and sea, and made all previous concentrations of Imperial force and wealth seem nursery trifles by contrast.

Then the Black Night shut down, never again to lift!

Thus stand briefly outlined the contents of Book II. In that Book I have set down the details.

The reader must not seek to know the author's name. Lest the Church learn it also!

AUTHOR OF "THE SECRET HISTORY OF EDDYPUS."

B3.   P. S.

AT the head of the manuscript Mark Twain wrote "To follow Xn Science in February N. A. Review." He had not yet quarreled with McCrackan, but by the time he submitted his February material the cordiality of this postscript was farthest from his mind. See the Explanatory Notes for an account of the quarrel.

P. S. *December* 10, 1902.

Mr. McCracken [McCrackan], Christian Science's chief writer, is going to answer me, or correct me, in the March number of this Review. The Harpers will issue these articles of mine in book form about the end of March or in April, and Mr. McCrackan asks that his

Rejoinder shall appear in that book. That hospitality he can have. It is not likely that the March Review can give him all the space he needs, but he can finish in the book; he can have half the room between the covers if he desires it. He is a straight and sincere man and a profoundly convinced and reverent Christian Scientist, and it may be that between us we can settle the Science question with the pen; though I doubt it, for the reason that we have orally tried it by the hour in my house and did not succeed. We finished where we began: he finding a meaning in the phrase "mortal mind," I only a fog; he believing that the mind, *with* Christian Science, can cure all ills, mental and physical, I believing that the mind can cure only half of them, and that it is able to do this powerful and beneficent work without being obliged to call in the help of Christian Science; he believing Mrs. Eddy discovered something, I believing she did not; he holding her in reverence, I holding her in irreverence. Times have changed, and for the worse. Three centuries ago these points of difference could have been settled with a shotgun; now one must resort to ink, and ink settles nothing.

M. T.

B4.   PORTRAITS OF MRS. EDDY

SOMEONE, probably Paine, dated the manuscript 1905, but it was almost certainly a first beginning of book 2, hence written in January 1903. The title was originally *Mrs. Eddy, as Portrayed by Herself.*

I

There are three portraits of Mrs. Eddy: one by her bitter enemies, one by her worshiping friends, and one by herself. The first-mentioned is done with black paint, the second with white paint and gilding, the third with what Mrs. Eddy intended for white. As a result, in the first we have the greediest and wickedest Christian since Judas, in the second we have a duplicate of the Savior, and in the third we have Jesus and Judas most naïvely and complacently mixed. If one wishes to prove to himself (or must I use that tiresome idiotism *oneself?*) that human estimates of human beings are of slight value and entitled to small respect, let him examine these portraits.

As a sample of the hostile portrait, I refer him to a pamphlet by Mr. Frederick W. Peabody of 15 Court Square, Boston, partly entitled "A Complete Exposé." The rest of the title engulfs 21 words; and as I am paid by the word I should consider it dishonorable in me to shovel those in and put that unearned $4.20 in my pocket. I should regard it as blood-money. The main part of the pamphlet is inside the covers; it is bitter, unsparing, fiendishly interesting, and would be worth the pamphlet's price—25 cents—just by itself, without the prodigal title. Samples of the friendly portrait are procurable at the C. S. Publishing Society's offices, 95 Falmouth street, Boston. They are to be had there in a variety of forms, the work of many eager and affectionate hands. For samples of Mrs. Eddy's portrait of herself, the reader is referred to her voluminous writings, which are likewise procurable at No. 95. Her features are scattered here and there through them, and have to be searched out; but they are all there, and collectible. I desire to plaster these three portraits together, one on top of another, in the composite-photograph style, and shall hope that the real Mrs. Eddy will develop from the combination. I shall expect to cull freely from Mr. Peabody, for when it comes to handling the controversial brush with true vindictiveness and charm, I regard him as the gayest of the gay. I shall cull as freely from Mrs. Eddy, likewise, for when it comes to putting 2 and 2 together and getting 46 out of it she is a solitaire, she is without a peer, and unapproachably fascinating.

I am not writing about her because I believe in her—for I don't; I am only writing about her because she is the most interesting figure in the world to-day. She is a portent. By and by there will hardly be room enough between the horizons for her name; and her shadow will fall across the whole earth. Fifty years from now I shall be spending the most of my holidays looking down over the balusters watching her cult spread about the earth, and thirty centuries from now I shall be at it still.

II

Her Youth

When she was about 70 years old, she published her autobiography (1891). It is a short 15,000 words, and Louis Stevenson could have written it in three days. In it she gives 17 pages to her childhood

and to her ancestry—the bulk of the 17 to the latter. Without warning
to the reader she now makes a jump of nearly half a century and lands
in the year 1878; certainly as surprising a sample of acrobatics as is to
be found in autobiographical literature anywhere. She compresses the
history of the next three years into five lines.

At this point she takes a rest, and pulls in a quite irrelevant poem
by the ears—two pages. It is she that calls it by that name, and I feel—
indeed I think I may say I know—that she does it innocently, and without intending to deceive. I will quote from it by and by.

After the refreshment of the Poem she vaults back from 1881 to
1843, a matter of about 40 years, and in three pages and a quarter tells
the reader about her marriages—an average of a page and two lines to
each. Instinct warns her that this is almost irreverently scanty; and she
—the shrewdness of it!—instead of apologising, makes a virtue of that
very scantiness:

"Mere historic incidents and personal events are frivolous and of
no moment, unless they illustrate the ethics of Truth. To this end, but
only to this end, such narrations may be admissible and advisable."
Retrospection and Introspection, p. 34.

Necessarily she is not meaning to mean what she means there. She
realizes that three marriages are historic incidents and personal events,
and that they illustrate the ethics of Truth if you stop there and do
not enlarge upon them; but that if you enlarge upon them those marriages then become frivolous and of no moment, and are no longer
competent material to illustrate the ethics of Truth with. I think that
is it. She goes on explaining the scantiness for a couple of pages, but it
is waste of space and I would there had been some more marriages.

We have now glanced at one-half of the autobiographical primer;
the other half of it springs around a good deal—for Mrs. Eddy is not
herself when she is not disconnected—but it furnishes glimpses of
the important features of the rest of her career. Only glimpses, merely
glimpses; it is plain that she [is] quite incapable of elaborating anything
except a something which she would mistake for a thought. She then
at once becomes garrulous and enthusiastic and ungrammatical and
incoherent beyond imagination.

B5.   [FRAGMENT ON UNFAMILIAR TEXTS]

THE place this manuscript might have had in the book is not clear. It is paged 1, 2, 3, with the letter "A" at top left of each leaf. The words "Human | Brutal | Bestial" follow the last sentence, and at the bottom of p. 3 an isolated note reads: "People think I have no reverence. I revered E. Cady Stanton. She *organized* her movement."

The Christian Scientist is surprised and affronted because people laugh at "Science and Health." People always laugh at what they do not understand, if it seems grotesque. It would be a strange thing if a Christian Scientist who was reading, for the first time, a learned Hindu's expositions of the sacred books of his people, or of the body of holy laws that have come down out of antiquity with them, did not find them fantastic and laughable. Every religion that is new to us has a terminology that is also new to us; and the strange words, being meaningless to us, and thundering along in what we take for an empty and ostentatious pretence of wisdom and profundity, acquire our derision on cheap and easy terms. Custom—not common sense, not fairness—permits us to laugh at the verbal costume of Science and Health: it is odd to us, and that is sufficient. Every disciple laughed at it at first; and continued to laugh until he believed he had discovered that there was a living and rational and respectworthy being inside of it. He did not arrive at his belief until he had mastered the book's specialized vocabulary—it was that that turned on the light for him. I do not know that vocabulary, therefore I laugh at the book by the privilege of ignorance, while quite well understanding that men with better heads than mine have learned it and stopped laughing. There is one German author whose books I feed upon with contentment and delight because they rest me and because I do not understand them. He uses the usual German words, but saddles them with meanings of his own that are not in the dictionary. I do not study him, I only just read him for the restfulness of it. I am reading Science and Health again, these days, and find it restful.

We laughed at Elizabeth Cady Stanton and her new dresses for

old words when she devoted her noble spirit and applied her fine powers to quite as valuable a work as the founding of a religion; after that,
whom shall we revere and what new thing shall we respect?

B6.   CONCERNING THE WORKS OF ART IN THIS BOOK

EVIDENTLY intended as an excursus or a postscript, depending on
where Mark Twain planned to insert his illustrations. Paine dated the
manuscript 1903 and wrote "C. S." at the head.

   The idea of illustrating this book with my own pencil is original
with me, it would have taken the publisher years to think of it; he said
so himself. A publisher does not think much of an idea which he did
not originate, so they do not get much chance to think. It keeps them
healthy, keeps them from getting careworn, you seldom see them going
to a health resort. This one says the pictures will inflame the reader.
   There is nothing in that argument. If a reader is so combustible,
let him take out a fire policy. But there is no fear; it is not going to
happen. When a reader understands a picture it does not inflame him.
Very well, he will understand these pictures, because I shall explain
them as I go along.
   It has taken me years to get recognition as an artist, but now that
I have got it I ought to be allowed to enjoy it, I think, and not be
crowded down and made unhappy. For years I could not get a picture
accepted at the Academy. I could get compliments, plenty of compliments, but not acceptance. Mr. Carrol Beckwith acknowledged, in so
many words, that there were no pictures like mine in the Academy; yet
after making this admission he was not able to explain why he could
not accept them, and showed embarrassment when asked to try. If
compliments could satisfy the hunger of the heart, I should have nothing to complain of, but they cannot. Mr. Sargent said I could infuse a
tenderness into a thunderstorm which he had not encountered in the
shedoovers of even the oldest of the old masters—his very words. Mr.
Dan Beard said that whenever I painted a dog you could tell it from
any other animal, often by just looking at it once. Mr. Robert Reed
said an impressionist picture by me contained all the emotions of a

jag, including those of next day. Mr. Simmons said he had seen works of mine that struck him speechless for hours. His club bought him one. Mr. Childe Hassam, Mr. Thulstrupp, Mr. Verryshoggin, Mr. Buggerroo, all said— But never mind what they said, it was all compliment, all praise, all enthusiasm, and harmonious with the above expressions; yet I could not get into the Academy just the same. Neither could I get any portraits to paint. The distinguished would not sit for me, the rich would not sit for me, although I offered to furnish the paint and do the work for nothing. For I was after reputation, I was longing for fame—I could charge later.

I was thoroughly discouraged. Why could I get no chance? What was the reason? I did not find out for myself; it was another and a wiser that whispered it to me. He said,

"It is because you are an American. Here you are, doing these immortal things for the cost of the frames and throwing the pictures in: those Works are worth twenty thousand dollars apiece—done by a foreigner."

A dark meaning seemed to lurk in his words. I asked him to continue.

"Go abroad," he said. "Change your name. Come back. And paint. Paint and charge. Charge like smoke."

"Ah," I sighed, disappointed, "but they will never have heard of me."

"That is nothing. You'll be foreign, that's a plenty. They'll swarm after you; they'll infest you; the professional Art Critics will deify you; you'll paint the President—ostensibly from life, really from a photograph; and thin? oh, thin to hell and gone! and it'll be exhibited in Fifth Avenue and be mistaken for a What-is-it or a Whatyoumaycallum disemboweled, disembodied and spiritualized; and it'll be hung in the White House to onkoorahj layzoters—the others that come over, you know. And then your fortune's made. The innocent rich will flock in, and you will do two of them a day for a fortnight, and sail back with three hundred thousand dollars in your gripsack. Go abroad, I tell you."

"It seems too good to be true."

"I beseech you, believe it. Go abroad. Foreignize your name. Come back. Paint. Paint and charge. Charge like Mrs. Eddy—she knows the American race."

"Indeed you almost persua—"

"Go abroad! Do you want to stay here and starve—like poor Twachtman? He could paint all around this invasion of obscure foreigners that's been buncoing New York of late years; and New York paid them two hundred thousand apiece and allowed him to go hungry to his grave. Go abroad. Frenchify your name. Come back. Paint. Paint and charge. Skin these people; they like it; they will bless you."

I went abroad three times, and came back with a new nationality each time. When I labor in my foreign capacities I am but a buccaneer, like the others, my aims are sordid and my reward prodigious; but when I illustrate a book I resume my nationality and paint for love, these being the established American art-terms.

SUPPLEMENT C

"THE TURNING POINT OF MY LIFE": FIRST VERSION

MARK TWAIN wrote this version late in 1909, apparently after his seventy-fourth birthday on 30 November. The manuscript and most of a typescript with author's revisions are in the Mark Twain Papers; a copy of another typescript fragment is at the University of Wisconsin. The copy was made in 1944 by the owner, Mr. Kenneth Gamet of Los Angeles, California, who represented Mark Twain's inscribed revisions and all other features of the original, including line lengths and revised pagination. The manuscript consists of "Pratt's" or similar tablet leaves. A Paine note is on the first page of the typescript in the Papers: "Read it aloud to Jean and me. We did not approve and it brought on one of his heart attacks" (see also Paine's less explicit account in *MTB*, p. 1528). A reference to Howells' *The Landlord at Lion's Head* (1897) as his "latest book" may indicate the seriousness of Mark Twain's physical decline, for Howells published several novels and other books between 1897 and 1909. It may rather indicate that Mark Twain wrote the passage in 1897 or 1898 (possibly designed for *What Is Man?*), because it occurs in three missing leaves labeled A, B, C which he asked to be inserted following a paragraph on the back of manuscript p. 15. The text is that of the manuscript, with the missing passage (526–527, the three paragraphs beginning "*Temperament* is the *source*. . . .") taken from the MTP typescript, which breaks off at the end of that passage, and with inscribed revisions taken from both typescript fragments. Part of the text (from 527, "I know the various," through 527, "settled it: my") is only in the manuscript; the Wisconsin typescript covers only the remainder. Contrary to his normal usage

Mark Twain put the title in quotes, evidently to characterize it as a familiar expression.

I

If I understand the idea, it is this: the Bazar invites several of us to write upon this subject, "The Turning Point of My Life."

I have no fault to find with the title, except the word "The." There is a plenty of turning-points in every person's life, and . . . but let me try to get at the thing I have in my mind by the help of a parable.

THE PARABLE OF THE TWO APPLES.

Once upon a time there were two apples hanging upon neighboring trees on the sharp apex of a mountain. Thomas Crab, and William Greening. Those were their names. Their ages were about the same. But not their circumstances. The Crabs were poor, ignorant, obscure, and not in society; it was just the other way with the Greenings. Nobody tried to improve the minds or bodies or morals of the Crabs, or endeavored to improve their condition in any way; but it was different with the Greenings. They were of old blood and established respectability; they were well to do; they were high up in society; their bodies and minds and characters were under painstaking cultivation all the time. Thomas Crab was undersized, pale, pinched, not quite round, and of a shrinking and timid disposition; whereas William Greening was large, perfect in sphericity and health, and bold and enterprising thereto.

It was by the accident of circumstance that Thomas was born on the crabtree instead of on the greening tree. It was by the accident of circumstance that William was born on the greening tree instead of on the crab.

Curiously enough, Thomas was ashamed of his birth, although he was in no way responsible for it; and William was just as absurdly *proud* of *his* birth, although he had had nothing to do with choosing his parentage.

Every day William and Thomas looked out admiringly over the vast landscape spread out below them, and longed for the time when they should be released from parental tutelage; for then they meant to travel and see the world.

The happy day came at last. The same wind blew both of them free at the same moment. But they struck the ground fifty feet apart. By just that small (yet all-determining) accident William fell upon a smooth slope and Thomas upon a slope that was less smooth. As a consequence William rolled easily and made good time, whereas Thomas didn't. William said to himself, complacently, "I chose well; this is the best road." Thomas said to himself, "I made a mistake; if it was to do over again, I would descend further to the left."

The conceit of those fate-fettered little Slaves of Circumstance! *they* had nothing to do with when they would fall, nor where they would fall, nor what road they would take.

William said to himself, "I fell in the right place; it is the turning-point of my life; much will come of it." Thomas said to himself, "I fell in the wrong place; it is the turning-point of my life; much will come of it."

By and by William saw an obstructive rock ahead, and was electing to go to the right of it, when he brushed against a small pebble which shied him to port and he passed down to the *left* of the rock. He congratulated himself, saying, "I chose well again; if I had gone down to the right I'd have passed under the very nose of that cow yonder, and straightway down her throat the next moment. This is the turning-point of my life."

By and by when Thomas came along he went down to the right of the rock. The cow was gone. But there was a bird there, and the bird nipped a piece out of him. The bird was disappointed, and used expurgative language, and spat out the piece. Thomas said, "I was going to take the other side, but was shied out of my course by a pebble which I didn't see till it was too late—and lo, the disastrous result! a wound which will never heal, and will disable me some day. My career is damaged; this is the turning-point of my life."

Such is life! You never could have convinced those apples that they had nothing to do with choosing their careers, nor with shaping them after the all-puissant Magician of Circumstance should choose them. And no one could have convinced them that the turning-point in a life is a thing that can't knowably happen; that it is never ascertainably a *the*, but only an *a*; that the *a* turning-points occur with great frequency; that you can't tell an important one from an unimportant one, because each does its own share in its own appointed place, toward bringing about a future more or less grand result, and it couldn't be left out of the chain without bringing about a totally *different* result—good? or bad?—there's no guessing which it would be.

Further down the mountain William came fearfully near rolling over a precipice when he was day-dreaming instead of watching, but a chance whiff of wind canted him to starboard and saved him. He said, "It was clever of me to take advantage of that wind; in another minute I'd have been mush in the bottom of the canyon. This is the turning-point of my life."

When Thomas came along he was brooding over his wound, and would have gone over the precipice, but he was not round, not perfectly spherical, and that defect saved him, for it made him wallow out of his course at the critical moment. Also it made him wallow over an ant-camp, and the ants swarmed to his wound and sucked it and gave thanks. He reproached himself, saying, "I ought to have steered to the left of that camp, it was foolish to run over it. Those creatures are digging into my vitals, a fateful future is before me. This is the turning-point of my life."

It was not just, it was not fair, to reproach himself: *he* had had no choice in the matter. It was Circumstance that chose his road and did his steering for him: the circumstance of his defective shape and the contour of the ground; it was not for *him* to choose whither he would go; and not for him to accomplish it after choosing—with Circumstance opposing, and in command of the situation. Circumstance being in sole command of *all* situations, without exception.

The apples continued their journey down the mountain. As often as once every hour they had an adventure apiece—invented, controlled and achieved by blind Circumstance: lucky ones for William, unlucky ones for Thomas. In each case, each remarked "This is the turning-point of my life."

They finally arrived in the valley. The King and his court came gorgeously processioning along. The King saw the apples, and sprang at them, and took them up in his hands, and broke into paeans of admiration over William, calling him beautiful, and wonderful, and all that; and handed him to the Lord High Admiral of the Bedchamber, saying, "Do him the highest honor: Place him in the view of all, at the royal banquet to-night!" Which made William purr with pride and contentment, and he said "This *is* the turning-point of my life,—at last and for sure!"

Then the King, examining Thomas, said, "Pah! this one's rotten!" and tossed him away. Thomas, lamenting, said, "Alas, *this* is the *real* turning-point of my life, the others were delusions. My life is a failure; I would that I were dead!"

Circumstance intruded again. The chief butler's pet monkey got into the banquet hall a little ahead of the dinner hour, and ate William, who said, thick-voiced and mushily, down in that dark stomach, "And so, all those apparently lucky and high-promising turning-points were painstakingly planned-out and hitched together to lead up to *this* result! I see the whole scheme, now. Those were only *temporary* turning-points, nothing permanent in any of them; no one of them of superior importance to the others, but *all* of them important to the grand end in view—the landing of me in the medulla-oblongata-major-maxillary of a monkey!" He added, coldly, "It may be humorous, but I fail to see the point."

Next morning Mr. Burbank of California came along and saw Thomas lying there neglected, forsaken, putrescent, heart-broken, envying William's splendidly-climaxed career and grieving over the shameful close of his own; and the wizard picked up the mourner and broke into sesquipedalian adjectives of delight over him, saying, "It is the priceless thing I have been searching the world for—found at last!"

And he took him home and planted him in a golden vase set with diamonds and rubies and emeralds, and watched over him night and day to dulcet measures of soft music, nourishing him the while with the juice of dissolved pearls and opals; until at last he saw Thomas rise up and burst into a giant spray of thitherto-unimaginable roses, the glory of the world, the wonder of the nations!

Thomas, oozing intoxicating fragrances, said, with feeling, "Heaven be praised, I see what those trifling and meaningless turning-points were *for*, now!"

II

When I look back over my seventy-four years and try to find the turning point of my life I am not able to succeed to my satisfaction. I find a great many incidents that were turning points. Each in its turn quite definitely—and always unexpectedly, I believe—changed my course, but there is no supreme "*the*" among them. Except that each in its turn was a "the;" a passing "the," a temporary "the," which soon accomplishes [accomplished] its small mission and went out of service, for good and all. These turning points begin with a person's birth; and the very first one is father to *all* the rest, I think—every one of them. If Napoleon's first act was to put his finger in the candle, that incident *produced* the next one, whatever it was, and the said next one produced the *next* one; and the procession of resulting events was now under way, to go on without a break to the end of his life. With no candle present there could be no burnt finger, and some other episode would take its place, and change Napoleon's entire career.

Temperament is the governing mechanism of a man's machinery and chief servant to the Magician of Circumstance, (and it is *born* in him and is unchangeable.) It determines what any given set of circumstances may and shall compel the man to do. Given the Circumstance of the battle of the Wilderness, General Grant's temperament required him to say "I will fight it out on this line if it takes all summer." And it made him *do* that desperate work. Whereas my temperament would not have required me to say it, and sixteen temperaments like mine couldn't have made me *do* it. They would have made me go away and get behind something.

Temperament is the *source* of *Character*. Temperament is the *instrument*, character is the *music*. Temperament inflexibly determines certain things; for instance, that the jewsharp temperament cannot be taught, nor persuaded, nor forced to produce piano-music—the jewsharp has its limitations, likewise the violin; and the bugle; and the flute; and the guitar; and the church organ, and so on. The instrument is permanent, the music produced is variable. *Circumstance* is the performer. There is a million of him; some bad, some good. The bad ones get bad music out of the instrument, better ones get better music, the best get the best the instrument is capable of. *That particular instrument*. But, as remarked before, no environment, no set of circumstances, can get organ-music out of a jewsharp. And no Circumstances can get anything more than a modified magnanimity out of a mean temperament, nor anything more than a modified warmth out of a cold one. Temperament is a tree, character is the fruit. Good soil, bad soil, wet weather, dry weather, cold weather, hot weather—these and a hundred other outside circumstances modify the *character* of the fruit for better or for worse, but they have to stop there: they can't ennoble crab apples into oranges.

Mr. Howells, in his latest book—his masterpiece, as I think*— makes Westover say to Durgin, "You were not r[e]sponsible for your *temperament*, but only for your *character*."

Necessarily Durgin was *not* responsible for his temperament, which was *born* to him—like the color of his eyes and as unchangeable —but as Durgin's temperament, *and* his situation and circumstances determined his *character* for him in spite of him, perhaps he wasn't very largely responsible for that, either. However, Westover tacitly admits this, five lines lower down, and so I have no fault to find with him except for not admitting it earlier: "*I always believed that if you had experienced greater kindness socially during your first year in college you would have been a better man.*" Without doubt. By born temperament Durgin was a dog, and a bad one; good treatment could not have made a canary out of him, but it would have made him a better dog.

I know the various turning points in my life, and how they came to happen, but if you should ask me how I came to be a literary person, I should in honor be obliged to say I became a literary person because I had the measles when I was twelve years old. And it would be true. I could go back of that, and tell you how I (most unnecessarily) came to get the measles. Also I could go back of that and . . .

But never mind, let us begin with the measles. I got the measles by getting into bed with a playmate who had them; I did it twice—surreptitiously and in disobedience to command. I did it because I had a terror of the measles, and wanted to get them and have it over, one way or the other. I had been a difficult boy, and that performance settled it: my mother put me in a printing office to keep me out of foolish and troublesome mischief.

That explains how I came to be in Keokuk, Iowa, ten years later; I went there on a job as printer.

Being there is how I came to find a fifty-dollar bill in the street one bitter morning in winter.

Finding that money explains how I came to start to Brazil—a

---

* "The Landlord at Lion's Head."

dream of mine which I had been obliged to put off and put off and put off, for lack of money. A person with a sane temperament would have invested the find in some sane way, but I had to do as *my* temperament commanded. Very well, I went down to New Orleans, proposing to sail from there—which I didn't, there being no ship bound for Brazil, and there never had *been* one.

Going down to New Orleans was another turning point. It made me acquainted with a pilot—Horace Bixby. Being stranded in New Orleans, I got Bixby to take me as an apprentice. Thus I became a pilot—the profession that stands out in my life as the pleasantest and the most desirable of all the occupations I have tried.

Being a pilot is how I came to be occupationless when the war broke out and the boats stopped running.

Being occupationless is how I came to enter the military service and do what I could to avoid danger during two fearful weeks. Then I resigned.

This brought me into contact with my brother, who had just been appointed Secretary of the new Territory of Nevada, and I eagerly crossed the plains with him to be his secretary.

That is how I came to be bitten with the silver fever. I went down to Esmeralda to make my fortune in the mines. Every man down there wrote large accounts of the prospects of his mining-claims, for publication in the Territorial Enterprise, and so I did the same. Then a principal officer of the Territorial government came down there to do an oration. Oratory was his specialty—his disease, I may say. It was of the superlatively flowery sort. I burlesqued his oration, and the Enterprise was pleased with my effort.

That is how I came to be a journalist. The Enterprise sent for me, and I served on the staff of that paper until I got into the preliminaries of a duel with the editor of the other paper. I got private word from the governor that I must vacate the Territory immediately or the utmost severities of the new law against dueling would be my portion.

That is how I came to go to California. And in such a hurry.

Being in California is how I came to get acquainted with the Sacramento Union editors.

Being acquainted with them is how I came to ask them to send me to the Sandwich Islands for five or six months as correspondent. Which they did. To write up the sugar interest. Which I did—and put in lots of entertaining stuff that wasn't strictly sugar. But it gave me a valuable notoriety.

And that is how I came to be a lecturer. San Francisco invited me to talk, and I did it. I became rich in a single night, but the doorkeeper got it. However, I got the next intake myself and was rich again. I had upwards of twelve hundred dollars.

That is why I was able to fructify an old dream of mine and become a traveler. I came to New York, attracted by an exciting advertisement mapping out a grand European excursion—the "Quaker City Excursion." I joined it, and sent some letters home to the Tribune, and one to the Herald. They attracted the attention of a publisher, and he asked me to write a book. Which I did. "The Innocents Abroad."

That is how I came to be a literary person.

I mean, that is the *last* link in the chain of apparently accidental circumstances which had been appointed and commissioned at the dawn of Creation to make me a literary person. But that is all it is— merely the last link. It hadn't any more to do with the result than its predecessors had. Not one link in the chain could have been left out and that result accomplished. If one single link had been left out I should not be a literary person to-day, but a burglar. I know it quite well.

I repeat: *I am a literary person because I had the measles when I was twelve years old.* It was The Turning Point of my Life wasn't it?

It was, if there ever was a *the* turning point of my life.

Reference Material

EXPLANATORY NOTES

THE numbers before all notes indicate page and line respectively. Epigraphs, quotations, and footnotes (but not titles) have been included in the line counts.

1.   SABBATH REFLECTIONS

37.16 *Golden Era* 'n' *Sund' Mercry*] The *Golden Era* and the *California Sunday Mercury*, two San Francisco literary miscellanies. The other publications were San Francisco newspapers—the *Alta California*, the *Morning Call*, and the *American Flag*. For a more extensive description of the street cries of San Francisco in that period, see B. E. Lloyd, *Lights and Shades in San Francisco* (San Francisco: A. L. Bancroft, 1876), pp. 357–363.

2.   REFLECTIONS ON THE SABBATH

39.1 The day of rest] The sketch appeared in the *Golden Era* on a Sunday—18 March 1866—but Mark Twain's later reference to "this morning" could not have meant the 18th, for he arrived in Hawaii on that day. The *Era* was regularly issued on Sundays only, and he may have written the piece weeks earlier, to be used at the editor's discretion. The *Era* possibly took it from the Virginia City *Territorial Enterprise*, but there was no acknowledgment of an earlier printing.

39.10 Michael Reese] (1815–1878), a well-known realtor and capitalist in San Francisco. In 1866 he was a frequent butt in the *Era*, which

ridiculed his vanity, pugnacity, and domestic troubles. Reese was un-
necessary to the argument, and Mark Twain may have mentioned him
to continue the *Era*'s running attack. This is the strongest evidence that
he wrote the piece for the *Era*, but for a claim that it first appeared
elsewhere, see Lawrence E. Mobley, "Mark Twain and *The Golden
Era*," *Papers of the Bibliographical Society of America* 58, no. 1
(January–March 1964): 21.

39.23 Dr. Wadsworth's] Rev. Charles Wadsworth (1814–1882), pastor of the Calvary Presbyterian Church in San Francisco. He went
west in 1862, after long service at the Arch Street Church in Philadelphia. It is presumed that Emily Dickinson met him in Philadelphia
in 1855, later developed a personal attachment, and suffered a severe
trauma upon his departure for California. The sermon Mark Twain
claims to have heard does not survive.

3.   Mr. Beecher and the Clergy

42.2 Rev. T. K. Beecher] Thomas Kinnicut Beecher (1824–1900),
friend of Clemens, pastor of the Independent Congregational Church
of Elmira. The epigraph and Clemens' letter contain most of the extant information about the controversy. On 8 April 1869 the Elmira
Daily Advertiser printed a letter from Jervis Langdon, Livy's father,
and on the day of Clemens' letter (10 April) it printed one from another correspondent. Neither was informative, and Beecher never
mentioned the episode in his regular column for the *Advertiser*. Other
news items confirm that he drew large crowds at the Opera House and
show that the Ministerial Union could not intimidate him. He replied
contemptuously to a rumor that he predicted the Second Coming in
1869, and shortly after the Union delivered its rebuke he announced
the engagement of the Opera House for another year. See the Elmira
Daily Advertiser, 16 and 19 April 1869. The epigraph is from the New
York *Evangelist and Religious Review* 40, no. 13 (1 April 1869): 4.
Jervis Langdon had already quoted it in his letter to the *Advertiser*,
which was probably Clemens' source.

43.18 Go ye into all the world] Compare Mark 16:15.

4.   ABOUT SMELLS

48.1   the Rev. T. De Witt Talmage] Thomas De Witt Talmage
(1832–1902), of the Central Presbyterian Church in Brooklyn, a popular preacher and regular contributor to the *Independent*.

48.4   I have a good Christian friend] Talmage's article first appeared
in the New York *Independent*, 9 December 1869. Mark Twain's source
was another religious weekly, the Chicago *Advance*, 6 January 1870,
which printed the passage he quoted and a long criticism of it. The
Advance and the *Independent* were unfriendly competitors, and the
Advance, knowing that popular sentiment favored free pews, saw a
chance to discredit its rival through Talmage. Thus it abused him as
though the passage expressed his true opinion. Talmage actually favored free pews, yet in his article he tried to conciliate both sides of the
issue through gentle ridicule. He argued that each had a right to its
preference but no right to impose it, and thus in the quotation he
represented the party of exclusiveness in sympathetic caricature. Mark
Twain could hardly be blamed for believing the *Advance*'s criticism
and its misleading quotation, which were all he had seen when he wrote
"About Smells," but after reading Talmage's entire article in the *Independent* he refused to apologize. In the Buffalo *Express* for 9 May
1870 he justified himself by denouncing Talmage's ambiguity and
other faults of style.

50.3   Son of the Carpenter] The first two lines of a Wesley hymn,
called "To Be Sung at Work"; see *The Poetical Works of John and
Charles Wesley* (London, 1868), 1:172–173.

5.   THE INDIGNITY PUT UPON THE REMAINS OF GEORGE HOLLAND
                      BY THE REV. MR. SABINE

51   *title*] See *MTB*, pp. 406–407, for an account of the incident.
George Holland (1791–1870) had been a respected comic actor; William Tufnell Sabine (1838–1913) was rector of the Episcopal Church
of the Atonement in New York.

51.4   Cardiff giant] In October 1869 a "petrified giant" was unearthed on a farm near Cardiff, New York. After a brief but profitable sensation, experts announced that the body was merely a piece of sculptured gypsum. The farmer's brother-in-law admitted starting the hoax, saying he wanted to embarrass clergymen who believed there were once "giants in the earth."

52   footnote] From the New York Times, 29 December 1870, p. 1.

53.4   five hundred William Tells] James Sheridan Knowles's William Tell had been a favorite on the American stage for forty-five years.

54.13   Black Crooks] The Black Crook, by Charles M. Barras, a spectacular stage show featuring beautiful girls in daring costumes, was a box-office sensation in 1866–1868 and was being successfully revived at Niblo's Garden in 1871.

54.15   Cooks, and Kallochs] Horace Cook (fl. 1870), a former pastor of the Seventh Street Methodist Episcopal Church, New York, and Isaac Smith Kalloch (1831–1887), a former Baptist pastor at Tremont Temple, Boston. Both men had scandalous reputations. Kalloch was tried for adultery in 1857, and Cook had recently lost his position because he seduced a parishioner's daughter. For Kalloch see M. M. Marberry, The Golden Voice (New York: Farrar, Straus, 1947); for Cook see the Buffalo Express, 3 September, 14 and 24 December 1870. In CG McElderry identifies Cook as Russell S. Cook (see DAB), of whom no scandal is known and who died in 1864.

6.   [THREE STATEMENTS OF THE EIGHTIES]

58.18   Thou shalt not commit adultery] See Exodus 20:14.

58.29   Straight is the gate] See Matthew 7:14. Mark Twain's "straight" was an acceptable spelling of the word now standardized as "strait."

58.31   multiply and replenish the earth] See, for example, Genesis 1:28.

7.   THE CHARACTER OF MAN

62.16   one single independent man] Henry Leavitt Goodwin (1821–
1899), whose courage and public spirit Mark Twain also praised in
deleted passages of *Life on the Mississippi* and *What Is Man?* (see
Supplement A6). For years Goodwin protested irregularities in the
Hartford transit system and the New York, New Haven, and Hartford
Railroad Company.

62.21   Asylum street crossing] A crossing in Hartford.

63.2   this year's] Mark Twain's note to the passage identifies James G.
Blaine (1830–1893), Grover Cleveland's opponent in 1884. A sarcastic
passage later in the article—"the Cid, and Great-Heart, and Sir Galahad, and Bayard the Spotless"—all but names him, for Blaine was
known as the "Plumed Knight."

63.15   A Hartford clergyman] Probably Matthew Brown Riddle
(1836–1916), an ordained minister of the Dutch Reformed Church
and Professor of New Testament Exegesis at the Hartford Theological
Seminary. Riddle was born at Pittsburgh, Pennsylvania, and Blaine
nearby at West Brownsville. Riddle's mother's name was Elizabeth
Blaine Brown Riddle. Riddle was the only member of the American
Revision Committee, New-Testament Company, who lived in Hartford. See Mark Twain's note; see also *DAB* and *Appletons' Annual
Cyclopaedia*, n.s., 10 (1886): 96.

64.13   The preacher who casts a vote] Joseph Hopkins Twichell
(1838–1918), one of Clemens' closest friends, pastor of the Asylum
Hill Congregational Church, Hartford. The reference is misleading
and is misleadingly explained in the Autobiographical Dictation of 24
January and 1 February 1906, for Twichell disapproved of Cleveland
as well as Blaine and voted for the Prohibition candidate. Though
some parishioners deplored his stand, there was no move to have him
dismissed; see *NF*, pp. 114–116.

64.17   Mr. Beecher may be charged with a *crime*] An allusion to the
famous adultery trial of Henry Ward Beecher (1813–1887) in 1875.

His congregation at Plymouth Church, Brooklyn, supported him during and after the civil court trial, which resulted in no verdict. In 1876 a council of Congregational ministers absolved him. But when Beecher endorsed Cleveland in 1884 he was subjected to ridicule in the press, heckling at his speeches, and threats from members of his church.

64.20 Take the editor so charged] Mark Twain's friend and collaborator Charles Dudley Warner (1829–1900), editor and part owner of the Hartford *Courant*. See the Autobiographical Dictation of 24 January 1906, which is again misleading, for Warner did not resign from the *Courant*; see *NF*, p. 115.

8.   [LETTER FROM THE RECORDING ANGEL]

65.3 Andrew Langdon] Mark Twain's hostility toward Langdon has never been explained satisfactorily. DeVoto supposed that he was shocked at the large profits of J. Langdon & Company and that Andrew Langdon shared in them: see "Letter from the Recording Angel," *Harper's Magazine* 192, no. 1149 (February 1946): 106. Wecter tried to prove DeVoto's suppositions, quoting notebook entries where Clemens listed company payments to Livy and where, in August 1887, he mentioned the success of the company's new colliery (see *RP*, p. xxv). On its face the DeVoto–Wecter argument seems weak, and it is irrelevant in light of the fact that Andrew Langdon had no connection with J. Langdon & Company.

Andrew Langdon (1835–1919), Livy's first cousin (DeVoto and Wecter believed he was her uncle), was perhaps best known in the 1870s and 1880s as a coal operator, but his enterprises already extended to banking and the metal industry. Later he became an officer in several communications and power companies. He took an active interest in Buffalo civic affairs, serving on the park commission and the grade-crossings commission. He was also president of the Buffalo Historical Society for fourteen years and held offices in the Academy of Fine Arts and the Society of Natural Sciences. He made several large gifts to the Historical Society and the city of Buffalo.

Clemens may have met Andrew Langdon by 1887, the probable year of composition, but their acquaintance could only have been slight. Even if Langdon committed such niggardly acts as appear in the satire, Livy and Clemens might not have heard about them, for the branches of the Langdon family were not in close or regular contact. Two letters from the author to Langdon are known to survive. One is a note written in 1900 shortly after the Clemenses returned to America, in which he cordially declines an unspecified invitation, perhaps a suggestion that the Clemenses visit Buffalo or renew residence there. The other is an equally cordial note of 1901 in which Clemens apologizes for being out when Langdon called. Though intense in 1887, his hostility had abated, and Langdon probably never knew of it.

Langdon's grandson, Mr. Andrew Langdon of Rochester, New York, suggests that Clemens tried unsuccessfully to enlist his grandfather among the backers of the Paige typesetter, and that in the extremity of his enthusiasm or need he could account for Langdon's refusal only by faults in his character. The suggestion seems plausible. Clemens was looking for backers in 1887, and he may well have turned to Langdon with the hope that the family tie would favorably affect his judgment. Following this hope, Langdon's refusal could have struck Clemens as an affront to himself and the family. It would have been typical of him to characterize Langdon as a gross egoist and hypocrite, already a common sort of figure in his vilifications after real or imagined insults. The important businessman and capitalist becomes a grasping "coal dealer." Though he is a Christian, his faith is all words and show. In refusing Clemens he has in effect refused his cousin Livy, and such a man would treat his cousin selfishly even if she were an impoverished widow making a direct appeal (compare the "Letter"). But a variety of causes could have led Mark Twain to make the same kind of personal attack, and without further evidence his motives in this instance cannot be known.

For an informative sketch of Langdon see his obituary in the Buffalo *Express*, 16 November 1919. The first letter mentioned above is dated 2 November 1900 and has been given to the Mark Twain Papers by Mr. Andrew Langdon of Rochester, New York. The second is a typescript copy dated 21 January 1901, in the Clifton Waller Barrett Library, University of Virginia.

69.4 John Wanamaker] Clemens' contempt for John Wanamaker, the Philadelphia merchant, was unremitting. Wanamaker (1838–1922), a lay leader of various Presbyterian endeavors, such as tem-

perance and Sunday schools, was a tough business competitor. Clemens
became furious when he discovered that Wanamaker was selling surreptitiously obtained copies of *Personal Memoirs of U. S. Grant*, the
most successful publication of Charles L. Webster & Co. In August
1886 Clemens lost a court suit to prohibit these sales; see *MTHL*,
p. 573.

9.   [BIBLE TEACHING AND RELIGIOUS PRACTICE]

73.7   we hear a pope] Leo XIII's encyclical on the abolition of African
slavery, 5 May 1888. Later that year the Pope openly supported Cardi-
nal Lavigerie, Archbishop of Algiers, in his militant campaign against
the slave trade; see *Harper's Weekly* 32, no. 1671 (29 December 1888):
1006.

73.23   John Hawkins] (1532–1595). After his voyage of 1565 he was
knighted by Elizabeth I and granted arms with the crest Mark Twain
describes.

74.7   an illegitimate Christian] William Wilberforce (1759–1833), a
member of the so-called "Clapham sect" of evangelical Christians. His
long campaign against the British slave trade finally succeeded in 1807,
when Parliament abolished it.

74.13   the visiting English critic] Mark Twain's reference is generic.
English travelers, including Hall, Marryat, and others whose accounts
of pre-Civil War travel he read, often felt such "distress."

75.10   the parson clung] Mark Twain probably means Cotton Mather
(1663–1728), in *The Wonders of the Invisible World* (1693). If so, he
exaggerates the immediate reaction against the witchcraft trials of
1692 or confuses the order of Mather's book and Samuel Sewall's confession of error in 1697.

75.14–17   the parson killed . . . the parson who came imploring] The
examples are nearly adjacent in chapter 5 of W. E. H. Lecky's *A History of England in the Eighteenth Century* (New York: D. Appleton,
1878–1890). A1911, p. 44, lists a set published in New York, 1887–
1888. The "witch" was Jane Corphar, lynched in 1705 at Pittenweem,

Fifeshire, with encouragement from the local minister. In 1736 the associated Presbytery denounced the repeal of the witchcraft laws as contrary to the word of God.

10.   [MACFARLANE]

76.7 Macfarlane] Mark Twain's only known reference to Macfarlane is in this work, and all descriptions of their relationship by subsequent scholars (beginning with Paine in *MTB*, pp. 114–115) have no other authority.

76.13 Sumner] While in Philadelphia in 1853–1854 Clemens wrote a sketch entitled "Jul'us Caesar," about a foolish resident of his boarding house who constantly uses "Jul'us Caesar" as an oath and who thinks himself a gifted individual. Clemens and a prankish friend named Sumner persuade this person that he is a natural poet and painter, but his performances in both arts are absurd. Thus there probably was an "Englishman Sumner," but nothing is known about him except his prankishness and his fondness for herring. The typescript (DV400) in the Mark Twain Papers was made from a manuscript formerly in the possession of Mrs. Samuel C. Webster.

11.   CONTRACT WITH MRS. T. K. BEECHER

79 *title*] Julia Jones Beecher (1826–1905), wife of Thomas Kinnicut Beecher (see note to 42.2 above). For circumstances of composition see the New York *Tribune*, 31 July 1895, p. 6; *MTB*, p. 1001; and *Parade*, 18 November 1962, p. 17. The *Tribune* said that Mark Twain wrote the poem at Mrs. Beecher's humorous suggestion; Paine implied that it was Mark Twain's idea; *Parade* did not argue either way. The *Tribune* account is suspect, though very close to the date of composition, for it also said that Mark Twain took the doubting side "playfully." Since the *Tribune* probably got the story from one of the Beechers, the implication is that he or she was protecting Mark Twain's reputation by denying the sincerity of his skepticism. From

the same motive may have come the claim that Mrs. Beecher suggested the poem.

79.8–9   no trace . . . of you and me] An echo of *The Rubaiyat of Omar Khayyam,* 33:
> . . . Some little talk awhile of ME and THEE
> There was—and then no more of THEE and ME.

Mark Twain once called the *Rubaiyat* "the only poem I have ever carried about with me" (*MTB*, p. 1295), and A1911, pp. 55–56, lists three copies acquired from the Hartford period until 1907, each with marginal notations. But the influence on Mark Twain's poem was only verbal, and his opinions determined his admiration for Omar, not the reverse. Characteristically, he burlesqued the *Rubaiyat* four years later in "My Boyhood Dreams."

12.   [MAN'S PLACE IN THE ANIMAL WORLD]

80   *title*] The first page of the manuscript is lost. It evidently contained the title and two newspaper clippings but none of Mark Twain's prose. The present title is an inscription by Mark Twain on an envelope in which he may have kept the manuscript (see the Textual Notes).

80.1   similar things were occurring] The reports heading the article concerned Turkish atrocities on Crete. See note to 83.21–22.

82.4   They killed seventy-two of those great animals] Source unknown. Mark Twain later used the same example in "God" (Supplement A4).

83.17   so does the monkey, as Mr. Darwin pointed out] See Charles Darwin, *The Descent of Man* (New York: D. Appleton, 1871), 1: 184. A copy of this edition with Mark Twain's marginalia is in MTP.

83.21–22   "three monks were burnt to death" . . . a prior "put to death with atrocious cruelty"] The quotations are probably from the London *Daily Telegraph,* 13 August 1896, which reads on p. 7: "On Monday [10 August] the convent of Agharatho was burnt by the Turks, and its *prior put to death with atrocious cruelty.* . . . Additional details continue to arrive about the atrocities at Anopolis, but, save the fact that *three monks were burnt alive,* they do not convey anything new" (editor's italics). Mark Twain evidently misread or misremembered the *Telegraph*'s "burnt alive," though the clippings may have come from a paper which shared in the dispatches but rephrased them. Clemens had been in London only two weeks, following his world tour of 1895–1896.

83.27 he uses a red-hot iron] See Shakespeare's *King John,* act 4, sc. 1, where Hubert de Burgh, King John's subordinate, contemplates blinding the nephew, Arthur, with a hot iron.

83.29 he shuts up a multitude of Jew families] The pogrom occurred at York in March 1190, shortly after the accession of Richard I. A1911, p. 39, lists a history that describes the atrocity: [W. Combe], *The History and Antiquities of the City of York from its Origin to the Present Times,* 3 vols. (London, 1785), 1:158–159.

83.31 he captures a family of Spanish Jews] The reference is too vague (and the atrocities under Ferdinand and Isabella too numerous) for identification.

83.32–33 a man is fined ten shillings . . . another man is fined forty shillings] It is doubtful that Mark Twain had recent incidents in mind. He had long resented the severity of English game laws. In 1891 he protested the execution of two poachers; see Arthur L. Scott, "*The Innocents Adrift* Edited by Mark Twain's Official Biographer," *PMLA* 78, no. 3 (June 1963): 235. Over a period of time he collected many clippings that illustrated the laxities and severities of English courts. One reported a fine of only ten shillings against a man who beat and kicked his mother. In "Labouchere's 'Legal Pillory' " (DV72) Mark Twain argued that Englishmen were more harshly punished for breaking game laws than for any other offense.

84.17 Prince Napoleon] Eugène Bonaparte (1856–1879), son of Napoleon III, joined Lord Chelmsford's expedition against the Zulus and was killed on 1 June 1879.

85.30 Among my experiments was this] The group of animals closely resembles P. T. Barnum's "Happy Family," a feature of his museum which Mark Twain ridiculed in 1867. See *Mark Twain's Travels with Mr. Brown*, ed. Franklin Walker and G. Ezra Dane (New York: Knopf, 1940), pp. 116–119.

14.   CORN-PONE OPINIONS

92.2   I had a friend] No more is known of the slave Jerry than appears in this article.

94.13–14   An Empress . . . A nobody] Empress Eugénie of France (1826–1920) and Amelia Jenks Bloomer (1818–1894), American feminist and reformer.

95.12   We are conforming in the other way, now] Mark Twain refers to a boom in historical fiction that began in the 1890s and lasted beyond 1900. The casualness of his statement indicates that he believed the vogue would be well-known among contemporary readers.

97.1   in silver lay salvation] An allusion to the controversy over the free coinage of silver, a major issue in the two McKinley-Bryan campaigns. Mark Twain's balance of the opinions was an exaggeration, for the presidential election of 1900 was not especially close in either the popular or the electoral vote.

15.   THE FIVE BOONS OF LIFE

98   *title*] Compare W. E. H. Lecky's exposition of stoicism in his *History of European Morals from Augustus to Charlemagne*, 3rd ed. (New York: D. Appleton, 1877), 1:204: "Death is the end of all sorrow. It either secures happiness or ends suffering. It frees the slave from his cruel master, opens the prison door, *calms the qualms of pain, closes the struggles of poverty. It is the last and best boon of nature . . .*" (editor's italics). Mark Twain approximates the phrases in italics, and he marginally lined pages of Lecky that included them; see the *Twainian* (July-August 1955): 1.

16.   "WAS THE WORLD MADE FOR MAN?"

101   *title*] Mark Twain derived the title and epigraphs from "Was the Universe Created for Man?," *Literary Digest* 26, no. 15 (11 April 1903): 539. The *Digest* had run articles on the same subject on 21 and 28 March: "The Universe for Man after All?" and "Our Place in the Universe." The three pieces were in response to an article by Alfred Russel Wallace, "Man's Place in the Universe," *Independent* 55, no. 2830 (26 February 1903): 473–483. Wallace (1823–1913) was one of the earliest and most famous evolutionary theorists.

102.10   Lord Kelvin] William Thomson, first Baron Kelvin (1824–1907), British physicist. The others were Sir Charles Lyell (1797–1875), British geologist, and, from Mark Twain's misidentification, Herbert Spencer (1820–1903), British philosopher. Modern science gives larger estimates for the age of the earth and the antiquity of man, but Mark Twain's probable source—S. V. Clevenger, *The Evolution of Man and his Mind* (Chicago: Evolution Publishing Company, 1903), p. 8—gives the figures he cites, though it does not say whether Kelvin agreed with Spencer. Clevenger uses only the last name "Spencer," from which Mark Twain inferred Herbert Spencer. Clevenger actually meant the Canadian-American geologist Joseph W. W. Spencer (1851–1921). Clemens acquired this book shortly before writing the article; the signature in his copy (MTP) is dated 1903. The other geological data (discounting Mark Twain's comic "amalekites," etc.) are too general and commonplace for attribution of particular sources.

105.5   'E isn't one o' the reg'lar Line] From Rudyard Kipling, "Soldier an' Sailor Too."

18.   AS CONCERNS INTERPRETING THE DEITY

109.1   This line of hieroglyphs] The Egyptian and Dighton Rock "inscriptions," together with their supposed histories and translations, constitute one of Mark Twain's most elaborate learned hoaxes. He took the Egyptian characters from some sort of lexicon and arranged them in meaningless sequences. The Dighton Rock figures are imaginary: see Emily C. Davis, *Ancient Americans* (New York: Holt, 1931), photograph between pp. 70 and 71. Jean François Champollion (1790–1832) solved the problem of the Rosetta Stone in 1822. Sir Henry Creswicke Rawlinson (1810–1895) was famous for his work in cuneiform inscriptions, not hieroglyphics, and he was only five years old when Napoleon escaped from Elba (1815). Grünfeldt (from Grotefend?) and Gospodin are invented or borrowed names. And demotic was a much later mode of writing than hieroglyphic, by no means a "phase of the language which had perished . . . 2500 years before the Christian era." Mark Twain drew the inscriptions in his manuscript, then cut them out and attached them to his typescript. They were reproduced in *WIM* (their source in the present text), but the originals do not survive.

109.5   *the worship of Epiphanes*] Mark Twain's hoax was probably suggested by the Rosetta Stone, which contains a decree honoring Ptolemy V Epiphanes (210?–181 B.C.).

111.26   *Bohn's Suetonius*] Suetonius, *The Lives of the Twelve Caesars*, Bohn's Classical Library (London, 1876); a copy with Mark Twain's marginalia is in MTP.

113.12   King Henry is dead] Henry I (1068–1135).

113.12   Stephen] (1097?–1154), nephew of Henry I. He took an oath to acknowledge Henry's daughter Matilda (1102–1167) as ruler of England and Normandy, but upon Henry's death he claimed the crown for himself.

113.14   Henry of Huntingdon] (1084?–1155), historian, and archdeacon of Huntingdon for about forty-five years. Mark Twain's source for the medieval English history was *The Chronicle of Henry of Huntingdon . . . Also, the Acts of Stephen*, trans. Thomas Forester, Bohn's Antiquarian Library (London, 1853), hereafter cited as *Chronicle*; see A1911, p. 40.

113.16   wherefore the Lord visited] *Chronicle*, p. 262.

113.22   The kingdom was a prey] *Chronicle*, p. 273.

115.17   King David of Scotland] *Chronicle*, pp. 266–267. David I

(1084–1153) initially supported Matilda's claim to the throne, and the brutalities described in the text passage resulted from his differences with Stephen.

115.27   Then the chief of the men] *Chronicle*, p. 269.

116.10   In the month of August] *Chronicle*, pp. 282–283. Robert Marmion (d. 1143) and Geoffrey de Mandeville (spelled Godfrey in the *Chronicle*) (d. 1144) were warriors in the days of Stephen.

117.22   Robert Fitzhildebrand's perfidy] Robert Fitz-Hildebrand (fl. 1141) betrayed his alliance with William de Pont de l'Arche and the Countess of Anjou, seduced William's wife and had William cast in a dungeon. The example is from *The Acts of Stephen*, by an unknown author, not by Henry of Huntingdon.

118.12   about to come] *Chronicle*, p. 75. The pope was Gregory I (540–604) in a letter to Ethelbert, King of Kent (552?–616).

118.18   sent before] *Chronicle*, pp. 75–76.

118.31   GOD BEHIND THIS WAR] The Russo-Japanese War of 1904–1905. The quotation is a clipping from the New York *Times*, 12 June 1905, p. 9, pinned to the manuscript. Rev. Newell Dwight Hillis (1858–1929) was pastor at Plymouth Church, Brooklyn.

20.   WHAT IS MAN?

124   *title*] From Psalms 8:4: "What is man, that thou art mindful of him? and the son of man, that thou visitest him?"

124.1   FEBRUARY, 1905] The dialogue had not received its final content or form by this date. Mark Twain inscribed the preface on the cover of the second typescript (see the Textual Notes), and Jean Clemens did not change the date when she prepared the printer's copy.

135.8   Take the case in the book here] Source unknown. Mark Twain put much of the example verbatim into "Which Was It?" (*WWD*, pp. 306–309). Allen Osgood, who has the Young Man's role in the adaptation, says he has just found the case in a St. Louis newspaper and that it happened in New York. A St. Louis newspaper is plausible under the circumstances of "Which Was It?" but Mark Twain was in Vienna when he first wrote the passage.

146.31   see episodes quoted by Parkman] In his copy of Francis Parkman's *The Jesuits in North America in the Seventeenth Century* (Boston: Little, Brown, 1880), pp. 97, 117 (copy in MTP), Mark Twain checked passages where Jesuit missionaries baptized sick Indian children while pretending to soothe them. The ruse was necessary because the parents objected to Christianity.

148.23   But here in this novel] The Young Man describes Florence Wilkinson's *The Strength of the Hills* (New York: Harper, 1901), listed in C1951. Much of the summary is correct, but Mark Twain misrepresents the novel to suit his argument that even generous action is selfish. For example, Holme's most powerful motive in going to New York is neither evangelism nor conceit but a half-conscious desire to be near a genteel woman he has met in the Adirondacks. Holme preaches unsuccessfully on the East Side but the immigrants do not scoff at him, nor is he disappointed in the way the Old Man claims. Holme supports his father, sponsors his sister's musical education in New York, and pays his brother Azrael's way to a technological college, yet he leaves the hills knowing that another brother will care for the father and that Azrael is safely away at school. The sister gives up her career not for lack of money but because Holme fears she has been or will be seduced by the husband of the woman whose attractions have brought him to New York. The "quotations" from the novel are Mark Twain's invention.

155.9   Take the case of the *Berkeley Castle*] Actually the sinking of H. M. S. *Birkenhead* in 1852 off the coast of South Africa, a famous incident of the Kaffir War. Mark Twain's misrecollection of the ship had a long history. In 1876, mistaking the war as well as the ship, he told Mrs. James T. Fields that poets had overlooked "the finest incident of the Crimean War. . . . That was the going down at sea of the man of war, Berkeley Castle." The account he proceeded to give was similar to the one in the text; see M. A. DeWolfe Howe, *Memories of a Hostess* (Boston: Atlantic Monthly Press, 1922), p. 254. Years later, early in 1897, he reminded himself in a notebook: "The ship was the Birkenhead, *not* the Berkeley Castle" (Notebook 32A, TS p. 6; and in another notebook shortly after: "The Birkenhead Birkenhead ship" [Notebook 32, TS p. 28]). Yet he reverted to his chronic error when the incident came to mind in this late addition of 1905, though Kipling had already celebrated it in "Soldier an' Sailor Too," one of Mark Twain's favorite poems for recitation among friends, quoted so recently as 1903 in " 'Was the World made for Man?' "

156.33 Take the case of a clergyman] Probably based on the Riddle incident (see note to 63.15). This text passage and the *Berkeley Castle* example were part of the same insertion in the printer's copy, written shortly before Mark Twain added his footnotes to "The Character of Man" in January 1906.

163.21 The accident of a broken leg] St. Ignatius Loyola (1491–1556), founder of the Society of Jesus, was a vain and self-indulgent soldier as a young man. In 1521 he suffered severe leg wounds at the siege of Pampeluna, and during his recovery underwent a religious conversion.

164.35 an honest man's the noblest work of God] From Alexander Pope, *An Essay on Man*, epistle 4, line 248.

165.23 We have an old servant] Mark Twain probably borrowed the examples from his experience with the Clemenses' servant Katy Leary (1856–1934). He wrote this text passage late in 1901 or early in 1902, when she had been with the family about twenty-two years. She was over twenty years younger than Clemens, yet he often called her "old" in the late period of her service: for example, "Katy Leary, our old housekeeper, who has been in our service more than 24 years. . . ." (SLC to Frank N. Doubleday [1904], *MTL*, p. 760). In *A Lifetime with Mark Twain* (New York: Harcourt, Brace, 1925) Mary Lawton has Katy admit to absent-mindedness (p. 204), though Mark Twain's instances do not occur in her narrative. If he based the examples on his experience with the servant, the "mother" probably was Livy.

176.1 When Mrs. W. asks] The foreword, dictated to Mark Twain's secretary Isabel V. Lyon and in her hand, is pinned to the title page of chapter 5 in the printer's copy. At the lower left, heavily canceled, are the place and date of dictation. "Dublin" (New Hampshire) is decipherable, and so is "Sept." The day and year are obscure but appear to be "Sept. 29 1905." The year must be 1905, for Clemens first spent a summer at Dublin in 1905, and the book was already printed by September 1906. Among Mark Twain's revisions was the substitution of "W." for the woman's name, which he also heavily canceled. Examination indicates that the name was "Aldrich"—Mrs. Thomas Bailey Aldrich (d. 1927), whom Clemens detested; see *MTE*, p. 293. Shortly before he dictated this note Mrs. Aldrich wrote him to ask for the name of H. H. Rogers' almoner, explaining that she wanted money for the improvement of a hospital, one of her various benevolent enterprises. Rogers later wrote that other obligations did not allow him to contribute. The letters are Lilian Aldrich to SLC, 15 September 1905, and H. H. Rogers to SLC, 27 September 1905, *MTHHR*, pp. 598–599, 601.

178.14   I saw Esau kissing Kate] In the Mark Twain Papers there is an unsent note consisting of this rhyme. Mark Twain first wrote the second line as it appears in the dialogue, then changed it to "In fact we all three saw." The latter was evidently the correct form; see E. O. Harbin, *The Fun Encyclopedia* (New York: Abingdon, 1940), p. 821. The note is not dated, but it is on stationery with the "21 Fifth Avenue" letterhead, and Clemens moved to that address in the fall of 1904. His correspondent is also unknown but was probably Andrew Carnegie, for Mark Twain's signature is preceded by a cross ("✝ Mark"), which suggests their routine of calling one another "Saint Andrew" and "Saint Mark."

178.22   In the Swee-eet By and By] A sentimental song by Joseph P. Webster and S. Fillmore Bennett, published in 1868. It was long and widely popular and became one of Mark Twain's favorite comic bores. In "The Loves of Alonzo Fitz Clarence and Rosannah Ethelton" the hero protested against hearing it too often. In *A Connecticut Yankee*, chapter 17, Morgan le Fay heard a band play a "crude first-draft" and had the composer hanged, and after hearing it twice the Yankee allowed her to hang the band.

179.10   Mr. Wells's man] In H. G. Wells, *The Invisible Man* (London: Harper, 1897).

180.15   if A owes B] Mark Twain enjoyed such puzzles. See, for example, *A Connecticut Yankee*, chapter 25. Susy's biography of her father contains a variant he proposed to his daughters: "If A byes a horse for $200 and B byes a mule for $140 and they join in copartnership and trade their creatures for a piece of land $480, how long will it take a lame man to borrow a silk umbrella?" (TS p. 9d).

180.31 an experience of mine of sixteen years ago] Mark Twain changed the number from "46" to "16" in the printer's copy (it is "46" in the manuscript also). The passage was part of another late addition to the dialogue—probably 1905—and it is suggestive that Clemens arrived in Virginia City nearly forty-six years earlier. Whether a desperado slapped him in Washoe or along the Mississippi River is not known, but in other cases he clearly gave his own experience and minor obsessions to the Young Man. Besides those already noted, in passages deleted from this section he gave him the involuntary repetition of the "Punch, brothers, punch" jingle, the recollection of being snowbound in the Humboldt Mountains, and the recurrent dream of appearing before a lecture audience without preparation (see the Textual Notes).

181.26 with Darwin's eyes] Charles Darwin, *Journal of Researches into the Natural History and Geology of the Countries Visited during the Voyage of H. M. S. Beagle round the World* (New York: D. Appleton, 1871), p. 216. C1951 lists a copy unidentified by place or date.

182.33 Watt] James Watt (1736–1819), perfecter of the steam-engine, whose boyhood observation of tea kettles was as legendary as Newton's experience with falling apples.

183.25–26 The astronomer . . . infers an invisible planet] The inference of the planet Neptune from perturbations in the orbit of Uranus, credited chiefly to the French astronomer Urbain Leverrier (1811–1877).

183 *footnote*] According to C1951, Clemens owned a copy of Henry Dircks, *The Life, Times, and Scientific Labours of the Second Marquis of Worcester* (London: Quaritch, 1865), in which there are extensive accounts of Worcester's so-called "water-commanding engine." Edward Somerset, second Marquis of Worcester (1601–1667), dabbled in several mechanical projects, as vaguely described in his "Century of Inventions" in Dircks. Worcester acquired a patent for his "water-commanding engine" in 1663, but it is not known that the machine was to be run by steam or that he ever designed any kind of steam-

engine. Mark Twain put too much faith in Dircks's characterization of Worcester as a technological pioneer.

190.14   Their heads are all turned in one direction] Mark Twain was long interested in this phenomenon. In the 1870s he described it in a marginal note to Darwin's *Descent of Man*, and in 1896 he mentioned it in a notebook (Notebook 30, TS p. 42). Mrs. Loftus tests Huck Finn's rural background by his knowledge of this trait in cattle (*Huckleberry Finn*, chapter 11).

191.13   an uncle of mine had an old horse] If Mark Twain borrows from his own experience again, the uncle probably is John A. Quarles (1801–1876), whose farm near Florida, Missouri, he often visited in his boyhood. For his recollections of the farm see 1*MTA*: 96–115, but he does not mention the horse incident.

191.31   Here, now, is the experience of a gull] This and the following example in the text appear in two adjacent letters to the *Spectator* (London) 81, no. 3654 (9 July 1898): 47. The letters are signed simply "George Nicolson" and "Henry Woodall"; in calling them naturalists Mark Twain uses the term informally or to give authority to the anecdotes. The examples were not crucial discoveries. Mark Twain wrote this part of the dialogue in the same month they were published, and he evidently found them just when he wanted them. Others were available at any time. The *Spectator* was one of several periodicals that regularly printed such anecdotes in the 1890s, almost always to prove the virtue and intelligence of animals.

196.7   Sir John Lubbock took ants] Mark Twain took his ant examples from Sir John Lubbock's *Ants, Bees, and Wasps* (New York: D. Appleton, 1882). Most of his account is faithful to Lubbock, but at one point, perhaps for comic effect, he misrepresents an experiment—where he says the sober ants tired of retrieving their drunken friends and "threw both friends and strangers overboard." The sober ants actually became proficient at retrieving friends and discarding strangers (Lubbock, pp. 112–117). In asserting the intelligence of ants Mark Twain is only slightly more insistent than Lubbock, who says "they have a fair claim to rank next to man in the scale of intelligence" (p. 1). For a somewhat different version of Franklin's experiment see Lubbock, pp. 155–156, and *The Papers of Benjamin Franklin*, ed. Leonard W.

Labaree and Whitfield J. Bell, Jr. (New Haven: Yale University Press, 1961), 4:59. Mark Twain was carefully studying Lubbock in 1896 (*MTB*, p. 1016), and in 1897 he included but later deleted the same examples in *Following the Equator* (DV330).

200.19   the Master inside of Pizarro] Francisco Pizarro (1471?–1541), conqueror of Peru, commonly execrated as a tyrant. In a copy of [Robert Calef and Cotton Mather,] *Salem Witchcraft* (Boston: William Veazie, 1865), p. 345, Mark Twain drew a marginal line beside Calef's description of Pizarro as "a bastard, dropt in a church-porch, put to suck a sow, and, being grown, ran away, and shipt himself for America; there so prospered as to command an army. . ." (MTP).

212.5   Henry Adams] In "The Lost America—The Despair of Henry Adams and Mark Twain," *Modern Age* 5, no. 3 (Summer 1961): 309, Tony Tanner suggests that Mark Twain alludes to the despair of the American historian Henry Adams (1838–1918): "[Mark Twain] must certainly have known too much about Adams to have used the name quite innocently. . . ." But Mark Twain had used the name "Henry Adams" in "The £1,000,000 Bank Note," and there is no allusion to the real Adams in that story. Mark Twain wrote this section of the dialogue in 1905, and thus the name "Burgess" is also a repetition (see "The Man That Corrupted Hadleyburg"). The two-fold repetition of names from his previous fictions implies that he conceived both characters as hypothetical illustrations, though his need for "genuine" friends of the Young Man made him avoid names like "John Smith."

21.   CHRISTIAN SCIENCE

215.2   matter written about four years ago] Mark Twain wrote the preface in 1903, when "about four years ago" was correct. He overlooked this reference when changing the date beneath the preface from March 1903 to January 1907.

215.8   Mrs. Eddy] Mary Baker G. Eddy (1821–1910), founder of the Christian Science movement. When Mark Twain first acquired a writing interest in Christian Science, around October 1898, Mrs. Eddy was entering a period of extreme disrepute. The movement was growing, and to many it seemed an insult to common sense and a threat to health and true religion. The death of the author Harold Frederic in October 1898—supposedly from inept treatment by Christian Science practitioners after a stroke—led to fierce editorials in newspapers and magazines, which continued the attack by broadcasting similar events after the Frederic scandal subsided. In the years 1898–1902 Mrs. Eddy suffered accusations and ridicule from several quarters—doctors, clergymen, politicians, laymen, and schismatics like Josephine Woodbury. They denounced Mrs. Eddy as a half-mad charlatan whose motives were power, prestige, and money. Though some critics never ceased their attacks, public opinion was relatively kind from 1903 until the fall of 1906. In the latter year, with the publication of unfavorable articles in the New York *World*, another spell of hostility began, culminating in 1907–1908 with Mark Twain's book and Georgine Milmine's biography of Mrs. Eddy in *McClure's Magazine*.

Throughout this decade Mrs. Eddy was living in seclusion and semi-retirement at Pleasant View, her home near Concord, New Hampshire. She still wrote for the *Christian Science Journal* and continued to revise her chief books, *Science and Health* and the *Manual of the Mother Church*. But her career as organizer of a movement was virtually over, and her critics were reacting to her past activities more than to anything she did in these years. For a convenient biographical sketch see *DAB*; for a favorable book see Lyman P. Powell, *Mary Baker Eddy: A Life Size Portrait* (New York: Macmillan, 1930); for unfavorable books see Edwin Franden Dakin, *Mrs. Eddy: The Biography of a Virginal Mind* (New York: Charles Scribner's Sons, 1929), and Ernest Sutherland Bates and John V. Dittemore, *Mary Baker Eddy, The Truth and the Tradition* (New York: Knopf, 1932).

216   *epigraph*] The quotation is from Mark Twain's own prose at 230.31–33.

218.16   her name was Fuller] Mrs. Fuller's appearance and the number of her marriages suggest that Mark Twain based her upon Mrs. Eddy and that he intended a joke which his contemporary readers might appreciate.

220.24   the fundamental propositions of Christian Science] From the cue words through the propositions Mark Twain slightly paraphrases

Mrs. Eddy. Since he wrote the first four chapters in 1898–1899, see *Science and Health with Key to the Scriptures,* 148th ed. (Boston: J. Armstrong, 1898), p. 7.

221.1 Disease sin evil death deny Good omnipotent God life] See *Science and Health,* p. 7: "The metaphysics of Christian Science, like the rules of mathematics, prove the rule by inversion." Although Mrs. Eddy pointed out the consistency between the normal and backward versions of her propositions, she carried the reversal no further than the cue words; Mark Twain completed it.

221.25 1. GOD—Principle] This and the next two definitions in the text are also from Mrs. Eddy (*Science and Health,* p. 9), though after the last she lists Webster as her source.

222.2 FIRST DEGREE: *Depravity*] This and the next two definitions in the text are from *Science and Health,* p. 9. Mrs. Fuller's first comment —"You see how ... anthropomorphous it all is"—is Mark Twain's invention, but her next—"In this Third Degree ... mortal mind disappears"—is a slight variant from *Science and Health,* p. 10.

222.26 in this Third Degree] From the cue words through the text paragraph, *Science and Health* verbatim, p. 10. The biblical citation is to Matthew 19:30.

223.13 Individuality is one] The sentence paraphrases *Science and Health,* p. 10.

223.20–29 Christian Science reverses . . . man co-exists with and reflects Soul] *Science and Health,* p. 13, slightly misquoted by Mark Twain. The rest of the text paragraph is his invention.

224.20 In the year 1866] This and the following quotation in the text are from *Science and Health,* p. 1.

225.16 This Apodictical Principle] The sentence paraphrases *Science and Health,* p. 1.

226.1 God had been graciously fitting me] See *Science and Health,* p. 1.

226.15 The twelfth chapter of the Apocalypse] See *Science and Health,* pp. 551–552; italics are Mark Twain's.

226.20   In the opening of the Sixth Seal] See *Science and Health*, p. 552, for the text sentence and the citation to Revelation 12:1.

226.28   Revelation xii.6] Cited in *Science and Health*, p. 557. Mrs. Eddy identifies the wilderness not as Boston but as "sense," through which one must pass on the way to "Soul."

227.2   And I saw another mighty angel] Revelation 10:1–2, cited in *Science and Health*, p. 550.

227.13–19   Then will a voice . . . its digestion bitter] See *Science and Health*, p. 551.

231.10–11   there came . . . a tract] Edward Anthony Spitzka, "Contributions to the Encephalic Anatomy of the Races," *American Journal of Anatomy* 2, no. 1 (29 November 1902): 25–71. Mark Twain clipped the quotation from p. 49. The donor is not known.

232.17   a farmer's wife] In 1*MTA*: 108, Mark Twain identifies her as Mrs. Utterback, a faith-doctor who specialized in toothaches.

233.6–7   Mind-Cure . . . Mental Science Cure] Though these practices did not include the use of medicines, they granted the existence of disease and trauma. For descriptions of Mind Cure and the other treatments, see a well-known contemporary book, James Monroe Buckley, *Faith-Healing, Christian Science and Kindred Phenomena* (New York: The Century Company, 1892).

233.27   I have personal . . . knowledge] Mark Twain means the case of Livy. See the Autobiographical Dictation of 13 February 1906.

237.35   with help of a polisher] Mark Twain inferred a "polisher" in his first Christian Science article, "Christian Science and the Book of Mrs. Eddy," *Cosmopolitan* 27, no. 6 (October 1899): 592. After publication of that work he received confirmation from one of Mrs. Eddy's editors, James Henry Wiggin (J. Henry Wiggin to SLC, 30 September and 1 November 1899). Wiggin (1836–1900) was a former Unitarian minister who turned free-lance ghost writer around 1875. In 1885 he was approached by Calvin A. Frye, Mrs. Eddy's assistant, and began his services with the 1886 edition of *Science and Health*. After 1891 Wiggin had little to do with Mrs. Eddy, but he claimed there were others who continued editing her works. See the New York *World*, 4–5 November 1906, and Dakin, pp. 223–233.

238 *epigraph*] From the *Christian Science Journal* 16, no. 7 (October 1898): 456. This passage and the three later quotations from a "Baptist clergyman" are from the lead article of the issue, "The Restoration," by Rev. E. R. Hardy. All citations in book 1, chapter 6 are to the same issue. Mark Twain often alters the original text—changing the order of sentences, replacing nouns with pronouns, and so forth. He misrepresents content only once, where he suggests that "little Gordon" learned to display his piety for adult approval. According to the boy's mother he continued to kiss the book only "until he became conscious of what he was doing, then it ceased" (p. 499).

238.26 This has been disputed by novices] The estimate was disputed by William Denison McCrackan (1864–1923), author of travel books and popular histories and director of the Christian Science literary bureau for the state of New York. Book 1, chapters 5 and 6, the first installment of Mark Twain's Christian Science series in the *North American Review*, appeared in the issue for December 1902, and Mc-Crackan wrote him soon after publication. He underscored several statements he thought incorrect, the one in question among them, removed the article from the journal and gave it to Mark Twain. The author used the same pages as copy for the book, with an instruction to the printer: "Pay no attention to the italics in this article when done with a pencil. S. L. C. The pencillings were made by McCrackan the Scientist—*indignantly*." In December Clemens and McCrackan argued about Christian Science in frequent conversations and several letters, with results painful and embarrassing to both men (see note to 250.30).

238.30 There is a dispute about that picture] McCrackan objected to the statement (W. D. McCrackan to SLC, 4 December 1902). Frederick William Peabody, though sympathetic toward Mark Twain's attacks on Mrs. Eddy, also denied it (F. W. Peabody to SLC, 13 December 1902). Peabody (b. 1862), a lawyer, wrote several attacks on Christian Science, including *The Religio-Medical Masquerade*, cited earlier (see note 67 to the Introduction). Another was a pamphlet called *A Complete Exposé of Eddyism or Christian Science and the Plain Truth in Plain Terms Regarding Mary Baker G. Eddy, Founder of Christian Science* (Boston, 1901), cited hereafter as "Peabody." It was the source for many of Mark Twain's examples, and through extensive correspondence Peabody was otherwise helpful. Material in the manuscript, altered before publication, discloses that Mark Twain heard of Mrs. Eddy's "picture or image" from an Austrian woman in Vienna in 1899. The manuscript does not give her name.

238.32 This suggestion has been scorned] In his *North American Review* copy McCrackan underscored "Christ" (238.25).

239.34 Through misinformation I doubled those figures] Evidently a correction supplied by McCrackan; the number was 500 in the *North American Review* text.

240.34 *That* has been disputed by a Christian Science friend] McCrackan again, who underscored *"a new personage to worship"* (240.26) in his copy. He also objected to Mark Twain's argument in an undated letter of December 1902.

241.5 Bellamy's "Nationalism"] In his novel *Looking Backward 2000–1887* (1888) Edward Bellamy (1850–1898) described an idyllic collectivist America in the twenty-first century. The wide appeal of *Looking Backward* led to the "Nationalist" movement, which advocated among other things the socialization of industry. Though there were many Nationalist Clubs in the United States during the 1880s and 1890s, they constituted a minority movement.

241.9 I believe it claims short of four millions] In 1899 the Spiritualists claimed 1,500,000 adherents in the United States and Canada; see *The World Almanac and Encyclopedia* (New York: Press Publishing Company, 1899), p. 328.

241.11 The few again] According to the census of 1890 there were 6,075 members of the Church of the New Jerusalem (the Swedenborgian Church) in the United States; *World Almanac*, p. 318.

242 *footnote*] The letter does not survive, but the correspondent may have been William A. Purrington (1852–1926), a lawyer by profession and a notable opponent of Christian Science in that day, who lectured on the relations of the law and medical practice at the Bellevue Hospital Medical College. A single letter from Purrington to Clemens is known to survive—25 January 1903—in which he enclosed a copy of his book, *Christian Science; An Exposition of Mrs. Eddy's Wonderful*

Discovery, Including its Legal Aspects; A Plea for Children and Other Helpless Sick (New York: E. B. Treat, 1900).

248 *footnote*] The only known letter containing the protest is Peabody to SLC, 10 December 1902, but Purrington may also have corresponded on the subject, which he treated fervently throughout his book.

248 *epigraph*] From "Christian Science: Its Practical Excellence," delivered at the Buffalo Music Hall, 22 November 1898, and printed in the Buffalo *Express*, 23 November 1898, p. 8, but in the absence of manuscript for book 1, chapter 7, Mark Twain's immediate source cannot be known. This quotation and the one in the footnote to p. 249 were probably among those Twichell sent the author in Europe in 1899; Twichell enclosed a clipping reporting another lecture on Christian Science in a letter of 8 April 1899. Mark Twain slightly misquotes the passage in the epigraph, in one place perhaps by accident: the second word should be "conscientiously" rather than "consciously."

249 *footnote*] Quotation probably from a reprint in the *Christian Science Sentinel* 1, no. 30 (23 March 1899): 13. A page from the *Sentinel* for 16 March 1899 is in the Mark Twain Papers; it contains Mark Twain's marginal lines near a discussion of the memorial-spoon (see 249.17).

250.30 I applied last month, but they returned my money] Mark Twain alludes to a cause of a serious quarrel with McCrackan. Early in January 1903, giving no reason, McCrackan returned Clemens' check and said he was countermanding his order for a copy of Mrs. Eddy's *Miscellaneous Writings*, an order he had accepted in December. Clemens became irate, denouncing both McCrackan and Mrs. Eddy to David A. Munro, associate editor of the *North American Review*. In *Harper's Weekly* for 24 and 31 January he placed an advertisement: "Mrs. Eddy's publishing agents having refused to sell me her book called 'Miscellaneous Writings,' to my great inconvenience, I have placed an order for this work with Messrs. Harper & Brothers, and shall hope that some one possessing an extra copy of it will be willing to sell it to them for me. Please communicate with them. MARK TWAIN." During this period he also wrote at least two offensive letters to McCrackan. Early in February, but after writing the footnote, he sent an eloquent apology, and McCrackan returned both letters with the comment that he had not taken offense. Clemens was touched; on McCrackan's envelope he wrote that he was a "very fine man." In March McCrackan even returned the letter of apology, with another courteous note. But in June, for reasons unknown, Clemens wrote Munro that McCrackan "has been playing sneak and spy in my house and I have told him so in a letter today." There was evidently no reply from McCrackan and no return of this letter. Those he returned do not survive in the Mark Twain Papers; Clemens probably destroyed them upon receipt. The following correspondence is relevant: W. D. McCrackan to SLC, [December 1902]; W. D. McCrackan to SLC, 7 January 1903; David A. Munro to SLC, 15 January 1903; W. D. McCrackan to SLC, 7 February and 2 March 1903; TS of portion of SLC to David A .Munro, 14 June 1903.

McCrackan refused Clemens' book order apparently because of a quarrel over their articles for the *North American Review* and because of ill feelings aroused through their conversations and correspondence of December 1902. During most of that month Clemens was amiable. He was willing to have McCrackan answer his series of articles, and he offered to reprint the answer in his book, which he thought would appear early in 1903. McCrackan's answer was finally planned for the March *North American Review,* but when he learned that Mark Twain might have an installment in the April issue, he tried to back down, evidently because he wanted to reply only to the completed series. Munro, who disliked McCrackan, told him in effect that Mark Twain's article projected for April was not his business and that he could use the March issue or none at all. McCrackan quickly gave in and prepared his answer for March. It was during the period of his exchanges with Munro that he countermanded Clemens' order. The following correspondence is relevant: W. D. McCrackan to SLC, 4 December 1902; SLC to W. D. McCrackan, 5 December 1902; SLC to David A. Munro, 6 December 1902; David A. Munro to SLC, 12 and 20 January 1903.

Paine's description of the Clemens-McCrackan relationship (*MTB*, pp. 1187–1188) is wrong in details and misleading in implication, and his entire chapter on Mark Twain and Christian Science suggests apology. It is possible that the author gave him a distorted account.

250.32 For one hundred, read *three* hundred] Mark Twain took the later figures from Peabody's tract, which cites the journal at p. 30.

251.13 say the By-Laws] The "By-Laws" Mark Twain cites throughout are in *Manual of the Mother Church; The First Church of Christ Scientist, in Boston, Massachusetts*, 11th ed. (Boston: Christian Science Publishing Society, 1899), not to be confused with three other editions published the same year. For the statement on "capitation-tax" see p. 32. Mark Twain's copy is now lost, as is his copy of the 28th edition (1903), which he heavily annotated.

253 *footnote*] A clipping from an unidentified American journal (MTP) lists the sums for voluntary offerings (actually for 1897 and 1898) as £7,051,778 and £7, 506,354—approximately $73,000,000 by the exchange rates of those years. The clipping contains Mark Twain's marginal note opposite the figures: "All by perhaps 2,000,000 families —10,000,000 individuals—$3.75 each? Then Xn S should contrib $3,500,000 to charity."

254.31 Without money and without price] See Isaiah 55:1.

254.32 A letter has come to me] The letter does not survive. Septimus James Hanna (1844–1921) was the editor of the *Christian Science Journal* and the *Christian Science Sentinel*, 1892–1902, and held various other church offices.

255.2 The laborer is worthy of his hire] Luke 10:7.

255.10 Exodus xxxii.4] "And [Aaron] received [the gold] at their hand, and fashioned it with a graving tool, after he had made it a molten calf: and they said, These be thy gods, O Israel, which brought thee up out of the land of Egypt."

255.34 the following letter has come] The letter survives only in its publication. The correspondent's allusion to "Uncle Silas" is to the denouement of "Tom Sawyer, Detective." Uncle Silas Phelps, mistakenly thinking he committed a murder, has become deranged because of guilt feelings. Tom exonerates him in a sensational courtroom episode, and Uncle Silas gradually regains his senses. As Huck says, the townspeople "loved the old man's intellects back into him again."

261.13 Huyler's candy] Mark Twain characteristically inserts a humorous item in a series; Huyler's ran comic advertisements in various periodicals during 1902–1903.

264   *epigraph*] Mark Twain wrote the "quotation," as revisions in the manuscript prove. He apparently invented it for the occasion; no work called "The Legend of the Man-Mystery" is known to survive.

265.20   Quimby] Phineas Parkhurst Quimby (1802–1866), considered the founder of mental healing in the United States and an important influence on Mrs. Eddy. She was his patient in 1862 and 1864.

266.21   She has revealed it in her autobiography] *Retrospection and Introspection* (Boston: W. G. Nixon, 1891). Citations in all notes are to the pagination of Clemens' copy (Boston: J. Armstrong, 1902) in the Mark Twain Papers.

266.31   an ancestor of mine was sent ambassador] See *SCH*, p. 2. For the "claimant to an earldom"—a second cousin of Jane Clemens' cousin James Lampton—see *MTHL*, p. 870, and *HH&T*, pp. 47–48.

267.14   And laud the land] The verses are from "Alphabet and Bayonet," *Retrospection and Introspection*, p. 21.

267.28   Here fame-honored Hickory] From "The Country Seat," *Retrospection and Introspection*, p. 28. Mark Twain was correct in suspecting a misprint (see his note); later editions read "bares."

268.10   Sir William Wallace] *Retrospection and Introspection*, pp. 8–9; Sir William Wallace (1272?–1305), Scottish general and patriot.

268.15   Hannah More] *Retrospection and Introspection*, p. 7; Hannah More (1745–1833), English poet, patroness, dramatist, and religious writer.

269.3   *After my discovery*] *Retrospection and Introspection*, p. 20; italics are Mark Twain's.

269.8   General Henry Knox] *Retrospection and Introspection*, p. 9. General Henry Knox (1750–1806) organized the Society of the Cincinnati after the Revolution and served as Secretary of War in Washington's first administration.

269.10   the late Sir John Macneill] *Retrospection and Introspection*, p. 9; Sir John McNeill (1795–1883), British diplomat.

269.14 Captain John Lovewell] *Retrospection and Introspection*, p. 10; John Lovewell (1691–1725), a famous Indian fighter, killed by Maine Indians in 1725.

269.18 John Macneil] *Retrospection and Introspection*, p. 10. John McNeil (1784–1850) fought at the battle of Chippewa and then at Lundy's Lane, during the War of 1812. Mrs. Eddy says only that Chippewa was "neighboring."

270.24 After his decease] From *Science and Health; with a Key to the Scriptures* (Boston: The author, 1883), 1: 3. Mark Twain calls this the "first revision," but it was at least the third. Elsewhere he makes the same mistake, as in Appendix A, where he calls the 1883 preface the "original first preface." Later he saw a copy of the 1881 edition, which has a different preface, but did not correct himself.

271.18 Man controlled by his Maker] *Science and Health*, 1: 65.

271.35 *Edition of 1902*] *Science and Health with Key to the Scriptures* (Boston: J. Armstrong, 1902).

272.10 What plague spot, or bacilli] This and the next two quotations in the text are from Mrs. Eddy's "A Narrative," *Christian Science Journal* 16, no. 10 (January 1899): 669–670.

273.12 well of English undefiled] Edmund Spenser's praise of Chaucer in *The Fairie Queene*, book 4, canto 2, stanza 32.

274.17 my babe was born] *Retrospection and Introspection*, p. 30.

278.25 Mr. Howells] William Dean Howells (1837–1920), American novelist and friend of Clemens. The "late Josh Billings" was Henry Wheeler Shaw (1818–1885), American humorist who practiced the comic convention of misspelling words; Jonathan Edwards (1703–1758) was an American clergyman and theologian; "Mr. Dooley" was Finley Peter Dunne (1867–1936), American humorist and friend of Clemens, familiarly called by the name of the comic character he invented. For Herbert Spencer see note to 102.10.

279.28 *Miscellaneous Writings of Mrs. Eddy*] *Miscellaneous Writings 1883–1896* (Boston: J. Armstrong, 1897). "554 pages of prose" is Mark Twain's error. In manuscript and printer's copy he correctly wrote that the book contained "471 pages," and after subtracting the seventeen pages of poetry he should have written "454" for the prose. In proof he evidently caught the discrepancy between 471 and 554, for "several hundred" replaces "471" in the 1907 text. Pages 401–471 of *Miscellaneous Writings* contain testimonials, not Mrs. Eddy's prose.

281.14   Mr. Peabody states] Peabody, p. 20.

282.19   She was not able to think of a "financial equivalent"] This and the other fragmentary quotations in the text paragraph are from *Retrospection and Introspection*, p. 71.

283.14   By-Laws] *Manual of the Mother Church . . .* , 11th ed. (Boston: Christian Science Publishing Society, 1899), hereafter cited as *Manual*; see note to 251.13.

283.16–17   The Board of Directors . . . is the property of Mrs. Eddy] According to the *Manual*, every candidate for the Board of Directors was subject to Mrs. Eddy's approval; the same was true of candidates for the Board of Lectureship.

283.33–34   before the Berne Convention and . . . our amended law of 1891] According to the Berne Convention of 1886, persons of each signatory country were to enjoy in the other signatory countries the same copyright privileges as their own citizens. In the 1891 revision of its copyright law, the United States (not a party to the Berne Convention) provided that foreign authors would be protected if their countries protected American authors.

284.32   I quote from Mr. Peabody's book] This and the following quotation in the text are from Peabody, p. 11.

286.7   It was not myself] Article entitled "Christian Science and the Episcopal Congress," *Christian Science Journal* 18, no. 10 (January 1901): 597. The sentence reads in full: "It was not myself, but the divine power of Truth and Love, infinitely above me, which dictated 'Science and Health with Key to the Scriptures.'"

287.20   impelled by a power not one's own] From a letter by Mrs. Eddy (*Miscellaneous Writings*, p. 148) used as a prefatory note to the *Manual*, p. [3].

287.25   *The Title of Mother*] *Manual*, p. 48.

288.1   I quote from Mr. Peabody's book again] Peabody, p. 21.

288.10   While we entertain decided views] *Miscellaneous Writings*, p. 3.

290.15   A year or two later she organized her first Christian Science "Association,"] See *Retrospection and Introspection*, p. 62.

290.18   She taught and healed gratis] See *Retrospection and Introspection*, p. 58.

290.22   aggrandize the "Association" to a "Church."] See *Retrospection and Introspection*, p. 62.

291.7   a Mind-healing Church] This and the other quotations in the text paragraph are from *Retrospection and Introspection*, p. 62.

291.14   the pathology of spiritual power] From *Retrospection and Introspection*, p. 61.

291.16–17   her husband . . . her adopted son] Asa G. Eddy (1832?–1882), Mrs. Eddy's third and last husband, whom she married in 1877, was a sewing-machine agent before studying under the then Mrs. Glover in 1875–1876. Dr. Eddy was the first person to adopt the title of "Christian Science Practitioner." Ebenezer J. Foster (b. 1847?), onetime homeopathic physician, became Mrs. Eddy's son by adoption in 1888. He held high office in the organization until he fell from favor in 1895. The men could not have been on the Metaphysical College staff at the same time, inasmuch as Eddy died before Foster Eddy entered the movement.

291.18   barely three weeks] *Retrospection and Introspection*, p. 71.

291.27   Preface to 1902 edition of *Science and Health*] The citation is to p. xii.

292.9–11   an advertisement . . . from the *Christian Science Journal*] From the *Christian Science Journal* 4, no. 6 (September 1886): 156. The quotation is selective and in a few places trivially wrong. It was probably among the many extracts Frederick W. Peabody lent Clemens in December 1902 and January 1903.

293.1   the horse-leech's daughter] See Proverbs 30:15.

293.8   in the spirit of Christ's charity] Condensed from the preface to *Science and Health*, edition of 1902, p. xii. See note to 271.35.

293   *footnote 2*] From *Science and Health; with a Key to the Scriptures* (Boston: The author, 1884), 2: 173. Clemens' copy of volume 2 (MTP) has his marginal checks opposite both quotations.

295.23   *except the candidate is approved*] *Manual*, p. 22; italics are Mark Twain's. The condition reads in full: "except the candidate is approved by the Pastor Emeritus and the remaining members of the Board." Unless otherwise stated, Mark Twain's subsequent statements of fact about the *Manual* are correct.

296.1   *This By-Law can neither be amended*] *Manual*, p. 22; italics are Mark Twain's.

296.5   *Subject to the approval*] *Manual*, p. 21; italics are Mark Twain's.

296.15   *or* upon the election of their successors] *Manual*, p. 21; italics are Mark Twain's.

296.30   imperative duty . . . at the place and time specified] *Manual*, p. 22.

297.8   if he fail] All quotations in the text sentence are from *Manual*, p. 22.

297.33   *except it be constituted*] *Manual*, p. 22; italics are Mark Twain's.

298.22   *They shall make no remarks*] *Manual*, p. 25; italics are Mark Twain's.

299.24   *Section 3*] Article IV, Section 3; *Manual*, p. 24; italics are Mark Twain's, and otherwise trivially misquoted.

300.16   *Naming Book and Author*] *Manual*, p. 25; italics are Mark Twain's.

300.27   important questions relative to Church members] *Manual*, p. 27.

300.31   fix the salaries of the Readers] *Manual*, p. 27.

301.3 shall be countersigned] *Manual*, p. 31. The 1907 text of *Christian Science* began the quotation at "Every recommendation," but since Mark Twain inserted "for membership in the Church" to clarify the passage, he specified in manuscript that the quotation should begin at "shall be."

301.8 transact any Church business] *Manual*, p. 27.

301.18 Before being elected] *Manual*, p. 26; italics are Mark Twain's.

302.15 Moody and Sankey and Sam Jones revivals] Dwight Lyman Moody (1837–1899), Ira David Sankey (1840–1908), and Samuel Porter Jones (1847–1906), three of the most famous evangelists of the late nineteenth century. Moody and Sankey were a team, Moody the speaker and Sankey the singer and organist. Jones was a vernacular Southerner whose speech and manners Mark Twain ridiculed in "A Singular Episode," a suppressed sketch of around 1890 (DV 329). In it Jones dies and goes to heaven, but the souls already there are so disgusted by him they depart for Sheol, leaving Jones in heaven by himself.

302 *footnote*] Clemens' "intellectual method" of curing a vice was to banish the vicious desire (see "Concerning a Reformed Pledge," Paine 154). The person he offered to cure of alcoholism was one of his servants, perhaps his butler Claude. In February 1903, apparently as a last resort, Clemens sent him to the Oppenheimer Institute in New York. Shortly after completing the cure the man turned up drunk again, and Clemens, who had paid the $150 for his treatment, complained unsuccessfully to the Institute. He added his footnote before the relapse, while he still thought the cure demonstrated the value and power of things difficult to attain. He inserted "(temporarily)" (303.35) in proof, after the relapse. For accounts see a draft of "Reverend and Dear Sirs" [1905], and Samuel Hopkins Adams, "The Scavengers," *Collier's* 37, no. 26 (22 September 1906): 18, 24. The article, one of a muckraking series called "The Great American Fraud" which Adams published in book form under that title, describes Clemens' experience with the Oppenheimer Institute in much the same way as the draft. Adams may have seen the finished letter, since both draft and article say the episode happened "two years ago"—correct in the draft, incorrect in the article.

303.12   Applications of students] Rephrased from *Manual*, p. 30.

303.15   one of Mrs. Eddy's loyal students] *Manual*, p. 30.

303.20   by invitation] *Manual*, p. 30.

303.30   *The candidates*] *Manual*, p. 31; italics are Mark Twain's.

304.15   good English scholars] *Manual*, p. 23.

304.15   thorough English scholars] *Manual*, p. 25.

304.22   *Understanding Communications*] *Manual*, Article II, p. 23.

304.28   Failing to adhere] *Manual*, p. 23; italics are Mark Twain's.

305.11   the Bible and the above-named book] *Manual*, p. 29.

305.18   I remember reading] *Retrospection and Introspection*, p. 7.

306.9   *In Any Church*] *Manual*, Article XXIII, p. 51; italics are Mark Twain's.

307.25   *This By-Law*] *Manual*, p. 51; italics are Mark Twain's.

307.33   *according to the platform*] *Manual*, p. 29; italics are Mark Twain's.

309.1   the Immaculate Conception] The Immaculate Conception of the Virgin Mary was pronounced by Pius IX on 8 December 1854.

309.8–9   the clergy . . . had a warm dispute] The dispute was over a sermon by Minot J. Savage of the Church of the Messiah, New York, on 21 December 1902. Savage argued against the virgin birth of Jesus, saying there was "no good reason in the New Testament, or in the early church history, for the belief that Jesus was God" (New York *Tribune*, 22 December 1902, p. 12). Letters on the issue continued in the New York newspapers well into January; thus Mark Twain could say around 15 January that the argument occurred "a week or two ago."

309.14   A week ago, another discussion broke out] The discussion actually began two weeks earlier, when Rev. Henry Frank of the Metropolitan Independent Church, New York, delivered an "Open Letter to John D. Rockefeller, Jr." The young Rockefeller (1874–1960) was well-known for his Sunday-school activities in the Baptist Church. Though praising his character and devotion, Frank asked: "In view of your conspicuous position both in religion and wealth I desire to learn from you your opinion as to the mutual relation which you think should exist between them" (New York *American*, 5 January 1903, p. 6). Frank's aim was clearly to embarrass Rockefeller, and he succeeded at least in getting an oblique reply. The following Sunday, 11 January, Rockefeller spoke on "Giving Up All for Christ" at the Fifth Avenue Baptist Church, using as his text the passage from Luke 18:22. His interpretation is the "verdict" Mark Twain quotes at 309.18 (New York *American*, 12 January 1903, p. 5). The next day, as Mark Twain says, the *American* printed ten clergymen's interpretations of the same passage. All but one—Rev. Thomas B. Gregory—substantially agreed with Rockefeller.

310.14 names in the following list] Mark Twain clipped the list from "Church Statistics for 1902," *Literary Digest* 26, no. 5 (31 January 1903): 158.

311.35 Mr. Lindh's optimistic article] See "The Problem of the 'Divided Church,'" *Literary Digest* 26, no. 7 (14 February 1903): 234, for an account of Lindh and for the journal's response.

312 *footnote 1*] Mark Twain may have derived the "Spiral Twist" image from Rev. Thomas B. Gregory's reply to Rockefeller. Gregory had said sarcastically: "[Rockefeller's] turnings and twistings are admirable. . ." (New York *American*, 13 January 1903, p. 5). The introduction of the "Spiral Twist" closely follows a deleted manuscript page to which is pinned a clipping of Gregory's attack (manuscript p. 106, Paine 42).

312 *footnote 2*] Leo XIII died on 20 July 1903, some time after Mark Twain first read proof on the book. He may not have added the footnote until he re-examined the book preparatory to its publication in 1907.

313.16 sacred revelations] *Manual*, p. 37.

313.21 from the poems of our Pastor Emeritus] *Manual*, p. 37.

313.30 Members shall also instruct] Both quotations in the text paragraph are from *Manual*, p. 37.

314 *title*] The transactions concerning the land and the church are described at length in Peabody, pp. 39–42.

314.9   *Sec. 10*] *Manual*, p. 93; italics are Mark Twain's.

316.4   a blaze of North Adams gauds] Cheap costume jewelry. Compare *Is Shakespeare Dead?*, section 11: "we are privately afraid we should find . . . that the jewels are of the sort that are manufactured at North Adams, Mass."

316.13   in . . . *Science and Health*, edition of 1902] For the first citation to this edition see note to 271.35. The passage cited here is on pp. 16–17.

316   *footnote*] The version of the "Lord's Prayer" Mark Twain quotes was the latest available at that time. He may have hoped to find a new one in the next edition of *Science and Health*, but it is more likely that his note resulted from a confusion. The only version among the appendixes is from the 1881 edition (Appendix C).

317.9   the Presbyterians extended the Calling and Election suffrage] At its General Assembly of May 1902 the Presbyterian Church adopted a liberal creed concerning the means and availability of salvation; see the *Nation* 74, no. 1926 (29 May 1902): 420–421.

317.17   *Working Against the Cause*] *Manual*, p. 48; italics are Mark Twain's.

317.31   It shall be the duty] *Manual*, p. 49; italics are Mark Twain's. The passage is part of the same sentence as the previous quotation.

318.10   *This rule cannot be changed*] *Manual*, p. 49; italics are Mark Twain's.

318.32   If a member is found] This and the other provisions are in *Manual*, p. 50.

319.6   his name shall be dropped] *Manual*, p. 50.

319.17   I possess *a spiritual sense*] From Septimus J. Hanna, *Christian Science History*, 1st ed. (Boston: Christian Science Publishing Society, 1899), p. 16; italics are Mark Twain's. A cancel later replaced the original pp. 15–16 and deleted the passage Mark Twain quotes. The example was probably among the extracts lent by Peabody in December 1902 and January 1903.

320.10   the Council of Ten and the Council of Three] The first a committee of public safety, the other an inquisition of state, in the Republic of Venice. In *The Innocents Abroad*, chapter 22, Mark Twain repeated a common exaggeration of their injustice and cruelty.

321.16   The By-Law . . . reads its transgressor] See *Manual*, p. 50.

321.26   *Silence Enjoined*] This and the other titles are sub-section heads under "Discipline," in the table of contents to *Manual*, p. 8; italics are Mark Twain's.

322.25   *but not unless approved*] *Manual*, p. 58; italics are Mark Twain's. The first two words were added by the author to make the quotation cohere with his own prose.

323.4–5   the sweet byanby . . . Tah-rah-rah boom-de-aye] For the first song see note to 178.22. Originally the other—a popular song by Henry J. Sayers, published in 1891—was also on the Young Man's list of tiresome pieces, but Mark Twain deleted it in proof.

323.16   if a solo singer shall neglect] *Manual*, p. 58.

324.9   in *Science and Health*] *Manual*, p. 68.

324.24   *Subject to the approval*] *Manual*, p. 70; italics are Mark Twain's.

326.4   perpetual copyright in Great Britain] In October 1907, after the publication of *Christian Science*, Frank N. Doubleday sent Clemens a correction of this statement by Dr. Hart, Controller of the University Press, Oxford. Dr. Hart said that though three presses in England were privileged to issue the Bible, they held the privilege only through sentiment and tradition, not copyright (Frank N. Doubleday to SLC, 16 October 1907).

327.3   it occurred to her to make somebody a present of it] The transaction is described in Peabody, pp. 43–44.

327.8   loyalty to our great cause] The citation (slightly rephrased) and other references in the same paragraph and the following text paragraph are to "Official Minutes of Fourth Annual Meeting, N. C. S. Association," *Christian Science Journal* 7, no. 4 (July 1889): 172–173. Probably a Peabody extract; the material does not appear in his book.

327.18   On assuming my duties] From "Publisher's Department,"

Christian Science Journal 10, no. 10 (January 1893): 479; a Peabody extract.

328.8 unique request] This and the other quotations in the text paragraph are from "Christian Science at the World's Religious Congress," *Christian Science Journal* 11, no. 8 (November 1893): 346; a Peabody extract.

328.17 she donated the Publishing Society] See Peabody, p. 43.

328.25 an almost countless number of private charities] From "A Gift to the Mother Church, and a Grant of Trusteeship," *Christian Science Journal* 15, no. 11 (February 1898): 662.

328.29 Let us endeavor to lift up our hearts] Peabody, p. 45. The "literary domestic" was Septimus J. Hanna.

329.2 Article XII] Mark Twain's error; it is Article XXIX.

329.13 *accepted by Mrs. Eddy*] Paraphrased from *Manual*, p. 63; italics are Mark Twain's.

329.15 *it shall be owned*] *Manual*, p. 63; italics are Mark Twain's.

330.16 *shall be officially controlled*] *Manual*, p. 59; italics are Mark Twain's.

330.31 *Local Self-Government*] *Manual*, p. 59.

332.25 *shall assume no official control*] *Manual*, p. 59; italics are Mark Twain's.

333.12 In its relation] *Manual*, p. 60.

334.7 *No First Members*] *Manual*, p. 60; italics are Mark Twain's.

334.32 *The article 'The' must not be used*] *Manual*, p. 59; italics are Mark Twain's.

335 footnote] The quotation (slightly condensed by Mark Twain) is in a clipping from "A Defense of the Jesuits," *Literary Digest* 24, no. 4 (25 January 1902): 121, pinned to the manuscript. The authority quoted in the clipping was Henri de Ladevèze. Note that the item was about a year old when Mark Twain used it.

336.29   A prominent Christian Scientist has assured me] W. D. Mc-
Crackan (see note to 238.26).

337.13   a hap which had not happened] Mark Twain claimed in the
North American Review that the December and January articles (book
1, chapters 5–6 and 7–8) were previously unpublished, yet both had
already appeared in the English *Hadleyburg.* There is no need to suspect disingenuousness there or in the book. He had intended the
Christian Science material for earlier publication in America (see the
Textual Notes), and he may have forgotten the omission by the summer of 1902—and may have forgotten the publication in *Hadleyburg*
altogether. He could legitimately regard the December and January
articles as first publication to an American audience, and he could
hardly believe his responsibility for the mistake about Mrs. Eddy's
portrait would be greater were it known that they had been printed
three years previously.

337.16   I said a lady told me "last night"] Mark Twain's December
article read: ". . . a lady told me last night that in the Christian
Science Mosque in Boston she noticed some things . . ." (*North
American Review,* 175: 759). He deleted the paragraph containing
this passage when preparing the book. The Christian Scientist who
asked for a retraction was McCrackan (see note to 238.26).

338.2   I will copy his newspaper account] Newspaper source unknown.
The item was one of Peabody's extracts. Mark Twain copied it in his
manuscript instead of inserting the clipping or transcription because
Peabody asked that it be returned. Peabody later published the same
account, with a few minor differences, in *The Religio-Medical Masquerade,* pp. 151–152. In a letter to Clemens of 12 January 1903 Peabody says he visited the "Holy of Holies" in the summer of 1899—by
no means so recently as Mark Twain claims. The newspaper item
probably dates from the same period.

339.22   *Science and Health* (ed. 1899)] *Science and Health with Key
to the Scriptures* (Boston: J. Armstrong, 1899).

340.2   His students then *received the Holy Ghost*] *Science and
Health,* pp. 351–352; italics are Mark Twain's.

341.16   go 'way back and set down] From a popular song—"Go 'Way Back and Sit Down"—by Elmer Bowman and Al Johns, published in 1901. The chorus indicates the tone of Mark Twain's allusion:

> Go way back and sit down.
> Coons in your class are easy found,
> You seldom have money, you never treat,
> Get in your place and take a back seat,
> Go way back and sit down.

341.24   Throughout the entire book] Quotation from "Editor's Table," *Christian Science Journal* 19, no. 12 (March 1902): 786.

342.10–13   Read the following *command* ... quoted by Mr. Peabody] Peabody, p. 33; also see Peabody, p. 34, for the next quotation in the text.

343.1   A Scientist out West] Person unknown.

350.35–351.1   she had been called . . . as had happened to little Samuel] See *Retrospection and Introspection*, pp. 17–19.

353.27   Madame de Rémusat] Madame Claire de Rémusat (1780–1821), lady-in-waiting to Empress Josephine. Clemens owned a copy of at least the third volume of her *Memoirs* (New York: D. Appleton, 1880); see A1911, p. 59.

356.13   when he sailed, when he sailed] Based upon a line from the ballad "Captain Kidd": " 'I'd a Bible in my hand, when I sailed, when I sailed.' "

358.8   O, islands there are] From the New York text of "The Pirate's Serenade" (ca. 1838), a song popular in Britain and America, by the Scottish composer John Thomson with words by William Kennedy. Helen Creighton included a Nova Scotia variant in *Maritime Folk Songs* (Toronto: Ryerson Press, 1962), p. 152. Mark Twain was perhaps reminded of the song by association with "Captain Kidd," quoted only five manuscript pages earlier, but he had been fond of these lines for many years. In 1866 he wrote them in a notebook shortly after arriving at Honolulu (Notebook 5, TS p. 20; *MTN*, p. 16) and in another notebook upon his return to San Francisco (Notebook 4, TS p. 44). In the 1880s he quoted them in a story fragment concerning Hawaii (DV111).

358.34 read the novel] [Anonymous,] *The Life Within* (Boston: Lothrop, 1903). The "two claims" are "the healing of the body" and "the healing of the spirit" (see 349.24–25).

359 *footnote 2*] Mark Twain's error; the citation appears in Appendix F. The quotation in Appendix B is from *Retrospection and Introspection* and illustrates a different reference.

363 APPENDIX A] From *Science and Health*, edition of 1883, 1: 3–8.

363.8 a mesmerist in Portland] P. P. Quimby, in Portland, Maine; see note to 265.20.

364.26 the issues of E. J. A.] In 1881 Edward J. Arens, a former pupil of Mrs. Eddy, published a booklet called *Theology; or, the Understanding of God, as Applied to Healing the Sick*, wherein he quoted and rephrased several passages from *Science and Health*. In 1883, the year of the preface, Mrs. Eddy successfully sued for infringement of copyright. She had broken with Arens before this controversy. In 1882, when Asa G. Eddy lay dying, both he and Mrs. Eddy thought Arens was slowly killing him by arsenic "mentally administered." See Georgine Milmine, "Mary Baker G. Eddy: The Story of Her Life and the History of Christian Science," *McClure's Magazine* 29, no. 5 (September 1907): 568, 579.

365.7 one of our youngest students, R. K——y] Richard Kennedy, a student of Mrs. Eddy's in the late 1860s, while still younger than twenty. He became her professional partner in 1870, employing manipulation to heal the sick, a method Mrs. Eddy taught and practiced in her early period. After several quarrels they ended their association in 1872. Mrs. Eddy repudiated manipulation and accused Kennedy of malpractice for continuing it. She also accused him of Malicious Animal Magnetism, adultery, theft, the torture and killing of his patients, and several other crimes. She attacked him in both the 1881 and 1883 editions of *Science and Health*.

367 APPENDIX B] From *Retrospection and Introspection*, pp. 34–35.

368 APPENDIX C] The introductory sentence and the prayer are from *Science and Health* (Lynn, Massachusetts: A. G. Eddy, 1881), 2: 176.

369 APPENDIX D] From *Science and Health*, edition of 1902, pp. 1–11.

377 APPENDIX E] From Richard Heber Newton, *Christian Science; The Truths of Spiritual Healing and their Contribution to the Growth of Orthodoxy* (New York: G. P. Putnam's Sons, 1899), pp. 8–12. Newton (1840–1914) was rector of All Souls' Episcopal Church, New York.

380 APPENDIX F] From *Science and Health*, edition of 1883, 1: 10–12.

382.3 a statement . . . on the 17th of January] Peabody clipped Mrs. Eddy's statement from the Boston *Herald* and sent it to Clemens on 17 January 1903, the day it appeared. Mark Twain pinned the clipping to his manuscript.

383.29 This is that Section 1] *Manual*, p. 48. William A. Purrington called the passage to Clemens' attention in his letter of 25 January 1903, but he had already quoted part of it (see 287.25).

384.18 a session of the National Christian Science Association] The page references in Mark Twain's footnotes suggest that someone sent him a separate reprint of the Association proceedings. No such reprint has been located, but the text is in the *Christian Science Journal* 8, no. 4 (July 1890): 139–149, 163–178. Mark Twain changes a few words for convenience, but he cites Mrs. Eddy's telegram verbatim. The official who said "there is but one Mary" was Mrs. Eddy's adopted son, E. J. Foster Eddy.

386.7 one who ought to be a very good authority] Person unknown.

386.8 verse 53 from the "Magnificat"] Luke 1:53.

390.12 *This By-Law shall not be changed*] For example, see *Manual*, p. 51, following the statement of Mrs. Eddy's right to dismiss readers.

390.30 Ask of the winds] A slight misquotation of "Casabianca," a well-known poem by Mrs. Felicia Hemans. Mark Twain quoted the same lines in *The Innocents Abroad*, chapter 44, also with the substitution of "away" for "around."

391.33 I quoted a lady] See notes to 238.30 and 337.16.

394.6 I quote from Mr. F. W. Peabody's book] Peabody, p. 21.

394.13 The following remark] From "Christian Science and its Revelator," *Christian Science Journal* 7, no. 1 (April 1889): 3. The quotation is not in Peabody's book; it was probably another extract he sent Clemens.

394.34   Mr. McCrackan's article appeared] "Mrs. Eddy's Relation to Christian Science," *North American Review* 176, no. 556 (March 1903): 349–364.

396.22   the last great municipal election in New York] In 1901 Seth Low, the Fusion candidate for mayor, defeated Edward M. Shepard, the Tammany candidate, by nearly 30,000 votes in a canvass of more than 500,000. Though Shepard was presumed to be honest, he would not disavow Tammany or its other candidates, among them several figures notorious in New York politics. For Mark Twain's involvement in the campaign see *MTB*, pp. 1145–1147.

22.   THINGS A SCOTSMAN WANTS TO KNOW

398   *title*] The title is a heading given two letters to the editor of *Harper's Weekly* 53, no. 2749 (28 August 1909): 6. The letters—one of them from E. Kaufman of Augusta, Maine, whom Clemens mentions in his own letter—were in reply to a list of theological questions submitted by a man named Donald Ross (*Harper's Weekly* 53, no. 2744 [24 July 1909]: 6). Ross, the "Scotsman," asked whether there were more gods than one, whether God was the author of evil, and so forth. Though Ross's letter was given the same heading, it is not known that Clemens saw more than the replies. He could have gotten the questions from Kaufman, who repeated them. Clemens was not in Augusta at that time; the location at the head was a support for the pseudonym he planned to use.

23.   LETTERS FROM THE EARTH

413.21   That innocent Bible tells about the Creation] The stories about the Creation, Adam and Eve, Cain and Abel, Noah and his sons, which Mark Twain uses as his narrative basis in this and the next several letters, are in Genesis 1–8.

414.31   the nearest star] Mark Twain's error. After the sun, the stellar system of Alpha Centauri is closest, at 4.3 light years. 61 Cygni is 11.1 light years distant, Arcturus about 33 light years. The condition of Mark Twain's memory for such details in 1909 is indicated by the fact that near the time he wrote "Letters from the Earth" he was reading an astronomer who gave the correct information on Alpha Centauri and 61 Cygni: Samuel G. Bayne, *The Pith of Astronomy* (New York: Harper, 1896); see *MTB*, p. 1542.

418.19   forgive them seventy-and-seven times] See Matthew 18:22.

421.15   Symmachus] Quintus Aurelius Symmachus (d. 405), Roman Senator. See, for example, Ludwig Friedländer, *Roman Life and Manners under the Early Empire* (London: G. Routledge & Sons, [1908]–1913), 2: 33–34.

421.29   it was Titus] Suetonius, p. 470; see note to 111.26.

425.29   I the Lord thy God am a jealous God] Exodus 20:5.

426.7   Thou shalt have no other gods] Exodus 20:3.

429.20   Constipation, O constipation] Based upon the following lines of Reginald Heber's "From Greenland's icy mountains":

> Salvation! oh, Salvation!
> The joyful sound proclaim,
> Till each remotest nation
> Has learn'd Messiah's name!

Heber's hymn was one of Mark Twain's favorites. In *Following the Equator*, chapter 55, he quoted the opening lines and said they were "beautiful verses, and . . . have remained in my memory all my life."

431.22   the Eye that never sleeps] Probably an allusion to the slogan of the Pinkerton Detective Agency, "We Never Sleep," which commonly appeared beneath a large open eye on the covers of Allan Pinkerton's books. Mark Twain had burlesqued Pinkerton many years earlier; see "Simon Wheeler, Detective," in *S&B*, p. 307; also "Tom Sawyer's Conspiracy," in *HH&T*, p. 152.

432.22   Dr. Charles Wardell Stiles] (1867–1941), zoologist. Stiles discovered the cause of hookworm disease in 1902 and from 1909 to 1914 served on the Rockefeller Commission for Eradication of Hookworm Disease in the southern states.

432.28 This morning's journals] From a public statement by the Rockefeller Commission. The quotation is in a clipping from the New York *Sun*, 29 October 1909, p. 1, pinned to the manuscript leaf. The closing phrase—"with God's help"—was Mark Twain's addition, and he changed "in fact largely due" to "in fact due."

434.5 Science has this to say] Source unknown; the quotation is in Mark Twain's hand. Sleeping sickness was a common news topic in that period, for the cause of the disease had recently been discovered, and there were serious epidemics in Africa. Starting in 1903 the Sleeping Sickness Commission of the Royal Society issued a series of reports, from which Mark Twain's immediate source probably derived. See *Reports of the Sleeping Sickness Commission*, no. 2 (London: Harrison and Sons, 1903), pp. 18–19.

434.28 *Man's* inhumanity to man] From Robert Burns, "Man Was Made to Mourn." Compare *MTN*, p. 344: "God's inhumanity to man makes countless thousands mourn."

439 *footnote*] The princess was Victoria Kamamalu (1838–1866). For details of her funeral see *Roughing It*, chapter 68, and *MTH*, pp. 328–334, 348–361. In an 1866 notebook Mark Twain wrote: "Pr. V. died in forcing abortion—kept half a dozen bucks to do her washing, and has suffered 7 abortions" (Notebook 4, TS p. 13).

444.11 And Israel abode in Shittim] Numbers 25:1; the verse following in the text is Numbers 25:4.

445.11 And the LORD spake unto Moses] Through verse 47 the quotations are from Numbers 31. They are in pages from a book of biblical selections which Mark Twain attached to the manuscript.

447.9 When thou comest nigh] This and the next four verses in the text are from Deuteronomy 20. Through the first half of verse 15 they are from the same book of biblical selections; the rest is in Mark Twain's hand.

447.23 *Thou shalt not kill*] Exodus 20:13.

448.4   the conduct of one Onan] For the references concerning Onan see Genesis 38:8–9.

449.5   I will cut off from Jeroboam] 1 Kings 14:10.

449.8   The same with the house of Baasha] See 1 Kings 16:11.

449.32 Thou shalt have a paddle] Deuteronomy 23:13; the next verse is Deuteronomy 23:14.

451.26 Père Hyacinth] Charles Jean Marie Loyson (1827–1912), commonly known as Père Hyacinth, before 1870 a well-known Carmelite, resigned his Church positions in protest against the decree of Papal Infallibility (1870). In 1872, with episcopal dispensation, he married an American widow. Thereafter, in Europe and America, he continued to be a popular lecturer and writer on religious and secular subjects. The charges adduced by Mark Twain have not been found in his works.

452.17 Twelve Indians broke into a farm house] The source was probably Col. Richard Irving Dodge's account of a very similar episode in The Plains of the Great West and Their Inhabitants, Being a Description of the Plains, Game, Indians, &c. of the Great North American Desert (New York: G. P. Putnam's Sons, 1877), pp. 420–422. A copy with Mark Twain's marginalia is in the Redding (Connecticut) public library.

453.15 Blessed are the poor in spirit] The group of verses is Matthew 5:3–11.

24.   "The Turning Point of My Life"

456.1   Coming up with his troops] Suetonius, p. 22; see note to 111.26.

456.17 While he was thus hesitating] The paragraph beginning with the cue words is also from Suetonius, p. 22, though until the present edition it has always been printed as if Mark Twain wrote it. In manuscript and typescript he asked that both Suetonius passages be set in small type, indicating quotation, yet the text type in Harper's Bazar was so small as to make that style impracticable. The printer compensated by setting the first passage in text type within quotation marks, but he forgot to put them around the second. No one caught the error in 1910, and it was perpetuated by *WIM* and all subsequent texts.

459.13 Among the books that interested me] William Lewis Herndon and Lardner Gibbon, *Exploration of the Valley of the Amazon* (Washington: R. Armstrong, 1853–1854). See *MTL*, p. 35, and *MTB*, p. 109.

460.24 Tweed] William Marcy Tweed (1823–1878), a former leader of Tammany Hall and one of the most notorious grafters of the post-Civil War period.

463.5 General Grant was asked a question] The question was asked by Mark Twain himself in 1885; see 2*MTA*: 144–145, and the variant at 463.5 in the Textual Notes.

TEXTUAL NOTES

1.   SABBATH REFLECTIONS

No manuscript is extant, nor any file of the Virginia City *Territorial Enterprise* for the period. The only text possibly authorized survives as a clipping from the *Territorial Enterprise* for 28 January 1866 in a scrapbook evidently kept by Orion Clemens, now in the Morse Collection, Yale University; see *MTCor*, pp. 5–6. The present text is based upon that printing, with the insertion of quotation marks after "broom!" (37.15) and before "*Alta*" (37.17), and with the omission of a period after the title. As necessary, periods have been dropped after the titles of other works in this volume.

Modern printings: *MTCor*, pp. 98–100; *Mark Twain's San Francisco*, ed. Bernard Taper (New York: McGraw-Hill, 1963), pp. 199–200.

2.   REFLECTIONS ON THE SABBATH

No manuscript extant. See the Explanatory Notes for consideration whether the piece first appeared in the *Golden Era* or the *Territorial Enterprise*. The present text is based upon the only text possibly authorized: *Golden Era* 14, no. 16 (18 March 1866): 3 (Bancroft Library, University of California). Two misprints in that text have been corrected, "Arevet" [emended to Brevet] (40.7) and "Prssbyterian" [Presbyterian] (40.9).

Modern printings: *The Washoe Giant in San Francisco*, ed. Franklin Walker (San Francisco: George Fields, 1938), pp. 115–116; Taper, pp. 235–237.

3.   Mr. Beecher and the Clergy

No manuscript extant. The present text is based upon the only text possibly authorized: Elmira *Daily Advertiser*, 10 April 1869, p. 1 (Micro Photo). Three misprints in that text have been corrected, "Jone's" [Jones'] (45.32), "pyrotenics" [pyrotechnics] (46.15), and "uniformerly" [uniformly] (46.20). The two-word formation "every body" (44.29) has been closed up in accordance with Mark Twain's known preference for this word.

Modern printing: *MTB*, pp. 1619–1623.

4.   About Smells

No manuscript extant. The present text is based upon the only text possibly authorized: *Galaxy* 9, no. 5 (May 1870): 721–722 (University of Iowa, University of Texas). Two misprints in that text have been corrected (a curved dash stands for the word previously quoted), "Terra" [Tierra] (48.15), "day," [~.] (49.24). "Saviour" (49.18) has been emended to "Savior"—Mark Twain's usual spelling. Compare the text at 43.26.

Facsimile of the *Galaxy* printing in *CG*, pp. 41–42. Modern printings: *The Curious Republic of Gondour and Other Whimsical Sketches* (New York: Boni and Liveright, 1919), pp. 25–29; Philip S. Foner, *Mark Twain: Social Critic* (New York: International Publishers, 1958), pp. 145–146; *Mark Twain: Life As I Find It*, ed. Charles Neider (Garden City: Hanover House, 1961), pp. 49–50; *Mark Twain on the Damned Human Race*, ed. Janet Smith (New York: Hill and Wang, 1962), pp. 36–38.

5.   The Indignity Put upon the Remains of George Holland
                    by the Rev. Mr. Sabine

No manuscript extant. The present text is based upon the only text possibly authorized: *Galaxy* 11, no. 2 (February 1871): 320–321

(University of Iowa, University of Texas). A garbled reading in that text has been emended, "to protest" [should protest] (55.7). An infinitive in the following sentence of the text suggests that the mistake resulted from an eye-skip. The emendation chosen here was also Paine's (*MTB*, p. 1627).

Facsimile of the *Galaxy* printing in *CG*, pp. 128–129. Modern printings: *MTB*, pp. 1624–1627; *Life As I Find It*, pp. 147–150.

6. [THREE STATEMENTS OF THE EIGHTIES]

The present texts are based upon three untitled manuscripts, DV274[5] and Paine 102d, the only phases under Mark Twain's control. In all three he used the same pen, ink (brown or faded to brown), handwriting, and brand of stationery. He probably wrote them at about the same time, perhaps on the same day, but even the decade of composition is conjectural. From evidence of hand and stationery Paine suggested a date in the early 1880s (*MTB*, p. 1582), which is plausible. The paper is a heavy white laid stationery torn into half-sheets measuring 4½" x 7", with a watermark reading "Pure [*crowned harp design*] Flax | Marcus Ward | & Co."

The pronoun "he" [He] (56.2), referring here to God, has been capitalized. In accordance with Mark Twain's usual style the present volume generally capitalizes pronouns referring to God and Jesus where manuscripts have lower case, but the words remain in lower case in most of "Letters from the Earth," where the style appears functional, and in quotations from writers whose practice differed. An erroneous duplication, "wisest & &" [wisest and] (58.8), has been corrected.

Previous printings: I: *MTB*, pp. 1583–1584. II (in part): *MTB*, p. 1584. III: previously unpublished.

7. THE CHARACTER OF MAN

The present text is based upon a heavily revised manuscript, DV32, the only phase under Mark Twain's control. According to the

Autobiographical Dictation of 24 January 1906, he wrote "The Character of Man" early in 1885, three or four months after Grover Cleveland's first election. Hand and paper are consistent with this date. The latter is Mark Twain's familiar buff laid paper with the "Keystone Linen" watermark, measuring 5½" x 8⅞". He discovered the manuscript among his papers around 11 January 1906, when he added the footnotes and a few revisions. It probably influenced "Taxes and Morals," a speech he delivered at Carnegie Hall on 22 January, wherein also he attacked party loyalty. On 23 January he inserted the piece in his Autobiographical Dictation, and Paine later published it in *Mark Twain's Autobiography*. No typescript survives, and Paine may have had only the instruction of the manuscript, which the state of some cancellations made confusing. Most of them were precisely indicated, however, and their reasons clear. The work was a compound of two fragments, and Mark Twain deleted passages in one that were substantially repeated in the other. He also canceled references to himself and a few anti-clerical and anti-Christian passages, probably because he thought of reading the manuscript before the Hartford Monday Evening Club, where he read a derivative but more politically oriented paper ("Consistency") in 1887. The work was first printed in 2MTA: 7–13 and was reprinted in 37Z: 7–13.

Three erroneous possessive forms have been corrected, "years' " [year's] (63.2), "conscience" [conscience'] (64.20), and "mens' " [men's] (64.25). Mark Twain inserted "Also—" (60.21) in 1906 but left "In" in upper case; the word is now in lower case. The compound "branch lies" at 61.19 has been emended to "branch-lies"; compare the text at 61.23 and 61.28.

The items that follow were Mark Twain's major revisions:

60.8   Creator....] This and all ellipses are Mark Twain's, following his deletion of long passages. The deletion at this point reads:

... Creator; that if he *was* made intentionally, it was not that he might be saved or damned, since he is conspicuously not worth that trouble, but was more probably merely intended as an annoyance—a thing to do for the Creator the office which other vermin do for *us*. If that is really what he was made for his creation does at last seem rational, explicable, even excusable, in a measure—for the office fits his bulk and his merit.

Mark Twain wrote the manuscript in ink. In pencil, probably when trying to convert the essay into a speech in 1885–1887, he softened the beginning:

> . . . Creator; that if he *was* made intentionally, he was probably merely intended. . . .

The proper state of the passage as a whole is somewhat unclear. At one time, in pencil, Mark Twain wrote "stet" near the matter deleted by the pencil revision, but the instruction is so large as to apply to the entire passage. At another time he canceled it in ink, and since the ink resembles that of the footnotes, which are dated 1906, the cancellation has been regarded as his final judgment.

61.5 . . . character.] The manuscript originally continued with the following paragraphs, which ended the first fragment:

> Upon what quality, what pretext, then, shall he arrogate to himself the position of the Deity's chosen creature?—His intellect? Will *that* enable him to adorn heaven? It is like the strained wisdom of discarding gas and electricity to pile decayed corpses in the family circle for the sake of the phosphorescent light that issues from them.
>
> Is it free will? He hasn't any more free will than the other creatures.
>
> He has the disposition to do mean and vicious things—and he restrains himself from doing them. Does that make him choicer company for the blest than the lamb, the calf, the horse, the bug that *hasn't* any such disposition? Look at him as you may, there is no rational argument in his favor. Yet he blandly shoves himself forward as the pet of the Deity—the Deity's chosen animal. We should not forget that the Deity has been accused of picking out the Jews for his favorite people. Those who know that race, know how wanton was that charge. This should make us modester; it should guard us from too readily jumping to gushy and grotesque conclusions from fantastic and irrational premises.
>
> Take one detail. Sham? or "Nature."

In 1885–1887 Mark Twain deleted the passage in pencil (except for the last line), wrote "stet" at the beginning, then in 1906 deleted the passage in ink, again excepting the last line. Then he struck out the last line also and added this transition to follow the cue word ("character") above:

So much by way of generalization, as regards man and his character. Let us strip him and examine him a little by detail:

He then canceled the transition.

61.6 .... There are] The second fragment begins here. The title is scarcely legible through Mark Twain's cancellation but seems to read "Accepted Lies."

62.7 .... Consider] Two manuscript pages (5 and 6) replaced by this ellipsis were destroyed.

63.14 If we would learn. . . .] The manuscript originally continued with the next paragraph ("And what a poor paltry lie. . . ."). The present paragraph, which concerns an immediate source of Mark Twain's anger, was nevertheless a second thought, as indicated by his changes of pagination. The paragraph "And what a poor paltry lie. . . ." began on a page originally numbered 12, then 14, then finally 15 after Mark Twain added more about Rev. Riddle. The interpolated paragraph was paged 12, 13, 14.

63.15 A Hartford clergyman. . . .] The manuscript originally read: "A Hartford clergyman—and the best man in this town, by long odds— met me. . . ." In pencil, when recasting the essay as a speech, Mark Twain changed the passage to read: "A Hartford clergyman—and one of the very best men in this town, prest c [present company] excepted —met me. . . ." He later deleted both versions.

64.3 ... of his life.] The sentence originally continued: ". . . of his life—the saving of souls; scraping them together, with a holy joy, to improve the society of heaven." Mark Twain deleted the passage in pencil after composition; someone else later wrote "stet" beneath it.

64.12 ... business.] Near the time of original composition Mark Twain deleted the remainder of the paragraph:

. . . business. If I may speak personally, take my own case. A year ago I had a friend in every newspaper in the land, and a reputation which was worth almost any commonplace man's having. I cast a vote for conscience' sake, and now if anybody values my reputation it is not I.

64.27 ...—selfishness.] Mark Twain deleted a continuation around
1885–1887:

What a fine irony it was to devise the Christian religion for such as he with
its golden array of impossibilities: Give *all* thou hast to the poor; if a man
smite thee on thy right cheek; if a man borrow thy coat of thee; if a man
require thee to go with him a mile; do unto others as you would that others
should do unto you; love thy neighbor as thyself. It has supplanted the old
religion which went before it—upon men's lips it has. But not in their
hearts. That old religion knew men better than this one, and must outlive
it: for it says, "Smite those people hip and thigh; burn all they possess with
fire; kill the cattle; kill the old men, and the women, and the young children, and the sucklings; spare nothing that has life; for their opinions are
not like ours."

64.28 Let us skip the other lies. . . .] The present last paragraph replaced the following fragment at the time of original composition:

Let us skip some of the lies, for brevity's sake. Truth is mighty, and
will prevail. I may be partial, but I think that that remark is in itself the
compactest and the most symmetrical lie that has been constructed by
man. It is pemmican. Why, we are so accustomed to feeding on lies, that
we can't

64.34 ... in death.] At the time of original composition Mark Twain
deleted a continuation:

What a poor little creature he is, with his airs and his importance, and his
wise cogitations about his Maker and the hereafter. Whereas if one would

The second fragment breaks off here.

8.   [LETTER FROM THE RECORDING ANGEL]

The present text is based upon an untitled manuscript, DV 53, the
only phase under Mark Twain's control. He could hardly have written
the satire after September 1887. A canceled fragment of A *Connecticut*

Yankee, DV22, paged 371–396, contains many of its passages, and by 15 August Mark Twain had completed 350 pages: see Howard G. Baetzhold, "The Course of Composition of *A Connecticut Yankee*: A Reinterpretation," *American Literature* 33, no. 2 (May 1961): 199. The manuscript of the present work was earlier, for it was revised to the text represented by fair copy in the *Yankee* fragment. Baetzhold thinks Mark Twain wrote the "Letter" in August (p. 203), reasoning from a notebook entry in that month which mentions profits of J. Langdon & Company, an entry Dixon Wecter cited to prove that Mark Twain resented Andrew Langdon's share of the profits. But since Langdon did not share in them (see the Explanatory Notes) this argument does not hold. The only reliable earliest date is the one Mark Twain used in the manuscript—20 January. He refers to December profits of Langdon's own company and to other circumstances suggesting that the season of his point of view was winter. His reference to the quarter just ended as "forty years later" than the quarter ending 31 December 1847 need not weaken the case for 20 January 1887, because he often gave such figures in round numbers and often miscalculated them. The paper (Keystone Linen), ink, and handwriting are consistent with a wide range of dates in the 1880s.

The title in the present edition, now standard, was DeVoto's invention for the first printing in *Harper's Magazine,* February 1946. Earlier he had prepared the text for publication as "Letter to the Earth," with Abner Scofield (the name in the *Yankee* fragment) in place of Andrew Langdon. This version was suppressed until publication of *LE* in 1962.

Three misspellings have been corrected, "dipththeria" [diphtheria] (65.18), "incerease" [increase] (66.10), and "nickle" [nickel] (70.2). A period has been supplied after "3" [3.] (65.15) and hyphens in "to wit" [to-wit] (66.32) and "Prayer Meeting" [Prayer-Meeting] (68.6). Mark Twain inserted "—for" (69.31) but left "You" in upper case; the word is now in lower case.

Previous printings: Bernard DeVoto, "Letter from the Recording Angel," *Harper's Magazine* 192, no. 1149 (February 1946): 106–109; *RP,* pp. 87–94; *Mark Twain: A Laurel Reader,* ed. Edmund Fuller (New York: Dell, 1958), pp. 361–366; *The Complete Essays of Mark Twain,* ed. Charles Neider (Garden City: Doubleday, 1963), pp. 685–689 (hereafter listed as Neider); as "Letter to the Earth," *LE,* pp. 117–122.

9.   [BIBLE TEACHING AND RELIGIOUS PRACTICE]

The present text is based upon an incomplete manuscript, DV354, the only phase under Mark Twain's control. On the first page Paine inscribed "written in 1890," a date supported by hand and paper. The green-tinted unwatermarked laid paper, 5½″ x 9″, often occurs around 1890—in at least two speeches of the late 1880s, correspondence from 1889 through 1891, part of *A Connecticut Yankee*, and all of *The American Claimant*.

The title is in Paine's hand. At the top left of the first page Mark Twain wrote "Bible-sick"; but if he was following his usual procedure, this was merely a reminder to use the word or notion in the article (compare "religion-sick" at 71.16). The manuscript ends with a broken sentence—". . . that if man"—at the bottom of a page. On the back of that page Paine completed it: "continues in the direction of enlightenment, his religious practice may, in the end, attain some semblance of human decency." That this was Paine's invention is evident from his erasing "continues to improve his religious practice" and substituting "continues in the direction of enlightenment."

First printed, as completed by Paine, in *Europe*, pp. 387–393; reprinted in 29Z: 387–393; derivative texts in Smith, pp. 41–45; Neider, pp. 568–572.

10.   [MACFARLANE]

The present text is based upon a manuscript, DV274, the only phase under Mark Twain's control. At the top of the first page Paine inscribed "written about 1898" (see 1MTA: 143). The phrase "about 1898" suggests he picked that year because he thought the work belonged with the brief autobiographical sketches Mark Twain wrote in 1897 and 1898, but the paper is not like that of the sketches. It is a white laid stationery torn into half-sheets normally measuring 4½″ x 7″, with an elaborate watermark: "Regina | Note | [*company emblem*]" and "Victoria | [*portrait of Victoria*] | Regina." Paper with this water-

mark has been found only in correspondence and manuscripts (for example, *Joan of Arc*) of 1894–1895. At the top of the first leaf, after
writing at least that page of "Macfarlane," Mark Twain wrote a reminder: "Coit? was that the name at Angel's Camp? No, Coon." Possibly he inscribed this note while preparing "The Private History of
the 'Jumping Frog' Story," which mentions Ben Coon (though not by
name) and which appeared in the *North American Review* for April
1894. The manuscript stops so abruptly as to seem incomplete, but it
ends at mid-page with a completed sentence.

The title appears to be in Paine's hand. He also inscribed two
emendations, the first disregarded and the other adopted in the present
text: "made" (76.3) to "made up" and "placid" to "placidly" (77.4).
Paine's other emendations first appeared in his edition of the autobiography; compare 1MTA: 143–147. The present text emends the solid
compound "boardinghouse" [boarding house] (77.9) in accordance
with Mark Twain's style elsewhere in "Macfarlane": compare 76.2 and
78.7.

First printed in 1MTA: 143–147; reprinted in 36Z: 143–147; in part:
The Autobiography of Mark Twain, ed. Charles Neider (New York:
Harper, 1959), pp. 95–97.

11.   CONTRACT WITH MRS. T. K. BEECHER

The present text is based upon three stone fragments Mark Twain
inscribed for Mrs. Beecher in 1895, the only phase known to have been
under his control. He had just begun his world lecture tour of 1895–
1896, and was somewhere between Crookston, Minnesota, and Butte,
Montana, when the poem appeared in the New York *Tribune* for 31
July 1895. Rev. Beecher or Mrs. Beecher was probably responsible for
this publication, and no known subsequent printing suggests Mark
Twain's return to the text. For accounts of composition see the New
York *Tribune,* 31 July 1895, p. 6; *MTB*, p. 1001; and *Parade,* 18 November 1962, p. 17. The "manuscript" is an ovoid stone split length-
wise into three pieces, the center piece containing stanza III on one
side and the title and date (Elmira, 2 July 1895) on the other. The

fragments remained in the Beecher home near Quarry Farm for many years and were finally donated to Elmira College in September 1962. The present text supplies periods after "face" (79.5) and "message" (79.12). The pronoun "his" [His] (79.6) referring to God has been capitalized.

Earliest known printing: New York *Tribune*, 31 July 1895, p. 6; text derivative of the *Tribune*: *Munsey's Magazine* 14, no. 1 (October 1895): 117; text revised probably by Paine: *MTB*, p. 1002; text set from the stone fragments: *Parade*, 18 November 1962, p. 17.

12. [MAN'S PLACE IN THE ANIMAL WORLD]

The present text is based upon a manuscript, DV11, the only phase under Mark Twain's control. He began it around 13 August 1896 and completed it about two months later; for details of composition see Paul Baender, "The Date of Mark Twain's 'The Lowest Animal,' " *American Literature* 36, no. 2 (May 1964): 174–179. The paper is of two kinds, a white laid (80.1–88.23, "rotting him") and a dark gray, heavy wove stationery (88.23, "killing him"-end), both unwatermarked and both torn into half-sheets respectively measuring 5" x 8" and 4⅜" x 6". The first leaf is lost, but it apparently contained only the title and the "telegrams" Mark Twain mentions in the text. De-Voto invented the title—"The Lowest Animal"—used in *LE*. The present title is a Mark Twain inscription on a manila envelope (DV127) dating from about 1896. The inscription seems to have been a title for a manuscript, possibly of the present work, once kept in the envelope. DeVoto's text is in *LE*, pp. 222–232; an excerpt of his text appeared in *Life*, 28 September 1962, pp. 121–122.

The manuscript leaves five alternative readings unresolved (the first words in the pairs are on the line, the second are off the line): "deeply"-"scientifically" (81.1), "never"-"not" (84.11), "were"-"was" (86.8), "He"-"The F" [The Frenchman] (87.14), and "festering offal"-"pestilent corruption" (88.19). Both alternative readings at 81.1 and "profoundly" in line 3 were deleted in pencil (the manuscript is in ink) in a way not characteristic of Mark Twain. Evidently DeVoto canceled them when preparing his edition. The present text keeps "profoundly" and selects "scientifically," "never," "was," "The Frenchman," and "festering offal" of the alternative readings.

Mark Twain inserted "But" (83.17) and "And" (84.26), leaving "So" and "He" in upper case; the latter are now in lower case. The present text capitalizes "defect" [Defect] (86.18; compare the text at 86.17 and 86.20), supplies a hyphen in "to wit" (81.22), and corrects "unpintable" to "unprintable" (88.14) and "bacilii" to "bacilli" (88.20).

The items that follow were Mark Twain's major revisions:

89.1 ... mistake.] The sentence originally concluded a paragraph on manuscript p. 28. It was followed on the remainder of the page:

Certain functions lodged in the other sex perform in a lamentably inferior way as compared with the performance of the same functions in the Higher Animals. In the human being, menstruation, gestation and parturition are terms which stand for horrors. In the Higher Animals these things are hardly even inconveniences.

Above this paragraph, as a continuation of the previous, Mark Twain then inserted the passage beginning "What is his beard. . . ." and ending ". . . it won't stay." (p. 28A). He next clipped off the paragraph quoted above, numbered it 28B to follow the sentence ending ". . . it won't stay." and attached it to a full half-sheet. At an undetermined point he wrote an alternative p. 28B on the back of this half-sheet:

Man is always admiring himself, always assuring himself that he is a wonder.

Before clipping off and numbering the first paragraph quoted above, Mark Twain wrote the present remainder of the paragraph following ". . . it won't stay." on a page originally numbered 28B. He changed it to 28C, probably after the quoted paragraph became p. 28B and probably as a continuation of that paragraph. Then he decided to suppress the quoted paragraph and its alternative, for he wrote "Run to 28C" at the bottom of p. 28A and "Run to 29" at the bottom of p. 28C. In pencil another hand—almost certainly DeVoto—wrote "Insert 28B" after the paragraph ending ". . . it has never seen." on p. 28C. At this point the first p. 28B quoted above appears in *LE*, p. 231.

13.   [SOMETHING ABOUT REPENTANCE]

The present text is based upon a manuscript, DV234, probably the only phase under Mark Twain's control. Two typescripts prepared in his lifetime are extant, yet neither shows correction or revision other than Paine's. On one of them Paine wrote "dictated in 1908," but it is merely a copy of the manuscript. The manuscript paper is a light double-ruled stationery of European manufacture which Mark Twain occasionally used in 1897–1898.

The present title is in Paine's hand in the typescript "dictated in 1908." It is preferred over "Repentance," which heads the manuscript in a hand other than Mark Twain's, because Paine may have been instructed to add it and because "Repentance" seems to be only a designation of subject. Mark Twain changed "minds." to "minds; but" (90.10), leaving "When" in upper case; the word is now in lower case.

Previous printing: *LE*, pp. 167–168.

14.   CORN-PONE OPINIONS

The present text is based upon a manuscript, Box 28 no. 7, probably the only phase under Mark Twain's control. A typescript possibly prepared in his lifetime is extant, but it lacks his correction and revision. The manuscript paper is a cream, unwatermarked wove, normally measuring $5\frac{3}{4}''$ x $9''$, from one of the tablets (in this instance possibly "Pratt's Greater New York Tablet") Mark Twain often used after his return to America in 1900. Paper from all tablets mentioned hereafter is unwatermarked wove. An entry in Mark Twain's 1901 notebook reads: "Thur. Jan. 31, 1901 Hoecake opinions (bread-and-butter) on religion and politics" (Notebook 34, TS p. 5). Later he wrote a marginal note on a clipping from the New York *Herald* for 18 February 1901: "Broadly speaking corn-pone stands for self-approval. Self-approval is acquired mainly from the approval of others. Conformity is the result. Corn-pone is Confor. Sometimes it has a sordid business interest back of it and is calculated; but mainly it is unconscious and not calculated" (Documents File, MTP). Mark Twain's opening reference—"Fifty years ago. . . ."—and his allusion to a recent election (the presidential election of 1900) indicate composition near the time of these notes.

In the manuscript an unknown hand, probably Paine, canceled in pencil (the manuscript is in ink) the last paragraph and the last word of the penultimate paragraph. Both items were omitted in the typescript, but both are retained in the present text. A period has been supplied after "tainted" (97.15).

First printed, as abridged by Paine, in *Europe*, pp. 399–406; reprinted in 29Z: 399–406; texts derivative of *Europe* in *The Family Mark Twain* (New York: Harper, 1935), pp. 1400–1403; *The Portable Mark Twain*, ed. Bernard DeVoto (New York: Viking, 1946), pp. 572–578; Smith, pp. 21–26; Neider, pp. 583–587.

15.   THE FIVE BOONS OF LIFE

No manuscript discovered. The present text is based upon the first printing in *Harper's Weekly*, 5 July 1902 (copies at the University of Iowa, University of Texas). Other printings in Mark Twain's lifetime show only variation in format, notably in heading the sections "Chapter I," etc., rather than "I," etc.

The title appears by itself in a notebook of 1897 (Notebook 32B, TS p. 36). Nearly five years later, 11 June 1902, Mark Twain wrote a more extensive note: "*The 5 Boons—death the best.* Remains unchosen —later they come one after the other and beg for it. Make each a separate tale. Beauty, Fame, Riches, Long Life, Death. (Wife and children?)" (Notebook 35, TS p. 17). A canceled beginning, with notes, is on the back of manuscript p. 86 of "Tom Sawyer's Conspiracy":

In the morning of life came the good fairy with her basket, and said—
"Here are gifts. Choose cautiously, choose wisely, for only one is
valuable. You may take but one at this time. Be wary; remember, only one
of them is precious.["]
Death, pleasure, love, fame, riches (which is power)
Old age. Men think it a benefaction—it is an insult.

Printings in Mark Twain's lifetime: "The Five Boons of Life," *Harper's Weekly* 46, no. 2376 (5 July 1902): 866; *The $30,000 Bequest
and Other Stories* (New York and London: Harper, 1906, BAL 3492),
pp. 160–165; *The $30,000 Bequest* . . . (Leipzig: Bernhard Tauchnitz,
1907, BAL 3671), pp. 130–135; *The $30,000 Bequest* . . . , in *The
Writings of Mark Twain*, "Autograph Edition" (Hartford: American
Publishing Company, 1907, BAL 3456), 24: 160–165. Modern printings: 24Z: 218–223; *The Complete Short Stories of Mark Twain*, ed.
Charles Neider (Garden City: Hanover House, 1957), pp. 470–472;
The Mysterious Stranger and Other Stories, ed. Edmund Reiss (New
York: New American Library, 1962), pp. 138–140.

16.   "WAS THE WORLD MADE FOR MAN?"

The present text is based upon a manuscript, DV12, the only
phase under Mark Twain's control. External evidence (see the Explanatory Notes) suggests composition around April 1903, and the
hand and paper (from a "Par Value" tablet; see *What Is Man?* table
below, item 5) are consistent with this date. Contrary to Mark Twain's
practice the title is in quotes in the manuscript, evidently to indicate
that the question was not so much his own as one of current interest.
In December 1903 Howells humorously recommended to him Alfred
Russel Wallace's *Man's Place in the Universe*, not knowing that he
was already aware of Wallace's argument (*MTHL*, p. 776). No reply
from Mark Twain is extant.

The only previous printing was in *LE*, pp. 211–216. The present
text selects "scientist" (103.4) from an unresolved alternative reading,
"man"-"scientist"; "prepation" has been corrected to "preparation"
(103.12).

The item that follows was Mark Twain's only major revision:

101.1   Headed by the second epigraph, a canceled beginning reads:

Land, it is just for the world the way I feel about it myself, sometimes, even when dry. And when not dry, even those warm words are not nearly warm enough to get up to what I am feeling, when I am holding on to something, and blinking affectionately at myself in the glass, and recollecting that I'm it.

And when I am feeling historical, there is nothing that ecstatifies me like hunting the Chief Love and Delight of God around and around just here on this tiny earth and watching him perform. I watch him progressing and progressing—always progressing—always mounting higher and higher, sometimes by means of the Inquisition, sometimes by means of the Terror, sometimes by eight hundred years of witch-burning, sometimes by help of a St. Bartholomew's, sometimes by spreading hell and civilization in China, sometimes by preserving and elevating the same at home by a million soldiers and a thousand battleships; and when he gets down to to-day I still look at him spread out over a whole page of the morning paper, grabbing in Congress, grabbing in Albany, grabbing in New York and St. Louis and all around, lynching the innocent, slabbering hypocrisies, reeking, dripping, unsavory, but always recognizable as the same old Most Sublime Existence in all the range of Non-Divine Being, the Chief Love and Delight of God; and then I am more gladder than ever that I am it.

This passage has twice been published separately, as though it were an independent work (*MTE*, pp. 383–384; and Smith, p. 68). But the following points show that it is a canceled fragment from the present manuscript:

(1) Manuscript p. 1 of " 'Was the World made for Man?' " contains the title, both epigraphs, and a fair copy of the first paragraph above, crowded at the bottom of the leaf and then deleted.

(2) The passage quoted above occupies two full leaves, numbered 2 and 3 at top center; the second epigraph is at the head of p. 2.

(3) The first four and a half paragraphs of " 'Was the World made for Man?' " occupy two full leaves, first numbered 2 and 3 at top left (all subsequent pages in the manuscript are also numbered at top left), then 3A and 3B, then 2 and 3 again at top center.

Mark Twain evidently wrote the piece with only the first epigraph and the present text. After writing it he noticed the passage that became the second epigraph (later in the *Literary Digest* article), put it at the head of deleted p. 2, and wrote the quoted fragment as a new beginning. To avoid renumbering all subsequent pages he changed original pp. 2 and 3 to 3A and 3B. Then he decided to cancel the insertion but to keep the second epigraph, which he copied under the first on p. 1. Pages 3A and 3B became 2 and 3 again. Then he chose to keep the first paragraph of the canceled insertion and crowded it at the bottom of p. 1. Finally he canceled this paragraph also, leaving the original text but with the addition of the second epigraph.

17.   GOD

The present text is based upon a manuscript, DV9, the only phase under Mark Twain's control. The paper is from a "Pratt's Greater New York Tablet." The date of composition is probably 1905, for Mark Twain's script follows the long dimension of the leaves (see description of Supplement A7). The present title is Mark Twain's; DeVoto invented the title for the only previous publication (*LE*, pp. 220–222), "The Intelligence of God." In pencil an unknown hand, probably DeVoto, inscribed brackets around the sixth sentence of the first paragraph. The sentence does not appear in *LE*. Mark Twain inserted "Daily" (107.8) but left "We" in upper case; the word is now in lower case. A period has been supplied after "exceptions" (108.35).

18.   As CONCERNS INTERPRETING THE DEITY

The present text is based upon Mark Twain's final holographic text, a manuscript (Paine 186) together with revisions he inscribed in a typescript prepared by Jean Clemens. In the manuscript the lines of writing again follow the long dimension of "Pratt's" tablet leaves. Mark Twain dated the manuscript June 1905 and the typescript "Summer-end" of 1905. The title in the manuscript is "Interpreting the Deity"; Mark Twain changed it to the present title in the typescript. See the Explanatory Notes for an account of the Egyptian and Dighton Rock "inscriptions."

First printed, revised and abridged by Paine, in *WIM*, pp. 265–274; reprinted in 26Z: 265–274; text derivative of *WIM*: Neider, pp. 523–529.

NOTES

The following notes include Mark Twain's major deletions in the manuscript; Mark Twain's revisions in the typescript; Paine's emendations of the typescript for his edition in *WIM*; and editorial changes in the present text.

Present text readings are at the left. Where the symbol MS follows a reading at the right, the present text reading is Mark Twain's revision in the typescript and the one at the right is the superseded manuscript reading. Where readings for both manuscript and typescript follow a present text reading, that of the present text is editorial, and if the typescript reading differs from the manuscript, it is Mark Twain's revision in the typescript. Where the symbol P follows a reading at the right, the rejected reading is Paine's inscription in the typescript. The symbol DP after a present text reading indicates a Paine deletion. A curved dash ($\sim$) stands for the word before or after the punctuation of the present text.

110.20–26	But the scholars. . . . *restricted to the clergy.*] DP
110.25–26	*decree of the Holy Synod*] decree MS
113.22	The] "$\sim$ MS, TS
113.24	quarter.] $\sim$." MS, TS
114.2	H. H.'s and] DP
114.6–20	Meantime, the remains. . . . *Huntingdon,* p. 262.] DP
114.21	This is] His was P
114.22–115.4	It is. . . . of the conditions.] DP
115.17	King] "$\sim$ TS

115.19   pregnant] DP

115.25   living.] MS ~." TS

115.27   Then] MS "~ TS

115.29   cobweb.] MS ~." TS

116.10   In] MS "~ TS

116.21   ages!] MS ~!" TS

116.28–32   I could sit. . . . different, I think.] DP

116.32   his] a man's P

117.2   fry,] ~ DP

117.8   . . . I get so little time.] *In the manuscript Mark Twain
                deleted a passage that followed the cue words:*

Here is the rest of that incident:
    While that Abbey was converted into a fortress, blood exuded from
the walls of the church and the cloister adjoining, witnessing the divine
indignation, and prognosticating the destruction of the impious. This was
seen by many persons, and I observed it with my own eyes. How then can
the wicked say that the Almighty sleeps? He woke indeed in this sign, and
that which it signified.
    He is just as certain about that as if it happened yesterday. But it does
not convince me.

117.22   . . . the] ". . . ~ MS

117.26   end;] ~." MS ~;" TS

117.30   Anyway, it has gone out, now, thanks be.] DP

117.32   Robert F.] He MS

118.12   . . . about] MS ". . . ~ TS

118.17   pass.] ~." MS

118.21   thirteen hundred] about thirteen hundred MS

118.22   Has the trade. . . .] *Paine indicated that this sentence
                of the text should begin a paragraph. Later he changed*

> *the text more radically, for in* WIM *his text ends with the preceding sentence.*

118.31   GOD BEHIND THIS WAR.] *Before deleting this section of the text Paine added a footnote to the headline:* "The Russo-Japanese—but of equal timeliness today applied to divine explanations of the Turko-Bulgarian conflict." *This last reference places the note in 1912–1913.*

119.16   fly] burst MS

119.32   Brooklyn praise. . . .] *Before deleting the section Paine canceled the paragraph ending here. He also changed* "me" (120.2) *to* "I."

120.4   God's] "~ MS

120.5   destroyed.] ~." MS

120.9   . . . centuries overdue.] *In the typescript Mark Twain deleted a footnote to this sentence of the text, cited here from the correct version in the manuscript:*

*And it is after the wrong party, anyway. The Czar and his Grand Dukes are the only oppressors, and nothing is happening to them: *they* don't go to the front to fight and get slaughtered, they stay at home and send the oppressed peasants to the butchery.

19.   IN THE ANIMAL'S COURT

The present text is based upon a manuscript, DV8, the only phase under Mark Twain's control. The paper is from a "Pratt's" tablet and the script placement is the same as for "God" and "As Concerns Interpreting the Deity"; the date of composition is probably 1905. Paine wrote "Gospel" at the top of the first leaf, meaning that the piece was a fragment of *What Is Man?*, but Mark Twain did not indicate where or whether it was to be inserted in the dialogue. The present text supplies "to" in "to say" (123.4), omitted in the manuscript.

Previous printing: LE, pp. 216–218.

20.   WHAT IS MAN?

All of the several pre-publication phases of *What Is Man?* (1906) survive except printer's proof: the first draft (1898), manuscripts added during the years 1898–1905, two passages Mark Twain dictated to his secretary, Isabel V. Lyon, and three typescripts in lineal descent, the last used as printer's copy for the first edition, and all containing Mark Twain's holograph revisions.

The development of *What Is Man?* was possibly the most intricate, and is surely the most amply documented, in Mark Twain's career. In 1898 he wrote what became the first two chapters, parts of chapters 4 and 5, and nearly half of the present chapter 6. At that time these were contiguous and in different positions. What became chapter 2 was chapter 1, and chapter 1 was chapter 2. Parts of what became chapters 4 and 5 followed as the conclusion of the original chapter 2, and what became part of chapter 6 was chapter 3. Also in 1898 he wrote "The Moral Sense" and "The Quality of Man" as chapters 4 and 5, which he later deleted. Upon completing this stint he had a typescript prepared (called the Vienna typescript in this summary), though "The Quality of Man" may not have reached this stage. For Mark Twain subsequently tore off "The Moral Sense" and all that may have followed it, and whereas "The Moral Sense" turns up in a later typescript, "The Quality of Man" does not.

He next wrote "Instances in Point" (but not "Further Instances") and a segment called "Notes upon Training. The Admonition," which originally made up a single manuscript paged 1–38. Later he decided to separate them. Using the Vienna typescript as the basis for his next typescript, he wrote at the end of chapter 1 (present chapter 2): "Here insert 'Instances in Point,' " and at the end of chapter 2: "Here insert 'Notes upon Training. The Admonition.' " Shortly after writing these sections he wrote "Further about Training," paged as a continuation, 39–41. To this he attached the section containing "A Parable" as still another continuation. The latter manuscript has its own pagination, 1–8, and he may have written it before returning to America in 1900. The other additions all date from the fall of 1901 at the earliest, since the novel he criticizes at the beginning of "Instances in Point" was first published in that season. The topic of "Further about Training" suggests he completed these additions around February 1902 (see note to 173.25, below).

The next stage was the preparation of another typescript (hereafter called the second typescript), based on the Vienna typescript and the later additions. It included the first stint of manuscript ("The Moral Sense" appears here but not "The Quality of Man"), the additions just described, and three pages of manuscript (the "Keno" fragment; see note to 133.14, below) inserted in the Vienna typescript. After the second typescript was prepared Mark Twain corrected errors and made minor changes, but there was one gross mistake he may not have caught until it was repeated in the preparation of the printer's copy. This was the duplication of "Notes upon Training. The Admonition," "Further about Training," and a segment containing "A Parable." What happened was that the typist, upon reading his instruction at the end of chapter 1 in the Vienna typescript, copied all these additions, which were evidently grouped together with "Instances in Point," then copied them again upon reading his instruction at the end of chapter 2. It is not certain when Mark Twain had this typescript prepared, but in 1907 he recollected that he finished *What Is Man?* in 1902. His writing the preface on the cover in February 1905, some time after he wrote even the latest manuscript represented in this typescript, also implies that he once considered it a final version, notwithstanding the duplicate passage. But the second typescript was merely the last complete instance of the early phase.

In 1905, after February, Mark Twain ordered still another typescript, and it commenced as another form of this phase, based upon the second typescript. But before it was completed he began the series of revisions that would produce nearly the text as published. Keeping the new pages but renumbering them, he transposed the first two chapters and determined their final substance, deleting long passages from the beginning of each and reserving portions of the new chapter

1 for chapters 4 and 5. He retitled the new first chapter from "Personal Merit" to "a. *Man the Machine*. b. *Personal Merit*." Chapter 2, originally untitled, became *"Man's Sole Impulse—The Securing of His Own Approval."* The latter was part of his systematic revision of the new chapter 2, the substitution of "spiritual comfort" and similar terms for "selfishness." And at the end of chapter 1 he replaced the "Keno" fragment with a more suitable transition to what now followed it. "Instances in Point," which had been part of the previous chapter, became chapter 3, with the addition of "Further Instances." A portion of the original chapter 2 introduced what now became chapter 4, followed by "Notes upon Training. The Admonition," "Further about Training," and the "Parable" segment, but Mark Twain deleted "Further about Training" after it was typed again. Two other portions of the old chapter 2 introduced and concluded chapter 5. Between them he put "After an Interval of Days," which was appearing in typescript for the first time although he had written the beginning of it earlier. Roughly the second half of this section was a continuation dating from 1905, and he dictated the preface of the chapter to Miss Lyon in September 1905.

Chapter 6 illustrates the additive process by which Mark Twain built up the dialogue as a whole. For the first part, almost down to the "Free Will" section, he used the material that constituted chapter 3— "Instinct and Thought"—in the original version. With "Free Will" he turned to a long manuscript which also included "A Difficult Question" and "Conclusion." This was a 1905 manuscript, but he had already prepared a typescript of it, paged 1–50, as though he did not immediately know where it might best belong. After repaging the "Free Will" typescript he inserted in manuscript "Not Two Values, But Only One," numbered to follow "Free Will." Upon repaging the rest of the typescript he placed "The Master Passion," another 1905 manuscript, after "A Difficult Question" and titled the remainder "Conclusion."

A descriptive table now follows for possible clarification of the composition to this point. Page numbers of manuscript written in 1898 are in roman type, all subsequent additions in italics. Words in column one indicate the beginning and conclusion of passages in the text that correspond to manuscripts in the second column, but these cue words do not necessarily indicate the first and last words on the manuscript page.

Present Text	*Manuscript*	*Description*
1. 124	*Preface*	In Mark Twain's hand on cover of second typescript; typed in printer's copy.
2. 125.5–133.13 (OLD MAN. What are . . . credit for it?)	26–47	Begins chapter 1, originally chapter 2; portions deleted from beginning and conclusion after transposition. Synopsis (125.1–4) added in proof. Paper for this and parts of items 4 and 7 a slick buff lightweight double-ruled stationery, wove and unwatermarked, torn into half-sheets normally measuring 5⅝″ x 8⅝″.
3. 133.14–134.7 (O.M. Your question . . . from it.)	20–22	Substitution for "Keno" fragment, following reversal of first two chapters. Script follows long dimension of leaves, indicating composition in 1905. Cream tablet paper, possibly "Pratt's," for this and items 6, 10, 13–14, 17–21.
4. 135.1–147.17 (O.M. There have been . . . you think.)	3–22G	Chapter 2, originally chapter 1; portion deleted from beginning after transposition. Pages 3–21, 22E–G on double-ruled stationery as above. Pages 22, 22A–D (141.21–143.17, "exasperating") and 0, 1–10 (143.17, "A while"–146.32) are on a white unwatermarked lightweight wove paper in half-sheets normally measuring 5¾″ x 9″. Items 11, 15, and 16 are on the same sort of paper.

Present Text	Manuscript	Description

5. 148.1–154.26
(O.M. Have you
... transaction.)

1–18

Begins chapter 3; "Instances in Point." This and items 8 and 12 are on "Par Value" tablet paper—the leaves slick and gray, normally measuring $5^{11}\!/_{16}''$ x $8^{15}\!/_{16}''$.

6. 154.27–157.3
(Y.M. Well, to
... and training.)

66–73

"Further Instances"; manuscript inserted in printer's copy, numbered to follow pagination of printer's copy after revisions of previous portion of typescript. Script follows long dimension.

7. 161.1–165.18
(Y.M. You keep
... concerned.)

49–60

Begins chapter 4, originally part of chapter 2 (present chapter 1). Double-ruled paper as above, except for pp. 53A (162.22, "They"–163.2, "impossible") and 60 (165.12, "thing"–165.18), which are on white wove paper as above.

8. 165.19–173.24
(Y.M. You have ...
community.)

19–38

Segment containing "Notes upon Training. The Admonition"; originally followed "Instances in Point."

9. 173.25–175.29
(Y.M. One's *every*
... quicksilver.)

1–8

Segment containing "A Parable"; "Further about Training" originally preceded this segment but was deleted in printer's copy. White unwatermarked laid paper torn into half-sheets normally measuring 5″ x 8″.

10. 176.1–10

Note

Preface to chapter 5, in hand of Miss Lyon.

Present Text	Manuscript	Description
11. 176.11–177.11 (Y.M. You really ... talk.)	60–63	Begins chapter 5, originally chapter 2 (present chapter 1). Last sentence of this section added in second typescript.
12. 177.13–179.34 (O.M. Now, dreams ... machine.)	111–118	"After an Interval of Days," written in 1904 at the latest, perhaps in 1902; numbered to follow "The Moral Sense," which is paged 102–110, and which Mark Twain deleted in 1904 (*MTE*, p. 242).
13. 179.34–182.24 (Have you ... product.)	118A–J	Continuation of preceding section, typed for the first time in printer's copy. Script follows long dimension.
14. 182.25–182.29 (Y.M. You really ... engine?)	119	Late copy and revision of material on manuscript p. 63, to serve as bridge between manuscript pp. 118J and 64. Script follows long dimension.
15. 182.30–185.13 (O.M. It takes ... approaches.)	64–70	Originally part of chapter 2 (present chapter 1).
16. 189.1–198.31 (Y.M. It is ... that.)	71–101	Begins chapter 6; constituted all of chapter 3 as late as the second typescript. Remaining portion of section, down to "Free Will," added in SLC to Frank N. Doubleday, 25 May 1906.
17. 199.5–201.35 (Y.M. What is ... decide.)	1–8	"Free Will," a late addition; begins segment of typescript originally numbered 1–50. Script follows long dimension.

Present Text	Manuscript	Description
18. 202.1–203.18 (Y.M. There is . . . worthless.)	156–160	"Not Two Values, But Only One"; manuscript inserted in printer's copy and paged according to it.
19. 203.19–206.2 (Y.M. You keep . . . else.)	9–16	"A Difficult Question"; continuation of manuscript begun with "Free Will"; script follows long dimension.
20. 206.3–207.29 (Y.M. What is . . . made.)	1–5	"The Master Passion"; manuscript inserted in printer's copy; script follows long dimension.
21. 207.30–214.3 (O.M. You have . . . troubled.)	16–35	"Conclusion"; originally continuous with "A Difficult Question"; script follows long dimension.

Each time an author's work is copied, the opportunities both for authorial revision and for unauthorized alterations (by typists, editors, and compositors) are multiplied. Recognizing this condition, modern editorial theory stipulates that an editor should choose forms of a work which most nearly embody the author's final textual intentions as to "substantives" (words and word order) and "accidentals" (paragraphing, punctuation, and word forms). If a work without surviving manuscript was set in type more than once, an editor normally chooses the earliest printing as his authority for the accidentals, since these are most liable to corruption in resetting and since the earliest printing generally must be regarded as closest in its accidentals to those of the lost manuscript. A printing so chosen is by convention termed the "copy-text." If later printings contain substantive or accidental variants which appear to represent authorial revision, an editor readily accepts them as emendations of the copy-text, since the choice of copy-text is independent of the question as to final substantive authority. If a manuscript survives, normally it is chosen as copy-text, and substantive

variants in the first and any later typesettings are accepted as emendations insofar as they appear to represent authorial revision.[1]

The preservation of several stages of composition for works like
What Is Man? and the next work in this volume, *Christian Science*,
introduces certain problems in the choice of copy-text. From his earliest
career, Mark Twain's habit was to pigeonhole work, resurrect it, recast
it, and rewrite it, for as long as circumstances gave him the opportunity.
His writing remained provisional until it was published. Before the
1880s, when he began to employ typists, his revisions were normally
incorporated into single manuscripts. He discarded superseded pages,
moved pages about, and integrated new pages—so that many of the
stages through which his work passed can no longer be reconstructed.
His use of the typewriter provided him with a more convenient means
for incorporating extensive revisions: his manuscripts became provisional drafts and the typescripts not so much potential printer's copy
as cleaner copy on which he could continue the process of revision more
conveniently than on the manuscript. Since the stages remained separate physical entities, the complete record often survives for the course
of composition of such works.

What Is Man? clearly illustrates this process. The initial manuscript covers only a portion of the text which Mark Twain finally sent
to his printer. Each typescript underwent extensive revision, including
shifts in order, the insertion of new holograph pages, and the deletion
of typed pages, in addition to changes of typed readings. Also, his
typists made mistakes, and Mark Twain revised the typescripts usually
without noticing the new readings produced by transcription error and
sophistication. The survival of an initial manuscript and later typescripts, more or less revised, thus means that no one form of the text is
both complete and completely authorial. The initial manuscript and
the intermediate typescripts lack Mark Twain's subsequent revisions.
The final typescript contains almost all the additions, in their latest

---

1. The common source of these principles is W. W. Greg, "The Rationale of
Copy-Text," *Studies in Bibliography* 3 (1950): 19–36. The substance of Greg's
theory is expressed in two key sentences: "The true theory is, I contend, that the
copy-text should govern (generally) in the matter of accidentals, but that the choice
between substantive readings belongs to the general theory of textual criticism and
lies altogether beyond the narrow principle of the copy-text. Thus it may happen
that in a critical edition the text rightly chosen as copy may not by any means be
the one that supplies most substantive readings in cases of variation" (p. 26).

order, and contains holograph revisions; but it also contains hundreds of transcription errors—the many originating in that typescript and the many others which had escaped the author's notice in the earlier typescripts.

Attempting to apply Greg's theory to a work thus complicated, one may designate the copy-text in four ways. Readings in the edited work would not be affected by any of the designations, but only one of them is fully appropriate.

(1) One may choose the initial manuscript as copy-text. These pages embody only slightly more than half of the text as printed, and they were later revised and reordered. By the logic of this choice all subsequent expansions, deletions, shifts in order, and verbal revisions in the typescripts would have to be listed as emendations—even though the author himself made them in pre-publication stages of the work. Such a list of emendations would present, in addition to its bulk, an insuperable practical problem, for the course of composition of *What Is Man?* was so elaborate and remains so fully documented that it cannot be encompassed in tabular form.[2] Moreover, the welter of detail would obscure the editor's genuine emendations—his rejection of known or inferred errors and his acceptance of variants he judges to be the author's revisions in missing proof stages.

(2) One may take the initial manuscript, reorder it into the arrangement of the corresponding sections in the final typescript, integrate into it the holograph pages which Mark Twain inserted in all the typescripts, and call the whole a "final manuscript," although the manuscript so produced would be one that never existed as a separate entity during the course of composition. Designating this synthetic manuscript as copy-text would limit the size of the emendations list. The editor would have to record there all the short verbal changes Mark Twain inscribed in the typescripts, but he could dispense with listing the many pages which were added, deleted, or shifted in the typescripts. The great liability is that this synthetic manuscript suggests that revisions inscribed on the typescripts have a different status from pages inserted in or deleted from the typescripts. The only difference between them is their length; Mark Twain often made the shorter revisions at the same time new passages were drafted, or altered a type-

2. Thus a full listing of Mark Twain's alterations, ordinarily a component of a definitive edition, is impossible in this volume.

script to make it cohere with a new addition, or was led to insert new manuscript material from having made short revisions on a typescript page. To treat the new pages as part of the "manuscript" and the typescript revisions that prompted or accompanied them as "emendations" would misrepresent the actual way the text grew.

(3) One may designate the printer's copy typescript as copy-text. To do so, however, would necessitate listing all corrections of typing errors in this and the other typescripts as emendations. Since there are hundreds of such errors in the *What Is Man?* typescripts, the true emendations which the editor seeks to provide his readers would again be obscured, here in the interest of giving information which is for the most part of no textual significance.[3]

(4) While there are serious objections to all three of these possible choices, there remains a fourth way of applying Greg's theory to *What Is Man?* and to other works for which no single document may satisfactorily serve as copy-text. This way, the one taken in the present volume, is to designate the author's final inscription as copy-text, whether it is located in the initial manuscript, in added manuscript pages, or in holograph changes on either manuscript or typed pages, together with Miss Lyon's transcription of the author's dictation. This decision recognizes the authority of the author's revisions in the typescript stages of composition, and in defining the author's final textual intentions does not invidiously segregate small holograph additions and changes from larger shufflings, deletions, and expansions. All final holographic readings remain in the edited text except for necessary corrections supplied by Mark Twain's typist or by the present editor or unless authority may be attributed to variants in the first edition. In practice the recovery of the full inscription from the documents in which it is embedded is simple. Typing errors are detectable through collation of each typescript against the copy from which it was prepared; no editorial inference is necessary. The reader may reconstruct the final holographic text from the edited text by using the list of emendations. This list contains only necessary corrections, and readings adopted from the first edition on the assumption that they were Mark Twain's changes in the lost proofs.

3. The source of substantive corruptions which persisted into the first edition may be found in Schedule B, Historical Collation.

The printer's copy typescript contains no editorial marks besides job and galley numbers and designations of type sizes and title styles.[4] The first edition (New York: The DeVinne Press, 1906) at times deviates unwarrantably from the accidentals of the printer's copy, but it capitalizes pronouns referring to God and Jesus[5] and in other ways follows copy styles which may not have been house policy, for example in the use of commas before and after parentheses. In a letter to Frank N. Doubleday (29 May 1906) J. W. Bothwell, DeVinne's superintendent, even requested the author's opinion before deleting a half title. The correspondence between Doubleday and Mark Twain during the typesetting shows that the printing was leisurely (see the Introduction) and that the author saw proofs at intervals, with no indicated deadlines for their return. The foregoing evidence, together with the nature of most variants originating in the first edition, supports the conclusion that the printers generally attempted to follow copy and that such variants were chiefly the result of Mark Twain's proof revision, for which he had ample time. This edition was the last phase under his control, for all subsequent typesettings were posthumous and without authority. They derived as follows: the first English (1910) from the first American; the second American (1917, in *What Is Man? and*

4. A company rule at DeVinne's probably still in force in 1906 required that editing be done in manuscript, not proof; see *Office Manual, for the Use of Workmen in the Printing House of Theo. L. DeVinne & Co.* (New York: Theo. L. DeVinne & Co., 1883), p. 8. The font of the first edition was Classic, the text type was 12-point. The book must have been set by linotype machine, for DeVinne's had linotype matrices in Classic but for handset work only one job case each of Classic roman and italic sorts. See *Types of the DeVinne Press* (New York: [The DeVinne Press], 1907), p. 243.

5. In 1883 DeVinne's house policy specified lower case: the "pronouns he, his, and him, when referring to Deity, will always begin with lower-case h, as is done in the Bible" (*Manual*, p. 9). Policy in this matter became flexible by 1906, for DeVinne later wrote: "The capitalizing of a pronoun is contrary to the general rules of English grammar, but for this purpose [of referring to Deity] capitals have found approval for many years, and when a compositor or proof-reader finds such pronouns consistently capitalized in manuscript he should not make or suggest their alteration to lower-case letters" (Theodore Low DeVinne, *Correct Composition*, 2nd ed. [New York: The Century Co., 1904], p. 110). But even in 1883 a more general company rule took precedence: "follow the fairly prepared copy of an educated writer, in spelling, punctuation, and use of capitals. . . . It is the author's undoubted right to go before the public in his own way" (*Manual*, p. 8; see *Correct Composition*, pp. 327–328, for a restatement of this principle).

Other Essays) from the first American; the second English (1930) from the first English; and the third American (1963, in *The Complete Essays of Mark Twain*; see Description of Texts, below) from the second American. The present edition adopts the following policies on variants in the first edition:

1. *Words and Word Order.* The present text accepts variants in the first edition that are most different from Mark Twain's holographic text—different in several adjacent words or different in the characters of single words—insofar as they could hardly have resulted from error or sophistication. The phrase "product of immoral commerce" (194.29), for example, must be considered a deliberate replacement of "low-down son of a thief," and the only person who engaged in deliberate revision was Mark Twain. An unusually high proportion of minor variants in the first edition, such as changes from plural to singular inflections, seem designed to improve or correct the text. Since the publication was private and did not entail editorial improvements, and since Mark Twain made numerous slight changes in all the typescripts, the present edition accepts several first-edition variants that might be rejected under different circumstances. Thus first-edition singular "performance" (126.31) and "heroism" (209.1), and plural "combinations" (197.25) and "temperaments" (213.12), all of them appropriate in context, are accepted as Mark Twain's proof revisions. But acceptance of substantive variants in the first edition always follows consideration of possible error or sophistication—whether the placement of words and other physical characteristics of the printer's copy and the first edition may imply error, and whether the nature of a variant may imply grammatical or other sophistication.

The present edition rejects variants in the first edition if they appear clearly erroneous, or if they cannot with assurance be attributed to Mark Twain even on the assumption that he read the proofs with unwonted care. First-edition "the sidestep," "a side-step" (181.18) in the pre-publication phases and the present text, is so pointless a change as to seem an improbable revision. Though Mark Twain may have been recalling an actual event, he could hardly have cared whether the pulpit had one or more than one side-step. First-edition "it" in "it can't be forced" (198.13) may have been Mark Twain's addition in order to establish a clause beginning with "and," yet the word occurs three times earlier in the sentence and is now rejected as a probable erroneous repetition. Two substantive omissions, "other" (174.20) and "thought" (190.10), seem clearly erroneous. In the first case, the context calls for a jet of steam mixed with vaporized quicksilver to be turned upon the "other ingot," the second of two mentioned earlier, to establish the basis for the analogy completed in "A Parable." In the second case, according to a printer's mark in the typescript, italicized "*thought*" (190.10) began galley 31, and the adjacent "thought" omitted in the first edition is at the right margin of the same typescript line. These conditions may have led the compositor to overlook "thought," a word essential to the parallelism with the following phrase, a parallelism implicit in the first-edition retention of a semicolon after "thought."

    2. *Paragraphing, Punctuation, Word Forms.* Though the first edition did not systematically edit Mark Twain's accidentals, in a few places it changed punctuation and spellings where authorial revision can hardly be posited. For example, three colons appear to have resulted from misreadings of Mark Twain's semicolons in manuscript inserted in the printer's copy, and one semicolon a misreading of a colon in the typescript portion of the printer's copy. Mark Twain's "offence" (126.32) became "offense," "up town" (135.9) became "up-town," and "toward" (193.23) became "towards." The present edition rejects all accidental variants in the first edition that misrepresent or sophisticate the holographic text in these ways. Only two kinds of variants are accepted as authoritative in the first edition—changes which correct obvious mistakes in the holographic text and changes which seem beyond reasonable doubt to have been authorial revisions. This second class of variants includes all changes of word forms and punctuation which affect stress—alterations of words from italic to roman or from roman to italic type styles and the change of an exclamation point to a period. Mark Twain habitually made stress changes as he reread his works; frequently he instructed his typists to omit the underscoring of a manuscript so that he could rehear the words and change their emphasis as he might wish. He made many such changes in the typescripts of *What Is Man?*, and the great number of stress variants in the first edition may thus be regarded as continuations of that practice through revision in proof. Otherwise accidental variants in the first edition are accepted only when they concur with policies of the present edition stated below, and though the symbol for the first edition may appear

as the source for emendations of accidentals, it does not imply an authority in that edition except for the two kinds of variants specified.

The present text is an unmodernized, critical edition of *What Is Man?* Idiosyncratic but historically acceptable word forms in the holographic text—such as "Shakspeare" [Shakespeare] and "Goliah" [Goliath]—have been retained, and Mark Twain's punctuation, often designed to suggest oral intonation, has been followed wherever it is not clearly defective and was not superseded by first-edition variants here accepted as authorial revisions. This policy, valid in general, is especially appropriate to Mark Twain, who commonly insisted that printers follow his idiosyncratic punctuation. However, the holographic text also contains ampersands, inconsistencies, and orthographic slips which, though characteristic of Mark Twain's drafts, were not among the accidentals he wished to preserve in print. On the contrary, he expected ampersands to be spelled out in print, and he often left to his publishers such matters as the styling of the "Y.M."-"O.M." rubrics in *What Is Man?* In certain word forms (such as "recognise"-"recognize") and placements of terminal punctuation (such as the quotation marks–question mark sequence) Mark Twain was often inconsistent, whether from oversight or indifference, but in these cases also the proper inference is that he expected their consistent rendering in print, rather than that they were among the idiosyncrasies he wished to be kept. Thus the present edition attempts to establish a texture of accidentals which is faithful to Mark Twain's holographic text and which, on the basis of preferences evident in the holographic text or in his contemporary practice, renders certain varying forms consistently when his inconsistencies were without apparent intention or function. Items covered in these policies are as follows :

I Punctuation
    Commas and periods are placed outside terminal parentheses, to make uniform Mark Twain's common usage in the holographic text.

II Word Forms
1. Compounds normally hyphenated and compounds normally not hyphenated in the holographic text are regularized according to their dominant form in *What Is Man?* or in other works of the period.
2. Variant spellings (such as "recognise"-"recognize") are styled ac-

cording to Mark Twain's dominant usage. Other variations in word forms remain if a variant form is functional, such as "Man" (normally "man" in the holographic text), or if the differences are justified contextually (compare "Democrat," 184.34, and "democrats," 212.24).

3. Numbers remain in the arabic numerals of the holographic text except when Mark Twain refers to years ("twenty-two years"). Mark Twain used lettered forms more often than arabic numerals when referring to years, and the arabic numerals in this case are emended to lettered forms.

All these policy changes, as well as corrections of obvious mistakes in the holograph, are noted in the list of emendations (Schedule A of Collation, below). Only the following changes are made without notation:

1. Ampersands are silently spelled out as "and"; periods are silently dropped from chapter headings and subtitles; chapter headings are in arabic rather than roman numerals.

2. Chapter headings are in italic type; subtitles and the designations of speakers are in small capital letters.

NOTES

The following notes include discussions of editorial choices; Mark Twain's major revisions in the manuscript and the typescripts; fragments related to the work; and comments on special features of the American editions.

124 *title*] The present title first appears typed on the cover of the printer's copy. The former title, *What Is the Real Character of Conscience?*—a replacement for *A Slandered Word* (that is, "selfishness") —last appears in the second typescript. The following manuscript fragment, never put into the text but probably intended as some sort of postscript, is the only passage of dialogue that refers to the final title. The first leaf contains an instruction: "Put these 2 pages on a page by itself, Jean."

Y.M. You said, one day, that the proper text for these disreputable talks of yours would be the question "What Is Man?" I think that your answer, as developed in them, amounts to about this: "Man is a Pigmy who imagines himself a Colossus." I could state it in another way—with permission.

o.m. Go on.

y.m. Thus: There is no such person as "I." The thing which we call "I" is a blend of three ingredients—temperament, training, and circumstance. They consider, they decide, they act; and they alone. When the body dies they cease to exist, and there is nothing left.

o.m. How can you say Nothing? A balloon is left, after it is punctured.

125 *title*] The titles and synopsis first appear in the printed text. The synopsis replaced the following passage, partly destroyed upon deletion from the printer's copy, here reproduced from its last complete version in the second typescript. All typescript citations have as necessary been corrected by the manuscripts.

II.

"PERSONAL MERIT."

YOUNG MAN. A while ago you claimed that there is no more merit in the philanthropist's acts than in the miser's. Now—

OLD MAN. Wait, you are giving me pain. You are committing a common fault—a fault which I commit, myself, but which I am trying diligently to train out of my disposition.

y.m. What fault is that?

o.m. The employment of inexact language—the careless use of words.

y.m. I thank you for your kindness in calling my attention to it. You do me a valuable service. And at heavy cost to your theory, I am glad to notice.

o.m. How?

y.m. You are trying to help me. That is not a selfish act.

o.m. You mistake. I am quite willing to help you; indeed I am very glad to help you—at *second hand*. But that is not what moved me. I said your fault gave *me* pain. I wish I could make you realize that in no circumstances are we ever (primarily) moved to help another except for the one sole reason—that by it we shall rid ourselves of a pain or procure for ourselves a pleasure.

y.m. But where was I inexact? Didn't you claim that there is no more merit in the philanthropist's acts than there is in the miser's?

o.m. I should have to refer to our notes to find out what my language was, but it is quite impossible that I could have used the word "merit" in such a connection.

Y.M. Why?

O.M. Because it would imply *personal* merit.

Y.M. Well?

O.M. There is no such thing as personal merit.—Why do you gasp like that?

Y.M. I was trying to get my breath. You caught me unexpectedly with this insane doctrine.

O.M. What is there insane about it?

Y.M. What is there sane about it? Do you mean to say that a good man is entitled to no credit for being good and for diligently and conscientiously striving to do right?

O.M. I must go carefully, now, or I shall hurt you, and I sincerely desire to avoid that—for two reasons: the most important one of the two being the old, old, all-powerful reason that in wounding you I should distress myself. Otherwise it would not occur to me to think about you at all. Now, then, let me work up the thing as inoffensively as I can. What are the. . . .

132.1 O.M.] As in the first typescript and all subsequent phases; the manuscript reads "Y.M." Corrections in the typescripts are also accepted at 171.16, 193.25, 197.12 (see Schedule A.1) and at 141.28, 146.3, 148.4, 211.10 (see Schedule A.2). Almost all other variants originating in the typescripts are rejected; for exceptions see discussions of 135 *title*, 182.7, 184.10, 190.15, and 197.33.

133.14 The present text, from 133.14 to the end of the chapter, was a substitution for the following passage, originally a manuscript insertion in the first typescript. The text is that of the second typescript.

O.M. Keno!

Y.M. Pray what do you mean?

O.M. "Keno" is an exclamation used by the winner in a certain game. It announces victory.

Y.M. Have you won a victory?

O.M. I think so. I think I may claim that your remark gave your whole case away, as regards Selfishness, and threw up the game.

Y.M. How?

O.M. In the discussion upon Selfishness, the other day, I claimed that a man never does *anything* (primarily) for duty's sake, or goodness' sake or the sake of his neighbor, but always works for himself *first*; that he must always be *bought and paid for*—with praise from the outside or from within, or from both, to an amount and degree that will overbid other competition and *come nearest to completely contenting his spirit*—or he will not stir a jot. You closed that discussion with the remark that you were "not convinced."

Y.M. Have I intimated that I have changed my mind, and am convinced now?

O.M. You are like everybody else: unconsciously, you have always lived the doctrine of Self, while ignorantly and stupidly repudiating it with your mouth. I say to you again, a man will do nothing until he has been bribed to it by the self-praise of his own approbation; and that in the great majority of cases this *self*-approval is the creation of another bribe, the praiseful approval of *other* people. Don't you think you gave your case away and accepted my bribery-position, a minute ago, when you used these disastrous words? "Hang it, where is the sense in a man's becoming brave if he is to get no *credit* for it?"

Y.M. I—well, yes, I—that is—

O.M. That is sufficient, you needn't go on if it is painful. Now then, in that remark you seek outside the man himself for the most prized and desirable bribe for bravery. It is the world's way—the world's mistaught way—to place it there, and it is a mistake.

134.7 Inserted in the first typescript, but probably written in 1905, is a working-note for a sequel:

(Insert this after "Personal Merit," for instance—to get it away from "Selfishness" and beguile the reader and make him perceive that that is often a false term and blameless.)

———————

(Make a dialogue examining into the moving impulses of each of these, showing that they were *good* ones, but in each case done to get self-approval, proving that most selfishnesses are slandered when that innocently-degraded term is applied to them:

Man comes with coal from *former* supplier.

Colored *Charles* has ordered it. Katy sorry for Ch. *and* the driver, whom Ch wanted to help.

Present supplier inquires why order didn't come to *him*.

Miss L. involved. } All trying to do a kindness to somebody and
I am involved. } mixing everything up. Each gets *momentary*
            } self-approval.

The reference at the beginning ("Insert this") is to a newspaper clipping once pinned to the sheet, concerning heroic acts by railroadmen. Katy (Leary) and Charles were family servants; Miss L. was Miss Lyon, Mark Twain's secretary.

135 *title*] The chapter heading first appears typed in the printer's copy, where it is styled as a half title. The words are here accepted as Mark Twain's, and the placement is accepted as having his approval (see discussion of 148 *title*, below).

135.1   The following passage, originally the beginning of the chapter and of the work, was deleted from the printer's copy and destroyed. It is reproduced from its last appearance in the second typescript.

WHAT IS THE REAL CHARACTER OF CONSCIENCE?

I.

YOUNG MAN. The man's act, as stated by you, has a fine and generous look, but I have no admiration to waste upon it. He did it from a purely selfish motive.

OLD MAN. That damages it in your eyes?

Y.M. Of course it does.

O.M. Why?

Y.M. Why? A strange question. Because selfish motives are base motives. They take away all merit from the act.

O.M. Are all selfish motives base motives?

Y.M. Certainly. But you are chaffing. It is a truism.

O.M. What makes you think so?

Y.M. I don't think anything about it, I know it. Everybody knows it. Everybody knows that selfishness is the most degraded and degrading of all the passions.

O.M. You are not merely using a random and heedless habit of speech inherited from books and schools and talk?

Y.M. Why—no.

O.M. You have thought it all out for yourself, and do actually know what Selfishness is?

Y.M. Know it? Of course I do. Everybody does.

O.M. What is it?

Y.M. Why, it is the quality which impels a person to do a thing because he expects to get a personal advantage out of it.

o.m. Then there is the opposite quality, I suppose—Unselfishness?
y.m. Certainly.
o.m. What is Unselfishness?
y.m. The sacrifice of self for others' good.
o.m. There have been instances. . . .

143.17 A while ago] The passage beginning with the cue words and
ending at 146.32 was an early insertion (manuscript pp. o, 1–10). A
sketch of "A Little Story" is in a notebook entry for July 1898:

An infidel takes away a dying boy's Christian faith and is reproached by
the mother. Remorse.
    To appease his tortures he devotes himself to missionary work and
gets back his peace of mind. Persuades away a dying pagan boy's faith in
his gods. Is reproached by the mother. Remorse again. Does not know what
to do now. (Notebook 32, TS p. 26)

148 title] In proof Mark Twain evidently requested a half-title page
before chapter 3. Such a page had been inserted in the printer's copy.
On 29 May 1906 J. W. Bothwell wrote Frank N. Doubleday: "On page
39 [pagination of the first edition] the author asks for a half title to
precede Chapter 3. I fail to see the reason . . . I don't see why there
should be a half title here any more than before the preceding and following chapters. . . . Will you kindly call the author's attention to
this. . . ." Doubleday forwarded the query to Mark Twain, recommending that he accept the suggestion. Apparently Mark Twain agreed, for
a half title did not appear before chapter 3 in the first edition. However,
a half title appeared before chapter 4 as requested in the printer's copy,
one requested before chapter 5 ("More About the Machine") was
styled as a chapter heading, and one appeared before chapter 6 though
not requested in the printer's copy. All these stylings of the first edition,
in addition to the title of chapter 2, are here accepted on the assumption that they were seen and passed by Mark Twain.

151.26 No—at least, not yet.] The dialogue originally continued as
follows:

y.m. No—at least, not yet. But I have not tried religions and sermons yet.
    o.m. And prayer. Try them all. None of them can budge the rule

from its place. There is but one *primary* impulse back of any act, be it a religious one or otherwise.

Y.M. I shall hope to disprove it in time.

O.M. You will have to suffer disappointment. All religions recognize the law of Selfishness, they all concede its supremacy, they all make offerings to it, they all bribe it; none of them asks a man to be good and do right without pay. He would never be good for nothing; he never is good for nothing. He is always paid for it—paid in every instance.

Y.M. How do you make out that religions appeal to selfishness?

O.M. "Believe on Me." Without pay? No; you get eternal life. "Come unto Me, you that are weary." You know the pay—rest. "Honor thy parents." For nothing? No, the pay is long life. Be righteous always, obey the commandments. For nothing? No, the pay is heaven. Blessed are the meek —for reasons; blessed are the pure in heart—for reasons; pray for your daily bread; pray that you may be protected from temptation. Somewhere in every prayer or back of it is an impulse which conforms to the rule. "If I should die before I wake," let my soul be cared for. Mahomet promised heaven for a devout life; Christian Science promises peace of mind here, and heaven hereafter, for loyalty to its teachings. No religion asks a man to be good merely for the *sake* of being good. They all recognize man's sole impulse, man's sole persuader, his only moving principle—Self.

Y.M. To come back to this world—

O.M. We haven't been out of it, yet.

Y.M. Take the case of servant-tipping. . . .

Mark Twain deleted the passage in the printer's copy and destroyed a page containing most of it. The citation is to the second typescript, with a revision from the surviving text in the printer's copy.

161.1 In the original sequence the following passage continued the dialogue after 133.13. When Mark Twain transposed the first two chapters, he split the original second chapter just before this passage, replaced the "Keno" fragment as indicated above, and deleted this passage from the beginning of the new chapter 4. The citation is to the second typescript.

Y.M. Explain.

O.M. Why should you be anxious first about ice-cream and ladyfingers? Roast beef is the real dinner. Friends' applause and the public applause are valuable, but they ought not to be of *first* value, and you should train yourself to push them to *second* place. *Your own* applause is the valuable thing, the essential thing, the inestimably precious thing. You should train yourself to acquire it *without* the public applause.

Y.M. You said, yourself, that Alexander Hamilton valued the public approbation—gave it place before his principles, his convictions, his affections, and—

O.M. Yes, gave it place before everything but *one*—his self-approbation. He gave it that high place merely because it secured something still higher for him—his *own* spiritual contentment. That all came of bad training. But the man that slaughtered the stranger—that case was the opposite of Hamilton's, yet it was another case of bad training. He acted in plain *defiance* of public opinion. He would have preferred to have the public approval, but he could not have it and follow the exacting requirements of his own training; he could not disobey those requirements and have peace of mind; he *had* to have peace of mind at all costs; so he killed the stranger to get it. I also reminded you that the challenged man who can get a larger measure of self-approval out of standing by his *anti*-dueling principles than he would get out of the public applause, *fights no duel.* It is a case of good training.

163.21   a profane and ribald soldier] A one-page manuscript fragment, never part of the text, also deals with Loyola:

Accidental Orientings.

O.M. Casual and unconsidered happenings often give a new trend to a person's moral drift and exert upon it a strong and lasting influence. The broken leg which brought Loyola into intercourse with the monks and resulted in his conversion is an instance in point. The religious spirit was in him from birth, and had been appealed to a thousand times without effect merely because the environment and atmosphere were of an unfavorable sort and were strong enough to have their way; but finally the atmosphere was favorable, and it soon did the work which the diligent warnings and admonitions of years had failed to do.

164.11   the comparatively innocent] In 1917 the compositor of WIM skipped from the cue words to "at times."—just to the right in the line below in the 1906 setting. Thus the words "However, all governments are hard on the inocent" were omitted. The third American edition repeated the elision: see *The Complete Essays of Mark Twain,* ed. Charles Neider (Garden City: Doubleday, 1963), p. 362.

173.26   In the second typescript the dialogue continues with the following segment. Mark Twain deleted and destroyed most of it in the printer's copy; the citation is to the second typescript.

Further about Training.

o.m. Jonathan Edwards is an extraordinary instance of what deliberate teaching along special lines, powerfully assisted by other and persistent *outside influences*—such as environment, association, and so on—can do with an apparently rational person. He had an acute and penetrating mind, but it was so shackled by his *training* that he had no free use of its large capacities.

y.m. How do you arrive at that?

o.m. He piles up a vast mountain of proof (to use his phrase) that before the Creation God appointed and decreed the fate—unalterably—of each and every man who was to be born in the earth while the earth should last. Each individual was to enter the world with his fate already decided, inalterably fixed: if he was appointed to be damned, nothing could save him, if he was appointed to be saved, nothing could damn him. Have I not correctly stated it?

y.m. You have.

o.m. Then Edwards tells how God came down to the earth to be crucified for man's sake—and this futile and romantic incident fills him with worshipping admiration. Why? Nobody knows. Edwards grants, quite enthusiastically, that nothing whatever could come of it; that it could not alter the fate of any man in the least degree; yet he rears mountains of "proof" again, that it was a most thoughtful and magnanimous thing to do. Nowhere is there a word to show that Edwards has even a suspicion that he is talking absurdities and insanities. Yet an ordinary school boy of to-day would perceive it. It is as striking an instance as I can call to mind, of the miracles which environment, association and specialized schooling can do with a person's intellect.

y.m. Those factors did it?

o.m. Necessarily. Edwards—like every one else—uttered not his own voice and mind, but the voice and mind of his *training and associations*. He remasticated old stale food, rebreathed old disoxygenated air, and probably thought he was "originating." And he was, as far as personal peculiarities of style, go—and no man gets nearer to originality than that. But if he had been reared in an atmosphere where 2 and 2 made 4 instead of 75, he would have scoffed at such "reasonings" as he puts on the market in his sermon called "The Freedom of the Will."

y.m. Did he ever scoff?

o.m. Yes—at the Arminians; he scoffed, but he did not laugh; for he was destitute of imagination, and had no more sense of humor than a tombstone.

The tone suggests a recent reading of Edwards' *The Freedom of the Will*, and the sequence of the writing suggests that Mark Twain wrote "Further about Training" around February 1902, when he sent Twichell the famous letter about Edwards (*MTL*, pp. 719–721). Mark Twain finds Edwards in agreement with the first two chapters of *What Is Man?* and claims that "Up to that point he could have written chapters III and IV of my suppressed 'Gospel' " (*MTL*, p. 720). At that time chapter 3 was what later became part of chapter 6, "Instinct and Thought" (189.1–198.31), and chapter 4 was "The Moral Sense." Mark Twain means that someone in agreement with the argument of the first two chapters would also agree with 3 and 4. The disagreement would begin with the assignment of responsibility for man's limitations—that is, with the argument of the "God" dialogue (Supplement A4).

176   *title*] There are in effect two titles. In the printer's copy, at the end of the previous chapter, Mark Twain added an instruction: "On page by itself: MORE ABOUT THE MACHINE," referring to the next page (108) of the typescript. He apparently forgot that under the manuscript of the foreword, which was pinned to p. 108, the title was already "THE MAN-MACHINE AGAIN." The printer set both titles in the order of their appearance.

176.3   bread; she] Miss Lyon's transcription reads "bread? She"—almost certainly a slip. The present reading first appears in the 1906 setting and is here accepted as Mark Twain's proof correction.

176.11   In the manuscript Mark Twain deleted the following passage, which begins on manuscript p. 60 and continues through two pages numbered 61 and 62. After the cancellation he replaced the latter with two pages bearing the same numbers. The replacement ends at 177.11, with "unconscious of him and his talk."

    Y.M. And that the machine is driven solely by forces outside and independent of the man?
    O.M. Yes.

Y.M. Then I should like you to tell me how the man is going to be responsible for the machine's performance.

O.M. I have not intimated that I thought him responsible.

Y.M. Well, isn't he?

O.M. Decidedly not, I think.

Y.M. This is monstrous. Who is?

O.M. None but the makers of machines can be responsible for their performance.

Y.M. Do you mean to suggest that God, and God alone, is responsible for every act of man, good or bad?

O.M. It is what I believe. If I make a watch and it doesn't keep time I am responsible for that, not the watch. The watch commits no sin; it is not capable of it.

Y.M. And man?

O.M. He can no more commit a sin than can a watch. He is not capable of it.

Y.M. God has said, in so many words, that man is a sinner and responsible for his sins.

O.M. I could say that of the watch. Saying it would not make it true.

Y.M. When God says it it makes it true.

O.M. Are you sure He said it?

Y.M. Certainly. I know it.

O.M. Perhaps you heard Him. When I hear Him say it I will believe He said it. And even then it will not be true, for there is no way to make it true.

Y.M. True or not, He holds the sinner responsible and will destroy him.

O.M. I could do that with the watch.

178.20 ...go crazy.] The "Punch, brothers, punch" jingle, which continues the text in the printer's copy, is elided in the first edition (see Schedule A.1). Mark Twain may have thought his familiar association with the jingle would reveal his authorship; the omission is accepted as his proof change.

178.24 awake,] The comma first appears in the 1906 setting. Evident authorial proof changes of substantive readings are near this variant, and the first-edition comma is accepted as Mark Twain's proof correction.

181.29 Did my mind stop to mourn with that nude black sister of mine?] A long passage concerning Clemens' escape from a snowstorm in the Humboldt Mountains is elided in the first edition and is replaced there by the cue words (see Schedule A.1). Again Mark Twain may have feared discovery of his authorship, for he had described the episode in *The Innocents Abroad*, chapter 27. The omission is accepted as his proof change.

181.35 . . . got there.] Another long passage, concerning an unpleasant recurrent dream, is elided in the first edition (see Schedule A.1). After deleting the previous passages Mark Twain need not have feared disclosure from this one, but he may have felt it too embarrassing to keep in the text. See *MTB*, p. 1368, and *MTN*, p. 351, for other descriptions of the dream. The omission is accepted as his proof change.

182.7 one way] The manuscript reads "a way." Jean Clemens omitted "a" in the printer's copy typescript, but though Mark Twain caught the error when proofing her work, he inserted "one" instead of "a." The later holographic reading is here accepted as a revision.

182.27–28 brain-machines . . . combine] As in the first edition; the reading of all earlier phases is "brain-machine . . . combines." The later reading is accepted as Mark Twain's proof revision, designed to make the subject-verb forms consistent with the first clause of the sentence, "Men perceive."

184.10 of necessity that] In the printer's copy Jean Clemens miscopied "that by necessity" as "by necessity that." The original reading has not been restored because Mark Twain apparently changed the phrase in proof to "of necessity that" to create a parallelism with his evident proof revision at 184.6 (see Schedule A.1).

190.15 one direction] The manuscript reads "in the direction from which the wind comes." In the first typescript Mark Twain crossed out the words after "direction" and inserted "one" before "direction," apparently forgetting to delete the definite article, which is not idiomatic in the context. The second typescript reads "the one direction"; Jean Clemens dropped the article in the next typescript, and the first edition thus has "one direction." The final reading is accepted because it probably represents what Mark Twain meant to produce in his revision.

190.31   and now and then breaks] As in the first edition; all earlier phases have "and then now and then it breaks." The final reading is accepted as Mark Twain's proof revision, designed to avoid awkwardness and excess words.

196.34   in procession] As in the first edition; all earlier phases read "procession." The first-edition variant is accepted as Mark Twain's proof correction of the idiom.

197.12   recognize] As in the second typescript and all later phases. The manuscript originally read "recognise him when he returns." Mark Twain crossed out the last four words to substitute "the returned absentee" but also crossed out "recognise." The first typescript corrected this obvious mistake, but the present edition accepts the spelling of the later phases.

197.25   deducing] As in the manuscript, the first typescript, and the printer's copy typescript. The agreement of the second typescript and the first edition in "deducting" was only a coincidence of errors.

197.33   hordes] As in all phases except the second typescript. Jean Clemens omitted "hordes" in that typescript, and Mark Twain inserted "gangs." The reversion of the next full typescript to "hordes" implies that a section of the fragmentary first typing of the printer's copy, no longer extant (see Description of Texts), restored the original.

198.32–199.4   Y.M. This is . . . assailable.] Not in the printer's copy, the passage survives in Miss Lyon's letterbook (from the collection of Bigelow Paine Cushman), with Mark Twain's instruction to Doubleday concerning its place in the dialogue: "Doubleday, please add the above pair of remarks after O.M.'s remark that he isn't 'hoisting' man up to the rat's moral level." The instruction may seem ambiguous, since Mark Twain's quotation of "hoisting" refers to "hoist" on p. 198, whereas the specific reference to rats is on p. 189: "The rat is well above him, there." But Mark Twain's quotation of "hoisting" and the likelihood that he could have relocated the insertion in proof if he was dissatisfied are here considered sufficient reasons for accepting the first-edition placement. Moreover, the Young Man's reply in the passage on p. 189—"Are you joking?"—could hardly follow the Old Man's speech in the insertion, which begins: "I am not jesting. . . ." The passage and the instruction were sent from Dublin, New Hampshire, 25 May 1906; Doubleday acknowledged receipt on 28 May 1906.

203.6 unsatisfied] As in the first edition; the manuscript insertion in the printer's copy has "unsatiated." The later reading is appropriate, for the passage concerns a man who is discontented rather than unsurfeited, and the change is accepted as Mark Twain's proof revision. Changes to italic stress in the same page of the first edition indicate his attention in proof to the immediate context.

204.31 crazy mind] As in the first edition; the manuscript and the printer's copy have "crazed mind." The final reading renders more clearly than "crazed mind" (a normal, temporary result of an injury) the idea of a relation of physical trauma to a mental condition not usually associated with such a cause—"A cracked skull has resulted in a crazy mind." Changes to italic stress in the same page of the first edition again indicate Mark Twain's attention in proof to the immediate context; the later reading is accepted as his proof revision.

205.8 the *physical* messenger] As in the first edition; the manuscript and the printer's copy have "a physical messenger." The later reading is accepted as Mark Twain's proof revision, designed to establish a generic character for "messenger" in appropriate contrast with "spiritual" (204.32).

205.25 To. . . .] As in the first edition; the manuscript and the printer's copy begin a new paragraph with the text sentence. The dialogue elsewhere has paragraph breaks within a speech only to set off internal quotations in "A Little Story" (chapter 2), and the variant is accepted as Mark Twain's proof correction.

208.14 within itself] As in the first edition; the manuscript and the printer's copy have "itself." The later reading is accepted as Mark Twain's proof revision, designed to emphasize the place of origination he wishes to deny—"a person's brain is incapable of originating an idea within itself"—and to prevent the misconstruction that "itself" qualifies "idea."

208.33 thinks about it.] The first-edition compositor omitted "it."— the only word in the last line of first-edition p. 131. Mark Twain caught the error when Doubleday sent him two copies of the book in late

August 1906. Mark Twain thought of adding the word by hand, but the printer inserted a cancel. Both copyright copies, already sent to the Library of Congress, show the error, but no other such defective text has been located. See *BAL* 3490; also Mark Twain's marginal notes on Frank N. Doubleday to SLC, 24 August 1906.

210.9 of which you spoke] As in the first edition; the manuscript and the printer's copy have "which you spoke of." The later reading is accepted as Mark Twain's proof revision, intended to give the Old Man a formality of speech. Two first-edition changes to italic stress are in the immediate context.

Collation

1. Description of Texts

MS   Manuscript; the symbol refers to all manuscripts 1898–1905 except those inserted in the printer's copy.

TS1   First typescript; covers present chapters 1 and 2, parts of present chapters 4 (161.1–165.18), 5 (176.11–177.12; 182.25–185.13), and 6 (189.1–198.31). This and the other typescripts show revision and partial correction by Mark Twain.

TS2   Second typescript; covers present chapters 1, 2, and 4, and parts of present chapters 3 (148.1–154.26), 5 (176.11–177.12), and 6 (189.1–198.31).

PCa   First typing of part of the printer's copy. Pagination variously revised, but in the original sequence the fragment covers parts of chapters 5 (176.11–177.12; 182.25–185.13), 4 (165.19–175.29), and 6 (189.1–193.7, "enable"). The portion covering chapter 4 is the erroneous duplicate copied from TS2 (see discussion above); this was discarded by Mark Twain and is ignored in collation. The other segments show authorial corrections and revisions later typed in corresponding portions of the printer's copy; these segments are included in collation.

PC   Printer's copy; typescript with manuscript insertions (see descriptive table above). Complete final text except for evident proof changes noted in Schedule A.

A   First American edition. New York: The DeVinne Press, 1906. BAL 3490. The two copies machine-collated are of one text state. Copies: University of Texas, Clemens 533, 533a; the present edition has been set from emended Xerox copies of Clemens 533.

Rejected as being of no authority are the first English edition (London: Watts, 1910; see BAL 3490); the second American edition, in *What Is Man? and Other Essays* (New York and London: Harper, 1917, BAL 3524; reissued, London: Chatto & Windus, 1919, see BAL 3524);

successive impressions of the second American edition in the "Definitive Edition" (New York: Gabriel Wells, 1923; *BAL* 3691) and the "Stormfield Edition" (New York: Harper, 1929; not in *BAL*); the second English edition (London: Watts, 1936; not in *BAL*); and the third American edition, in Charles Neider, ed., *The Complete Essays of Mark Twain* (Garden City: Doubleday, 1963; not in *BAL*).

2. Collation Schedules

Schedule A: Emendations of the Copy-text

This collation presents emendations of Mark Twain's final holographic text and of Miss Lyon's transcriptions. Accepted readings, their sources identified by symbols, are at the left; rejected readings are at the right. The letter I follows emendations for which the editor of this volume is the source. Dashes link the first and last texts which agree in a reading, and indicate that there are intervening texts which also agree. Where symbols are separated by commas, either no texts intervene or those which do have different readings. Where the earliest phase noted is a typescript (such as TS1) though there is manuscript for the passage, the typescript reading represents Mark Twain's holograph revision in that phase. In A.1 the expression *not in* indicates the absence of first-edition words in the earlier phases. Where only a present text reading appears in A.2, all phases before the first edition which contain the passage style the reading for roman type if this text is in italic, and for italic if this text is in roman. In collations of punctuation curved dashes ($\sim$) stand for the words before the punctuation of this text. The curved dashes are followed by the punctuation of the variant texts; if no punctuation appears, the variant texts have none. A dagger (†) precedes entries which are discussed in Notes, above.

1. WORDS AND WORD ORDER

†124 *title*	*What Is Man?* I	WHAT IS THE REAL CHARACTER OF CONSCIENCE? MS–TS2 WHAT IS MAN? PC, A

	Iowa-California Readings	Rejected Readings
†125 *title*	a. Man . . . Merit I	"Personal Merit." MS–TS2 *not in* PC a. *Man . . . Merit.* A
†125.1–4	[The . . . position.] A	*not in* MS–PC
126.31	performance A	performances MS–PC
†132.1	o.m. TS1–A	Y.M. MS
†135 *title*	Man's . . . *Approval* PC, A	*not in* MS–TS2
146.4	they A	it TS2, PC
†148 *title*	3 I	*not in* MS–PC III A
155.8	than he would for A	than for PC
161 *title*	4 | *Training* I	*not in* MS–PC IV | *Training* A
168.31	*hand* I	*hands* MS–A
171.16	are arriving TS2–A	arriving MS
172.10	incapable A	on my uppers MS–PC
176 *title*	5 I	*not in* MS–PC V A
†178.20	crazy. A	crazy. The same with "A pink trip-slip for a 3-cent fare, a blue trip-slip for a 5-cent fare, a buff trip-slip for an 8-cent fare, punch! in the presence of the passenjaire! Punch, brothers, punch with care! punch in the presence of the passenjaire!"

Iowa-California Readings	*Rejected Readings*
	It rode me—oh, days and nights! till I was nothing but skin and bone. MS, PC
178.22 etc. A	"Tah-rah-rah boom de aye!" "There'll be a hot time in the Old Town to-night!" MS, PC
178.29 ingeniously-constructed A	wonderfully-constructed MS, PC
179.2 out, and get it accepted? A	out? MS, PC
†181.29–30 Did my mind stop to mourn with that nude black sister of mine? A	The gaunt rocks, the frosty air, the bitter wind and the flying snow transported my mind to a gorge in the Humboldt mountains, and I saw our party of young wayfarers wake up aghast at two in the morning in the fright of an ominous warning—snow falling in our faces; I heard the excited shouts, "Hurry! hurry! it's our graveyard, we're going to get snowed-in!" —I saw the vague figures frantically scrambling and stumbling around in the dark, gathering up blankets, harnessing the horses—and so on. I saw it all, strong and vivid,

Iowa-California Readings   *Rejected Readings*

and felt all the terror and despair again. One of the boys couldn't find his hat, and left it behind. My memory faltered for a moment: wasn't it his shirt, and not his hat? Did my mind stop to discuss that? MS, PC

†181.35   there. And so on ... A   there. Wondering and suffering. This swept my mind to another recurrent dream—a dream which comes frequently and always fills me with humiliation and distress. In this dream I find myself before a lecture audience, with no lecture, no notes, no subject; I cannot think of anything to talk about; I struggle along, talking at random to gain time and find a topic; I make silly jokes, and see pity and contempt rise in the faces of the people; see anger follow, and disgust; at length see the house get up and turn their backs and move out, and leave me solitary, dumb, petrified, ashamed, disgraced. This picture of retreating backs flung another pic-

	Iowa-California Readings	*Rejected Readings*
		ture upon the canvas of my mind, the massed backs of the hosts of Israel retreating before Pharaoh, between the walled waters of the Red Sea—and so on . . . MS, PC
†182.7	one way PC, A	a way MS
†182.27–28	brain-machines . . . combine A	brain-machine . . . combines MS–PC
184.6	what he does, it follows of necessity that he A	his achievements, a man MS–PC
†184.10	of necessity that A	that by necessity MS–PCa by necessity that PC
189 *title*	6 I	III MS–PC VI A
†190.15	one direction PCa–A	the one direction TS1, TS2
†190.31	now A	then now MS–PC
†190.31	breaks A	it breaks MS–PC
191.17	insert A	stick-in MS–PC
193.25	several TS1–A	several several MS
194.9	to—to— A	to— MS–PC
194.29	product of immoral commerce A	low-down son of a thief MS–PC
194.29	fly A	fly for you MS–PC
194.34	hundred A	thousand MS–PC
†196.34	in procession A	procession MS–PC

	Iowa-California Readings	Rejected Readings
†197.12	recognize TS2–A	*not in* MS recognise TS1
197.25	combinations A	combination MS–PC
199.15	the two appeals A	the two MS, PC
199.23	Will: A	Will, he had no free choice: MS, PC
†203.6	unsatisfied A	unsatiated PC
204.6	You think so? A	Yes, everybody grants that. MS, PC
†204.31	crazy A	crazed MS, PC
†205.8	the *physical* A	a physical MS, PC
207.18	so-called material A	material PC
†208.14	within itself A	itself MS, PC
209.1	heroism A	heroisms MS, PC
†210.9	of which you spoke A	which you spoke of MS, PC
213.12	temperaments A	temperament MS, PC

2. PARAGRAPHING, PUNCTUATION, WORD FORMS

124.2	twenty-five A	25 TS2, PC
124.2	twenty-seven A	27 TS2, PC
124.3	seven A	7 TS2, PC
130.21	sewing-machine I	sewing machine MS–A
131.6	sewing-machines I	sewing machines MS–A
141.6	account), I	~,) MS–A
141.16	definition), I	~,) MS–A
141.28	teachers, TS1–A	~ MS

	Iowa-California Readings	*Rejected Readings*
146.3	⟪ The TS1–A	The MS
148.4	was TS2–A	wa MS
148.16	primarily). A	~.) PC
156.28	recognizing A	recognising PC
165.12	*him* TS2, A	him MS, TS1, PC
170.16	*first hand* I	first-hand MS, TS2
		first-hand PC, A
173.33	*single* TS2, A	single MS, PCa, PC
174.26	*single* A	
175.15	Sunday-school A	Sunday school MS–PC
†176.3	bread; she A	~? She PC
†178.24	awake, A	~ MS–PC
180.31	sixteen I	16 PC, A
182.29	steam-engine I	steam engine MS–A
184.4	*personal* A	
184.16	Truth Seeker I	Truth-Seeker MS–A
192.23	maneuvers I	maneuvres MS, TS1
		manoeuvres TS2, PC
		manœuvers A
194.17	*has* A	
197.14	recognized TS1–A	recognised MS
197.17	recognized TS2–A	recognised MS, TS1
197.19	recognized TS2–A	recognised MS, TS1
200.7	*select, choose,*	
	point out A	
200.24	*moral* A	

	Iowa-California Readings	Rejected Readings
200.26	mind's A	
200.30	knows A	
200.31	bound A	
201.2	right A	
201.5	right A	
201.18	right A	
201.23	see A	
201.28	intellectual perceptions of right and wrong A	
202.2	material A	
202.2	spiritual A	
202.6	material A	
202.8	spiritual A	
202.10	all A	
202.11	spirit A	
202.16	spiritual desire A	
202.29	material A	
203.2	material A	
203.12	material A	
203.17	material A	
203.17	spirit A	
203.24	the whole thing in one A	
203.30	the whole thing A	
204.1	mind A	
204.2	you A	
204.18	feeling A	

	Iowa-California Readings	Rejected Readings
204.22	*physical* A	
204.29	*is* A	
204.32	*independent* A	
†205.8	*physical* A	
205.12	*mental* A	
205.13	*moral* A	
205.15	*and* A	
205.20	*independently* A	
205.20	recognize PC, A	recognise MS
205.22	*definite and indisputable "I,"* A	
†205.25	To A	⟨ To MS, PC
205.29	*one* A	
206.23	instinct A	
206.31	means A	
207.16	*realize* A	
208.5	twenty PC, A	20 MS
209.13	*elementals* A	
210.11	*you* A	
210.14	*You* A	
210.31	*I* A	
211.1	*expose* A	
211.10	achievements PC, A	achievents MS
212.4	Easily. A	~! MS, PC
212.10	fifty PC, A	50 MS

	Iowa-California Readings	Rejected Readings
212.34	*acquirements* A	
213.1	*born* A	
213.11	*think* A	
213.11	*feel* A	
213.14–15	*any kind of government or religion that can be devised* A	
213.34	*I* A	

Schedule B: Historical Collation

This collation presents substantive variants among the phases identified by symbols in Description of Texts. Rejected readings in Mark
Twain's holographic text have already appeared in Schedule A.1, and
citations of pages and lines for these entries are italicized. All texts with
corresponding passages agree with the present text if their symbols do
not appear after rejected readings. The expression *not in* indicates the
absence in early phases of words later added; the abbreviation *om.*
(omitted) indicates words elided in phases after the manuscript and
after an insertion in the second typescript (see entry for 195.24). A
dagger (†) precedes entries which are discussed in Notes, above.

†124 *title*	*What Is Man?*	WHAT IS THE REAL CHARACTER OF CONSCIENCE? MS–TS2 WHAT IS MAN? PC, A
†125 *title*	a. *Man . . . Merit*	"Personal Merit." MS–TS2 *not in* PC a. *Man . . . Merit.* A
†125.1–4	[The . . . position.]	*not in* MS–PC
126.29–30	a man	man TS2–A
126.31	performance	performances MS–PC

	Iowa-California Readings	*Rejected Readings*
127.30	those	these TS1–A
127.32	stronger	strong TS1–A
128.5	himself—not even an opinion,	*om.* TS1–A
128.15	ten	*om.* TS1–A
†132.1	O.M.	Y.M. MS
132.16	speech	speak TS1–A
133.7	the flags	flags TS2–A
†135 *title*	*Man's . . . Approval*	*not in* MS–TS2
135.9–10	blowing hard,	*om.* TS2–A
136.8	suffering old	old suffering PC, A
136.17–18	This able trader got a hundred dollars' worth of clean profit out of an investment of twenty-five cents.	*om.* TS1–A
137.27	to the wars	to the war TS1, TS2 to war PC, A
138.22	the duel	that duel TS1–A
138.23	the *public*	*public* TS1–A
138.24	could	would PC, A
139.6	in trying	*om.* PC, A
140.24	always he	he always TS2–A
141.11	his	a TS1–A
141.12	this	his TS1–A
142.29	like	*om.* PC, A
143.6	which	*om.* TS2–A

	Iowa-California Readings	*Rejected Readings*
143.23	a guest	guest TS1–A
144.3	*had*	*have* TS2–A
145.1	and presently with tenderness,	*om.* TS1–A
146.4	they	it TS2, PC
†148 *title*	3	*not in* MS–PC III A
148.14	you have	have you PC, A
150.27	dull and	dull TS2, PC dull, A
153.25	a quite	quite a PC, A
154.22	secure	get PC, A
155.8	than he would for	than for PC
161 *title*	4 | *Training*	*not in* MS–PC IV | *Training* A
161.12	a law	the law TS1–A
162.23	a nicely	nicely TS1–A
162.32	his Truth	the Truth TS1–A
164.22	all his opinions,	*om.* TS1–A
165.9	to tell me	*om.* PC, A
165.14–15	To train men to lead virtuous lives is an inestimably important thing.	*om.* PC, A
166.33	was so intent	so intent PC, A
167.5	jumped suddenly	suddenly jumped PC, A
167.7	instant	instance PC, A
168.10	remember	remember that PC, A

	Iowa-California Readings	*Rejected Readings*
168.31	hand	hands MS–A
170.19	and to do *unselfish* things;	om. PC, A
171.16	are arriving	arriving MS
171.20	pride's	his pride's TS2–A
171.34	nursed	used to nurse PC, A
172.1	risk	the risk PC, A
172.10	incapable	on my uppers MS–PC
173.29	came	comes PC, A
174.20	other ingot	ingot A
174.29–30	rotten with quicksilver,	om. PC, A
174.33	with	of PC, A
176 *title*	5	*not in* MS–PC V A
177.2	on	upon PCa–A
177.19	about	of.PC, A
†178.20	crazy.	crazy. The same with "A pink trip-slip for a 3-cent fare, a blue trip-slip for a 5-cent fare, a buff trip-slip for an 8-cent fare, punch! in the presence of the passenjaire! Punch, brothers, punch with care! punch in the presence of the passenjaire!" It rode me—oh, days and nights! till I was nothing but skin and bone. MS, PC

	Iowa-California Readings	Rejected Readings
178.22	etc.	"Tah-rah-rah boom de aye!" "There'll be a hot time in the Old Town to-night!" MS, PC
178.29	ingeniously-constructed	wonderfully-constructed MS, PC
179.2	out, and get it accepted?	out? MS, PC
179.15	which	that PC, A
181.18	a side-step	the sidestep A
181.20–21	dissatisfied; saw her go on struggling, on her back and getting more and more dissatisfied,	dissatisfied, PC, A
†181.29–30	Did my mind stop to mourn with that nude black sister of mine?	The gaunt rocks, the frosty air, the bitter wind and the flying snow transported my mind to a gorge in the Humboldt mountains, and I saw our party of young wayfarers wake up aghast at two in the morning in the fright of an ominous warning—snow falling in our faces; I heard the excited shouts, "Hurry! hurry! it's our graveyard, we're going to get snowed-in!"—I saw the vague figures frantically scrambling and stumbling around in the dark, gathering up blankets, harnessing the horses—and so on. I saw

Iowa-California Readings   *Rejected Readings*

it all, strong and vivid, and felt all the terror and despair again. One of the boys couldn't find his hat, and left it behind. My memory faltered for a moment: wasn't it his shirt, and not his hat? Did my mind stop to discuss that? MS, PC

†181.35   there. And so on . . .   there. Wondering and suffering. This swept my mind to another recurrent dream—a dream which comes frequently and always fills me with humiliation and distress. In this dream I find myself before a lecture audience, with no lecture, no notes, no subject; I cannot think of anything to talk about; I struggle along, talking at random to gain time and find a topic; I make silly jokes, and see pity and contempt rise in the faces of the people; see anger follow, and disgust; at length see the house get up and turn their backs and move out, and leave me solitary, dumb, petrified, ashamed, disgraced. This picture of retreating

	Iowa-California Readings	*Rejected Readings*
		backs flung another picture upon the canvas of my mind, the massed backs of the hosts of Israel retreating before Pharaoh, between the walled waters of the Red Sea—and so on . . . MS, PC
†182.7	one way	a way MS
182.10–11	to talk	talking PC, A
†182.27–28	brain-machines . . . combine	brain-machine . . . combines MS–PC
183.8	creative	creating TS1–A
183.18–19	The elaborate Shakspearean play was the final outcome.	om. PC, A
184.6	what he does, it follows of necessity that he	his achievements, a man MS–PC
†184.10	of necessity that	that by necessity MS–PCa by necessity that PC
184.30	hunting for	hunting TS1–A
189 *title*	6	III MS–PC VI A
189.6–7	the rat	a rat TS2–A
189.28	a merely	merely TS2–A
190.7	the outside	outside TS2–A
190.10	thought solidified	solidified A
†190.15	one direction	the one direction TS1, TS2

	Iowa-California Readings	Rejected Readings
190.26	a part	part PC, A
†190.31	now	then now MS–PC
†190.31	breaks	it breaks MS–PC
191.1	ever	*om.* TS2–A
191.16	heedlessly	had heedlessly PCa–A
191.17	insert	stick-in MS–PC
191.20	pulled out the pin	pulled the pin out PCa–A
192.17	English gentleman	Englishment TS2 Englishman PCa–A
193.21	creatures	animals PC, A
193.25	several	several several MS
194.9	beast	beasts TS1–A
194.9	to—to—	to— MS–PC
194.29	product of immoral commerce	low-down son of a thief MS–PC
194.29	fly	fly for you MS–PC
194.34	hundred	thousand MS–PC
195.23	all be	be TS1–A
195.24	much above what he is,	*om.* PC, A
196.9	this nest	the nest TS1–A
196.12	while	time PC, A
†196.34	in procession	procession MS–PC
197.11	that after	after TS1–A
†197.12	recognize	*not in* MS recognise TS1
197.13	were	are TS1–A

	Iowa-California Readings	Rejected Readings
197.19	one	same TS1–A
197.24	for putting	of putting PC, A
†197.25	deducing	deducting TS2, A
197.25	combinations	combination MS–PC
†197.33	hordes	gangs TS2
198.13	can't	it can't A
198.17	intellectually	intellectuality PC, A
198.25	haven't	haven't got PC, A
199.15	the two appeals	the two MS, PC
199.23	Will:	Will, he had no free choice: MS, PC
†203.6	unsatisfied	unsatiated PC
204.6	You think so?	Yes, everybody grants that. MS, PC
†204.31	crazy	crazed MS, PC
†205.8	the *physical*	a physical MS, PC
207.18	so-called material	material PC
†208.14	within itself	itself MS, PC
209.1	heroism	heroisms MS, PC
†210.9	of which you spoke	which you spoke of MS, PC
210.31	things	thing A
210.34	a fact	the fact PC, A
212.21	Now	And PC, A
213.12	temperaments	temperament MS, PC

21.   CHRISTIAN SCIENCE

All of the original manuscript of *Christian Science* (1907) sur-
vives except book 1, chapters 7–8.[1] Chapters 1–4 of book 1 were printed
four times, under the title "Christian Science and the Book of Mrs.
Eddy," before the preparation of the first-edition printer's copy: in the
Cosmopolitan (October 1899); in unpublished pages from an uniden-
tified book setting with predominantly American spellings; in *The
Man That Corrupted Hadleyburg and Other Stories and Sketches*
(London: Chatto & Windus, 1900); and in a resetting of the English
Hadleyburg text (Leipzig: Bernhard Tauchnitz, 1900). Chapters 5–8
of book 1 were also printed four times before the preparation of the
printer's copy: in pages from the unidentified setting, in the English
Hadleyburg and its Leipzig reprint, and in the *North American Review*
(December 1902 and January 1903). Chapter 9 of book 1 had one
earlier printing, in the *North American Review* (February 1903). "Mrs.

1. However, three footnotes and part of a fourth first appeared in the 1907
edition. The following table lists the first appearance of all footnotes in the present
edition. The term "Typescript" refers to the printer's copy typescript for the *North
American Review* publication of "Mrs. Eddy in Error"; footnotes first in that
phase and in "Printer's Copy" were Mark Twain's holograph additions. Page
numbers are those of this edition; numbers in parentheses distinguish notes where
more than one are on a page. A portion of a note, beginning on p. 255 and dated
12 March 1903, first appears in the 1907 edition, which is designated "1907" in
the table. The notes to Appendix E are from the source quoted. All footnotes first
appearing in the pages of the unpublished setting, the *North American Review*,
and the 1907 edition are accepted in this edition.

Manuscript: 267, 268, 273, 276, 293(1–2), 335, 341, 356, 359(1–2), 360(1), 386
Unpublished Pages: 249, 253(1–2)
Typescript: 394
North American Review: 248(2), 250(2)
Printer's Copy: 230, 233(1–2), 234, 238(1–3), 239, 240, 242, 248(1), 250(1),
251(1–2), 252, 254, 255, 258(1), 302, 312(1), 315, 316, 358, 360(2)
1907: 258(2), 312(2), 391

The manuscript paper is of two kinds. The first, for book 1, chapters 1–6, is a
white unwatermarked lightweight wove torn into half-sheets normally measuring
5½" x 8⁹⁄₁₆". Book 1, chapter 9, and all of book 2 consist of leaves from "Par
Value" tablets (see *What Is Man?* table above, item 5). A cover of one of these
tablets, crowded with Mark Twain's notes on Christian Science, is in MTP.

Eddy in Error" (in book 2) also appeared in the *North American Review* (April 1903).

The printer's copy for the first edition, lacking only the conclusion, also survives. Book 1 in the printer's copy consists of pages from the unidentified setting (chapters 1–4) and of tearsheets from the *North American Review* (chapters 5–9), in which Mark Twain made copious holograph revisions and additions. Book 2 in the printer's copy consists of a typescript, copied from the manuscript, and of page proof for the *North American Review* publication of "Mrs. Eddy in Error." The typescript portion of book 2, further pages from the unidentified setting used as printer's copy for the *North American Review* publication of book 1, chapters 5–8, and a typescript used as printer's copy for the *North American Review* publication of "Mrs. Eddy in Error" contain numerous revisions and additions in Mark Twain's hand. As is the case for *What Is Man?*, the survival of printer's copy bearing the author's holograph revisions means that no one phase of the text is both complete and completely authorial. Thus for the present edition the copy-text corresponds to no single physical document but is Mark Twain's final holographic text—his inscriptions in the manuscript and on the tearsheets and typescripts used as printer's copy.[2] Since no manuscript survives for chapters 7–8 of book 1, the earliest known surviving phase, in the pages from the unidentified setting, augmented by Mark Twain's printer's copy revisions, is copy-text, but certain word forms evidently resulting from faulty transcription or house styling have been emended to conform with Mark Twain's usage in the manuscript.

Only partial printer's copy and printer's proof survive for the earlier publications of book 1, but little remains conjectural concerning its development through the printer's copy for the edition of 1907. The pages from the unidentified setting (chapters 1–8) are numbered 1–65. In chapters 1–4 (pp. 1–30) these pages repeat the *Cosmopolitan* substantive variants from the manuscript and introduce only one new reading ("Bible" for "Book," 230.26). The text in the English *Hadleyburg* also has "Bible," but it contains three indifferent substantive variants not in the *Cosmopolitan* or the unidentified setting. Since the *Cosmo-*

2. For a detailed discussion of the theory of copy-text employed here see the commentary for *What Is Man?*

politan edition was the first printing of this portion, and since the *Hadleyburg* edition followed in the next year, the safest conjecture is that the unidentified setting followed the *Cosmopolitan* and preceded the English *Hadleyburg*. Similarly, in book 1, chapters 5–6, the manuscript and the unpublished pages (pp. 31–52) agree in three places where the *Hadleyburg* text again has indifferent substantive variants. The verso of p. 65 of the unpublished pages contains the beginning of "About Play-Acting," first collected in the American and English editions of *Hadleyburg*. But since the unpublished pages begin with page number 1, Mark Twain probably first contemplated a book with the Christian Science material as the feature and perhaps titular item, which he later replaced with "The Man That Corrupted Hadleyburg." In any event, the pages from the unidentified setting may legitimately be regarded as preceding the English *Hadleyburg* throughout book 1, chapters 1–8.

The unpublished pages agree with the English *Hadleyburg* in many substantive and accidental variants from the extant portion of the manuscript—in so many as to suggest that *Hadleyburg* derived from a set of the unpublished pages or that each derived from a common original, such as a typescript and carbon possibly containing both transcription errors and author's revisions. The latter hypothesis is supported by the appearance in *Hadleyburg* of several colons where the unpublished pages have clear semicolons, because extant typescripts prepared for Mark Twain around 1900 often have semicolons barely distinguishable from colons. But the safest conjecture is that *Hadleyburg* derived from a set of the unpublished pages, for comparison with an inaccurate and revised contemporary typescript (the first typescript of *What Is Man?*) indicates that these texts have in common more accidental variants from the manuscript than may convincingly be explained by transcription error and authorial revision combined, and that a factor of house styling should be added. The relation of the unpublished pages to the *North American Review* publication of book 1, chapters 5–8, requires no conjecture. On 30 October 1902 Mark Twain mailed a set of the pages, with his inscribed revisions and with copy for book 1, chapter 9, to the editor of the *North American Review*. The copy was assigned to a subordinate editor who made extensive changes of Mark Twain's punctuation and word forms and even several changes of his language. The *North American Review* printing was set from these altered pages, and Mark Twain made further changes in proof.[3]

The first edition of *Christian Science* (New York and London: Harper and Brothers) was issued in February 1907. The book was first set in type in 1903 (see the Introduction), and statements in the text suggest that it was not reset in 1906 (see explanatory notes to 215.2 and 312 *footnote* 2). The best assumption is that it was set, edited in proof, revised in proof by the author, and plated in 1903; and that the plates were then stored until printing in late 1906 or early 1907.[4] There was no English typesetting; the English issue of 1907 was printed in the United States from plates of the first American edition and differs only in ordering the cities of publication (see Description of Texts, below, and Merle Johnson, *A Bibliography of the Works of Mark Twain*, rev. ed. [New York: Harper and Brothers, 1935], p. 87). In Mark Twain's

3. Mark Twain could have supplied a set of the unpublished pages for the English *Hadleyburg* in addition to the one he sent to the *North American Review*, inasmuch as the Mark Twain Papers have two sets of book 1, chapters 1–4, in the same typesetting—the one containing Mark Twain's revisions used in the printer's copy for the 1907 edition and another without inscriptions. The only set of the pages for book 1, chapters 5–8, known to survive is the one used as printer's copy for the *North American Review*. It is at the University of Virginia, together with the envelope in which it was mailed and final, unmarked, page proof for the installment of December 1902. The material also includes Mark Twain's itemized list of the copy, in which he describes the unpublished pages as "reprint." Clearly he means reprint in the sense of "offprint," for at the head of the first page of this copy he wrote "hitherto unpublished." See 337.11–14 of the text (and explanatory note on the same passage), where again he seems to have forgot the *Hadleyburg* publication of book 1, chapters 5–8. In his list Mark Twain describes book 1, chapter 9 (the installment of February 1903), as "type-written." This portion has not been located. The name "Brown" was written and circled on the mailing envelope; apparently this was the editor to whom the copy was assigned. Similarity of handwriting in the printer's copy for "Mrs. Eddy in Error" (the installment of April 1903) indicates that the same editor worked on all of Mark Twain's Christian Science articles for the *North American Review*.

4. Editing was almost certainly done in proof, for the printer's copy contains few editorial marks affecting the text, whereas the punctuation of the book indicates systematic editorial styling. The second footnote on p. 312 reveals that Mark Twain examined the text after 20 July 1903; he probably saw it in proofs stored with the copy in the Harper office (for the location of the copy in 1906 see *MTHHR*, pp. 607, 610). The only known account of the Harper plant near the period offers no relevant information except that the company always printed from stereotype or electrotype plates; see *Visitor's Guide to Harper & Brothers' Establishment* ([New York: Harper and Brothers, 1891]), p. vii.

lifetime the only other typesetting was a German edition (Leipzig: Bernhard Tauchnitz) issued in July 1907, entirely a derivative of the first American edition. The second American edition (New York: Gabriel Wells, 1923) was likewise derivative and without authority.

Authorial revision in missing stages may be posited for the following printed texts—the *Cosmopolitan* (book 1, chapters 1–4), the pages from the unidentified setting (book 1, chapters 1–8), the *North American Review* (book 1, chapters 5–9, and book 2, "Mrs. Eddy in Error"), and the American edition of 1907. Mark Twain could hardly have seen proof for the *Cosmopolitan* printing, since he was abroad during its preparation, but the copy he submitted to the journal was not the original manuscript; in that period it would probably have been a typescript. Since he apparently forgot that the English *Hadleyburg* contained book 1, chapters 5–8, he was probably not closely involved in its preparation. Only one substantive variant first occurred in the setting of the unidentified pages for book 1, chapters 1–4, but its character suggests Mark Twain's revision rather than imposition or error ("Bible" for "Book," 230.26). In book 1, chapters 5–6, the unpublished pages contain several substantive variants from the manuscript, implying that Mark Twain had introduced revisions in a fair copy (again, probably a typescript) now lost. The author almost certainly saw proof for all of the *North American Review* articles, and certain readings first in those printings must be accepted as his proof changes. A note on the cover of the book 2 printer's copy indicates that he wanted to see proofs for purposes of revision rather than correction: "Please send me no first proofs nor second proofs—I do not wish to see the wig until the very finest fine-tooth comb has been through it. Through it for *Sunday*." And a footnote added in the 1907 edition, dated 12 March 1903, shows that he saw these late proofs: "While I am reading the final proofs of this book . . ." (255.34). The present edition adopts the following policies on variants in these printed texts:

1. *Words and Word Order*. The present text accepts printing variants that are most different from Mark Twain's holographic text—different in several adjacent words or different in the characters of single words—insofar as they could hardly have resulted from error or sophistication. For example, a phrase first in the unpublished pages, "In large measure, yes." (241.25; manuscript, "I think so."), must be considered a replacement made by the author for aesthetic reasons, and

not a likely intrusion by a house editor. Similarly, the shift from "exactly the same as" to "merely" (324.4) in the 1907 edition could hardly have resulted from misreading and is of a kind more likely authorial than editorial. The present edition also accepts certain linked variants, for example, the replacement in the unpublished pages of manuscript "were" and "before" with "are" and "now" (234.12–13, ". . . which are involved in haunting and harassing difficulties now."), and the 1907 edition readings "History," "itself," and "history" instead of the manuscript readings "She," "herself," and "she" (321.5–7, "History is always repeating itself. . . . history always gets a duplicate product."). Substantive variants in the printings are accepted if they correct clear errors in the holograph, for example, the correction of manuscript "imagining" by "imaginary" first in the unpublished pages (242.32, ". . . inventing imaginary diseases. . . .") and the correction of numerical references in the 1907 edition (such as 261.18, "five" for "four"). Acceptance of substantive variants in the printings always follows consideration of possible error or sophistication—whether the placement of words and other physical characteristics of the manuscript and the printings may imply error, and whether the nature of a variant may imply grammatical or other sophistication.

The present edition rejects variants in the printings if they cannot with assurance be attributed to Mark Twain, if they appear indifferent, or if they produce a grammatical conformity which is unnecessarily scrupulous and beyond Mark Twain's usual concern. Several variants in the *North American Review* publication of book 1, chapter 9, though they clarify the text, are rejected because they resemble the editor's known changes in book 1, chapters 5–8. The error of many indifferent variants in quotations is confirmed by the sources (see Schedule B of Collation, entries for 223.22, 226.29, 227.5, 246.6, 246.7, 269.11, 319.19, 338.5, 365.5, 369.17, 385.7). The reading "one another's," first in the unpublished pages, is better grammatically than "each other's" (236.25, "This should move us to be charitable toward each other's lunacies."), but the variant may at least as well be attributed to an editor as to the author. Similarly, the reading "There are the Mind-Cure, the Faith Cure. . . ." (*Cosmopolitan* through 1907 edition; manuscript, 233.6, "There is . . .") does not necessarily imply revision by Mark Twain, who always allowed himself idiomatic freedoms with grammar, and may have been an editorial sophistication.

2. *Paragraphing, Punctuation, Word Forms*. All the printings for which authorial revision may be posited show both editorial change and erroneous transcription of Mark Twain's accidentals, especially the *North American Review* and 1907 texts. The latter printing was most systematic in changing the punctuation to conventional usage—for example, through the introduction of commas before and after modifiers and through the deletion of commas after verbs that were followed by subordinate clauses. Also, many of Mark Twain's preferred spellings (such as "worshiped" and "worshiping") were changed in the unpublished pages, *Hadleyburg*, the *North American Review*, and the 1907 text to English styles or to styles preferred by the house (to "worshipped" and "worshipping," and in the 1907 edition from Mark Twain's "boulder" to "bowlder"). The present edition rejects all accidental variants in the printings that sophisticate the holographic text in these ways. Only two kinds of variants are accepted as authoritative in the printings—changes which correct obvious mistakes in the holographic text and changes which seem beyond reasonable doubt to have been authorial revisions. As in the case of *What Is Man?*, this second class of variants includes all changes of word forms and punctuation which affect stress—alterations of words from italic to roman or from roman to italic type styles, changes in stress capitalization, the introduction of quotation marks around phrases and single words in Mark Twain's own prose, and the introduction of exclamation points. The authoritative Christian Science printings show several stress changes, and these may be regarded as Mark Twain's revisions, characteristic of his alterations in typescripts, in missing phases between the holographic text and the printings. Otherwise accidental variants in the printings are accepted only when they concur with policies of the present edition stated below, and though symbols for the printings may appear as sources for emendations of accidentals, they do not imply an authority in those texts except for the two kinds of variants specified.

The present text is an unmodernized, critical edition of *Christian Science*. Obsolete but historically acceptable word forms in the holographic text—such as "Klondyke" [Klondike] and "Kuran" [Koran]—have been retained, and Mark Twain's punctuation, often designed to suggest oral intonation, has been followed wherever it is not clearly defective and was not superseded by printing variants here accepted as authorial revisions. This policy, valid in general, is especially appropriate to Mark Twain, who commonly insisted that printers follow his idiosyncratic punctuation. However, the holographic text also contains abbreviations, inconsistencies, misspellings, and orthographic slips which, though characteristic of Mark Twain's drafts, were not among the accidentals he wished to preserve in print. On the contrary, he expected many abbreviations and other short forms, such as ampersands, to be spelled out in print, and since he honored distinctions between "correct" and "incorrect" spellings, one cannot assume that he wished even his habitual misspellings (for example, "sieze") to be preserved. In certain word forms (such as title stylings and variant spellings of a given word) Mark Twain was often inconsistent, whether from oversight or indifference, but in these cases also the proper inference is that he expected their consistent rendering in print, rather than that they were among the idiosyncrasies he wished to have kept. Thus the present edition attempts to establish a texture of accidentals which is faithful to Mark Twain's holographic text and which, on the basis of preferences evident in the holographic text or in his contemporary practice, renders certain varying forms consistently when his inconsistencies were without apparent intention or function. In addition, preferred spellings and other preferred accidentals in the holographic text replace variants found only or preponderantly in the unpublished pages for book 1, chapters 7–8. Items covered in these policies are as follows:

I Punctuation

1. Question marks and exclamation points remain inside quotation marks though they are not part of the quotation; semicolons are placed inside quotation marks. The placement in the first two cases follows Mark Twain's practice throughout the holographic text; the placement of semicolons makes uniform the dominant usage of this holographic text, which is the dominant usage of Mark Twain's manuscripts in general.

2. Commas and periods are placed outside terminal parentheses, again to make uniform Mark Twain's common usage in the holographic text.

3. Dashes are inserted after "P.S.," before "M. T.," and in other places where the holographic text does not always designate formal separations of headnotes and citations.

4. The holographic text generally has colons at the end of paragraphs when the following paragraphs are simply being introduced, and dashes when the following paragraphs are continuations or interruptions of the preceding matter (for example, 333.10–13, "The By-Law . . . says— ⟨['In its relation . . . " and 333.17–18, " 'Therefore—' ⟨[Therefore no branch Church . . ."). The present edition accordingly emends a few end-paragraph dashes to colons, mostly in the early portion of the text, where Mark Twain's practice was not yet stable.

II Word Forms

1. Compounds normally hyphenated and compounds normally un-hyphenated in the holographic text are regularized according to their dominant form. The unpublished pages for book 1, chapters 7–8, used as printer's copy for the *North American Review*, are emended in agreement, most often "Christian Science" and "Christian Scientist" when used as adjectives.

2. Variant spellings and other variations in word forms (such as "per centage"-"percentage") are styled according to Mark Twain's domi-nant usage, except when a variant form is functional, such as "byanby" [by and by]. The spelling "recognise" (used only in the portion Mark Twain wrote abroad) becomes "recognize," but other words with "-ise" suffixes remain so spelled if they do not also appear as "-ize" in the holographic text (for example, "itemised").

3. Abbreviations are spelled out unless there is reason to believe Mark Twain wished them to remain. His common "C. S." [Christian Sci-ence] as an adjective is kept, since it was also used in Christian Science publications (see explanatory note to 327.8), but this abbreviation is normally spelled out in the title "*Christian Science Journal.*"

4. Numbers remain in the arabic numerals of the holographic text when the context stresses quantities or proportions. Mark Twain used lettered forms more often than arabic numerals when referring to years ("forty years"), and the arabic numerals in this case are emended to lettered forms.

5. Variations in capitalization (such as "dollar"-"Dollar") remain when the occasional capitalization is meaningful as honorific or pejora-tive stress, and when Mark Twain indicates religious institutions and congregations, as distinguished from buildings, by styling "Church" in upper case. The few instances where lower-case "church" has the same reference are emended to upper case. Other words normally capitalized

in the holographic text, such as "Protestant" and "Catechism" (in "Westminster Catechism"), are now uniformly in upper case.

6. All book, play, journal, and newspaper titles are in upper- and lower-case italics. Mark Twain's usage included, besides this style, instructions for roman type both with and without quotation marks.

All these policy changes, as well as corrections of obvious mistakes in the holograph, are noted in the list of emendations (Schedule A). Only the following changes are made without notation:

1. Punctuation and other accidentals in quoted matter are in general silently restored to their originals where Mark Twain misquoted in the holographic text. Misquotations of punctuation occasionally remain where Mark Twain incorporates quotations in his own sentences and where changes of the originals are necessary in the incorporation. (His misquotations of substantive readings remain unless there is reason to believe he wished to quote correctly. Restorations of substantives in quotations are fully noted in Schedule A.1.)

2. Ampersands are silently spelled out as "and"; periods are silently dropped from chapter headings and subtitles; chapter headings are in arabic rather than roman numerals.

3. The citation form "—M. T." after Mark Twain's footnotes is silently adopted from the edition of 1907, in order to distinguish his footnotes from those of his quotations (see his Appendix E). The present edition adds this citation form to five footnotes which lack it in the 1907 printing; all five are noted in the list of emendations.

NOTES

The following notes include discussions of editorial choices; Mark Twain's major revisions in the manuscript and the printer's copy for the 1907 edition; and comments on special features of the manuscript and the 1907 edition.

215.13 *January, 1907*] The date "March, 1903" is uncanceled in the printer's copy. The present reading, first in the 1907 edition, is accepted as Mark Twain's proof change, designed to adapt the time reference. Substantive variants at 259.25 and 391.33 are accepted for the same reason. In the unpublished pages used as printer's copy for the *North*

American Review Mark Twain changed "In the past two years the
membership . . . have given" to "In two years (1898–99) the membership . . . gave" (253.33–34).

216   *epigraph*] The epigraph, from Mark Twain's own prose on p.
230, first appeared in the *Cosmopolitan* article, "Christian Science and
the Book of Mrs. Eddy."

216.10   large] First in the *Cosmopolitan* article, "large" replaces manuscript "huge" in "a large . . . sitting room." Although "huge" in Mark
Twain's hand could have been misread by his typist as "large," the word
is accepted as a revision typical of Mark Twain, in that it diminishes
an extreme statement. Compare the change from "at no expense" to
"at small expense" (230.26–27).

218.24   Return it to its receptacle. We deal] The *Cosmopolitan* sentence break is accepted as a probable revision in the printer's copy for
that publication (manuscript: ". . . receptacle, we"). Elsewhere also
Mrs. Fuller's speech acquires abruptness through the use of periods
and semicolons after brief sentences and clauses.

219.18   Just at that point] The sentence begins a two-page pencil insertion (11A–B) in the original manuscript, ending at 220.7 ("do you
an injury."). The first page is on the back of p. 10 of a discarded article
on Spain, Cuba, and the Philippines; p. 11B is on the back of a discarded p. 181 of "Tom Sawyer's Conspiracy."

223.22   to Mind] As in the manuscript, the English *Hadleyburg,* and
Science and Health (see explanatory note to 220.24). The *Cosmopolitan,* the printer's copy for the 1907 edition, and the 1907 edition have
"to the Mind." The correction in *Hadleyburg* was evidently fortuitous;
the present reading is adopted only on the authority of the manuscript
and *Science and Health.*

223.32   equal."] Mark Twain deleted a paragraph in the printer's copy
for the 1907 edition:

. . . equal."
    (It is very curious, the effect which Christian Science has upon the
verbal bowels. Particularly the Third Degree; it makes one think of a
dictionary with the cholera. But I only thought this; I did not say it.)

The paragraph was in all printings before 1907, but Mark Twain probably thought it too coarse for the book.

236.28   as insane as he—] The omission of manuscript "is" after "he," first in the unpublished pages used as printer's copy for the North American Review, is accepted as a typical Mark Twain trimming of grammatical structure. The change from the manuscript colon to a dash appears correlative and also acceptable.

237.3   Opinions that prove nothing] In the manuscript the cue words are followed by the phrase "and judgments that decide nothing." But in the context Mark Twain's topic is only "opinions," and the elision of the manuscript phrase, first in the unpublished pages used as printer's copy for the North American Review, is therefore accepted as his deletion of irrelevant material.

237.31   book;"] In the unpublished pages used as printer's copy for the North American Review the editor deleted "—the one described in the previous article;" and inserted a semicolon after "book." He made a similar change at 247.28 (see Schedule B). Both deletions are accepted as necessary adaptations. Though the references remained in the unpublished pages and the English Hadleyburg, they were appropriate only to Mark Twain's plan in 1899 for a sequel or sequels to the Cosmopolitan article.

238.13   planet.] In the printer's copy for the 1907 edition Mark Twain deleted a long paragraph following the text paragraph. It was followed by the epigraph of what only in the printer's copy became a separate chapter. See the North American Review 176, no. 554 (January 1903): 759–760.

240.4–5   religion,] The manuscript has a dash after "religion"; the unpublished pages used as printer's copy for the North American Review, and all subsequent phases, have a comma. The dash makes parenthetical the words "and show its hand later, when strong and prosperous" and thus links "religion" with "like Mohammedanism"— nonsense in the context. Mark Twain may have first intended to close the sentence with "prosperous," for the dash after "religion" would have been appropriate in that case. The later punctuation is accepted as his correction.

241.22   *clientèle*] The word is italicized in the English *Hadleyburg,* but the authority for this word form derives from Mark Twain's underscoring in the unpublished pages used as printer's copy for the *North American Review.*

248.14–15   would have essentially died thirty times more, in the three years which have since elapsed.] In the 1907 edition the first seven of the cue words follow the other eight and end the sentence. Both groups of words occupy full lines in that printing, and the transposition is here regarded as an error possibly occurring during proof correction.

251.19   by 1930] Through apparent error the *North American Review* has "in" rather than "by." Mark Twain changed "1920" to "1930" in the tearsheets used as printer's copy for the 1907 edition but overlooked the variant.

253.5   city missions,] The earliest extant phase, the unpublished pages used as printer's copy for the *North American Review,* has "foreign missions" after "city missions"; the item was not deleted in those pages by Mark Twain or the editor but was dropped in the *North American Review* and thereafter. Between the printing of the unpublished pages (probably 1900) and of the *North American Review* article for January 1903 Mark Twain had severely attacked American missionaries abroad, and the omission is therefore accepted as his deletion in early journal proof of a cause he no longer believed might appeal "to a human being's purse through his heart" (253.6).

258   *title*] In the manuscript and the *North American Review* "LAT-ER." appears as a subtitle (compare "LATER STILL." in Supplement B2). The manuscript chapter number is ten, possibly because at the time of writing Mark Twain still considered section 4 of the *Cosmopolitan* article (see Supplement B1) a part of the text. The chapter number in the *North American Review* was four, to follow the sequence in the previous installments (December contained number one, January contained numbers two and three). Mark Twain changed to nine when revising the *North American Review* tearsheets in the printer's copy for the 1907 edition.

259.1   Facts are nothing to him,] The cue words are followed by "history is nothing to him," in the manuscript. Mark Twain may have intended to amplify both charges, but he took up only the first. The elision, first in the *North American Review,* is therefore accepted as his revision.

262.2 Buddhist] In the manuscript a comma follows "Buddhist," and originally the succeeding words were "or the Republican or the Democrat, it is environment." Mark Twain deleted "or the Republican or the Democrat" and substituted "or the Mormon," leaving the comma after "Buddhist." But the comma was clearly meant to separate the series of sects after "Presbyterian" from the political parties, and it is now deleted as an oversight.

266.8 calculated to] The manuscript lacks "to"; the typist supplied the word in the typescript, creating a split infinitive typical of Mark Twain's style in this and other works ("calculated to satisfactorily demonstrate"). The present edition also accepts the typist's corrections of slips at 276.7, 282.27, 283.15, 293.18–19, 324.2–3, 330.5, 332.2, 332.5, 332.7, and 348.16. For the cue item see Schedule A.1; for the others see Schedule A.2, except for 330.5, a change of *"siezed"* to *"seized"* first noted as a recurrent emendation in the entry for 260.20. All other variants originating in the typescripts are rejected except where Mark Twain adapted revisions to errors (see discussions of 384.21 and 385.11, below).

267.23 autobiography] In the 1907 edition a confusion began with this instance of "autobiography" that lasted through the rest of the book. The manuscript and the printer's copy for that edition correctly read "autobiography," but the Harper compositor or editor evidently thought the word was Mrs. Eddy's title, which was actually *Retrospection and Introspection.* The confusion was abetted by Mark Twain, who later capitalized and underscored the word. The present text consistently styles it as a common noun when the reference is to Mrs. Eddy's book.

276.24 This is too extraneous for me.] The sentence derived from the close of a long passage which Mark Twain deleted in the manuscript:

> Overcoming evil with Good brings out the nothingness of evil. I don't understand it, and I am not going to bet against it with the hand I hold; but I wish to double the ante and draw five cards on the other proposi-

tion. While I do not know what the eternal Somethingness is, I do believe it vindicates the Divine Principle, although I do not know the process, because I think it stands to reason that if anything can vindicate it the eternal Somethingness is the bird. I quite understand that the eternal Somethingness presupposes a similarly eternal Unsomethingness, otherwise spiritual harmony could not subtend on account of the absence of ostracism, hence the projection of the eternal Somethingness into an arena thitherto occupied by an incomplete and evanescent Unsomethingness would almost or at least in a measure it seems to me. That is, that is my impression. But then, on the other hand—Let us have a new deal, this subject is too extraneous for me.

In the manuscript Mark Twain also canceled two sentences that concluded the text paragraph at 276.27:

I have not made good my attack upon the eternal Somethingness, and honor requires me to confess defeat, but I will not concede that they "improve the race of Adam." On that I stand pat and pass the buck.

279.29   several hundred] As in the 1907 edition; the manuscript and the printer's copy typescript for the 1907 edition read "471." See the Explanatory Notes for an account of this variant.

303.35   (temporarily) cured] As in the 1907 edition; Mark Twain inscribed the footnote in the printer's copy typescript, where "(temporarily)" does not appear. See the Explanatory Notes for an account of this variant.

304.2   is *herself*] The present text has the word order of the manuscript and Mark Twain's italicization in the printer's copy typescript for the 1907 edition; the typist transposed the words in the typescript.

326.11–12   ... what Congress of ours—] Mark Twain deleted a passage in the printer's copy typescript for the 1907 edition:

... what Congress of ours—that august body which is always overwhelmingly and showily pious—that impressive and imposing Cemetery of Whited Christian Sepulchres, pension-mongers, Grosvenors, bunco-steerers —what Con—
    But this is unparliamentary. One must not get excited when considering grave matters of state.

328.8 unique request] In the printer's copy typescript for the 1907 edition Mark Twain added and deleted a footnote:

Necessarily she means a strange request, a request of an unsual sort; she couldn't mean that it was a request of a sort which was absolutely new in the world and had never been made before under like conditions. However, upon reflection it seemed best for me to make sure that it is never permissible to use the word unique in the sense of strange, unusual, odd—a sense in which it is used (misused?) by every English-speaking human being forty-four times every day in speaking, and eleven in writing, for it is much the hardest-worked word that exists in any language. Very well, then, in order to save myself the humiliation of finding fault with a person who might chance to be right, I consulted two Unabridged Dictionaries: Webster's, (edition of 1890) and the Standard, (edition of 1900.) The word isn't in either of them! Yet it is a word which falls (misused) out of everybody's mouth several times every day. Next, I became doubtful about the word exequatur. It was absent from both of those Dictionaries. By consequence, it will not be found in my book, now; I expelled it, and substituted a word whose meaning I could risk money on in case of challenge. M. T.

338.35 . . . on the Chair.] In the manuscript Mark Twain deleted a passage following the cue words:

. . . on the Chair. The Rocking-Chair. Horse-hair Rocking-Chair. Spiritualized Oil Picture of the Horse-hair Rocking-Chair. In a Shrine, with Electric Carbons Flooding It with up-to-date Sacred Light. Four years ago, it was worship of Mrs. Eddy's portrait; now it is worship of her Chair. It is a good deal of a descent. Next, it will be her Galoshes.

The text sentence which follows the cue words, "At the same time . . . choose the Chair." (338.35–339.2), is inscribed on the back of the manuscript leaf, and on the front Mark Twain wrote "over" after ". . . on the Chair." Thus the insertion may have been a replacement for the deleted passage.

355.13 We may take that up, now.] The original chapter title ("The 'If' ") was omitted in the 1907 edition, and the text sentence becomes clear only from what follows it. Almost all chapter titles were dropped in the 1907 edition; the action could hardly have been taken without Mark Twain's choice or concurrence.

382.1 Mark Twain inscribed the text paragraph and title in the printer's copy typescript of "Mrs. Eddy in Error" he sent to the *North American Review*. In the manuscript the title and opening paragraph read:

"Self-Deification."

Mrs. Eddy—without her knowledge or consent—is helping me do this portrait of her. I do not want any other help. She furnishes the paint, I furnish the canvas; everything is fair and right. I put the paint on, but that is a trifle, and does not count. She has lately furnished some more paint, and I find it in the associated press dispatches of the date of January 17th:

384.21   24,] The present text accepts a comma supplied by the typist in the printer's copy typescript of "Mrs. Eddy in Error," for Mark Twain deleted "of the" after "24," producing the form in this text parenthesis which he had used in all subsequent parentheses of the manuscript.

385.9–10   The confusions being now dispersed, we have this clarified result:] From the manuscript through the printer's copy for the 1907 edition (*North American Review* page proof of "Mrs. Eddy in Error") the cue words followed the text paragraph at 385.11–14. In the text order of the 1907 edition the cue words acquire a sarcastic reference to the preceding quotation and properly introduce the following paragraph. The transposition is accepted as Mark Twain's proof revision.

385.11   at one time,] The typist added the comma in the printer's copy typescript for "Mrs. Eddy in Error." The comma remains in the present text because Mark Twain inscribed a comma in the typescript after the parallel "at one time" which follows.

386.32   ... protest.] In the manuscript Mark Twain deleted a passage following the cue word:

... protest. I think that the convention that listened without remark to the wildly metamorphosed v. 53 would have found no fault with the next change which she is going to make, and which, to my mind, will seriously mar the grace and charm of the beautiful verse in which she has resolved to make it. I had a revelation about this, for I often have revelations when I eat indiscreetly, and it was in that way that I found out the new wording which she has arranged in her mind and will deliver to her people in June. As follows:

"Consider the microbe of the corpuscle; he toils not, neither does he spin, yet Vanderbilt with all his capital cannot extend his business like one of these."

It has a profane sound to me, but that is because I have not had Mrs. Eddy's practice in mending the Scriptures. It will sound differently when she promulgates it and adds it to her new arrangements in behalf of those Christianly-Scientific non-existent "sick" whom she has put in a place which had been so disadvantageous to the "rich" before.

388.5   chapter] As in the 1907 edition; the manuscript, the typescript printer's copy for "Mrs. Eddy in Error," and the *North American Review* have "magazine"; compare the manuscript word at 391.25.

391.25   chapter] As in the manuscript and the typescript printer's copy for "Mrs. Eddy in Error"; the *North American Review* and the 1907 edition read "article." Mark Twain forgot to restore "chapter" before submitting the printer's copy for the 1907 edition (page proof for the *North American Review*).

392.17   . . . harmonious."] When "Mrs. Eddy in Error" was part of book 2, chapter 8, it ended with the text sentence, which was followed by Mark Twain's signature. He added the remainder after making "Mrs. Eddy in Error" a separate chapter to follow book 2, chapter 9 (see the Introduction).

395.1   appeared (in the March number of the *North American Review*)] Mark Twain added the postscript in the typed printer's copy for "Mrs. Eddy in Error." There and in the *North American Review* the corresponding passage reads: ". . . has appeared (in the last number of this Review)." Someone other than Mark Twain, probably a Harper editor, inscribed the changes in the *North American Review* page proof used as printer's copy for the 1907 edition. Though the later reading adapts the earlier only for the publication date originally planned (spring 1903), it is accepted as a necessary revision.

395   CONCLUSION] A manuscript fragment (University of Virginia) contains the title ("Christian Science—Conclusion") and Mark Twain's advice to F. A. Duneka: "This is a most damn good Conclusion—put it in, Duneka." Mark Twain evidently wrote the conclusion after sending him the rest of the copy.

Collation

1. Description of Texts

MS   Manuscript; chapters 7–8 of book 1 missing.

A1   "Christian Science and the Book of Mrs. Eddy," *Cosmopolitan* 27, no. 6 (October 1899): 585–594. Copy: University of Iowa. First printing of what became book 1, chapters 1–4 (216–234), with omission of section 4 of the article (see Supplement B1; *Cosmopolitan*, pp. 592–593).

UP   Unpublished pages from unidentified typesetting used as printer's copy for the *North American Review*. Copy: University of Virginia. First printing of what became book 1, chapters 5–8 (234–258); contains author's and editor's inscribed revisions.

Q2   *The Man That Corrupted Hadleyburg and Other Stories and Sketches*. London: Chatto & Windus, 1900. BAL 3460. "Christian Science and the Book of Mrs. Eddy," pp. 92–143; covers book 1, chapters 1–8 (216–258). Copies: University of Iowa, University of Texas [hereafter TxU].

TS   Typescript printer's copy of "Mrs. Eddy in Error" for the *North American Review*. Copy: Washington University (St. Louis). Covers pp. 382–395 of the text; contains author's and editor's inscribed revisions.

A2   "Christian Science," *North American Review* 175, no. 553 (December 1902):756–768. Copy: MTP. Resetting of what became book 1, chapters 5–6 (234–248); tearsheets of this printing used in the printer's copy for the 1907 edition.

"Christian Science—II," *North American Review* 176, no. 554 (January 1903):1–9. Copy: MTP. Resetting of what became book 1, chapters 7–8 (248–258); tearsheets of this printing used in the printer's copy for the 1907 edition.

"Christian Science—III," *North American Review* 176, no. 555 (February 1903):173–177. Copy: MTP. First printing of what became book 1, chapter 9 (258–263), with omission of "Eddypus" continuation (see Supplement B2; *North American Review*, pp. 177–184); tearsheets of this printing used in the printer's copy for the 1907 edition.

"Mrs. Eddy in Error," *North American Review* 176, no. 557 (April 1903):505–517. Copy: MTP. First printing of this section (382–395); page proof of this publication, containing no printed variants from the journal issue, used in the printer's copy for the 1907 edition.

PC Printer's copy for the 1907 edition. Preface: typescript; book 1, chapters 1–4: pages from unidentified setting; book 1, chapters 5–9: tearsheets from the *North American Review*; book 2, pp. 264–381: typescript; book 2, "Mrs. Eddy in Error": page proof for the *North American Review*; Conclusion: in manuscript only.

A First American edition. New York and London [TxU, Clemens 557: London and New York]: Harper and Brothers [and another imprint], 1907, [1917?]. *BAL* 3497. The eight copies machine-collated are of two text states:
   Aa 1907 (TxU, Clemens 544, 550, 557; BX6955/C6/1907, University of Iowa; the present edition has been set from emended Xerox copies of Clemens 544). First edition, first text state (distinguished by 275.31: *Autobiograyhy*).
   Ab 1907 (TxU, Clemens 553; *The Writings of Mark Twain*, "Autograph Edition" [Hartford: American Publishing Company; *BAL* 3456], TxU, Groves Collection); n.d. [1917?] (TxU, 817/C59/A1/v.25/cop.4; PS1300/E99/v.25, University of Iowa). First edition, second text state (distinguished by 275.31: *Autobiography*).

Rejected as being of no authority are *The Man That Corrupted Hadleyburg and Other Stories and Sketches* (Leipzig: Bernhard Tauchnitz, 1900; see *BAL* 3460), book 1, chapters 1–8, in 1: 124–190; the German edition of *Christian Science* (Leipzig: Bernhard Tauchnitz, 1907; see *BAL* 3497); the second American edition, in the "Definitive Edition" (New York: Gabriel Wells, 1923; *BAL* 3691); another impression of the second American edition, in the "Stormfield Edition" (New York: Harper, 1929; not in *BAL*).

2. Collation Schedules

Schedule A: Emendations of the Copy-text

This collation presents emendations of Mark Twain's final holographic text and, for book 1, chapters 7–8, of the unpublished pages from the unidentified typesetting used as printer's copy for the *North American Review*. Accepted readings, their sources identified by symbols, are at the left; rejected readings are at the right. The letter I follows emendations for which the editor of this volume is the source. Dashes link the first and last texts which agree in a reading, and indicate that there are intervening texts which also agree. Where symbols are separated by commas, either no texts intervene or those which do have different readings. Where the earliest phase noted is printer's copy (PC or TS) though there is manuscript for the passage, the printer's copy reading represents Mark Twain's holograph revision in that phase. The symbol UPE indicates readings inscribed by the *North American Review* editor in the unpublished pages. In A.1 the expression *not in* indicates the absence of words in phases before the phases of accepted readings; the abbreviation *om.* (omitted) indicates words elided in quoted matter and in variant texts. The entry in A.1 and B for 219.34 represents a word chosen in the first printing from alternative readings uncanceled in the manuscript. For the phases in which Mark Twain's footnotes originate see footnote 1 above. In A.2 the first instances of recurrent and consistent changes are indicated by asterisks (*); subsequent instances are not noted. Readings in A.2 followed only by a plus sign (+) represent instances where the copy-text agrees with the forms chosen in recurrent changes. In collations of punctuation curved dashes (~) stand for the words before or after the punctuation of the present text. The curved dashes are followed or preceded by the punctuation of the variant texts; if no punctuation appears, the variant texts have none. A dagger (†) precedes entries which are discussed in Notes, above.

1. WORDS AND WORD ORDER

[Relevant texts, p. 288: MS (manuscript); PC (typescript used as printer's copy for the 1907 edition); A (1907 edition)]:

	Iowa-California Readings	Rejected Readings
†215.13	*January, 1907* A	March, 1903 PC

[Relevant texts, pp. 216–234: MS (manuscript); A1 (*Cosmopolitan*); PC (unpublished pages with holograph revision used as printer's copy for the 1907 edition); Q2 (*Hadleyburg*); A (1907 edition)]:

†216.1–3	*"It . . . command."* A1–A	*not in* MS
†216.10	large A1–A	huge MS
219.34	pity A1–A	compassion/charity/pity MS
221.14	"It A1–A	"Yes, it has that look. It MS
221.34	strong. A1–A	strong. Uncommon. MS
223.6	viz., ease A1–A	ease MS
226.31	it, madam. A1–A	it. MS
230.26	Bible PC–A	Book MS, A1
230.27	small A1–A	no MS
230.27	and no expense of A1–A	nor MS
230.33	command. A1–A	command. It has been said to me by people who would compliment me, that I possess the sense of humor, and to me that compliment is precious and I would not lightly do anything to bring it under suspicion of being undeserved; yet precious as it is I am willing to peril it upon the assertion that

	Iowa-California Readings	*Rejected Readings*
		this is the very funniest book that any person, sane or insane, has ever written. And the most pathetic, in its honest unconsciousness of the fact. MS
232.1	client's A1–A	subject's MS
232.9	own A1–A	proper MS
232.16	patient? A1–A	patient? Genuine and remarkable cures are constantly being made at Lourdes. The patient believes that a personage from heaven appeared there and gave medicinal properties to the waters of a spring. But it is not claimed by the Church that a *personage* appeared there, or even the shadow or spectre of a personage, but only an apparition which figured, not an entity but an *abstraction*— the Immaculate Conception. Faith, then, in the curative powers of water made holy by the visit of a sacred Abstraction, would seem to be as effective as faith in the powers of a doctor or a King or other entity. MS

	Iowa-California Readings	*Rejected Readings*
232.16	patient? A1, Q2, A	patient?[1]
		[1]When Professor Buckland, the eminent osteologist and geologist, discovered that the relics of St. Rosalia, at Palermo, which had for ages cured diseases and warded off epidemics, were the bones of a goat, this fact caused not the slightest diminution of their miraculous power. ANDREW D. WHITE: *A History of the Warfare of Science with Theology.* PC
233.9	Differing A1–A	Various MS
233.13	achieve A1–A	procure MS
233.24	much. A1–A	much. I know it can cure any kind of a surgical case that can be imagined, but I am well convinced that it can neither cure nor modify even the simplest forms of human disease. MS
233.24–25	ought to A1–A	ought to come down from its arrogant cure-all summit and MS
233.35	radically A	quite PC
234.9	inconsistent. A1–A	inconsistent. NOTE. This article is already long enough, but as it has not yet touched up-

Iowa-California Readings *Rejected Readings*

on two or three of the largest features of the Christian Science cult, I will cut it short at this point and take up those features in another article. One of those features is the probable future of the movement. I think there are reasons for suspecting that Christian Science is a permanency; also, that its spread in the earth will be one of the wonders of the twentieth century. This surmise is not much of a compliment to the human race, but that cannot be helped. M. T.   MS

[Relevant texts, pp. 234–248: MS (manuscript); UP (unpublished pages with holograph revision used as printer's copy for the *North American Review*); Q2 (*Hadleyburg*); A2 (*North American Review*); PC (tearsheets of A2 with holograph revision used as printer's copy for the 1907 edition); A (1907 edition)]:

234.14	are UP–A	were MS
234.15	now UP–A	before MS
234.21	several UP–A	a good many MS
235.4–5	are; just as insane as Shakespeare was, just as insane as the Pope is. Q2	are. MS are; just as insane as Shakspeare was, just as insane as the Pope is. UP are; just as . . . was. UPE–A

	Iowa-California Readings	Rejected Readings
†236.28	he— UP–A	he is: MS
†237.3	nothing UP–A	nothing, and judgments that decide nothing, MS
237.4	but a dead person UP–A	flathead MS
†237.31	book;" UPE–PC	book"—the one described in the previous article; MS–Q2 book"; A
237.34–35	English (with help of a polisher) UP–A	English MS
238.20	Mosque UP–A	Temple MS
239.28	not yet five UP–A	only ten MS
240.16	the bulk UP–A	all MS
241.25	In large measure, yes. UP–A	I think so. MS
241.33	gloomy UP–A	cloudy MS
242.32	imaginary UP–A	imagining MS
243.5	dump-pit UP–A	dump-tank MS
244.16	C. S. magazine UP–A	magazine MS
245.16	St. Vitus's dance UP, Q2	child-birth MS St. Vitus's dance is UPE–A
246.13	rat UP–A	thing MS
247.28	surgeon. UPE–A	surgeon. I can believe this, because my own case was somewhat similar, as per my former article. MS–Q2

	Iowa-California Readings	*Rejected Readings*
248.22	side. UP–A	side.
		Mark Twain
		NOTE. Space-limits will not at this time allow me to statistically explain why I think the new religion may achieve a wide and marvelous conquest, so I will leave that for next month. M. T. MS

[Relevant texts, pp. 248–258: UP (unpublished pages with holograph revision used as printer's copy for the *North American Review*); Q2 (*Hadleyburg*); A2 (*North American Review*); PC (tearsheets of A2 with holograph revision used as printer's copy for the 1907 edition); A (1907 edition)]:

†251.19	by 1930 I	by 1920 UP, Q2
		in 1920 A2
		in 1930 PC, A
†253.5	city missions, A2–A	city missions, foreign missions, UP, Q2

[Relevant texts, pp. 258–263: MS (manuscript); A2 (*North American Review*); PC (tearsheets of A2 with holograph revision used as printer's copy for the 1907 edition); A (1907 edition)]:

†258 *title*	CHAPTER 9 I	X	LATER. MS
		IV.—LATER. A2
		Chapter IX.	—LATER. PC
		CHAPTER IX A
†259.1	him, A2–A	him, history is nothing to him, MS
259.25	four A2–A	three MS
261.18	five A	four MS–PC

	Iowa-California Readings	Rejected Readings
262.33	alert and diligent A2–A	wily MS

[Relevant texts, pp. 264–361: MS (manuscript); PC (typescript with holograph revision used as printer's copy for the 1907 edition); A (1907 edition)]:

265 *title*	CHAPTER 1 I	Chapter 1. | MRS. EDDY PC CHAPTER I A
266.3–4	Eiffel tower A	Eiffel MS, PC
†266.8	calculated to PC, A	calculated MS
275.9	silenced A	silence MS, PC
†279.29	several hundred A	471 MS, PC
281 *title*	CHAPTER 4 I	Chapter IV. | DIVINE AUTHORSHIP? MS, PC CHAPTER IV A
286 *title*	CHAPTER 5 I	Chapter V. | WHAT IS HER CELESTIAL RANK? MS, PC CHAPTER V A
292.30	reduction I	deduction MS–A
†303.35	(temporarily) cured A	cured MS, PC
309.34	nine A	ten MS, PC
310.3	nine A	ten MS, PC
310.9	nine A	ten MS, PC
311.24	139 A	138 PC
316.23	us I	*om.* MS–A
321.5	History A	She MS, PC
321.5	itself A	herself MS, PC
321.7	history A	she MS, PC

	Iowa-California Readings	Rejected Readings
324.4	merely A	exactly the same as MS, PC
326.1–2	copyright (a fact not known to twenty people in the world). A	copyright, and only just that one. MS, PC
329 *title*	CHAPTER 8 I	Chapter VIII | PERSONAL AGGRANDIZEMENTS. MS, PC CHAPTER VIII A
332.34	thing as death. A	thing. MS, PC
340.7	eternal I	*om.* MS–A
344.3	can be let A	can let PC
344 *title*	CHAPTER 9 I	Chapter IX | SUMMING UP OF MONOPOLIES. MS, PC CHAPTER IX A
354 *title*	CHAPTER 14 I	Chapter XIV | THE PAPACY. MS, PC CHAPTER XIV A
†355 *title*	CHAPTER 15 I	Chapter XV | THE "IF." MS, PC CHAPTER XV A
360.34	is to A	is PC

[Relevant texts, pp. 363–381: PC (typescript used as printer's copy for the 1907 edition); A (1907 edition)]:

365.5	past I	last PC, A
369 *title*	APPENDIX D A	APPENDIX D | PRAYER. PC
369.21	who I	that PC, A
380.19	of either I	by either PC, A

[Relevant texts, pp. 382–395: MS (manuscript); TS (typescript with holograph revision used as printer's copy for the *North American Review* publication of "Mrs. Eddy in Error"); A2 (*North American Review*); PC (page proof of A2 used as printer's copy for the 1907 edition); A (1907 edition)]:

†385.9–14	The confusions . . . her." A	There . . . result: MS–PC
†388.5	chapter A	magazine MS–PC
389.10	She carries the key. A2–A	*not in* MS, TS
391.33	recently published A2–A	recent MS, TS
391.33	article A	article (written four years ago) MS–PC
†395.1	appeared (in the March number of the *North American Review*) A	has appeared (in the last number of this Review) TS has . . . REVIEW) A2, PC
395.6	*North American Review* A	Review TS REVIEW A2, PC

2. PARAGRAPHING, PUNCTUATION, WORD FORMS

[Relevant texts, pp. 216–234: MS (manuscript); A1 (*Cosmopolitan*); PC (unpublished pages with holograph revision used as printer's copy for the 1907 edition); Q2 (*Hadleyburg*); A (1907 edition)]:

218.23	passion: A1–A	~— MS
†218.24	receptacle. We A1–A	~, we MS
219.18	imaginings." A1, PC, A	~. MS ~,' Q2
219.20	caution: A1–A	~— MS
219.34	His A	his MS–PC
220.8	recognize A1, PC, A	recognise MS, Q2

	Iowa-California Readings	Rejected Readings
220.25	summarized A1, PC, A	summarised MS, Q2
220.32	hesitancy: A1–A	~— MS
223.6	ease A1–A	~, MS
224.12–13	*Science and Health, with Key to the Scriptures* *A	'Science and Health, with Key to the Scriptures' MS–PC
226.10	prophesied A1–A	prophecied MS
226.11	St. A1–A	St MS
226.16	*century* A1–A	century MS
226.24	a *woman* clothed with the sun A1–A	*a woman clothed with the sun* MS
226.31	recognize A1, PC, A	recognise MS, Q2
227.7	importance A1–A	immortance MS
227.19	bitter.' A1–A	~." MS
230.19	Evidence, PC–A	~; MS, A1
230.20	*mentioning* A1–A	mentioning MS
230.30	light!" A1–A	Light" MS
230.30	have A1–A	*have* MS
232.1	*imagination* A1–A	imagination MS
232.2	recognized A1, PC, A	recognised MS, Q2
233.9	*the patient's imagination* A1–A	the patient's imagination MS
233.14	Prayer-Cure I	Prayer Cure MS–A
233.32	forty-one A	41 PC
234.10	NOTE.— A	~. PC
234.10–11	*Cosmopolitan Magazine* A	Cosmopolitan Magazine PC

[Relevant texts, pp. 234–248: MS (manuscript); UP (unpublished pages with holograph revision used as printer's copy for the *North American Review*); Q2 (*Hadleyburg*); A2 (*North American Review*); PC (tearsheets of A2 with holograph revision used as printer's copy for the 1907 edition); A (1907 edition)]:

234.26	eight UP–A	8 MS
235.6–7	*it is where his opinion differs from ours* UP–A	it is where his opinion differs from ours MS
235.12	Catechism UP–A	catechism MS
235.19	republicans UP, Q2	Republicans MS, UPE–A
236.15	Mugwumps), UP–A	~,) MS
236.26	recognize UP, A2–A	recognise MS, Q2
237.13	fifteen UP–A	15 MS
237.13	recognize UP, A2–A	recognise MS, Q2
237.23	picturesquely UP–A	*picturesquely* MS
237.28	*have* UP–A	have MS
237.28–29	when it is not violent UP–A	*when it is not violent* MS
238.12	Protestant UP–A	protestant MS
239.15	which has special reference to the present age UP–A	*which has special reference to the present age* MS
†240.4	religion, UP–A	~— MS
240.25	*beginning* UP–A	beginning MS
241.4	admissible UP–A	admissable MS
241.12	organized UP, A2–A	organised MS, Q2

	Iowa-California Readings	Rejected Readings
242.4–5	the *Christian Science Journal* *I	*The Christian Science Journal* MS, UP, A 'The Christian Science Journal' Q2 "The Christian Science Journal" UPE–PC
244.2	*his* UP–A	his MS
246.5	*seemed* UP–A	seemed MS
246.20	Two UP–A	two MS
246.21	Two UP–A	two MS
247.14	tooth-ache I	toothache MS–A
247.31	recognize UP, A2–A	recognise MS, Q2
247.33	*he* demonstrate UP–A	he demonstrate MS
247.33	he do UP–A	*he* do MS

[Relevant texts, pp. 248–258: UP (unpublished pages with holograph revision used as printer's copy for the *North American Review*); Q2 (*Hadleyburg*); A2 (*North American Review*); PC (tearsheets of A2 with holograph revision used as printer's copy for the 1907 edition); A (1907 edition)]:

249.12	worshiped I	worshipped UP–A
249.19	Christian Science I	Christian-Science UP–A
249.23	Christian Science I	Christian-Science UP–A
249.27–28	Christian Science I	Christian-Science UP–A
249.28	Mother Church I	Mother-Church UP–A
250.2	Christian Science I	Christian-Science UP–A
250.12	*Miscellaneous Writings* *A	"Miscellaneous Writings" UP, A2, PC 'Miscellaneous Writings' Q2

	Iowa-California Readings	Rejected Readings
250.14–15	*Christ and Christmas* *A	"Christ and Christmas" UP, A2, PC 'Christ and Christmas' Q2
250.16	it!— A	~— UP–PC
250.20–21	the *Christian Science Journal*	+
250.22	Christian Science I	Christian-Science UP–A
250.30	*February,* A	Feb. PC
250.36	*Christian Science Journal*	+
251.11	Christian Scientist I	Christian-Scientist UP–A
251.13	"capitation-tax" I	"capitation tax" UP–A
252.7–8	by and by I	by-and-by UP–A
253.23	heaven I	Heaven UP–A
253.35	benevolent Q2–A	benevoleut UP
254.14	per cent I	~~. UP–A
254.34	Septimus I	Septimius PC, A
255.7	heaven-commanded I	Heaven-commanded UP–A
255.16	price (A	~, (PC
255.16	calling). A	~.) PC
255.28	practise A	practice PC
257.26	Mind-Curist I	Mind Curist UP–A
257.30	Christian Scientist I	Christian-Scientist UP–A

[Relevant texts, pp. 258–263: MS (manuscript); A2 (*North American Review*); PC (tearsheets of A2 with holograph revision used as printer's copy for the 1907 edition); A (1907 edition)]:

	Iowa-California Readings	Rejected Readings
258.31	1898.—M. T. I	~. A
259.17	reason A2–A	*reason* MS
260.20	seize *A2–A	sieze MS
261.34	*Environment* A2–A	Environment MS
†262.2	Buddhist I	~, MS–A
262.3	*environment* A2–A	environment MS
262.33–34	(while ... schools) A2–A	~ ... ~ MS

[Relevant texts, pp. 264–361: MS (manuscript); PC (typescript with holograph revision used as printer's copy for the 1907 edition); A (1907 edition)]:

264.29	experts."— A	~." MS, PC
268.18	*Hamlet* I	Hamlet MS, PC "Hamlet" A
271.11	*Health* (1883). A	Health," (~.) PC
272.11	it [the heart] on A	~" (~ ~) "~ MS, PC
276.7	judgment PC, A	judgement MS
277.22	forty A	40 MS, PC
277.23	forty A	40 MS, PC
278.26	Spot-Bacilli A	Spot Bacilli MS, PC
281.22	autobiography *I	*Auto.* MS Autobiography PC *Autobiography* A
281.25	His A	his MS, PC
282.27	led PC, A	"~ MS
283.15	70.) PC, A	~). MS
283.26	me), A	~,) MS, PC

	Iowa-California Readings	Rejected Readings
284.33–34	(*Eddyism, or Christian Science*; Boston: 15 Court Square, price 25 cents): I	("*Eddyism, or Christian Science;*" Boston: 15 Court Square), price 25 cents: PC (*Eddyism, or Christian Science*. Boston: 15 Court Square, price twenty-five cents): A
285.30	rest). A	~.) MS, PC
293.18–19	always and PC, A	~, ~ MS
293.33	*Health.*—M. T. I	Health. MS, PC *Health.* A
293.34	only."— A	~." MS, PC
298.17	it from MS, A	it *from* PC
298.18	*Science and Health*	+
298.20	Sec. A	sec. MS, PC
302.17	is;" I	~"; MS–A
302.33	think A	~, PC
305.18	autobiography), I	Autobiography,) MS, PC *Autobiography*): A
307.10	Reader A	reader MS, PC
307.15	Readers A	readers MS, PC
307.21	quoted) A	~), PC
308.16	book A	~, MS, PC
308.17	author," A	~, MS, PC
308.17	text-books A	~" MS, PC
309.33	percentage A	per centage MS, PC

	Iowa-California Readings	Rejected Readings
310.20	*Christian Advocate*: A	Christian Advocate: MS, PC
311.26	*Transcript* A	Transcript MS, PC
311.34	The *Literary Digest* I	The Literary Digest MS, PC The *Literary Digest* A
311.34	February 14th A	Feb. 14 MS, PC
312.15	percentage A	per centage MS, PC
312.16	percentage A	per centage MS, PC
312.16	percentage A	per centage MS, PC
314.9	*deed*). A	~.) PC
314.22	and- A	~ MS, PC
315.35	January 17th A	Jan. 17 PC
316 *title*	PRAYER— A	~. MS, PC
318.12	naïvely A	naively MS, PC
319.16	*Christian Science History,* A	"Christian Science History," MS, PC
320.22	say: A	~ MS, PC
322.15	Race). A	~.) PC
323.18	Directors A	~" MS, PC
323.32	Sec. A	sec. PC
324.2–3	that is PC, A	~ ~, MS
324.4	herself). A	~.) MS, PC
324.10	*Christian Science Practice,* A	"Christian Science Practice," MS, PC
325.1	*The branch Churches are strictly forbidden to use them* A	The branch Churches are strictly forbidden to use them MS, PC

	Iowa-California Readings	*Rejected Readings*
325.25	forty-two-year A	42-year MS, PC
326.15	twenty-eight PC, A	28 MS
327.15	*Journal* A	Journal PC
327.22	*Journal* A	Journal MS, PC
327.26	*Journal* A	Journal MS, PC
328.9	*Christian Science* A	C. S. MS, PC
328.23	*Christian Science* A	C. S. MS Christian Science PC
329.8	*Christian Science* A	C. S. MS, PC
331.5	Churches I	churches MS–A
331.5	Churches I	churches MS–A
331.22	Church A	church MS, PC
332.2	C. S. PC, A	C S MS
332.5	C. S. child PC, A	C S ~ MS
332.7	Church PC, A	church MS
332.14	Church A	church MS, PC
332.15	Church A	church MS, PC
332.18	Church-function A	church-function MS, PC
333.18	Church A	church MS, PC
334.2	Limited). A	~.) MS, PC
334.7	*Members.* A	~." MS, PC
335.6	article), A	~,) PC
336.19	Church A	church MS, PC
336.26	*self*-worship I	self-worship MS, PC *self* worship A
337.14–15	*North American* *Review* *A	North American Review MS, PC

	Iowa-California Readings	Rejected Readings
341.17	*Christian Science* A	C. S. MS, PC
341.35	Prayer.) A	~) PC
342.12	*Christian Science* A	C. S. MS, PC
342.20	the Mother Church I	The Mother Church MS, PC The Mother-Church A
344.10	canvass A	canvas PC
344.10	*Health* A	Health," PC
344.11	words). A	~.) PC
344.28–29	etc.—New York *Sun*, February A	~. N. Y. Sun, Feb. PC
345.20	Church A	~; MS, PC
346.20	*nature* A	nature MS, PC
348.14	mental-healing I	mental healing MS–A
348.16	mental-healing PC, A	mental healing MS
353.25	naïvely A	naively MS, PC
353.27	Rémusat A	Remusat MS, PC
356.13	Captain A	Capt. MS, PC
358.8	"O A	~ MS, PC
358.29	systematized A	systematised MS, PC
358.35	*The Life Within* A	"The Life Within" PC
359.20	Mother Church's I	Mother-Church's MS–A
360.35	April, 1903. A	~/o3 PC

[Relevant texts, pp. 367–368: PC (typescript with holograph revision used as printer's copy for the 1907 edition); A (1907 edition)]:

368.11	paragraphs.—M. T. A	~. M. T. PC
368.29	practice.—M. T. A	~. M. T. PC

[Relevant texts, pp. 382–395: MS (manuscript); TS (typescript with holograph revision used as printer's copy for the *North American Review* publication of "Mrs. Eddy in Error"); A2 (*North American Review*); PC (page proof of A2 used as printer's copy for the 1907 edition); A (1907 edition)]:

†384.21	24, TS–A	~ MS
†385.11	time, TS–A	~ MS
386.8	verse A2–A	v. MS, TS
386.35	imagination.—M. T. I	~. MS–A
388.23	*Manual of The First Church of Christ, Scientist* A	"Manual of The First Church of Christ, Scientist" MS–PC
390.29	says: A2–A	~— MS, TS
390.31	sea! A	~. MS–PC
391.33	article, A	~ MS–PC
391.35	1902.—M. T. I	~. A
394.34	P. S.— A2–A	~. MS, TS
394.35	Square.—M. T. I	~. TS–A
395.23	percentage A2–A	per centage TS
395.25	Ananias. A2–A	~. M. T. TS

Schedule B: Historical Collation

This collation presents substantive variants among the phases identified by symbols in Description of Texts. Rejected readings in the copy-text have already appeared in Schedule A.1, and citations of pages and lines for these entries are italicized. All texts with corresponding passages agree with the present text if their symbols do not appear after rejected readings. The expression *not in* indicates the absence of words in phases before the phases of accepted readings; the abbreviation *om.* (omitted) indicates words elided in quoted matter and in variant texts. The entry for 219.34 represents a word chosen in the first printing from alternative readings uncanceled in the manuscript. The symbols UPE and TSE indicate readings inscribed by the *North American Review* editor in the unpublished pages used as printer's copy for what became book 1, chapters 5–8, and in the printer's copy typescript of "Mrs. Eddy in Error." For the phases in which Mark Twain's footnotes originate see footnote 1, above. A dagger (†) precedes entries which are discussed in Notes, above.

[Relevant texts, p. 215: MS (manuscript); PC (typescript used as printer's copy for the 1907 edition); A (1907 edition)]:

| †215.13 | *January, 1907* | March, 1903 PC |

[Relevant texts, pp. 216–234: MS (manuscript); A1 (*Cosmopolitan*); PC (unpublished pages with holograph revision used as printer's copy for the 1907 edition); Q2 (*Hadleyburg*); A (1907 edition)]:

†216.1–3	"It . . . command."	not in MS
†216.10	large	huge MS
216.13	and on	on A1–A
217.21	off of	off A1–A
218.3	functionable	functional Q2
219.22	mind	the mind Q2
219.26	imagination	imagining A
219.32	a real	real Q2
219.34	pity	compassion/charity/pity MS
220.23	was	were A1–A
221.14	"It	"Yes, it has that look. It MS
221.17	a wonderful	wonderful A1–A
221.34	strong.	strong. Uncommon. MS
223.6	viz., ease	ease MS

	Iowa-California Readings	Rejected Readings
†223.22	Mind	the Mind A1, PC, A
226.29	hath	had A1–A
226.31	it, madam.	it. MS
226.32	those	these A1–A
227.5	had	held A
227.24	influences	influence A1–A
227.27	quite	om. A
228.3	excepting	except A1–A
229.20	a horse-doctor	the horse-doctor A
230.26	Bible	Book MS, A1
230.27	small	no MS
230.27	and no expense of	nor MS
230.33	command.	command.

It has been said to me by people who would compliment me, that I possess the sense of humor, and to me that compliment is precious and I would not lightly do anything to bring it under suspicion of being undeserved; yet precious as it is I am willing to peril it upon the assertion that this is the very funniest book that any person, sane or insane, has ever written. And the most pathetic, in its honest unconsciousness of the fact. MS

	Iowa-California Readings	*Rejected Readings*
231.21	on	upon A
232.1	client's	subject's MS
232.9	own	proper MS
232.16	patient?	patient? Genuine and remarkable cures are constantly being made at Lourdes. The patient believes that a personage from heaven appeared there and gave medicinal properties to the waters of a spring. But it is not claimed by the Church that a *personage* appeared there, or even the shadow or spectre of a personage, but only an apparition which figured, not an entity but an *abstraction*—the Immaculate Conception. Faith, then, in the curative powers of water made holy by the visit of a sacred Abstraction, would seem to be as effective as faith in the powers of a doctor or a King or other entity. MS
232.16	patient?	patient?[1]

[1]When Professor Buckland, the eminent osteologist and geologist, discovered that the relics of St. Rosalia, at Palermo,

Iowa-California Readings *Rejected Readings*

which had for ages cured diseases and warded off epidemics, were the bones of a goat, this fact caused not the slightest diminution of their miraculous power. ANDREW D. WHITE: A *History of the Warfare of Science with Theology.* PC

232.31	demands	demand A1–A
233.3	past	last A1–A
233.6	is	are A1–A
233.9	Differing	Various MS
233.13	achieve	procure MS

233.24   much.

much. I know it can cure any kind of a surgical case that can be imagined, but I am well convinced that it can neither cure nor modify even the simplest forms of human disease. MS

233.24–25   ought to

ought to come down from its arrogant cure-all summit and MS

233.25	itself strictly	itself A1–A
233.35	radically	quite PC

234.9   inconsistent.

inconsistent. NOTE. This article is already long enough, but as it has not yet touched up-

Iowa-California Readings   *Rejected Readings*

on two or three of the largest features of the Christian Science cult, I will cut it short at this point and take up those features in another article. One of those features is the probable future of the movement. I think there are reasons for suspecting that Christian Science is a permanency; also, that its spread in the earth will be one of the wonders of the twentieth century. This surmise is not much of a compliment to the human race, but that cannot be helped. M. T. MS

[Relevant texts, pp. 234–248: MS (manuscript); UP (unpublished pages with holograph revision used as printer's copy for the *North American Review*); Q2 (*Hadleyburg*); A2 (*North American Review*); PC (tearsheets of A2 with holograph revision used as printer's copy for the 1907 edition); A (1907 edition)]:

234.14	are	were MS
234.15	now	before MS
234.21	several	a good many MS
234.29	them	them him UPE–A
234.31	them	them him UPE–A
235.4–5	are; just as insane as Shakespeare was, just as insane as the Pope is.	are. MS are; just as insane as Shakspeare was. UPE–A

	Iowa-California Readings	Rejected Readings
235.30	other 115	115 UPE–A
236.25	each other's	one another's UP–A
†236.28	he—	he is: MS
†237.3	nothing	nothing, and judgments that decide nothing, MS
237.4	but a dead person	flathead MS
237.25	much	om. Q2
†237.31	book;"	book"—the one described in the previous article; MS–Q2
237.34–35	English (with help of a polisher)	English MS
238.11	it	the Bible UPE–A
238.20	Mosque	Temple MS
238.23	image	picture or image UPE–A
239.9	poverty	as poverty Q2
239.26	prove it	prove it is Q2
239.28	not yet five	only ten MS
240.16	the bulk	all MS
†241.22	clientèle	clientage A2–A
241.25	it	so UPE–A
241.25	In large measure, yes.	I think so. MS
241.26	are	is UP–A
241.33	gloomy	cloudy MS
242.18	in and	in UP, Q2 in, UPE–A
242.32	imaginary	imagining MS

	Iowa-California Readings	Rejected Readings
243.4	thus	this A2–A
243.5	dump-pit	dump-tank MS
244.16	C. S. magazine	magazine MS
245.9	farther	further A
245.16	St. Vitus's dance	child-birth MS St. Vitus's dance is UPE–A
246.6	in	to A
246.7	*shall*	*will* UP–A
246.13	rat	thing MS
246.33	It	This UPE–A
247.28	surgeon.	surgeon. I can believe this, because my own case was somewhat similar, as per my former article. MS–Q2
248.3	a plenty	plenty A
248.5	it	the Science UPE–A
†248.14–15	would have . . . elapsed.	in the . . . more. A
248.17	time that	time UP–A
248.21	be far	be UP–A
248.22	side.	side. Mark Twain NOTE. Space-limits will not at this time allow me to statistically explain why I think the new religion may achieve a wide and marvelous conquest, so I will leave that for next month. M. T. MS

[Relevant texts, pp. 248–258: UP (unpublished pages with holograph revision used as printer's copy for the *North American Review*); Q2 (*Hadleyburg*); A2 (*North American Review*); PC (tearsheets of A2 with holograph revision used as printer's copy for the 1907 edition); A (1907 edition)]:

249.21	only cash	cash only Q2
250.17	highwayman's	highwaymen's Q2
251.6	possess	possesses A
†251.19	by 1930	by 1920 UP, Q2 in 1920 A2 in 1930 PC, A
†253.5	city missions,	city missions, foreign missions, UP, Q2
253.33	Church in	Church of Q2
253.34	$73,000,000	seventy-three millions of dollars A
254.19	business	its business A2–A
257.26–27	Mind-Curist, Lourdes Miracle-Worker,	Mind Curist, UPE–A
257.27–28	Expert, or Hypnotist,	Expert, Q2

[Relevant texts, pp. 258–263: MS (manuscript); A2 (*North American Review*); PC (tearsheets of A2 with holograph revision used as printer's copy for the 1907 edition); A (1907 edition)]:

†258 *title*	CHAPTER 9	X | LATER. MS IV.—LATER. A2 Chapter IX. | —LATER. PC CHAPTER IX A
†259.1	him,	him, history is nothing to him, MS

	Iowa-California Readings	*Rejected Readings*
259.25	four	three MS
260.16	those	these A2–A
260.17	them	these limits A2–A
260.21	it	value A2–A
260.33	these	these two A2–A
260.34	the three	these three A2–A
261.14	sausage	sausages A2–A
261.18	five	four MS–PC
261.25	plant	plan A2–A
262.9	that cult	the cult A2–A
262.26	get it	get that A2–A
262.27	gets it	gets that A2–A
262.28	to begin to get	to get A2–A
262.33	alert and diligent	wily MS
263.2	secured it	secured that chance A2–A
263.4	created it	created an environment A2–A
263.15	numbers 400 now	now numbers 400 A
263.21	makes it	makes Christian Science A2–A

[Relevant texts, pp. 264–361: MS (manuscript); PC (typescript with holograph revision used as printer's copy for the 1907 edition); A (1907 edition)]:

265 *title*	CHAPTER 1	Chapter 1. | MRS. EDDY PC
		CHAPTER I A

	Iowa-California Readings	*Rejected Readings*
265.28	also	and also PC, A
266.3–4	Eiffel tower	Eiffel MS, PC
†266.8	calculated to	calculated MS
267.20	note that	note PC, A
269.11	Grandmother	Grandfather A
271.30	that	*om.* PC, A
272.15	electric street cars	electric-cars PC, A
274.4	went	came PC, A
275.9	silenced	silence MS, PC
276.10	43	42 PC, A
276.31	one	we PC, A
277.3	me	us PC, A
277.15	had it it	had it PC, A
278.9	those	these A
279.7	evidences show	evidence shows A
†279.29	several hundred	471 MS, PC
281 *title*	CHAPTER 4	Chapter IV. | DIVINE AUTHORSHIP? MS, PC CHAPTER IV A
281.27	in place	instead PC, A
282.29	strong	pretty strong PC, A
283.9	highest	brightest PC, A
286 *title*	CHAPTER 5	Chapter V. | WHAT IS HER CELESTIAL RANK? MS, PC CHAPTER V A
288.20	find	feel PC, A
289.28	behind	behind them PC, A

	Iowa-California Readings	*Rejected Readings*
290.24	suggested	suggests A
291.21	college's	*om.* PC, A
292.30	reduction	deduction MS–A
295.1	office	the office A
295.29	was	is PC, A
296.12	is	are A
297.25	further	farther A
297.26	the ambitious	ambitious PC, A
297.27	mighty	*om.* PC, A
300.1	a year	one year PC, A
300.32	is, candidates	is, PC, A
302.10	neighbors	neighbor A
†303.35	(temporarily) cured	cured MS, PC
†304.2	is *herself*	is herself MS *herself* is PC, A
307.15	office	offices A
308.11	improvements upon them,	*om.* PC, A
308.34	during	*om.* PC, A
309.34	nine	ten MS, PC
310.3	nine	ten MS, PC
310.9	nine	ten MS, PC
311.24	139	138 PC
315.9	think	think that PC, A
316.9	furthest	farthest A
316.23	us	*om.* MS–A

	Iowa-California Readings	*Rejected Readings*
318.19	word	*om.* PC, A
319.10	say not	not say PC, A
319.19	purpose	purposes A
320.23	amongst	among A
321.5	History	She MS, PC
321.5	itself	herself MS, PC
321.7	history	she MS, PC
323.16	By-Law says	By-laws say A
324.4	merely	exactly the same as MS, PC
325.7	further	farther A
326.1–2	copyright (a fact not known to twenty people in the world).	copyright, and only just that one. MS, PC
326.23	gilt-edged	gilt-edges A
327.35	of her	of the PC, A
328.4	believed	believed that PC, A
328.30	a generosity	generosity PC, A
329 *title*	CHAPTER 8	Chapter VIII | PERSONAL AGGRANDIZEMENTS. MS, PC CHAPTER VIII A
329.23	for what	what PC, A
330.12	she is autocrat over them all,	*om.* PC, A
331.3	By-Law	By-laws PC, A
332.13	can	*om.* PC, A

	Iowa-California Readings	*Rejected Readings*
332.34	thing as death.	thing. MS, PC
333.20	the one	one PC, A
336.14–15	not a	nor a A
337.1	really	*om.* PC, A
337.7	that	any A
338.5	at	on A
340.7	eternal	*om.* MS–A
344.3	can be let	can let PC
344 *title*	CHAPTER 9	Chapter IX | SUMMING UP OF MONOPOLIES. MS, PC CHAPTER IX A
349.20	dominion	domination A
349.28	to be	*om.* PC, A
354 *title*	CHAPTER 14	Chapter XIV | THE PAPACY. MS, PC CHAPTER XIV A
†355 *title*	CHAPTER 15	Chapter XV | THE "IF." MS, PC CHAPTER XV A
356.22	all	*om.* PC, A
357.32	the ages	ages PC, A
360.18	upon	on PC, A
360.34	is to	is PC

[Relevant texts, pp. 363–381: PC (typescript used as printer's copy for the 1907 edition); A (1907 edition)]:

365.5	past	last PC, A
365.19	is	it A

	Iowa-California Readings	*Rejected Readings*
369 *title*	APPENDIX D	APPENDIX D | PRAYER. PC
369.17	loss	less A
369.21	who	that PC, A
380.19	of either	by either PC, A

[Relevant texts, pp. 382–395: MS (manuscript); TS (typescript with holograph revision used as printer's copy for the *North American Review* publication of "Mrs. Eddy in Error"); A2 (*North American Review*); PC (page proof of A2 used as printer's copy for the 1907 edition); A (1907 edition)]:

383.14	is it	it is TS–A
385.7	was	is A
†385.9–14	The confusions . . . her."	There . . . result: MS–PC
387.20	he said	the secretary said TSE–A
387.20	his	the TSE–A
387.21	his	the TSE–A
388.4	before been	been before A
†388.5	chapter	magazine MS–PC
389.10	She carries the key.	*not in* MS, TS
389.27	title	little A
†391.25	chapter	article A2–A
391.33	recently published	recent MS, TS
391.33	article	article (written four years ago) MS–PC
392.5	object	only object TS–A
392.8	does seem	seems A2–A
392.23	she	it A

	Iowa-California Readings	*Rejected Readings*
392.25	It	This TSE–A
393.22	has either	either has TSE–A
393.25	know	*om.* TS–A
394.14	the	her A
394.24	true	*om.* TS–A
†395.1	appeared (in the March number of the *North American Review*)	has appeared (in the last number of this Review) TS has . . . REVIEW) A2, PC
395.6	*North American Review*	Review TS REVIEW A2, PC

22.   THINGS A SCOTSMAN WANTS TO KNOW

The present text is based upon a manuscript previously unpublished, DV263, the only extant phase. External evidence (see the Explanatory Notes) suggests that the date at the head—31 August [1909]—was the actual date of composition. Mark Twain used a cream tablet paper, probably the "Pratt's" brand, for this and the next two works of this volume, "Letters from the Earth" and " 'The Turning Point of My Life'." The pronoun "he" [He] (398.12), which refers to God, has been capitalized; one misspelling has been corrected, "dipththeria" [diphtheria] (399.12).

23.   LETTERS FROM THE EARTH

The present text is based upon two manuscripts, DV33a, the only phases under Mark Twain's control, here grouped under the title of the second. The first manuscript, untitled and covering pp. 401–406 of this volume, has its own pagination (1–13) and breaks off in mid-sentence at the end of the last leaf. On p. 13 Paine wrote: "This is all he ever wrote of this M. S. Letters from the Earth was suggested by it, but is *not* a continuance of it." But the fragment was clearly meant to introduce a commentary by Satan so like "Letters from the Earth" that the two manuscripts belong together (see DeVoto's similar argument, *LE*, p. 289). Mark Twain inscribed relatively few revisions in either manuscript. Most cancellations, substitutions, and insertions were brief and trivial style changes, averaging two or three to a leaf, and the leaves normally contained about 130 words. Revisions of this kind were the substitution of "them" for "these performers" (409.28), the deletion of "wholly" before "without offence" (416.1), and the insertion of "Whereupon" (417.3). Another feature of the second manuscript was the appearance of Mark Twain's customary marginal notes, designed to introduce ideas for later development or revision. The letters contain six of these reminders, a large number for so brief a work. Mark Twain may not have trusted his memory in 1909, or he may have believed the structure was too vagarious to suggest continuations he had planned earlier.

In the introductory fragment Mark Twain irregularly capitalized pronouns referring to God; the present text uniformly capitalizes them. In the second manuscript he everywhere used lower case, which is kept in the present text because he seems to have chosen the style to suit Satan's derogation of God in that manuscript. The only previous printing of the entire work was in *LE*, pp. 3–55. The many variants in that edition derived from transcription errors in the printer's copy typescript prepared under DeVoto. Excerpts of that edition were published in *Life*, 28 September 1962, pp. 109–121.

NOTES

The following notes include Mark Twain's major revisions and his marginal reminders.

410.8–9 ... southward; as quaint ... I take it.] Mark Twain's substitution for the following:

... southward; and at times, in an access of rapture, waves his sceptre two up two down, two right two left, conducting the music.

At the top of manuscript p. 10 (which begins "as quaint") Mark Twain wrote: "looking down into hell."

410.22   change] The cue word begins manuscript p. 11, at the top of which Mark Twain wrote:

immodesty	must be
sexual-in	done in
is indecent—	the dark.

412.27   the one I have been speaking of.] Mark Twain's substitution for "the one that was conducting the music, you remember. Let us grant it. He could have done it, I think." Compare his revision at 410.8–9.

413.31   darkness] The cue word begins manuscript p. 20, originally numbered 18. Mark Twain also renumbered the next eight leaves, 19 becoming 21, etc. He did not make a two-page insertion that required these changes but rather misread 19 as 17 and thus first numbered p. 20 as 18, 21 as 19, etc., until he caught the error at p. 29.

417.1   Her lad] The cue words begin manuscript p. 28, at the top of which Mark Twain wrote and canceled: "savages do it publicly."

422.10   . . . no Gila Monster,] The series originally continued:

. . . no Gila Monster, and no Jersey mosquito, and no yellow-fever mosquito, and no malaria-mosquito, and no dipththeria germ, and no hydrophobia germ, and no typhoid germ, and no black-plague germ, . . .

Mark Twain gives these items extensive treatment later in the text; see pp. 424, 429.

425.4   permanent] The cue word begins manuscript p. 52, at the top of which Mark Twain wrote: "decorations and character of fly."

436.4   [forni]cation] The last part of the cue word begins manuscript p. 85, at the top of which Mark Twain wrote: "tempera [temperament] born in man."

438.20–21   . . . adultery and all.] After the text paragraph Mark Twain wrote and canceled: "(Go back. Solomon 700 w 300 con." Instead of going back he developed the material later; see p. 440.

438.30 27 days] Mark Twain apparently inscribed "7" over "3," but
DeVoto's typist thought the reverse; compare *LE*, p. 40. Only "27" is
consistent with Mark Twain's statement at 439.16–17.

442.29 sensuality] Mark Twain's substitution for "sexual intercourse."

    The following table records emendations of the manuscripts.
Present text readings are at the left; manuscript readings are at the
right. A curved dash (∼) stands for the word before or after the
punctuation of the present text.

401.1	Him	him
401.3	Him	him
401.9	He	he
401.11	His	his
406.26	to take	take
407.33	recognize	recognise
411.13–14	them hates	them they hates
412.20–21	hundreds of	hundred of
413.10	either	ether
415.2	its	it's
417.3	they adopt	They adopt
420.29	most	the most
422.10	ornithorhynchus	ornothorhyncus
422.31	harem	harum
423.21	monsters	mosters
425.27	naïvely	naievely
426.26	How	How a

	Iowa-California Readings	Rejected Readings
427.3	heartbreaks	heart breaks
427.16	cradle	crdle
428.12	concedes	conceds
429.10	family	families
430.27	Shem	Seth
432.13	Shem	Seth
434.29	thousands	thousand's
435.8	gonorrhea	gonnorhea
435.24	concedes	conceds
435.29	immune	immne
436.5	contend	contends
436.26	Thou	Thous
437.2	temperament,	~
437.27	50.	~
437.31	90.	~
438.12	hey-day	hey-dey
439.30–31	and defeat	and & defeat
443.31	than	that
445.11	Lord	Lord
447.19	16 But	But
447.19	Lord	Lord
449.8	house	"~
451.26	Père	Pere
453.15	theirs	their's
453.25	theirs	their's

24.   "THE TURNING POINT OF MY LIFE"

For all except the last two paragraphs the present text is based upon Mark Twain's final holographic text, a manuscript (Paine 13, 14) together with revisions he inscribed in a typescript (University of Wisconsin) evidently prepared by Jean Clemens. The last two paragraphs, not in manuscript, typescript, or proof (proofs also at the University of Wisconsin), are taken from the first publication of the work in *Harper's Bazar* for February 1910. The circumstances of composition are described in *MTB*, pp. 1528, 1545, and in Robert A. Rees and Richard Dilworth Rust, "Mark Twain's 'The Turning Point of My Life,'" *American Literature* 40, no. 4 (January 1969): 524–535. Mark Twain wrote this version late in 1909, after Paine and Jean Clemens disapproved of his previous draft (see Supplement C). For what amounts to a still earlier draft see the Autobiographical Dictation of 2 October 1906 (*MTE*, pp. 385–393). The present edition accepts the judgment of Rees and Rust that Mark Twain did not revise in proof or after submitting the last two paragraphs and that all variants in the first printing were unauthorized changes, introduced for the most part by an editor at *Harper's Bazar*, Elizabeth Jordan. The title is in quotation marks in the manuscript, evidently to indicate that it was a familiar expression.

Previous printings: *Harper's Bazar* 44, no. 2 (February 1910):118–119; *WIM*, pp. 127–140; reprinted in 26Z: 127–140; texts derivative of *WIM* in *The Family Mark Twain*, pp. 1129–1135; *The Favorite Works of Mark Twain* (New York: Garden City Publishing Co., 1939), pp. 1129–1135; Neider, pp. 477–485.

The following table records Mark Twain's revisions in the typescript; substantive errors in the typescript repeated in *Harper's Bazar*; editorial changes in the present text; and readings in *Harper's Bazar* rejected editorially or in favor of the manuscript.

Present text readings are at the left. Where the symbol MS follows a reading at the right, the present text reading is Mark Twain's revision in the typescript and the one at the right is the superseded manuscript reading. Where the symbols TS and B follow a reading at the right, the present text reading is that of the manuscript and the reading at the right is common to the typescript and *Harper's Bazar*. Where the symbols MS and TS follow a reading at the right, the present text reading is editorial. Where the symbol *B* follows a reading at the right, the rejected reading first appears in *Harper's Bazar*. A curved dash (∼) stands for the word before the punctuation of the present text.

455.1	*Bazar*	Bazar MS, TS BAZAR *B*
455.5	was *itself*, individually,	*itself* was *B*
455.9	weighty	grand MS
455.9	weighty	cardinal *B*
456.32–33	him, and thence go piping down the aisles of history forever.	him. MS
458.28	once a day,	once, MS
459.4	Also	∼, MS
459.7	man's master—	man's master—man's only master here below— MS
460.14	eyes	∼, MS
460.30	elevate him	polish him, improve him, exalt him, *B*
461.3	things first	things TS, *B*
461.6–7	afterward. Always violently. When I am reflecting, on those occasions, even deaf persons can hear me think.	afterward. Always My reflections would attract attention in Sunday school, but they would do no real good there. MS
461.11	had *been*	*had* been MS

	Iowa-California Readings	*Rejected Readings*
461.11–14	Para. I reflected. A policeman came and asked me what I was doing, and I told him. He made me move on; and said if he caught me reflecting in the public street again he would run me in.	Para. That settled it. MS
461.20	a stage	another stage B
461.26	office. I accepted.	office. MS
461.28	fortune and enter the ministry.	fortune. MS
461.28	fortune and enter the ministry.	fortune. B
461.29	move	advance B
461.31	*Enterprise*	Enterprise MS, TS
461.33	unconsciously	quite unconsciously MS
462.1	*Enterprise*	Enterprise MS, TS
462.4	*Union*	Union MS, TS
462.6	of extraneous matter	of matter MS
462.11	the platform had	Circumstance had most kindly and unexpectedly hurled me upon the platform and B
462.14	link:	link—the conspicuous, the consummating, the victorious link: B
462.14	*write a book*	write a book MS
462.15	*The Innocents Abroad*	"The Innocents Abroad" MS, TS

	Iowa-California Readings	Rejected Readings
462.15	at last I became	I became at last TS, B
462.30	being—	~, MS
462.31	marvel—	~, MS
463.2	circumstances	circumstance TS, B
463.5	Once General Grant was asked	Once I asked General Grant MS
463.26–27	A gang of patriots throws	Some patriots throw B
463.27	it destroys	some other patriots destroy B
463.34	turning point	turning-point B
464.12	kill	Kill B

WORD DIVISION

1. End-of-line hyphenation in this volume

The following possible solid compounds are hyphenated at the ends
of lines in this volume. They are listed as they would appear in this
volume if not broken at the ends of lines.

40.18	pro-gress
70.11	hand-shakings
74.35	thumb-screws
85.9	graveyard
94.3	hoop-skirt
108.24	falsehood
114.10	bystanders
116.25	lifetime
118.23	time-worn
133.5	tear-choked
165.32	safeguarded
182.1	ever-changing
190.30	far-off
192.21	mother-bird
218.20	hand-bag
231.24	subcentral
248.16	life-long
255.29	law-breaker
259.27	aforesaid
264.4	every-day
264.17	mean-minded
305.2	forecast
334.18	outclasses
338.25	drain-pipes
341.18	half-soling
352.13	thenceforth
373.6	wrong-doing
386.16	bombshell
425.27	outspokenly

431.33	hookworms
435.6	almshouse
442.18	sandpaper
456.27	life-chain
485.2	caterpillar
519.28	Whatyoumaycallum
526.27	jewsharp

2. End-of-line hyphenation in the copy-texts

The following possible solid compounds are hyphenated at the ends of lines in the copy-texts. They are listed as they appear in this volume.

38.18	overtake
53.30	wire-drawn
57.6	brimstone
61.30	tail-end
76.14	nightcap
80.20	week-days
89.6	bald-headed
89.13	earth-worm
104.21	far-flung
118.8	forecasts
132.23	sweetheart
192.29	mother-bird
208.28	second-hand
231.4	medicine-man
233.23	horse-doctor
234.19	healthy-minded
250.24	trade-mark
252.9	book-shop
257.31	out-prospers
272.21	grown-up
273.3	long-range
307.11	grave-digger
336.28	lifetime
339.11	drain-pipes
421.21	caterpillars
452.6	storm-swept

486.19	heart-breaks
486.22	to-morrow
490.8	grave-yard
498.6	stock-holders

3. Special Cases

The following possible solid compounds are hyphenated at the ends of lines in the copy-texts and in this volume. They are listed as they would appear in this volume if not broken at the ends of lines.

140.14	thousandfold
507.5	*Eddypus*